BATV

RC
480.5
.H54

The History of psychotherapy : from healing
magic to encounter / edited by Jan Ehrenwald.
-- New York : J. Aronson, c1976 (1991
printing)

589 p. ; 24 cm.

Bibliography: p. [577]-583.
Includes index.
ISBN 0-87668-280-8

1. Psychotherapy--History. 2.
Psychotherapy. 3. Healing--History. 4.
Medicine, Magic, mystic, and spagiric. I.
Ehrenwald, Jan, 1900-

To Renew Books
PHONE (925) 969-3100

THE
HISTORY
OF
PSYCHOTHERAPY

COMMENTARY

"This work is more than a book of readings. Its author has combined historical scholarship with understanding derived from extensive clinical experience to present a meaningful, unified, and comprehensive anthology. With prefatory and concluding statements, Ehrenwald has placed each selection in historical context and provided, where necessary, summaries of theoretical systems. . . . Through his presentation and interpretation of history Ehrenwald has gone far to explain the conflicting and seemingly paradoxical reports of successful outcomes of psychotherapy made by opposing schools."
—Carol E. McMahon

"Ehrenwald has admirably succeeded in presenting in an appealing fashion the tortuous and at times cyclic development of psychotherapeutic principles and techniques, mainly by excerpting from written sources. This volume can be of tremendous help to anyone interested in acquiring a much wider and more balanced perspective on the field of psychiatry—from the psychiatric resident to the practicing psychiatrist, regardless of school or technique."
—George Mora, M.D.

"There appears to be an inverse relation between the rich and varied history of psychotherapy and the extent to which this history is known to modern practitioners of the art. Dr. Ehrenwald, in a style that is eminently readable, incisive, and discriminatingly appreciative, orients us to this heritage. He has chosen his excerpts carefully and with a scholar's concern for highlighting the connection between past and present. The passages he quotes serve not only to whet our appetite, often the case with anthologies, but also to satisfy those appetites in large measure. Ehrenwald's grappling with the question of where we as psychotherapists came from can help us better understand where we are now."
—Montagu Ullman, M.D.

THE
HISTORY
OF
PSYCHOTHERAPY

edited by
JAN EHRENWALD, M.D.

JASON ARONSON INC.
Northvale, New Jersey
London

New Printing 1991

ISBN 0-87668-280-8
Library of Congress Catalog Number 76-25782

Manufactured in the United States of America. Jason Aronson Inc. offers books and cassettes. For information and catalog write to Jason Aronson Inc., 230 Livingston Street, Northvale, New Jersey 07647.

Preface

Psychotherapy on the contemporary scene seems headed in all directions at once. Freudian analysis is challenged by gestalt therapy, transactional analysis, screaming cures, nude marathons; the proliferation of diverse "pop" therapies duplicates the recent trend toward chronic avant-gardism in art and literature. Disenchanted and alienated youth, suffering from symptoms of an acute demythologization of our culture—comparable to dream deprivation in laboratory experiments—seeks solace in new myths, esoteric cults, or media-manufactured gimmicks to fill their spiritual void. Despairing over their inability to alter the state of world affairs—or the affairs of state—they experiment with altered states of consciousness or mind-expanding and will-constricting drugs. Some proclaim the dawn of an age of do-it-yourself mind-control through biofeedback, transcendental meditation, or chemical shortcuts to peace of mind, happiness, and mental health. Others try to make their way back to the dark ages of witchcraft and demonology: to regress from Freud to the Medicine Man, as it were.

More than that. Thomas Szasz and his followers are questioning the very existence of mental disease and describe psychiatric diagnosis and treatment as nothing but veiled attempts to stigmatize, penalize, and control helpless minorities who are unable or unwilling to conform to social norms dictated by the majority. At the other end of the spectrum are various devices for electronic behavior control, and such miracle drugs as Thorazine, Valium, and Lithium, that are supposed to eradicate the scourge of mental disease, if not existential anxiety, with one stroke once and for all.

But we shall see that if there is a lesson to be learned, here and now, from the past, it is that man is the most important therapeutic agent for man, and that psychotherapy is the time-tested accretion and codification of a social expedient to meet universal human needs. Mental healing, psychotherapy, or encounter groups, had they not evolved over the milennia as necessary psychosocial regulatory devices, would have had to be invented as surely as the tranquilizers and other nostrums of our medical armamentarium. Indeed, they continue to be invented and reinvented in our day over and over again.

Twenty years ago a briefer version of this guided tour through the history of psychotherapy was published; it was entitled *From Medicine Man to Freud*. But history is not in the habit of grinding to a halt even at major milestones of the road. Psychoanalysis, once in the avant garde of Western man's quest for understanding of himself and of his society, has become a universally accepted exploratory tool, the classical prototype of a medical model of mental healing and of a dynamically oriented psychotherapeutic approach.

But developments since 1956 reflect the same breathless scramble for change as do science, technology, and culture. Both the ultimate concerns of religion, and the intrinsic value of scientific progress and rational insight are being questioned, and the medical model faces the challenge of a new nonmedical, psychosocial or humanistic model.

It is wholly consistent with such a trend that the earlier version, devoted to the two or three millenia stretching "from medicine man to Freud," ran to barely more than four hundred pages, while nearly the same space is now being allotted in the present volume to accommodate the wealth of material which has accrued in the past two or three decades. It may well be that such a lopsided arrangement is due merely to the editor's personal bias. But it may also reflect the intellectual ferment, the accelerated place of inquiry and quest for innovation so characteristic of our time.

At this point it may be well to note that in compiling the original texts for my pilgrimage through the history of psychotherapy. I was aided by those whose pioneering efforts have brought the vast historic pageant reviewed here within my reach. I am indebted to Gregory Zilboorg's monumental *History of Psychotherapy*; to Henri Ellenberger's *The History of the Unconscious*; to Gardner Murphy's *Historic Introduction to Modern Psychology*; and to Walter Bromberg's *Man Above Humanity*. Pierre Janet's *History of Mental Healing* still maintains its place as an invaluable source of information about the development of psychotherapy up to the advent of psychoanalysis. For the history of psychoanalysis itself, Ernest Jones's *The Life and Work of Sigmund Freud*, Clara Thompson's *Psychoanalysis—Evolution and Development*, L. L. Havens *Approaches to the Mind*, and *The Freud-Jung Letters* have been highly illuminating reading. Leslie Weatherhead's *History of Religion and Psychology* has been equally useful for a better understanding of religious aspects, while C. J. S. Thompson's *Magic and Healing* served as a welcome guide in the search for ancient medical texts. Other important contributions are included in the bibliography.

J.E.

Acknowledgments

The editor and publisher have made every effort to determine and credit the holders of copyright of the selections in this book. Any errors or omissions may be rectified in future editions.

For permission to use these selections, the editor and publisher make grateful acknowledgment to the following authors, publishers, and agents, who reserve all rights to the matter reprinted:

from *Magic and Healing* by C. J. S. Thompson, by permission of Rider & Company, London.

from *Magic to Science* by Charles Singer, © Copyright 1928 by Ernest Benn Ltd., London, by permission of the author.

from *The Golden Bough* by James G. Frazer, © Copyright 1922 by The Macmillan Company, © Copyright 1950 by Barclay Banks, by permission of The Macmillan Company, New York.

from *Magic, Science and Religion* by Bronislaw Malinowski, by permission of Madame Malinowska.

from *Black Magic Reborn* by Albert Schweitzer, gathered and set down by Robert Amadou in the *Revue Metapsychique*, by permission of Robert Amadou.

from *Totem and Taboo* by Sigmund Freud, by permission of W. W. Norton & Company, Inc., New York, © Copyright 1950 by Routledge & Kegan Paul, Ltd., London.

from *Upanishads*, translated by Swami Prabhavananda and Frederick Manchester, by permission of the Vedanta Press, Hollywood.

from *Bhagavad Gita*, by permission of Marcel Rodd Incorporated.

from *The Yellow Emperor's Classic on Internal Medicine*, translated by I. Veith, © Copyright 1949 by the Williams and Wilkins Company, by permission of the Williams and Wilkins Company, Baltimore.

from *Malleus Maleficarum* by Kramer and Sprenger, translated by Montague Summers, by permission of the Pushkin Press, London.

from *The Voyage to Lourdes* by Alexis Carrel, © Copyright 1950 by Anne Carrel; and from *Christian Science* by Mark Twain, © Copyright 1907

by Harper & Bros., © Copyright 1935 by Clara Clemens Gabrilowitsch;
by permission of Harper & Bros., New York.

from *Mental Healers* by Stefan Zweig, © Copyright 1932 by Dr. Richard
Friedenthal, by permission of Dr. Friedenthal and Mrs. Eva Alberman.

from *The Genuine Works of Hippocrates*, translated by Francis Adams, by
permission of the Williams and Wilkins Company, Baltimore.

from *Avicenna's Psychology*, translated and edited by F. Rahman, by permission of the Clarendon Press, Oxford.

from *Four Treatises of Paracelsus*; and from *Asclepius*, by E. J. and L. E.
Edelstein; by permission of the John Hopkins University Press, Baltimore.

from *A History of Medical Psychology* by Zilboorg and Henry, © Copyright 1941 by W. W. Norton and Company, Inc., by permission of W.
W. Norton and Company, Inc., New York.

from *Mesmerism* by Anton Mesmer, edited by Gilbert Frankau, by permission of Macdonald & Co. (Publishers) Ltd., and the Executors of the Estate of Gilbert Frankau.

from *Suggestive Therapeutics* by H. Bernheim, © Copyright 1880, by permission of G. P. Putnam's Sons.

from *Outline of Psychoanalysis* by Sigmund Freud, © Copyright 1949 by
W. W. Norton and Company, Inc., by permission of W. W. Norton and
Company, Inc., New York.

from *What Life Should Mean to You* by Alfred Adler, © Copyright 1931 by
Dr. Kurt Adler, by permission of Sanford J. Greenburger.

from *The Basic Writings of Sigmund Freud*, translated and edited by Dr.
A. A. Brill, Copyright 1938 by Random House, Inc., New York, by permission of the Trustees of the Brill Estate.

from *Origins of Psychoanalysis* (Freud's letter to W. Fliess) by Sigmund
Freud, by permission of Basic Books, Inc., New York.

from *Sigmund Freud: An Autobiographical Study*, translated by J.
Shackey, © Copyright 1952 by W. W. Norton and Company, Inc., by
permission of W. W. Norton and Company, Inc., New York.

from *Conceptions of Modern Psychiatry* by Harry Stack Sullivan, ©
Copyright 1947 by the William Alanson White Psychiatric Foundation,
by permission of W. W. Norton and Company, Inc., New York.

from *The Collected Works of C. G. Jung*, © Copyright 1953 by Pantheon
Books, Inc., by permission of the Bollingen Foundation, New York.

from *Freud or Jung* by Edward Glover, by permission of W. W. Norton and
Company, Inc., New York, Published 1950. All rights reserved.

from *Escape from Freedom* by Erich Fromm, © Copyright 1941 by Erich
Fromm, by permission of Rinehart and Company, Inc., New York.

from *The Neurotic Personality of Our Time* by Karen Horney, by permission of W. W. Norton and Co., New York 1937, © copyright renewed by Renate Mintz and Marianne von Eckardt 1964.

from *Science and Psychoanalysis*, Vol. 3, ed. J. Masserman, *Psychoanalytic Thought and Eastern Wisdom* by Harold Kelman, permission of Grune and Stratton, New York and by permission of the author.

from *Games People Play* by Eric Berne, Grove Press, New York.

from "Freud versus Jung—The Mythophobic versus the Mythophilic Temper in Psychotherapy," by Jan Ehrenwald, by permission of *The Israel Annals of Psychiatric and Related Disciplines*, Vol. 6, No. 2, 1968.

from *Being in the World*, Selected Papers, transl. and with a critical psychoanalysis by J. Needleman, by Ludwig Binswanger, in Ausgewahlte Vortrage und Aufsatze, Berne 1955, Vol. II, and Basic Books, New York 1963, by permission of Francke Verlag, CH-3000 Bern 26. Switzerland.

from *Psychoanalysis and Daseinsanalysis* by Medard Boss, by permission of Basic Books, New York, copyright 1963.

from *Existence: A New Dimension in Psychiatry and Psychology*, by Rollo May, Ernest Angel, Henri F. Ellenberger, editors, by permission Basic Books, New York, copyright 1958.

from *The Politics of Experience* by R. D. Laing, Penguin Books Ltd. England, copyright R. D. Laing, 1967.

from "Dreams and the Occult" in New Introductory Lectures (chapter 30), by Sigmund Freud, by permission of W. W. Norton and Co., New York, Copyright 1952 and the Institute of Psycho-Analysis, and the Hogarth Press Ltd. to quote from New Introductory Lectures, Vol. 22 of *The Standard Edition of the Complete Psychological Works of Sigmund Freud*, revised and edited by James Strachey.

from "A Presumptively Telepathic Precognitive Dream During Analysis," by Emilio Servadio, by permission of *International Journal of Psychoanalysis, Vol. 36, part 1, 1955, and by the author.*

from *New Dimensions of Deep Analysis, A Study of Telepathy in Interpersonal Relationships* by Jan Ehrenwald, by permission of Grune and Stratton, New York, 1955.

from *PSI and Psychoanalysis* by Jule Eisenbud, permission by Grune and Stratton, New York, © copyright 1970 and by the author.

from *Dream Telepathy* by Montague Ullman, Stanley Krippner and Alan Vaughan, permission by Macmillan Publishing Co., New York, © copyright 1973, and by the authors.

from *The Effects of Psychotherapy* by Hans Eysenck, by permission of International Science Press, New York, 1966, and by the author.

from *Evaluating Psychoanalysis* by Hans Eysenck, by permission of Medical Tribune, April 4, 1973, New York.

from *Conditioning Therapies* by J. Wolpe, A. Salter, L. Reyna, by permission of Holt, Rinehart and Winston Company, New York 1964.

from *Clinical Behavior Therapy*, ed. A. A. Lazarus, by Thomas Kraft, permission by Brunner Mazel Inc., New York, 1972.

from *Behavior Therapy* by Thomas S. Szasz, permission by Thomas Szasz, 1967.

from the *Journal of American Academy of Psychoanalysis*, Vol. 1, No. 1 *On Behavior Therapy* by Irving Bieber, 1973, by permission of John Wiley and Sons, New York, and by the author and the editor.

from *Dynamic Psychotherapy and Behavior Therapy* by Judd Marmor, Vol. 24, Jan. 1971, by permission of the author, *Archives of General Psychiatry*, © Copyright 1971, American Medical Association.

from *Character Analysis*, third enlarged edition, by Wilhelm Reich, translated by Vincent R. Carfagno, in *History of Psychotherapy*, © copyright 1945, 1949, 1972 by Mary Boyd Higgins, as Trustee of the Wilhelm Reich Infant Trust Fund, by permission of Farrar, Straus and Giroux.

from *Gestalt Therapy: Excitement and Growth in the Human Personality* by Frederick Perls, M.D., Ph.D., Ralph F. Hefferline, Ph.D., Paul Goodman, Ph.D., permission of The Julian Press, New York, 1951, Delta paperback 1964.

from "The Psychoanalysis of Groups," in the *American Journal of Psychotherapy*, Vol. 3, No. 4, Oct. 1949, and Vol. 4, No. 1, Jan. 1950, by Alexander Wolf, permission of editor, Dr. Stanley Lesse, and author.

from *Psychotherapy and Group Therapy, Practicum of Group Psychotherapy*, by S. H. Foulkes, ed. Asya Kadis, J. D. Kramer, and C. Winnick, 1963, permission Harper and Row, New York, and the author.

from "The Philosophy of the Third Psychiatric Revolution with Special Emphasis on Group Psychotherapy and Psychodrama" by J. L. Moreno in *Progress in Psychotherapy*, Vol. 1, permission of Beacon House, Inc., and Grune and Stratton, New York, 1956.

from *Carl Rogers on Encounter Groups*, by Carl Rogers, © copyright 1970 by Carl Rogers, and Harper and Row, New York, by permission.

from chapter 2 of *Encounter Groups: First Facts*, by Morton A. Lieberman, Irvin D. Yalom, and Matthew B. Miles, © copyright 1973 by the authors, by permission Basic Books, New York.

from "The Group Can Comfort But It Can't Cure," by Kurt W. Bak, December 1972, in *Psychology Today* Magazine, December 1972, © copyright 1972, Ziff-Davis Publishing Company, New York.

The editor also wishes to thank the Ralph E. Ogden Foundation, Inc., for a grant supporting the publication of this book.

But for her reluctance to occupy the pride of place, Anny should, as usual, head this list of thanks and acknowledgments.

J.E.

Contents

PART ONE: MAGIC
or the Quest for Omnipotence

PART TWO: RELIGION
or the Quest for Salvation

PART THREE: SCIENCE
or the Quest for Knowledge and Mastery

Contents 13

chapter 1

Introduction

If mental healers were to be summoned to the patient's bedside in the order of their appearance in history, the magician or medicine man would be the first one to answer the call. He would be followed by the philosopher-priest of various religious denominations, who would, in turn, yield his place to the scientifically oriented psychotherapist. There would be a world of difference between their underlying philosophies and the way they minister to their patients' needs. But their goal would be the same: to cure psychological (and sometimes physical) ills by essentially psychological means.

The term *mental healing* as it is applied here thus covers a vast field. It extends from the analyst's couch and from the meeting halls of modern faith healers and miracle men to the shrines of worship of ancient Greece and Judea, to the thatched-roof huts of the primitive shaman or witch doctor. For mental healing in its broader sense includes the humble origins of contemporary psychology and psychiatry in the dawn of recorded history as well as the latest exploits of scientific psychotherapy as it is practiced in the major centers of treatment in Europe and in the United States.

Our frame of reference has to be still further extended if we are to include the principal trends which can be discerned in cultures alien to our Western Greco-Judean civilization. The student of ancient Hindu and Chinese texts will be struck by their vastly different approach toward health and disease. Buddhist and Taoist doctrines are less concerned with a "healthy" adjustment to the demands of everyday life than with devising a method of escape from their pressures. They place their main emphasis on self-denial and mortification of the flesh as the surest way toward salvation. Clearly, such an approach can hardly be correlated with Western concepts of mental healing. Even our own Greco-Judean tradition has shown little concern for the mental health of the individual as compared with the welfare of the group.

In the early Christian era the concepts of health, wholeness and holiness were closely related. The word *salvation* itself implied the idea of relief from anguish, suffering and all the rest of the calamities which the flesh is heir to. On the other hand, the word *salvation* as it was applied by the medieval church fathers, or by Lutheran or Calvinist theologians respectively, carried different connotations. All this goes far to show that we must not try to arrive at a literal translation of psychological attitudes toward the Good Life, toward salvation, from one culture to another. We cannot calibrate our concepts of health and disease, of mental hygiene and mental healing, with what we assume to be the corresponding ideas in the mind of an African native, in the texts of the Vedic Hymns, in the Bhagavad Gita, or in Freud's *Introductory Lectures on Psychoanalysis*.

The difficulties increase when we try to go back into prehistoric times. Archeologists have found fragments of human skulls dating from the Paleolithic era which suggest that Stone Age man was familiar with the art of trephining. But another theory is that the fragments were worn as fetishes to protect the wearer from disease. If so, the Stone Age practitioner of magic acted as a primitive psychotherapist rather than as a neurosurgeon in the modern sense.

In fact, we learn from the anthropologists that African or Australian natives, those modern counterparts of Stone Age man, may derive considerable benefit from their magic rites and rituals. One may hesitate to refer to these practices in terms of modern psychotherapy; but there can be little doubt that whatever beneficial effects do result from them are chiefly psychological.

The motivations of the Hindu religious practitioner and of the Christian mystic are of an entirely different order. These people are not seekers of mental or physical health, but of their respective brands of spiritual salvation. We hinted that their answer to the problem of pain and suffering lies in the power of renunciation and self-denial. Psychologically speaking, theirs is a method of prevention rather than cure. Measured by Western standards, the classic Buddhist doctrine would seem to seek deliverance from suffering by an attitude of withdrawal that is comparable to the mechanisms of escape seen in certain neurotic or psychotic patients in our time. One may well wonder how, in these circumstances, a religious system basically hostile to life can have survived for thousands of years. Presumably the answer is that its extreme prohibitions and injunctions, imposed on the very strong and the very weak alike, are precisely what have helped to maintain the balance of a society otherwise threatened by social disintegration.

It is in this way that the doctrine of nonaction and nonviolence may have had a tempering effect on Hindu society. At the same time it has served as a rich source of spiritual consolation to countless millions of far eastern religious devotees from Buddha to Gandhi. And one should add at this point that one of the side effects of the Christian quest for salvation was perhaps of an essential similar order: whether by accident or by purpose, it had a tempering influence upon the lives of the faithful. If this is true, even the essentially other-worldly, transcendental orientation of the Hindu or Christian mystic, although entirely lacking in what can be described as psychotherapeutic intent, may ultimately result in an attitude conducive to the common good. Thus even in the eyes of the agnostic it may possess a modicum of "survival value."

The incidents of miraculous healing described in the New Testament seem to come closer to our modern concepts of mental healing. Yet here too, more emphasis is placed on the theological implications of the healing miracles than on the achievement of an individual cure. The paramount goal is redemption and deliverance from evil. Each of the four Gospels emphasizes Christ's deep reluctance to "work miracles" and to use outward signs of divine power as his credentials. Much the same considerations apply to the modern miracles attributed to the healing powers of Lourdes.

Shifting our focus to yet another period of history, the spectacular "magnetic" cures effected by Mesmer and his followers were but a revival of the primitive magic are, adjusted to the temper of eighteenth-century romanticism. In this case, a false theory, based on essentially prescientific, astrological concepts, produced striking psychological effects. The same is true— though to a lesser degree—for such cultist or sectarian movements as Rudolf Steiner's Anthroposophy or Mary Baker Eddy's Christian Science.

All these many and varied techniques of allaying anxiety and relieving suffering must be contrasted with the principles of modern scientific psychotherapy. In scientific psychotherapy (as in science in general) magic has been replaced by reliance on the laws of nature. The principle of trial and error which seems to be responsible for the paradoxical survival of certain ineffectual or even harmful magic practices—as well as of certain mystic attitudes of self-denial and renunciation—has given way to the austere discipline of empirical observation, experimentation and statistical analysis of results achieved. Does man's physical well-being seem to be imperiled by the implacable forces of nature? If so, the scientific mind is confident that the operation of these forces can be properly understood and made subservient to man's physical requirements. Does his psychological welfare appear to be threatened by powers residing within his own nature? They, too, can be reduced to the operation of natural forces, subject to the same laws that govern nature at large. Once these laws, the principles of psychodynamics and learning theory have been discovered, the way is cleared for the ultimate control of our emotional life, comparable to the measure of control already achieved on the level of technological progress.

Yet we indicated that in the last analysis the goal of the magic, the religious and the scientific approaches remains the same; only the way by which they seek to reach the goal is different. And despite their vast differences in method, the magic, the religious and the scientific approaches to human suffering have something else in common: their remedy is of an essentially psychological nature. The witch doctor practices psychotherapy using his charms and fetishes as the physical vehicles for his cure. The priestly healer achieves the same end through the believer's faith in his ministrations. The modern psychotherapist relies chiefly on his dynamic understanding—magical or imaginary—of the patient's mental processes, and on their purposeful manipulation by purely psychological means.

According to these *three major avenues* of mental healing, selections for this anthology have been arranged under four headings: (1) Magic or the Quest for Omnipotence; (2) Religion or the Quest for Salvation; (3) Science or the Quest for Knowledge and Mastery; The fourth heading, (4) Beyond Psychoanalysis, focuses on the contemporary scene.

It is, however, needless to say that such an organization is largely a matter of convenience. A strict discrimination between magic and religion is not always possible. Seen from the vantage point of the modern Western observer, magic has been described as a pseudo science, a confused welter of false beliefs and crude misconceptions regarding the laws of nature. James Frazer called magic a "bastard sister of science" and E. B. Tylor condemned its underlying philosophy as a "monstrous farrago." Students of comparative religion have pointed out, on the other hand, that what in one society is considered magic may proudly claim the status of religion in another. Conversely, religious beliefs held in high esteem in one society may with the decline and fall of the society in which they flourished be relegated into the realm of magic. Magic, one could state, is the discredited religion of a past era. And to this a religious skeptic might retort that religion itself is nothing but magic triumphant. What future generations will have to say about our present-day faith in science is another question.

Indeed, we must realize that the demarcation line between contemporary science and magic is not as sharp as Frazer or Tylor would have it. The precise separation of the two is still but a distant goal of truly scientific psychotherapy. The fact is that while science is based on the firm foundations of controlled and repeatable laboratory experiments, modern psychiatry still lags behind in such accomplishments. The psychotherapist trying to control, to change and to predict the behavior of his patients may find himself in much the same predicament as the primitive medicine man seeking to control, to change or to foretell the weather. Unable to achieve this end, the psychotherapist—like the rainmaker—may easily yield to the temptation of looking for a magical shortcut to his goal. He may fall back on the tradition of his primitive forerunner.

Yet despite the difficulties in the way of scientific psychotherapy, the gradual shift from the magic to the rational approach is an unmistakable feature in the development of mental healing in every civilization. Men of many cultures and many cultural epochs have moved in this direction with varying success. Some have never made the grade and have failed to emerge from the twilight of an essentially magico-mystical outlook. Other civilizations—including our own—seem to follow an irresistible urge toward growing rationalization in the field of both natural and "mental" sciences.

The history of mental healing up to our day could be described as the record of unremitting efforts by the ancestors of the modern psychotherapist to distill from the primordial brew of primitive magic a product of ever increasing scientific purity. This formulation has, in effect, served as the guiding principle in compiling the present anthology.

In pursuing this trend it was not always possible to follow the chronological order of events, nor to avoid major gaps in the continuity of their documentation. Occasional duplications caused by the changing focus on magical, religious and scientific aspects were equally unavoidable. These three aspects of the historical process are closely interrelated—they are three different ways of looking at the same thing. The reader will probably not be surprised, therefore, to discover the same underlying trend from whatever angle he approaches the material reviewed here.

Part 1

MAGIC
or
The Quest
for
Omnipotence

chapter 2

Healing Magic,
Ancient Oriental Version

ASSYRIAN AND BABYLONIAN TABLETS . . .
THE PAPYRUS EBERS

*Perhaps the earliest writings in medical history are found in Assyrian tab-
lets dating from about 2500 B.C. Some of these contain incantations addressed by the magician to his tribal gods; others are a direct challenge to
the evil demon or disease to yield to the magician's superior powers and to
depart from his victim. Both varieties are illustrated by these cuneiform
texts quoted from C. J. S. Thompson's* Magic and Healing.

Sickness of the head, of the teeth, of the heart, heartache;
Sickness of the eye, fever, poison;
Evil-spirits, evil-demons, evil-ghost, evil-evil, evil-god,
    evil-fiend;
Hag, demon, ghoul, robber sprite;
Phantom of night, night wraith, hand-maid of the phantoms;
Evil pestilence, noisome fever, baneful sickness;
Pain, sorcery or any evil,
Headache, Shivering,

Evil spell, witchcraft, sorcery,
Enchantment and all evil:
Drive from the house; go forth, Unto the man, the son of his god, come not
    into,
    Get thee hence.

*Another tablet contains a prayer directed to the Babylonian god Ea, the
Lord of the Deep.*

[To be said over a sick man:]
He that stilleth all to rest, that pacifieth all,
By whose incantation everything is at peace
He is the great Lord Ea.

By whose incantation everything is at peace,
When I draw nigh into the sick man
All shall be assuaged.
I am the magician born of Eridu
Begotten in Eridu and Subari
When I draw nigh unto the sick man
May Ea, King of the Deep, safeguard me.

[Then the magician is thus to address the deity sought:]
O Ea, King of the Deep, see
I am the magician, am thy slave.
March thou on my right hand,
Assist (me) on my left,
Add thy pure spell to mine;
Vouchsafe (to me) pure words
Make fortunate the utterances of my mouth,
Ordain that my decisions may be happy,
Let me be blest where'er I tread,
Let the man whom I now touch be blessed.

The boundless self-confidence of the magician—his claim to omnipotence —is clearly expressed in this fragment. At the same time he bows to the superior powers of the deity and concedes that all his powers derive from the divinity itself.

For sickness of the head, of the teeth or the heart,
Sickness of the eye, fever, poison,
Come my sorceress or enchantress
Over a nulukhkha-plant shalt thou recite.
Upon the fumigation bowl which is at the head of the bed
Shalt thou place it with an upper garment
Shalt thou envelop the bed.

Whether it be an evil spirit or an evil demon
Or an evil ghost or an evil devil or an evil god or an evil fiend
Or a hag-demon, or a ghoul or a robber sprite
Or an evil spirit that holdeth the man in his grip
Or an evil ghost that hath seized the man,
Or an evil man, or one whose face is evil, whose mouth is evil, whose
    tongue is evil,
That incantation at his head, may they be removed.

Passages like these are graphic illustrations of the magic approach to illness. The curative agent is the spoken or written word, the solemn ritual—and both the patient's and the magician's belief in their efficacy.

But the references to fumigation and other physical paraphernalia forming part of the ceremony show that psychological means were not the only ones by which the primitive medicine man sought to help his patient. Even in the oldest writings handed down to us, we can see magic operating alongside the principle of trial and error which ultimately paved the way for the advent of the scientific method.

The following fragment shows how the magician sought to prevent a demon from entering a house by placing bitumen under the doorstep:

I am the messenger of Marduk
As I perform the pure incantation
I put bitumen on the door beneath,
That Ea may rest within the house
May a kindly spirit, a kindly Guardian
Enter the house,
May no evil Spirit or evil Demon
Or evil ghost or evil Devil
That thou mayest depart.

In this incantation water is used as the vehicle of magic:

A sorcerer of Eridu whose mouth is purified (am I)
The sick man upon whom sickness has seized,
Fever hath taken up its seat upon him.
When I draw near unto the sick man,
When I examine the muscles of the sick man,
When I compose his limbs,
When I sprinkle the water of Ea on the sick man,
When I subdue the sick man,
When I bring low the strength of the sick man
Nor evil god or evil fiend
Draw nigh unto the King
By Heaven be ye exorcised! By Earth be ye exorcised!

Such passages illustrate two more characteristics of magic medicine: the belief in possession by evil spirits as the cause of disease and in the power of incantations to drive the spirits out of the body of the possessed.

This demoniacal theory of illness is a recurrent theme in many cultures. In the Middle Ages it was largely confined to explaining the origin of mental

*disease. We shall see later how exorcism by prayer, torture and ultimately
burning at the stake became standard procedures of the Inquisition.*

*The following tablet includes in its plea a comprehensive list of all con-
ceivable parts of the body that may be affected by illness. This is to make
sure that no loophole was left in the healing magic of the exorcist.*

Sickness of the head, of the teeth, of the heart, heartache,
Sickness of the eye, fever, poison,
Evil Spirit, evil Demon, evil Ghost, evil Devil, evil God, evil Fiend,
Hag-demon, Ghoul, Robber sprite,
Phantom of night, Night wraith, Hand maiden of the Phantom,
Evil pestilence, noisome fever, baneful sickness,
Pain, sorcery or any evil,
Headache, shivering,
Roaming the streets, dispersed through dwellings, penetrating bolts,
Evil man, he whose face is evil, he whose mouth is evil, he whose tongue is
     evil,
Evil spell, witchcraft, sorcery,
Enchantment and all evil,
From the house go forth!
Unto the man, the son of his god come not nigh,
Get thee hence!

In his seat sit thou not,
On his couch lie thou not,
Over his fence rise thou not,
Into his chamber enter thou not,
By Heaven and Earth I exorcise thee,
When I recited an incantation over the sick man,
When I perform the incantation of Eridu,
May a kindly spirit at my side,
Whether thou art an evil Spirit or an evil Demon
Or an evil Ghost, or an evil Devil.

Or an evil pestilence or noisome fever,
Or pain or sorcery or any evil,
Or headache or shivering or an evil man or evil face,
Or evil spell or evil tongue or evil mouth or sorcery,
Or any evil, be thou removed from before me,
By Heaven be thou exorcised! By Earth be thou exorcised!

One of the most celebrated documents of medical history, the Papyrus Ebers, illustrates the same need for an anti-inclusive formula, making sure that all parts of the body are protected from disease. The Papyrus was discovered in 1874 in Luxor by the German egyptologist G. M. Ebers. In an excellent state of preservation, it is sixty feet long and contains a wealth of information about Egyptian medicine of around 1500 B.C., part of it going back to still earlier times. Here are the introductory passages of the Papyrus:

Here begins the book of the preparation of medicines for all parts of the body of a person. I was born in Heliopolis with the priests of Het-Aat, the lords of protection, the kings of eternity and of salvation. I have my origin in Sais with the maternal goddesses who have protected me. The Lord of All has given me words to drive away the diseases of all the gods and mortal sufferings of every kind. There are chapters for this my head, for this my neck, for these my arms, for this my flesh, and for these my limbs, so that [disease] enters unto this my flesh, placing a spell on these my limbs, whenever Ra has taken mercy and has said "I protect him against his enemies." It is his guide Hermes who gave him the word, who created the books and gave glory to those who know everything and to the physicians who follow him to decipher that which is dark. He whom the god loves is made alive; I am the one whom the god loves, me he makes alive, to pronounce words in the preparation of medicine for all parts of the body of a person who is sick. As it should be a thousand times. This is the book of the healing of all diseases.

The Papyrus Ebers is not, however, exclusively concerned with magic spells and incantations. It contains a wealth of rational medical advice, from the prescription of purgatives and poultices to a simple recipe for the treatment of crocodile bite. Without assuming responsibility for its effectiveness, the remedy is as follows:

If thou meetest with a crocodile bite and thou findest the flesh equally fallen away, cover the site of his bite with raw meat.

chapter 3

Healing Magic,
Western Style

The far-reaching resemblance of magic ritual and mythical concepts found in various cultures widely separated in space and time has puzzled historians, anthropologists and psychologists alike. This similarity is high-lighted by a fragment from an ancient Anglo-Saxon or Celtic document known as the Lorica de Gildas. *It was composed in the seventh or eighth century A.D. and was written in an early medieval Latin idiom. The Lorica was a magic coat which was supposed to protect the devotee from the influence of demons and evil spirits. The list of the parts of the body included in the prayerful incantation reproduced below is reminiscent of a similar Egyptian text included in the previous chapter.*

Oh God, with thy inscrutable saving power defend all my parts, deliver the whole trunk of my body with thine own protecting shield that foul demons may not hurl, as is their wont, their darts at my flanks, skull, head with hair and eyes, forehead, tongue, teeth and nose, neck, breast, side and reins, thighs, under-rump and two hands. To my head, with hairs on top of it, be a helmet of protection, to forehead, eyes and triformed brain, to nose, lip, face and temple, to chin, beard, eyebrows, ears, cheeks, lips, internasal septum and nares, to the round pupils, eyelids and eyelashes, gums, breath, jaws, fauces, to the teeth, tongue, mouth and throat, uvula, larynx and frenum of the tongue, to head-pan, brain and gristly, and to my neck be thou a protector in thy mercy; I beseech thee, O Lord Jesus Christ, for the nine orders of holy angels. Be thou a secure lorica both to my members and to my viscera. So that thou turn back from me the invisible points of the shafts which transfix the abhorred. Cover me then, O God, Thou strong lorica, as to my shoulders, arms and forearms; Cover arms with elbows and hands, fists, palms, fingers with nails. Cover the spine and ribs with their joints, the rear and back with nerves and bones. Cover skin, blood with kidneys, haunches and rump with thighs. Cover hams, calves and thigh parts with knuckle-bones, poplites and knees. Cover the tenfold branches [of the feet] with toes and their twice five nails. Cover ankles with shanks and heels, legs, feet, soles with insteps. Cover breast, peritoneum and breast bone, mammae, stomach and navel. Cover belly, groin, genital parts and paunch and vital parts of the heart. Cover the trifid liver and ilia, scrotum, kidneys, intestines and rete mirabile. Cover tonsils, thorax with lung, vessels, sinews, gall with pericardium. Cover flesh, groin with marrow, spleen with tortuous intestines. Cover bladder fat and all the innumerable sorts of structures. Cover hairs and the other members the names of which I have perchance omitted. Cover all of me with my five senses, and with the ten doors that were contrived [for their use], that from the soles to the top of the head in no member, without or within, may I be sick; that there may not thrust the life from my body neither pest not fever nor languor nor pain, while by God's grace I may reach old age and may wipe out my sins with good deeds, and leaving the flesh I may be blameless and may be worthy to pass on high and by God's pity I may rise happy to the refreshing ether of His Kingdom. Amen. Amen.

The laying on of hands is another procedure which was widely used in antiquity and through the Middle Ages in the Western world. It differs in one important point from most of the practices reviewed thus far: It dispenses altogether with the use of other external physical or chemical paraphernalia. Bodily contact between the patient and the healer is all that is needed. But this in itself emphasizes the paramount importance of their personal relationship.

The moving mystical and religious aspects of the ritual of the laying on of hands are illustrated by the following account of miraculous healings attributed to St. Francis of Assisi. It is taken from the compilation The Little Flowers of St. Francis of Assisi, *translated by Abby Langdon Alger.*

That true disciple of Christ, Saint Francis, living in this miserable life, with all his strength strove ever to follow Christ, the Perfect Way, whence it ofttimes befell by divine action what whereas he healed a man's body, God did heal his soul in that selfsame hour, even as we read of Christ. And inasmuch as He not only freely became the servant of Lepers, but furthermore ordered that the Brothers of his Order, whether journeying or sojourning anywhere in this world, should become the servants of lepers for the love of Christ, who for our love was fain to be held a Leper, it fell out that on a time at a Convent near which Saint Francis was then abiding, the Brethren were serving in a hospital for Lepers and infirm; in which was a Leper so peevish, so intolerable, and so arrogant that all men assuredly deemed, and so indeed it was, that he was possessed of a Devil, forasmuch as alike with words and with blows he terribly reviled all them that served him; nay, yet worse, he scandalously blasphemed against the blessed Christ and his most Holy Mother the Virgin Mary, so that none could in any wise be found who could or would serve him. And albeit the Brethren truly study meekly to endure injuries and insults to themselves, to the end that patience may have her perfect work, nevertheless, those to Christ and his Mother their consciences could not suffer, and every man among them determined to leave the said Leper: but this they would not do before they had duly declared their purpose unto Saint Francis, who was then abiding at a Convent hard by. And having signified to him their purpose, Saint Francis came unto that perverse Leper; and drawing nigh to him, he greeted him, saying: "God grant thee peace, my beloved Brother." The Leper made answer, "What peace can I have of God, Which hath robbed me of peace and of every good thing, and hath made me all corrupt and stinking?" And Saint Francis said, "Son, have patience, forasmuch as the infirmities of the body are given us of God in this world for the salvation of our soul, they being of exceeding merit when they are borne meekly." The sick man replied, "And can I endure the continual Pain that torments night and day? And not only am I afflicted by mine infirmity, but far worse do I suffer from the Brethren whom you have given me to wait upon me, and they serve me not as they should." Then Saint Francis knowing by a revelation that this Leper was possessed of an evil spirit, went out and prayed, and entreated God piously for him. And his prayer ended, he returned to him again and spake these words: "My Son, I myself will serve you, since you are ill-content with the others." "It pleaseth me well," said the sick man; "But what can you do for me more than the others?" St. Francis answered, "Whatsoever you would that I should do." Said the Leper, "I would that you wash me, every inch of me; forasmuch as so terribly I stink that I myself can ill endure it." Then Saint Francis straight commanded water to be heated with many sweet-smelling herbs; then stripping him, he began to wash him with his own hands, another Brother pouring on the water; and by a divine miracle, wheresoever Saint Francis laid his holy hands upon him the Leprosy left him and his flesh remained perfectly sound. And even as his flesh began to heal, so too his soul began to be made whole; hence the Leper seeing himself beginning to be cured, began to have great compunction and repentance for his sins, and began to weep very bitterly; for as his body was cleansed of the Leprosy from without by the washing of the water, even so his soul was cleansed of Sin from within by correction and tears. And being wholly healed, alike in body and in soul, he humbly confessed himself guilty, and cried aloud, weeping: "Woe unto me, for I am worthy of Hellfire for the injuries and insults which I have heaped upon the Brethren, and for the peevishness and blasphemy which I have manifested towards God."

The ideas underlying healing by the laying on of hands differ from culture to culture. They have, however, one thing in common: belief in a healing power which is transmitted from the person of a Christ-like healer or some royal personage through physical contact to a diseased part of the stricken person. Plutarch describes the exploits of Pyrrhus, King of Epirus, who healed colics and other illnesses by passing his toes over the bodies of patients brought before him. The Emperor Vespasian has been described as a reluctant healer in the magic tradition. Yet despite his reluctance and disbelief it is said that he cured blindness and lameness by touching patients with his saliva.

The Royal Touch as it was practiced by the kings of the medieval Christian world is a variation on the same theme. More clearly than its ancient prototype it shows the hidden psychological meaning of the ritual—the kindly king representing the image of a benevolent parent. His healing touch conveys to the patient the idea of loving care reminiscent of his childhood years. This aspect of medieval healing magic thus contains a factor well known in the modern psychotherapeutic approach, the factor described as "rapport" or psychoanalytic "transference" between patient and therapist. Whatever cures were effected by the Royal Touch were obviously due to the psychological qualities in this ancient magico-religious ritual.

Here is an account of the practice of the Royal Touch given by William of Malmesbury. It tells the story of Edward the Confessor (1042-1066) and a young woman apparently suffering from scrofula.

A young woman who had a husband about the same age as herself, but having no child got into an ill state of health by an overflowing of humors in her neck which broke out in great nobbs. She was commanded in a dream to apply to the King to wash it. So to Court she goes and the king being at his devotions all alone, dipped his fingers in water and dabbled the woman's neck and he had no sooner taken away his hand than she found herself better. The loathsome scabb dissolved but the lips of the ulcers remaining wide and open. She remained at Court till she was well which was in less than a week's time; the ulcers being so well closed, the skin so fair, that nothing of her former disease could be discovered and in less than a year's time she was brought to bed with Twins.

A special form of religious service devoted to healing by the Royal Touch was instituted in Henry VII's time and was continued down to the year 1719. It was included in the English Prayer Book until that period. The document begins:

The Ceremonies for Healing Them That Be Diseased
With the King's Evil in the Time of King Henry VII

The King shall be crossing the sore of the sick person with an angel of Gold Noble and the sick person to have the same angel hang'd about his neck and wear it until he be full whole.

Then the following prayer was to be said secretly after the sick person departed from the King, at his pleasure:

Almighty God, Ruler and Lord by whose goodness the blind see, the deaf hear, the dumb speak, the lame walk, the lepers are cleansed, and all sick persons are healed of their infirmities; by whom also the gift of healing is given to mankind and so great a grace, thro' Thine unspeakable goodness towards this Realm is granted unto the Kings thereof, that by the sole imposition of their hands a most grievous and filthy disease should be cured, mercifully grant that we may give thanks therefore for this Thy singular benefit conferred on us, not to ourselves but to Thy name, let us daily give glory and let us always exercise ourselves in piety, that we may labour not only diligently to conserve, but every day more and more to increase Thy grace bestowed upon us; And grant that on those bodies soever we have imposed hands in Thy name, thro' this Thy virtue working in them and thro' our ministry, may be restored to their former health, and being confirmed therein, may perpetually with us give thanks unto Thee, the Chief Physician and Healer of all diseases, and that henceforth they may so lead their lives, as not their bodies only from sickness but their souls also from sin may be perfectly purged and cured.

The following is a description of a ceremony of healing carried out at Whitehall in 1672:

The tickets being delivered out, His Majestie does generally appoint the day of Healing of which the Chirurgeon is to acquaint those who are to be Touch'd, the which for the most part does happen on Sundays or other days it matters not which, the effecte of his Cure being as good at one time as another. The Day being come, before his Majestie doth approach to his Royal Chair, which is generally after morning prayers, the Chief Officer of the Yeomen of the Guard doth place the sick people in very convenient order for their approaching the King without trouble or noise. The which done, His Majestie enters his Royal Chair, uncovered, at whose beginning there are generally two chaplains attending; one of which reading the ceremonies appointed for this Service, His Majestie all the while being surrounded by his Nobles and many other spectators. The Sick and Diseased people being kept back by the Chirurgeon till the appointed time, where, having made three obeisances, they do bring them up in order. The chief-in-waiting delivering them one by one to the King to be touched the which done, the other receives him or her from him, and this method is used throughout the whole number which come to be healed.

C. J. S. Thompson, who quotes this report in Magic *and* Healing, *remarks that:*

Close enquiries were made into the success of the practice by investigators at the time, some of whom were by no means believers in any actual royal virtue, but who yet admitted unhesitatingly the reality of many of the claimed cures. Some persons are said to have been cured immediately they were touched, while others did not get rid of their swellings until they had been treated a second time. Cases are related of persons who had been quite blind for several weeks and were even obliged to be led to Whitehall yet recovered their sight immediately on being "touched"; others, unable to walk, were carried on their beds and after the rite are said to have received immediate relief.

William Beckett, F.R.S., a well-known surgeon, in 1732, and Dr. Douglas, Bishop of Salisbury, in 1754, both admit that cures did result from the King's touch, and the latter states that he knew a man personally who had been healed. Beckett points out how likely it was that "the excitement of the visit to the Court both in anticipation and realization, and the impressive ceremony there conducted, would in many instances so affect the constitution, causing the blood to course through the veins more quickly as to effect a cure."

Dr. Beckett's point is certainly well taken. We shall see on a later page that some of the miraculous cures reported from Lourdes or attributed to Christian Science and other healing cults may be due to similar factors.

The late eighteenth century was a more enlightened age. It was the time which saw the growing influence of Hume's skeptical philosophy upon the English speaking world. It was the era of the German Aufklaerung or Enlightenment, which culminated in Kant's monumental Critique *of* Pure Reason. *It was the age of Voltaire, Diderot and the Encyclopedists, who paved the way for the holocaust of the French revolution. And it was certainly a period when kings, once they happened to incite the wrath of their disillusioned subjects, were apt to lose not only their healing powers but also their heads.*

Yet the need for a magic shortcut to health and happiness remained un-diminished on both sides of the English Channel. While Anton Mesmer (see chapter 17) the discoverer of so-called animal magnetism, attracted an increasing number of patients to the darkened rooms of his clinic in Paris, James Graham, a self-styled doctor of medicine, opened his Temple of Health in London. Conceived in the traditions of an ancient shrine, it was equipped with an electrical throne and a metal cylinder, the source of "vivifying celestial fires" and magnetic vapors. All this was claimed to cure various illnesses—sterility among them. In addition it promised to insure the health and bounty of the patient's offspring.

The most important furnishings of Dr. Graham's Temple of Health was his Celestial Bed, which he described in the following way:

The Grand Celestial Bed, whose magical influences are now celebrated from pole to pole and from the rising to the setting of the sun, is twelve feet long by nine feet wide, supported by forty pillars of brilliant glass of the most exquisite workmanship, in richly variegated colours.

The super-Celestial Dome of the bed which contains the odoriferous balmy and ethereal spices, odours and essences, which is the grand reservoir of those reviving and invigorating influences which are exhaled by the breath of the music and by the accelerating force of electrical fire, is covered on the other side with brilliant panes of looking glass.

On the upmost summit of the dome are placed two exquisite figures of Cupid and Psyche, with a figure of Hymen behind, with his torch flaming with electrical fire in one hand, and with the other, supporting a celestial crown sparkling over a pair of great living turtledoves, on a little bed of roses.

The other elegant groups of figures which sport on the top of the dome having each of them musical instruments in their hands, which by the most expensive mechanism, breathe forth sounds corresponding to their instruments, flutes, guitars, violins, clarinets, trumpets, horns, oboes, kettledrums, etc.

The post or pillars, too, which support the grand dome, are groups of musical instruments, organ pipes, etc., which in sweet concert, breathe forth celestial sounds, lulling with visions of Elysian joys.

At the head of the bed appears sparkling with electrical fire the great first commandment: "Be fruitful, multiply and replenish the earth"; Under that is an elegant sweet-toned organ in the front of which is a fine landscape of moving figures, priests, brides and a fine procession entering the Temple of Hymen.

In some respects the magic of James Graham's establishment is indeed reminiscent of ancient shrines and the healing powers attributed to sleeping

*in the precincts of a Greek or Egyptian temple. In other respects Dr.
Graham was far ahead of his time. He charged five hundred guineas for one
night's occupancy of his Celestial Bed.*

*Our next selection illustrates still another aspect of the magic approach. It
is an approach in which the magic element is concealed under a cloak of
pseudo-scientific, essentially alchemistic and astrological concepts that still
flourished in the late seventeenth century. Sir Kenelm Digby (1603-1665)
emphatically disavowed his adherence to primitive demonology and other
medieval superstitions. Author, seafarer, courtier and chief protagonist of
the* Powder of Sympathy, *he regarded himself as a man of science and
sought to account for the striking properties of his remedy in what he considered purely rationalistic terms.*

What is the Powder of Sympathy? *Digby describes it as a concoction of
copper sulfate and other ingredients prepared according to various alch-
mistic and astrological formulas. As its most astonishing property he
claimed the capacity to heal wounds at a distance. Digby states that the
formula of the powder was handed to him by an anonymous Carmelite
monk who had brought it to the west from Persia or India. One thing Sir
Kenelm Digby fails to mention in his report is the fact that the great Ren-
naissance physician Theophrastus Bombastus Paracelsus (see chapter 14)
had employed a similar remedy, his celebrated* Weapon Salve, *some hundred years before. It was credited with the same magic properties as Digby's*
Powder of Sympathy. *In effect, both are direct derivatives from a long line
of magic remedies whose effect depends largely on psychological factors:
on the faith in their efficacy of those using them.*

*Whether or not an added, conceivably telepathic, factor was involved in
their claimed action must remain an open question. R. Amadou, in a recent
study devoted to the* Powder of Sympathy, *is inclined to believe in the operation of such a factor. Other scholars have offered a more pedestrian explanation. The treatment of wounds in the times of Paracelsus and Digby
consisted of dressing them with such dubious materials as dried cow's dung,
mummy's powder or preparations made from powderized toads. The result
was the dreaded secondary infection of wounds. Little wonder that any
treatment at a distance was superior to the local mistreatment of wounds
according to the precepts of the medieval dirt-pharmacy.*

*The following are excerpts from Sir Kenelm Digby's Address to the Uni-
versity of Montpellier in a translation by R. White (London, 1658).*

A LATE DISCOURSE
MADE IN A SOLEMNE ASSEMBLY OF NOTABLES AND
LEARNED MEN AT MONTPELLIER IN FRANCE
By Sir Kenelm Digby, Knight And C.

Touching the Cure of Wounds by the Powder of Sympathy;
with Information how to Make the Said Powder;
Whereby May Other Secrets of Nature Are Unfolded

. . . I should be very sorry, that having dome my uttermost to make it clear, how the Powder which they call the Powder of Sympathy, doth naturally, and without any magick, cure wounds without handling them, yea, without seeing of the patient; I say I should be very sorry that it should be doubted, whether such a cure may effectually be performed or no.

In matter of fact, the determination of existence, and truth of a thing, depends upon the report which our senses make us. This businesse is of that nature; for they who have seen the effects, and had experience thereof, and have been careful to examine all the necessary circumstances, and satisfied themselves afterwards, that there is no imposture in the thing, do nothing doubt but that it is real, and true. But they who have not seen such experiences, ought to referre themselves to the Narrations, and authority of such, who have seen such things; I could produce divers, whereof I was an ocular witness, nay, *Quorum pars magna fui*: But as a certain, and an averred example in the affirmative, is convincing to determine the possibility, and truth of a matter which is doubtful: I shall content myself, because I would not trespass too much upon your patience at this time, to make instance in one only; but it shall be one of the clearest, the most perspicuous, publick, & the most averred that can be, not only for the remarkable circumstances thereof, but also for the hands, which are above the Vulgar, through which the whole businesse passed. For the cure of a very sore hurt was perfected by this Powder of Sympathie, upon a *person* that is famous, as well for his Learning, as for his severall imployments. All the circumstances were examined, and sounded to the bottom, by one of the greatest, and most knowing Kings of his time, viz. King *James*, of *England*, who had a particular talent, and marvellous sagacity, to discuss natural things, and penetrate them to the very bottom; as also by his Son, the late King *Charles*, and the late Duke of *Buckingham*, their prime Minister. And in fine, all was registered among the observations of the great *Chancelor Bacon*, to be added by the way of Appendix, unto his Naturall History. And I believe, Sirs, when you shall have understood this History, you will not accuse me of vanity, if I attribute unto my self the introducing into this Quarter of the World this way of curing. Now the businesse was thus.

Mr. *James Howel*, (well known in *France*, by his Writings, and particularly by his Dendrologia, translated into French by *Monsieur Baudoin*) coming by chance as two of his best friends were fighting in Duel, he did his endeavour to part them, and putting himself between them, seized with his left hand upon the hilt of the sword of one of the Combatants, while with his right hand he laid hold of the blade of the other: they being transported with fury one against the other, strugled to rid themselves of the hindrance their friend made that they should not kill one another; and one of them roughly drawing the blade of his sword, cuts to the very bone the nerves, the muscles, and tendons of Mr. *Howels* hand; and then the other disingaging his hilts, gave a crosse blow on his adversaries head, which glanced towards his friend, who heaving up his sore hand to save the blow, he was wounded on the back of his hand, as he had been before within. It seems some strange Constellation reigned then against him, that he should lose so much blood by parting two such dear friends, who had they been themselves, would have hazarded both their lives to have preserved his: but this unvoluntary effusion of blood by them, prevented that which they should have drawn one from the other: For they seeing Mr. *Howels* face besmeared with blood, by heaving up his wounded hand, they both ran to embrace him; and having searched his hurts, they bound up his hand with one of his garters, to close the veines which were cut, and bled abundantly. They brought him home, and sent for a Surgeon. But this being heard at Court, the King sent one of his own Surgeons, for his Majesty much affected the said Mr. *Howel*.

It was my chance to be lodged hard by him; and four or five dayes after, as I was making my self ready, he came to my House, and prayed me to view his wounds, for I understand, said he, that you have extraordinary remedies upon such occasions, and my Surgeons apprehend some fear, that it may grow to a Gangrene, and so the hand must be cut off. In effect, his countenance discovered that he was in much pain, which he said was unsupportable, in regard of the extream inflammation: I told him that I would willingly serve him, but if haply he knew the manner how I would cure him, without touching or seeing him, it may be he would not expose himself to my manner of curing, because he would think it peradventure either ineffectual, or superstitious: he replied, "That the wonderful things which many have related unto me, of your way of curing, makes me nothing doubt at all of its efficacy; and all that I have to say unto you, is comprehended in the Spanish Proverb, *Hagafe el milagro, y hagalo Mahoma*, Let the miracle be done though *Mahomet* do it."

I asked him then for any thing that had the blood upon it, so he presently sent for his Garter, wherewith his hand was first bound: and having called for a Bason of water, as if I would wash my hands; I took a handful of Powder of Vitrol, which I had in my study, and presently dissolved it. As soon as the bloody garter was brought me, I put it within the Bason, observing in the interim what Mr. *Howel* did, who stood talking with a Gentleman in a corner of my Chamber, not regarding at all what I was doing: but he started suddenly, as if he had found some strange alteration in himself; I asked him what he ailed? I know not what ailes me, but I find that I feel no more pain, methinks that a pleasing kind of freshnesse, as it were a wet cold Napkin did spread over my hand, which hath taken away the inflammation that tormented me before; I replyed, since that you feel already so good an effect of my medicament, I advise you to cast away all your playsters onely keep the wound clean, and in a moderate temper twixt heat and cold. This was presently reported to the Duke of *Buckingham*, and a little after to the King, who were both very curious to know the issue of the businesse, which was, that after dinner I took the garter out of the water, and put it to dry before a great fire; it was scarce dry, but Mr. *Howels* servant came running, and told me, that his Master felt as much burning as ever he had done, if not more, for the heat was such, as if his hand were twixt coales of fire: I answered, that although that had happened at present, yet he should find ease in a short time; for I knew the reason of this new accident, and I would provide accordingly, for his Master should be free from that inflammation, it may be, before he could possibly return unto him: but in case he found no ease, I wished him to come presently back again, otherwise, he might forbear coming. Thereupon he went, and at the instant I did put again the garter into the water; thereupon he found his Master without any pain at all. To be brief, there was no sense of pain afterward; but within five or six days the wounds were cicatrized, and entirely healed. King *James* required a punctuall information of what had passed touching this cure: and after it was done and perfected, his Majesty would needs know of me how it was done, having drolled with me first (which he could do with a very good grace) about a Magician and a Sorcerer. . . .

Behold now, Sirs, the Genealogie of the Powder of Sympathy in this part of the World, with a notable History of a cure performed by it. It is time now to come to the discussion, which is, to know how it is made. It must be avowed that it is a marvellous thing, that the hurt of a wounded person should be cured by the application of a remedy put to a rag of cloth, or a weapon, at a great distance. And it is not to be doubted, if after a long and profound speculation of all the oeconomy and concatenation of naturall Causes, which may be adjudged capable to produce such effects, one may fall at last upon the true causes which must have subtill resorts and means to act. Hitherto they have been wrapped up in darknesse, and adjudged so inaccessible, that they who have undertaken to speak or write of them (at least those whom I saw) have been contented to speak of some ingenious gentilenesse, without diving into the bottom, endeavouring rather to show the vivacity of their spirit, and the force of their eloquence, than to satisfie their Readers and Auditors how the thing is really to be done. They would have us take for ready mony some terms which we understand not, nor know what they signifie. They would pay us with conveniences, with re-semblances, with Sympathies, with Magnetical virtues, and such terms, without explicating what these terms mean. They think they have done enough, if they feebly perswade any body that the businesse may be per-formed by a naturall way, without having any recourse to the intervention of Daemons and spirits: but they pretend not in any sort to have found out the convincing reasons, to demonstrate how the thing is done. . . .

. . . 'Tis an ordinary thing, when one finds himself burnt as in the hand, he holds it a good while as near the fire as he can, and by this means the ig-nited atomes of the fire, and of the hand mingling together, and drawing one another, and the stronger of the two, which are those of the fire, having the mastery, the hand finds it self much eased of the inflammation which it suffered. 'Tis an ordinary remedy, though a nasty one, that they who have ill breaths hold their mouths open at the mouth of a Privy, as long as they can, and by the reiteration of this remedy, they find themselves cured at last, the greater stink of the Privy drawing unto it, and carrying away the lesse, which is that of the mouth. They who have been pricked, or bit by a Viper, or Scorpion, hold over the bitten, or prickled place, the head of a Viper or Scorpion bruised, and by this means the poyson, by a kind of fil-tration, going on to gaine the heart of the party, returns back to its prin-ciples, and so leaves the party well recovered. In time of common contag-ion, they use to carry about them the powder of a toad, and sometimes a living toad or spider shut up in a box; or else they carry Arsnick, or some other venomous substance, which draws unto it the contagious air, which otherwise would infect the party: and the same powder of a toad draws unto it the poyson of a plague-soar. . . .

It is hard to think of Sir Kenelm Digby as a contemporary of Galileo, Kepler and Descartes. The only way they seem to have affected his work was to make him couch his magical beliefs in a cloak of pseudo-scientific phraseology. Otherwise his Discourse is a typical example of the survival of magic in the midst of the newly awakened scientific spirit of his age. Never-theless, his colorful personality, his suave manners and his fanatical faith in his remedy had a powerful impact upon his contemporaries—and some of this impact may well have been therapeutic. In this respect we find him in direct line of descent from the primitive medicine man.

At the same time he is, however, a forerunner of a long line of healers, self-styled or genuine, who grope for new and unorthodox cures of mental and physical ailments. The Mesmerists, homeopaths, absent-healers and other cultists of the past and present may owe more to Sir Kenelm's Powder *of sympathy than they like to realize—or to admit. He is in effect one of the forerunners of modern placebo research and placebo therapy.*

chapter 4

Healing Magic in
Sleep and Dream

THE TABLETS OF EPIDAURUS . . .
ARTEMIDORUS OF DALDIS . . .
THE NAVAHO MEDICINE MAN'S INTERPRETATION
OF DREAMS

Civilizations in a state of transition from magic to a more empirical orientation regard magic as no longer the rule but the exception. They relegate magic to such extraordinary psychological states as sleep, trance or ecstasy. This principle is illustrated by the sacred shrines of ancient Greece, dedicated to Apollo or Asclepius, and by the Oracles of Delphi and Dodona.

The healing powers of the Temple of Epidaurus were held in particularly high esteem. Pilgrims attending the shrine first went through a ritual of fasting, ablutions and communal prayers. Subsequently they were made to fall asleep in the temple and asked to relate their dreams to the officiating priest. The dream itself was regarded as a source of higher revelation, containing clues to the necessary treatment.

The quotations below contain graphic accounts of cure attributed to the shrine. They are taken from votive tablets found among the remains of the Temple of Epidaurus.

A man whose fingers, with the exception of one, were paralyzed, came as a supplicant to the god. While looking at the tablets in the temple he expressed incredulity regarding the cures and scoffed at the inscriptions. But in his sleep he saw a vision. It seemed to him that, as he was playing at dice below the Temple and was about to cast the dice, the god appeared, sprang upon his hand, and stretched out his [the patient's] fingers. When the god had stepped aside it seemed to him [the patient] that he [the patient] bent his hand and stretched out all his fingers one by one. When he had straightened them all the god asked him if he would still be incredulous of the inscriptions on the tablets in the Temple. He answered that he would not. "Since, then, formerly you were incredulous of the cures, though they were not incredible, for the future," he said, "your name shall be 'Incredulous.'" When day dawned he walked out sound.

Ambrosia of Athens, blind of one eye. She came as a supplicant to the god. As she walked about in the Temple she laughed at some of the cures as incredible and impossible, that the lame and the blind should be healed by merely seeing a dream. In her sleep she had a vision. It seemed to her that the god stood by her and said that he would cure her, but that in payment he would ask her to dedicate to the Temple a silver pig as a memorial of her ignorance. After saying this, he cut the diseased eyeball and poured in some drug. When day came she walked out sound.

A voiceless boy. He came as a supplicant to the Temple for his voice. When he had performed the preliminary sacrifices and fulfilled the usual rites, thereupon the temple servant who brings in the fire for the god, looking at the boy's father, demanded he should promise to bring within a year the thank-offering for the cure if he obtained that for which he had come. But the boy suddenly said, "I promise." His father was startled at this and asked him to repeat it. The boy repeated the words and after that became well.

Pandarus, a Thessalian, who had marks on his forehead. He saw a vision as he slept. It seemed to him that the god bound the marks round with a headband and enjoined him to remove the band when he left the Abaton and dedicate it as an offering to the Temple. When day came he got up and took off the band and saw his face free of the marks; and he dedicated to the Temple the band with the signs which had been on his forehead.

Echedorus received the marks of Pandarus in addition to those which he already had. He had received money from Pandarus to offer to the god at Epidaurus in his name, but he failed to deliver it. In his sleep he saw a vision. It seemed to him that the god stood by him and asked if he had received any money from Pandarus to set up as an offering an Athena in the Temple. He answered that he had received no such thing from him, but if he [the god] would make him well he would have an image painted and offer it to him [the god]. Thereupon the god seemed to fasten the headband of Pandarus round his marks, and ordered him upon leaving the Abaton to take off the band and to wash his face at the fountain and to look at himself in the water. When day came he left the Abaton, took off the headband, on which the signs were no longer visible. But when he looked into the water he saw his face with his own marks and the signs of Pandarus in addition.

Euphanes, a boy of Epidaurus. Suffering from stone he slept in the temple. It seemed to him that the god stood by him and asked: "What will you give me if I cure you?" "Ten dice," he answered. The god laughed and said to him that he would cure him. When day came he walked out sound.

The following account is a good example of the combination of magic with more or less rational methods of treatment as they are practiced in many healing shrines throughout antiquity.

In the Priesthood of Poplius Aelius Antiochus

I, Marcus Julius Appelas, an Idrian from Mylasa, was sent for by the god, for I was often falling into sickness and was suffering from dyspepsia. In the course of my journey, in Aegina, the god told me not to be so irritable. When I arrived at the temple, he told me for two days to keep my head covered, and for these two days it rained; to eat cheese and bread, celery with lettuce, to wash myself, without help, to practice running, to take lemon-peels, to soak them in water, near the [spot of the] *akoai* in the bath to press against the wall, to take a walk in the upper portico, to take some passive exercise, to sprinkle myself with sand, to walk around barefoot, in the bathroom, before plunging into the hot water, to pour wine over myself, to bathe without help and to give an Attic drachma to the bath attendant, in common to offer sacrifice to Asclepius, Epione and the Eleusinian goddesses, to take milk with honey. When one day I had drunk milk alone he said, "Put honey in the milk so that it can get through." When I asked of the god to relieve me more quickly I thought I walked out of the Abaton near the [spot of the] *akoai* being anointed all over with mustard and salt, while a small boy was leading me holding a smoking censer, and the priest said: "You are cured but you must pay up with thank-offerings." And I did what I had seen, and when I anointed myself with the salts and the moistened mustard I felt pains, but when I bathed I had no pain. That happened within nine days after I had come. He touched my right hand and also my breast. The following day as I was offering sacrifice the flame leapt up and scorched my hand, so that blisters appeared. Yet after a little the hand got well. As I stayed on he said I should use dill along with olive oil against my headaches. I usually did not suffer from headaches. But it happened that after I had studied, my head was congested. After I used the olive oil I got rid of the headache. To gargle with a cold gargle for the uvula—since about that too I had consulted the god—and the same also for the tonsils. He bade me also inscribe this. Full of gratitude I departed well.

The Interpretation of Dreams *by Artemidorus of Daldis is an example of attempts at divining the secret meaning of dreams, which had wide currency at the time of the Emperor Hadrian. The book itself is generally considered a compilation of earlier works, but it gives, in the words of the Encyclopedia Britannica, "valuable insight into ancient superstitions." Artemidorus himself appears as the Sophist of Cnidos in Shakespeare's tragedy, warning Caesar of Brutus and Cassius:*

> *If thou read this, O Caesar, thou mayst live;*
> *If not, the fates with traitors do contrive.*

There is, however, another reason to include Artemidorus's book in this anthology. His work was one of the sources which inspired Freud in writing his Interpretation of Dreams. *Indeed, Artemidorus's "ancient superstitions" had by no means lost their hold over the mind of Western man in the course of centuries. R. Wood, his translator, a contemporary of Shakespeare, introduces Artemidorus as follows:*

To the Reader

Some Authors are of Opinion that dreams arise of natural and carnal affection; but our Author Artemidorus, doth not agree with them, but saith Dreams of an Importance come of God. In the Holy Scripture we have experience both in the Old and New Testament: Joseph and son of Jacob, and Joseph the Husband of the Virgin Mary; and St. Peter in the Acts; repeateth the prophecy of Joel, whereby he sheweth that it was god sent Visions and Dreams.

In ancient histories you may see much of the issues and experience of Dreams: Hecuba, Queen of Troy, when with child of Paris, dreamed that she should bring forth a firebrand, that should consume the whole country, which proved true; for the said Paris, of whom she was delivered, was the cause of the burning Troy; which was interpreted by his sister Cassandra, to whom they gave no credit: Whereupon the mischief seized not only the King and Queen, father and mother to the said Paris, but the whole Kingdom whose miserable destruction is recorded to this day. Also Socrates, Cicero, Hannibal, Calphurnia, and many others, had Dreams and Visions by night, and their effects came to pass as divers histories do verify.

And it seemeth great arrogance in any man to say all Visions and Dreams are of none effect; which hath already been proved false, by many histories both divine and human.

I doubt not but some persons, when they read this book, will think it a frivolous thing; for I, before I had considered it, thought as much; but after I had compared these things with experience, I could not but reverence and admire the Author. And therefore I commit it to thy perusal, and rest,

Thy loving Friend,

R. Wood

The following passage is an exposition of Artemidorus's theory of dreams as paraphrased by Wood in 1644:

ARTEMIDORUS

His Exposition of Dreams

Dreams and Visions are infused into men for their advantage and instruction. And both sacred and prophane Histories furnish such a variety of examples concerning the true event of Dreams, that it would argue incredulity and ignorance not to credit them. Hippocrates is of opinion, that whilst the body sleeps, the spirit is awake, and transported to all places where the body could have access; and it sees and knows all things which the body could know and see when awake, and touches all that it could touch: In short, that it hath all the operations that the body, now asleep, can be capable of when awake.

There are Five Sorts of Dreams, that have different qualities. The first is a Dream: The second a Vision: The third an Oracle: The fourth a Phantasy or vain Imagination: The fifth an Apparition.

That is called a Dream which discovers the truth under a hidden figure; as when Joseph interpreted Pharaoh's Dream of the seven lean kine that should devour the seven fat ones, and the same of the ears of corn, &c.

A Vision is this: When a man really sees awake, what he did asleep; as it happened to Vespatian, when he saw the Surgeon that drew out Nero's tooth.

An Oracle is a revelation or advertisement made to us in our sleep by some Angel, or other Saint, to perform God's will according to their informations; as it happened to Joseph, the husband of the Holy Virgin, and the Three Wise Men.

The Phantasy, or vain Imagination, happens in that instant when the affections are so vehement that they ascend up to the brain during our sleep, and meet the more watchful spirits; thus what the thoughts are employed about in the day, we fancy in the night; so a lover, who in the day-time thinks on his fair-one, in the night when asleep meets with the same thoughts. It happens also, that he that fasts all day, dreams at night that he is feeding; or if thirsty in the day-time, in the night time he dreams of drinking, and is very much delighted with it. And the miser and usurer dream of bags, nay, will discourse of them in their sleep.

An Apparition is not other than a nocturnal Vision that presents itself to weak infants and ancient men, who fancy they see chimeras approaching to intimidate or offend them.

There are Two principal kinds of Dreams: First, Speculative or Contemplative. The Second is Allegorical or Figurative.

Speculative Dreams have an immediate event; but the Allegorical not so soon, for there is a day or two between a Dream and the event thereof.

Sometimes there are Dreams which cannot possibly happen; as when you dream that you fly, have horns, go down into Hell, and the like:—These are Allegorical, and carry a different signification.

Dreams are proportioned according to the condition of the party dreaming. Thus those of eminent persons, will be great, as, if good, they signify great benefit, and, on the contrary, great misery. If the party that dreams be of a mean condition, the dreams, with their events, will be mean also; if poor, their dreams will be very inconsiderable; for the rules of dreaming are not general, and therefore cannot satisfy all persons, seeing they often, according to times and persons, admit of various interpretations.

And thus, having given a short History of the variety of Dreams, will proceed accordingly.

In some respects this "Exposition of Dreams" has a modern ring, as when Artemidorus remarks that the hungry and thirsty may dream of food and drink, while the miser's dream life is full of money bags. Still more significant is the general belief held in ancient times—from Plato to Artemidorus —that the deeper, symbolic meaning of dreams is not accessible to the dreamer himself. This is why the professional interpreter had to come to his aid. Unfortunately, in trying to unravel the hidden meaning of what psychoanalysis today calls the manifest content of the dream, the primitive dream interpreter was apt to bring in his own associations instead of the dreamer's. Needless to say, in doing so he was bound to miss the crucial point of modern dream interpretation. A further factor discrediting his method—at least in modern eyes—was his implied belief in the divinatory or veridical aspects of dreams. Yet if more recent reports of apparently telepathic or precognitive dreams by a number of psychiatrists are further substantiated our current views may well be in need of revision (see chapter 24).

Be that as it may, the following samples from Artemidorus's book show that despite the few grains of truth contained in it, a deep gulf exists between ancient and modern approaches to dream interpretation:

Of Births

If any one dreams that he comes out of a woman's belly, as to be born into the world, it is good for him that he is poor, for he shall have many friends, who will maintain him: But if rich, it signifieth that he shall have no rule in his house, but be governed by others. To a sick man it signifies death.

He that dreams he comes out of his mother's womb, will in a short time be free from some unlucky business, and raised to preferment.

If any one dreams he re-enters his mother's womb, if he be in remote parts, that denotes a speedy return into his native country.

If a man dreams he is big with child, that signifies wealth, gain, and profit, which will soon fall to him.

If a man dreams his wife is big with child, and that it really proves so, it a sign the child will live and that he will have a son that resembles the father.

To him whose wife is not with child, it signifieth that he shall lose his wife.

When a man dreams he sees a woman brought to bed, that denotes unto him joy and prosperity.

He that dreams he sees two or three children born, shall have cause of joy and success in his business.

If a woman dreams she is delivered of a child, and yet is not big with child, it is a sign she will happily accomplish her designs.

If a maid has the same dream, it signifies banquetting, joy, revelling, and nuptials; and sometimes fear and grief to the mother. . . .

Of Actions of Men and Women

Flying. To dream of flying a little height from the earth, being upright, is good, for as much as one is lifted higher than those that are about him, so much the greater and more happy shall he be. It were better for him not to be in his own country, for it signifieth wandering, or not resting, or returning to his country. To fly with wings, is good generally for all. To fly very high from the earth, and without wings, is fear and danger. To fly over the houses, and through the streets and forlorn ways, is trouble and sedition. To fly into Heaven, is for servants to enter into rich houses, and especially the Court. To those which would be secret, it is ill. To fly with the birds, is to keep company with strangers, and pain and punishment to malefactors. It is always good, after having flown on high, to descend low, and after that to awake: But it is best of all to fly when one will, and come down when one will; for it is a sign of faculty and good disposition in affairs. But to fly by constraint, or being pursued by men, spirits, or beasts, is not good; for they are great uneasiness and dangers. To fly backwards is not ill to these that would sail; for commonly in a ship which goeth her course without tempest, the people take their ease, and lie backward; to others it is for want of work and business; for those which be so, are idle; to the sick, it is death. It is very ill to desire to fly and cannot; or to fly with the head lowermost, and the feet upwards; and in what kind soever the sick fly it is death. To fly is ill to those which have a trade that requireth no removing out of his place; but it is good for captives. To fly in a chair or bed, or being set in any under prop for the better sustaining of himself, is great sickness; but it is not so ill to him that should travel; for it is a sign that he should travel with his family, with his tools and moveables, in a cart or coach.

Running. To run is good to all except to sick persons; for when they dream they come well to the end of their race, it signifieth that shortly they shall come to the end of their life.

Riding. To dream you ride a horse nimbly, is good for all. To ride a horse through a town is good for a sick man; for he shall be healed; but to ride out of town is quite contrary. To dream of riding a wild horse, if he be able to govern him, and to keep the saddle, is good; for this dream signifies rule and dignity; but if he fall, or be thrown out of the saddle, it is ill, and signifieth disgrace, dishonour or reproach. To lead or guide chariots through woods and deserts, signifieth death to all at hand. To ride in a cart signifieth to a sick person death; as also to ride in a chariot of four wheels.

Carrying or being carried. To carry another, is better than to be carried, as it is more honour to give than to take: For he which carrieth represents him which doth good; and he which is carried, him which receiveth. To be carried by a woman, a child, or a poor person, is means of profit and support. It is good for a servant to be carried by his master, and for the mean man to be carried by the rich.

Travelling. If any one dream that he is travelling through a wood, and that he sticketh in the briars and bushes, this dream is evil, for it betokeneth many troubles and hindrances in important affairs. Also to travel over high hills and mountains, and rocky places, signifieth advancement, but with much difficulty obtained; notwithstanding, if he meet with any one that seemeth to direct him the right way, it betokeneth some friends that will be helpers to him.

Fighting. To dream of fighting with any one, is ill to all men; for besides shame, he shall have hurt. Likewise it signifieth much strife and contention: And to be wounded in fight betokeneth shame and dishonour. Notwithstanding it is good for such as live by blood-shed, as surgeons, butchers, and cooks.

Also fighting signifieth noise or lawsuits, which resemble the pains and labour of the combatants: Sometimes this dream hath foretold marriages.

Fighting, with friends or strangers, is not good: But to the sick it shall be danger of raving and loss of sense. To fight with great personages, as Kings, Princes, or Magistrates, is very bad. To dream to hate, or be hated, whether of friends or enemies, is ill; for one may have need of friendship of all the world.

Gaming. To dream to play at Dice, is noise and debate for money; but it is always good to win: To the sick it is ill if one gives over in play. The Dice or Tables simply seen in a dream is sedition and noise; but loss of them is end of noise and sedition. To see a child play at Dice is not ill. To a perfect man, it is ill to play at Dice, except he hopes for some succession by the death of another, for the Dice are made of the bones of the dead.

To dream that you play at Chess, is gain by lying and deceit. To see another play, is, that he shall sustain loss by cheating.

Drinking. To dream of drinking cold water, is good to all; but hot, signifieth sickness and hindrance of affairs. To drink wine with reason, and not to be drunk, is good. But to drink too much, and without reason, signifieth much evil. To drink sweet wine, or to see fair women, or to sleep under shady trees, to him that would take a wife betokeneth a good success in love. All compounded wines, and potions mingled otherwise than naturally, are good for rich men, because of their delicacy; but it is evil for poor folks, which never drink them but in sickness. To drink urine, signifieth sickness. To drink oil signifieth poison or sickness. To thirst and find no drink, neither in wells, fountains, or rivers, is ill; and a sign not to finish his business; but to find drink is good.

The Conclusion of Our Author, Artemidorus, Upon His Book of Dreams

If peradventure any of those who shall have had my book in their hands suppose that I have put any thing therein which I have not known by experience, he abuseth himself. Moreover if any one hath an opinion contrary to any speech by me recited, because it shall have (as I think) some probability; he must know for answer, that I know already that he will find whereof to speak, and that which shall be very likely, which I myself can set also: But I seek not to complain, as those which seek applause or favour at theatres, or which do their words to sale. But always I call to witness for me Experience and the rule of Reason: Wherefore I have set down nothing at all but what I have gained (with much travel and industry) by experience. For I have done no other thing day and night, but meditate and spent my spirit in the judgment and Interpretation of Dreams. But I must request one little favour of the Reader, that he would neither add nor diminish any thing of my present work. If any one thinks that he can add, he may as well make another book: If he thinks any thing superfluous, let him use only that which he shall find good, leaving the rest for others.

I therefore desire all courteous Readers, who are desirous to peruse my book, not to accuse or blame it before they have diligently read and understood it; for I am confident, and dare affirm with great security, that my book will not be rejected by the learned and judicious, nor by those who are either studious, diligent, or friendly Readers.

Certain Examples of Dreams, With Their Effects Which Followed

A man dreamt that he drank Mustard so well stampt, and so clear, that it was potable: It fell out that one practised and coined a certain accusation in case of a crime of manslaughter, wherewith he was so well charged, and so attained to the quick, that he received Sentence of Death and was executed by Justice.

Another man dreamt, that the water of the River Xanthus, which is near Troy the Great, was all changed into blood: (A dream very fearful and marvellous.) What then fell out: He cast blood at divers times for ten years together, and died thereof: By which appears, that great Rivers stay not, but continue and hold their course.

A man dreamt that his cushion or feather-bed was full of corn instead of feathers. He had a wife which never before had any child, and that year conceived and bare him a son.

Another dreamt he lighted a candle at the moon, and he became blind: For he dreamt a thing impossible: Besides the moon hath no light of her own.

A woman dreamt that she saw within the moon three images, or resemblances like herself: She bare three daughters, which in a month died; for a moon hath a month's life.

A man dreamt he saw his image or representation in the moon, and he made long voyages, wandering this way and that way a long time: For the continual change of the moon signified that he should often change his place and habitation.

A man dreamt his privy members were of massy iron; and he had afterwards a son, by whom he was slain; for iron by its own rust consumes itself.

A man dreamt an Olive-tree came out of his head; and he followed the study of philosophy with great courage and got everlasting knowledge and honour: For this is a tree always green and sound, and by all dedicated to the Goddess Minerva, reputed the Goddess of Wisdom.

Another dreamt that from his stomach there came ears of corn, and there was one which plucked them out: He had two sons which soon after him died.

One dreaming on a time by mischance he slipped into a pit of water, whereupon forthwith the small of his leg was turned into white marble, and after a while deceased of a dropsy. Who sees not by this plain example that

recourse of waterish humours to the weakest part had made a certain coldness and stiffness in the place, which the party felt more easily in sleep, for
divers reasons which before have been declared.

Another dreaming that he swam against a bloody stream, was cured of a
pleurisy.

Another dreaming that he appeared all on fire, like Hercules's furies upon
a stage, fell that very day into a burning fever.

One dreaming over night, before he should run at Olympus, that he was
an eagle, met with an interpreter, who concluded hereupon, because an
eagle was the prince and leader of all birds, he should prevail. Another took
not so great hold upon the quality and kind of the bird, which shews a
courage to attempt; as of his place in coming after all the flock. Which declares a kind of heavy metal, with want of agility.

*Belief that dreams contain clues as to the proper way of treatment can be
found all over the world, from classical antiquity to the present. The following example comes right from the doorstep of our culture. It is an account of a white man's dream interpreted by a Navaho medicine man. The
story is taken from Jackson S. Lincoln's dissertation on* The Dream in Primitive Culture.

The dreamer went to the medicine man's *hogan* hut in the heart of the
Navaho reservation in Arizona and seated on a sheepskin before the central
fire he told him his dream.

The Dreamer: "I dreamed of a very large egg made of a hard rocky substance. I cracked open the egg and out flew a young but full-grown eagle. It
was indoors and the eagle flew all around trying to fly out but it could not
get out because the window was shut."

The Interpretation: "The eagle belongs to the bird group of the higher
spirits which is one of a group of three allied spirits, namely, the wind,
the lightning and the birds, all of which live on the top of San Francisco
mountain. These spirits can wreak great havoc and destruction when offended. They can also be friendly. The eagle cannot fly out because you
must have offended the bird spirit, possibly by walking on its nest, or perhaps your father had committed the offense."

The Dreamer then offered the old man a polished abalone shell as a gift.
The latter turned it over and over murmuring something about the wide
water from which it came, said, "That is what I need, thank you!" After this
simple expression of appreciation he requested to have sent him for his
medicine collection a certain fleshy growth to be secured from the groin of a
beaver dried in the sun. Following a long pause he mentioned that sometimes white doctors had cure Indians where medicine men had failed, and

Indian medicine men had cured white men where the white doctors had failed, and suggested that the dreamer return on the following day and he would hold a medicine "sing" to appease the offended spirit, and give the dreamer as a cure for bad dreams a medicine drink to be drunk from the abalone shell.

Returning the next day, the dreamer seated himself on the left of the old man in the hogan. There ensued a period of silence before the latter announced his opinion that there was no reverence any more for the great spirits and because of that, the great destructive forces like the whirlwind were let loose. After a simple meal the dreamer was told that the bad dream would be cured before nightfall and that he would be given full rights as a Navaho which would be necessary in order that the medicine be effective. The eagle "sing" was chosen to be sung in order to "blow away the wings" and release the eagle spirit of the dream. . . . Communion with the eagle spirit having once been established the song went on at the same high pitch of intensity, and he turned toward the dreamer with the bundle of eagle feathers and struck him with them on the head, the hands, the abdomen, the knees and the feet. Some of the herb-sprinkled water from the gourd was offered to the dreamer to drink, followed by a similar drink from the abalone shell. From the shell some of the aromatic smelling liquid was poured on his hands and rubbed on his face and hair, and he was instructed to look up toward the smoke hole and blow hard, to "blow away the wings of the eagle spirit on the wind." Four times he was struck with the feathers, and four times he took the curing drinks, and four times he blew up toward the smoke hole. At this point in the ceremony, the nature and tone of the singing changed and took on a lighter, airy, more released quality, and seemed to have the joyous sound of a bird soaring, flying to freedom.

"It is gone," said Nanai (the medicine man) when he stopped singing. From out of his medicine bundle he took a few grains of pollen mixed with honey and gave them to the dreamer to eat. Afterwards he took a sharp pointed object which he called a petrified eagle's claw and inserted it and extracted it four times from the latter's mouth. As a final act of the treatment, a chain of shells, wildcat claws and eagle claws were pressed to his head, hands, knees and chest. There followed a prayer and the dreamer was told he would have no more bad dreams.

Navaho Indians, up to our days, have been greatly concerned with matters of health. The anthropologist Ralph Linton called them a society for hypochondriacs. Such an attitude may well account for their marked interest in the secret meaning of dreams. But one may also wonder whether or not a similar tendency current among their contemporary neighbors is the result of some subtle psychological contagion flowing from one culture to the other.

chapter 5

Healing Magic: Survival and Revival in Modern Times

JAMES FRAZER: MAGIC AND THE ART OF HEALING . . .
BRONISLAW MALINOWSKI: MAGIC AND THE PROFILE
OF A MAGICIAN . . .
ALBERT SCHWEITZER: REVIVAL OF BLACK MAGIC IN AFRICA . . .
SIGMUND FREUD: A PASSAGE FROM "TOTEM AND TABOO"

James Frazer (1854-1941), one of the founders of modern anthropological research, has paid particular attention to the survival of magic beliefs and practices in modern times. His celebrated work The Golden Bough, *first published in 1890, contains a classical description of magic. It has served as an important point of departure for later researchers in the field and was of decisive influence upon Sigmund Freud's psychoanalytic inquiry into the prehistory of the human mind contained in his* Totem *and* Taboo.

The following selections are taken from Frazer's chapters on sympathetic and homeopathic magic.

The Principles of Magic

If we analyze the principles of thought on which magic is based, they will probably be found to resolve themselves into two: first, that like produces like, or that an effect resembles its cause; and, second, that things which have once been in contact with each other continue to act on each other at a distance after the physical contact has been severed. The former principle may be called the Law of Similarity, the latter the Law of Contact or Contagion. From the first of these principles, namely the law of Similarity, the magician infers that he can produce any effect he desires merely by imitating it: from the second he infers that whatever he does to a material object will affect equally the person with whom the object was once in contact, whether it formed part of his body or not. Charms based on the Law of Similarity may be called Homeopathic or Imitative Magic. Charms based on the Law of Contact or Contagion may be called Contagious Magic. To denote the first of these branches of magic the term Homeopathic is perhaps preferable, for the alternative term Imitative or Mimetic suggests, if it does not imply, a conscious agent who imitates, thereby limiting the scope of magic too narrowly. For the same principles which the magician applies in the practice of his art are implicitly believed by him to regulate the operations of inanimate nature; in other words, he tacitly assumes that the Laws of Similarity and Contact are of universal application and are not limited to human actions. In short, magic is a spurious system of natural law as well as a fallacious guide of conduct; it is a false science as well as an abortive art. Regarded as a system of natural law, that is, as a statement of the rules which determine the sequence of events throughout the world, it may be called Theoretical Magic: regarded as a set of precepts which human beings observe in order to compass their ends, it may be called Practical Magic. At the same time it is to be borne in mind that the primitive magician knows magic only on its practical side; he never analyzes the mental processes on which his practice is based, never reflects on the abstract principles involved in his actions. With him, as with the vast majority of men, logic is implicit, not explicit: he reasons just as he digests his food in complete ignorance of the intellectual and physiological processes which are essential to the one operation and to the other. In short, to him, magic is always an art, never a science; the very idea of science is lacking in his undeveloped mind. It is for the philosophic student to trace the train of thought which underlies the magician's practice; to draw out the few simple threads of which the tangled skein is composed; to disengage the abstract principles from their concrete applications; in short, to discern the spurious science behind the bastard art.

If my analysis of the magician's logic is correct, its two great principles turn out to be merely two different misapplications of the association of ideas. Homeopathic magic is founded on the association of ideas by similarity: contagious magic is founded on the association of ideas by contiguity. Homeopathic magic commits the mistake of assuming that things which resemble each other are the same: contagious magic commits the mistake of assuming that things which have once been in contact with each other are always in contact. But in practice the two branches are often combined; or, to be more exact, while homeopathic or imitative magic may be practised by itself, contagious magic will generally be found to involve an application of the homeopathic or imitative principle. Thus generally stated, the two things may be a little difficult to grasp, but they will become intelligible when they are illustrated by particular examples. Both trains of thought are in fact extremely simple and elementary. It should hardly be otherwise, since they are familiar in the concrete, though certainly not in the abstract, to the crude intelligence not only of the savage, but of ignorant and dull-witted people everywhere. Both branches of magic, the homeopathic and the contagious, may conveniently be comprehended under the general name of Sympathetic Magic, since both assume that things act on each other at a distance through a secret sympathy, the impulse being transmitted from one to the other by means of what we may conceive as a kind of invisible ether, not unlike that which is postulated by modern science for a precisely similar purpose, namely to explain how things can physically affect each other through a space which appears to be empty.

It may be convenient to tabulate as follows the branches of magic according to the laws of thought which underlie them.

Sympathetic Magic
(Law of Sympathy)

Homeopathic Magic   Contagious Magic
(Law of Similarity)   (Law of Contact)

I will now illustrate . . . sympathetic magic by examples (of) homeopathic magic.

Homeopathic or Imaginative Magic

Perhaps the most familiar application of the principle that like produces like is the attempt which has been made by many peoples in many ages to injure or destroy an enemy by injuring or destroying an image of him, in the belief that, just as the image suffers, so does the man, and that when it perishes he must die. A few instances out of many may be given to prove at once the wide diffusion of the practice over the world and its remarkable persistence through the ages. Thousands of years ago it was known to the sorcerers of ancient India, Babylon and Egypt, as well as of Greece and Rome, and at this day it is still resorted to by cunning and malignant savages in Australia, Africa and Scotland. Thus the North American Indians, we are told, believe that by drawing the figure of a person in sand, ashes, or clay, or by considering any object as his body, and then pricking it with a sharp stick or doing it any other injury, they inflict a corresponding injury on the person represented. For example, when an Ojebway Indian desires to work evil on any one, he makes a little wooden image of his enemy and runs a needle into his head or heart, or he shoots an arrow into it, believing that wherever the needle pierces or the arrow strikes the image, his foe will the same instant be seized with a sharp pain in the corresponding part of his body; but if he intends to kill the person outright, he burns or buries the puppet, uttering certain magic words as he does so. The Peruvian Indians moulded images of fat mixed with grain to imitate the persons whom they disliked or feared, and then burned the effigy on the road where the intended victim was to pass. This they called burning his soul.

A Malay charm of the same sort is as follows. Take parings of nails, hair, eyebrows, spittle, and so forth of your intended victim, enough to represent every part of his person, and then make them up into his likeness with wax from a deserted bees' comb. Scorch the figure slowly by holding it over a lamp every night for seven nights, and say:

> "It is not wax that I am scorching,
> It is the liver, heart, and spleen of So-and-so
>   that I scorch."

After the seventh time burn the figure, and your victim will die. This charm obviously combines the principles of homeopathic and contagious magic; since the image which is made in the likeness of an enemy contains things which once were in contact with him, namely, his nails, hair, and spittle. Another form of the Malay charm, which resembles the Ojebway practice still more closely, is to make a corpse of wax from an empty bees' comb and of the length of a footstep; then pierce the eye of the image, and your enemy is blind; pierce the stomach, and he is sick; pierce the head and his head aches; pierce the breast and his breast will suffer. If you would kill him outright, transfix the image from the head downwards; enshroud it as you would a corpse; pray over it as if you were praying over the dead; then bury it in the middle of a path where your victim will be sure to step over it. In order that his blood may not be on your head you should say:

> "It is not I who am burying him,
> It is Gabriel who is burying him."

Thus the guilt of the murder will be laid on the shoulders of the archangel Gabriel, who is a great deal better able to bear it than you are.

If homeopathic or imitative magic, working by means of images, has commonly been practiced for the spiteful purpose of putting obnoxious people out of the world, it has also though far more rarely, been employed with the benevolent intention of helping others into it. In another words, it has been used to facilitate childbirth and to procure offspring for barren women. Thus among the Bataks of Sumatra a barren woman, who would become a mother, will make a wooden image of a child and hold it in her lap, believing that this will lead to the fulfillment of her wish. In the Babar Archipielago, when a woman desires to have a child, she invites a man who is himself the father of a large family to pray on her behalf to Upulero, the spirit of the sun. A doll is made of red cotton, which the woman clasps in her arms, as if she would suckle it. Then the father of many children takes a fowl and holds it by the legs to the woman's head saying, "O Upulero, make use of the fowl, let fall, let descend a child, I beseech you, I entreat you, let a child fall and descend into my hands and on my lap." Then he asks the woman, "Has the child come?" and she answers, "Yes, it is suckling already."

After that the man holds the fowl on the husband's head, and mumbles some form of words. Lastly the bird is killed and laid, together with some betel, on the domestic place of sacrifice. When the ceremony is over, word goes about in the village that the woman has been brought to bed, and her friends come and congratulate her. Here the pretence that a child has been born is a purely magical rite designed to secure, by means of imitation or mimicry, that a child really shall be born. But an attempt is made to add to the efficacy of the rite by means of prayer and sacrifice. To put it otherwise, magic is here blent with and reinforced by religion.

Bronislaw Malinowski (1889-1942), the Polish-born anthropologist, is the first representative of the so-called functional school of anthropology. His description of the lives of the Trobriand Islanders has become a classic of anthropologic literature, taking the reader from the closed study of the theorist into the wide-open spaces of the anthropological "field."

The following passage gives a vivid description of a sorcerer observed by Malinowski performing an act of "black magic." It should be noted, however, that essentially the same emotional factors are involved in the operation of "white" or healing magic.

The Rite and the Spell

Let us have a look at a typical act of magic, and choose one which is well-known and generally regarded as a standard performance—an act of black magic. Among the several types which we meet in savagery, witchcraft by the act of pointing the magical dart is, perhaps, the most widespread of all. A pointed bone or a stick, an arrow or the spine of some animal, is ritually, in a mimic fashion, thrust, thrown, or pointed in the direction of the man to be killed by sorcery. We have innumerable recipes in the oriental and ancient books of magic, in ethnographic descriptions and tales of travelers, of how such a rite is performed. But the emotional setting, the gestures and expressions of the sorcerer during the performance, have been but seldom described. Yet these are of the greatest importance. If a spectator were suddenly transported to some part of Melanesia and could observe the sorcerer at work, not perhaps knowing exactly what he was looking at, he might think that he had either to do with a lunatic or else he would guess that here was a man acting under the sway of uncontrolled anger. For the sorcerer has, as an essential part of the ritual performance, not merely to point the bone dart at his victim, but with an intense expression of fury and hatred he has to thrust it in the air, turn and twist it as if to bore it in the wound, then pull it back with a sudden jerk. Thus not only is the act of violence, or stabbing, reproduced, but the passion of violence has to be enacted.

We see thus that the dramatic expression of emotion is the essence of this act, for what is it that is reproduced in it? Not its end, for the magician would in that case have to imitate the death of the victim, but the emotional state of the performer, a state which closely corresponds to the situation in which we find it and which has to be gone through mimetically.

I could adduce a number of similar rites from my own experience, and many more, of course, from other records. Thus, when in other types of black magic the sorcerer ritually injures or mutilates or destroys a figure or object symbolizing the victim, this rite is, above all, a clear expression of hatred and anger. Or when in love magic the performer has really or symbolically to grasp, stroke, fondle the beloved person or some object representing her, he reproduces the behavior of a heartsick lover who has lost his common sense and is overwhelmed by passion. In war magic, anger, the fury of attack, the emotions of combative passion, are frequently expressed in a more or less direct manner. In the magic of terror, in the exorcism directed against powers of darkness and evil, the magician behaves as if himself overcome by the emotion of fear, or at least violently struggling against it. Shouts, brandishing of weapons, the use of lighted torches, form often the substance of this rite. Or else in an act, recorded by myself, to ward off the evil powers of darkness, a man has ritually to tremble, to utter a spell slowly as if paralyzed by fear. And this fear gets hold also of the approaching sorcerer and wards him off.

All such acts, usually rationalized and explained by some principle of magic, are *prima facie* expressions of emotion. The substances and paraphernalia used in them have often the same significance. Daggers, sharp-pointed lacerating objects, evil-smelling or poisonous substances, used in black magic; scents, flowers, inebriating stimulants, in love magic; valuables, in economic magic—all these are associated primarily through emotions and not through ideas with the end of the respective magic.

Besides such rites, however, in which a dominant element serves to express an emotion, there are others in which the act does forecast its result, or, to use Sir James Frazer's expression, the rite imitates its end. Thus, in the black magic of the Melanesians recorded by myself, a characteristic ritual way of winding-up the spell is for the sorcerer to weaken the voice, utter a death rattle, and fall down in imitation of the rigor of death. It is, however, not necessary to adduce any other examples, for this aspect of magic and the allied one of contagious magic have been brilliantly described and exhaustively documented by Frazer. Sir James has also shown that there exists a special lore of magical substances based on affinities, relations, on ideas of similarity and contagion, developed with a magical pseudo-science.

But there are also ritual proceedings in which there is neither imitation nor forecasting nor the expression of any special idea or emotion. There are rites so simple that they can be described only as an immediate application of magical virtue, as when the performer stands up and, directly invoking the wind, causes it to rise. Or again, as when a man conveys the spell to some material substance which afterwards will be applied to the thing or person to be charmed. The material objects used in such ritual are also of a strictly appropriate character—substances best fitted to receive, retain, and transmit magical virtue, coverings designed to imprison and preserve it until it is applied to its object.

But what is the magical virtue which figures not only in the last-mentioned type of act but in every magical rite? For whether it be an act expressing certain emotions or a rite of imitation and foreshadowing or an act of simple casting, one feature they have always in common: the force of magic, its virtue, must always be conveyed to the charmed object. What is it? Briefly, it is always the power contained in the spell, for, and this is never sufficiently emphasized, the most important element in magic is the spell. The spell is that part of magic which is occult, handed over in magical filiation, known only to the practitioner. To the natives knowledge of magic means knowledge of spell, and in an analysis of any act of witchcraft it will always be found that the ritual centers around the utterance of the spell. The formula is always the core of the magical performance.

The study of the texts and formulas of primitive magic reveals that there are three typical elements associated with the belief in magical efficiency. There are, first, the phonetic effects, imitations of natural sounds, such as the whistling of the wind, the growling of thunder, the roar of the sea, the voices of various animals. These sounds symbolize certain phenomena and thus are believed to produce them magically. Or else they express certain emotional states associated with the desire which is to be realized by means of the magic.

The second element, very conspicuous in primitive spells, is the use of words which invoke, state, or command the desired aim. Thus the sorcerer will mention all the symptoms of the disease which he is inflicting, or in the lethal formula he will describe the end of his victim. In healing magic the wizard will give word pictures of perfect health and bodily strength. In economic magic the growing of plants, the approach of animals, the arrival of fish in shoals are depicted. Or again the magician uses words and sentences which express the emotion under the stress of which he works his magic, and the action which gives expression to this emotion. The sorcerer in tones of fury will have to repeat such verbs as "I break—I twist—I burn—I destroy," enumerating with each of them the various parts of the body and internal organs of his victim. In all this we see that the spells are built very much on the same pattern as the rites and the words selected for the same reasons as the substances of magic.

Thirdly there is an element in almost every spell to which there is no counterpart in ritual. I mean the mythological allusions, the references to ancestors and culture heroes from whom this magic has been received.

Our next selection is taken from an article by Dr. Albert Schweitzer published in the first issue of Tomorrow Magazine. *Albert Schweitzer (1875-1965), physician, theologian, virtuoso organist and winner of the 1972 Nobel Prize for peace, describes his personal observations about the part played by black magic among the natives of Lambarene in the African bush. His article, "Black Magic Reborn," brings our condensed survey of the vicissitudes of the magic art up to date. Dr. Schweitzer's conclusion from his observations is striking: he attributes the revival of magic among his flock of African natives to European influence.*

In broad outline, we may define . . . magical faith as follows: being of a non-religious nature, it rests essentially on the belief in a supernatural force placed above all other forces, even that of divinities and fetishes—a supernatural force which the initiate can compel to serve him once he has mastered the means. One of my hospital attendants, Joseph, had an uncle who was supposed to possess this power. When he went walking in the woods, if he wished to touch the leaves of a palm tree, he could order it to bend down before him. However, he did not make use of this power in the presence of the uninitiated.

The origin of this belief is to be sought in the experience of ecstasy, and the aim of native secret societies is to communicate this experience, to codify its practices and to bring together those who share it. Whereas in certain civilizations it is opium, peyotl, or hashish that induces ecstasy, for the Negroes of the Lambarene it is IBOGA. This plant is turned to profane as well as sacred ends. For instance, paddlers frequently drug themselves with Iboga merely to gain increased physical strength and a momentary stimulation. I have from time to time received at my hospital patients who showed grave symptoms of disequilibrium because they had overdrugged themselves with this stimulant. Such accidents occur in secret societies as well, but there they are exploited for a mystic and magical purpose. Indeed, the essential activity of the secret societies consists of using incantatory rites and the absorption of Iboga in order to reach a state of ecstasy producing a feeling of supernatural strength which can be disposed of at will. The important role played by Iboga is demonstrated moreover in the admission test which the secret societies require of their candidates. When they have absorbed a certain quantity of Iboga the ecstatic visions induced by it are studied. If white birds appear in the native's vision he is admitted to the fraternity; if not, he is rejected. These societies do not operate in public; they have no name; their assemblies are not open to the uninitiated: they are secret in a real sense. Their adepts are content with the knowledge that they have risen above the ordinary condition of humanity. By means of their ecstasy they get to know the other, the true world, compared to which the daily world is nothing more than an illusion. It is incidentally interesting to note that this belief has crept into the Vedas, and it may be worthy of mention that I myself have been able to understand Brahmanism only after my contact with the natives. Like the latter, the Brahmans are convinced that they have found the truth about the universe, beings and things, and ecstasy is the great event which raises them above the human condition: a marvelous power is within their reach. But contrary to the Brahmans, who were led by the Indian caste-system to make use of their magical power, the natives of the Gaboon are content with the knowledge that such power exists and that it is at their disposal. They do not think it necessary to make any kind of use of it.

It would be an absolute error to assume that these primitive, non-religious, magical beliefs, rooted in the experience of ecstasy, disappear with the infiltration of occidental and so-called civilized ideas. Indeed, within the last years a new flourishing of these beliefs has become evident. The first European missionaries arrived in the Lambarene region of the Gaboon in 1874. By 1890 they were solidly entrenched and developing their apostolate with great rapidity. Hence, when I arrived in the Gaboon in 1913, all magical beliefs had practically disappeared. They had been retained only by the forest tribes, by the "savages" in the native sense of the term: men who lived fifty kilometers away! But today an evolution is apparent the origins of which I was able to discern around 1924. Under European influence, a native nationalism has been aroused and the core of this nationalism is magical belief. In his attempt to oppose the invasion of occidental ideas, the native returns to his primitive faith. Like the Greek mysteries of the second century, the traditional beliefs are reborn, and are perfected through contact with a foreign civilization. Furthermore, coming upon the Daily Horoscope as well as ads for protection stones or talismans in the European newspapers—and in general all the publicity put out by the professional "magi" of the ruling country—the natives discover that the whites share the very ideas which they tried to root out of the Negro mentality. Thenceforth, they set about giving the white man some real lessons in occultism; they are overjoyed to find that the Europeans practice magic, but they see here good grounds for asserting their own superiority. "You are right," they say to them, "to believe in magic; but yours is a poor kind of magic; you imitate us, but you imitate us badly." This argument is so persuasive that white men occasionally have themselves initiated into secret societies and become faithful and absolutely believing members of such groups. In sum, we are

witnessing today in the Gaboon a considerable new wave of traditional and
magical ideas. A renaissance rather than a true evolution: the natives return
to their most ancient beliefs; no progress can be discerned in the development of these ideas. The notion of salvation, of dependency in relation to a
divine being—in a word, the notion of religion, remains unknown or at best
secondary. The primitive beliefs show no sign of real spiritualization.
Whether or not it is put to use, it is always the notion of power on which the
native's faith rests. The movement which transforms the Brahma into a
supernatural force, a divinity, never took place among the natives living
along the shores of the Gaboon.

Along with the secret societies which practice the cult of ecstasy giving
their adherents a power of which they make little use, we find the fetishists.
The latter must be carefully distinguished from the members of secret societies. They belong, in a certain sense, to a much lower category: their
powers are not the superior ones bestowed by ecstasy. Fetishism is a profession, and its functions are numerous. To begin with, the fetishists do not
predict the future; no native ever does, nor is this knowledge of any concern to him. The future is of no more interest to the natives than the past:
they live in the present. The fetishists do, however, claim they have the
power to chase away evil spirits. They practice their exorcism in public ceremonies, the rites of which go back to very ancient times . . .

Magic medicine practiced by fetishists is a well-known phenomenon: its
frequent successes are, to my mind, due solely to a psychotherapy which
dares not say its name—or rather does not know its name. In like manner, I
believe, the undeniable results of sympathetic magic (employing nail and
hair clippings of the person on whom one wants to act) and of taboos can be
attributed to a subtle psychological process. But the essential nature of this
process still escapes us; rather than risk an as yet premature general interpretation, I shall cite one or two cases from my personal experience, cases of
which I have already had the occasion to speak in my *Stories of the Virgin
Forest*.

The idea of taboo is of first rank importance in the life of the primitive
man. The word means a forbidding of certain things or of certain gestures
because they would result in a misfortune or in death. Some taboos are
valid for everyone, without distinction, others only for those on whom they
have been imposed. In the first category let us mention the strange prohibitions which face the husband of a pregnant woman: he must not eat gamy
meat, nor touch a chameleon, nor hammer nails, nor fill in holes in the
ground, etc. . . . Anything can become the object of a taboo. A taboo imposed on one of the pupils of the missionary school of Samkita consisted of
his being forbidden to eat bananas; he was not even to touch food prepared
in a pot where bananas had previously been cooked. One day his school-

mates announced to him that the fish he was eating came out of a pot which still contained some left-over bananas. He was immediately overcome with convulsions and died in a few hours. Such deaths are explainable, no doubt, by the fact that the natives stand in so great an awe of taboos that they are subject to psychological shocks the violence of which we cannot imagine; but it is possible for a white man who has gained the confidence of the natives to bring his moral influence to bear upon such cases with a certain amount of success. Here is another case in which a taboo violation resulted in violent death: a man had received from his father the following taboo: in order to escape an early death he would be obliged to have a numerous progeny. He had been married for several years and had only three children. One day his father came to see him to remind him of his taboo. As soon as he had finished speaking the son fainted, fell to the ground, and began having convulsions. They kept him in the village for a few days and then brought him to our hospital. It soon became clear that the medicaments normally used to stop convulsions had no effect: he died soon thereafter.

Sigmund Freud's Totem and Taboo *is the first significant psychoanalytic contribution to the problem of primitive mentality. Not satisfied with Frazer's theory, which merely sought to explain "the path that magic travels," Freud tried to account for its operation in dynamic terms. The dynamic factor in question is what Freud describes as the wish for omnipotence of thought, characteristic of primitive man, the neurotic and the child.*

The motives which impel one to exercise magic are easily recognized; they are the wishes of men. We need only assume that primitive man had great confidence in the power of his wishes. At bottom everything which he accomplished by magic means must have been done solely because he wanted it. Thus in the beginning only his wish is accentuated.

In the case of the child which finds itself under analogous psychic conditions, without being as yet capable of motor activity, we have elsewhere advocated the assumption that it at first really satisfies its wishes by means of hallucinations, in that it creates the satisfying situations through centrifugal excitements of its sensory organs. The adult primitive man knows another way. A motor impulse, the will, clings to his wish and this will, which later will change the face of the earth in the service of wish fulfilment, is now used to represent the gratification so that one may experience it, as it were, through motor hallucination. Such a *representation* of the gratified wish is altogether comparable to the *play* of children, where it replaces the purely sensory technique of gratification. If play and imitative representation suffice for the child and for primitive man, it must not be taken as a sign of modesty, in our sense, or of resignation due to the realization of their impotence; on the contrary, it is the very obvious result of the excessive valuation of their wish, of the will which depends upon the wish and of the paths the wish takes. In time the psychic accent is displaced from the motives of the magic act to its means, namely to the act itself. Perhaps it would be more correct to say that primitive man does not become aware of the over-valuation of his psychic acts until it becomes evident to him through the means employed. It would also seem as if it were the magic act itself which compels the fulfilment of the wish by virtue of its similarity to the object desired. At the stage of animistic thinking there is as yet no way of demonstrating objectively the true state of affairs, but this becomes possible at later stages when, though such procedures are still practiced, the psychic phenomenon of scepticism already manifests itself as a tendency to repression. At that stage men will acknowledge that the conjuration of spirits avails nothing unless accompanied by belief, and that the magic effect of prayer fails if there is no piety behind it. (The King in *Hamlet*—Act III, Scene 4: "My words fly up, my thoughts remain below, Words without thoughts never to heaven go.")

The possibility of a contagious magic which depends upon contiguous association will then show us that the psychic valuation of the wish and the will has been extended to all psychic acts which the will can command. We may say that at present there is a general over-valuation of all psychic processes, that is to say there is an attitude towards the world which according to our understanding of the relation of reality to thought must appear like an over-estimation of the latter. Objects as such are over-shadowed by the ideas representing them; what takes place in the latter must also happen to the former, and the relations which exist between ideas are also postulated as to things. As thought does not recognize distances and easily brings together in one act of consciousness things spatially and temporally far removed, the magic world also puts itself above spatial distance by telepathy, and treats a past association as if it were a present one. In the animistic age the reflection of the inner world must obscure that other picture of the world which we believe we recognize.

Let us also point out that the two principles of association, similarity and contiguity, meet in the higher unity of contact. Association by contiguity is contact in the direct sense, and association by similarity is contact in the transferred sense. Another identity in the psychic process which has not yet been grasped by us is probably concealed in the use of the same word for both kinds of associations. It is the same range of the concept of contact which we have found in the analysis of taboo. . . .

In summing up we may now say that the principle which controls magic, and the technique of the animistic method of thought, is "Omnipotence of Thought."

I have adopted the term "Omnipotence of Thought" from a highly intelligent man, a former sufferer from compulsion neurosis, who, after being cured through psychoanalytic treatment, was able to demonstrate his efficiency and good sense. He had coined this phrase to designate all those peculiar and uncanny occurrences which seemed to pursue him just as they pursue others afflicted with this malady. Thus if he happened to think of a person, he was actually confronted with this person as if he had conjured him up; if he inquired suddenly about the state of health of an acquaintance whom he had long missed, he was sure to hear that this acquaintance had just died, so that he could believe that the deceased had drawn his attention to himself by telepathic means; if he uttered a half-meant imprecation against a stranger, he could expect to have him die soon thereafter and burden him with the responsibility for his death. He was able to explain most of these cases in the course of the treatment, he could tell how the illusion had originated, and what he himself had contributed towards furthering his superstitious expectations . . . All compulsion neurotics are superstitious in this manner and often against their better judgment.

The existence of omnipotence of thought is most clearly seen in compulsion neurosis, where the results of this primitive method of thought are most often found or met in consciousness. But we must guard against seeing in this a distinguishing characteristic of this neurosis, for analytic investigation reveals the same mechanism in the other neuroses. In every one of the neuroses it is not the reality of the experience but the reality of the thought which forms the basis for the symptom formation. Neurotics live in a special world in which, as I have elsewhere expressed it, only the "neurotic standard of currency" counts, that is to say, only things intensively thought of or affectively conceived are effective with them regardless of whether these things are in harmony with outer reality. The hysteric repeats in his attacks, and fixates through his symptoms, occurrences which have taken place only in his fantasy, though in the last analysis they go back to real events or have been built up from them. The neurotic's guilty conscience is just as incomprehensible if traced to real misdeeds. A compulsion neurotic may be oppressed by a sense of guilt which is appropriate to a wholesale murderer, while at the same time he acts towards his fellow beings in a most considerate and scrupulous manner, a behavior which he evinced since his childhood. And yet his sense of guilt is justified; it is based upon intensive and frequent death wishes which unconsciously manifest themselves towards his fellow beings. It is motivated from the point of view of unconscious thoughts, but not of intentional acts. Thus the omnipotence of thought, the over-estimation of psychic processes as opposed to reality, proves to be of unlimited effect in the neurotic's affective life and in all that emanates from it. But if we subject him to psychoanalytic treatment, which makes his unconscious thoughts conscious to him, he refuses to believe that thoughts are free and is always afraid to express evil wishes lest they be fulfilled in consequence of his utterance. But through this attitude as well as through the superstition which plays an active part in his life he reveals to us how close he stands to the savage who believes he can change the outer world by a mere thought of his.

The primary obsessive actions of these neurotics are really altogether of a magical nature. If not magic they are at least antimagic and are destined to ward off the expectation of evil with which the neurosis is wont to begin. Whenever I was able to pierce these secrets it turned out that the content of this expectation of evil was death. According to Schopenhauer the problem of death stands at the beginning of every philosophy; we have heard that the formation of the soul conception and of the belief in demons which characterize animism are also traced back to the impression which death makes upon man. It is hard to decide whether these first compulsive and protective actions follow the principle of similarity, or of contrast, for under the conditions of the neurosis they are usually distorted through displacement upon some trifle, upon some action which in itself is quite insignificant. The protective formulae of the compulsion neurosis also have a counterpart in the incantations of magic. But the evolution of compulsive actions may be described by pointing out how these actions begin as a spell against evil wishes which are very remote from anything sexual, only to end up as a substitute for forbidden sexual activity, which they imitate as faithfully as possible.

If we accept the evolution of man's conceptions of the universe mentioned above, according to which the *animistic* phase is *succeeded* by the *religious*, and this in turn by the *scientific*, we have no difficulty in following the fortunes of the "omnipotence of thought" through all these phases. In the animistic stage man ascribes omnipotence to himself; in the religious he has ceded it to the gods, but without seriously giving it up, for he reserves to himself the right to control the gods by influencing them in some way or other in the interest of his wishes. In the scientific attitude towards life there is no longer any room for man's omnipotence; he has acknowledged his smallness and has submitted to death as to all other natural necessities in a spirit of resignation. Nevertheless, in our reliance upon the power of the human spirit which copes with the laws of reality, there still lives on a fragment of this primitive belief in the omnipotence of thought.

Part 2

RELIGION
or
The Quest
for
Salvation

chapter 6

Salvation Through Renunciation

SELECTIONS FROM THE SACRED BOOKS
THE EAST : THE UPANISHADS ;
THE BHAGAVAD GITA ; BUDDHA'S FIRE SERMON . . .
"THE YELLOW EMPEROR'S MEDICINE" . . .
ST. FRANCIS DE SALES

Religion means many different things to different people. We have seen how, according to Freud, the religious man merely transfers the illusion of his own omnipotence to the gods, "but without seriously giving it up." Thus to Freud, the religious skeptic, religion is barely distinguishable from magic. It is an escape into what he describes as the Oceanic feeling, in which the faithful are apt to lose sight of the shores of reality. Freud considers the ritualistic taboos and observances of religion as symptoms of a collective compulsion neurosis which may at best save the individual from developing a compulsion neurosis of his own. Otherwise he regards religion as of little value to man's mental welfare.

For C. G. Jung, religion is a factor indispensable to our culture. It is needed as an outlet for the unruly forces of the Collective Unconscious. It channels these forces into dogma and ritual and in so doing it serves as a safety valve for the "Perils of the Soul" that would otherwise threaten to disrupt man's personality structure. Rabbi Joshua Liebman seems to be in far-reaching agreement with such a thesis when he says that the Jews, in prayers, in songs and in dances, in home festivals and synagogue rites, "acted out in unison their own inner needs and passions, finding collective health and enormous powers of resistance as by-products of this wise emotional strategy." But to both the Jewish and Christian theologian—or for that matter, to the Moslem or Hindu believer—religion is much more than that. It is a means toward the mystic union with the godhead. It is the promise of redemption from sin; it is "the kingdom which is not of this world." It is the narrow path toward salvation, the quest for a spiritual goal that transcends the boundaries of rational human experience.

What is the relevance of such a quest to the problem of mental health and mental healing? From this point of view it represents a new technique to deal with pain, suffering and all the rest of the calamities of life. While magic confines itself to spiritual first-aid, as it were, ancient Buddhist, Taoist and early Christian doctrine seek a long-term solution. If life is beset with

pain, suffering and frustration, all this can be countered by bracing oneself
with a particular attitude to minimize their impact. This approach is well illustrated by ancient Hindu religious doctrine, which, like the early Christian church, has been quite outspoken in repudiating the magic heritage of a
preceding era.

Our first selection is taken from the Upanishads, one of the oldest Hindu
religious texts. Written in archaic Sanskrit, it originated some time between
800 and 300 B.C. Our text illustrates the peculiar spiritual discipline by
which ancient Hindu doctrine sought to achieve the goal of emancipating
the self from attachment to the physical world. It is a blend of timeless
meditation, prayer—often confined to the muttering of the sacred syllable
OM—and the assumption of a variety of bodily attitudes. The latter form
part of various Yoga practices which have since found their way into the
Western world. All these devices, mental and physical, should lead to states
of trance and ecstasy, culminating in the mystic union with the deity and
the loss of self.

To realize God, first control the outgoing senses and harness the mind.
Then meditate upon the light in the heart of the fire—meditate, that is, upon
pure consciousness as distinct from the ordinary consciousness of the intellect. Thus the Self, the Inner Reality, may be seen behind physical appearance.

Control your mind so that the Ultimate Reality, the self-luminous Lord,
may be revealed. Strive earnestly for eternal bliss.

With the help of the mind and the intellect, keep the senses from attaching
themselves to objects of pleasure. They will then be purified by the light of
the Inner Reality, and that light will be revealed.

The wise control their minds and unite their hearts with the infinite, the
omniscient, the all-pervading Lord. Only discriminating souls practice
spiritual disciplines. Great is the glory of the self-luminous being, the Inner
Reality.

Hear, all ye children of immortal bliss, also ye gods who dwell in the high
heavens: Follow only in the footsteps of the illuminated ones, and by continuous meditation merge both mind and intellect in the eternal Brahman.
The glorious Lord will be revealed to you.

Control the vital force. Set fire to the Self within by the practice of meditation. Be drunk with the wine of divine life. Thus shall you reach perfection.

Be devoted to the eternal Brahman. Unite the light within you with the
light of Brahman. Thus will the source of ignorance be destroyed and you
will arise above karma.

Sit upright, holding the chest, throat, and head erect. Turn the senses and
the mind inward to the lotus of the heart. Meditate on Brahman with the

help of the syllable OM. Cross the fearful currents of the ocean of worldliness by means of the raft of Brahman—the sacred syllable OM.

With earnest effort hold the senses in check. Controlling the breath, regulate the vital activities. As a charioteer holds back his restive horses, so does a persevering aspirant hold back his mind.

Retire to a solitary spot, such as a mountain cave or any sacred spot. The place must be protected from the wind and rain, and it must have a smooth, clean floor, free from pebbles and dust. It must not be damp, and it must be free from disturbing noises. It must be pleasing to the eye and quieting to the mind. Seated there, practice meditation and other spiritual exercises.

As you practice meditation you may see in vision, forms resembling snow, crystal, wind, smoke, fire, lightning, fireflies, the sun, the moon. These are signs that you are on your way to the revelation of Brahman.

As you become absorbed in meditation, you will realize that the Self is separate from the body and for this reason will not be affected by disease, old age or death.

The first signs of progress on the path of yoga are health, a sense of physical lightness, clearness of complexion, a beautiful voice, an agreeable odor of the person, and freedom from craving.

As a soiled piece of metal, when it has been cleaned, shines brightly, so the dweller in the body, when he has realized the truth of the Self, is freed from sorrow and attains bliss.

The yogi experiences directly the truth of Brahman by realizing the light of the Self within. He is freed from all impurities—he is pure, the birthless, the bright.

The same thought is expressed in this passage from another Upanishad:

A man acts according to the desires to which he clings. After death he goes to the next world, bearing in his mind the subtle impressions of his deeds; and after reaping there the harvest of his deeds, he returns again to this world of action. Thus he who has desire continues subject to rebirth.

But he in whom desire is stilled suffers no rebirth. After death, having attained to the highest, desiring only the Self, he goes to no other world. Realizing Brahman, he becomes Brahman.

When all the desires which once entered into his heart have been driven out by divine knowledge, the mortal, attaining to Brahman, becomes immortal.

As the slough of a snake lies cast off on an anthill, so lies the body of a man at death; while he, freed from the body, becomes one with the immortal spirit, Brahman, the Light Eternal.

Immortality as a reward for renouncing the desires of the flesh is also promised in the following fragment:

When all the senses are stilled, when the mind is at rest, when the intellect wavers not—that, say the wise, is the highest state.

This calm of the senses and the mind has been defined as yoga. He who attains it is freed from delusion.

In one not freed from delusion this calm is uncertain, unreal: it comes and goes. Brahman words cannot reveal, mind cannot reach, eyes cannot see. How, then, save through those who know him, can he be known?

There are two selves, the apparent self and the real self. Of these it is the real Self, and he alone, who must be felt as truly existing. To the man who has felt him as truly existing he reveals his innermost nature.

The mortal in whose heart desire is dead, becomes immortal. The mortal in whose heart the knots of ignorance are untied, becomes immortal. These are the highest truths taught in the scriptures.

Our next selection is taken from the Bhagavad Gita, The Song of God. *It is part of the monumental Hindu epic* Mahabharata *(about 500 B.C.). It shows how in Hindu doctrine the quest for magic omnipotence is replaced by an attitude of nonviolence, of passivity, sometimes amounting to total surrender and self-effacement. If mastery over the forces of nature and over one's own destiny is still the objective, this is no longer sought through direct attack upon the world of objects. It is sought in a roundabout way, as it were, through mastery over one's own impulses and instinctual drives. Its guiding principle could be described as strength through weakness. Yet at the same time it affirms the hope of conquering the infirmities of human nature through something like compensatory spiritual development. This, the Hindu sages assert, holds the promise of ultimate emancipation from the shackles of material existence and paves the way to immortality on a higher mystical plane.*

The illumined soul
Whose heart is Brahman's heart
Thinks always: 'I am doing nothing.'
No matter what he sees,
Hears, touches, smells, eats;
No matter whether he is moving,
Sleeping, breathing, speaking,
Excreting, or grasping something with his hand,
Or opening his eyes,
Or closing his eyes:

This he knows always:
'I am not seeing, I am not hearing:
It is the senses that see and hear
And touch the things of the senses.

He puts aside desire,
Offering the act to Brahman.
The lotus leaf rests unwetted on water:
He rests on action, untouched by action.

To the follower of the yoga of action,
The body and the mind,
The sense-organs and the intellect
Are instruments only:
He knows himself other than the instrument
And thus his heart grows pure.

United with Brahman,
Cut free from the fruit of the act,
A man finds peace
In the work of the spirit.
Without Brahman,
Man is a prisoner,
Enslaved by action,
Dragged onward by desire. . . .

. . . The enlightened, the Brahman-abiding,
Calm-hearted, unbewildered,
Is neither elated by the pleasant
Nor saddened by the unpleasant.

His mind is dead
To the touch of the external:
It is alive
To the bliss of the Atman,
Because his heart knows Brahman
His happiness is for ever.

When senses touch objects
The pleasures therefrom
Are like wombs that bear sorrow.
They begin, they are ended:
They bring no delight to the wise.

Already, here on earth,
Before his departure,
Let Man be the master
Of every impulse
Lust-begotten
Or fathered by anger:
Thus he finds Brahman,
Thus he is happy.

Only that yogi
Whose joy is inward,
Inward his peace,
And his vision inward
Shall come to Brahman
And know Nirvana.

All consumed
Are their imperfections,
Doubts are dispelled,
Their senses mastered,
Their every action
Is wed to the welfare
Of fellow-creatures:
Such are the seers
Who enter Brahman
And know Nirvana.

Self-controlled,
Cut free from desire,
Curbing the heart
And knowing the Atman,
Man finds Nirvana
That is in Brahman,
Here and hereafter.

Shutting off sense
From what is outward,
Fixing the gaze
At the root of the eyebrows,
Checking the breath-stream
In and outgoing
Within the nostrils,

Holding the senses,
Holding the intellect,
Holding the mind fast,
He who seeks freedom,
Thrusts fear aside,
Thrusts aside anger
And puts off desire :
Truly that man
Is made free for ever.

The passage quoted above, taken from the Yoga of Renunciation, can convey only the most rudimentary idea of Yogi techniques. Their exposition has been the topic of countless volumes of ancient Hindu literature. But many and varied though they are, they all have one aim in common: to expand the range of human consciousness into what is now called the unconscious sphere. At the same time they aim at extending volitional control into organs and bodily systems usually outside the range of will power. In this respect ancient Yogi techniques may well be compared with modern techniques of hypnotic treatment, therapeutic suggestion and relaxation exercises.

The sermons of Gautama Buddha (about 563-483 B.C.), founder of the Buddhist religion, reiterate the same theme of self-discipline and renunciation as the best antidote against human suffering. Here is part of his Fire Sermon, which has been hailed as one of the greatest religious utterances and one of the most eloquent documents deploring the frailties of human nature.

All things, O priests, are on fire. Forms are on fire. Eye-consciousness is on fire. Impressions received by the eye are on fire. And whatever sensation, pleasant or unpleasant or indifferent, originates in dependence or impressions received by the fire, that also is on fire. And with what are these on fire?

With the fire of passion, say I, with the fire of hatred, with the fire of infatuation. With birth, old age, death, sorrow, lamentation, misery, grief, and despair are they on fire.

The ear is on fire. Sounds are on fire. . . . The nose is on fire. Odours are on fire. . . . The tongue is on fire. Tastes are on fire. . . . The body is on fire. Things tangible are on fire. . . . The mind is on fire. Ideas are on fire. . . . Mind consciousness is on fire. Impressions received by the mind are on fire. And whatever sensation, pleasant or unpleasant, or indifferent, originates in dependence on impressions received by the mind, that also is on fire. And with what are these on fire?

With the fire of passion, say I, with the fire of hatred, with the fire of infatuation. With birth, old age, death, sorrow, lamentation, misery, grief,
and despair are they on fire.

Perceiving this, O priests, the learned and noble disciple conceives an
aversion for the eye, conceives an aversion for forms, conceives an aversion
for eye-consciousness, conceives an aversion for impressions received by
the eye; and whatever sensation, pleasant or unpleasant, or indifferent,
originates in dependence on impressions received by the eye, for that also he
conceives an aversion. . . . And in conceiving this aversion, he becomes di-
vested of passion, and by the absence of passion he becomes free, and when
he is free, he becomes aware that he is free; and he knows that rebirth is exhausted, that he has lived the holy life, that he has done what it behoved
him to do, and that he is no more for this world.

*Other teachings of Buddha emphasize, however, the need for striking a
happy balance between indulgence and mortification of the flesh. They are
in far-reaching agreement with the Taoist doctrine, and show close resemblance to the plea for moderation found in Plato's and Epicurus's writings
(see chapter 11).*

The following passage from The Yellow Emperor's Classic of Internal
Medicine *may seem to be out of place in this section. It should perhaps be
included among the earliest documents of the scientific approach to the art
of healing, in Part III of this anthology. Yet its underlying philosophy is essentially religious. It reflects the Taoist attitude toward the Good Life. It
cautions against extreme indulgence in both sensual desire and ascetic withdrawal from reality. The earliest version of the treatise has been dated as far
back as 1000 B.C. and is attributed to a learned physician. Its main body
deals with such ancient Chinese medical techniques as acupuncture, blood-
letting and other physiological methods of treatment. More relevant to our
subject is the discussion of the merits of action versus nonaction in the early
part of the book. It shows the close connection which exists between ancient
Chinese Taoist philosophy and the principal themes of some of the Hindu
and Buddhist texts quoted in the preceding pages. It is interesting to note
that both Buddha, the Hindu religious reformer, and Laotse, the founder of
the Chinese religious system of Taoism, flourished in the period of the sixth
and seventh century, B.C., that is, about the time of the highest bloom of
ancient Greek religious thought.*

This fragment is from a recent translation by I. Veith.

Treatise on the Natural Truth in Ancient Times

In ancient times when the Yellow Emperor was born he was endowed
with divine talents; while yet in early infancy he could speak; while still

very young he was quick of apprehension and penetrating; when he was grown up he was sincere and comprehending; when he became perfect he ascended to Heaven.

The Yellow Emperor once addressed T'ien Shih, the divinely inspired teacher: "I have heard that in ancient times the people lived (through the years) to be over a hundred years, and yet they remained active and did not become decrepit in their activities. But nowadays people reach only half of that age and yet become decrepit and failing. Is it because the world changes from generation to generation? Or is it that mankind is becoming negligent (of the laws of nature)?"

Ch'i Po answered: "In ancient times those people who understood Tao [the way of self cultivation] patterned themselves upon the Yin and the Yang [the two principles of nature] and they lived in harmony with the arts of divination.

"There was temperance in eating and drinking. Their hours of rising and retiring were regular and not disorderly and wild. By these means the ancients kept their bodies united with their souls, so as to fulfill their allotted span completely, measuring unto a hundred years before they passed away.

"Nowadays people are not like this; they use wine as beverage and they adopt recklessness as usual behaviour. They enter the chamber (of love) in an intoxicated condition; their passions exhaust their vital forces; their cravings dissipate their true (essence); they do not know how to find contentment within themselves; they are not skilled in the control of their spirits. They devote all their attention to the amusement of their minds, thus cutting themselves off from the joys of long (life). Their rising and retiring is without regularity. For these reasons they reach only one half of the hundred years and then they degenerate.

"In the most ancient times the teachings of the sages were followed by those beneath them; they said that weakness and noxious influences and injurious winds should be avoided at specific times. They [the sages] were tranquilly content in nothingness and the true vital force accompanied them always; their vital (original) spirit was preserved within; thus, how could illness come to them?

"They exercised restraint of their wills, and reduced their desires; their hearts were at peace and without any fear; their bodies toiled and yet did not become weary.

"Their spirit followed in harmony and obedience; everything was satisfactory to their wishes and they could achieve whatever they wished. Any kind of food was beautiful (to them); and any kind of clothing was satisfactory. They felt happy under any condition. To them it did not matter whether a man held a high or a low position in life. These men can be called pure at heart. No kind of desire can tempt the eyes of those pure people and their mind cannot be misled by excessiveness and evil.

"(In such a society) no matter whether men are wise or foolish, virtuous or bad, they are without fear of anything; they are in harmony with Tao, the Right Way. Thus they could live more than one hundred years and remain active without becoming decrepit, because their virtue was perfect and never imperiled."

The quest for Laotse's Right Way, for Buddha's Middle Path, or for the Golden Mean preached by Confucius was not, however, confined to the great religions of the East. It is implied in the classical Platonic concept of Temperance; it is one of the propositions of Stoic philosophy; it is contained in many Talmudic writings and in some passages of the Sermon on the Mount.

The following quotation from St. Francis de Sales expresses a seventeenth-century Western version of the same thought.

Disquietude is the greatest evil which happens to the soul except sin. For as the seditious and internal troubles of a State ruin it entirely and prevent it from being able to resist the foreigner, so our heart, being troubled and disquieted in itself, loses not only the force to maintain the virtues it has acquired, but more than this, even the means of resisting the temptations of the enemy, who thereupon makes all sorts of efforts to fish, as is said, in troubled waters.

Disquietude arises from an immoderate desire to be freed from an evil which we feel, or to gain the good which we hope for. And yet there is nothing which makes the evil worse and which removes the good to a greater distance than disquietude and worry. Birds are caught in nets and snares because when they find themselves entrapped, they struggle and move immoderately to escape from it, and in so doing they entangle themselves so much the more. When, then, you are pressed with the desire of being freed from some evil, or of attaining some good, before all things, place your spirit in a state of repose and tranquillity, calm your judgment and your will. And then, quite softly and gently, pursue the end of your desire, taking in order the means which will be suitable. And when I say quite softly, I do not wish to say negligently, but without worry, trouble, and disquietude. Otherwise, in place of giving effect to your desire, you will spoil everything and will embarrass yourself very greatly.

chapter 7

Scriptural Demonology and the Healing Miracles of the Bible

THE OLD AND NEW TESTAMENTS

Perhaps the greatest historic message contained in the Old Testament is its clear formulation of the monotheistic creed and its rejection of magic. Yet many passages in both the Old and New Testaments show once more the difficulties of drawing a sharp line of demarcation between magic and the higher religions. The archaic heritage of magic continued to keep its hold over man's mind in biblical times.

This is illustrated by a passage from Genesis XX, which tells the story of Abraham's healing prayer to revoke the spell cast on Abimelech as a punishment for his evil designs on Sarah, Abraham's wife. By the standards of a medieval court of inquisition this incident might well have brought Abraham under the suspicion of sorcery or black magic.

And Abraham journeyed from thence toward the south country, and dwelled between Kadesh and Shur, and sojourned in Gerar. And Abraham said of Sarah his wife, She is my sister: and Abimelech king of Gerar sent, and took Sarah. But God came to Abimelech in a dream by night, and said to him, Behold, thou art but a dead man, for the woman which thou has taken; for she is a man's wife. But Abimelech had not come near her: and he said, Lord wilt thou slay also a righteous nation? Said he not unto me, She is my sister? and she, even she herself said, He is my brother: in the integrity of my heart and innocence of my hands have I done this. And God said unto him in a dream, Yea, I know that thou didst this in the integrity of thy heart; for I also withheld thee from sinning against me: therefore suffered I thee not to touch her. Now therefore restore the man his wife; for he is a prophet, and he shall pray for thee, and thou shalt live: and if thou restore her not, know thou that thou shalt surely die, thou, and all that are thine. Therefore Abimelech rose early in the morning, and called all his servants, and told all these things in their ears: and the men were sore afraid. Then Abimelech called Abraham, and said unto him, What hast thou done unto us? and what have I offended thee, that thou has brought on me and

on my kingdom a great sin? thou has done deeds unto me that ought not to
be done. And Abimelech said unto Abraham, What sawest thou, that thou
has done this thing? And Abraham said, Because I thought, Surely the fear
of God is not in this place; and they will slay me for my wife's sake. And
yet indeed she is my sister; she is the daughter of my father; but not the
daughter of my mother; and she became my wife.

And it came to pass, when God caused me to wander from my father's
house, that I said unto her, This is thy kindness which thou shalt shew unto
me; at every place whither we shall come, say of me, He is my brother. And
Abimelech took sheep, and oxen, and menservants, and womenservants,
and brought them unto Abraham, and restored him Sarah his wife. And
Abimelech said, Behold, my land is before thee: dwell where it pleaseth
thee. And unto Sarah he said, Behold, I have given thy brother a thousand
pieces of silver: behold, he is to thee a covering of the eyes, unto all that are
with thee, and with all other: thus she was reproved.

So Abraham prayed unto God and God healed Abimelech and his wife,
and his maidservants; and they bare children. For the Lord had fast closed
up all the wombs of the house of Abimelech, because of Sarah, Abraham's
wife.

*II Kings, XX, contains another example of healing powers attributed to
the prayer of a prophet. In this case, however, the effect of prayer was supported by a half-magical, half-rational ministration, the application of a
"lump of figs" to a boil.*

In those days was Hezekiah sick unto death. And the prophet Isaiah the
son of Amoz came to him, and said unto him, Thus saith the Lord, Set thine
house in order; for thou shalt die, and not live. Then he turned his face to
the wall, and prayed unto the Lord, saying, I beseech Thee, O, Lord, remember now how I have walked before thee in truth and with a perfect
heart, and have done that which is good in thy sight. And Hezekiah wept
sore. And it came to pass, afore Isaiah was gone out into the middle court,
that the word of the Lord came to him, saying, Turn again, and tell Hezekiah the captain of my people, Thus saith the Lord, the God of David thy
father, I have heard thy prayer, I have seen thy tears: behold, I will heal
thee: on the third day thou shalt go up unto the house of the Lord. And I
will add unto thy days fifteen years; and I will deliver thee and this city out
of the hands of the king of Assyria; and I will defend this city for mine own
sake, and for my servant David's sake. And Isaiah said, Take a lump of
figs. And they took and laid it on the boil, and he recovered.

In Leviticus XIV we see a similar combination of magic with thoroughly rational procedures of preventive hygiene, characteristic of ancient Hebrew law:

And the Lord spake unto Moses and unto Aaron, saying, When ye be come into the land of Canaan, which I give to you for a possession, and I put the plague of leprosy in a house of the land of your possession; And he that owneth the house shall come and tell the priest, saying, It seemeth to me there is as it were a plague in the house: Then the priest shall command that they empty the house, before the priest go into it to see the plague, that all that is in the house be not made unclean: and afterward the priest shall go in to see the house; And he shall look on the plague, and behold it, if the plague be in the walls of the house with hollow strakes, greenish or reddish, which in sight are lower than the wall; Then the priest shall go out of the house to the door of the house, and shut up the house seven days: And the priest shall come again the seventh day, and shall look: and behold, if the plague be spread in the walls of the house; Then the priest shall command that they take away the stones in which the plague is, and they shall cast them into an unclean place without the city: And he shall cause the house to be scraped within round about, and they shall pour out the dust that they scrape off without the city into an unclean place. . . .

And he that lieth in the house shall wash his clothes; and he that eateth in the house shall wash his clothes. And if the priest shall come in, and look upon it, and behold, the plague hath not spread in the house, after the house was plaistered: then the priest shall pronounce the house clean, because the plague is healed. And he shall take to cleanse the house two birds, and cedar wood, and scarlet and hyssop: And he shall kill the one of the birds in an earthen vessel over running water: And he shall take the cedar wood, and the hyssop, and the scarlet, and the living bird, and dip them in the blood of the slain bird, and in the running water, and sprinkle the house seven times: And he shall cleanse the house with the blood of the bird, and with the running water, and with the living bird, and with the cedar wood and with the hyssop, and with the scarlet: But he shall let go the living bird out of the city into the open fields, and make an atonement for the house: and it shall be clean.

The healing miracles described in the New Testament follow the same unbroken line of healing magic that can be seen in the Old Testament. The figure of Christ the Healer himself seems to be a reincarnation of the healing gods worshiped in ancient Babylonian, Egyptian and Greco-Roman times. It therefore depends on one's attitude toward the authority of the Scriptures whether one considers his feats of miraculous healing as incontrovertible facts; as accounts of historic events of doubtful authenticity; or merely as added documentations of the ancient belief in magic. But whatever our attitude toward them, they had a profound effect upon the whole Western approach to healing. Jung has described the figure of Christ the Healer as one of the eternal images or archetypes deeply rooted in the minds of all people reared in the Christian tradition. It recurs in the dreams and fantasies of men and women of various cultures and historic epochs. Accounts of miraculous healings, real or imaginary, are a frequent theme in the lives of the apostles and of the saints, from St. Bernard of Clairveaux and St. Catherine of Siena to Bernardette Soubirou—and Mary Baker Eddy.

The same motifs, although in a distorted form, appear over and over again in the grandiose delusions of omnipotence in certain schizophrenic patients seen in the mental hospitals of our day. They may have been equally frequent in the Middle Ages and in the late Hellenistic period.

The following selection of incidents described in the Gospels follows the classification suggested by Leslie Weatherhead in his Psychology, Religion, and Healing.

CURES WHICH INVOLVE THE MECHANISM OF SUGGESTION

The Cleansing of a Leper:
Mark I: 40-45

And there cometh to Him a leper, beseeching Him, and kneeling down to Him, and saying unto Him, If Thou wilt, Thou canst make me clean. And being moved with compassion, He stretched forth His hand and touched him, and saith unto him, I will; be thou made clean. And straightway the leprosy departed from him, and he was made clean. And He strictly charged him, and straightway sent him out, and saith unto him, See thou say nothing to any man: but go thy way, show thyself to the priest, and offer for thy cleansing the things which Moses commanded, for a testimony unto them. But he went out, and began to publish it much, and to spread abroad the matter, insomuch that Jesus could no more openly enter into a city, but was without in desert places: and they came to Him from every quarter.

The Woman with Hemorrhage:
Mark V: 25-34

And a certain woman, which had an issue of blood twelve years, and had suffered many things of many physicians, and had spent all that she had, and was nothing bettered, but rather grew worse, When she had heard of Jesus, came in the press behind, and touched His garment. For she said, If I may touch but His clothes, I shall be whole. And straightway the fountain of her blood was dried up; and she felt in her body that she was healed of that plague. And Jesus, immediately knowing in Himself that virtue had gone out of Him, turned Himself about in the press, and said, Who touched my clothes? And His disciples said unto Him, Thou seest the multitude thronging Thee, and sayest Thou, Who touched me? And He looked round about to see her that had done this thing. But the woman fearing and trembling, knowing what was done in her, came and fell down before Him, and told Him all the truth. And He said unto her, Daughter, thy faith hath made thee whole; go in peace, and be whole of thy plague.

The Blind Man at Bethsaida:
Mark VIII: 22-26

And He cometh to Bethsaida; and they bring a blind man unto Him, and besought Him to touch him. And He took the blind man by the hand, and led him out of the town; and when He had spit on his eyes, and put His hands upon him, He asked him if he saw ought. And he looked up, and said, I see men as trees, walking. After that He put His hands again upon his eyes, and made him look up: and he was restored, and saw every man clearly. And He sent him away to his house, saying, Neither go into the town, nor tell it to any in the town.

The Man with the Withered Hand:
Mark III: 1-6

And he entered again into the synagogue; and there was a man there which had a withered hand. And they watched Him, whether He would heal him on the sabbath day; that they might accuse Him. And He saith unto the man, which had the withered hand, Stand forth. And He saith unto them, Is it lawful to do good on the sabbath days, or to do evil? to save life, or to kill? But they held their peace. And when He had looked round about on them with anger, being grieved for the hardness of their hearts, He saith unto the man, Stretch forth thine hand. And he stretched it out: and his hand was restored whole as the other.

CURES WHICH INVOLVE A MORE COMPLICATED TECHNIQUE

The Gerasene Demoniac:
Mark V: 1-20

And they came to the other side of the sea, into the country of the Gerasenes. And when He was come out of the boat, straightway there met Him out of the tombs a man with an unclean spirit, who had his dwelling in the tombs; and no man could any more bind him, no, not with a chain; because that he had been often bound with fetters and chains and the chains had been rent asunder by him, and the fetters broken in pieces: and no man had strength to tame him. And always, night and day, in the tombs and in the mountains, he was crying out, and cutting himself with stone. And when he saw Jesus from afar, he ran and worshipped Him; and crying out with a loud voice, he said, What have I to do with Thee, Jesus, Thou Son of the most High God? I adjure Thee by God, torment me not. For He said unto him, Come forth, thou unclean spirit, out of the man. And He asked him, What is thy name? And he saith unto Him, My name is Legion; for we are many. And he besought Him much that He would not send them away out of the country. Now there was there on the mountain side a great herd of swine feeding. And they besought Him, saying, Send us into the swine, that we may enter into them. And He gave them leave. And the unclean spirits came out, and entered into the swine: and the herd rushed down the steep into the sea, in number about two thousand; and they were choked in the sea. And they that fed them fled, and told it in the city, and in the country. And they came to see what it was that had come to pass. And they came to Jesus, and beheld him that was possessed with devils sitting, clothed and in his right mind, even him that had the legion: and they were afraid. And they that saw it declared unto them how it befell him that was possessed with devils, and concerning the swine. And they began to beseech Him to depart from their borders. And as He was entering into the boat, he that had been possessed with devils besought Him that he might be with Him. And He suffered him not, but saith unto him, Go to thy house unto thy friends, and tell them how great things the Lord hath done for thee, and how He had mercy on thee. And he went his way, and began to publish in Decapolis how great things Jesus had done for him: and all men did marvel.

CURES WHICH INVOLVE THE INFLUENCE OF A PSYCHIC "ATMOSPHERE" OR THE "FAITH" OF PEOPLE OTHER THAN THE PATIENT

The Paralytic at Capernaum:
Mark II: 1-12

And when He entered again into Capernaum after some days, it was noised that He was in the house. And many were gathered together, so that there was no longer room for them, no, not even about the door: and He spake the word unto them. And they came, bringing unto Him a man sick of the palsy, borne of four. And when they could not come nigh unto Him for the crowd, they uncovered the roof where He was: and when they had broken it up, they let down the bed whereon the sick of the palsy lay. And Jesus seeing their faith saith unto the sick of the palsy, Son, thy sins are forgiven. But there were certain of the scribes sitting there, and reasoning in their heart, Why doth this Man thus speak? He blasphemeth: who can forgive sins but One, even God? And straightway Jesus perceiving in His spirit that they so reasoned within themselves, saith unto them, Why reason ye these things in your hearts? Whether it is easier, to say to the sick of the palsy, Thy sins are forgiven; or to say, Arise, and take up thy bed, and walk? But that ye may know that the Son of man hath power on earth to forgive sins (He saith to the sick of the palsy), I say unto thee, Arise, take up thy bed, and go into thy house. And he arose, and straightway took up the bed, and went forth before them all; insomuch that they were all amazed, and glorified God, saying, We never saw it on this fashion.

The Epileptic Boy:
Mark IX: 14-29

And when He came to His disciples, He saw a great multitude about them, and the scribes questioning with them. And straightway all the people, when they beheld Him, were greatly amazed, and running to Him saluted Him. And He asked the scribes, What question ye with them? And one of the multitude answered and said, Master, I have brought unto Thee my son, which hath a dumb spirit; And wheresoever he taketh him he teareth him: and he foameth, and gnasheth with his teeth, and pineth away: and I spake to Thy disciples that they should cast him out; and they could not. He answered him, and saith, O faithless generation, how long shall I be with you? how long shall I suffer you? bring him unto me. And they brought him unto Him; and when he saw Him, straightway the spirit tare him; and he fell on the ground, and wallowed foaming. And He asked his father, How long is it ago since this came unto him? and he said, Of a child. And ofttimes it hath cast him into the fire, and into the waters, to destroy him: but if Thou canst do any thing, have compassion on us and help us. Jesus said unto him, If thou canst believe, all things are possible to him that believeth. And straightway the father of the child cried out, and said with tears, Lord I believe; help Thou mine unbelief. When Jesus saw that the people came running together, He rebuked the foul spirit, saying unto him, Thou dumb and deaf spirit, I charge thee, come out of him, and enter no more into him. And the spirit cried, and rent him sore, and came out of him: and he was as one dead; insomuch that many said, He is dead.

But Jesus took him by the hand, and lifted him up; and he arose. And when He was come into the house, His disciples asked Him privately, Why could not we cast him out? And He said unto them, This kind can come forth by no thing, but by prayer and fasting.

chapter 8

The Bonfires of the Inquisition or the Witches' Hammer Versus Mental Disease

KRAMER AND SPRENGER'S "MALLEUS MALEFICARUM"

In our next selection the focus shifts from the mountain slopes and the orchard groves of India, and from the idyllic landscape of Palestine, the scenes of the healing miracles described in the Bible, to a totally different setting. The place is Germany, the time 1484, when two Dominican monks, Heinrich Kramer and James Sprenger, published the first edition of the Malleus Maleficarum, also known as the Witches' Hammer. This book has been described as the "most prominent, the most important, the most authoritative volume in the vast literature of witchcraft." It is at the same time the book which has served generations of inquisitioners as a handy manual in sending hundreds of thousands of innocent women to their deaths at the stake.

The Malleus Maleficarum is an amazing document inflated by the scholarly pretentions and the fanatical zeal of its authors. On many pages it reveals more than that: their sadistic hostility toward women, which can only be understood as the manifestation of an underlying personality disorder. Maleficarum reflects the spirit of their time. It shows that even at the height of the Renaissance and at the threshold of the Reformation, the conflict between paganism and Christianity—between magic and a more enlightened monotheistic outlook—had not ceased to be a burning issue in more than one sense of the word. The ancient idols and deities, torn down from their pedestals a long time ago, had not altogether lost their grip on men's minds. Relegated to the role of fallen angels, devils and evil demons residing in the netherworld of the unconscious, they continued to be a threat to Western man.

In their introductory passages Kramer and Sprenger develop the basic principles of their theory of witchcraft. This, they felt, should explain the persistence of evil in a Christian universe ruled by the will of God. At the same time it should alert the faithful to the dangers of doubt and heresy.

MALLEUS MALEFICARUM

The First Part Treating of the Three Necessary Concomitants of Witchcraft, Which Are the Devil, a Witch, and the Permission of Almighty God

Certain writers, pretending to base their opinion upon the words of S. Thomas, have tried to maintain that there is not such a thing as magic, that it only exists in the imagination of those men who ascribe natural effects, the causes whereof are not known, to witchcraft and spells. There are others who acknowledge indeed that witches exist, but they declare that the influence of magic and the effects of charms are purely imaginary and phantasmical. A third class of writers maintain that the effects said to be wrought by magic spells are altogether illusory and fanciful, although it may be that the devil does really lend his aid to some witch.

The errors held by each one of these persons may thus be set forth and thus confuted. For in the very first place they are shown to be plainly heretical by many orthodox writers, and especially by S. Thomas, who lays down that such an opinion is altogether contrary to the authority of the saints and is founded upon absolute infidelity. Because the authority of the Holy Scriptures says that devils have power over the bodies and over the minds of men, when God allows them to exercise this power, as is plain from very many passages in the Holy Scriptures. Therefore those err who say that there is no such thing as witchcraft, but that it is purely imaginary, even although they do not believe that devils exist except in the imagination of the ignorant and vulgar, and the natural accidents which happen to a man he wrongly attributes to some supposed devil. For the imagination of some men is so vivid that they think they see actual figures and appearances which are but the reflection of their thoughts, and then these are believed to be the apparitions of evil spirits or even the spectres of witches. But this is contrary to the true faith, which teaches us that certain angels fell from heaven and are now devils, and we are bound to acknowledge that by their very nature they can do many wonderful things which we cannot do. And those who try to induce others to perform such evil wonders are called witches. And because infidelity in a person who has been baptized is technically called heresy, therefore such persons are plainly heretics.

As regards those who hold the other two errors, those, that is to say, who do not deny that there are demons and that demons possess a natural power, but who differ among themselves concerning the possible effects of magic and the possible operations of witches: the one school holding that a witch can truly bring about certain effects, yet these effects are not real but phantastical, the other school allowing that some real harm does befall the person or persons injured, but that when a witch imagines this damage is the effect of her arts she is grossly deceived. This error seems to be based upon two passages from the Canons where certain women are condemned who falsely imagine that during the night they ride abroad with Diana or Herodias. This may be read in the Canon. Yet because such things often happen by illusion and merely in the imagination, those who supposed that all the effects of witchcraft are mere illusion and imagination are very greatly deceived. Secondly, with regard to a man who believes or maintains that a creature can be made, or changed for better or for worse, or transformed into some other kind or likeness by anyone save by God, the Creator of all things, alone, [that man] is an infidel and worse than a heathen. Wherefore on account of these words such an effect if wrought by witchcraft cannot be real but must be purely phantastical.

It is useless to argue that any result of witchcraft may be a phantasy and unreal, because such a phantasy cannot be procured without resort to the power of the devil, and it is necessary that there should be made a contract with the devil, by which contract the witch truly and actually binds herself to be the servant of the devil and devotes herself to the devil, and this is not done in any dream or under any illusion, but she herself bodily and truly cooperates with, and conjoins herself to, the devil. For this indeed is the end of all witchcraft; whether it be the casting of spells by a look or by a formula of words or by some other charm, it is all of the devil, as will be made clear in the following question.

In truth, if anyone cares to read the words of the Canon, there are four points which must particularly strike him. And the first point is this: It is absolutely incumbent upon all creatures and Priests, and upon all who have the cure of souls, to teach their flocks that there is one, only, true God, and that to none other in Heaven or earth may worship be given. The second point is this, that although these women imagine they are riding (as they think and say) with Diana or with Herodias, in truth they are riding with the devil, who calls himself by some such heathen name and throws a glamour before their eyes. And the third point is this, that the act of riding abroad may be merely illusory, since the devil has extra-ordinary power over the minds of those who have given themselves up to him, so that what they do in pure imagination, they believe they have actually and really done in the body. And the fourth point is this: Witches have made a compact to obey the devil in all things, wherefore that the words of the Canon should be extended to include and comprise every act of witchcraft is absurd, since witches do much more than these women, and witches actually are of a very different kind. . . .

Whether It Be a Heresy to Maintain that Witches Exist

This then is our proposition: devils by their art do bring about evil effects through witchcraft, yet it is true that without the assistance of some agent they cannot make any form, either substantial or accidental, and we do not maintain that they can inflict damage without the assistance of some agent, but with such an agent diseases, and any other human passions or ailments, can be brought about, and these are real and true. How these agents or how the employment of such means can be rendered effective in co-operation with devils will be made clear in the following chapters. . . .

With regard to operations of witchcraft, we find that some of these may be due to mental influence over others, and in some cases such mental influence might be a good one, but it is the motive which makes it evil. . . .

But in order yet more fully to attempt a solution of these matters we may consider certain difficulties from a discussion of which we shall yet more clearly arrive at the truth. First, spiritual substances cannot change bodies to some other natural form unless it be through the mediumship of some agent. Therefore, however strong a mental influence may be, it cannot effect any change in a man's mind or disposition. Moreover, several universities, especially that of Paris, have condemned the following article: That an enchanter is able to cast a camel into a deep ditch merely by directing his gaze upon it. And so this article is condemned, that a corporeal body should obey some spiritual substance if this be understood simply, that is to say, if the obedience entails some actual change or transformation. For in regard to this, it is God alone Who is absolutely obeyed. Bearing these points in mind we may soon see how that fascination, or influence of the eyes of which we have spoken, is possible. For it is not possible that a man through the natural powers of his mind should direct such power from his eyes that, without the agency of his own body or of some other medium, he should be able to do harm to the body of another man. Nor is it possible that a man through the natural powers of his mind should at his will bring about some change, and by directing this power through the mediumship of his eyes entirely transform the body of a man, upon whom he fixes his gaze, just as his will and pleasure may be. . . .

So far we have set down our opinions absolutely without prejudice and refraining from any hasty or rush judgment, not deviating from the teachings and writings of the Saints. We conclude, therefore, that the Catholic truth is this, that to bring about these evils which form the subject of discussion, witches and the devil always work together, and that in so far as these matters are concerned one can do nothing without the aid and assistance of the other.

What, then, are the evil things witches, in co-operation with the devil, can bring about? They range from the practice of black magic to corrupting man's mind so as to betray his Christian faith. They may cause illness, mental and physical. And they may, above all, entice man to indulge in all sorts of sexual deviations. The witches themselves are the chief perpetrators of such crimes; they copulate with devils and other demons and are capable of begetting children with them. In any case, the root of the evil lies in man's carnal desires, or, anatomically speaking in his—or her—"privy parts."

Witches, by the exercise of no natural power, but only by the help of the devil, are able to bring about harmful effects. And the devils themselves can only do this by the use of material objects as their instruments, such as bones, hair, wood, iron, and all sorts of objects of this kind, concerning which operation we shall treat more fully a little later. . . .

Moreover, witchcraft differs from all other harmful and mysterious arts in this point, that of all superstition it is essentially the vilest, the most evil and the worst, wherefore it derives its name from doing evil, and from blaspheming the true faith.

Let us especially note too that in the practice of this abominable evil, four points in particular are required. First, most profanely to renounce the Catholic Faith, or at any rate to deny certain dogmas of the faith; secondly, to devote themselves body and soul to all evil; thirdly, to offer up unbaptized children to Satan; fourthly, to indulge in every kind of carnal lust with Incubi and Succubi and all manner of filthy delights. . . .

Now there are two circumstances which are certainly very common at the present day, that is to say, the connexion of witches with familiars, Incubi and Succubi, and the horrible sacrifices of small children. Therefore we shall particularly deal with these matters, so that in the first place we shall discuss these demons themselves; secondly, the witches and their works, and thirdly, we will inquire wherefore such things are suffered to be. Now these demons work owing to their influence upon man's mind and upon his free will, and they choose to copulate under the influence of certain stars rather than under the influence of others, for it would seem that at certain times their semen can more easily generate and beget children. Accordingly, we must inquire why the demons should act at the conjunction of certain stars. . . .

Whether Children Can Be Generated by Incubi and Succubi

At first it may truly seem that it is not in accordance with the Catholic Faith to maintain that children can be begotten by devils, that is to say, by Incubi and Succubi; for God Himself, before sin came into the world, instituted human procreation, since He created woman from the rib of man to be a helpmeet unto man: And to them He said: Increase and multiply. In the time of the new law also, Christ confirmed this union: Have ye not read, that he who made man from the beginning, made them male and female? Therefore man cannot be begotten in any other way than this.

But it may be argued that devils take their part in this generation not as the essential cause, but as a secondary and artificial cause, since they busy themselves by interfering with the process of normal copulation and conception by obtaining human semen, and themselves transferring it. . . .

Now the Theologians have ascribed to the devils certain qualities, as that they are unclean spirits, yet not by very nature unclean. For according to Dionysius there is in them a natural madness, a rabid concupiscence, a wanton fancy, as is seen from their spiritual sins of pride, envy, and wrath. For this reason they are the enemies of the human race: rational in mind, but reasoning without words; subtle in wickedness, eager to so hurt; ever fertile in fresh deceptions, they change the perceptions and befoul the emotions of men, they confound the watchful, and in dreams disturb the sleeping; they bring diseases, stir up tempests, disguise themselves as angels of light, bear Hell always about them; from witches they usurp themselves the worship of God, and by this means magic spells are made; they seek to get a mastery over the good, and molest them to the most of their power; to the elect they are given as a temptation, and always they lie in wait for the destruction of men.

And although they have a thousand ways of doing harm, they have tried ever since their downfall to bring about schisms in the Church, to disable charity, to infect with the gall of envy the sweetness of the acts of the Saints, and in every way to subvert and perturb the human race; yet their power remains confined to the privy parts and the navel. For through the wantonness of the flesh they have much power over men; and in men the source of wantonness lies in the privy parts since it is from them that the semen falls just as in women it falls from the navel. . . .

But the reason that devils turn themselves into Incubi or Succubi is not for the cause of pleasure, since a spirit has not flesh and blood; but chiefly it is with this intention, that through the vice of luxury they may work a twofold harm against men, that is, in body and in soul, that so men may be more given to all vices. And there is no doubt that they know under which stars the semen is most vigorous, and that men so conceived will be always perverted by witchcraft. . . .

But if it is asked why the devil is allowed to cast spells upon the venereal act, rather than upon any other human act, it is answered that many reasons are assigned by the Doctors, which will be discussed later in the part concerning the divine permission. For the present the reason that has been mentioned before must suffice, namely, that the power of the devil lies in the privy parts of men. For of all struggles those are the hardest where the fight is continuous and victory rare. And it is unsound to argue that in that case the work of the devil is stronger than the work of God, since the matrimonial act instituted by God can be made void: for the devil does not make it void by violence, since he has no power at all in the matter except as he is permitted by God. Therefore it would be better to argue from this that he is powerless.

Secondly, it is true that to procreate a man is the act of a living body. But when it is said that devils cannot give life, because that flows formally from the soul, it is true; but materially life springs from the semen, and an Incubus devil can, with God's permission, accomplish this by coition. And the semen does not so much spring from him as it is another man's semen received by him for this purpose.

For the devil is Succubus to a man, and becomes Incubus to a woman. . . .

Therefore we make three propositions. First, that the foulest venereal acts are performed by such devils, not for the sake of delectation, but for the pollution of the souls and bodies of those to whom they act as Succubi or Incubi. Second, that through such action, complete conception and generation by women can take place, inasmuch as they can deposit human semen in the suitable place of a woman's womb where there is already a corresponding substance. In the same way they can also collect the seeds of other things for the working of other effects. Third, that in the begetting of such children only the local motion is to be attributed to devils, and not the actual begetting, which arises not from the power of the devil or of the body which he assumes, but from the virtue of him whose semen it was; wherefore the child is the son not of the devil, but of some man.

And here there is a clear answer to those who would contend that there are two reasons why devils cannot generate children: First, that generation is effected by the formative virtue which exists in semen released from a living body; and that because the body assumed by devils is not of such a sort, therefore, etc. The answer is clear, that the devil deposits naturally formative semen in its proper place, etc. Secondly, it may be argued that semen has no power of generation except as long as the heat of life is retained in it, and that this must be lost when it is carried great distances. The answer is that devils are able to store the semen safely, so that its vital heat is not lost; or even that it cannot evaporate so easily on account of the great speed at which they move by reason of the superiority of the mover over the thing moved.

In the following pages the authors ask a question which has since been raised over and over again by historians and psychologists. "Why is superstition"—that is to say, witchcraft—"chiefly found in women?" Or to put the question more specifically: "Why did the Witches' Hammer confine its blows to the female sex, and deal only gingerly with an occasional male wizard or sorcerer?" We have already hinted at the probable explanation for this state of affairs. It lies in the essentially antifeminine attitude of the writers, who were in turn able to support their position by ample quotations from the classics, from the Old Testament, and from authorities of the early Paulinian church. All this had undoubtedly become part and parcel of the Christian tradition. Their attitude may have been further reinforced by socioeconomic factors operating in medieval feudal society, which allotted a generally inferior role to the "weaker sex."

But the decisive motive must have been their fanatical hatred of women, based on what can only be attributed to a sadistic streak in their own mental make-up. The authors themselves sought to rationalize this hatred by the well-known device of projection and displacement, characteristic of the paranoid patient and, to a lesser degree, of the latent homosexual. To them, as to the Catholic Church of their times, woman was the initiator and arch perpetrator of Original Sin. This accounts for her innate wickedness. She and only she is the eternal temptress inciting the carnal desires of man.

But it is interesting to note that at one point of their indictment they come out with a surprisingly astute observation. "Women," they assert, "are naturally more impressionable and more ready to receive the influence of a disembodied spirit; and that when they use this quality well, they are very good, but when they use it ill they are very evil."

Here, in a nutshell, is the theory of women's greater sensitiveness, the idea that their intuitive capacities are higher than those commonly seen in men. This is the same hypothesis the French historian Michelet has proposed in the introduction to his volume Satanism and Witchcraft. It has, in a different context, been suggested by anthropologists, clinical psychologists and workers in psychical research or parapsychology. Whether or not this ostensibly sex-linked "psychic" faculty of women is actually due to biological factors is debatable. It may well be that it is a natural corollary of motherhood: the result of woman's lifelong dedication to the care of the young and to the necessity of keeping alert to the slightest "subliminal" clues to the infants' physical and emotional needs.

There is another question which can be raised at this point. Why, one may ask, did the fury of the witch hunters, resulting in the fiery death of hundreds of thousands of innocent women, reach its highest pitch at that particular period of history? The striking fact is that it came at a juncture when the "Dark Ages" were receding and giving way to a new outlook on life. Dogma and superstition were gradually yielding to a more rationalistic attitude; Martin Luther has already launched his crusade against the infallibility of the Catholic Church. Yet it is one of the paradoxes of this *situation that both the Church and the Protestant movement that rallied against her found themselves in perfect agreement in their determination to purge the Western world from the scourge of witchcraft. In terms of this overriding purpose, there were no major theological differences between the Grand Inquisitioner of Catholic Spain and the witch hunters of Salem in Protestant New England.*

This peculiar alignment of forces suggests the answer to our question. Seen from the vantage point of the twentieth century, the inquisitions staged by the Catholic Church were desperate attempts to rid itself of the vestiges of magic and demonology which had survived within the Christian tradition. It was fully consistent with this trend that the Protestant movement and the very forces of the new humanistic and scientific spirit felt committed to continuing this struggle. Witches and sorcerers had to be burned not only for the greater glory of God but also in the interest of scientific progress. The burning of witches was meant to be the death knell of magic. It was superstition to end all "superstitions."

The period of the witch hunts was thus an era of transition. It was an era in which Western man had his "last fling," as it were, at the "monstrous farrago" of paganism—of magic and countermagic. Once the bonfires of the Inquisition were extinguished and the smoke of burning flesh cleared from the village greens and market places of Europe and the New World, the stage was set for the advent of a new humanistic era, followed by the spectacular technological and scientific achievements of Western culture. From now on, devils and witches were relegated to the realm of folklore and fairy tale; the Church itself was anxious to repudiate the embarrassing chapter of witch trials as one of the tragic fallacies of the Dark Ages.

This concept of a miscarried rationalistic overreaction of Western man to his heritage of magic is further borne out by the fact that other civilizations have nothing, or next to nothing, comparable to the frenzy of organized Western witch trials. It is true that such technologically backward oriental cultures as the ancient Hindu and Chinese were not averse to sending an occasional witch in their midst to her death at the stake. Nor can there be any denying of the venerable Brahman custom of giving the same treatment to women who had the misfortune to outlive their husbands. But meeting such a fate never became the foremost professional risk of a Hindu Yogi or a Chinese sage.

In effect the holy man of the East was held in high esteem by both the common man and the nobility. He was accepted as a living paragon of the good life and his alleged magic or supernatural powers envied and emulated by countless disciples and followers.

This, then, is the answer to our second question. It is the fundamentally different attitude toward the heritage of magic which seems to account for the conspicuous absence in the histories of China and India of anything like the witch trials that have disgraced the annals of Western civilization.

It is one of the paradoxes of history that the same factor may also be responsible for the considerable lag in technological and scientific progress which has, up to recent years, been characteristic of Far Eastern cultures. Apparently, intolerance of magic is one of the prices the West had to pay for its achievements. Conversely, the price paid by the East for its greater tolerance of the "irrational," metaphysical, aspects of existence has been the slowness of its technological development and the dearth of scientific know-how.

The answer given by Kramer and Sprenger themselves is, however, altogether different. Their interpretation is as follows:

Why Superstition is Chiefly Found in Women

As for the first question, why a greater number of witches is found in the fragile feminine sex than among men; it is indeed a fact that it were idle to contradict, since it is accredited by actual experience, apart from the verbal testimony of credible witnesses. And without in any way detracting from a sex in which God has always taken great glory that His might should be spread abroad, let us say that various men have assigned various reasons for this fact, which nevertheless agree in principle. Wherefore it is good, for the admonition of women, to speak of this matter; and it has often been proved by experience that they are eager to hear of it, so long as it is set forth with discretion.

For some learned men propound this reason; that there are three things in nature, the Tongue, an Ecclesiastic, and a Woman, which know no moderation in goodness or vice; and when they exceed the bounds of their condition, they reach the greatest heights and the lowest depths of goodness and vice. When they are governed by a good spirit, they are most excellent in virtue; but when they are governed by an evil spirit, they indulge the worst possible vices. . . .

Now the wickedness of women is spoken of in Ecclesiasticus XXV: There is no head above the head of a serpent; and there is no wrath above the wrath of a woman. I had rather dwell with a lion and a dragon than to keep house with a wicked woman. And among much which in that place precedes and follows about a wicked woman, he concludes: All wickedness is but little to the wickedness of a woman. Wherefore S. John Chrysostom says on the text, It is not good to marry: What else is woman but a foe to friendship, an unescapable punishment, a necessary evil, a natural temptation, a desirable calamity, a domestic danger, a delectable detriment, an evil of nature painted with fair colours! Therefore if it be a sin to divorce her when she ought to be kept, it is indeed a necessary torture; for either we commit adultery by divorcing her, or we must endure daily strife. Cicero in his second book of The Rhetorics says: The many lusts of men lead them into one sin, but the one lust of women leads them into all sins; for the root of all women's vices is avarice. And Seneca says in his Tragedies: A woman either loves or hates; there is no third grade. And the tears of a woman are a deception, for they may spring from true grief, or they may be a snare. When a woman thinks alone, she thinks evil. . . .

Others again have propounded other reasons why there are more superstitious women found than men. And the first is that they are more credulous; and since the chief aim of the devil is to corrupt faith, therefore, he rather attacks them. He that is quick to believe is light-minded, and shall be diminished. The second reason is, that women are naturally more impressionable, and more ready to receive the influence of a disembodied spirit; and that when they use this quality well they are very good, but when they use it ill they are very evil.

The third reason is that they have slippery tongues, and are unable to conceal from their fellow-women those things which by evil arts they know; and, since they are weak, they find an easy and secret manner of vindicating themselves by witchcraft. See Ecclesiasticus as quoted above: I had rather dwell with a lion and a dragon than to keep house with a wicked woman. All wickedness is but little to the wickedness of a woman. And to this may be added that, as they are very impressionable, they act accordingly.

But because in these times this perfidy is more often found in women than in men, as we learn by actual experience, if anyone is curious as to the reason, we may add to what has already been said in the following: that since they are feebler both in mind and body, it is not surprising that they should come more under the spell of witchcraft.

For as regards intellect, or the understanding of spiritual things, they seem to be of a different nature from men. . . .

But as the natural reason is that she is more carnal than a man, as is clear from her many carnal abominations. And it should be noted that there was a defect in the formation of the first woman, since she was formed from a bent rib, that is, a rib of the breast, which is bent as it were in the contrary direction to a man. And since through this defect she is an imperfect animal, she always deceives. . . .

And as to her other mental quality, that is, her natural will; when she hates someone whom she formerly loved, then she seethes with anger, and impatience in her whole soul, just as the tides of the sea are always heaving and boiling. Many authorities allude to this cause. There is no wrath above the wrath of a woman. And Seneca: No might of the flames or of the swol-

len winds, no deadly weapon, is so much to be feared as the lust and hatred
of a woman who has been divorced from the marriage bed. . . .

To conclude. All witchcraft comes from carnal lust, which is in women
insatiable. There are three things that are never satisfied, yea, a fourth
thing which says not, It is enough; that is the mouth of the womb.
Wherefore for the sake of fulfilling their lusts they consort even with devils.
More such reasons could be brought forward, but to the understanding it is
sufficiently clear that it is not matter for wonder that there are more women
than men found infected with the heresy of witchcraft.

*There is another ominous theme which runs through many chapters of
the* Malleus Maleficarum: *it is the theme of the witch "obstructing the generative forces of men" and "removing the members accommodated to that
act." It is an early version of what contemporary psychoanalysis describes
as the emasculating or castrating woman.*

*This leads the authors to a digression of considerable psychological inter-
est. In effect, they propose a theory of the unconscious, in which the operation of instinctual drives, sexual or otherwise, is attributed to the machina-
tion of the devil—and of his willing instrument, the witch. If there is an
element of truth in the macabre case histories which emerge from their text,
it indicates that more often than not the witch or sorceress was a woman
who constituted a threat to the vanity or masculine prowess of her lover. It
was a threat to which, for reasons of their own, her confessors and execu-
tioners seemed to be equally apt to succumb. And their answers to it were
the rationalizations of the* Witches' Hammer *justifying the branding iron,
the torturing rack and capital punishment of their victims.*

Now there are seven methods by which they infect with witchcraft the
venereal act and the conception of the womb: First, by inclining the minds
of men to inordinate passion; second, by obstructing their generative force;
third, by removing the members accommodated to that act; fourth, by
changing men into beasts by their magic art; fifth, by destroying the generative force in women; sixth, by procuring abortion; seventh, by offering
children to devils, besides other animals and fruits of the earth with which
they work much harm. And all these will be considered later; but for the
present let us give our minds to the injuries towards men. . . .

But indeed such hatred is aroused by witchcraft between those joined in
the sacrament of matrimony and such freezing up of the generative forces,
that men are unable to perform the necessary action for begetting offspring.
But since love and hate exist in the soul, which even the devil cannot enter,
lest these things must seem incredible to anyone, they must be inquired
into; and by meeting argument with argument the matter will be made
clear. . . .

Whether Witches Can Sway the Minds of Men to Love or Hatred

All sins are not committed at the instigation of the devil, but some are of our own choosing. For Origen says: Even if the devil were not, men would still lust after food and venery and such things. And from these inordinate lusts, much may result, unless such appetites be reasonably restrained. But to restrain such ungoverned desire is the part of man's free will, over which even the devil has no power. . . .

To return to the question. The apparitions that come in dreams to sleepers proceed from the ideas retained in the repository of their mind, through a natural local motion caused by the flow of blood to the first and inmost seat of their faculties of perception; and we speak of an intrinsic local motion in the head and the cells of the brain.

And this can also happen through a similar local motion created by devils. Also such things happen not only to the sleeping, but even to those who are awake. For in these also the devils can stir up and excite the inner perceptions and humours, so that ideas retained in the repositories of their minds are drawn out and made apparent to the faculties of fancy and imagination, so that such men imagine these things to be true. And this is called interior temptation.

And it is no wonder that the devil can do this by his own natural power; since any man by himself, being awake and having the use of his reason, can voluntarily draw from his repositories the images he has retained in them; in such a way that he can summon to himself the images of whatsoever things he pleases. And this being granted, it is easy to understand the matter of excessive infatuation in love.

Now there are two ways in which devils can, as has been said, raise up this kind of images. Sometimes they work without enchanting the human reason, as has been said in the matter of temptation, and the example of voluntary imagination. But sometimes the use of reason is entirely chained up; and this may be exemplified by certain naturally defective persons, and by madmen and drunkards. Therefore it is no wonder that devils can, with God's permission, chain up the reason; and such men are called delirious, because their senses have been snatched away by the devil. And this they do in two ways, either with or without the help of witches. . . .

This, then, is the theory of the causation of mental illness as it was proposed by Kramer and Sprenger. Taken in a metaphorical and not in a literal sense it would seem to miss Freud's discovery of the disrupting effects of repressed unconscious motivations by a hair's breadth. At the same time it shows, however, the unbridgeable gulf between the ancient demonological concept of mental disease and modern etiological concepts.

The fact is that despite the apparent progress made since the pre-Christian era, little has changed in Western man's understanding of the unconscious forces within himself. Theological writings from the early church fathers to St. Augustine abound with examples showing that by the late Middle Ages the iconoclastic fervor of the Catholic Church has still fallen short of its objective. Both the clergy and the laity continued to be haunted by fear of the deposed gods and goddesses of ancient times. They held on to the old belief in demoniacal possession as the principal cause of disease, mental and physical, while their attempts at "cure" became even more savage than they had been in the past.

The close resemblance of some of Kramer and Sprenger's ideas to his own discoveries has not escaped the watchful eyes of Sigmund Freud. In a letter dated January 17, 1897, to his friend Wilhelm Fliess, he remarks that his "whole brand-new theory" of the origins of hysteria has already been adumbrated by the inquisitioners. "Do you remember," he asked, "my always saying that the medieval theory of possession, that held by the ecclesiastical courts, was identical with our theory of a foreign body and the splitting of consciousness?"

He even notes that some of the confessions extorted from the victims of the inquisition were "so very much like what my patients tell me under psychological treatment." Freud seems to anticipate at this point some of the objections critics were to level against him many years later: the objection of "observer contamination" or "doctrinal compliance" as a potential source of error in the behavioral sciences (R. Rosenthal, 1971, J. Ehrenwald, 1966).

                                                        17. 1. 97 IX Berggasse 19.
My dear Wilhelm,

. . . By the way, what have you got to say to the suggestion that the whole of my brand-new theory of the primary origins of hysteria is already familiar and has even been published a hundred times over, though several centuries ago? Do you remember my always saying that the medieval theory of possession, that held by the ecclesiastical courts, was identical with our theory of a foreign body and the splitting of consciousness? But why did the devil who took possession of the poor victims invariably commit misconduct with them, and in such horrible ways? Why were the confessions extracted under torture so very like what my patients tell me under psychological treatment? I must delve into the literature of the subject. Incidentally, the cruelties practiced served to illuminate some hitherto obscure symptoms of hysteria. The pins which appear in such astonishing ways, the needles for which the poor creatures have their breasts cut open, though they are invisible with X-rays, can all be found in the stories of seduction! . . .

The inquisitors now again search with needles for diabolical stigmata, and the victims again invent the same gruesome stories (aided perhaps by the seducer's disguise). Thus victim and torturer alike recall their earliest youth . . .

Your
Sigm.

In the following passages Kramer and Sprenger go into more clinical details of their particular brand of "Psychopathia Sexualis."

Whether Witches Can Hebetate [Inhibit] the Powers of Generation or Obstruct the Venereal Act

The devil obstructs the genital power, not intrinsically by harming the organ, but extrinsically by rendering it useless. Therefore, since it is an artificial and not a natural obstruction he can make a man impotent towards one woman but not towards others: by taking away the inflammation of his lust for her, but not for other women, either through his own power, or through some herb or stone or some occult natural means.

Besides, since impotence in this act is sometimes due to coldness of nature, or some natural defect, it is asked how it is possible to distinguish whether it is due to witchcraft or not. Hostiensis gives the answer in his Summa (but this must not be publicly preached): When the member is in no way stirred, and can never perform the act of coition, this is a sign of frigidity of nature; but when it is stirred and becomes erect, but yet cannot perform, it is a sign of witchcraft.

It is to be noted also that impotence of the member to perform the act is not the only bewitchment; but sometimes the woman is caused to be unable to conceive, or else she miscarries.

Note, moreover, that according to what is laid down by the Canons, whoever through desire of vengeance or for hatred does anything to a man or a woman to prevent them from begetting or conceiving must be considered a homicide. And note, further, that the Canon speaks of loose lovers who, to save their mistresses from shame, use contraceptives, such as potions or herbs that contravene nature, without any help from devils. And such penitents are to be punished as homicides. But witches who do such things by witchcraft are by law punishable by the extreme penalty, as has been touched on above in the First Question. . . .

Wherefore the Catholic Doctors make the following distinction, that impotence caused by witchcraft is either temporary or permanent. And if it is temporary, then it does not annul the marriage. Moreover, it is presumed to be temporary if they are able to be healed of the impediment within three years from their cohabitation, having taken all possible pains, either through the sacraments of the Church, or through other remedies, to be cured. But if they are not then cured by any remedy, from that time it is presumed to be permanent.

Whether Witches May Work Some Prestidigitatory Illusion so that the Male Organ Appears to be Entirely Removed and Separate from the Body

Here is declared the truth about diabolic operations with regard to the male organ. And to make plain the facts in this matter, it is asked whether witches can with the help of devils really and actually remove the member, or whether they only do so apparently by some glamour or illusion. And that they can actually do so is argued a fortiori; for since devils can do greater things than this, as killing them or carrying them from place to place . . . therefore they can also truly and actually remove men's members. . . .

There is no doubt certain witches can do marvelous things with regard to male organs, for this agrees with what has been seen and heard by many, and with the general account of what has been known concerning that member through the senses of sight and touch. And as to how this thing is possible, it is to be said that it can be done in two ways, either actually and in fact, as the first arguments have said, or through some prestige or glamour. But when it is performed by witches, it is no illusion in the opinion of the sufferer. For his imagination can really and actually believe that something is not present, since by none of his exterior senses, such as sight or touch, can he perceive that it is present. . . .

And we can illustrate this from certain natural phenomena. For sweet wine appears bitter on the tongue of the fevered, his taste being deceived not by the actual fact, but through his disease. So also in the case under consideration, the deception is not due to fact, since the member is still actually in its place; but it is an illusion of the senses with regard to it. . . .

Again, as has been said above concerning the generative powers, the devil can obstruct that action by imposing some other body of the same colour and appearance in such a way that some smoothly fashioned body of the colour of flesh is interposed between the sight and touch, and between the true body of the sufferer, so that it seems to him that he can see and feel nothing but a smooth body with its surface interrupted by no genital organ. . . .

Like all conscientious clinicians, Kramer and Sprenger sought to illustrate *their point by more or less detailed case histories:*

Of the Several Methods by Which Devils Through Witches Entice and Allure the Innocent to the Increase of That Horrid Craft and Company

There is a place in the diocese of Brixen where a young man deposed the following facts concerning the bewitchment of his wife.

"In the time of my youth I loved a girl who importuned me to marry her; but I refused her and married another girl from another country. But wishing for friendship's sake to please her, I invited her to the wedding. She came, and while the other honest women were wishing us luck and offering gifts she raised her hand and, in the hearing of the other women who were standing round, said, You will have few days of health after to-day. My bride was frightened, since she did not know her (for, as I have said, I had married her from another country), and asked the bystanders who she was who had threatened her in that way; and they said that she was a loose and vagrom woman. None the less, it happened just as she had said. For after a few days my wife was so bewitched that she lost the use of all her limbs, and even now, after ten years, the effect of witchcraft can be seen on her body."

If we were to collect all the similar instances which have occurred in one town of that diocese, it would take a whole book; but they are written and preserved at the house of the Bishop of Brixen, who still lives to testify to their truth, astounding and unheard-of though they are.

But we must not pass over in silence one unheard-of and astounding instance. A certain high-born Count in the ward of Westerich, in the diocese of Strasburg, married a noble girl of equal birth; but after he had celebrated the wedding, he was for three years unable to know her carnally, on account, as the event proved, of a certain charm which prevented him. In great anxiety, and not knowing what to do, he called loudly on the Saints of God. It happened that he went to the State of Metz to negotiate some business; and while he was walking about the streets and squares of the city, attended by his servants and domestics, he met a certain woman who had formerly been his mistress. Seeing her, and not at all thinking of the spell that was on him, he spontaneously addressed her kindly for the sake of the old friendship, asking her how she did, and whether she was well. And she, seeing the Count's gentleness, in her turn asked very particularly after his health and affairs; and when he answered that he was well, and that everything prospered with him, she was astonished and was silent for a time. The Count seeing her thus astonished, again spoke kindly to her, inviting her to converse with him. So she inquired after his wife, and received a similar reply, that she was in all respects well. Then she asked if he had any children; and the Count said he had three sons, one born in each year. At that she

was more astonished, and was again silent for a while. And the Count asked
her, Why, my dear, do you make such careful inquiries? I am sure that you
congratulate me on my happiness. Then she answered, Certainly I congratulate you; but curse that old woman who said she would bewitch your
body so that you could not have connexion with your wife! And in proof of
this, there is a pot in the well in the middle of your yard containing certain
objects evilly bewitched, and this was placed there in order that, as long as
its contents were preserved intact, for so long you would be unable to co-
habit. But see! it is all in vain, and I am glad, etc. On his return home the
Count did not delay to have the well drained; and, finding the pot, burned
its contents and all, whereupon he immediately recovered the virility which
he had lost. Wherefore the Countess again invited all the nobility to a fresh
wedding celebration, saying that she was now the Lady of that castle and
estate, after having for so long remained a virgin. For the sake of the
Count's reputation it is not expedient to name that castle and estate; but we
have related this story in order that the truth of the matter be known, to
bring so great a crime into open detestation.

From this it is clear that witches use various methods to increase their
numbers. For the above-mentioned woman, because she had been supplanted by the Count's wife, cast that spell upon the Count with the help of
another witch; and this is how one witchcraft brings innumerable others in
its train.

The methods advanced by Kramer and Sprenger to "destroy and cure"
witchcraft are a bizarre mixture of magic and counter-magic aided by the
powers of persuasion, prayer and the sacraments. When all this had met
with failure—well, they had to resort to the branding iron, the torturing
rack and the ultimate remedy: the burning at the stake.

Some of the procedures used by the inquisitors are illustrated by the fol-
lowing passage:

Prescribed Remedies, to Wit, the Lawful Exorcisms of the
Church, for all Sorts of Infirmities and Ills Due to Witchcraft;
and the Method of Exorcising Those who Are Bewitched

It has already been stated that witches can afflict men with every kind of
physical infirmity; therefore it can be taken as a general rule that the various verbal or practical remedies which can be applied in the case of those
infirmities which we have just been discussing are equally applicable to all
other infirmities, such as epilepsy of leprosy, for example. And as lawful
exorcisms are reckoned among the verbal remedies and have been most
often considered by us, they may be taken as a general type of such remedies; and there are three matters to be considered regarding them.

First, we must judge whether a person who has not been ordained as an exorcist, such as a layman or a secular cleric, may lawfully exorcise devils and their works. Bound up with this question are three others: namely; first, what constitutes the legality of this practice; secondly, the seven conditions which must be observed when one wishes to make private use of charms and benedictions; and thirdly, in what way the disease is to be exorcised and the devil conjured.

Secondly, we must consider what is to be done when no healing grace results from the exorcism.

Thirdly, we must consider practical and not verbal remedies; together with the solution of certain arguments. . . .

This then is the significance of the words that are used in exorcism, as when it is said, "Depart, O Satan, from him"; and likewise of the things that are then done.

To return, then, to the actual point, when it is asked whether the disease is to be exorcised and the devil adjured and which of these should be done first; it is answered that not the disease but the sick and bewitched man himself is exorcised: just as in the case of a child, it is not the infection of the former which is exorcised, but the child itself. Also, just as the child is first exorcised, and then the devil is adjured to depart, so also is the bewitched person first exorcised, and afterwards the devil and his works are bidden to depart. Again, just as salt and water are exorcised, so are all things which can be used by the sick man, so that it is expedient to exorcise and bless chiefly his food and drink. In the case of baptism the following ceremony of exorcism is observed: the exsufflation towards the West and the renunciation of the devil; secondly, the raising of the hands with a solemn confession of the faith of the Christian religion; thirdly, prayer, benediction, and the laying on of hands; fourthly, the stripping and anointing with Holy Oil; and after baptism the communion and the putting on of the chrisom. But all this is not necessary in the exorcism of one who is bewitched; but that he should first have made a good confession and if possible he is to hold a lighted candle, and receive the Holy Communion; and instead of putting on a chrisom, he is to remain bound naked to a Holy Candle of the length of Christ's body or of the Cross. And then may be said the following:

I exorcise thee, Peter, or thee, Barbara, being weak but reborn in Holy Baptism, by the living God, by the true God, by God Who redeemed thee with His Precious Blood, that thou mayest be exorcised, that all the illusion and wickedness of the devil's deceit may depart and flee from thee together with every unclean spirit; adjured by Him who will come to judge both the quick and the dead, and who will purge the earth with fire. Amen.

The Witches' Hammer *represents one of the most tragic documents in the history of mental healing. Some of its passages amount to a vivid clinical* description of mental disorders and aberrations of various kinds. But its dogmatic, superstitious approach made it impossible to draw the right conclusions from some of its basically correct observations. It fought its battles against the enormity of "superstitions" by equally superstitious means. In effect, the persecution of witches was itself the product of collective mental derangement, a symptom of mass hysteria. It projected the sadistic drives of the persecutors upon the pathetic figures of witches and sorcerers, thus creating an artificial minority group to serve as a scapegoat for the majority. As it happened, many members of the minority group were themselves sufferers from mental illness of one kind or another. Yet far from recognizing their plight for what it was, the witch hunters and exorcists fought the witches' delusions on the level of the deluded, and whenever the patient failed to respond to exorcism by persuasion, prayer or the sacraments, they saw no choice but to resort to their own brand of shock treatment: burning at the stake. This, they felt, was the ultimate remedy to save the soul of the obstinate heretic from eternal damnation.

At the same time we find three significant by-products of the exorcist's labors: his emphasis on the sexual origin and implications of many mental and neurotic disorders; his vague realization of the part played by unconscious drives in the causation of mental illness in general; and the emergence of the clinical picture of the emasculating or castrating woman as the psychoanalytic prototype of the witch. On taking a closer look at her picture one may even recognize the self-portrait of the artist himself painted in the corner of the canvas: medieval man in his frenzied, fear-ridden reaction to her threat.

chapter 9

Modern Miracles

LOURDES, AS BELIEVERS AND SKEPTICS HAVE SEEN IT:
DR. BOISSARIE; EMILE ZOLA; ALEXIS CARREL

The healing miracles attributed to sacred shrines, to the apostles and saints and to other mediators between man and the Godhead, bring the truly religious, charitable aspects of the Catholic Church back into focus. The cures claimed by Lourdes are among the most famous examples of such healing recorded in modern times. They are associated with the Grotto of Massabieille, in which, it is said, the Holy Virgin appeared to a little shepherd girl, Bernadette Soubirou, in 1858.

The story of Lourdes has been told many times: by Emile Zola in his monumental trilogy, Three Cities; by Franz Werfel in his Song of Bernadette; by the surgeon Alexis Carrel; and by other less celebrated visitors to the holy shrine. The number of pilgrims seeking cures for all kinds of organic and functional diseases has been estimated at several millions. In 1884 ecclesiastical authorities appointed a Bureau de Constatations Médicales—a Medical Fact-finding Board—to investigate cases in which the claim of miraculous cures had been raised. It is housed at present in a well-run hospital building under the supervision of a professor of medicine at the University of Bordeaux. Yet despite the labors of the Bureau and the cooperation of hundreds of doctors, the nature of the cures observed at Lourdes has remained largely controversial. The Bureau itself has not claimed more than forty-nine genuine "miracles" to the credit of the shrine.

Our first view of Lourdes is taken from a book entitled Lourdes, Les Guérisons (The Cures of Lourdes), which was published in Paris in 1911 under the imprimatur of Catholic ecclesiastical authorities. Its author, Dr. Boissarie, had for many years been the chief of the Medical Bureau of Lourdes. Alexis Carrel describes him as an experienced physician who published his account "in all good faith." Yet while he testifies to Dr. Boissarie's character and intelligence he also notes that he "did not find the doctor exacting enough in his scientific standards." Apparently this criticism refers to some of Boissarie's case reports, in which he was satisfied with the miraculous nature of cures of such diverse organic diseases as gangrenous wounds, malignant tumors and various tubercular lesions.

The excerpts that follow are given in the editor's translation.

The Doctors of Lourdes

On November 17, 1858, the year when the Holy Virgin appeared to Bernadette, a Commission nominated by Msgr. Laurence, Bishop of Tarbes, went to Lourdes in order to make a thorough examination of all the extraordinary cures which were accomplished by the water of the Grotto.

At this moment a physician of unquestioned authority enters the scene: Dr. Vergez, Superintendent of the Baths of Bareges, Associate Professor of the Medical Faculty of the University of Montpellier. . . . The inquiry made by this careful observer proved of the highest order. For more than twenty years he was to remain both witness and judge of significant events. Surprised by facts so new to him, he saw the light of truly striking developments and he recorded his first impressions in a magnificent language. "Casting a brief glance," he wrote, "upon the manifestations of healing, one is struck, above all, by the facility, the promptness, the instantaneousness with which they spring into being out of the matrix of their underlying cause. One is tempted to speak of an open violation, of a total overturn of therapeutic methodology, of a flagrant contradiction to the established principles of science. There seems to be a tendency to play disdainful tricks with the perennial and irresistible nature of illness. Everything points to a carefully arranged plan operating in the effected cures, transgressing the laws of nature. They virtually reach beyond the scope of the spirit of man. How should we comprehend such opposites as the simplicity of the means used and the greatness of results achieved? How should we account for the uniformity of the remedy applied and for the diversity of illnesses upon which it can be brought to bear? How for the short period of time during which the therapeutic agent was employed, as compared with the long time during which attempts at scientific treatments had been made? How should we explain the immediate efficacy of one by contrast to the utter uselessness of the other? And what about the chronic nature of the illness as contrasted with the suddenness of the cures effected?

If you asked me what I have seen at Lourdes I could answer: On examining the best authenticated factual evidence surpassing the scope of orthodox science and of the healing arts, I have seen, I have touched the work of the divinity—the miracle. . . .

This is how Boissarie describes the work of the Bureau de Constatations Médicales:

We have never ceased to maintain closest contact with contemporary science. Never was a clinic more open than ours to a year by year increasing

number of physicians attending the shrine during the time of the pilgrim-
ages. There were, in addition, the politicians frequently coming to visit our
clinics. We have had senators, congressmen, officials of the Belgian government, representatives of the army, navy and various governmental organizations. Protestants themselves did not stay outside this movement which
attracts to Lourdes people of the most divergent opinions and diverse countries. The clinic of Lourdes is one of the most astonishing institutions of our
epoch. It was founded in the midst of the most hostile crosscurrents. From
the secular point of view it was a foolish undertaking. It seemed absurd to
subject the miraculous to a scientific inquiry; tantamount to opening a
breach in the closed system of the scientific method. . . .

Less than twenty years later the clinic of Lourdes opened its gates to 400-
600 physicians. It now has its interns, its chiefs of service; its offices are
open for six months in the year and in its archives are the entries of more
than 100 records of cures effected per year. The clinic has voluntary corre-
spondents all over the world and countless publications from the clinic are
widely circulated. The Bureau of Lourdes collects the material, sifts documentary evidence, answers all questions and offers guidance to the public.
In so doing it prevents the possibility of misguiding public opinion. The violent attacks of Zola came to grief on the methodical and conscientious
studies of the Bureau. . . .

What Dr. Boissarie describes as Zola's "violent attacks" appeared in his
celebrated novel Lourdes, *published in Paris in 1893. A short time before it*
was published, Zola was interviewed on the subject by his friend and biog-
rapher, Robert H. Sherard. This is what Zola had to say about the circum-
stances in which he became interested in the problem of Lourdes:

Lourdes came to be written by mere accident. In 1891 I happened to be
travelling for my pleasure, with my wife, in the Basque country and by the
Pyrenees, and being in the neighborhood of Lourdes, included it in my tour.
I spent fifteen days there, and was greatly struck by what I saw, and it then
occurred to me that there was material here for just the sort of novel that I
like to write—a novel in which great masses of men can be shown in motion
—*un grand mouvement de foule*—a novel the subject of which stirred up
my philosophical ideas.

It was too late then to study the question, for I had visited Lourdes late in
September, and so had missed seeing the best pilgrimage, which takes place
in August, under the direction of the Péres de la Miséricorde, of the Rue de
l'Assomption in Paris—the National Pilgrimage, as it is called. These fathers are very active, enterprising men, and have made a great success of
this annual national pilgrimage. Under their direction thirty thousand pil-

grims are transported to Lourdes, including over a thousand sick persons.

So in the following year I went in August, and saw a national pilgrimage, and followed it during the three days which it lasts, in addition to the two days given to travelling. After its departure, I stayed on ten or twelve days, working up the subject in every detail. My book is the story of such a national pilgrimage, and is, accordingly, the story of five days. It is divided into five parts, each of which is limited to one day.

There are from ninety to one hundred characters in the story: sick persons, pilgrims, priests, nuns, hospitallers, nurses, and peasants; and the book shows Lourdes under every aspect. There are the piscinas, the processions, the Grotto, the churches at night, the people in the streets. It is, in one word, Lourdes in its entirety. In this canvas is worked out a very delicate central intrigue, as in Dr. Pascal, and around this are many little stories or subsidiary plots. There is the story of the sick person who gets well, of the sick person who is not cured, and so on. The philosophical idea which pervades the whole book is the idea of human suffering, the exhibition of the desperate and despairing sufferers who, abandoned by science and by man, address themselves to a higher Power in the hope of relief; as where parents have a dearly loved daughter dying of consumption, who has been given up, and for whom nothing remains but death. A sudden hope, however, breaks in upon them: "supposing that after all there should be a Power greater than that of man, higher than that of science." They will haste to try this last chance of safety. It is the instinctive hankering after the lie which creates human credulity.

I will admit that I came across some instances of real cure. Many cases of nervous disorders have undoubtedly been cured, and there have also been other cures which may perhaps be attributed to errors of diagnosis on the part of doctors who attended the patients so cured. Often a patient is described by his doctors as suffering from consumption. He goes to Lourdes, and is cured. However, the probability is that the doctor made a mistake. In my own case I was at one time suffering from a violent pain in my chest, which presented all the symptoms of angina pectoris, a mortal malady. It was nothing of the sort. Indigestion, doubtless, and, as such, curable. Remember that most of the sick persons who go to Lourdes come from the country, and that the country doctors are not usually men of either great skill or great experience. But all doctors mistake symptoms. Put three doctors together to discuss a case, and in nine cases out of ten they wil disagree in their diagnosis. Look at the quantities of tumors, swellings, and sores, which cannot be properly classified. These cures are based on the ignorance of the medical profession. The sick pretend, believe, that they suffer from such and such a desperate malady, whereas it is from some other malady that they are suffering. And so the legend forms itself. And, of course, there must be cures out of so large a number of cases. Nature often cures without medical aid. Certainly, many of the workings of Nature are wonderful, but they are not supernatural. The Lourdes miracles can neither be proved nor denied. The miracle is based on human ignorance. And so the doctor who lives at Lourdes, and who is commissioned to register the cures and to tabulate the miracles, has a very careless time of it. A person comes, and gets cured. He has but to get three doctors together to examine the case. They will disagree as to what was the disease from which the patient suffered, and the only explanation left which will be acceptable to the public, with its hankering after the lie, is that a miracle has been vouchsafed.

I interviewed a number of people at Lourdes, and could not find one who would declare that he had witnessed a miracle. All the cases which I describe in my book are real cases, in which I have only changed the names of the persons concerned. In none of these instances was I able to discover any real proof for or against the miraculous nature of the cure. Thus, in the case of Clementine Trouve, who figures in my story as Sophie—the patient who, after suffering for a long time from a horrid open sore on her foot, was suddenly cured, according to current report, by bathing her foot in the piscina, where the bandages fell off, and her foot was entirely restored to a healthy condition—I investigated that case thoroughly. I was told that there were three or four ladies living in Lourdes who could guarantee the facts as stated by little Clementine. I looked up those ladies. The first said No, she could not vouch for anything. She had seen nothing. I had better consult somebody else. The next answered in the same way, and nowhere was I able to find any corroboration of the girl's story. Yet the little girl did not look like a liar, and I believe that she was fully convinced of the miraculous nature of her cure. It is the facts themselves which lie.

Lourdes, the Grotto, the cures, the miracles, are, indeed, the creation of that need of the lie, that necessity for credulity, which is a characteristic of human nature. At first, when little Bernadette came with her strange story of what she had witnessed, everybody was against her. The Prefect of the Department, the Bishop, the clergy, objected to her story. But Lourdes grew up in spite of all opposition, just as the Christian religion did, because suffering humanity in its despair must cling to something, must have some hope; and, on the other hand, because humanity thirsts after illusions. In a word, it is the story of the foundation of all religions.

The violence of the controversy touched off by Zola's statement is illustrated by a further passage from Dr. Boissarie's Lourdes, Les Guérisons:

What strikes me most in Zola is his ignorance, conscious or unconscious, of the subjects he treats. He stayed at Lourdes for a fortnight or so, occupied his time by incessant visits, surrounded by a cloud of reporters and preoccupied by his concern for his popularity. There is no woman who would take so much care for her beauty as Zola seemed to be taking for the staging of his appearances. This was always more important to him than objective considerations. These, then, are the conditions in which he has seen everything and passed judgment on everything.

Zola spent ten hours in the Bureau de Constatations. He did not take one single note, he did not follow up any of the cures he had witnessed, he has not made one inquiry and he has written more than two hundred pages in his book about the healings. He criticizes our methods of controls and he traces for us a program which, he says, will save us from all future error.

His ignorance may well be astonishing but he cannot be credited with good faith. If one refuses to study the evidence, if one escapes discussion of the most obvious data regarding the healings of wounds, if one claims patients who are doing fine to be dead and if one creates types completely outside the realm of probability, then it is impossible to find justification for such a procedure.

It is unworthy of a writer to replace a frank and loyal argument by constant insinuations and unwarranted doubts, question marks and by the presentation of evidence in a false light, deliberately mutilating the facts. This however, has been Zola's mode of procedure. . . .

Leslie Weatherhead, author, psychologist and Lutheran minister, visited Lourdes in 1949 and gave a vivid account of his impressions in his Psychology, Religion, and Healing. *He left deeply moved by what he had seen, though he had found no evidence of supernormal healing. "Lourdes," he writes, "can no doubt provide a great spiritual experience. As a healing agency its proportion of cures makes it negligible. Few of its cures brought to our notice could possibly be regarded as miracles and those few did not depend on the paraphernalia of Lourdes." And he adds, "There is probably no stream in Britain which could not boast as high a proportion of cures as the stream of Lourdes if patients came in the same numbers and in the same psychological state of expectant excitement."*

Among recent testimonies to the healing powers of Lourdes, a report made by the New York psychiatrist, Dr. Smiley Blanton, is of special interest. In 1937 he studied the striking recovery from surgical tuberculosis of an Irishman named McDonald. Summing up his impressions, Dr. Blanton speaks of a "quickening of the healing process" which he attributes to the emotions aroused by "the transference to an all-powerful, all-loving Virgin Mother."

Our next selection deals with a similar case, described in detail by Alexis Carrel (1873-1944). Dr. Carrel, surgeon and biologist, winner of the Nobel

Prize for medicine in 1912, one-time Fellow of the Rockefeller Foundation in New York and author of Man the Unknown, *visited Lourdes in 1903 and was apparently convinced of the miraculous effects of the shrine. His account appeared posthumously in 1952, edited by Mrs. Carrel. Written in the third person, the report is attributed to Dr. Lerrac, that is, the author's name spelled backward. Although his pilgrimage was undertaken long before Carrel had reached the height of his fame, he never disavowed in public the conclusions reached by the young surgeon, Dr. Lerrac. The book itself contains a graphic description of the case of Marie Ferrand, a young girl who was brought to Lourdes apparently dying from tubercular peritonitis and who left it restored to health, a living testimony to its remarkable powers of healing.*

The following is an extract from Dr. Alexis Carrel's posthumous report on The Voyage to Lourdes.

Louis Lerrac had come on the journey to examine the sick, in order to learn whether or not the reports from Lourdes of radical improvements were authentic.

As a faculty member of the Medical School at the University of Lyons, Lerrac specialized in dissection for anatomy classes and in experimental sciences, but he was also much interested in certain problems bordering on the field of pathology. Long ago, his attention had been attracted by the stories of the cures in Lourdes. From what he had read of the two books by Dr. Boissarie, head of the Lourdes clinic, and aside from the wild claims published by Catholic periodicals, Lerrac was convinced that the Lourdes phenomena deserved scientific investigation. After all, Emile Zola himself, the last man to be suspected of a pro-Catholic bias, had seen and reported astounding facts.

This is how Carrel describes the condition of one of the patients on the way to the shrine:

Marie Ferrand was lying on her mattress, half-dressed; her face was green, but she had regained consciousness. There was only a dim light in the compartment. The heat was overwhelming. Lerrac lowered the window and the gusts of fresher air brought her completely to her senses.

"I shall never reach Lourdes," she sighed in distress.

Every time the long train jolted to a stop, the passengers were thrown against each other and these repeated shocks inflicted uninimaginable suffering upon the sick.

"She looked agonized," the nurse said, "each time the train came into a station. I kept thinking she was going to faint and I did not know what to do for her."

"We shall give her an injection, anyway," said Lerrac.

The nurse drew up the sleeve from Marie Ferrand's wasted arm. Lerrac filled the Pravaz hypodermic syringe with a morphine solution and, since he had no alcohol lamp, held the needle to a lighted match; then he thrust it under the white skin where the smoke-tinged needle made a small black smudge.

"In five minutes the pain will be gone," he said. "Meanwhile, let me have a look at your abdomen and put some laudanum on it."

Skillfully, the nurse laid bare Marie Ferrand's distended belly. The glistening skin was stretched tight and at the sides the ribs protruded sharply. The swelling was apparently caused by solid masses, and there was a pocket of fluid under the umbilicus. It was a classic case of tubercular peritonitis. Lerrac touched the abdomen with the back of his forefinger and his middle finger. The temperature was above normal. The legs were swollen, too. Both the heartbeat and the breathing were accelerated. . . .

[At the shrine] Lerrac sat down on a bench near the door of the women's pool. A little wind fluttered the dark leaves of the plane trees. Patches of sunlight trembled on the paved ground. From beneath the somber foliage, he could see the fields stretching away beyond the stream on the other side, the chain of low hills dotted with white-walled farms, and the intense blue sky with its occasional light clouds.

Marie Ferrand lay on her back, all shrunken beneath the dark brown blanket which made a mound over her distended abdomen. Her breath came quick and short. Over the deathly mask of her face Mlle. d'O was holding a white parasol. The sight of such misery, commonplace in any hospital, made a shocking impression outdoors, where each detail was so clearly etched.

For a moment, before going to the pool, they lowered the stretcher to the ground. The sick girl was apparently unconscious. Lerrac put his hand on her wrist. Her pulse was more rapid than ever. Her face was ashen. A green fly had lit in the opening of her nostril. Mlle. d'O. fanned it away with her handkerchief. . . .

How utterly impossible it was, he thought, to prophesy the exact moment when life ends. It was obvious that this young girl was about to die. But he could not say whether her death would come in an hour or in three or four days. He wondered how it would affect the pilgrims if she died in the pool. What would they think of miracles, then?

The church clock struck two. Groups of little carts drawn by the stretcher-bearers were approaching, followed by more and more pilgrims. . . .

A longing now swept over Lerrac to believe, with these unhappy people among whom he found himself, that the Virgin Mary was not merely an exquisite creation of the human brain. Lerrac was praying, now, praying for

Marie Ferrand who had suffered so unendurably; he was asking the Virgin Mary to restore her to life, and himself to faith.

Lerrac's exaltation did not last. He forced himself back into the safe paths of methodical scientific investigation and determined to be completely objective. He knew that Marie Ferrand was incurable, that recovery from advanced tubercular peritonitis was impossible. However, Lerrac kept his detachment and was prepared to accept the evidence of any phenomenon he might observe himself. . . .

It was now about half-past two. Beneath the rock of Massabieille, the Grotto glittered in the light of its thousand candles. The entrance and the walls were hung with rosaries and crutches. Beyond the high iron grille was a statue of the Virgin, standing in the hollowed rock where Bernardette once saw the glowing vision of the lady in white, the Immaculate Conception.

Before the statue of the Virgin, a large square space was fenced off; it was reserved as the place of honor for the sick. Volunteers of Our Lady of Salvation were on duty to prevent crowding and confusion among the little carts and stretchers.

Lerrac glanced again at Marie Ferrand. Suddenly he stared. It seemed to him that there had been a change, that the harsh shadows on her face had disappeared, that her skin was somehow less ashen.

Surely, he thought, this was a hallucination. But the hallucination itself was interesting psychologically, and might be worth recording. Hastily he jotted down the time in his notebook. It was twenty minutes before three o'clock.

But if the change in Marie Ferrand was a hallucination, it was the first one Lerrac had ever had. He turned to M.

"Look at our patient again," he said. "Does it seem to you that she has rallied a little?"

"She looks much the same to me," answered M. "All I can see is that she is no worse."

Leaning over the stretcher, Lerrac took her pulse again and listened to her breathing.

"The respiration is less rapid," he told M. after a moment. "That may mean that she is about to die," said M.

A non-believer, the young intern could see nothing miraculous in this change.

Lerrac made no reply. To him it was obvious that there was a sudden improvement of her general condition. Something was taking place. He stiffened to resist a tremor of emotion. Standing against the low wall near the stretcher, he concentrated all his powers of observation on Marie Ferrand. He did not lift his eyes from her face. A priest was preaching to the assembled throngs of pilgrims and patients; hymns and prayers burst out sporadically; and in this atmosphere of fervor, under Lerrac's cool, objective gaze, the face of Marie Ferrand slowly continued to change. Her eyes, so dim before, were now wide with ecstasy as she turned them toward the Grotto, the change was undeniable. Mlle. d'O. leaned over and held her.

Suddenly, Lerrac felt himself turning pale. The blanket which covered Marie Ferrand's distended abdomen was gradually flattening out.

"Look at her abdomen!" he exclaimed to M.

M. looked.

"Why yes," he said, "it seems to have gone down. It's probably the folds in the blanket that give that impression."

The bell of the basilica had just struck three. A few minutes later, there was no longer any sign of distension in Marie Ferrand's abdomen.

Some time later Lerrac visited Marie in the hospital ward.

With mute astonishment, he stood and gazed. The change was overpowering.

Marie Ferrand, in a white jacket, was sitting up in bed. Though her face was still gray and emaciated, it was alight with life; her eyes shone; a faint color tinted her cheeks. The lines at the corners of her mouth, etched there by years of suffering, still showed. But such an indescribable serenity emanated from her person that it seemed to illuminate the whole sad ward with joy.

"Doctor," she said, "I am completely cured. I feel very weak, but I think I could even walk."

Lerrac put his hand on her wrist. The pulse beat was calm and regular, eighty times a minute. Yet a few short hours ago it had been so accelerated, so fluttering, that he could hardly count it. Her respiration had also become completely normal; her chest rose and fell with slow regularity.

Confusion flooded Lerrac's mind. Was this merely an apparent cure, an extraordinary functional improvement, the result of the violent stimulus of autosuggestion? Or had the lesions really healed? Was this a rare, but accepted phenomenon in nature, or was it a new fact, an astounding, unacceptable event—a miracle? . . .

It is not likely that Carrel's moving description of Marie Ferrand's case will dispel the doubts of the skeptics. Several questions may be raised to weaken the validity of his report as a scientific statement. He did not write it under his own name but chose to use a pseudonym, and the book appeared after his death, leaving the question open whether or not Alexis Carrel, the world-famous scientist, would have upheld the conclusions drawn by the young surgeon, Dr. Lerrac, at the age of thirty.

Doubts might also be raised as to the diagnosis of the case. Measured by the standards of up-to-date clinical medicine, the diagnosis of tubercular peritonitis would at least be open to debate. The findings of a distended stomach, of fluid in the abdominal cavity, etc., may conceivably be attributed to heart trouble or some other disease. This brings a number of unknown factors into the evaluation of the patient's recovery.

In fact, in an undated postcript to his book Carrel seems to be less emphatic in affirming the miraculous nature of Marie Ferrand's case. And if he had witnessed the striking therapeutic results that have recently been achieved with cortisone and similar "miracle" drugs, he might conceivably have been still more guarded in his judgment. Despite uncertainty as to the mode of action of such drugs, one thing has been established: some of them act in the same way as the hormone produced in situations of stress by the cortex of the adrenal gland. This includes physical as well as emotional stress; stress which accompanies such bodily efforts as climbing a mountain peak or standing up to the horrors of an artillery barrage.

In the light of the available clinical and experimental evidence, the "stressful" effect of such an emotional experience as a pilgrimage to Lourdes cannot possibly be overrated. Carrel gives an excellent description of its profound impact upon all those participating in the ceremony, including the stretcher-bearers, the nurses and the doctors themselves. We learn from his report that Marie had been looking forward to her pilgrimage for months, and that the arduous journey on the train brought her expectations literally to fever pitch. On her arrival Marie's condition appeared to take a sudden turn for the worse. She seemed to collapse like an exhausted mountain climber on arriving at his destination. But what to the clinical observer had appeared to be a collapse was instead like the pulling back of a recoiling spring, ready to leap into action on release. Hers was a reculer pour mieux sauter—a recoiling so as to be better able to leap—as Dr. Lerrac would probably have put it. This, in effect, was Marie's supreme moment of crisis. It was the moment when, according to the faithful believer, the Virgin Mary herself stepped into the picture and brought the dying girl back to life: a miracle in the ecclesiastical sense. But it also may have been the moment when, after a period of "recoiling," her adrenal cortex—or pituitary gland— suddenly leaped into action to pour out some life-giving hormone into her circulatory system. If so, Marie Ferrand's miraculous recovery was the effect of thoroughly natural factors, brought into operation by a highly complicated chain of events that consisted of physical, psychological and so-called spiritual factors.

It is true that such an explanation could be applied to Dr. Lerrac's case only if his original diagnosis were to be disproved. So far tubercular peritonitis has failed to respond to treatment with cortisone or similar preparations. If a hormone was responsible for the changes observed in Marie's condition it has yet to be discovered by science. Nor can the rapidity of her recovery be matched by the exploits of the "miracle" drug known to contemporary medicine. Alexis Carrel remarks in his postcript: "If we are able to determine the causes scientifically; if we can establish these things as facts, every man is free to interpret the events of our work as he pleases."

It should be noted in closing that a more recent study of Eleven Lourdes Miracles, by Donald West, published in London in 1957, has arrived at wholly negative conclusions as far as the miraculous nature of the cures is concerned.

chapter 10

Mary Baker Eddy's Christian Science

SIBYL WILBUR, MARK TWAIN, STEFAN ZWEIG

It is one of the paradoxes of the late nineteenth century that it was an era when extreme scientific materialism existed side by side with such a radically anti-materialistic crusade as Mary Baker Eddy's movement and with the rise of such cultist or sectarian fads as spiritualism, theosophy and anthroposophy, both in Europe and in the United States.

Mary Baker Eddy's Science and Health with Key to the Scriptures was first published in Boston in 1875. To millions of Americans it is not an ordinary book. It is the sacred text of a new religion: Christian Science. It was hailed by her followers as a new revelation and it was denounced by her adversaries as the fabrication of a disturbed mind, compiled with the help of secretaries and ghost writers who gave it its final literary shape. It has been accused of plagiarism and described as a hodge-podge of early Christian mysticism, Hegelian philosophy and Mesmerian astrological speculations, presented in the flowery language of the period. But despite the logical inconsistencies of its reasoning and the absurdities of some of its statements, Science and Health must be classed among the most influential books of the late nineteenth century.

Part of this influence is undoubtedly due to certain flashes of intuitive insight which it contains. There is, first and foremost, Mary Baker Eddy's emphasis on the part played by what she called the mortal mind, both conscious and unconscious, in the origin of disease, functional as well as organic. There is, secondly, her assertion that every disease, regardless of its nature, can be cured by spiritual, that is to say, psychological methods of treatment. There is, thirdly, her profound distrust of purely mechanical, impersonal methods of treatment, which were widely current in her time. Unfortunately, these flashes of insight were vitiated by exaggerated claims of cures and some caustic attacks against the rules of hygiene, preventive inoculation, surgery and the medical profession in general.

Seen in historical perspective, Christian Science is one of the latest offshoots of the ancient magico-religious approach, following in the footsteps *of medieval astrological and alchemistic medicine and of Mesmer's theories of animal magnetism (see Chapter XVII). There is, however, at least one way in which Christian Science marked a new departure. It dispensed with most of the outer paraphernalia of magic and confined itself to a direct appeal to the faith and suggestibility of the believer. Mary Baker Eddy's mind cure thus represents a resolute attempt at curing disease by purely psychological means.*

There are two flagrantly contradictory versions of Mary Baker Eddy's personal history. There is, on the one hand, the legend circulated by her admirers, and there is, on the other hand, the version offered by her enemies, hell-bent on destroying the myth, on calling her bluff, on "debunking" the Christian Science doctrine. There are the pious chronicles of the life of a modern saint—if not of a second advent of Christ—and there are the accounts of an eccentric personality, half fraud, half fanatic, suffering first from hysteric paralysis of the leg and later from ideas of grandeur and delusions of persecution.

This is what Sibyl Wilbur, her official biographer, had to say in The Life of Mary Baker Eddy *(1821-1910):*

I have a life story to relate and I plant myself unreservedly on the methods of St. Mark. St. Mark, I believe, was a scribe who related what he had been able to gather from witnesses in a direct and unvarnished way. Now I shall endeavor to do simply that. It is not for me to explain or to expound. The facts of this life shall be left to elucidate themselves when set in an orderly and unembellished array before the world; the import must carry to that consciousness able to receive it. I shall concern myself only to report the truth.

The connection between Christ and Mary Baker Eddy is clearly implied here, and the faithful disciple goes on to say:

She had come to understand that, where the Hebrew prophets had occasionally and sporadically made God's will prevail in a so-called miracle, Jesus of Nazareth had never failed in invoking health and sustenance. He had cured the most desperate diseases with the same readiness as the mildest; he had blessed the few loaves, and abundance had been found to feed the multitude. Yet, here she, Mary Baker, lay on a bed of pain and in sore need of means. Did God withhold from her His bounty because she was a sinner? Like Job, she knew in her heart this was not true. Then where was the fault and what was the law?

Mary Baker had performed certain cures from which she argued as from the sure ground of experience, but these healings were incidental and accidental and she scarcely knew how they had occurred except that she knew they had happened when her thoughts were associated with God. She pondered after this fashion: Laws of God are immutable and universal. Then because His laws are so fixed and so infinitely operative, man by studying them has built up the sciences, as mathematics and mechanics. But in physics he is still crying out for the philosopher's stone and in medicine for the elixir of life. "I know there is cause and effect in the spiritual world as in the natural!" she would exclaim to herself. "I know there is a science of health, a science of life, a divine science, a science of God."

But it did not enter Mary Baker's mind in that hour that by this assertion she had declared herself the discoverer of a great truth, that by this affirmation of faith she had pledged herself to find the way and prove what she had declared. She was to herself only a woman in extremity, hungering for truth.

Mark Twain was one of the spokesmen for the opposite camp. The following are fragments from his book Christian Science, *published in 1910:*

For of all the strange and frantic and incomprehensible and uninterpretable books which the imagination of man has created, surely [*Science and Health*] is the prize sample. It is written with a limitless confidence and complacency, and with a dash and stir and earnestness which often compel the effects of eloquence, even when the words do not seem to have any traceable meaning. There are plenty of people who imagine they understand the book; I know this, for I have talked with them; but in all cases they were people who also imagined that there were no such things as pain, sickness, and death, and no realities in the world; nothing actually existent but Mind. It seems to me to modify the value of their testimony. When these people talk about Christian Science . . . they do not use their own language, but the book's; they pour out the book's showy incoherences, and leave you to find out later that they were not originating, but merely quoting; they seem to know the volume by heart, and to revere it as they would a Bible—another Bible, perhaps I ought to say. . . .

When you read it you seem to be listening to a lively and aggressive and oracular speech delivered in an unknown tongue, a speech whose spirit you get but not the particulars; or, to change the figure, you seem to be listening to a vigorous instrument which is making a noise which it thinks is a tune, but which, to persons not members of the band, is only the martial tooting of a trombone, and merely stirs the soul through the noise, but does not convey a meaning.

The book's serenities of self-satisfaction do almost seem to smack of a heavenly origin—they have no bloodkin in the earth. It is more than human to be so placidly certain about things, and so finely superior, and so airily content with one's performance. Without ever presenting anything which may rightfully be called by the strong name of Evidence, and sometimes without even *mentioning* a reason for a deduction at all, it thunders out the startling words, "I have *Proved*" so and so. It takes the Pope and all the great guns of his Church in battery assembled to authoritatively settle and establish the meaning of a sole and single unclarified passage of Scripture, and this at vast cost of time and study and reflection, but the author of this work is superior to all that: she finds the whole Bible in an unclarified condition, and at small expense of time and no expense of mental effort she clarifies it from lid to lid, reorganizes and improves the meanings, then authoritatively settles and establishes them with formulas which you cannot tell from "Let there be light!" and "Here you have it!" It is the first time since the dawn-days of Creation that a Voice has gone crashing through space with such placid and complacent confidence and command. . . .

Yet Mark Twain adds on a later page:

In several ways she is the most interesting woman that ever lived, and the most extraordinary. The same may be said of her career, and the same may be said of its chief result. She started from nothing. Her enemies charge that she surreptitiously took from Quimby [a Mesmerist who treated her] a peculiar system of healing which was mind-cure with a Biblical basis. She and her friends deny that she took anything from him. . . . Whether she took it or invented it, it was—materially—a sawdust mine when she got it, and she has turned it into a Klondike; its spiritual dock had next to no custom, if any at all: from it she has launched a world-religion which has now six hundred and sixty-three churches, and she charters a new one every four days. When we do not know a person—and also when we do—we have to judge his size by the size and nature of his achievements, as compared with the achievements of others in his special line of business—there is no other way. Measured by this standard, it is thirteen hundred years since the world has produced any one who could reach up to Mrs. Eddy's waistbelt.

Later statements attributed to Mark Twain show him in a still more conciliatory mood toward Mary Baker Eddy. Those expressing outright admiration may, however, have been made with his tongue in his cheek.

Stefan Zweig, (1881-1942), in his brilliant though partly fictional book, Mental Healers, *sought to strike a balance between these two contradictory pictures of her personality:*

But who was Mary Baker Eddy? Mrs. Anybody, unattractive, by no means beautiful, not particularly sincere, rather stupid, one whom it would be a compliment to describe as even half-educated, isolated, unknown, and utterly without position, money, friends, or what the Americans call "pull." There was no group or sect for her to appeal to: she had nothing in her hand but a pen, and nothing in her mediocre brain but one solitary idea. Everything was against her: science, religion, the school, the universities, common sense. Nor, at first sight, could any land seem more unfavourable to the spread of so abstract a doctrine than her homeland, the United States, the most matter-of-fact, cold-blooded, and unmystical country in the world. The only force at her disposal to aid her in overcoming all these obstacles was her tenacious, her mulish faith in her own faith, her own creed; and, simply by advocating it with the persistency of a monomaniac she made the improbable true. Her success was utterly illogical. Well, what is the most salient characteristic of miracle? Surely it is the conquest of truth by the inane!

She had nothing but an idea, and an extremely questionable one, but she thought of absolutely nothing else. She had only this one standpoint, but to this she clung as if her feet had been rooted to the earth. Motionless, unshakable, deaf to every objection, with her frail lever she moved the world. In twenty years out of a maze of metaphysical confusion she created a new method of healing; established a doctrine counting its adherents by the myriad, with colleges and periodicals of its own, and promulgated in textbooks credited with inspiration; established a Church and built numerous churches; appointed a sanhedrin of preachers and priests; and won for herself private wealth amounting to three million dollars. Over and above all this, by her very exaggerations she gave contemporary psychology a vigorous forward thrust, and ensured for herself a special page in the history of mental science. In the breadth of her influence, in the swiftness of her success, in the number of her supporters, this old woman scarcely more than half-witted, always ailing and of very dubious character, outstripped all the leaders and investigators of our time. Never beneath the eyes of us moderns has spiritual and religious disturbance emanated from any one to the same marvellous extent as from this daughter of an American farmer, whom her countryman Mark Twain angrily terms "the most daring and masculine and masterful woman that has appeared on earth in centuries." . . .

In truth, the allurement exercised by the complicated mind of Mrs. Eddy depends upon the mingling of opposing characteristics; upon a union between extreme foolishness and a good measure of what in her native land is often called "horse-sense"; upon the way in which hysteria is wedded to calculation.

Just as carbon and salpetre, utterly dissimilar ingredients, make an explosive powder when mixed with sulphur in the right proportions, so has the strange admixture of mystical and commercial, of hysterical and psychological trends produced a wonder-working compost. Not even Ford or Lincoln, not even Washington or Edison, is a more striking example than Mary Baker Eddy of the strange fusion of American idealism and American shrewdness.

It is only fair to note that Stefan Zweig, too, seems to have had second thoughts after his rather skeptical evaluation of Mary Baker Eddy's accomplishments. Frederike Zweig, in Stefan Zweig, Wie Ich Ihn Erlebte, *writes, "He was afraid he had overshot his mark with his vehemence and he was not a little touched by the special courtesy with which some of the adherents of Christian Science answered him." However, Zweig did not go so far as Mark Twain, who is said to have described her on a later occasion as "the benefactor of the age."*

By contrast to the Old and New Testaments, to the Koran or the Vedic hymns, carefully protected copyrights dating back to 1875, and repeatedly extended since, stand in the way of reprinting uncensored passages from Mary Baker Eddy's Science and Health with Key to the Scriptures. *Still, a few brief quotations may suffice to convey at least a flavor of the spiritual zeal, the missionary fervor and the sense of apodictic certainty with which every page of the book is imbued. Stating that she discovered the "Christ Science or divine laws of Life, Truth, and Love" in a flash, she describes how the discovery prepared her for the "divine Principle of mental healing." One of its basic propositions, she declares, is that "matter possesses neither sensation nor life; that human experiences show the falsity of all material things," and that they establish "the truism that the only suffering is in mortal mind, for the Divine Mind cannot suffer."*

This insight led her in turn to the thesis that by a sufficiently strong faith in the unreality of illness and death—or even of error and sin—these illusions can be made to disappear or to give up their hold over the "mortal mind." In effect, it is the "erring, misnamed, mortal mind" that "produces all the organism and action of the mortal body" and thereby all the infirmities of the flesh. "There is no pain in Truth and no Truth in pain," she asserts. This is why it is wrong to mix inferior and unspiritual with spiritual methods of healing. "The two," she cautions, "will not mingle scientifically" —that is to say, not in terms of Christian Science. To illustrate the point, Mrs. Eddy notes that "you may say a boil is painful," but her retort is that this is not possible since, according to her a priori proposition, "matter without mind is not painful."

An added important dimension are the prayers and the reassuring presence of the Christian Science practitioner—or even the intercession of an absent healer. Whether or not a paranormal (e.f., telepathic) factor is involved in such ministrations must remain an open question.

In any case, it seems to be the combination of these ingredients that accounts for the therapeutic exploits of Christian Science. We have seen in preceding chapters that similar considerations apply to virtually all forms of unorthodox healing. They are contingent on the combined effects of three major factors: (1) a properly motivated healer (magician, priest or lay practitioner), (2) a hopeful and trusting patient, and (3) a favorable cultural setting; e.g., an animated tribal, cultist or sectarian group, a devout congregation, sharing the experience and getting in on the act. Apparently dramatic cures or the alleviation of the patient's sufferings may then give rise to a spate of enthusiastic eyewitness accounts, self-reports, testimonials or laudatory letters, which in turn are apt to enhance and reinforce the requisite tripartite psychological configuration in the next round.

There is reason to believe that some of the striking exploits of Edgar Cayce, the Sleeping Prophet, were drawn from a similar concatenation of circumstances. They flowed from his unique charismatic personality, meeting halfway, as it were, the wishes and expectations of those who sought his aid and advice. At the same time he drew part of his arcane powers from the cultural climate of his native Kentucky and home base in Virginia Beach in the forties and fifties of this century. On the other hand, Cayce's overall philosophy came closer to the medical model. He included various nostrums and chemical agents in his armamentarium and relied heavily on intuitive, if not clairvoyant, diagnostic hunches or "readings" produced in his trancelike states. With all that, however, there can be no doubt that his overall impact on the American scene has remained on a more modest scale than that of the Christian Science movement.

Much has been said about the part played by Quimby, the Mesmerist, in the development of the theory of Christian Science. *His influence was quite obvious in the early editions of* Science and Health, *and it can still be traced in later editions including references to animal magnetism. Other passages sound like Coue's formulae for autosuggestion elevated to a more lofty metaphysical plane.*

How can we account for Mary Baker Eddy's impact upon the American scene? What is the explanation of the spectacular success of her movement which has been compared to that achieved within an equally short period of time by no lesser religious reformer than Mohammed, the founder of Islam? Leslie Weatherhead has rightly pointed out that Christian Science met a need which had remained sorely unfulfilled by the materialistic culture of the late nineteenth and early twentieth centuries. Pierre Janet, on the other hand, emphasized the very realistic concern of the average American not only for physical health but also for material wealth and economic security.

*Christian Science, he remarks, ministers to the sense of satisfaction and
well-being characteristic of the prosperous classes in the United States. Stefan Zweig, in a similar vein, points to the boundless optimism of Mrs. Eddy's philosophy. This, he asserts, appealed to a nation that had just succeeded in conquering the vast expanses of an undeveloped continent and in
turning it into a powerful empire, reaching unprecedented heights of technological progress and economic prosperity. Such a nation, he holds, could
not help being fascinated by a promise to add to this achievement the conquest of human suffering, illness, old age, and death itself. It is only fair to
add to these considerations Mary Baker Eddy's genuine contribution to
which reference has already been made: her intuitive insight into the part
played by the mind in the cause and cure of disease, both mental and physical.*

*But if this is so, how did a small-town girl, daughter of a New England
farmer, lacking in formal education and training, hit upon her discovery?
From where did she draw the power of conviction that made her capable of
"selling" Christian Science to the American public on a scale comparable to
the sales of Ford's Model T or Edison's incandescent lamp? If it is permissible to cut through the luxuriant growth of conflicting biographical data
and highly colored legendary accounts which have been woven around her
personality, there is one hypothesis which suggests itself.*

In Chapter VI of Science and Health, *Mary Baker Eddy touches briefly on
her sudden discovery of the science of metaphysical healing. More about
this can be found in her autobiography, in which she describes her miraculous cure following an injury sustained on a slippery street in Lynn, Massachusetts, on February 3, 1866. But her biographers have a different story
to tell. It is the story of her cure from a prolonged period of hysterical paralysis by Dr. Quimby, the Mesmerist and self-styled medical practitioner
whom she had consulted in 1862, while she was still married to her first
husband, Dr. Patterson. This is Zweig's account of her consultation:*

Quimby's new practice, though it often seemed magical in its effects, was
not really magical in the least. The good fellow, grey-haired now and well
on in years, one whose fee already inspired confidence, sat down in front of
the patient, stroked the latter's head with moistened fingers (these last vestiges of magnetic or hypnotic methods being designed to promote concentration), asked for an account of the symptoms, and then gave the invalid a
talking-to. He made no attempt at any scientific examination, it being
enough for him to deny the reality of the illness, his aim being not to give
medicinal palliatives for the relief of pain, but to cure suggestively by modifying the patient's own feeling about the matter. Rather cheap, rather primitive, the reader may think, to cure in this way by simply telling the sick

man that what he thinks hurts him does not really hurt. Rather too easy, is it not, to deny the existence of the disease instead of seriously treating it? Yet it was but a step from the practice of Quimby the clockmaker in 1860 to that of Coué the apothecary in 1920—and the use of suggestion and auto-suggestion is today accepted as scientific. Moreover, the now forgotten Quimby was quite successful as the Nancy healer whose fame recently circled the world. In New England seventy years ago Quimby became the vogue. So many thousands wanted to enjoy the benefit of his "mind cure," that in the end his consulting-room was overcrowded, and he had to deal with the overflow by letters and circulars—by the methods which the Christian Scientists afterwards developed into what they called "absent treatment."

The renown of this wonderful healer had reached the Pattersons in their little New Hampshire village. They had heard wonderful things about the new "science of health" as taught by the ex-clockmaker. The result had been that in 1861, under date October 14th, shortly before leaving to join up with the Northern army, "Dr." Patterson had written to ask "Dr." Quimby whether it would not be possible for him to visit Concord. "My wife has been crippled for a number of years by spinal paralysis. She is barely able to sit up, and we shall be so glad, if it is at all possible, to try your wonderful powers in her case." But the local exigencies of his gigantic practice made it impossible for Quimby to undertake the proposed journey, and he courteously declined. Mrs. Patterson, however, still clung to the thought of Quimby as her last hope. A year later, when Patterson was already interned in the South, the despairing patient sent an S.O.S. call, begging the healer to come to her rescue. Here is the letter of the woman who in later years expunged the name of Quimby from all her writings: "Above all I must see you in person! I have full confidence in your philosophy, as expounded in your circulars. Can you, will you come to see me? I shall die unless you can save me. My illness is chronic; I can no longer even turn over, and no one but my husband is able to lift me. I am bedridden, and suffer horrible pain. Please, please, come to my aid! You will pardon all the defects of this letter, which I am writing in bed and without the proper conveniences." Again Quimby was forced to refuse. Then, when she was at the hydropathic institute in New Hampshire, she wrote to him once more, asking him whether he approved of her idea to visit him. "Do you think I can reach you without sinking from the effects of the journey?" Quimby replied encouragingly. Let her undertake the venture!

But there was a material obstacle, the lack of money for the journey. Abigail, who had already done so much to help her sister, had not the least confidence in the report of the cures effected by this "mental healer." Weary of the invalid's whims, she declared that nothing would induce her to spend a cent upon such obvious humbug. But when Mary Baker had determined to do anything, she could make short work of obstacles. Beseeching the help of friends, acquaintances, and strangers, laboriously adding dollar to dollar, she found herself, towards the end of October 1862, after she had been several months at the hydropathic, in possession of enough for the journey to Portland. We have no details concerning the remove, but are informed that she was in very poor case when she reached her goal. It might have been well for her, one would think, to rest awhile before visiting Quimby. But to her rest was impossible in such circumstances, and she could always find energy to do anything she really wanted. She made her way straight to the International Hotel, where Quimby had his consulting-room, and was actually strong enough to walk up the first flight of stairs. Then her forces gave out, and, half carried, half supported, she achieved the second flight and the entry into the waiting-room. Emaciated, her face pale and worn and her eyes sunken, shabbily dressed, she dropped into a chair, the mere broken vestiges of a human being. At this moment Quimby, whom she had come so far to see, emerged from the inner office. As her eyes lighted on the kindly face of the small greyhaired man, confidence and hope began to flow back to her.

A week or two later, and Mary Baker, given up by all her doctors as an incurable invalid, had been restored to health. Once more she had the full use of her limbs, and was able without difficulty to climb the 182 steps to the dome of the City Hall. She talked, she questioned, she rejoiced, she glowed with ardour; she was rejuvenated and almost beautified; she was bubbling over with activity and inspired with renewed energy—an energy unexampled even in America. She was inspired with an energy which, ere long, was to make numberless retainers subservient to her will.

This spectacular cure by purely mental means of a chronic affliction which the patient as well as her doctors considered organic and virtually incurable may have been the great turning point in Mary Baker Eddy's life. It hit her with the impact of a sudden religious experience, carrying with it the illuminating insight that her illness—nay, illness in general—was due to psychological causes and to nothing else. The surest way of conquering it therefore called for essentially psychological means. More than that: if her illness (and illness in general) was solely in the mind, it was not a real illness —or rather, it was not real at all. Consequently, she reasoned, all that was needed was to convince the sufferer from any disease of the unreality, the fictitious nature, of his affliction—and he would be cured.

Certainly, this was an unwarranted oversimplification of a highly complicated state of affairs—a wholly illicit exploitation of a grain of truth contained in her reasoning. She did not say to herself, "I have been the victim of an incapacitating disease, largely imaginary in nature." She did not argue, "My legs only seemed to me to be paralyzed. There was really nothing the matter with my locomotor system or with my spinal cord, and once I made a supreme effort to snap out of my inertia I was cured—or allowed myself to be cured by good Dr. Quimby, the watchmaker turned magnetopath." Instead, Mrs. Eddy, barely able to stand on her feet, wasted from lack of exercise, literally jumped to a conclusion of staggering import. In the blissful moment of her newly restored health, it became a "self-evident" truth to her that not only her illness, but all illnesses, regardless of their nature, were but matters of the mind, errors of man's misguided imagination. They were, in effect, unreal, nonexistent, and could therefore be conquered by a mere act of will, like the one mustered by herself some time in October, 1862 (or was it February, 1866 when she fell on a slippery street in Lynn?) in her great moment of illumination.

This may have been the way in which Mary Baker Eddy arrived at what to her and her followers appeared as a new and revolutionary insight, bound to save the world from the dream of ill health and suffering and from the avoidable error of death. Thus her discovery of a cure-all for every woe was the result of a generalization—which gradually grew to cosmic proportions—of an originally wholly private experience. It was valid, within certain limits, to her particular case, and it may apply to a number of cases similar to her own—but not to others.

Part 3

SCIENCE
or
The Quest
for Knowledge and Mastery

chapter 11

Prelude to Psychotherapy

PLATO'S "DIALOGUES" . . .
EPICURUS'S PRESCRIPTION FOR THE GOOD LIFE

We have seen in Part One of this anthology how the magic approach to mental healing was guided by primitive man's faith in the omnipotence of thought—both the medicine man's and his own. Part Two showed the mellowing of this attitude through religious experience: the Far Eastern or Christian devotee ready to surrender his quest for omnipotence to a superior power, to renounce the gratification of his desires in return for salvation.

Scientific psychotherapy reverts once more to the quest for mastery and control. Yet in doing so it differs from the magic approach in the more realistic attitude with which it pursues this goal. The man of science, in contrast to the magician, bases his actions on premises which can be tested and verified in the light of practical experience. On coming to grips with an object in the outside world he asks himself: What is it? What is it for? How can I make it subservient to my purpose? The scientifically oriented psychotherapist approaches the mental state of his patients in much the same way. He too wants to know how they "tick," and above all, he too seeks to devise a technique for the deliberate manipulation and control of their minds so as to effect their cure on an empirical basis.

The first step on this road was the development of the conceptual tools needed for such a task. These concepts were first formulated by the great thinkers of classical antiquity, especially by Socrates, Plato and Aristotle. Part Three, then, takes the Dialogues of Plato as its point of departure.

Plato lived in the fifth century B.C. and spent his life meditating and teaching in the famous academy which he founded in 387 B.C. in his native city, Athens. It was the time when ancient Greek civilization had reached the peak. Philosophy, poetry, playwriting, sculpture and architecture flourished as never before, and great statesmen helped the city to attain a position of leadership unparalleled in the Western world.

Plato was a contemporary of Pericles, Thucydides, Phidias, Sophocles, Aristophanes and Hippocrates. He was a disciple of Socrates and the *teacher of Aristotle. All this must have played an important part in molding his outlook. Yet he was undoubtedly also influenced by Far Eastern religious philosophers like those we quoted in Part Two. Plato's system of thought focused on the world of ideas and the nature of the soul. He was a speculative philosopher and had little use for the objective "behavioral" aspects of the human mind. But some of his intuitions regarding the part played by instinctual drives—about the nature of dreams and unconscious "reminiscences"—have had a profound influence upon our Western thinking—including modern psychoanalytic concepts. A classical example is Plato's metaphorical picture of the "soul."*

Of the nature of the soul, though her true form be ever a theme of large and more than mortal discourse, let me speak briefly, and in a figure. And let the figure be composite—a pair of winged horses and a charioteer. Now the winged horses and the charioteer of the gods are all of them noble and of noble descent, but those of other races are mixed; the human charioteer drives his in a pair; and one of them is noble and of noble breed, and the other is ignoble and of ignoble breed; and the driving of them of necessity gives a great deal of trouble to him. I will endeavor to explain to you in what way the mortal differs from the immortal creature. The soul in her totality has the care of inanimate being everywhere, and traverses the whole heaven in divers forms appearing;—when perfect and fully winged she soars upward, and orders the whole world; whereas the imperfect soul, losing her wings and drooping in her flight at last settles on the solid ground— there, finding a home, she receives an earthly frame which appears to be self-moved, but is really moved by her power; and this composition of soul and body is called a living and mortal creature. . . .

At the beginning of this tale, I divided each soul into three—two horses and a charioteer; and one of the horses was good and the other bad: the division may remain, but I have not yet explained in what the goodness or badness of either consists, and to that I will now proceed. The right-hand horse is upright and cleanly made; he has a lofty neck and an aquiline nose; his colour is white, and his eyes dark; he is a lover of honour and modesty and temperance, and the follower of true glory; he needs no touch of the whip, but is guided by word and admonition only. The other is a crooked lumbering animal, put together anyhow; he has a short thick neck; he is flat-faced and of dark colour, with grey and bloodshot eyes; the mate of insolence and pride, shag-eared and deaf, hardly yielding to whip and spur. Now when the charioteer beholds the vision of love, and has his whole soul warmed through sense, and is full of the prickings and tinglings of desire, the obedient steed, then as always under the government of shame, refrains from leaping on the beloved; but the other, heedless of the pricks and of the blows of the whip, plunges and runs away, giving all manner of trouble to his companion and the charioteer, whom he forces to approach the beloved and to remember the joys of love. They at first indignantly oppose him and will not be urged on to do terrible and unlawful deeds; but at last, when he persists in plaguing them, they yield and agree to do as he bids them. And now they are at the spot and behold the flashing beauty of the beloved; which when the charioteer sees, his memory is carried to the true beauty, whom he beholds in company with Modesty like an image placed upon a holy pedestal. He sees her, but he is afraid and falls backwards in adoration, and by his fall is compelled to pull back the reins with such a violence as to bring both the steeds on their haunches, the one willing and unresisting, the unruly one very unwilling; and when they have gone back a little the one is overcome with shame and wonder, and his whole soul is bathed in perspiration; the other, when the pain is over which the bridle and fall had given him, having with difficulty taken breath, is full of wrath and reproaches, which he heaps upon the charioteer and his fellow-steed, for want of courage and manhood, declaring that they have been false to their agreement and guilty of desertion. Again they refuse, and again he urges them on, and will scarcely yield to their prayer that he would wait until another time. When the appointed hour comes, they make as if they had forgotten, and he reminds them, fighting and neighing and dragging them on, until at length he on the same thoughts intent, forces them to draw near again. And when they are near he stoops his head and puts up his tail, and takes the bit in his teeth and pulls shamelessly. Then the charioteer is worse off than ever; he falls back like a racer at the barrier, and with a still more violent wrench drags the bit out of the teeth of the wild steed and covers his abusive tongue and jaws with blood, and forces his legs and haunches to the ground and punishes him sorely. And when this has happened several times and the villain has ceased from his wanton way, he is tamed and humbled, and follows the will of the charioteer, and when he sees the beautiful one he is ready to die of fear. And from that time forward the soul of the lover follows the beloved in modesty and holy fear.

This passage may well be compared with the following quotation from Freud's The Ego and the Id:

The Ego represents what we call reason and sanity, in contrast to the id which contains the passions. . . . Thus in its relation to the id it is like a man on horseback, who has to hold in check the superior strength of the horses, with the difference, that the rider seeks to do so with his own strength while the ego uses borrowed forces. The illustration may be carried further. Often

a rider if he is not parted from his horse, is obliged to guide it where it wants
to go; so in the same way the ego constantly carries into action the wishes
of the id as if they were its own. . . .

The following selections from Timaeus *show Plato's attempts to develop
a theory of physical and mental disease on purely speculative grounds. In
these attempts he was influenced by his great contemporary, Hippocrates,
the "Father of Medicine" (see Chapter XII). But the crude misconceptions
regarding autonomy and physiology of the human body current in his time
greatly detract from the value of Plato's intuitions. Some of the fallacies
contained in his writings were passed on from generation to generation of
theologians, philosophers and physicians up to modern times. Timaeus
contains the famous passage attributing various diseases seen in women to
the wanderings of the womb (hysteros) in the female body. This was supposed to be at the root of what is now known as hysteria. Charcot and
Freud, nearly two and a half millenia later, were still hard put to dislodge
this misconception from the minds of their colleagues.*

*Plato's thesis about what he calls the right proportion in the relationship
between body and soul is, however, of more than merely historic importance. It is the first formulation of the principle that a healthy body and
healthy mind go together.*

There is no proportion or disproportion more productive of health and
disease, and virtue and vice, than that between soul and body. This however we do not perceive nor do we reflect that when a weak or small frame
is the vehicle of a great and mighty soul, or conversely, when a little soul is
encased in a large body, then the whole animal is not fair, for it lacks the
most important part of all symmetries; but the due proportion of mind and
body, is the fairest and loveliest of all sights to him who has the seeing eye.
Just as a body which has a leg too long, or which is unsymmetrical in some
other repsect, is an unpleasant sight, and also when doing its share of work,
is much distressed and makes convulsive efforts, and often stumbles
through awkwardness, and is the cause of infinite evil to its own self—in
like manner we should conceive of the double nature which we call the living being; and when in this compound there is an impassioned soul more
powerful than the body, the soul, I say, convulses and fills with disorders
the whole inner nature of man; and when eager in the pursuit of some sort
of learning or study, causes wasting; or again, when teaching or disputing
in private or in public, and strifes and controversies arise, inflames and dis-
solves the composite frame of man and introduces rheums; and the nature
of this phenomenon is not understood by most professors of medicine, who
ascribe it to the opposite of the real cause. And once more, when a body

large and too strong for the soul is united to a small and weak intelligence, then inasmuch as there are two desires natural to man—one of food for the sake of the body, and one of wisdom for the sake of the diviner part of us— then, I say, the motions of the stronger, getting the better and increasing their own power, but making the soul dull, and stupid, and forgetful, engender ignorance, which is the greatest of diseases. There is one protection against both kinds of disproportions: that we should not move the body without the soul or the soul without the body, and thus they will be on their guard against each other, and be healthy and well balanced. And therefore the mathematician or any one else whose thoughts are much absorbed in some intellectual pursuit, must allow his body also to have due exercise, and practice gymnastic; and he who is careful to fashion the body, should cultivate music and all philosophy, if he would deserve to be called truly fair and truly good. And the separate parts should be treated in the same manner, in imitation of the patterns of the universe.

The following passage shows Plato's naive attempt at presenting a systematic picture of mental disorders. They are supposed to be of two kinds: madness and ignorance. Both madness and vice are largely attributed to bodily causes.

The disorders of the soul, which depend upon the body, originate as follows. We must acknowledge disease of the mind to be a want of intelligence; and of this there are two kinds; to wit, madness and ignorance. In whatever state a man experiences either of them, that state may be called disease; and excessive pains and pleasures are justly to be regarded as the greatest disease to which the soul is liable. For a man who is in great joy or in great pain, in his unreasonable eagerness to attain the one and to avoid the other, is not able to see or to hear anything rightly; but he is mad, and is at the time utterly incapable of any participation in reason. He who has the seed about the spinal marrow too plentiful and overflowing, like a tree overladen with fruit, has many throes, and also obtains many pleasures in his desires and their offspring, and is for the most part of his life deranged, because his pleasures and pains are so very great; his soul is rendered foolish and disordered by his body; yet he is regarded not as one diseased, but as one who is voluntarily bad, which is a mistake. The truth is that the intemperance of love is a disease of the soul due chiefly to the moisture and fluidity which is produced in one of the elements by the loose consistency of the bones. And in general, all that which is termed the incontinence of pleasure and is deemed a reproach under the idea that the wicked voluntarily do wrong is not justly a matter for reproach. For no man is voluntarily bad; but the bad become bad by reason of an ill disposition of the body and bad education, things which are hateful to every man and happen to him against his will. And in the case of pain too in like manner the soul suffers much evil from the body.

This is what Plato, the advocate of "platonic" love, had to say about sex:

And the seed having life, and becoming endowed with respiration, produces in that part in which it respires a lively desire of emission, and thus creates in us the love of procreation. Wherefore also in men the organ of generation becoming rebellious and masterful, like an animal disobedient to reason and maddened with the sting of lust, seeks to gain absolute sway; and the same is the case with the so-called womb or matrix of women; the animal within them is desirous of procreating children, and when remaining unfruitful long beyond its proper time, gets discontented and angry, and wandering in every direction through the body, closes up the passages of the breath, and, by obstructing respiration, drives them to extremity, causing all varieties of disease, until at length the desire and love of the man and the woman, bringing them together and as it were plucking the fruit from the tree, sow in the womb, as in a field, animals unseen by reason of their smallness and without form; these again are separated and matured within; they are then finally brought out into the light, and thus the generation of animals is completed.

The following quotation from The Republic *contains one of Plato's striking passages on dreams. Freud, on his own admission, became acquainted with Plato's writings only in later life. Yet the philosopher's references to the "savage and rude parts of the soul" which manifest themselves during sleep may well have seeped down in the course of centuries to the author of* Interpretation of Dreams.

Such as are excited in sleep, when the rest of the soul—which is rational, mild and its governing principle—is asleep, and when that part which is savage and rude, being satisfied with food and drink, frisks about, drives away sleep, and seeks to go and accomplish its practice: in such a one, you know, it dares to do everything, because it is loosed and disengaged from all modesty and prudence: for, if it pleases, it scruples not at the embraces, even of a mother, or of any one else, whether gods, men, or beasts; nor to commit murder, nor abstain from any sort of meat—and in one word, it is wanting neither in folly nor shamelessness. You speak most truly, replied he. But when a man is in good health, methinks, and lives temperately, and goes to sleep after exciting his reason, and feasting it with noble reasonings and investigations, having thus attained to an internal harmony, and given up the appetites neither to want nor repletion, that they may be at rest, either by joy or grief, but suffer it by itself alone without interruption to inquire and long to apprehend what it knows not—either something of what has existed, or now exists, or will exist hereafter; and so also having soothed the spirited part of the soul, and not allowed it to be hurried into transports of anger, or to fall asleep with agitated passion; but after having quieted these two parts of the soul, and roused to action that third part, in which wisdom dwells, he will thus take his rest; you know, that by such a one the truth is best apprehended, and the visions of his dreams are then least of all portrayed contrary to the law. I am quite of this opinion, said he. We have digressed indeed a little too far in talking of these things; but what we want to know is this, that in every one resides a certain species of desires that are terrible, savage, and irregular, even in some that we deem ever so moderate: and this indeed becomes manifest in sleep.

In Charmides *Plato makes a fascinating digression into psychosomatic medicine. Indeed, his caution against the physician's confining his treatment to the "part" while neglecting the "whole" definitely has a modern ring. This too was presumably influenced by the teachings of Hippocrates. Similarly, Plato's plea to use "fair words," or "beautiful logic," as an integral part of medical treatment has been interpreted as an intimation of the part played by persuasion and suggestion in modern psychotherapy.*

I dare say that you have heard eminent physicians say to a patient who comes to them with bad eyes, that they cannot cure his eyes by themselves, but that if his eyes are to be cured, his head must be treated; and then again they say that to think of curing the head alone, and not the rest of the body also, is the height of folly. And arguing in this way they apply their methods to the whole body, and try to treat and heal the whole and the part together. Did you ever observe that this is what they say?

Yes, he said.

And they are right, and you would agree with them?

Yes, he said, certainly I should.

His approving answers reassured me, and I began by degrees to regain confidence, and the vital heat returned. Such, Charmides, I said, is the nature of the charm, which I learned when serving with the army from one of the physicians of the Thracian king Zamolxis, who are said to be so skillful that they can even give immortality. This Thracian told me that in these notions of theirs, which I was just now mentioning, the Greek physicians are quite right as far as they go; but Zamolxis, he added, our king, who is also a god, says further, 'that as you ought not to attempt to cure the eyes without the head, or the head without the body, so neither ought you to attempt to cure the body without the soul; and this,' he said, 'is the reason why the cure of many diseases is unknown to the physicians of Hellas, because they are ignorant of the whole, which ought to be studied also; for the part can never be well unless the whole is well.' For all good and evil, whether in the body or in human nature, originates, as he declared, in the soul, and overflows from thence, as if from the head into the eyes. And therefore if the head and body are to be well, you must begin by curing the soul; that is the first thing. And the cure, my dear youth, has to be effected by the use of certain charms, and these charms are fair words; and by them temperance is implanted in the soul, and where temperance is, there health is speedily imparted, not only to the head, but to the whole body. And he who taught me the cure and the charm at the same time added a special direction: 'Let no one,' he said, 'persuade you to cure the head, until he has first given you his soul to be cured by the charm. For this,' he said, 'is the great error of our day in the treatment of the human body, that physicians separate the soul from the body.' And he added with emphasis, at the same time making me swear to his words, 'let no one, however rich, or noble, or fair, persuade you to give him the cure, without the charm.' Now I have sworn, and I must keep my oath, and therefore if you will allow me to apply the Thracian charm first to your soul, as the stranger directed, I will afterwards proceed to apply the cure to your head. But if not, I do not know what I am to do with you, my dear Charmides.

The Greek philosopher Epicurus (341-270 B.C.) was born a few years after Plato's death. He is popularly known as the advocate of a life of pleasure and idle contemplation. More accurate is the description of his philosophy as a guide to a tranquil life, equally averse to the extremes of debachery and those of asceticism. In 310 B.C. he founded the School of Mitylene, which some have compared to a modern sanatorium for the treatment of nervous disorders, others to a medieval monastic community. Later on, Epicurus moved his school to Athens. It consisted of a group of faithful disciples, including their friends and relatives, both male and female, who gathered around him in the garden of what may have been a modest Athenian suburban house. Their discussions ranged far and wide over such subjects as the material nature of the soul, the freedom of will and the folly of superstition. But the most important topic was the question of how to establish reason as the sole guide of human conduct, so as to avoid pain and suffering and irrational fears of the gods and of an imaginary afterlife.

Epicurus wrote some three hundred books, only fragments of which have been preserved—and they are of doubtful authenticity. Their influence cannot be compared with that of Plato's Dialogues. Yet what Epicurus says about "fortitude against discontent of mind" has more direct relevance to our subject. It shows him as one of the first practitioners of "moral thera-peutics" in the history of mental healing—that is, of an essentially moral-istic and rationalistic approach, reinforced by the therapist's personal im-pact upon his patients.

These passages are taken from the translation by Walter Charleton (1654), based on his compilation of existing fragments.

On the Means to Procure Felicity

As for the Diseases of the Mind, against them Philosophy is provided of Remedies; being, in that respect, justly accounted the Physick of the Mind: but it is not with equal facility consulted, nor applied by those who are sick in Mind. And this, because we judge of the Diseases of the body, by the Mind: but the diseases of the Mind we neither feel in the body, nor know or judge of them as we ought; because that, whereby we should judge, is dis-tempered.

Hence it appears, that the Diseases of the Mind are more grievous and dangerous than those of the Body: as among Diseases Corporeal, those are most dangerous, which deprive us of our senses; such are the Apoplexy, Lethargy, Phrensie, etc. Again, that the Diseases of the Mind are more per-nicious than those of the Body, is manifest from the same reason, which demonstrateth that the Pleasures of the mind are much better than those of the body, which is this, that we feel in the body nothing but what is present, but in our mind we are sensible of also what is past, and what's to come. For, as the Anxiety of the mind arising by consent from the pains of the body, may be very much aggravated, if we have possessed our selves with a conceit, that some Eternal and Infinite Evil is impendent over us: so may it be very much mitigated, if we fear no such Evil. And this likewise is mani-fest; that the greatest Pleasure or Trouble of the mind, doth more conduce to an happy or miserable life; than either of the other two, though it should be equally lasting in the body.

Now, because there are two Capital diseases of the Mind, namely Cupid-ity and Fear, with their several branches, and with discontent or trouble conjoyned, after the same manner as pain is adjoyned to the diseases of the body; therefore is it the part of Philosophy to apply such Remedies, as may prevent them from invading the mind; or at least overcome and expel them, when they have invaded it. Such chiefly are the vain Desires of Wealth, of Honours, of Dominion, etc. and the Fear of Celestial Powers, of Death, etc. which having once assaulted and taken possession of the mind, they leave no part thereof sound or unshaken.

Of Fortitude Against Pain of the Body

Corporal Pain is that alone, which deserves the name of Evil in it self, and which indeed would carry the Reason of the Greatest of Evils, if so be our own delusive opinions had not created and pulled upon our heads another sort of pain, called the pain of the Mind; which many times becomes more grievous and intolerable than any pain of the Body whatever, as we have formerly deduced. For Discontent of mind, conceived upon the loss of Riches, Honours, Friends, Wife, Children, and the like doth frequently grow to that height, that it exceeds the sharpest pains of the Body: but still that which gives it both being and growth, is our own Opinion, which if right and sound, we should never be moved by any such loss whatever; in regard that all such things are without the circle of our selves, and so cannot touch us by the intervention of Opinion, which we coin to our selves. And thereupon we may infer, that we are not subject to any other real Evil, but only the pain of the body: and that the mind ought to complain of nothing, which is not conjoyned to some pain of the body, either present or to come.

The wise man, therefore will be very cautious, that he do not wittingly draw upon himself any Corporal pain; nor do any action, whereupon any such pain may be likely to ensue: unless it be in order either to the avoidance of some greater pain, that would otherwise certainly invade him; or the comparation (causing) of some Greater pleasure dependent thereupon; as we have formerly inculcated. This considered, we may very well wonder at those philosophers who accounting Health, which is a state of Indolency, a very great Good as to all other respects; do yet, as to this respect, hold it to be a thing merely Indifferent: as if it were not an indecent playing with words, or rather a high piece of Folly, to affirm, that to be in pain, and to be free of pain, is one and the same thing.

But, in case of Necessity either of his native Constitution, in respect whereof his body is infirm and obnoxious to Diseases; or of any External violence done him, which he could not prevent or avoid; (for experience attesteth that a Wise man and Innocent person may be wounded by his malicious Enemies; or called to the bar, impleaded, condemned and beaten with Rods, or otherwise cruelly tormented by Tyrants) we say, in case either of these shall have brought pain upon him: then is it his part, to endure that pain with Constancy and Bravery of mind, and patiently to expect either the Solution, or Relaxation of it.

For, certainly, Pain doth never continue long in the Body; but, if it be Great and Highly intense, it ceaseth in a short time, because either it is determined of its self, and succeeded if not by absolute Indolency, yet by very great mitigation; or is determined by Death, in which there can be no pain. And as for that pain, which is lasting; it is not only gentle and remiss in it self, but also admits many lucid intervals, so that there are not many days, nay, nor hours, in which the body may enjoy not only ease, but very much pleasure also.

And may we not observe, that all long or Chronique Diseases have many more hours of Ease and quiet, than of pain and trouble? For (to omit this, that if a Disease increase our Thirst, it doth as much increase our pleasure in drinking) they give us time for our Reflection, frequent respites to hold comfortable Conferences with our Friends, leasure to recreate our selves wtih some gentle Game, and admit many and long intervals of ease, in which we may apply our selves to our studies and any other necessary affairs. Whereupon it is most evident, that Great pain cannot be Long; nor Long pain Great: and so, we may console our selves against the Violence of pain, by an assurance of the shortness of it; and with the Remissness against the Diuturnity of it. . . .

Of Fortitude Against Discontent of Mind

We said now, that all Discontent of Mind is conceived of such things, that are External Evils, and the Contraries to those Goods that we most love and desire. For, men usually call some things Adverse, and others Prosperous: and we may generally observe, that the Mind, which is elevated and insolent with Prosperity, and dejected with Adversity; is low, abject and base. This considered, you may easily collect, that all we should in this place say, concerning Evils inducing Discontent, and in respect whereof we have need of Fortitude; may be sufficiently inferred from what we formerly said, concerning those Goods, that are the General Objects of our Desires or Cupidities, and in respect whereof we have need of Temperance.

Let this General Axiom, therefore, suffice; that Discontent of Mind is not grounded upon Nature, but upon mere Opinion of Evil; and in respect thereof it becomes necessary, that every man be in Discontent, who conceives himself to be under some Evil, whether only prevised and expected, or already come upon him. For, how comes it, that a Father whose Son is killed, is not a whit less cheerful or merry, if he know not of the death of his Son, than if he were yet alive and in health? or, that he who hath lost much of his good fame abroad, or all his goods and cattle by robbery at home; is not at all sensible of either loss till he hears of it? Is it not Opinion alone, which makes him sad and discontented thereupon? Certainly, if Nature itself were the Author of that sadness, the Father's mind would be struck with a sense of the loss of his Son in the same moment wherein he was slain: and in like manner, he that hath suffered Detraction from his honour, or been robbed of his Goods and Cattle, would in the same instant receive intelligence of his loss from the secret Regret impressed upon his mind. . . .

Hence it is a perspicuous Truth, that those things, for which the mind becomes malcontent and contristate, are not Real Evils to us; forasmuch as they are without the orb of our Nature, and can never touch us immediately or of themselves, but by the meditation of our own Opinion. And this was the Ground of our former Assertion that it is Reason alone which makes life happy and pleasant, by expelling all such false Conceptions or Opinions, as may any way occasion perturbation of mind. For it is Discontent alone, that perturbs the mind, and wholly subverts the Tranquillity, and so the Jucundity thereof.

Plato and Epicurus were both spokesmen of a highly sophisticated culture, unprecedented in the sweep and depth of its philosophical inquiry. But their approach to psychological problems remained essentially rationalistic, with a tendency to overestimate the power of reason and verbal exhortation. Perhaps to counteract his own propensity to flights of mystical fancy, Plato himself seemed to seek the "soul's salvation through laborious intellectual discipline," as the historian W. G. de Burgh put it. This intellectual discipline became an integral part of the scholastic philosophy of the ensuing centuries, and it supplied the basic concepts of the gradually evolving science of psychology. But its exclusive emphasis on reason left it helpless in the face of pain and suffering stemming from deeper levels of human personality. Mankind had to wait two more millennia for a new, truly scientific attack upon the problem.

chapter 12

Hippocrates
and
the Not-So-Sacred Disease

Hippocrates was a contemporary of Plato—which means that he lived at a time of unprecedented concentration of genius in ancient Greek civilization, or for that matter, in any other period of history. Hippocrates's contribution to this civilization was that of the medical man drawing on a vast store of clinical experience based on methodical clinical observation.

Born in the fifth century B.C., the son of a Greek physician, he is called the "Father of Medicine." But more important than this widely acclaimed paternity is the fact that Hippocrates was the first medical man to make a deliberate attempt to separate his art—or his science—from philosophy and from magico-religious beliefs. Although his approach was mainly concerned with the physical and environmental aspects of illness, he achieved a degree of psychological understanding of mental disease that few had before him. This is best illustrated by his essay On the Sacred Disease, *with its emphasis on the natural origin of epileptic disorders and, by implication, of many other disturbances usually attributed to demoniacal possession.*

ON THE SACRED DISEASE

It is thus with regard to the disease called Sacred: it appears to me to be nowise more divine nor more sacred than other diseases, but has a natural cause from which it originates like other affections. Men regard its nature and cause as divine from ignorance and wonder, because it is not at all like other diseases. And this notion of its divinity is kept up by their inability to comprehend it, and the simplicity of the mode by which it is cured, for men are freed from it by purifications and incantations. But if it is reckoned divine because it is wonderful, instead of one there are many diseases which would be sacred; for as I will show, there are others no less wonderful and prodigious, which nobody imagines to be sacred.

. . . The quotidian, tertian, and quartan fevers, seem to me no less sacred and divine in their origin than this disease, although they are not reckoned so wonderful. And I see men become mad and demented from no manifest cause, and at the same time doing many things out of place; and I have known many persons in sleep groaning and crying out, some in a state of suffocation, some jumping up and fleeing out of doors, and deprived of their reason until they awaken, and afterward becoming well and rational as before, although they be pale and weak; and this will happen not once but frequently. And there are many and various things of the like kind, which it would be tedious to state particularly. And they who first referred this disease to the gods, appear to me to have been just such persons as the conjurors, purificators, mountebanks, and charlatans now are, who give themselves out for being excessively religious, and as knowing more than other people. Such persons, then, using the divinity as a pretext and screen of their own inability to afford any assistance, have given out that the disease is sacred; adding suitable reasons for this opinion, they have instituted a mode of treatment which is safe for themselves, namely, by applying purifications and incantations, and enforcing abstinence from baths and many articles of food which are unwholesome to men in disease. Of sea substances, the sur-mullet, the blacktail, the mullet, and the eel; for these are the fishes most to be guarded against. And of fleshes, those of the goat, the stag, the sow, and the dog; for these are the kinds of flesh which are aptest to disorder the bowels. Of fowls, the cock, the turtle, and the bustard, and such others as are reckoned to be particularly strong. And of pot-herbs, mint, garlic, and onions, for what is acrid does not agree with a weak person. And they forbid to have a black robe, because black is expressive of death; and to sleep on a goat's skin, or to wear it, and to put one foot upon another, or one hand upon another; for all these things are held to be hindrances to the cure. All these they enjoin with reference to its divinity, as if possessed of more knowledge, and announcing beforehand other pretents, so that if the person should die, they would have a certain defense, as if the gods, and not they, were to blame, seeing they had administered nothing either to eat or to drink as medicines, not had overheated him with baths, so as to prove the cause of what had happened. But I am of opinion that (if this were true) none of the Libyans, who live in the interior, would be free from this disease, since they all sleep on goats' skins, and live upon goats' flesh; neither have they couch, robe, nor shoe that is not made of goat's skin, for they have no other herds, but goats and oxen. But if these things, when administered in food, aggravate the disease, and if it be cured by abstinence from them, then is God not the cause at all; nor will purifications be of any avail, but it is the food which is beneficial and prejudicial, and the influence of the divinity vanishes. Thus then, they who attempt to cure these diseases in this way, appear to me neither to reckon them sacred nor divine. For when they are removed by such purifications and this method of cure, what is to prevent them from being brought upon men and induced by other devices similar to those? So that the cause is no longer divine, but human. For whoever is able, by purifications and conjurations to drive away such an affection, will be able, by other practices to excite it; and, according to this view, its divine nature is entirely done away with. By such sayings and doings, they profess to be possessed of superior knowledge, and deceive mankind by enjoining lustrations and purifications upon them, while their discourse turns upon the divinity and the godhead. And yet it would appear to me that their discourse savors not of piety, as they suppose, but rather of impiety, and as if there were no gods, and that what they hold to be holy and divine, were impious and unholy. This I will now explain. For, if they profess to know how to bring down the moon, and darken the sun, and induce storms and fine weather, and rains and droughts, and make the sea and land unproductive, and so forth, whether they arrogate this power as being derived from mysteries or any other knowledge or consideration, they appear to me to practice impiety, and either to fancy that there are no gods, or, if there are, that they have no ability to ward off any of the greatest evils. How, then, are they not enemies to the gods? For if a man by magical arts and sacrifices will bring down the moon, and darken the sun, and induce storms, or fine weather, I should not believe that there was anything divine, but human, in these things, provided the power of the divine were overpowered by human knowledge and subjected to it. But perhaps it will be said, these things are not so, but, men being in want of the means of life, invent, many and various things, and devise many contrivances for all other things, and for this disease, in every phase of the disease, assigning the cause to a god. Nor do they remember the same things once, but frequently. For, if they imitate a goat, or grind their teeth, or if their right side be convulsed, they say that the mother of the gods is the cause. But if they speak in a sharper and more intense tone, they resemble this state to a horse, and say that Poseidon is the cause. Or if any excrement be passed, which is often the case, owing to the violence of the disease, the appellation of Enodius is adhibited; or, if it be passed in smaller and denser masses, like bird's, it is said to be from Apollo Nomius. But if foam be emitted by the mouth, and the patient kick with his feet, Ares gets the blame. But terrors which happen during the night, and fevers, and deliriums, and jumpings out of bed, and frightful apparitions, and fleeing away—all these they hold to be the plots of Hecate, and the invasion of the Heroes, and use purifications and incantations, and, as appears to me, make the divinity to be most wicked and most impious.

If the secretion from the whole brain be greater than natural, the person, when he grows up, will have his head diseased, and full of noises, and will neither be able to endure sun nor cold. Or, if the melting take place from any one part, either from the eye or ear, or if a vein has become slender, that part will be deranged in proportion to the melting. Or, if the depuration do not take place, but it accumulates in the brain, it necessarily becomes phlegmatic. And such children as have an eruption of ulcers on the head, on the ears, and along the rest of the body, with copious discharges of saliva and mucus—these, in after life, enjoy best health; for in this way the phlegm which ought to have been purged off in the womb, is discharged and cleared away and persons so purged, for the most part, are not subject to attacks of this disease. But such as have had their skin free from eruptions, and have had no discharge of saliva or mucus, nor have undergone the proper purgation in the womb, these persons run the risk of being seized with this disease. But if the defluxion be determined to the heart, the person is seized with palpitation and asthma, the chest becomes diseased, and some also have curvature of the spine. For when a defluxion of cold phlegm takes place on the lungs and heart, the blood is chilled, and the veins, being violently chilled, palpitate in the lungs and heart, and the heart palpitates, so that from this necessity, asthma and orthopnoea supervene. For it does not receive the spirits until the defluxion of phlegm be mastered, and being heated is distributed to the veins, then it ceases from its palpitation and difficulty of breathing, and this takes place as soon as it obtains an abundant supply; and this will be more slowly, provided the defluxion be more abundant, of if it be less, more quickly. And if the defluxions be more condensed, the epileptic attacks will be more frequent, but otherwise if it be rarer. Such are the symptoms which the defluxion is upon the lungs and heart; but if it be upon the bowels, the person is attacked with diarrhoea. And if, being shut out from all these outlets, its defluxion be determined to the veins I have formerly mentioned, the patient loses his speech, and chokes, and foam issues by the mouth, the teeth are fixed, the hands are contracted, the eyes distorted, he becomes insensible, and in some cases the bowels are evacuated. And these symptoms occur sometimes on the left side, sometimes on the right, and sometimes both. . . .

The defluxion also takes place in consequence of fear, from any hidden cause, if we are frightened at any person's calling aloud, or while crying, when one cannot quickly recover one's breath, such as often happens to children. When any of these things occurs, the body immediately shivers, the person becoming speechless cannot draw his breath, but the breath stops, the brain is contracted, the blood stands still, and thus the excretion and defluxion of the phlegm take place. In children, these are the causes of the attack at first. But to old persons winter is most inimical. For when the head and brain have been heated at a great fire, and then the person is brought into cold and has a rigor, or when from cold he comes into warmth, and sits at the fire, he is apt to suffer in the same way, and thus he is seized in the manner described above. And there is much danger of the same thing occurring if in spring his head be exposed to the sun, but less so in summer, as the changes are not sudden. When a person has passed the twentieth year of his life, this disease is not apt to seize him, unless it has become habitual from childhood, or at least this is rarely or never the case. For the veins are filled with blood, and the brain consistent and firm, so that it does not run down into the veins, or if it do, it does not overpower the blood, which is copious and hot. But when it has gained strength from one's childhood, and become habitual, such a person usually suffers attacks, and is seized with them in changes of the winds, especially in south winds, and it is difficult of removal. . . .

Thus is this disease formed and prevails from those things which enter into and go out of the body, and it is not more difficult to understand or to cure than the others, neither is it more divine than other diseases. And men ought to know that from nothing else but thence [from the brain] come joys, delights, laughter and sports, and sorrows, griefs, despondency and lamentations. And by this, in an especial manner, we acquire wisdom and knowledge, and see and hear, and know what are foul and what are fair, what are bad and what are good, what are sweet, and what unsavory; some we discriminate by habit, and some we perceive by their utility. By this we distinguish objects of relish and disrelish, according to the seasons; and the same things do not always please us. And by the same organ we become mad and delirious, and fears and terrors assail us, some by night and some by day, and dreams and untimely wandering, and cares that are not suitable, and ignorance of present circumstances, desuetude, and unskillfulness. All these things we endure from the brain, when it is not healthy, but is more hot, more cold, more moist, or more dry than natural, or when it suffers any other preternatural and unusual affliction. And we become mad from humidity [of the brain]. For when it is more moist than natural, it is necessarily put into motion, and the affection being moved, neither the sight nor hearing can be at rest, and the tongue speaks in accordance with the sight and hearing. As long as the brain is at rest, the man enjoys his reason, but the depravement of the brain arises from phlegm and bile, either of which you may recognize in this manner: Those who are mad from phlegm are quiet, and do not cry out nor make a noise; but those from bile are vociferous, malignant, and will not be quiet, but are always doing something improper. If the madness be constant, these are the causes thereof. But if terrors and fears assail, they are connected with derangement of the brain, and derangement is owing to its being heated. And it is heated by bile when it is determined to the brain along the blood-vessels running from the trunk; and fear is present until it returns again to the veins and trunk, when it ceases. He is grieved and troubled when the brain is unseasonably cooled and contracted beyond its wont. This it suffers from phlegm, and from the same affection the patient become oblivious. He calls out and screams at night when the brain is suddenly heated. The bilious endure this. But the phlegmatic are not heated, except when much blood goes to the brain, and creates an ebullition. Much blood passes along the aforesaid veins. But when the man happens to see a frightful dream and is in fear as if awake, then his face is in a greater glow, and the eyes are red when the patient is in fear. And the understanding meditates doing some mischief, and thus it is affected in sleep. But if, when awakened, he returns to himself, and the blood is again distributed along the aforesaid veins, it ceases. In these ways I am of opinion that the brain exercises the greatest power in the man. This is the interpreter to us of those things which emanate from the air, when it [the brain] happens to be in sound state. But the air supplies sense to it. And the eyes, the ears, the tongue and the feet, administer such things as the brain cogitates. For inasmuch as it is supplied with air, does it impart sense to the body. It is the brain which is the messenger to the understanding. . . .

But the diaphragm has obtained its names [phrenes] from accident and usage, and not from reality or nature, for I know no power which it possesses, either as to sense or understanding, except that when the man is affected with unexpected joy or sorrow, it throbs and produces palpitations, owing to its thinness, and as having no belly to receive anything good or bad that may present themselves to it, but it is thrown into commotion by both these, from its natural weakness. It then perceives beforehand none of those things which occur in the body, but has received its name vaguely and without any proper reason, like the parts about the heart, which are called auricles, but which contribute nothing towards hearing. Some say that we think with the heart and that this is the part which is grieved and experiences care. But it is not so; only it contracts like the diaphragm, and still more so for the same causes. For veins from all parts of the body run to it, and it has valves, so as to perceive if any pain or pleasurable emotion befall the man. For when grieved the body necessarily shudders, and is contracted, and from excessive joy it is affected in like manner. Wherefore the heart and the diaphragm are particularly sensitive, they have nothing to do, however, with the operations of the understanding, but of all these the brain is the cause. Since, then, the brain, as being the primary seat of the sense and of the spirits, perceives whatever occurs in the body, if any change more powerful than usual takes place in the air, owing to the seasons, the brain becomes changed by the state of the air. For, on this account, the brain first perceives, because I say, all the most acute, most powerful, and most deadly diseases, and those which are most difficult to be understood by the inexperienced, fall upon the brain. And the disease called the Sacred arises from causes as the others, namely those things which enter and quit the body, such as cold, the sun, and the winds, which are ever changing and are never at rest. And these things are divine, so that there is no necessity for making a distinction, and holding this disease to be more divine than the others, but all are divine, and all human. And each has its own peculiar nature and power, and none is of an ambiguous nature, or irremediable. And the most of them are curable by the same means as those by which they were produced. For any other thing is food to one, and injurious to another. Thus, then, the physician should understand and distinguish the season of each, so that at one time he may attend to the nourishment and increase, and at another to abstraction and diminution. And in this disease as in all others, he must strive not to feed the disease, but endeavor to wear it out by administering whatever is most opposed to each disease, and not that which favors and is allied to it. For by that which is allied to it, it gains vigor and increase, but it wears out and disappears under the use of that which is opposed to it. But whoever is acquainted with such a change in men, and can render a man humid and dry, hot and cold by regimen, could also cure this disease, if he recognizes the proper season for administering his remedies, without minding purifications, spells, and all other illiberal practices of a like kind.

Airs, Waters and Places is another famous work of the "Father of Medicine." It examines the influence of climatic, geological and other environmental factors upon the "races" of man, that is, upon men of various cultural and ethnological backgrounds. Hippocrates, like Toynbee, holds that the physical and emotional make-up of the inhabitants of a certain area are decisively influenced by those factors.

Describing the Scythian race, Hippocrates says that it is impossible for persons of their type to be prolific, "for with the men, the sexual desires are not strong owing to the laxity of their constitution, the softness and coldness of their bellies, from all which causes it is little likely that a man should be given to venery." And he goes on to say:

There are many eunuchs among the Scythian, who perform female work, and speak like women. Such persons are called effeminates. The inhabitants of the country attribute the cause of their impotence to a god, and venerate and worship such persons, every one dreading that the like might befall himself; but to me it appears that such affections are just as much divine as all others are, and that no one disease is either more divine or more human than another, but that all are alike divine, for that each has its own nature, and that no one arises without a natural cause. But I will explain how I think that the affection takes its rise. From continued exercises on horseback they are seized with chronic defluxions in their joints, owing to their legs always hanging down below their horses; they afterwards become lame and stiff at the hip-joint, such of them at least, as are severely attacked with it. . . . Such persons afterwards, when they go in to women and cannot have connection with them, at first do not think much about it, but remain quiet; but when, after making the attempt two, three, or more times, they succeed no better, fancying they have committed some offence against the god whom they blame for the affection, they put on female attire, reproach themselves for effeminacy, play the part of women, and perform the same work as women do. This the rich among the Scythians endure, not the basest, but the most noble and powerful, owing to their riding of horseback; for the poor are less affected, as they do not ride on horses. And yet, if this disease had been more divine than the others, it ought not to have befallen the most noble and the richest of the Scythians alone, but all alike, or rather those who have little, as not being able to pay honors to the gods, if, indeed, they delight in being thus rewarded by men, and grant favors in return; for it is likely that the rich sacrifice more to the gods, and dedicate more votive offerings, inasmuch as they have wealth, and worship the gods; whereas the poor, from want, do less in this way, and, moreover, upbraid the gods for not giving them wealth, so that those who have few possessions were more likely to bear the punishments of these offences than the rich. But, as I formerly said, these affections are divine just as much as others, for each springs from a natural cause, and this disease arises among the Scythians from such a cause as I have stated. But it attacks other men in like manner, for whenever men ride much and very frequently on horseback, then many are affected with rheums in the joints, sciatica, and gout, and they are inept at venery. But these complaints befall the Scythians, and they are the most impotent of men for the aforesaid causes, and because they always wear breeches, and spend the most of their time on horseback, so as not to touch their privy parts with the hand, and from the cold and fatigue they forget the sexual desire, and do not make the attempt until after they lose their virility. Thus it is with the race of the Scythians.

Following this somewhat debatable discourse about the causes of impotence in the Scythians, Hippocrates makes a fascinating excursion into what today would be described as cultural anthropology, again seeking to account for the differences in the mentality of European and Asian races along wholly naturalistic lines. His praise of free people ready to "undertake dangers on their own account" could be from a modern treatise extolling the virtues of democracy.

The other races in Europe differ from one another, both as to stature and shape, owing to the changes of the seasons, which are very great and frequent, and because the heat is strong, the winters severe, and there are frequent rains, and again protracted droughts, and winds, from which many and diversified changes are induced. These changes are likely to have an effect upon generation in the coagulation of the semen, as this process cannot be the same in summer as in winter, nor in rainy as in dry weather; wherefore, I think, that the figures of Europeans differ more than those of Asiatics; and they differ very much from one another as to stature in the same city; for vitiations of the semen occur in its coagulation more frequently during frequent changes of the seasons, than where they are alike and equable. And the same may be said of their dispositions, for the wild and unsociable, and the passionate occur in such a constitution; for frequent excitement of the mind induces wildness, and extinguishes sociableness and mildness of disposition, and therefore I think the inhabitants of Europe more courageous than those of Asia; for a climate which is always the same induces indolence, but a changeable climate, laborious exertions both of body and mind; and from rest and indolence, cowardice is engendered, and from laborious exertions and pains, courage. On this account the inhabitants of Europe are more warlike than the Asiatics, and also owing to their institutions, because they are not governed by kings like the latter, for where men are governed by kings there they must be very cowardly, as I have stated before; for their souls are enslaved, and they will not willingly, or readily undergo dangers in order to promote the power of another; but those that are free undertake dangers on their own account, and not for the sake of others; they court hazard and go out to meet it, for they themselves bear off the rewards of victory, and thus their institutions contribute not a little to their courage.

Like Plato and Aristotle, Hippocrates believed in the prophetic or divinatory nature of certain dreams. This is illustrated by the following passage from a short book on Dreams *which has been attributed to Hippocrates but whose true authorship, like that of many other writings in the so-called Hippocratic Collection, is controversial.*

He who forms a correct judgment of those signs which occur in sleep, will find that they have a great efficacy in all respects; for the mind is awake when it ministers to the body, being distributed over many parts; it is not then master of itself, but imparts a certain portion of its influence to every part of the body, namely, to the senses, to the hearing, seeing, touch, walking, action, and to the whole management of the body, and therefore its cogitations are not then in its power. But when the body is at rest, the soul, being in a state of movement, steals over the organs of the body, manages its own abode, and itself performs all the actions of the body; for the body, being asleep, does not perceive, but the soul, being awake, beholds what is visible, hears what is audible, walks, touches, is grieved, reflects, and in a word, whatever the offices of the soul or body are, all these the soul performs in sleep. Whoever, then, knows how to judge of these correctly, will find it a great part of wisdom. But with regard to such dreams as are divine, and prognosticate something, either good or evil, to cities or to a particular people, there are persons who have the art of judging of them accurately, without falling into mistakes. But such affections of the body as the soul prognosticates, namely, such as are connected with repletion and evacuation, from the excess of customary things or the change of unusual things, on these also persons pronounce judgment, and sometimes they succeed, and sometimes they err, and understand neither how this happens, that is to say, how it comes that sometimes they are right, and sometimes they fall into mistakes; but warning people to be upon their guard lest some mischief befall them, they do not instruct them how to guard themselves, but direct them to pray to the gods; and to offer up prayers is no doubt becoming and good, but while praying to the gods a man ought also use his own exertions. With regard to these, then, the matter stands thus: Such dreams as represent at night a man's actions through the day, and exhibit them in the manner in which they occur, namely, as performed and justly deliberated, these are good to a man, and prognosticate health, inasmuch as the soul perseveres in its diurnal cogitations, and is not weighed down by any repletion, evacuation, or any other external accident. But when the dreams are the very opposite to the actions of the day, and when there is a conflict between them—when this happens, I say, it indicates a disorder in the body; when the contrast is great, the evil is great, and when the one is small the other is small also.

One of Hippocrates' most celebrated aphorisms may be quoted here in conclusion: "Life is short but art reaches far; the favorable moment is transient, experiment is deceptive and decision difficult."

His reference to Kairos, the favorable moment, has more recently gained growing attention. It points to the temporal aspects of both illness and the therapeutic process which are thought to occur outside the flow of chronological time. It can be grasped only within an existential or theological frame of reference as conceived by Paul Tillich, Abraham Maslow, and Harold Kelman in this country or by A. Kielholz in Switzerland.

chapter 13

Light in the Dark Ages

SELECTIONS FROM BARTHOLOMAEUS ANGELICUS,
AVICENNA, AND MOSES MAIMONIDES

With the decline and fall of Greco-Roman civilization, the progress made by Hippocratic medicine came to standstill. In the ensuing centuries it was to remain in a state of suspended animation. Once more Europe's learned doctors of theology took the place of the physician in his specialty, and more often than not, the theologian himself proved to be a magician in disguise, committed to the ancient demonological theory of the origin of mental illness.

This was illustrated by the tragic excesses of the Inquisition and its notorious manual the Witches' Hammer *(see Chapter VIII). It would be wrong, however, to conclude from such aberrations that the Dark Ages were really all darkness and superstition. The Catholic Sacrament of Penance—contrition, confession, and active penance—was an important empirical step toward a future "cathartic" type of psychotherapy. In the late thirteenth century Pope Innocent III took the initiative in founding the healing orders of the Catholic Church. This marked the beginning of monastic medicine, which brought loving care and true understanding to those sick in body and mind. It amounted, among other things, to a first attempt at "intramural" treatment of the mentally ill and spread sweetness and light in a period often considered to be governed solely by the crude superstitions of medieval man.*

Bartholomaeus Angelicus, the English-born Franciscan theologian and encyclopedist, is a scholarly representative of this trend. The fragments that follow are taken from his De Proprietatibus Rerum *(Concerning the Properties of Things), published about 1275. Consisting of nineteen volumes, it shows the influence of the thinkers of antiquity recently rediscovered in the Western world. Book VII deals specifically with the body and its ailments. In contrast to that of Kramer and Sprenger, Bartholomaeus's approach is wholly naturalistic; even his treatment of mental disease lacks any reference to witches, devils or sorcerers. His contribution shows once more the closeness of medieval Christian thought to science and philosophy.*

These be the signs of frenzy, woodness [wildness] and continual waking, moving, casting about eyes, raging, stretching, casting out of hands, moving and wagging of the head, grinding and gnashing together of the teeth; always they will arise out of their bed, now they sing, now they weep, and they bite gladly and rend their keeper and their leech: seldom be they still, but cry much. And these be most perilously sick, and yet they wot not then that they be sick. Then they must be soon holpen lest they perish, and that both in diet and in medicine. The diet shall be full scarce, as crumbs of bread, which must many times be wet in water. The medicine is, that in the beginning the patient's head be shaven, and washed in lukewarm vinegar, and that he be well kept or bound in a dark place. Diverse shapes of faces and semblance of painting shall not be shewed tofore him, lest he be tarred with woodness. All that be about him shall be commanded to be still and in silence; men shall not answer to his nice words. In the beginning of medicine he shall be let blood in a vein of the forehead, and bled as much as will fill an egg-shell. Afore all things (if virtue and age suffereth) he shall bleed in the head vein. Over all things, with ointments and balming men shall labour to bring him asleep. The head that is shaven shall be plastered with lungs of a swine, or of a wether, or of a sheep; the temples and forehead shall be anointed with the juice of lettuce, or of poppy. If after these medicines are laid thus to, the woodness dureth three days without sleep, there is no hope of recovery.

Madness is infection of the foremost cell of the head, with privation of imagination, like as melancholy is the infection of the middle cell of the head, with privation of reason.

Madness cometh sometimes of passions of the soul, as of business and of great thoughts, of sorrow and of too great study, and of dread: sometime of the biting of a wood hound, or some other venomous beast: sometime of melancholy meats, and sometime of drink of strong wine. And as the causes be diverse, the tokens and signs be diverse. For some cry and leap and hurt and wound themselves and other men, and darken and hide themselves in privy and secret places. The medicine of them is, that they be bound, that they hurt not themselves and other men. And namely, such shall be refreshed, and comforted, and withdrawn from cause and matter of dread and busy thoughts. And they must be gladded with instruments of music, and somedeal be occupied.

A discording voice and an inordinate troubleth the accord of many voices. But according voices sweet and ordinate, gladden and move to love, and show out the passions of the soul, and witness the strength and virtue of the spiritual members, and show pureness and good disposition of them, and relieve travail, and put off disease and sorrow. And make to be known the male and the female, and get and win praising, and change the affection of the hearers; as it is said in fables of one Orpheus, that pleased trees, woods, hills, and stones, with sweet melody of his voice. Also a fair voice is according and friendly to kind. And pleaseth not only men but also beasts, as it fareth in oxen that are excited to travail more by sweet song of the herd, than by strokes and pricks.

Also by sweet songs of harmony and accord or music, sick men and frantic come oft to their wit again and health of body. Some men tell that Orpheus said, "Emperors pray me to feasts, to have liking of me; but I have liking of them which would bend their hearts from wrath to mildness, from sorrow to gladness, from covetousness to largeness, from dread to boldness." This is the ordinance of music, that is known above the sweetness of the soul.

The rediscovery and revival of the achievements of classical antiquity was by no means confined to the Christian world. It was in effect initiated by a number of Arabic and Jewish scholars, some of them greatly renowned medical men in their own right. At least a few passages from the works of two representatives of these groups should be included in this anthology: one Moslem, Avicenna; and one Jewish, Moses Maimonides.

Avicenna (979-1037) was one of the great sages of the Moslem world. He was a noted physician, scientist, philosopher and poet. Born in Persia, he was equally versed in the Iranian and the Islamic traditions of his time, and was thoroughly familiar with the great legacy of classical antiquity. It was to a considerable extent through his labors that the Western world became acquainted with the works of Plato and Aristotle. His own writings comprise a monumental encyclopedia of medicine, containing about one million words. With all these accomplishments, it is difficult to assign him a proper place in medieval Western civilization. Modern oriental scholars have described him as the product and intellectual fulfillment of the Golden Age of Islamic culture which began about the middle of the eighth century A.D., and as a universal genius of oriental vintage.

This fragment from his Book of Salvation *can convey only the vaguest idea of the range and depth of Avicenna's learning. It discusses the immortality and incorruptibility of the soul in unmistakably Aristotelian terms. But Avicenna's emphasis on the unity of the soul, on the part played by the consciousness of the self, is said to have gone beyond traditional Aristotelian concepts.*

As for the proposition that the soul does not admit of corruption at all, I say that there is another conclusive reason for the immortality of the soul.

Everything which might be corrupted through some cause has in itself the potentiality of corruption and the actuality of persistence; its potentiality of corruption cannot be due to its actual persistence; for the concept of potentiality is contrary to that of actuality. Also the relation of this potentiality is opposed to the relation of this actuality, for the one is related with corruption, the other with persistence. These two concepts, then, are attributable to two different factors in the concrete thing. Hence we say that the actuality of persistence and the potentiality of corruption may be combined in composite things and in such simple things as subsist in composite ones. But these two concepts cannot come together in simple things whose essence is separate. I say in another absolute sense that these two concepts cannot exist in a simple thing whose essence is unitary. This is because everything which persists and has the potentiality of corruption also has the potentiality of persistence, since its persistence is not necessary. When it is not necessary, it is possible; and possibility is of the nature of potentiality.

It goes without saying that philosophical speculation of this order was not conducive to a sound empirical approach to problems of psychopathology. Yet as a practicing physician Avicenna was apparently able to break out of the grip of metaphysical speculations which considered the "soul" as basically incorruptible and therefore not subject to disease. This is illustrated by an anecdote which has recently been retold by Professor Arthur Upham Pope: Avicenna was once challenged to cure, on the instant, a girl serving in the royal apartments who had bent over and could not straighten up again. "Take off her veil." prescribed Avicenna. This was done, putting the girl in an anguish of embarrassment; yet her body was still locked immobile. "Out with the skirt," commanded Avicenna, and the girl, in a spasm of emotional shock, straightened up and disappeared. Avicenna thus obtained a cure within the hour and at the same time, although there are some antecedents to the story, scored one of the earliest recorded triumphs for psychotherapy.

Moses Maimonides (1135-1204) was one of the great Jewish physicians and philosophers of the Middle Ages. Born in Spain, educated by Arabic masters, yet faithful to the Jewish tradition, he sought to harmonize ancient rabbinical doctrine with the teachings of Aristotle. His contributions to mental healing are of a largely rationalistic nature. To him, the soul, just as much as the body, may be the seat of disease. If so, it is in need of treatment by spiritual means: by exhorting the patient to avoid all extremes, to practice moderation in all walks of life. Yet Maimonides's writings reveal a dawning insight into the limitations of the intellect and into the part played by the passions in the origin of both illness and vice. In this respect he sounds very much like a forerunner of the great Jewish philosopher Baruch Spinoza. At a time when most of the Western world was still in the clutches of ancient superstitions, Maimonides spoke to his patients and disciples with the voice of reason, appealing to their consciences and sense of personal responsibility in overcoming emotional difficulties. He scorned the use of physical remedies in these conditions and was one of the early advocates of "moral therapy" in patients suffering from diseases of the "soul."

The selection that follows is taken from the Eight Chapters of Maimonides on Ethics, *originally written in Arabic.*

The ancients maintained that the soul, like the body, is subject to good health and illness. The soul's healthful state is due to its condition, and that of its faculties, by which it constantly does what is right, and performs what is proper, while the illness of the soul is occasioned by its condition, and that of its faculties, which results in its constantly doing wrong, and performing actions that are improper. The science of medicine investigates the health of the body. Now, just as those, who are physically ill, imagine that, on account of their vitiated tastes, the sweet is bitter and the bitter is sweet—and likewise fancy the wholesome to be unwholesome—and just as their desire grows stronger, and their enjoyment increases for such things as dust, coal, very acidic and sour foods, and the like—which the healthy loathe and refuse, as they are not only not beneficial even to the healthy, but possibly harmful—so those whose souls are ill, that is the wicked and the morally perverted, imagine that the bad is good, and the good is bad. The wicked man, moreover, continually longs for excesses which are really pernicious, but which, on account of the illness of his soul, he considers to be good. Likewise, just as when people, unacquainted with the science of medicine, realize that they are sick, and consult a physician, who tells them what they must do, forbidding them to partake of that which they imagine beneficial, and prescribing for them things which are unpleasant and bitter, in order that their bodies may become healthy, and that they may again choose the good and spurn the bad, so those whose souls become ill should consult the sages, the moral physicians, who will advise them against indulging in those evils which they (the morally ill) think are good, so that they may be healed by that art of which I shall speak in the next chapter, and through which the moral qualities are restored to their normal condition. But, if he who is morally sick be not aware of his illness, imagining that he is well, or, being aware of it, does not seek a remedy, his end will be similar to that of one, who, suffering from bodily ailment, yet continuing to indulge himself, neglects to be cured, and who in consequence surely meets an untimely death.

Those who know that they are in a diseased state, but nevertheless yield to their inordinate passions, are described in the truthful Law which quotes their own words, "Though I walk in the stubbornness of my heart, in order that the indulgence of the passions may appease the thirst for them." This means that, intending to quench the thirst, it is, on the contrary, intensified. He who is ignorant of his illness is spoken of in many places by Solomon, who says, "The way of the fool is straight in his own eyes, but he who hearkeneth unto counsel is wise." This means that he who listens to the counsel of the sage is wise, for the sage teaches him the way that is actually right, and not the one that he (the morally ill) erroneously considers to be such. Solomon also says, "There is many a way which seemeth even before a man; but its ends are ways unto death." Again, in regard to these who are morally ill, in that they do not know what is injurious from that which is beneficial, he says, "The way of the wicked is like darkness; they do not know against what they stumble."

The art of healing the diseases of the soul will, however, form the subject-matter of the fourth chapter. . . .

Concerning the Cure of the Diseases of the Soul

Good deeds are such as are equibalanced, maintaining the mean between two equally bad extremes, the *too much* and the *too little*. Virtues are psychic conditions and dispositions which are mid-way between two reprehensible extremes, one of which is characterized by an exaggeration, the other by a deficiency. Good deeds are the product of these dispositions. To illustrate, abstemiousness is a disposition which adopts a mid-course between inordinate passion and total insensibility to pleasure. Abstemiousness, then, is a proper rule of conduct, and the psychic disposition which gives rise to it is an ethical quality; but inordinate passion, the extreme of excess, and total insensibility to enjoyment, the extreme of deficiency, are both absolutely pernicious. The psychic dispositions, from which these two extremes, inordinate passion and insensibility, result—the one being an exaggeration, the other a deficiency—are alike classed among moral imperfections.

Likewise, liberality is the mean between sordidness and extravagance; courage, between recklessness and cowardice; dignity, between haughtiness and loutishness; humility, between arrogance and self-abasement; contentedness, between avarice and slothful indifference; and magnificence, between meanness and profusion. [Since definite terms do not exist in our language with which to express these latter qualities, it is necessary to explain their content, and tell what the philosophers meant by them. A man is called magnificent whose sole intention is to do good to others by personal service, by money, or advice, and with all his power, but without meanwhile bringing suffering or disgrace upon himself. That is the medium line of conduct. The mean man is one who does not want others to succeed in anything, even though he himself may not thereby suffer any loss, hardship, or injury. That is the one extreme. The profuse man, on the contrary, is one who willingly performs the above-mentioned deeds, in spite of the fact that thereby he brings upon himself great injury, or disgrace, terrible hardship, or considerable loss. That is the other extreme.] Gentleness is the mean between irascibility and insensibility to shame and disgrace; and modesty, between impudence and shamefacedness. [The explanation of these latter terms, gleaned from the sayings of our sages (may their memory be blessed!) seems to be this. In their opinion, a modest man is one who is very bashful, and therefore modesty is the mean. This we gather from their saying "A shamefaced man cannot learn." They also assert, "A modest man is worthy of Paradise," but they do not say this of a shamefaced man. Therefore, I have thus arranged them.] So it is with the other qualities. One does not necessarily have to use conventional terms for these qualities, if only the ideas are clearly fixed in the mind.

It often happens, however, that men err as regards these qualities, imagining that one of the extremes is good, and is a virtue. Sometimes, the extreme of the *too much* is considered noble, as when temerity is made a virtue, and those who recklessly risk their lives are hailed as heroes. Thus, when people see a man, reckless to the highest degree, who runs deliberately into danger, intentionally tempting death, and escaping only by mere chance, they laud such a one to the skies, and say that he is a hero. At other times, the opposite extreme, the *too little*, is greatly esteemed, and the coward is considered a man of forbearance; the idler, as being a person of a contented disposition; and he, who by the dullness of his nature is callous to every joy, is praised as a man of moderation [that is, one who eschews sin]. In like manner, profuse liberality and extreme lavishness are erroneously extolled as excellent characteristics. This is, however, an absolutely mistaken view, for the really praiseworthy is the medium course of action to which every one should strive to adhere, always weighing his conduct carefully, so that he may attain the proper mean.

Know, moreover, that these moral excellences or defects cannot be acquired, or implanted in the soul, except by means of the frequent repetition of acts resulting from these qualities, which, practiced during a long period of time, accustoms us to them. If these acts performed are good ones, then we shall have gained a virtue; but if they are bad, we shall have acquired a vice. Since, however, no man is born with an innate virtue or vice, . . . and, as every one's conduct from childhood up is undoubtedly influenced by the manner of living of his relatives and countrymen, his conduct may be in accord with the rules of moderation; but, then again, it is possible that his acts may incline towards either extreme, as we have demonstrated, in which case, his soul becomes diseased. In such a contingency, it is proper for him to resort to a cure, exactly as he would were his body suffering from an illness. So, just as when the equilibrium of the physical health is disturbed, and we note which way it is tending in order to force it to go in exactly the opposite direction until it shall return to its proper condition, and, just as when the proper adjustment is reached, we cease this operation, and have recourse to that which will maintain the proper balance, in exactly the same way must we adjust the moral equilibrium. Let us take, for example, the case of a man in whose soul there has developed a disposition [of great avarice] on account of which he deprives himself [of every comfort in life], and which, by the way, is one of the most detestable of defects, and an immoral act, as we have shown in this chapter. If we wish to cure this sick man, we must not command him merely [to practice] deeds of generosity, for that would be as ineffective as a physician trying to cure a patient consumed by a burning fever by administering mild medicines, which treatment would be inefficacious. We must, however, induce him to squander so often, and to repeat his acts of profusion so continuously until that propensity which was the cause of his avarice has totally disappeared. Then, when he reaches that point where he is about to become a squanderer, we must teach him to moderate his profusion, and tell him to continue with deeds of generosity, and to watch out with due care lest he relapse either into lavishness or niggardliness.

If, on the other hand, a man is a squanderer, he must be directed to practice strict economy, and to repeat acts of niggardliness. It is not necessary, however, for him to perform acts of avarice as many times as the mean man should those of profusion. This subtle point, which is a canon and secret of the science of medicine, tells us that it is easier for a man of profuse habits to moderate them to generosity, than it is for a miser to become generous. Likewise, it is easier for one who is apathetic [and eschews sin] to be excited to moderate enjoyment, than it is for one, burning with passion, to curb his desires. Consequently, the licentious man must be made to practice restraint more than the apathetic man should be induced to indulge his passions; and, similarly, the coward requires exposure to danger more frequently than the reckless man should be forced to cowardice. The mean man needs to practice lavishness to a greater degree than should be required of the lavish to practice meanness. This is a fundamental principle of the science of curing moral ills, and is worthy of remembrance.

On this account, the saintly ones were not accustomed to cause their dispositions to maintain an exact balance between the two extremes, but deviated somewhat, by way of [caution and] restraint, now to the side of exaggeration, and now to that of deficiency. Thus, for instance, abstinence would incline to some degree towards excessive denial of all pleasures;

valor would approach somewhat towards temerity; generosity to lavishness; modesty to extreme humility, and so forth. This is what the rabbis hinted at, in their saying, "Do more than the strict letter of the law demands."

When, at times, some of the pious ones deviated to one extreme by fasting, keeping nightly vigils, refraining from eating meat or drinking wine, renouncing sexual intercourse, clothing themselves in woolen and hairy garments, dwelling in the mountains, and wandering about in the wilderness, they did so, partly as a means of restoring the health of their souls, as we have explained above, and partly because of the immorality of the townspeople. When the pious saw that they themselves might become contaminated by association with evil men, or by constantly seeing their actions, fearing that their own morals might become corrupt on account of contact with them, they fled to the wilderness far from their society, as the prophet Jeremiah said, "Oh that some one would grant me in the wilderness the dwelling of a wanderer, and I would quit my people and abandon them; for they are all adulterers, a troop of faithless evil-doers." When the ignorant observed saintly men acting thus, not knowing their motives, they considered their deeds of themselves virtuous, and so, blindly imitating their acts, thinking thereby to become like them, chastised their bodies with all kinds of afflictions, imagining that they had acquired perfection and moral worth, and that by this means man would approach nearer to God, as if He hated the human body, and desired its destruction. It never dawned upon them, however, that these actions were bad and resulted in moral imperfection of the soul. Such men can only be compared to one who, ignorant of the art of healing, when he sees skillful physicians administering to those at the point of death [purgatives known in Arabic as] colocynth, scammony, aloe, and the like, and depriving them of food, in consequence of which they are completely cured and escape death, foolishly concludes that since these things cure sickness, they must be all the more efficacious in preserving the health, or prolonging life. If a person should take these things constantly, and treat himself as a sick person, then he would really become ill. Likewise, those who are spiritually well, but have recourse to remedies, will undoubtedly become morally ill.

The perfect Law which leads us to perfection—as one who knew it well testifies by the words, "The Law of the Lord is perfect restoring the soul; the testimonies of the Lord are faithful making wise the simple"—recommends none of these things (such as self-torture, flight from society, etc.). On the contrary, it aims at man's following the path of moderation, and living among people in honesty and uprightness, but not dwelling in the wilderness or in the mountains, or clothing oneself in garments of hair and wool, or afflicting the body.

chapter 14

Paracelsus,
the Magician Turned Scientist

The waning of the Middle Ages and the advent of the Renaissance had two important effects upon the development of medicine. The Renaissance broke the hold of ancient classical tradition and medieval dogma upon the mind of the practitioner. At the same time it opened up new paths for intellectual adventure and bold inquiry both into human nature and nature at large.

The German physician Theophrastus Bombastus Paracelsus (1493-1541) was one of the towering figures of the Renaissance. Some of his biographers compare his stature to that of his contemporaries—or near contemporaries Leonardo da Vinci, Copernicus, Luther and Shakespeare. Others see in him little more than an imaginative adventurer and charlatan, and are inclined to discount his contributions to scientific medicine. His attempts at testing the effects of chemical agents—such as mercury, which he used to treat syphilis, and of the opiate laudanum—which he administered for convulsions—are a matter of historical record. Yet at the same time he was an advocate of the notorious Weapon Salve, which, he held, was capable of healing wounds at a distance. He was a firm believer in divination from the stars; in the "correspondences" between Man and the Universe—between microcosm and macrocosm—and in the healing powers of a preparation made of powdered mummies. He was an alchemist and astrologer and served as a model for Goethe's celebrated Dr. Faustus. Yet when he took time out from his magico-mystical flights of fancy to give a factual account of his wide medical experience he spoke with the voice of the seeker for scientific truth, in rebellious defiance of ancient Galenic tradition or scholastic dogma.

Fifty years before Johann Weyer (see Chapter XV), he denounced the cruelties of the Inquisition and asserted: "There are more superstitions in the Roman church than in all these women and witches." Hundreds of years before the development of modern psychiatry he declared: "There are two kinds of diseases in all men: one material and one spiritual . . . against

material diseases material remedies should be applied. Against spiritual dis-
eases spiritual remedies." He was well aware of the value of the experimen-
tal method when he stated: "Every experiment should be used according to
its specific function—as a spear is used to thrust, or a club to batter." Nor
was he unaware of the deeper meaning of dreams, "wherever they may
come from: from fantasy, from the elements, or from another inspiration."

Paracelsus's books, written in a quaint medieval German idiom, make
difficult reading and are open to various interpretations. The selection that
follows is taken from his Treatise On Diseases that Deprive Men of Health
and Reason. It is reproduced here in Gregory Zilboorg's translation.

ON DISEASES THAT DEPRIVE MEN
OF HEALTH AND REASON

Preface

In nature there are not only diseases which afflict our body and our
health but many others which deprive us of sound reason, and these are
most serious. While speaking about the natural diseases and observing to
what extent and how seriously they afflict various parts of our body, we
must not forget to explain the origin of the diseases which deprive men of
reason, as we know from experience that they develop out of man's disposition. The present-day clergy of Europe attributes such diseases to ghostly
beings and threefold spirits; we are not inclined to believe that. For nature
proves that such statements by earthly gods are quite incorrect and, as we
shall explain . . . that nature is the sole origin of diseases. . . .

After these introductory remarks Paracelsus discusses the clinical picture
of mania, melancholia, and other mental diseases which he tries to distin-
guish from the former two. Although basically opposed to the
demonological theory of insanity, he seems to be inclined at one point to
give the devil his due in the origin of at least one form of mental illness.
Likewise, his emphasis on the influence of the stars and the moon was fully
in line with the astrological concepts of his time. Many forms of insanity he
attributed to the operation of purely physiological or hereditary causes.
Others he sought to explain in terms of love potions or poisoned foods ad-
ministered by evil women to their reluctant lovers.

On Mania

Now we must speak about mania which is a transformation of reason and
not of senses. Perception is forced upon the senses, and there is no judgment

at all. Mania has the following symptoms: frantic behavior, unreasonableness, constant restlessness, and mischievousness. It may be recognized by the fact that it subsides by itself and reason returns; mania may disappear and recur several times, or it may never recur. Some patients suffer from it depending on the phases of the moon, others after some external accident. Thus we have two kinds of mania and, likewise, two causes: one coming from the healthy body and one from other diseases. . . .

There is also a mania which does not indicate the nature of man; on the contrary, his nature is against it and rebels. Therefore, watch how the nature of man displays itself, for it often happens that the constitution of man becomes manic and he attempts to expel the mania. In such cases the natural qualities of mania are also seen. It follows that, as we stated in the beginning, mania does not result from the qualities, as it appears to. Those manias which develop from sublimation of *spiritus vitae* and the like are not due to melancholy, but merely show the same symptoms as melancholia, etc.

On The Origin Of Truly Insane People

In previous chapters I have spoken of the deprivation of reason, but it is not the case that patients remain without reason until they die. They suffer from attacks time and again, so that they lose their reason and then regain it, as we have indicated. Now we shall speak of those who are permanently insane and of insane body, rather than of those subject to recurring attacks. The period is irregular, once long, then short, in correspondence with the starts; it does not always occur, behave, and stay in the same way, but is irregular in accordance with the course of the stars.

There are four kinds of insane people: *Lunatici, Insani, Vesani and Melancholici. Lunatici* are those who get the disease from the moon and react according to it. *Insani* are those who have been suffering from it since birth and have brought it from the womb as a family heritage. *Vesani* are those who have been poisoned and contaminated by food and drink, from which they lose reason and sense. *Melancholici* are those who by their nature lose their reason and turn insane. We must, however, note that apart from these four kinds there is another kind: these are the *Obessi* who are obsessed by the devil; the various ways in which this happens are treated by us in *De Spiritibus*. But here we deal with those who are insane by nature, and sufferers of these four kinds cannot become obsessed by the devil and his company, as many people say; for the devil and his crew do not enter an insane body which is not being ruled by the entire reason according to its quality. Therefore, the devil does not enter those four kinds of insane people for, due to causes that will be explained later, they have no power of reason. While they are out of their senses they are possessed by, but safe against, the devils. . . .Although there are four kinds of insanity, each with a separate origin and derivation, they all end in depriving man of his reason . . . but without any other disease, so that there is no pain, as in epilepsy, in *mania*, in *chorea lasciva*, in *suffocationis intellectus;* but these people always live in madness and, in the cases in which it is apparent that there is going to be another sick day, increasing insanity. When reason announces such sick days, death is not far, because the origin of the disease is so violent that it hurts the *spiritus vitae* and poisons it, and death results.

Now we shall take up the lunatics and the reason for their disease. . . . The stars have the power to hurt and weaken our body and to influence health and illness. They do not fall into us materially or substantially, but influence reason invisibly and insensibly, like a magnet attracting iron, or a scarab dust, or asphalt fibers and wood. Such power of attraction is possessed by the moon, which tears reason out of man's head by depriving him of humors and cerebral virtues. The moon does not enter us and work in us, as has been affirmed, for no star has the power to possess us, as many . . . state falsely; but we must believe that it takes reason from us as the stars do, by virtue of their powers of attraction. Just so the sun takes the humidity of the earth, not by entering the earth and driving out the water as if it had been poured into fire, but by attracting it. Not only the moon acts thus; many planets deprive the organs of the whole body of their humors. . . .

In the same way we can explain those people who have received insanity from the mother's womb as a heritage, such as a family which is insane or a child who has been born insane: the seed and its function may be defective, or it may be inherited from the part of father or mother. . . . The moon can take away man's reason at birth; when, however, this is hereditary, the circumstance is such that if there is insanity in the brain, the child's mother also has some deficiency in her brain, for the brain of the parents is continued in the brain of the son, . . . because the nature and qualities of the one originate in those of the other. This does not always happen, because the sperma become mixed, and either the man or the woman may or may not be insane, and the child may follow the insanity or take after the one who has the greater influence. It may even happen that if both are insane they still would give birth to a healthy child. This is due to the power of nature, which drives out the impediments and adversities.

Now we must also speak about *Vesani* who become insane from eating and drinking. It often happens that food offered by whores causes deprivation of the senses, and this in many ways. Such insanity may lead to love, so that the *Vesani* put all their being into the whores; some are bent on war only, and therefore they have to do with war only, and there is no sanity; some climb and run; some act in various ways which we do not wish to enumerate and shall not describe, but which should be remembered. Let us not be amazed that it should be possible for food to cause this, for it is possible; and much less should we be astonished at the effects they produce. And why? Because food and drink have affected them greatly. Now we shall describe the fourfold insanity that comes from food and drink. . . .

First of all, there are those that have so eaten and drunk that they have to and are compelled to love a woman. We shall leave out a few points here. If a person offers something to eat to another, whether man or woman, unbreakable, eternal love is the result; for this reason some servants give food to their masters so as to flatter them and to make love spring up in them, with the result that servants are above masters. . . . Further, unreasonable animals, dogs and others, can be brought to such love for those who offer it to them. It is natural that women should give such things to men, so that the latter should think only of making love to them; and they have no reason, and their melancholy is directed toward those women who have offered it. We shall leave it at that, because of other proposed topics.

The others who are bent only on war have been given some food intended to make them insane, and if they are choleric by nature they think only of war; their insane behavior has been given them through the food. We must also speak about the melancholic and phlegmatic ones, who exhibit their nature and constitution in like behavior.

The third, who jump up and run around all the time, have received their insanity from eating the kind of thing that gives them an urge to mount and climb; this comes from the nature of this food and not from that of man. If it were up to us to write about it we would reveal everything here, but some things must remain unmentioned as there exists a great body of philosophy and contemplation on the nature of this insanity, and that must suffice.

The introductory paragraph of his chapter on St. Vitus' dance shows Paracelsus at his best. It is a first intimation to the sexual origin of certain hysteric behavior disorders which he describes under the misleading name of chorea lasciva or lascivious chorea. It was a disease largely due to emotional contagion, comparable to the Rock'n'Roll craze of our days, and occurred in his time in epidemic form all over Europe.

On St. Vitus's Dance

We do not wish to admit, in this chapter, that the saints can cause a plague or the diseases which eventually are named after them. In our opinion, such diseases have nothing to do with the works of the saints. There are many who connect great sufferings with saints and attribute their sufferings to God rather than nature. This is idle talk. We dislike talk behind which there is no proof but mere belief. Belief is an inhuman thing and the gods do not think much of it. As this disease is known under the name of a saint, we do not intend to change the name; it should, however, rather be called *chorea lasciva*, for reason which will be given. We discard unproven words which speak of God without knowing Him and digress from His given path by which he may be recognized. Thus the cause of the disease, *chorea lasciva*, is a mere opinion and idea assumed by the imagination, affecting those who believe in such a thing. This opinion and idea are the origin of the disease both in children and adults. In children the cause is also an imagined idea, based not on thinking but on perceiving, because they have heard or seen something. The reason is this: their sight and hearing is so strong that unconsciously they have fantasies about what they have seen or heard. And in such fantasies their reason is taken and perverted into the shape imagined. Moreover, in adults who do not imagine the dance but hear and see it, hearing and sight become stronger than reason.

Even people who do not have such sight and hearing are afflicted with the dance; they are overcome by this kind of dancing and joy. The cause is in the laughing veins which comprehend their spirit in such a subtle way that they are tickled into dancing and joy. There are two causes for this disease, for this dance: a natural one from the laughing veins, and an incidental one from the imagination. The natural origin of the dance is this: everyone has laughing veins; if these veins are opened and bled, the person begins to laugh and cannot stop while he is bleeding. If the bleeding continues he will laugh until he dies. Such veins are the cause and origin of this disease, and this is what happens: the veins remain complete and uninjured unless the *spiritus* in them on which they live and feed should be modified and separated and thus digress from its course and order; then it jumps and makes the blood rage; this causes a ticklish feeling, then laughter, which in turn makes the spirit in the veins stir more and more, for the veins lie at ticklish ends and spots and it is in their disposition and nature to make one laugh. The reason for the *spiritus vitae's* moving and breaking is the fact that it is a fine *spiritus*. The life of those veins can no longer be regarded as natural. Just as brandy left to itself becomes sharper, finer, and lighter from the warmth in the wineskin, the *spiritus vitae* in the veins becomes fine and sharp from natural warmth, and as a result the blood changes so that it has the same quality as ordinary wine after its substance has been changed by mixture with brandy. . . .

Another kind of dance may result from stimulation which originates from vision and hearing, in this way: joy in man comes from the heart; vision and hearing are things that go to the heart. If I hear someone whistling, something I like by nature, I feel joy in my heart. This joy is twofold: I have a feeling of pleasure as is my natural disposition, and, besides, I have the image in my senses as if I see the person whistling before me. And while I am pressing that whistling into my thoughts it gives me pleasure, and joy prevails in my heart; as it stands before me it impresses itself upon me while all other qualities, blood, and dispositions are driven from me, so that they are suppressed and have no further effect. This is followed by the deprivation of senses, but not of reason. If my power of reason is taken from me and, due to my imagination, I act in the same way as I would if I had noticed or watched the whistling, my lack of will is the cause of my disease. And it is natural that such lack of will, in which a person indulges with joy and with all his heart, causes such imaginations, as we have described in *De Imaginationibus*. This obviously is one of the reasons why whores and scoundrels who take pleasure in guitar and lute playing, who satisfy all voluptuousness, bodily pleasure, imagination and fancy, never escape but become ill in such a way that they jump and dance, thus applying what has been their occupation.

This is what Paracelsus has to say about the treatment of chorea lasciva:

If a choreic man or woman develop St. Vitus dance through a voluptuous urge to dance—and this happens more frequently to women than to men since women have more imagination and restlessness and are more easily conquered by the very strength of their nature—there is nothing better for expelling this than thoughts and actions against it. Their thoughts are free, lewd and impertinent, full of lasciviousness and without fear or respect. These thoughts may be expelled in the following way: shut the patients into a dark, unpleasant place and let them fast on water and bread for some time, without mercy. Thus hunger will compel them to adopt a different nature and different thoughts, so that the lasciviousness is driven out by abstinence. This is the best way, since their immodest actions and blood settle down, the *spiritus vitae* changes and slows down, and the heart becomes sad because of the sadness of the place and the changed, imprisoned way of living. So the old disease vanishes and sadness becomes the master. There is no joy, no laughing, no dancing, no howling. When this result has been accomplished, then you should begin to mollify the hard life a little day by day, to improve the food a little every day, to ease the confinement until melancholia too has been consumed, so that the patient may come back to his senses. This prescription is against the thoughts and actions of these people, and it is foolish to give in to such dancing and to their will and way of life, with its singing and dancing. Such giving in only stimulates and furthers the disease. Some think they would die if they could not act in such a way (singing, dancing, etc.) but it is not so. It is better to take a good stick and give the patients a good beating and lock them in as has been described

above. It should be noted, however, that if they are beaten, such a rage
arises within them that they may die of it; therefore, one should be careful
to observe moderation. The best cure, and one which rarely fails, is to
throw such persons into cold water.

What, then, is the contribution of Paracelsus to the history of psycho-
therapy? He set observation before slavish adherence to dogma. He dis-
carded the old Galenic concepts of medicine which sought the causes of ill-
ness in essentially innate factors: in a disturbance of the "four humours"
(blood, phlegm, black bile and yellow bile), which were in turn thought to
be determined by unalterable astrological constellations. Paracelsus chal-
lenged this defeatist belief in predetermination. To him the causes of mental
disorders were only partly due to physical factors. Some were of an essen-
tially functional nature. He believed in the possibility of psychological
change, although he expressed it more in terms of mysterious alchemistic
transmutations than in dynamic, psychological terms. This is why C.G.
Jung hailed him as one of the great pioneers of modern psychiatry.

If, in addition to these concepts, he also believed in the beneficial effect of
throwing a mentally disturbed person into cold water, this does not neces-
sarily make him also a pioneer of modern methods of shock treatment.

chapter 15

Johann Weyer,
or the Twilight of the Witches

*The decisive attack against ancient and medieval belief in magic and de-
monology came from the camp of the humanists, philosophers and physicians of the Renaissance. One of the most prominent figures in this group
was Johann Weyer (1512-1576), also known as Wierus. He was a disciple of
Cornelius Agrippa who himself had denounced "the vanity" of the sciences
—both medical and theological—of his time. Weyer was a devoted physician and at the same time a loyal churchman. But his clear clinical insight
could not help bringing him into direct conflict with the superstitions held
by most of his contemporaries. To him, apparent diabolical possession was
an indication of a disordered metabolism and a deranged mind. So were the
fantasies of "melancholic women" who "while lying on their backs asleep
thought they were raped by an evil spirit." Our selection is taken from his
work De Praestigiis Daemonum (1563), in which he spoke in defense of
these wretched "little women" who were wrongly charged with witchcraft
and sorcery. In taking this position he laid the foundations of the modern
scientific approach to insanity. Gregory Zilboorg has called him the "first
descriptive and clinical psychiatrist."*

*Dedicating his book to his sponsor, Duke William of Juelich, Johann
Weyer wrote:*

Of all the misfortunes which the various fanatical and corrupt opinions,
through Satan's help, have brought in our time to Christendom, not the
smallest is that which, under the name of witchcraft, is sown as a vicious
seed. The people may be divided against themselves through their many
disputes about the Scriptures and church customs while the old Snake stirs
the blast, still no such great misfortune results from that as from the thereby
inspired opinion that childish old hags, whom one calls witches or wizards,
can do any harm to men and animals. Daily experience teaches what cursed
apostasy, what friendship with the Wicked One, what hate and fighting
among fellow creatures, what dissension in city and in country, what

numerous murders of innocent people through the devil's wretched aid, such belief in the power of witches brings forth. No one can more correctly judge about these things than we physicians whose ears and hearts are being constantly tortured by this superstition.

I notice more from day to day that the bog of Camarina blows its plague-laden breath stronger than ever. For a time one hoped that its poison would be gradually eliminated through the healthy teaching of the word of God; but I see that in these stormy days it reaches farther and wider than ever. In the meantime, the pastors sleepily allow him to continue. Almost all the theologians are silent regarding this godlessness, doctors tolerate it, jurists treat it while still under the influence of old prejudices; wherever I listen, there is no one, no one who out of compassion for humanity unseals the labyrinth or extends a hand to heal the deadly wound.

Therefore, I, with my limited means, have undertaken to dare to measure myself with this difficult affair, which disgraces our Christian Belief. It is not arrogance which impels me. I know that I know nothing, and my work allows me little free time. I know too that many others could do this work better than I. I would like to incite them to out-do me; I will gladly listen to reason.

My object is chiefly of a theological nature: I have to set forth the artfulness of Satan according to Biblical authority and to demonstrate how one can overcome it; next, my object is philosophical, in that I fight with natural reason against the deceptions which proceed from Satan, and the crazy imagination of the so-called witches; my object is also medical, in that I have to show that those illnesses, whose origins are attributed to witches, come from natural causes; and finally, my object is legal, in that I shall have to speak of the punishment, in another than the accustomed way, of sorcerers and witches.

But in order that I shall not meet with the reproach that I have overstepped the borders of my intellectual power and the limits of my profession with too great a faith in my own intelligence, I have submitted my seemingly paradoxical manuscript to men of Your Highness' family as well as to theologians, lawyers, and the excellent physicians, that it may be read in a critical sense. The manuscript shall remain protected through their authority if it is founded on reason; it shall fall if it is convicted of error; it shall become better if it needs supplement or revision. For there is nothing in the world which can be made immediately and at once completely perfect.

One could rejoin here that the *Malleus Maleficarum* has already fulfilled this mission. But one has only to read in that book the silly and often godless absurdities of the theologians Heinrich Kramer and Johann Sprenger and to compare these quietly with the contents of my manuscript. Then it will be clearly seen that I expound and advocate a totally different, even an opposite point of view.

To you, Prince, I dedicate the fruit of my thought. For thirteen years your physician, I have heard expressed in your Court the most varied opinions concerning witches; but none so agree with my own as do yours, that witches can harm no one through the most malicious will or the ugliest exorcism, that rather their imagination—inflamed by the demons in a way not understandable to us—and the torture of melancholy makes them only fancy that they have caused all sorts of evil. For when the entire manner of action is laid on the scales, and the implements therefore examined with careful scrutiny, then soon there is shown clearly before all eyes and more lucid than the day, the nonsense and the falsity of the matter. You do not, like others, impose heavy penalties on preplexed, poor old women. You demand evidence, and only if they have actually given poison, bringing about the death of men or animals, do you allow the law to take its course.

When a Prince of such virtues protects me, then I have faith that I can make short work of the snapping teeth of insolent quarrelers; especially since it is certain that on my side stands invincible truth. I implore God, the Highest and Best, the Father of our Lord Jesus Christ, that He may profitably extend through greater employment of the Holy Spirit, what in His Benevolence He has so happily begun in Your Highness, to the honor of His Name, to the glory of Your Highness, and to the flourishing happiness of your country. Your Highness' most obedient servant, Johann Weyer, Physician.

Addressing himself to a wider audience, Weyer continues:

To all you to whom the King of Kings has entrusted the sword with which to punish the bad and to protect the good among us, I humbly submit this modest book; from the very depths of my heart and on bended knees, I pray that it will not be met with scorn as you read it and learn the views of your humblest and most respectful ward. The misdeeds of the demons whom Satan uses to shut the eyes of man and keep him in dire darkness have covered our Christian Europe with a fetid blot of shame; they have led man into the most insane error, frequent murder of innocent people, and truly severe injury of the conscience of governments. Should this manuscript meet with your disapproval, I shall at once humbly recall it, though its suppression endow me with an over-coming determination to demonstrate the truth. Should it however gain corroboration in the strength of your opinion, I shall consider myself duly rewarded for my labors. In the latter case, I would pray that people should bow to your opinion, that they should throw down their heathen views, and that the prejudices which they have absorbed through centuries be destroyed. This will come about if and when in all your countries, provinces, and estates, whenever a question of witchcraft arises, the various devilish cases be properly judged. The eye of reason will come out victorious over the misdeeds of the evil-minded; the blood of innocent people will then stop flowing so profusely, the edifice of public peace will stand firmer, the needle of conscience will sting our hearts less frequently, the rule of the devil will sink further and further away into the depths, and the Kingdom of Christ will broaden and widen its borders.

Johann Weyer was a quiet, soft-spoken man, quite unlike his compatriot, the rebellious and unruly Dr. Paracelsus. Yet he did not lack the revolutionary fervor of the humanistic pioneer, nor the courage to defy openly the cruelty and superstitious dogmatism of his contemporaries. Although he was not apparently subjected to persecution, we learn that he died in isolation, "tired of the age he lived in, but with invincible faith in Christ surrendered his soul to the Maker."

chapter 16

Philippe Pinel, Who Took the Chains Off the Insane

Johann Weyer's impassioned plea for the innocence of witches and his advocacy of a sober scientific approach to mental illness came two thousand years after Hippocrates's treatise on the Sacred Disease. Philippe Pinel (1745-1826) who "took the chains off the insane," came more than two centuries after Weyer, Juin Ives and other humanists of the Renaissance. Philippe Pinel was himself a humanist inspired by the ideals of the French Encyclopedists. He was a man of science, courage and integrity. But it was the turmoil of the French Revolution which sparked him to action and made him the great liberator of the mentally ill. A contemporary of William Tuke, who stood for the same cause in England, Pinel abolished the dark dungeons of the Bicêtre in Paris that had served as a prison rather than as a hospital for generations of mental patients unable to afford private care.

But while it was the spirit of the French Revolution that threw open the doors of both the Bastille and the Bicêtre, it was Pinel's scientific vision that paved the way for the further progress that was to come in the wake of the great psychiatric revolution of his time. His Traité Medico-Psychologique *(1801) stands at the threshold of the modern approach to mental illness. Gregory Zilboorg calls his introduction to the first edition "one of the most valuable texts in the history of psychiatry." The quotation that follows is Dr. Zilboorg's translation.*

Introduction to the First Edition

As one takes up mental alienation as a separate object of investigation, it would be making a bad choice indeed to start a vague discussion on the seat of reason and on the nature of its diverse aberrations; nothing is more obscure and impenetrable. But if one wisely confines one's self to the study of the distinctive characteristics which manifest themselves by outward signs and if one adopts as a principle only a consideration of the results of enlightened experience, only then does one enter a path which is generally followed

by natural history; moreover, if in doubtful cases one proceeds with reserve, one should have no fear of going astray. . . .

   In medicine there are few topics as fruitful as insanity, because of its
many points of contact and because of the necessary relation of this science
to moral philosophy and to the history of human understanding. But there
are even fewer topics against which there are as many prejudices to be rectified and errors to be destroyed. Derangement of the understanding is generally regarded as the result of an organic lesion of the brain and therefore
as incurable—which in many cases is contrary to anatomic observations.
Public mental asylums have been considered places of confinement and isolation for dangerous patients and pariahs. Therefore their custodians, who
in most cases are inhuman and unenlightened, have taken the liberty of
treating these mentally sick in a most despotic, cruel, and violent manner,
though experience continually shows the happy results of a conciliating attitude, of a kind and compassionate firmness.

   Empiricism has often profited from this realization due to the establishing
of asylums suitable for mental patients; numerous cures were discovered,
but no substantial literary contributions to the progress of science were
made. On the other hand, the blind routine of a great number of medical men
has moved always within the narrow circle of numerous blood-lettings, cold
baths, and violent and repeated showers, with almost no attention paid to the
moral side of the treatment. Thus in all aspects of the subject, man has
neglected the purely philosophical viewpoint of the derangement of understanding, the knowledge about the physical or moral causes likely to produce
it, the distinction between the various kinds of mental derangement, the
exact history of the precursory symptoms, the course and end of the attack
if it is an intermittent one, the rules of interior policy in the hospitals, the
careful definition of those circumstances which make certain remedies necessary and of those which make them superfluous. For in this illness as in
many others the skill of the physician consists less in the repeated use of
remedies than in the careful art of using them or avoiding them at the right
moment. . . .

   The habit of living constantly in the midst of the insane, of studying their
habits, their different personalities, the objects of their pleasures or their
dislikes, the advantage of following the course of their alienation day and
night, during the various seasons of the year, the art of directing them without effort and sparing them excitement and grumbling, the gift of being able
to assume at the right time a tone of kindness or of authority, of being able
to subdue them by force if methods of kindness fail, the constant picture of
all the phenomena of mental alienation, and finally the functions of supervision itself—the combination of all these must give an intelligent and zeal-
ous man an immense number of facts and minute details usually lacking in

the narrow-minded physician unless he has taken a special interest during fleeting visits to asylums. Can such men—otherwise unacquainted with the study of medicine, and without preliminary knowledge of the history of the human understanding—bring order and precision into their observation, or even rise to a language appropriate for the rendering of their ideas? Can they distinguish one kind of alienation from another and then describe it and correlate several observed facts? Will they ever be able to link the experience of past centuries to the phenomena they see, or hold themselves within the boundaries of philosophic doubt in uncertain cases, or adopt a firm and sure course to direct their research, or last but not the least, arrange a series of objects in systematic order?

It is as important in medicine as in other science to value sound judgment, a natural shrewdness, and an inventive mind unspoiled by any prejudice. It is hardly necessary to determine whether a man with such a mind has made certain routine studies or complied with certain formalities; it is only necessary to determine whether he has really contributed to some branch of medical science or discovered some useful truth. During almost two years of practicing medicine at the Bicêtre I have become acutely aware that these ideas must be realized for the sake of further progress of the doctrine of mental alienation. . . .

I abandoned the dogmatic tone of the physician; frequent visits, sometimes lasting several hours a day, helped me to familiarize myself with the deviations, shouting, and madness of the most violent maniacs. I held repeated conversations with whatever men knew best their former condition and their delirious ideas. Extreme care is necessary to avoid all pretensions of self-esteem and many questions on the same subject if the answers are obscure. I never object if patients make equivocal or improbable remarks but postpone my questions to a later examination, for the purpose of enlightenment and correction. I take careful notes on the facts observed with the sole object of having as many accurate data as possible. Such is the course I have followed for almost two years.

These passages are from the English translation of Pinel's Treatise on Insanity, *published in 1806 in Sheffield, England:*

**Maxims of Lenity and Philanthropy Applicable
To the Management of Lunatics**

To apply our principles of moral treatment, with undiscriminating uniformity, to maniacs of every character and condition in society, would be equally ridiculous and unadviseable. A Russian peasant, or a slave of Jamaica, ought evidently to be managed by other maxims than those which would exclusively apply to the case of a well bred irritable Frenchman, un-used to coercion and impatient of tyranny. Of the unhappy influence upon the French character of needless and vexatious opposition, my experience has furnished me with too many instances, in the paroxysms of rage and indignation, which have been occasioned at the Asylum de Bicêtre, by the thoughtless jests and barbarous provocations of idle and unfeeling visitors. In the lunatic infirmary, which is insulated from the body of the hospital, and which is not subject to the control of the governor, it has frequently happened that lunatics, who were perfectly composed and in a fair way of recovery, have, in consequence of the silly raillery and rude brutality of their attendants, relapsed into the opposite condition of violent agitation and fury. Maniacs, on the other hand, who have been transferred from the infirmary to the asylum, and represented upon their arrival as more than commonly furious and dangerous, rendered so no doubt by severe treat-ment, have, upon being received with affability, soothed by consolation and sympathy, and encouraged to expect a happier lot, suddenly subsided into a placid calmness, to which has succeeded a rapid convalescence. To render the effects of fear solid and durable, its influence ought to be associ-ated with that of a profound regard. For that purpose, plots must be either avoided or so well managed as not to be discovered; and coercion must al-ways appear to be the result of necessity, reluctantly resorted to and com-mensurate with the violence or petulance which it is intended to correct. Those principles are strictly attended to at Bicêtre. . . . I can assert, from ac-curate personal knowledge, that the maxims of enlightened humanity pre-vail throughout every department of its management; that the domestics and keepers are not allowed, on any pretext whatever, to strike a madman; and that straight waistcoats, superior force, and seclusion for a limited time, are the only punishments inflicted. When kind treatment, or such pre-parations for punishment as are calculated to impress the imagination, pro-duce not the intended effect, it frequently happens, that a dexterous strata-gem promotes a speedy and an unexpected cure.

A Happy Expedient Employed in the Cure of a Mechanician

A celebrated watchmaker, at Paris, . . . was infatuated with the chimera of perpetual motion, and to effect this discovery, he set to work with inde-fatigable ardour. From unremitting attention to the object of his enthusiasm coinciding with the influence of revolutionary disturbances, his imagination was greatly heated, his sleep was interrupted, and, at length, a complete derangement of the understanding took place. His case was marked by a most whimsical illusion of the imagination. He fancied that he had lost his head on the scaffold; that it had been thrown promiscuously among the heads of many other victims; that the judges, having repented of their cruel sentence, had ordered those heads to be restored to their respective owners, and placed upon their respective shoulders; but that, in consequence of an unfortunate mistake, the gentlemen, who had the management of that business, had placed upon his shoulders the head of one of his unhappy companions. The idea of this whimsical exchange of his head, occupied his thoughts night and day; which determined his relations to send him to the Hotel de Dieu. Thence he was transferred to the Asylum de Bicêtre. Nothing could equal the extravagant overflowings of his heated brain. He sung, cried, or danced incessantly; and, as there appeared no propensity in him to commit acts of violence or disturbance, he was allowed to go about the hospital without control, in order to expend, by evaporation, the effervescent excess of his spirits. "Look at these teeth," he constantly cried; —Mine were exceedingly handsome; —these are rotten and decayed. My mouth was sound and healthy: this is foul and diseased. What difference between this hair and that of my own head." To this state of delirious gaiety, however, succeeded that of furious madness. He broke to pieces or otherwise destroyed whatever was within the reach or power of his mischievous propensity. Close confinement became indispensable. Towards the approach of winter his violence abated; and, although he continued to be extravagant in his ideas, he was never afterwards dangerous. He was, therefore, permitted, when ever he felt disposed, to go to the inner court. The idea of the perpetual motion frequently recurred to him in the midst of his wanderings; and he chalked on all the walls and doors as he passed, the various designs by which his wondrous piece of mechanism was to be construed. The method best calculated to cure so whimsical an illusion, appeared to be that of encouraging his prosecution of it to satiety. His friends were, accordingly, requested to send him his tools, with materials to work upon, and other requisites, such as plates of copper and steel, watch-wheels, & c. The governor, permitted him to fix up a work-bench in his apartment. His zeal was now redoubled. His whole attention was rivetted upon his favourite pursuit. He forgot his meals. After about a month's labour, which he sustained with a constancy that deserved better success, our artist began to think that he had followed a false rout. He broke into a thousand fragments the piece of machinery which he had fabricated at so much expense of time, and thought, and labour; entered on the construction of another, upon a new plan, and laboured with equal pertinacity for another fortnight. The various parts being completed, he brought them together, and fancied that he saw a perfect harmony amongst them. The whole was now finally adjusted: —his anxiety was indescribable: —motion succeeded: —it continued for some time: —and he supposed it capable of continuing for ever. He was elevated to the highest pitch of enjoyment and triumph, and ran as quick as lightning into the interior of the hospital, crying out like another Archimedes, "At length I have solved this famous problem, which has puzzled so many men celebrated for their wisdom and talents." But, grievous to say, he was disconcerted in the midst of his triumph. The wheels stopped! The perpetual motion ceased! His intoxication of joy was succeeded by disappointment and confusion. But, to avoid a humiliating and mortifying confession, he declared that he could easily remove the impediment, but tired of that kind of employment, that he was determined for the future to devote his whole time and attention to his business. There still remained another maniacal impression to be counteracted;—that of the imaginary exchange of his head, which unceasingly recurred to him. A keen and an unanswerable stroke of pleasantry seemed best adapted to correct this fantastic whim. Another convalescent of a gay and facetious humour, instructed in the part he should play in this comedy, adroitly turned the conversation to the subject of the famous miracle of Saint Denis. Our mechanician strongly maintained the possibility of the fact, and sought to confirm it by an application of it to his own case. The other set up a loud laugh, and replied with a tone of the keenest ridicule: "Madman as thou art, how could Saint Denis kiss his own head? Was it with his heels?" This equally unexpected and unanswerable retort, forcibly struck the maniac. He retired confused amidst the peals of laughter, which were provoked at his expense, and never afterwards mentioned the exchange of his head. Close attention to his trade for some months, completed the restoration of his intellect. He was sent to his family in perfect health; and has, now for more than five years, pursued his business without a return of his complaint.

The Treatment of Maniacs to be Varied According to the Specific Characters of Their Hallucination

Of all the powers of the human mind, that of the imagination appears to be the most subject to injury. The fantastic illusions and ideal transformations, which are by far the most frequent forms of mental derangement, are solely ascribable to lesions of this faculty. Hence the expediency of a great variety of schemes and stratagems for removing these possessions. Of the numerous illusions to which the imagination is subject, the most difficult to be eradicated are those originating in fanaticism. My experience on this subject agrees with the reports of English authors. How extremely difficult to level, with his real situation, the ideas of a man swelled up with morbid pride, solely intent on his high destinies, or thinking himself a privileged being, an emissary of heaven, a prophet from the Almighty, or even a divine personage. What measures are likely to counteract the influence of mystic visions or revelations, of the truth of which he deems it blasphemy to express a doubt?

How Far May Lenient Measures Suffice to Calm the Violence and Fury of Acute Mania?

To detain maniacs in constant seclusion, and to load them with chains; to leave them defenceless, to the brutality of underlings, on pretence of danger to be dreaded from their extravagances: in a word, to rule them with a rod of iron, as if to shorten the term of an existence considered miserable, is a system of superintendence, more distinguished for its convenience than for its humanity or its success. Experience proves that acute mania, especially when periodical, may be frequently cured by measures of mildness and moderate coercion, conjoined to a proper attention to the state of the mind. The character of a superintendent, who is in the habit of discharging the important duties of his office, with integrity, dignity and humanity, is itself a circumstance of great weight and influence in a lunatic establishment. As instances of the truth of this remark, may be cited the names of Willis, Fowler, Haslam in England; Dicquemare, Poution, Pussin in France; and the keeper of the madhouse at Amsterdam. A coarse and unenlightened mind, considers the violent expressions, vociferation and riotous demeanour of maniacs as malicious and intentional insults. Hence the extreme harshness, blows and barbarous treatment which keepers, if not chosen with discretion and kept within the bounds of their duty, are disposed to indulge in towards the unfortunate beings confided to their care. A man of better feeling and consideration, sees in those effervescences of a maniac but the impulses of an automaton, or rather the necessary effects of a nervous excitement, no more calculated to excite anger than a blow or a crush from a stone propelled by its specific gravity. Such an observer, on the contrary, is disposed to allow his patients all the extent of liberty consistent with their own safety and that of others; he conceals with great address the means of constraint to which he is compelled to resort; yields to their caprices with apparent complacency; eludes with dexterity their inconsiderate demands; soothes with coolness and kindness their intemperate passions; turns to advantage every interval of their fury; and meets with force their otherwise incoercible extravagances.

Is Close Confinement Requisite in all Cases and Throughout the Whole Term of Acute Mania?

Dr. Ferriar observes; that in their paroxysms of violent fury, maniacs ought to have their arms and legs effectually secured; but that we should only have recourse to those measures where it is impossible to avoid them. It is that gentleman's practice in cases of refractory conduct, to confine the offenders to their apartments, where, with their windows closed, they are left in darkness, supplied only with water gruel and dry bread, until they show signs of repentance, which is seldom long delayed. But before the adoption of that decided measure, he always tries the means of mildness and remonstrance: "For in general," adds the same author, "lunatics have a deep sense of honour, which is more efficacious than coercion in reducing them to propriety of conduct."

Close confinement, solitude, darkness and a spare diet, may no doubt be recurred to occasionally, and for a short time, as a punishment for the improper demeanour of maniacs. But when the paroxysms are of long duration or the disorder of a continued form, restriction in the article of food might be exceedingly prejudicial.

A state of dependence and constraint may greatly accelerate the cure of a madman who is elated to improprieties of behaviour, by imaginary consequence, or by the recollection of dignities and power once possessed.

chapter 17

Anton Mesmer: The Healing Power That Was Only in the Patient's Imagination

Anton Mesmer (1734-1815), the Austrian-born physician, discoverer of "animal magnetism" as a new principle of psychotherapy, was a contemporary of Philippe Pinel, the great French reformer of psychiatry and advocate of more humanitarian care for the mentally ill. But the gulf between the two men seems unbridgeable. Mesmer was little concerned with mental disease. He regarded all illnesses as the manifestations of disturbances in a mysterious ethereal fluid which linked together animate and inanimate things alike, and which made man equally subject to the influences of the stars and to those influences emanating from Dr. Mesmer himself. This is what Mesmer described as animal, in contrast to "ordinary," magnetism. His theories thus reach back to ancient astrological and magical concepts. But it was in his practical approach to the patient that Mesmer hit upon a discovery of prodigious consequences. It was the discovery that by applying what he believed to be magnetic passes or other manipulations, he was capable of inducing peculiar trancelike conditions—or else convulsive crises—in his patients. Sometimes these magnetic influences resulted in spectacular cures of such apparently organic disorders as blindness, convulsions, paralyses or "congestions" of the liver or spleen.

One of the by-products of Mesmer's labors was his discovery of a peculiar "rapport" between the therapist and his patient. This too he ascribed to the operation of his all-pervading animal magnetism. He was not aware of the essentially psychological nature of the bond. One of his patients, a Miss Paradis, aged eighteen, whose blindness he claimed he had cured with his magnetic method, apparently fell in love with him. Mesmer himself, caught in the trap of her devotion—her "positive transference"—incurred the wrath of her outraged family and the censure of the medical profession. As a result of the ensuing scandal he had to leave his beautiful mansion in Vienna with its famous fishpond and magnetized trees. He fled to Paris in 1778. There he rose once more to fame—and notoriety—until in 1784 the French Academy of Science passed a devastating verdict on the claims made by him and his pupil Dr. d'Eslon.

The committee included such famous names as Jean Sylvain Bailly, Benjamin Franklin and Dr. Guillotin. They found that his results were essentially based on his patients' imagination or due to mechanical friction, imitation and the like. But there is one important fact which the learned committee (and subsequent equally learned committees) failed to realize: Mesmerism, although it was founded on thoroughly unscientific premises, was, in effect, a new method of psychotherapy. It was the first step toward the development of scientific hypnotism, hypnoanalysis and our current psychoanalytic methods of treatment.

History has been more generous in acknowledging Mesmer's share in this development than the various committees appointed to investigate his claims. There are few authors in the annals of mental healing whose contributions to the field have been quoted by so many as those of the discoverer of animal magnetism. But few have been read so little. This is why the selection that follows contains the major part of his Dissertation on Animal Magnetism, published in Paris in 1779. It is reproduced here in a translation by V. R. Myers, edited by Gilbert Frankau in 1948.

DISSERTATION ON THE DISCOVERY
OF ANIMAL MAGNETISM

It may . . . be asserted that among the vulgar opinions of all ages, whose principles are not rooted in the human heart, there are but few which, however ridiculous and even extravagant they may appear, cannot be regarded as the remains of an originally recognized truth.

Such are my reflections . . . on the fate of the doctrine of the influence of celestial bodies on the planet we inhabit. These reflections have induced me to seek, among the ruins of that science, brought so low by ignorance, what it might have contained that was useful and true.

In accordance with my ideas on this subject, I published at Vienna in 1766 a thesis on the influence of planets on the human body. According to the familiar principles of universal attraction, ascertained by observations which teach us how the planets mutually affect one another in their orbits, how the sun and moon cause and control the ocean tides on our globe and in the atmosphere, I asserted that those spheres also exert a direct action on all parts that go to make up animate bodies, in particular on the nervous system, by an all-penetrating fluid. I denoted this action by the *Intensification and the Remission* of the properties of matter and organic bodies, such as gravity, cohesion, elasticity, irritability, electricity.

I maintained that just as the alternate effects, in respect of gravity, produce in the sea the appreciable phenomenon which we term ebb and flow, so the *Intensification and Remission* of the said properties, being subject to the action of the same principle, cause in animate bodies alternate effects similar to those sustained by the sea. By these considerations I established that the animal body, being subjected to the same action, likewise underwent a kind of ebb and flow. I supported this theory with different examples of periodic revolutions. I named the property of the animal body that renders it liable to the action of heavenly bodies and of the earth *Animal Magnetism*. I explained by this magnetism the periodical changes which we observe in sex, and in a general way those which physicians of all ages and in all countries have observed during illnesses.

My object then was only to arouse the interest of physicians; but, far from succeeding, I soon became aware that I was being taxed with eccentricity, that I was being treated like a man with a system and that my tendency to quit the normal path of Medicine was being construed as a crime.

I have never concealed my manner of thinking in this respect, being unable to convince myself that we have made the progress of which we boast in the art of healing.

Indeed, I have held that the further we advanced in our knowledge of the mechanism and the economy of the animal body, the more we were compelled to admit our insufficiency. The knowledge that we have gained today about the nature and action of the nerves, imperfect though it be, leaves us in no doubt in this respect. We know that they are the principal agents of sensation and movement, but we are unable to restore them to their natural order when this has been interfered with. We confess this to our shame. The ignorance of bygone centuries on this point has sheltered physicians. The superstitious confidence which they had and which they inspired in their specifics and formulae made them despotic and presumptuous.

I have too much respect for Nature to be able to convince myself that the individual preservation of Man has been left to the mere chance of discovery and to the vague observations that have been made in the course of a number of centuries, finally becoming the domain of the few.

Nature has provided everything for the existence of the individual. Propagation takes place without "system" and without trickery. Why should preservation be deprived of the same advantage? The preservation of animals affords proof that the contrary is the case.

A non-magnetised needle, when set in motion, will only take a determined direction by chance, whereas a magnetised needle, having been given the same impulse, after various oscillations proportional to the impulse and magnetism received, will regain its initial position and stay there. Thus the harmony of organic bodies, when once interfered with, goes through the uncertainties of my first hypothesis, unless it is brought back and determined by the *General Agent*, whose existence I recognize: it alone can restore harmony in the natural state.

Thus we have seen, in all ages, maladies which become worse or are cured with and without the help of Medicine, in accordance with different systems and by the most conflicting methods. These considerations have removed all doubt from my mind that there exists in Nature a universally acting principle which, independently of ourselves, operates what we vaguely attribute to Art *and* Nature.

These reflections have caused me to stray imperceptibly from the beaten track. I have subjected my ideas to experience for over twelve years, which I have devoted to the most accurate observations of all types of disease, and I have had the satisfaction of seeing the maxims I had forecast being borne out time and time again.

It was chiefly in the years 1773 and 1774 that I undertook in my house the treatment of a young lady aged twenty-nine named Oesterline, who for several years had been subject to a convulsive malady, the most troublesome symptoms of which were that the blood rushed to her head and there set up the most cruel toothache and earache, followed by delirium, rage, vomiting and swooning. For me it was a highly favorable occasion for observing accurately that type of ebb and flow to which *Animal Magnetism* subjects the human body. The patient often had beneficial crises, followed by a remarkable degree of alleviation; however, the enjoyment was always momentary and imperfect.

The desire to ascertain the cause of this imperfection and my own uninterrupted observations brought me time and time again to the point of recognizing Nature's handiwork and of penetrating it sufficiently to forecast and assert, without hesitation, the different stages of the illness. Encouraged by this first success, I no longer had any doubts as to the possibility of bringing it to perfection, if I were able to discover the existence, among the substances of which our globe is made, of an action that is also reciprocal and similar to that of the heavenly bodies, by means of which I could imitate artificially the periodic revolutions of the ebb and flow just referred to.

I possessed the usual knowledge about the magnet: its action of iron, the ability of our body fluids to receive that mineral. The various tests carried out in France, Germany and Britain for stomach ache and toothache were known to me. These reasons, together with the analogy between the properties of this substance and the general system, induced me to regard it as being the most suitable for this type of test. To ensure the success of this test, in the interval of the attacks, I prepared the patient by the continuous use of chalybeates.

My social relations with Father Hell, Jesuit and Professor of Astronomy at Vienna, then provided me with an opportunity of asking him to have made for me by his craftsmen a number of magnetised pieces, of convenient shape for application. He was kind enough to do this for me and let me have them.

On 28th July 1774, after the patient had had a renewal of her usual attacks, I applied three magnetised pieces to the stomach and both legs. Not long afterwards, this was followed by extraordinary sensations; she felt inside her some painful currents of a subtle material which, after different attempts at taking a direction, made their way towards the lower part and caused all the symptoms of the attack to cease for six hours. Next day, as the patient's condition made it necessary for me to carry out the same test again, I obtained the same success with it.

My observation of these effects, coupled with my ideas on the general system, provided me with fresh information. While confirming my previous ideas about the influence of the *General Agent*, it taught me that another principle was causing the magnet to act, the magnet itself being incapable of such action on the nerves, and I saw that I only had a short way to go in order to arrive at the *Imitative Theory*, which formed the subject of my research.

A few days afterwards, having met Father Hell, I mentioned to him in the course of conversation that the patient was in a better state of health, also the good effects of my process and the hopes that I had, on the strength of this operation, of soon finding a means of curing nerve sufferers.

I found out not long afterwards, from the public and from the newspapers, that this man of religion, abusing his fame in astronomy and wishing to appropriate for himself a discovery of whose nature and benefits he was entirely ignorant, had taken upon himself to publish the fact that by means of some magnetised pieces, to which he attributed a specific virtue depending on their shape, he had obtained the means of curing the gravest nerve disorders. To lend support to this opinion, he had sent to a number of Academies some sets consisting of magnetised pieces of all shapes, mentioning according to their outline their analogy with the various maladies.

This is how he expressed himself: "I have discovered in these shapes, which agree with the magnetic vortex, a perfection on which depends their specific virtue in cases of illness; it is owing to the lack of this perfection that the tests carried out in England and France have met with no success." And by affecting to confuse the manufacture of the magnetised shapes with the discovery I had mentioned to him, he finished by saying "that he had communicated everything to the physicians, and particularly to myself, and would continue to avail himself of them for his tests."

The repeated writings of Father Hell on this subject inspired the public, which is always eager for a specific against nervous disorders, with the ill-founded opinion that the discovery in question consisted in the mere use of the magnet. I in my turn wrote to refute this error, by publishing the existence of *Animal Magnetism*, essentially distinct from the Magnet; however, as the public had received its information from a man of high repute, it remained in its error.

I continued my experiments with different disorders so as to generalize my knowledge and perfect the application thereof.

I knew particularly well Baron de Stoerck, President of the Faculty of Medicine at Vienna and Chief Physician to Her Majesty. It was moreover seemly for him to be acquainted with the nature of my discovery and its purpose. I consequently placed before him the circumstantial details of my operations, particularly as regards the communication and currents of animal magnetic matter, and I invited him to verify them for himself, stating that it was my intention to report to him in future all progress that I might make in this new science. To give him certain proof of my good faith, I made known my methods to him without reserve.

The natural timidity of this physician, no doubt based on motives which it is not my intention to penetrate, induced him to reply that he wished to have nothing to do with what I was telling him about, and he begged me not to compromise the Faculty by giving publicity to an innovation of this kind.

Public prejudice and uncertainty as to the nature of my methods decided me to publish, on 5th January 1775, a Letter to a Foreign Physician, in which I gave an exact idea of my theory, the success I had hitherto obtained and the success I had reason to hope for. I set forth the nature and action of *Animal Magnetism* and the analogy between its properties and those of the magnet and electricity. I added "that all bodies were, like the magnet, capable of communicating this magnetic principle; that this fluid penetrated everything and could be stored up and concentrated, like the electric fluid; that it acted at a distance; that animate bodies were divided into two classes, one being susceptible to this magnetism and the other to an opposite quality that suppresses its action." Finally, I accounted for the various sensations and based these assertions on experiments which enabled me to put them forward.

A few days prior to the publication of this Letter, I heard that Mr. Ingenhousze, member of the Royal Academy of London and Inoculator at Vienna, by entertaining the nobility and distinguished personages with experiments in electricity, and by the skill with which he varied the effects of the magnet, had acquired the reputation of being a physician. I heard, as I said, that when this gentleman learned of my operations, he treated them as vain imaginings, going so far as to say that only the English genius was capable of such a discovery, if it could be done. He came to see me, not to gain information, but with the sole intention of persuading me that I was laying myself open to error and should suppress all publicity with a view to avoiding inevitable ridicule.

I replied that he was not sufficiently talented himself to give me this advice, and that I should moreover have pleasure in convincing him at the first opportunity. This presented itself two days afterwards.

Miss Oesterline took fright and contracted a chill, causing a sudden stoppage, and she relapsed into her former convulsions. I invited Mr. Ingenhouse to call. He came, accompanied by a young physician. The patient was then in a fainting fit with convulsions. I told him that it was the most favourable opportunity for convincing himself of the existence of the principle I announced, and the property which it has to communicate. I told him to approach the patient, while I withdrew from her, instructing him to touch her. She made no movement. I recalled him to me, and communicated animal magnetism to him by taking him by the hands; I then bade him approach the patient once more, while I kept at a distance, telling him to touch her a second time. This resulted in convulsive movements. I made him repeat this touching process several times, which he did with the top of his finger, changing the direction each time. Always, to his great astonishment, he brought about a confulsive effect in the part touched.

When this operation was over, he told me he was convinced, and I suggested a second visit. We withdrew from the patient, so as not to be perceived even had she been conscious. I offered Mr. Ingenhousze six china cups and asked him to tell me to which one he wished me to communicate the magnetic quality. I touched the one of his choice and then applied the six cups to the patient's hand in succession; on reaching the cup that I had touched, the hand made a movement and gave signs of pain. Mr. Ingenhousze obtained the same result when he applied the six cups.

I then had these cups taken back to the place whence they had come, and after a certain interval, holding him by one hand, I asked him to touch with the other any cup he wished; he did so, the cups were brought to the patient, as before, with the same result.

The communicability of the principle was now well-established in Mr. Ingenhousze's eyes, and I suggested a third experiment to show its action at a distance and its penetrating quality: I pointed my finger at the patient at a distance of eight paces; the next instant, her body was in convulsion to the point of raising her on her bed with every appearance of pain. I continued, in the same position, to point my finger at the patient, placing Mr. Ingenhousze between herself and me. She underwent the same sensations.

Having repeated these tests to Mr. Ingenhousze's satisfaction, I asked him if he was convinced of the marvellous properties about which I had told him, offering to repeat our proceedings if he were not. His reply was to the effect that he wished for nothing further and was convinced; but owing to his friendship with me, he entreated me not to make any public statement on this subject, so as not to lay myself open to public incredulity. We parted, and I went back to the patient to continue the treatment, which was most successful. That same day I managed to restore the normal course of nature, thereby putting an end to all the trouble brought about by stoppage.

Two days later I was astonished to hear that Mr. Ingenhousze was making statements in public that were quite the reverse of his utterance in my house, and was denying the success of the different experiments he had witnessed. He effected to confuse *Animal Magnetism* with the magnet and was endeavoring to damage my reputation by spreading the report that with the aid of a number of magnetised pieces which he had brought with him, he had succeeded in unmasking me, proving that it was nothing but a ridiculous, prearranged fraud.

I must confess that such words at first seemed to me to be unbelievable, and I had some difficulty in bringing myself to regard Mr. Ingenhousze as their author. However, his association with the Jesuit Hell, and the latter's irresponsible writings in support of such odious insinuations, aimed at ruining the effect of my letter of 5th January 1775, removed all doubt from my mind that Mr. Ingenhousze was the guilty party. I refuted Father Hell and I was about to draw up an indictment when Miss Oesterline, who had been informed of Mr. Ingenhousze's procedure, was so affronted at finding herself thus compromised that she relapsed into her former state, which was aggravated by a nervous fever.

Miss Oesterline's condition claimed the whole of my attention for a fortnight. In these circumstances, by continuing my research, I was fortunate in overcoming the difficulties which stood in the way of my progress and of giving my theory the desired perfection. The cure of this young lady represented the first fruits of my success, and I had the satisfaction of seeing her henceforth in excellent health. She married and had some children.

It was during this fortnight that, being determined to justify my conduct and to give the public a correct idea of my abilities by unmasking Mr. Ingenhousze's behaviour, I informed Mr. de Stoerck, requesting him to obtain orders from the Court for a Commission of the Faculty to be acquainted with the facts, so that it might verify and make them known to the public. This step appeared to be agreeable to the senior physician; he seemed to share my viewpoint and promised to act accordingly, remarking, however, that he could not be on the Commission.

I suggested several times that he should come and see Miss Oesterline and satisfy himself as to the success of my treatment. His replies in this matter were always vague and uncertain. I explained to him how it would benefit humanity to have my method adopted by the hospitals, and asked him to demonstrate its utility forthwith at the Spanish Hospital. He agreed to this and gave the necessary instructions to Mr. Reinlein, physician at that hospital.

The latter was a witness of the effects and usefulness of my visits over a period of eight days. On several occasions he expressed surprise and reported to Mr. de Stoerck. However, I soon became aware that different impressions had been given to this leading physician. I met him almost every day and insisted on my request for a Commission, reminding him of the interesting matters about which I had told him, but saw nothing but indifference, coldness and reserve in his attitude whenever the topic was broached.

Being unable to obtain any satisfaction, and as Mr. Reinlein had ceased reporting to me (I moreover found out that his change of front was the result of steps taken by Mr. Ingenhousze), I realized my inability to stem the course of the intrigue, and sought consolation in silence.

Emboldened by the success of his plans, Mr. Ingenhousze acquired fresh vigour; he vaunted his incredulity and it was not long before he succeeded in having those who suspended judgment or who did not share his opinion classed as feebleminded. It will readily be understood that all this was quite enough to alienate the masses and have me looked upon at least as a visionary, especially as the indifference of the Faculty appeared to support that opinion.

What I felt to be most strange was that the same opinion should be shared the following year by Mr. Klinkosch, Professor of Medicine at Prague, who, without knowing me and without the slightest idea of the true state of the matter, was sufficiently foolish (to use no stronger term), as to publish in the public journals the curious details of the impostures attributed to me by Mr. Ingenhousze.

Whatever public opinion might be, I felt that truth could not find better support than in facts. I undertook the treatment of various disorders, including a hemiplegia, the result of apoplexy; stoppages, spitting of blood, frequent colics and convulsive sleep from childhood, with spitting of blood and normal ophthalmia. Mr. Bauer, Professor of Mathematics at Vienna and a man of outstanding merit, was attacked by this latter malady. My work was crowned with the best possible success, and Mr. Bauer himself was honest enough to make public a detailed report on his cure. However, prejudice had the upper hand. Nevertheless, I had the satisfaction of being quite well known to a great Minister, a Privy Councillor and an Aulic Councillor, friends of humanity, who had often recognized truth for themselves, seeing that they upheld and protected it. They even made several attempts to lighten the shadows in which it was being wrapped. They met with little success, however, it being objected that only the opinion of physicians was capable of deciding, and their good will was thus confined to their offers to give my writings the necessary publicity in foreign lands.

It was through this channel that my explanatory Letter of 5th January 1775 was transmitted to the majority of the scientific institutions, and to a few scientists. Only the Berlin Academy, on the 24th March that year, made a written reply in which by confusing the properties of *Animal Magnetism* which had expounded with those of the magnet, which I only spoke of as a conductor, it incurred a number of errors and its opinion was that I was the victim of illusion.

This Academy was not the only one to make the mistake of confusing *Animal Magnetism* with mineral magnetism, although I have always stressed in my writings that the use of the magnet, however convenient, was always imperfect without the assistance of the theory of *Animal Magnetism*. The physicians and doctors with whom I have been in correspondence, or who have endeavoured to find out my methods in order to usurp this discovery, have taken upon themselves to spread about either that the magnet was the only means I employed, or else that I used electricity as well, because it was well known that I had availed myself of both. Most of them have been undeceived by their own experience, but instead of realizing the truth I was expounding, they have concluded from the fact that they obtained no success from the use of these two agents that the cures announced by myself were imaginary and that my theory was nothing but an illusion.

The desire to refute such errors once and for all, and to do justice to truth, determined me to make no further use of electricity or of the magnet from 1776 onwards.

The poor reception given to my discovery and the slight hopes it held out to me for the future made me resolve to undertake nothing of a public nature at Vienna, but instead to travel to Swabia and Switzerland and add to my experience, thus arriving at the truth through facts. Indeed, I had the satisfaction of making some striking cures in Swabia, and of operating in the hospitals, before the eyes of doctors from Berne and Zurich. They were left in no doubt as to the existence of *Animal Magnetism* and the usefulness of my theory, which corrected the error into which they had been led by my opponents.

Between the years 1774 and 1775 an ecclesiastic, a man of good faith but of excessive zeal, was operating in the diocese of Ratisbon on various disorders of a nervous nature, using means that appeared to be supernatural to the less well informed in that district. His reputation extended to Vienna, where society was divided into two halves: one regarded his methods as imposture and fraud, while the other looked upon them as miracles performed by Divine power. Both, however, were wrong, and my experience at once told me that the man in question was nothing but a tool of Nature. This was because his profession, assisted by fate, had furnished him with certain natural talents enabling him to find out the periodical symptoms of maladies without knowing their cause. The end of such paroxysms was held to be a complete cure, and time alone could undeceive the public.

On returning to Vienna towards the end of 1775, I passed through Munich, where His Highness the Elector of Bavaria was kind enough to consult me on this subject, asking me whether I could account for these pretended miracles. I carried out before his eyes some experiments that removed any prejudices he may have had and left him in no doubt as to the truth I announced. Shortly afterwards, the Scientific Institution of that city paid me the honour of admitting me as a member.

In 1776 I again visited Bavaria and secured similar success there in illnesses of different kinds. In particular, I effected the cure of an imperfect amaurosis, accompanied by paralysis of the limbs, which was afflicting Mr. d'Osterwald . . . director of the Scientific Institution of Munich; he was kind enough to make public mention of this and of the other results he had witnessed.

After returning to Vienna, I persisted until the end of that year in undertaking no further work; neither would I have altered my mind if my friends had not been unanimous in opposing my decision. Their insistences, together with my desire to see the truth prevail, aroused in me the hope of accomplishing this by means of fresh successes, particularly through some striking cure. With this end in view, among other patients I undertook the treatment of Miss Paradis, aged eighteen, whose parents were well known; she herself was known to Her Majesty the Queen-Empress, through whose bounty she received a pension, being quite blind since the age of four. It was a perfect amaurosis, with convulsions in the eyes. She was moreover a prey to melancholia, accompanied by stoppages in the spleen and liver, which often brought on accesses of delirium and rage so that she was convinced she was out of her mind.

I also undertook the treatment of one Zwelferine, a girl nineteen years of age who had been blind since the age of two owing to amaurosis accompanied by a very thick, wrinkled albugo with atrophy of the ball; she was also afflicted with periodic spitting of blood. I found this girl in the Vienna orphanage and her blindness was attested by the Governors.

At the same time I also treated Miss Ossine, aged eighteen, who was in receipt of a pension from Her Majesty, as being the daughter of an officer in her armies. Her malady consisted of purulent phthisis and irritable melancholia, accompanied by fits, rage, vomiting, spitting of blood and fainting. These three patients and other besides were accommodated in my house so that I might continue my treatment without interruption. I was fortunate in being able to cure all three.

The father and mother of Miss Paradis, who witnessed her cure and the progress she was making in the use of her eyesight, hastened to make this occurrence known and how pleased they were. Crowds flocked to my house to make sure for themselves, and each one, after putting the patient to some kind of test, withdrew greatly astonished, with the most flattering remarks to myself.

The two Presidents of the Faculty, at the head of a deputation of their corps, came to see me at the repeated instances of Mr. Paradis; and, after examining the young lady, added their tribute to that of the public. Mr. de Stoerck, one of these gentlemen who knew this young person particularly well, having treated her for ten years without the slightest success, expressed to me his satisfaction at so interesting a cure and his regret at having so far deferred his acknowledgment of the importance of my discovery. A number of physicians, each for himself, followed the example set by our leaders and paid the same tribute to truth.

After such authentic recognition, Mr. Paradis was kind enough to express his gratitude in his writings, which went all over Europe. It was he who afterwards published the interesting details of his daughter's recovery in the newspapers.

Among the physicians who came to see me to satisfy their curiosity was Mr. Barth, professor of anatomy of diseases of the eye, and cataract specialist; he had even admitted on two occasions that Miss Paradis was able to use her eyes. Nevertheless, this man's envy caused him to state publicly that the young lady could not see, and that he had satisfied himself that she could not. He founded this assertion on the fact that she did not know or confused the objects shown to her. He was answered from all quarters that he was therein confusing the necessary inability of those blind from birth or at a very tender age with the knowledge acquired by blind persons operated on for cataract. How, he was asked, is it that a man of your profession can be guilty of so obvious an error? His impudence, however, found an answer to everything by asserting the contrary. It was in vain that the public told him again and again that a thousand witnesses had given evidence of the cure; he alone held the opposite view, in which he was joined by Mr. Ingenhousze, the Inoculator of whom I have spoken.

These two individuals, who were at first regarded as fanatics by sensible, honest folk, succeeded in weaving a plot to withdraw Miss Paradis from my care, her eyes still being in an imperfect state, and made it impossible for her to be presented to Her Majesty, as was to have been the case. This inevitably lent credence to their assertion of imposture. To this effect they worked on Mr. Paradis, who began to be afraid that his daughter's pension and several other advantages held out to him might be stopped. He consequently asked for his daughter back.

The latter, supported by her mother, showed her unwillingness and fear lest the cure might be imperfect. The father insisted, and this dispute brought on her fits again and led to an unfortunate relapse. However, this had no effect on her eyes, and she continued to improve the use of them. When her father saw she was better, being still egged on by the conspirators, he returned to the charge. He demanded his daughter with some heat and compelled his wife to do likewise.

The girl resisted for the same reasons as before. Her mother, who had hitherto supported her, and had apologized for the lengths to which her husband had gone, came to tell me on 29th April 1777 that she intended to remove her daughter instantly. I replied that she was free to do so, but if fresh accidents were the result, she could not count on my help.

These words were overheard by the girl, who was so overcome that she went into a fit. . . . Her mother, who heard her cries, left me abruptly and seized her daughter angrily from the hands of the person who was assisting her, saying: "Wretched girl, you too are hand in glove with the people of this house!" as she flung her in a fury head-first against the wall.

Immediately all the troubles of that unfortunate girl recommenced. I hastened towards her to give her assistance, but her mother, still livid with rage, hurled herself upon me to prevent me from doing so, while she heaped insults on me. I had the mother removed by certain members of my household and went up to the girl to assist her. While I was so engaged, I heard more angry shouts and repeated attempts to open and shut the door of the room where I was.

It was Mr. Paradis who, having been warned by one of his wife's servants, now invaded my house sword in hand with the intention of entering the room where I was, while my servant was trying to remove him by guarding the door. The madman was at last disarmed, and he left my house breathing imprecations on myself and my household.

Meanwhile, his wife had swooned away. I had her given the necessary attention, and she left some hours afterwards, but the unhappy girl was suffering from attacks of vomiting, fits and rages, which the slightest noise, especially the sound of bells, accentuated. She had even relapsed into her previous blind state through the violence of the blow given her by her mother, and I had some fears for the state of her brain.

Such were, for my patient and for me, the sinister effects of that painful scene. It would have been easy for me to take the matter to court, on the evidence of Count de Pellegrini and eight persons who were with me, to say nothing of other neighbours who could have acted as witnesses too, but, as I was solely concerned with saving Miss Paradis, if possible, I refrained from availing myself of legal redress. My friends remonstrated in vain, pointing out the ingratitude exhibited by her family and the wasted expenditure of my labours. I adhered to my first decision and would have been content to overcome the enemies of truth and of my peace of mind by good deeds.

Next day I heard that Mr. Paradis, in an endeavour to cover up his excesses, was spreading about the most wicked insinuations regarding myself, always with a view to removing his daughter and proving, by her condition, the dangerous nature of my methods. I did indeed receive through Mr. Ost, Court physician, a written order from Mr. de Stoerck, in his capacity as head physician, dated Schoenbrunn, 2nd May 1777, who called upon me "to put an end to the imposture" (his own expression) "and restore Miss Paradis to her family, if I thought this could be done without risk."

Who would have believed that Mr. de Stoerck, being so well informed by the same physician of all that had taken place in my house and, after his first visit, having come twice to convince himself of the patient's progress and the success of my methods, could have taken upon himself to use such offensive and contemptuous language to me? I had indeed reason to expect the contrary, because being well placed for recognizing a truth of this kind, he should have been its defender. I would even go so far as to say that as the repository of Her Majesty's confidence, one of his first duties under these circumstances should have been to protect a member of the Faculty whom he knew to be blameless, and to whom he had time and time again given assurances of his affection and esteem. I made answer to this irresponsible order that the patient was not in a position to be moved without running the risk of death.

Miss Paradis's critical condition no doubt made an impression on her father, and caused him to reflect. Through the intermediary of two reputable persons, he begged me to continue attending his daughter. I told him that I would do so on condition that neither he nor his wife ever again appeared in my house. My treatment indeed exceeded my hopes, and nine days sufficed to calm down the fits entirely and put an end to the disorders. But her blindness remained.

Fifteen days' treatment cured the blindness and restored the eye to its condition prior to the incident. To this period I added a further fortnight's attention to improve and restore her health. The public then came to obtain proof of her recovery, and everybody gave me, even in writing, fresh evidence of satisfaction. Mr. Paradis, being assured of the good health enjoyed by his daughter through Mr. Ost, who, at his request and by my permission, followed the progress of the treatment, wrote a letter to my wife in which he thanked her for her motherly care.

He also wrote thanking me and apologizing for the past; he finished by asking me to send back his daughter so that she might enjoy the benefit of country air. He said that he would send her back to me whenever I might think necessary, so as to continue the treatment, and he hoped that I would attend her. I believed him in all good faith, and returned his daughter to him on the 8th of June.

Next day I heard that her family asserted that she was still blind and subject to fits. They showed her thus and compelled her to imitate fits and blindness. This news evoked some contradictions by persons who were convinced of the contrary, but it was upheld and accredited by the obscure intriguers who used Mr. Paradis as their tool, and I was unable to check its spread by the highest testimony, such as that of Mr. de Spielmann, Aulic Councillor of Their Majesties and Director of the State Chancellery; Their Majesties' Councillors, Messrs de Molitor and de Umlauer, physician to Their Majesties; the Boulanger, the Heufeld and Baron de Colnbach and Mr. de Weber, who, independently of several other persons, had almost every day followed for themselves my processes and results.

Thus in spite of my perseverance and my work, I have little by little seen relegated to the position of a conjecture, or at least of something uncertain, a truth that has been authentically proven.

It is easy to imagine how I might have been affected by the relentlessness of my enemies to do me harm and by the ingratitude of a family on which I had showered kindnesses. Nevertheless, during the last half of 1777 I continued with the cure of Miss Ossine and the aforementioned Zwelferine whose eyes, it will be remembered, were in an even more serious condition than Miss Paradis's. I also persevered successfully with the treatment of my remaining patients, in particular Miss Wipior, aged nine, who had in one eye a growth on the cornea, known by the name of staphyloma; this cartilaginous excrescence, of 3 to 4 lines, prevented her from seeing with that eye.

I succeeded in removing the excrescence to the extent that she was able to read sideways. There only remained a slight albugo in the centre of the cornea, and I have no doubt that I would have caused it to disappear entirely, had circumstances permitted me to continue the treatment. However, being wearied by my labours extending over twelve consecutive years and still more so by the continued animosity of my adversaries, without having reaped from my research and efforts any satisfaction other than that of which adversity could not deprive me, I felt that I had done my duty by my fellow-citizens.

With the conviction that justice would one day be done me, I decided to travel for the sole purpose of securing the relaxation I so much needed. However, to guard against prejudice and insinuations as far as possible, I arranged matters so as to leave at home in my absence Miss Ossine and the girl Zwelferine. I next took the precaution of telling the public of the reason for this arrangement, stating that these persons were in my home so that their condition could be ascertained at any moment and thereby lend support to truth. They remained there eight months after my departure from Vienna and only left on orders from a higher authority.

On arriving at Paris in February 1778, I began to enjoy the delights of repose there, in the interesting company of the scientists and physicians of that capital. However, acceding to their requests and to repay the kindness shown to me, I decided to satisfy their curiosity by speaking of my system. They were astonished at its nature and results and asked me for an explanation. I gave them my concise assertions in nineteen articles. They seemed to them to bear no relation to established knowledge. I felt indeed how difficult it was, by reason alone, to prove the existence of a principle of which people had not the slightest conception. With this in mind, I therefore yielded to the request made to me to show the reality and the usefulness of my theory by the treatment of a few serious maladies.

A number of patients placed their trust in me. Most were in so desperate a plight that it required all my desire to be of use to make me decide on attending them. Nevertheless, I cured a vaporous melancholia with spasmodic vomiting, a number of longstanding stoppages in the spleen, liver and mesentery, an imperfect amaurosis, to the extent of preventing the patient from moving about alone, and a general paralysis with trembling which gave the patient (aged forty) every appearance of old age and drunkenness. This malady was the result of frost-bite; it had been aggravated by the effects of a putrid and malignant fever which the patient had contracted six years before in America.

I also obtained the same success in a case of total paralysis of the legs, with atrophy; one of chronic vomiting, which reduced the patient to a state of progressive emaciation; one of general scrofulous debility, and finally in a case of general decay of the organs of perspiration.

These patients, whose condition was known and verified by the physicians of the Paris Faculty, were all subject to considerable crises and evacuation, on a par with the nature of their maladies, without making use of any medicaments. After completing their treatment, they gave me detailed declarations.

That should have been more than enough to prove beyond all doubt the advantages of my method. I had reason to flatter myself that recognition would follow. However, the persons who had induced me to undertake the foregoing treatments were not enabled to see their effects, owing to considerations and reasons which it would be out of place to enumerate in this dissertation.

The result is that the cures which, contrary to my expectation, were not communicated to bodies whose duty it might have been to call the attention of the public to them, only imperfectly fulfilled the task I had set myself, and for which I had been praised.

This induces me to make a fresh effort today in the cause of truth, by giving more scope and the publicity which they have hitherto lacked to my original Assertions.

Propositions Asserted

1. There exists a mutual influence between the heavenly Bodies, the Earth and Animate Bodies.

2. A universally distributed and continuous fluid, which is quite without vacuum and of an incomparably rarefied nature, and which by its nature is capable of receiving, propagating and communicating all the impressions of movement, is the means of this influence.

3. This reciprocal action is subordinated to mechanical laws that are hitherto unknown.

4. This action results in alternate effects which may be regarded as an Ebb and Flow.

5. This ebb and flow is more or less general, more or less particular, more or less composite according to the nature of the causes determining it.

6. It is by this operation (the most universal of those presented by Nature) that the activity ratios are set up between the heavenly bodies, the earth and its component parts.

7. The properties of Matter and the Organic Body depend on this operation.

8. The animal body sustains the alternate effects of this agent, which by insinuating itself into the substance of the nerves, affects them at once.

9. It is particularly manifest in the human body that the agent has properties similar to those of the magnet; different and opposite poles may likewise be distinguished, which can be changed, communicated, destroyed and strengthened; even the phenomenon of dipping is observed.

10. This property of the animal body, which brings it under the influence of the heavenly bodies and the reciprocal action of those surrounding it, as shown by its analogy with the Magnet, induced me to term it *Animal Magnetism*.

11. The action and properties of Animal Magnetism, thus defined, may be communicated to other animate and inanimate bodies. Both are more or less susceptible to it.

12. This action and properties may be strengthened and propagated by the same bodies.

13. Experiments show the passage of a substance whose rarefied nature enables it to penetrate all bodies without appreciable loss of activity.

14. Its action is exerted at a distance, without the aid of an intermediate body.

15. It is intensified and reflected by mirrors, just like light.

16. It is communicated, propagated and intensified by sound.

17. This magnetic property may be stored up, concentrated and transported.

18. I have said that all animate bodies are not equally susceptible; there are some, although very few, whose properties are so opposed that their very presence destroys all the effects of magnetism in other bodies.

19. This opposing property also penetrates all bodies; it may likewise be communicated, propagated, stored, concentrated and transported, reflected by mirrors and propagated by sound; this constitutes not merely the absence of magnetism, but a positive opposing property.

20. The Magnet, both natural and artificial, together with other substances, is susceptible to Animal Magnetism, and even to the opposing property, without its effect on iron and the needle undergoing any alteration in either case; this proves that the principle of Animal Magnetism differs essentially from that of mineral magnetism.

21. This system will furnish fresh explanations as to the nature of Fire and Light, as well as the theory of attraction, ebb and flow, the magnet and electricity.

22. It will make known that the magnet and artificial electricity only have, as regards illnesses, properties which they share with several other agents provided by Nature, and that if useful effects have been derived from the use of the latter, they are due to Animal Magnetism.

23. It will be seen from the facts, in accordance with the practical rules I shall draw up, that this principle can cure nervous disorders directly and other disorders indirectly.

24. With its help, the physician is guided in the use of medicaments; he perfects their action, brings about and controls the beneficial crises in such a way as to master them.

25. By making known my method, I shall show by a new theory of illnesses the universal utility of the principle I bring to bear on them.

26. With this knowledge, the physician will determine reliably the origin, nature and progress of illnesses, even the most complicated; he will prevent them from gaining ground and will succeed in curing them without ever exposing the patient to dangerous effects or unfortunate consequences, whatever his age, temperament and sex. Women, even in pregnancy and childbirth, will enjoy the same advantage.

27. In conclusion, this doctrine will enable the physician to determine the state of each individual's health and safeguard him from the maladies to which he might otherwise be subject. The art of healing will thus reach its final stage of perfection.

Although there is not one of these Assertions regarding which my constant observation over a period of twelve years leaves me in any uncertainty, I quite realize that compared with old-established principles and knowledge, my system may appear to contain as much illusion as truth. I must, however, ask the enlightened to discard their prejudices and at least suspend judgment, until circumstances enable me to furnish the necessary evidence of my principles. Consideration for those languishing in pain and unhappiness through the very inadequacy of known methods is well calculated to inspire the desire for and even the hope of more useful methods.

Physicians, being the repositories of public trust for everything connected with the preservation and happiness of mankind, are alone enabled, by the knowledge on which their profession is founded, to judge of the importance of the discovery I have just announced and realize its implications. In a word, they alone are qualified to put it into practice.

As I have the privilege of sharing the dignity of their profession, I am in no doubt whatever that they will hasten to adopt and spread principles intended to alleviate the sufferings of humanity, as soon as they realize the importance of this Dissertation, written essentially for them, on the true conception of *Animal Magnetism*.

These samples from Mesmer's writings are perhaps more helpful in understanding his failure as a scientist than in accounting for his success as a healer. The fact is that the cleavage between the rationalistic aspirations and the still lingering astrological and mystical beliefs characteristic of his age runs right through his own personality. He was torn between the austere scientific standards set by his profession and his inability to explain his personal impact upon his patients in professionally satisfactory terms. The result was a poorly organized, rambling presentation of his thesis, together with his tendency to answer critics in terms of ill-tempered controversy and petty personal invective.

Mesmer was undoubtedly right in his claim of having hit upon a major medical discovery. But like Christopher Columbus, he remained unaware that his discovery had in effect opened up a New World—a hitherto unknown continent of psychological treatment—which had nothing to do with the discredited magical and astrological concepts of a past era. It was for generations of psychologists and psychiatrists who came after Mesmer to discover what his discovery was really "all about." But in so doing they did one more thing: they destroyed what was left of his lingering myth.

chapter 18

Hypnotism, Suggestion, and the Power of Ideas

SELECTIONS FROM BRAID, LIÉBEAULT,
BERNHEIM, CHARCOT, AND JANET

The Manchester surgeon James Braid (1795-1860) owes his place in the history of psychotherapy to a two-fold discovery: one negative and one positive. His negative discovery was the fact that animal magnetism, which Mesmer and his followers held responsible for the so-called Mesmeric phenomena, did not in reality exist. His positive discovery was the fact that the phenomena of trance, somnambulism, etc., could be induced by such physiological means as fatigue of the eye muscles, or by mere suggestion and its appeal to the subject's imagination, without resort to Mesmer's "baquet," magnetic "passes," or the like. He described the phenomena with the terms neuro-hypnotism and neurypnology, and finally settled for the term hypnosis, which has by now become a common word in many languages.

Braid's discovery earned him both the hostility of the remaining followers of Mesmer and the distrust of his medical colleagues, who refused to have any dealings with a method tainted with the heritage of what the Lancet *called the "gross humbug" of Mesmerism. Braid made his position still more precarious by his excursions into the field of phrenology. Phrenologists sought to discover—and to influence—a person's mental faculties by examining and manipulating minor and major protuberances of the skull. In these pursuits Braid's hypnotic influence upon his subjects may have set the trap for the spurious confirmation of his phrenological theories. His subjects obliged by producing all the phenomena he had looked for.*

Nevertheless, Braid's basic contribution, his discovery of hypnotism, is a matter of historic record. It is an important stepping stone for the work of Liébeault, Bernheim and Charcot, and for the early experiments in hypnosis and hypnoanalysis by Breuer and Freud.

The selection which follows is taken from Braid's principal work, Neurypnology, or the Rationale of Nervous Sleep, considered in Relation with Animal Magnetism, *published in London in 1843.*

In November, 1841, I was led to investigate the pretensions of animal magnetism, or mesmerism, as a complete sceptic, from an anxiety to discover the source of fallacy in certain phenomena I had heard were exhibited at M. Lafontaine's conversazioni. The result was, that I made some discoveries which appeared to elucidate certain of the phenomena, and rendered them interesting, both in a speculative and practical point of view. I considered it a most favourable opportunity for having additional light thrown upon this subject, to offer a paper to the medical section of the British Association, which was about to meet in Manchester. Gentlemen of scientific attainments might thus have had an opportunity of investigating it, and eliciting the truth, unbiassed by local or personal prejudice. I hoped to learn something from others, on certain points which were extremely mysterious to me, as to the *cause* of some remarkable phenomena. I accordingly intimated my intention to the secretaries, by letter, on 18th May, and on the morning of Wednesday, the 22nd June, 1842, sent the paper I proposed reading for the consideration of the committee, intimating also, by letter, my intention to produce before them as many of the patients as possible, whose cases were referred to in proof of the curative agency of Neuro-Hypnotism, so that they might have an opportunity of ascertaining, for themselves, the real facts of the cases, uninfluenced by any bias or partiality that I might exhibit as the discoverer and adapter of this new mode of treatment. The committee of the medical section, however, were pleased to decline entertaining the subject.

Many of the most eminent and influential members of the Association, however, had already witnessed and investigated my experiments in private, and expressed themselves highly gratified and interested with them. In compliance with the repeated desire of these gentlemen, and many other eminent members of the Association to whom I could not possibly afford time to exhibit my experiments in private, and who were anxious to have an opportunity afforded them of seeing, hearing, and judging of the phenomena for themselves, I gave a gratuitous conversazione, when I read the "Rejected Essay," and exhibited the experiments in a public room, to which all the members of the Association had been respectfully invited. The interest with which the subject was viewed by the members of the Association generally, was sufficiently testified by the number and high respectability of those who attended on that occasion; in reference to which the chairman requested the reporters to put on record, "that he had been in the habit for many years of attending public meetings, and he had never in his life seen a more unmixed, a more entirely respectable assembly in Manchester." It was also manifested by their passing a vote of thanks at the conclusion of the conversazione, for my having afforded an opportunity to the members of the British Association of witnessing my experiments, to which they had previously borne testimony as having been "highly successful."

On that occasion I stated, there was certain phenomena, which I could readily induce by particular manipulations, whilst I candidly confessed myself unable to explain the *modus operandi* by which they were induced. I referred particularly to the extraordinary rapidity with which dormant functions, and a state of cataleptiform rigidity may be changed to the extreme opposite condition, by a simple waft of wind, either from the lips, a pair of bellows, or by any other mechanical means. I solicited information on these points, both privately and publicly, from all the eminently scientific gentlemen who honoured me with their company during the meetings of the British Association in this town; but no one ventured to express a decided opinion as to the causes of these remarkable phenomena. I now beg to assure every reader of this treatise, that I shall esteem it a great favour to be enlightened on points which I confess are, at present, still above my comprehension.

It will be observed, for reasons adduced, I have now entirely separated Hypnotism from Animal Magnetism. I consider it to be merely a simple, speedy, and certain mode of throwing the nervous system into a new condition, which may be rendered eminently available in the cure of certain disorders. I trust, therefore, it may be investigated quite independently of any bias, either for or against the subject, as connected with mesmerism; and only be the facts which can be adduced. I feel quite confident we have acquired in this process a valuable addition to our curative means; but I repudiate the idea of holding it up as a universal remedy; nor do I even pretend to understand, as yet, the *whole range of diseases* in which it may be useful. Time and experience alone can determine this question, as is the case with all other new remedies.

When we consider that in this process we have acquired the power of raising sensibility to the most extraordinary degree, and also of depressing it far below the torpor of natural sleep; and that from the latter condition, any or all of the senses may be raised to the exalted state of sensibility referred to, almost *with the rapidity of thought,* by so simple an agency as a puff of air directed against the respective parts; and that we can also raise and depress the force and frequency of the circulation, locally or generally, in a most extraordinary degree, it must be evident we have thus an important power to act with. Whether these extraordinary physical effects are produced through the imagination chiefly, or by other means, it appears to me quite certain, that the imagination has never been so much under our control, or capable of being made to act in the same beneficial and uniform manner, by any other mode of management hitherto known. . . .

I am aware great prejudice has been raised against mesmerism, from the idea that it might be turned to immoral purposes. In respect to the Neuro-Hypnotic state, induced by the method explained in this treatise, I am quite certain that it deserves no such censure. I have proved by experiments, both in public and in private, that during the state of excitement, the judgment is sufficiently active to make the patients, if possible, even *more* fastidious as regards propriety of conduct, than in the waking condition; and from the state of rigidity and insensibility, they can be roused to a state of mobility, and exalted sensibility, either by being rudely handled, or even by a breath of air. Nor is it requisite this should be done by the person who put them into the Hypnotic state. It will follow equally from the manipulations of any one else, or a current of air impinging against the body, from any mechanical contrivance whatever. And, finally, the state cannot be induced, in any stage, unless with the knowledge and consent of the party operated on. This is more than can be said respecting a great number of our most valuable medicines, for there are many which we are in the daily habit of using, with the best advantage in the relief and cure of disease, which may be, and have been rendered most potent for the furtherance of the ends of the vicious and cruel; and which can be administered *without the knowledge of the intended victim.* It ought never to be lost sight of, that there is the use and *abuse* of every thing in nature. It is the *use*, and only the *judicious use* of Hypnotism, which I advocate.

It is well known that I have never made any secret of my modes of operating, as they have not only been exhibited and explained publicly, but also privately, to any professional gentleman, who wished for farther information of the subject. Encouraged by the confidence which flows from a consciousness of the honesty and integrity of my purpose, and a thorough conviction of the reality and value of this as a means of cure, I have persevered, in defiance of much, and, as I think, unwarrantable and capricious opposition.

In now unfolding to the medical profession generally—to whose notice, and kind consideration, this treatise is more particularly presented—my views on what I conceive to be a very important, powerful, and extraordinary agent in the healing art; I beg at once distinctly to be understood, as repudiating the idea of its being, or ever becoming, a universal remedy. On the contrary, I feel quite assured it will require all the acumen and experience of medical men, to decide in what cases it would be safe and proper to have recourse to such a mean; and I have always deprecated, in the strongest terms, any attempts at its use amongst unprofessional persons, for the sake of curiosity, or even for a nobler and more benevolent object—the relief of the infirm; because I am satisfied it ought to be left in the hands of professional men, and of them only. I have myself met with some cases in which I considered it unsafe to apply it at all; and with other cases in which it would have been most hazardous to have carried the operation so far as the patients urged me to do.

In now submitting my opinions and practice to the profession in the following treatise, I consider myself as having discharged an imperative duty to them, and to the cause of humanity. In future, I intend to go on quietly and patiently, prosecuting the subject in the course of my practice, and shall leave others to adopt or reject it, as they shall find consistent with their own convictions.

As it is of the utmost importance, in discussing any subject, to have a correct knowledge of the meaning attached to peculiar terms made use of, I shall now give a few definitions, and explain my reasons for adopting the terms selected.

Neurypnology is derived from the Greek words *neuron*, nerve; *hypnos*, sleep; *logos*, a discourse; and means the *rationale*, or *doctrine* of *nervous* sleep, which I define to be, "a peculiar condition of the nervous system, into which it can be thrown by artificial contrivance:" of thus, "a peculiar condition of the nervous system, induced by a fixed and abstracted attention of the mental and visual eye, on the one object, not of an exciting nature."

By the term "Neuro-Hypnotism," then, is to be understood "nervous sleep;" and, for the sake of brevity, suppressing the prefix "Neuro," by the terms—

Hypnotic,	Will be understood,	The state or condition of *nervous* sleep.
Hypnotize,		To induce *nervous* sleep.
Hypnotized,		One who has been put into the state of *nervous* sleep.
Hypnotism,		*Nervous* sleep.
Dehypnotize,		To restore from the state or condition of *nervous* sleep.
Dehypnotized,		Restored from the state or condition of *nervous* sleep.
and *Hypnotist,*		One who practices Neuro-Hypnotism.

Whenever, therefore, any of these terms are used in the following pages, I beg to be understood as alluding to the discovery I have made of certain peculiar phenomena derived and elicited by my mode of operating; and of which, to prevent misconception, and intermingling with other theories and practices on the nervous system, I have thought it best to give the foregoing designation.

I regret, as many of my readers may do, the inconvenient length of the name; but, as most of our professional terms, and nearly all those of a *doctrinal* meaning, have a Greek origin, I considered it most in accordance with good taste, not to deviate from an established usage. To obviate this in some degree, I have struck out two letters from the original orthography, which was Neuro-Hypnology. . . .

Neurypnology

Having presented a cursory view of certain points, and given a few explanatory remarks, I shall now proceed to a more particular and detailed consideration of the subject. I shall explain the course I have pursued in prosecuting my investigation; the phenomena which I discovered the result from the manipulations I had recourse to; the inferences I was consequently led to deduce from them; the method I now recommend for inducing the hypnotic condition, for applying it in the cure of various disorders, and the result of my experience, as to the efficacy of hypnotism as a curative agent.

By the impression which hypnotism induces on the nervous system, we acquire a power of rapidly curing many functional disorders, most intractable, or altogether incurable, by ordinary remedies, and also many of those distressing affections which, as in most cases they evince no pathological changes of structure, have been presumed to depend on some peculiar condition of the nervous system, and have therefore, by universal consent, been denominated "*nervous complaints;*" and as I felt satisfied it was not dependent on any special agency or emanation, passing from the body of the operator to that of the patient, as the animal magnetizers allege is the case by their process, I considered it desirable, for the sake of preventing misconception, to adopt new terms, as explained in the introduction.

I was led to discover the mode I now adopt with so much success for inducing this artificial condition of the nervous system, by a course of experiments instituted with the view to determine the cause of mesmeric phenomena. From all I had read and heard of mesmerism, (such as, the phenomena being capable of being excited in so few, and these few individuals in a state of disease, or naturally of a delicate constitution, or peculiarly susceptible temperament, and from the phenomena, when induced, being said to be so exaggerated, or of such an extraordinary nature; I was fully inclined to join with those who considered the whole to be a system of collusion or delusion, or of excited imagination, sympathy, or imitation.

The first exhibition of the kind I ever had an opportunity of attending, was one of M. Lafontaine's conversazioni, on the 13th November, 1841. That night I saw nothing to diminish, but rather to confirm, my previous prejudices. At the next conversazione, six nights afterwards, *one* fact, the inability of a patient to *open his eyelids,* arrested my attention. I considered that to be a *real phenomenon,* and was anxious to discover the physiological cause of it. Next night, I watched this case when again operated on, with intense interest, and before the termination of the experiment, felt assured I had discovered its cause, but considered it prudent not to announce my opinion publicly, until I had had an opportunity of testing its accuracy, by experiments and observation in private.

In two days afterwards, I developed my views to my friend Captain Brown, as I had also previously done to four other friends; and in his presence, and that of my family, and another friend, the same evening, I instituted a series of experiments to prove the correctness of my theory, namely, that the continued fixed stare, by paralyzing nervous centres in the eyes and their appendages, and destroying the equilibrium of the nervous system, thus produced the phenomenon referred to. The experiments were varied so as to convince all present, that they fully bore out the correctness of my theoretical views.

My first object was to prove, that the inability of the patient to open his eyes was caused by paralyzing the levator muscles of the eyelids, through their continued action during the protracted fixed stare, and thus rendering it *physically* impossible for him to open them. With the view of proving this, I requested Mr. Walker, a young gentleman present, to sit down, and maintain a fixed stare at the top of a wine bottle, placed so much above him as to produce a considerable strain on the eyes and eyelids, to enable him to maintain a steady view of the object. In three minutes his eyelids closed, a gush of tears ran down his cheeks, his head drooped, his face was slightly convulsed, he gave a groan, and instantly fell into profound sleep, the respiration becoming slow, deep and sibilant, the right hand and arm being agitated by slight confulsive movements. At the end of four minutes I considered it necessary, for his safety, to put an end to the experiment.

This experiment not only proved what I expected, but also, by calling my attention to the spasmodic state of the muscles of the face and arm, the peculiar state of the respiration, and the condition of the mind, as evinced on rousing the patient, tended to prove to my mind I had got the key to the solution of mesmerism. The agitation and alarm of this gentleman, on being roused, very much astonished Mrs. Braid. She expressed herself greatly surprised at his being so much alarmed about nothing, as she had watched the whole time, and never saw me near him, or touching him in any way whatever. I proposed that she should be the next subject operated on, to which she readily consented, assuring all present that she would not be so easily alarmed as the gentleman referred to. I requested her to sit down, and gaze on the ornament of a china sugar basin, placed at the same angle to the eyes as the bottle in the former experiment. In two minutes the expression of the face was very much changed; at the end of two minutes and a half the eyelids closed convulsively; the mouth was distorted; she gave a deep sigh, the bosom heaved, she fell back, and was evidently passing into an hysteric paroxysm, to prevent which I instantly roused her. On counting the pulse I found it had mounted up to 180 strokes a minute.

In order to prove my position still more clearly, I called up one of my men-servants, who knew nothing of mesmerism, and gave him such directions as were calculated to impress his mind with the idea, that his fixed attention was merely for the purpose of watching a chemical experiment in the preparation of some medicine, and being familiar with such he could feel no alarm. In two minutes and a half his eyelids closed slowly with a vibrating motion, his chin fell on his breast, he gave a deep sigh, and instantly was in a profound sleep, breathing loudly. All the persons present burst into a fit of laughter, but still he was not interrupted by us. In about one minute after his profound sleep I roused him, and pretended to chide him for being so careless, said he ought to be ashamed of himself for not being able to attend to my instructions for three minutes without falling asleep, and ordered him down stairs. In a short time I recalled this young man, and desired him to sit down once more, but to be careful not to go to sleep again, as on the former occasion. He sat down with this intention, but at the expiration of two minutes and a half his eyelids closed and exactly the same phenomena as in the former experiment ensued.

I again tried the experiment by causing Mr. Walker to gaze on a different object from that used in the first experiments, but still, as I anticipated, the phenomena were the same. I also tried him *à la Fontaine*, with the thumbs and eyes, and likewise by gazing on my eyes without contact, and still the effects were the same, as I fully expected.

I now stated that I considered the experiments fully proved my theory; and expressed my entire conviction that the phenomena of mesmerism were to be accounted for on the principle of a derangement of the state of the cerebro-spinal centres, and of the circulatory, and respiratory, and muscular systems, induced, as I have explained, by a fixed stare, absolute repose of the body, fixed attention, and suppressed respiration, concomitant with the fixity of attention. That the whole depended on the physical and psychical condition of the patient, arising from the causes referred to, and not at all on the volition, or passes of the operator, throwing out a magnetic fluid, or exciting into activity some mystical universal fluid or medium. I farther added, that having thus produced the *primary* phenomena, I had no doubt but the others would follow as a matter of course, time being allowed for their gradual and successive development.

For a considerable time I was of opinion that the phenomena induced by my mode of operating and that of the mesmerizers, were identical; and, so far as I have yet personally seen, I still consider the condition of the nervous system induced by both modes to be at least analogous. It appeared to me that the fixation of the mind and eyes was attained occasionally during the monotonous movements of the mesmerizers, and thus they succeeded sometimes, and as it were, by chance; whereas, by insisting on the eyes being fixed in the most favourable position, and the mind thus rivetted to one idea, as the *primary and imperative conditions*, my success was consequently general and effects intense, while theirs was feeble and uncertain.

The French country doctor, A. A. Liébeault (1823-1904), has the distinction of having developed a consistent psychological theory of hypnotism based on a proper evaluation of the part played by suggestion in inducing hypnotic sleep. Setting up his practice in Nancy, he treated the poor free of charge if they were willing to submit to his hypnotic experiments. His friend and disciple, H. Bernheim, hails his book, Concerning Sleep and Analogous States, Considered from the Angle of the Mind-Body Relationship *(1866), as "the most important work that has ever been published on Braidism." Another of his disciples reported that, nevertheless, only one copy of Liébeault's book had been sold.*

Liébeault puts great emphasis on the similarity of sleep and hypnosis. Both states, he insists, result from a withdrawal of the person's attention from reality, and both presuppose the subject's willingness or consent to fall asleep. Some of his formulations have a surprisingly modern ring and seem to anticipate Freud's concept of the mobility of libidinal charge—or sexual energy—as an important factor in our mental life.

This quotation is from an article in the Journal du Magnetisme *(June, 1881) summarizing Liébeault's methods as they were originally described in his principal work. It is given here in the editor's translation.*

The method of suggestion consists of the transmission by word or gesture of certain ideas to the mind of a sleeping subject. The ideas are aimed at bringing about certain physical and above all, certain mental processes in the organism. This method of modifying, in part or as a whole, the bodily functions of a sleeping person had been widely used for a long time in order to analyze the peculiarities of artificial sleep, to investigate the coordinated or separate functioning of organs, to enhance or to diminish their vital functions and, in case of illness, to bring disturbed functions back to normal again. Our present technique of inducing artificial sleep is derived from two principles. First, the sleeper's mind is focused in the direction of one specific train of thought, that is, in the direction of meditation. Secondly, from his invariable acceptance of our assurances regarding the forthcoming hypnotic phenomena, that is, of our suggestions. The subject—usually a patient— keeps his gaze fixed on our eyes. While doing so his senses are shut off from both internal and external stimuli, his brain becomes increasingly sluggish and accessible to our suggestion (suggestibility is by no means confined to the sleeping state). Throughout this procedure we impress on him to think of nothing but of falling asleep and of getting well. We announce to him the premonitory symptoms of sleep: the bodily relaxation, drowsiness, heaviness of eyelids, general anesthesia, etc. Soon we note that his eyelids begin to twitch or become heavy, his eyes assume a surprised expression, his pupils fluctuate in size or dilate. Then we utter the magic word: "Sleep!" If the eyes fail to close at once following this command we repeat the same litany of assurances, if need be several times. Finally, we press down the upper lids with our thumbs which have been held in position on both sides of the eyes beforehand, all the time continuing with our suggestions. Workmen, peasants, children and former military men, accustomed to obey commands, close their eyes readily as soon as we utter the word "Sleep." Failing to achieve the desired result after a minute or so we adjourn the hypnotic session till the next day. After a few days of this procedure a few seconds suffice as a rule for our patients to pass into some degree of sleep. Soon they develop hypnotic states of increasing depth.

As you can see, here, again, there is nothing new under the sun. We simply add the method of suggestion . . . to the practices of the magnetisers. But this is not all. Cognisant of the compulsive nature of imitation, as well as of the sleep inducing power of rest and idleness, we always hypnotize our patients in groups of 15-20, following a wait of at least one or two hours. During this period of waiting they have time to adjust themselves to our ways. They make themselves comfortable, chat with their neighbors, get used to their environment, take an interest in our success, forget all about themselves and obey gently and unconsciously a powerful urge to yield by way of imitation to the desire to sleep as it continuously enfolds itself before their very eyes. They are all the more inclined to yield to this urge since they are well aware of the fact that falling asleep is to their best advantage, holding as it does the promise of cure.

Hyppolite Bernheim (1837-1919), a disciple of Liébeault, raised the study of hypnotism to the status of academic respectability. A professor at the University of Nancy, he hypnotized close to 10,000 subjects in the course of years. Not content with studying hypnotic suggestion—and its close relationship to sleep—he made methodical use of "positive" and "negative" suggestions for the purpose of treatment; e.g., he suggested a sense of wellbeing or the disappearance of symptoms to his patients. But he tried to go further than that. He sought to understand man and his motivations on the basis of psychological phenomena discovered in the hypnotic state, especially those described as automatisms and post-hypnotic suggestion. A contemporary of Charcot (see below), he refused to bow to the authority of his illustrious colleague and became the main spokesman of the Nancy School of hypnotism in its controversy with what is known as the Paris School.

The selection that follows is taken from Bernheim's Suggestive Therapeutics, A Treatise on the Nature and Uses of Hypnotism, first published in 1886. Unfortunately, the translation reproduced here does not do full justice to the original text.

There is no fundamental difference between spontaneous and induced sleep. M. Liébeault has very wisely established this fact. The spontaneous sleeper is in relationship with himself alone; the idea which occupies his mind just before going to sleep, the impressions which the sensitive and sensorial nerves of the periphery continue to transmit to the brain, and the stimuli coming from the viscera, become the point of departure for the incoherent images and impressions which constitute dreams. Have those who deny the psychical phenomena of hypnotism, or who only admit them in cases of diseased nervous temperament, ever reflected upon what occurs in normal sleep, in which the best balanced mind is carried by the current, in which the faculties are dissociated, in which the most singular ideas, and the most fantastic conceptions obtrude? Poor human reason is carried away, the proudest mind yields to hallucinations, and during this sleep, that is to say, during a quarter of its existence, becomes the plaything of the dreams which imagination calls for.

In induced sleep, the subject's mind retains the memory of the person who has put him to sleep, whence the hypnotizer's power of playing upon his imagination, of suggesting dreams, and of directing the acts which are no longer controlled by the weakened or absent will.

Moreover, owing to this paresis of the psychical activity of the voluntary regulator of the cerebro-spinal automatism, the latter becomes exaggerated and dominant. Thus sleep favors the production of suggestive phenomena, by suppressing or weakening the moderating influence, but it is not indispensable to their production. I repeat the fact that it is itself a phenomenon of suggestion. Certain subjects who reach the condition in which the cataleptiform closure of the eyelids occurs, resist the idea of sleep. In one case in my service, I cannot induce either sleep or closure of the contracted hand. Hypnotism is not then the necessary prelude to suggestion; it facilitates suggestion when it can be induced; but other suggestions may sometimes succeed when the suggestion of sleep is inefficacious. . . .

The doctrine of suggestion, as we have established it according to the facts gained from observation, raises the most throbbing questions on all sides. In psychology it means revolution. Though still in its infancy, what problems is not this study called upon to solve? To what degree may not suggestion influence the most widely different minds, chosen from among the intelligent classes, refined by the power of education, as well as from the lower classes where less cerebral resistance is offered? To what extent may not the subject's instincts, tastes, and psychical faculties be modified by a prolonged and cleverly managed suggestion, whether in the waking or in the hypnotic condition? Have we not, indeed, a veritable suggestion in the waking condition in the child's education, in the notions and principles inculcated by word and example, in the philosophical and religious teachings by which it is surrounded from the earliest age,—a suggestion which often works with an irresistible force if practiced methodically, directed in a uniform manner, and not thwarted by contradictory ideas or examples? Mature men, whose minds have been rendered liberal by personal experience, in spite of the intelligent action of their reasoning powers often reserve a stock of old ideas from which they cannot escape, because, through previous and long continued suggestion, these have become part of the mind, although they may seem to disagree with its present working. M. Liébeault says: "Without being aware of it, we acquire moral and political predispositions, prejudices, etc.; we are impregnated with the mental atmosphere about us. We honestly believe and defend as we would our own welfare, social and religious principles which may be opposed to common sense, not to say reason. These principles were held by our ancestors, they are also national, and they descend from father to son. It is impossible to destroy them by argument, and dangerous to do so by force. Their fallacy is pointed out in vain. Man thinks by imitation, and however absurd his thoughts may be, they form part of the man, and are finally transmitted from generation to generation as instincts are." . . .

I come now to the study of therapeutic suggestion. If, in the waking condition, violent moral emotions, lively religious faith, everything which strikes the imagination, can drive away functional troubles and work cures, it must nevertheless be said that active therapeutics does not often reap advantage from this means. In the waking condition, many imaginations are refractory to the suggestive shock of the moral emotions. Credulity is moderated by the superior faculties of the understanding. Hypnotism, like natural sleep, exalts the imagination, and makes the brain more susceptible to suggestion. The strongest minds cannot escape from the hallucinatory suggestions of their dreams. It is a physiological law, that sleep puts the brain into such a psychical condition that the imagination accepts and recognizes as real the impressions transmitted to it. To provoke this special psychical condition by means of hypnotism, and to cultivate the suggestibility thus artificially increased with the aim of cure or relief, this is the role of psychotherapeutics.

The brain, influenced by suggestion, tends to realize the phenomena commanded with an energy varying according to the individuality; in some it is already docile in the waking condition; it becomes so in almost all cases when the hypnotic condition, or a condition analogous to it, has put to sleep or dulled the faculties of reason, judgment, and control which moderate and restrain the cerebral automatism. Then the brain, more powerfully impressed by the formulated order, accepts the idea and transforms it into action. We have seen hypnotic suggestion cause paralysis, contracture, anaesthesia, pains, cough, nausea, etc.; we have seen these dynamic effects of suggestion persist when the subject is awakened, or appear only after the awakening [post-hypnotic suggestion]. The brain refuses to perceive the centripetal impressions of tactile, visceral, or sensorial sensibility; it refuses to set the motor cells of the spinal cord into activity; hence, psychical motor paralysis, anaesthesia, blindness, deafness, which are phenomena of inhibition. Or, on the contrary, it perceives the centripetal impression with greater vividness. It sends extra activity to the motor cells, hence, sensitiveness and sensorial hyperaesthesia, and more energetic muscular work, or contracture; these are dynamogenic phenomena. Other psychical [moral emotions], or experimental proceedings may put both the cerebral mechanism of inhibition and of dynamogeny into play; as for example, paralysis of speech produced by fear, or the increase of strength caused by anger or unusual excitement.

Observations having thus shown what the simple hypnotic suggestion can perform in the healthy condition, it was natural to apply these qualities to pathological states, and to make use of the nervous activity concentrated by means of suggestion, in neutralizing morbid phenomena. It was natural to say to oneself—if, in a hypnotized subject, anaesthesia, contracture, movements, pains, can be produced at will by an analogous mechanism, it ought to be possible in some cases to suppress anaesthesia, contracture, or paralysis caused by disease, to increase the weakened muscular force, to modify favorably or to restore the functional force perverted or diminished by the pathological condition, as far, of course, as the organic condition permits this restoration.

J. M. Charcot (1825-1893) is one of the great clinicians of the late nineteenth century. His field of research included neuropathology, psychiatry and the study of neuroses, with special emphasis upon hysteria. As chairman of the Department of Psychiatry at the Salpêtrière in Paris, he organized one of the first postgraduate centers for the teaching of psychiatry.

Charcot's primary interest was in the field of neurology and it was from this vantage point that he turned to the study of hysteria. He was anxious to draw a strict demarcation line between hysteric disorders and simulation and was only satisfied with the true hysteric nature of his patient's complaints when they displayed abnormal muscular symptoms or variations of reflexes and sensory functions which could not be brought about by will power alone. Yet his patients seemed particularly susceptible to hypnosis. They produced what Charcot described as the "grand hypnotisme." This was supposed to manifest itself in three different stages: lethargy, catalepsy and somnambulism. Charcot sought to correlate the three consecutive stages of hypnosis with various manifestations of hysteria. In effect, he regarded hypnotic phenomena as a form of artificial hysteria, which he believed, was ultimately based on hereditary predisposition. This, he held, made the patient particularly susceptible to suggestion and autosuggestion, which in turn would trigger off the symptoms of "major" and "minor" hysteria.

Thus in spite of his dawning insight into the psychological factors involved in the origin of functional disorders, Charcot held on to the organic theory of their causation. His treatment consisted of such conventional methods as electrization, hydrotherapy and isolation of the patient from his family.

The following selection from his Clinical Lectures on the Diseases of the Nervous System, *published in 1889, contains Charcot's description of the three stages of the "great hypnotism."*

We know that in subjects in a state of hypnotic sleep it is possible—and this is a notorious fact now—to originate by the method of suggestion, or of intimation, an idea, or a coherent group of associated ideas, which possess the individual, and remain isolated, and manifest themselves by corresponding motor phenomena. If this be so, we know that if the idea suggested be one of paralysis, a real paralysis virtually ensues, and we see in such case that it will frequently manifest itself in as accentuated a form as that deriving from a destructive lesion of cerebral substance. These assertions I am about to try and justify by placing before you cases of paralysis produced by suggestion, and which we may consider as typical of psychical paralysis. . . .

I would remind you that in the lethargic phase of what is called the great hypnotism, the mental inertia is so absolute that in general it is impossible to enter into relation with the hypnotized subject or to communicate any idea to him by any process whatever. But it is not thus in the other two phases of hypnotism. Thus in catalepsy—I speak here only of the true catalepsy, such as I have described—certain phenomena of suggestion are easily obtained, and owing to their simplicity and their small tendency to become generalized, they are relatively easy of analysis. Here, then, evidently, the study of hypnotic suggestions ought to commence. Here, as in the preceding phase, there is mental inertia, but it is less profound, less absolute; it has become possible, indeed, to produce a sort of partial waking in the organ of the psychic faculties. Thus one can call into existence an idea, or a group of ideas connected together by previous associations. But this group set in action will remain strictly limited. There will be no propagation, no diffusion of the communicated movement; all the rest will remain asleep. Consequently the idea, or group of ideas suggested, are met with in a state of isolation, free from the control of that large collection of personal ideas long accumulated and organized, which constitute the conscience properly so-called, the ego. It is for this reason that the movements which exteriorly represent the acts of unconscious cerebration, are distinguished by their automatic and purely mechanical character. Then it is truly that we see before us the human machine in all its simplicity, dreamt of by De la Mettrie.

In this cataleptic condition, in the greater number of individuals, the only means by which we can enter into relation with the person hypnotized is through the muscular sense. The gesture alone, or the attitude in which we put the subject, suggests to him the idea which we wish to transmit to him. By shutting, for example, his fists in an aggressive attitude you observe the head carried backwards, and the forehead, the eyebrows and the root of the nose become corrugated with a menacing expression. Or, again, if you place the tips of his stretched-out fingers on his mouth, then the lips relax, he smiles and all the face assumes an expression of softness totally opposed to what it just manifested. . . .

We now come to the third phase, the somnambulistic, which is the only one that will engage our attention today. We have here to do solely with a state of obnubilation [clouding], mental torpor more or less accentuated. Here, again, without doubt, the awakening determined by suggestion remains partial, but the number of elements called into operation is less limited than in the preceding case, and frequently a diffusion occurs of the induced psychical phenomena sufficiently extensive to manifest a certain tendency to the reconstitution of the ego. Hence, it sometimes happens under these circumstances that the injunction, the suggestion, becomes the occasion of a certain amount of resistance on the part of the subject. In all cases this yields to a little insistence. Nevertheless, it does not always do so without a preliminary discussion. Let me add that the movements in connection with the ideas suggested are consequently often very complex; they have not, therefore, that character of mechanical precision which they present in the preceding form; on the contrary, they assume the likeness of voluntary acts, more or less premeditated, even to the extent of leading one astray.

Further, in the somnambulistic stage all the senses are intact, and it may be said, indeed, that although the conscience is in abeyance, the sensibility to communicated impressions is exalted. It consequently becomes easier to enter in relation by diverse means with the hypnotized person. If he be urged to look at some object, the simple view of that object will arouse in that patient a certain number of ideas associated with the nature of the object, and those ideas will manifest themselves objectively in the form of corresponding acts. If, by significant gesture, an object or an animal is figured in space, that animal or that imaginary object will appear to the eyes of the hypnotized person as real, and will call into action a corresponding series of ideas and movements. And again, in a manner still more perfect, suggestion can be effected by the aid of speech, either alone or better, combined with gestures.

This is enough, gentlemen, to remind you in a general way of the chief characters of hypnotic suggestion in the somnambulic period, and how unlimited our power is in this domain, for really we can vary our action almost without end. Hence you will not be surprised to find that, in suggesting to a somnambulic subject the idea of a morbid state, for example motor paralysis of the extremities, the paralysis becomes objectively manifest, and thus lends itself to our clinical investigation.

This, in brief, is Charcot's description of the stages of hypnotism. His theories themselves were attacked and ultimately demolished by Bernheim's Nancy School of Hypnotism. Bernheim pointed out that the three stages studied by Charcot and his disciples were artifacts. They were the result of unconscious suggestion emanating from the hypnotist; they were due to the patients' readiness to "oblige" the experimenter by producing all the many and varied symptoms which he expected them to produce; they were "cultivated hypnotism"—by-products of the "Mesmeric" influence of the Wizard of the Salpêtrière upon his subjects. It may well be that a considerable part of Charcot's therapeutic impact upon his patients was due to similar factors. The same subtle personal influence that made them produce the three stages of hypnotism to order, as it were, may have contributed to their temporary clinical improvement.

Thus Charcot's successes as a psychotherapist may not have been of an altogether different order from those achieved by the Mesmerists, although his theories were supported by considerably sounder and better organized clinical observations. That they were nevertheless largely mistaken is another matter.

This is how Bernheim, in the book quoted on an earlier page, stated his case against Charcot and the Paris School:

I have never been able to induce in any of my cases, the three phases of the Salpêtrière school, and it is not for want of trial. I add, that even in three hospitals in Paris, I have seen subjects hypnotized in my presence and they acted as our subjects do, and the doctors who were treating them fully confirmed our observations.

Once only did I see a subject who exhibited perfectly the three periods of lethargy, catalepsy and somnambulism. It was a young girl who had been at the Salpêtrière for three years, and why should I not state the impression which I retained of the case? Subjected to a special training by manipulations, imitating the phenomena which she saw produced in other somnambulists of the same school, taught by imitation to exhibit reflex phenomena in a certain typical order, the case was no longer one of natural hypnotism, but a product of false training, a true suggestive hypnotic neurosis.

Even if I am mistaken, and these phenomena are met with primarily, and without any suggestion, we must recognize that this "grande hypnose" is a rare condition. Binet and Féré say that only a dozen of these cases have occurred at the Salpêtrière in ten years. Should these cases, opposed to thousands of cases in which these phenomena are wanting, serve as the basis for the theoretical conception of hypnotism?

It would be a curious thing in the history of hypnotism to see so many distinguished minds misled by an erroneous first conception, and carried into a series of singular errors which no longer permit them to see the truth. Grievous errors they are, for they hinder progress by obscuring a question which is so simple that everything explains itself, when it is known that suggestion is they key to all hypnotic phenomena!

From this point of view, there is nothing more curious to read than the many transfer experiments of MM. Binet and Féré. These authors conclude from their experiments, that the application of a magnet to a hypnotized subject can transfer to the side to which it is applied,—for example, to the upper left limb,—such phenomena as anaesthesia, contracture, paralysis, etc. which have been provoked on the opposite side,—for example, in the upper right limb. In the same way, the magnet is supposed to transfer sensorial anaesthesia, hallucinations of the senses, of smell, hearing, sight, taste, and touch. This transfer is supposed to take place without the intervention of suggestion, by a simple physical phenomenon in which the subject's brain, considered as the psychical organ, takes no part.

These authors think they have eliminated suggestion because they have made their experiments in the conditions known as lethargy and catalepsy. They say, "These are unconscious states in the 'grande hypnose,' states in which the condition of the senses and intelligence renders the subject a complete stranger to what is going on around him. Experiment, however, shows that in these conditions the magnet transfers a large number of phenomena." This is a fundamental error, which has been the source of all the experimental illusions of these authors.

I repeat that the subject remains conscious in all degrees of hypnotism, as we have observed in thousands of cases in Nancy.

If, in the twelve only cases in which, during the space of ten years, the phenomena of what is called "great hypnotism" to distinguish it from what is known as the "little hypnotism," of the Nancy School, have been observed; if in these cases, an apparent unconsciousness during what is called the lethargy state has been noticed, I believe that it was only an illusion. The subject, unconsciously educated in this suggestion, cannot react in this condition, because he believes he cannot, because the idea has been introduced into his brain, that as the necessary manipulation has not been made upon him he cannot emerge from this state, and cannot accept any suggestion. Nothing is easier than to artificially create an analogous condition in all somnambulistic cases.

The controversy ended in favor of Bernheim's position. But this did little to detract from Charcot's stature as one of the great psychiatrists of his time. Sigmund Freud, who came to Paris in 1885 to attend his famous Wednesday Lectures at the Salpêtrière, wrote in his obituary for Charcot: "It is unavoidable that with the progress of our science and with the expansion of our knowledge, some of Charcot's teachings should have become invalid. But no change in the times or in opinions will ever diminish the glory of the man whose passing we here, in France and elsewhere, all deplore."

Pierre Janet (1859-1947) was a disciple of the great Charcot and a contemporary of Freud (1856-1939). Nevertheless, Janet is usually described as a pre-Freudian psychiatrist, a forerunner of the discoverer of the Unconscious, with a capital U. This, at least, is the verdict of such psychoanalytically committed writers as Gregory Zilboorg, the Russian-born historian of psychotherapy, and Ernest Jones, the English psychoanalyst and biographer of Freud. Yet Janet certainly deserves a niche of his own in the pantheon of psychiatric pioneers. He presented a lucid description of somnambulism, fugues, hypnosis and hypnoidal states, and diverse forms of hysteria. His discovery of motor and sensory automatisms, of two coexisting or alternating states of consciousness, of "forgetfulness" of "abandoned psychological phenomena," paved the way for Freud's revolutionary formulation of personality structure and the distinction between ego, id, and superego. In a similar vein, Janet's concept of the "lowering of the level of mental functioning" anticipated some of Freud's ideas about psychic energies. Janet's metaphor about "mental disinfection" and the dislodging of idées fixes adumbrates the Freudian theory of catharsis. On the other hand, Janet's term sentiment d'infériorité is a direct counterpart of Alfred Adler's "inferiority complex."

In the early years of psychoanalysis, Janet generously acknowledged the originality of Breuer's and Freud's contributions. But mutual respect soon gave way to increasingly caustic controversy. Janet considered the Freudian unconscious merely as a facon de parler. He denied the usefulness or even the feasibility of free association and ridiculed the length of time needed for psychoanalytic exploration and treatment.

Freud, in turn, became more and more critical of his rival. "I always treated Janet with respect," he remarked, "since his discoveries coincided to a considerable extent with those of Breuer which had been made earlier, but published later than his. But when in the course of time psychoanalysis became a subject of discussion in France, Janet behaved ill, showed ignorance of the facts and used ugly arguments. . . . "

There can be little doubt today that Janet stopped short of plumbing the whole depth of the psychic apparatus that he had touched upon in his researches. His clinical observations and emphasis on the dual—or even multiple—organization of human personality have entered the mainstream of modern dynamic psychiatry. Some of his brilliant case studies, like the history of Nadia, have been compared with Freud's Wolf-Man or with Binswanger's case of Ellen West. His case history of Achilles, a man suffering from diabolical possession with marked hysterical features, is a model of sensitive clinical observation and reporting. But most of his interpretations are by now of largely historical interest, and his belief in the part played by hereditary factors in the origin of hysteria has proved to be erroneous.

Still, some of Janet's objections to the Freudian method have anticipated those of contemporary critics and are still being echoed by post-Freudian dissenters from the psychoanalytic school of thought. Ellenberger ranks him among the first pioneers of modern dynamic psychiatry.

The following selection is taken from Janet's État Mental des Hysteriques *(1901). It includes brief references to his distinction between hysteria and obsessive-compulsive states, described as "psychasthenic conditions."*

The most important work that has come to confirm our earlier studies is, without contradiction, the article of MM. Breuer and Freud, which recently appeared in the *Neurologisches Centralblatt.*

We are very glad that these authors, in their independent researches, have been able to verify ours with so much precision, and we thank them for their kindly reference to us. They show by numerous examples that the various symptoms of hysteria are not spontaneous manifestations, idiopathic of the disease, but are in close connection with the provocative trauma. The most common accidents of hysteria, even hyperaesthesias, pains, commonplace attacks, should be interpreted in the same way as the accidents of traumatic hysteria—namely, by the persistency of an idea or a dream. The relation between the provocative idea and the accident may be more or less direct, but it exists always. We should, however, establish the fact that the patient often, in his normal state, knows nothing of this provocative idea, which is not clearly found again except during the periods, natural or provoked, of the second state, and it is precisely to their isolation that these ideas owe their power. The patient is cured, say these authors, when he succeeds in finding again the clear consciousness of his fixed idea.

"This division of the consciousness, which has been clearly established in some celebrated cases of double existence, exists in a rudimentary state in every hysterical; the disposition to this dissociation and at the same time to the formation of abnormal states of consciousness, which we propose to bring together under the name of hypnoid states, constitutes the fundamental phenomenon of this neurosis." This definition goes to confirm those . . . which seek to group all the symptoms of the disease around a principal phenomenon, the undoubling of the personality.

Retraction of the Field of Consciousness

The preceding definitions are certainly quite general; they apply to the great majority of hysterical accidents, but, on the other hand, it is evident that they pass by almost completely other characters equally numerous and very important—namely, the stigmata.

Certain authors have tried to apply to the stigmata the same explanation as to accidents, and equally to connect them with fixed ideas. This explanation would be simple, and conforms to the principles we have adopted, but it has been seen that there could not be established in anaesthesias either evolution or the characteristics of fixed ideas. We may consider them as the proof of a lessening of the nervous functions, an exhaustion of the organs. This is not a theory; it is the expression, as just as it is common, of the fact itself; it remains now to interpret the nature of this exhaustion.

We can hardly discuss here an exact theory, for most authors who speak of this exhaustion have expressed themselves in the most vague and confused manner. The question presents itself to us as follows: Is this exhaustion,—the primitive causes of which we have not here to look for, be they heredity, degeneracy, intoxication, or accidental lesions,—is it localised in such or such sensory organ, or does it bear, in a general way, upon the superior parts of the brain? Can we say that tactile anaesthesia, the contraction of the visual field, are precisely related to a stoppage of the function of the nervous centres which serve this tactile or visual sensation, or, rather, are those anaesthesias only a special manifestation of an enfeeblement bearing on all the functions of the cerebral cortex, and do they consequently connect themselves with a general disturbance of the psychological functions?

We do not believe that the stigmata are due to local lesions of the sensory apparatus, of the muscles, nerves, or centres. (1) The stigmata are too mobile; they disappear too easily as soon as you modify somewhat the thought of the subject; the suggestion, the association of the ideas, especially the attention, suppress as if by enchantment these insensibilities and these muscular impotencies; (2) the stigmata are contradictory—that is to say, the function of the organs is real and continues to the very moment at which it seems to be suppressed. We have shown in numerous studies that the tactile sensation, the visual sensation, even at the periphery of the visual field, continued to be exercised, despite anaesthesia; that the remembrances were reproduced despite apparent amnesia, that the movements were possible, and that they had even preserved their strength despite the weakness, the amyosthenia indicated by the dynamometer. These facts can be demonstrated by a great number of exact experiments, but they may be established by the simplest clinical observation. Hystericals walk, run without falling, without knocking against any obstacles, as real anaesthetics should do, — patients, namely, who have their visual field truly reduced to a point. You see them work, lift burdens, exercise for a long time when they are not conscious of being observed, while they exhibit an astonishing muscular weakness, an extremely rapid fatigue, as soon as you subject them to an examination. . . .

We purposed formerly to study a psychological phenomenon, which was already pointed out more or less vaguely among the disturbances of the character of the hystericals, and which seemed to us the principal expression of this insufficiency. The question is a feebleness of attention or rather a state of perpetual absent-mindedness easily established among most of these patients. The attention is painfully slow in fixing itself, is accompanied with accidents of all sorts, is quickly exhausted, and gives but a minimum of results; it forms but vague, doubtful, surprising, and unintelligible ideas. If we consider attention under its motor aspect, when it is applied to actions, we find again the same characteristics. Voluntary acts are slow, painful, of short duration, interspersed with innumerable stoppages. Often this so feeble attention seems even to disappear entirely; all attention, all voluntary acts become then impossible; the subject is no longer able to understand what he reads, nor even what he hears; he can no longer make the smallest voluntary motion. Abulia, aprosexia, hesitation, doubt, —we think we should insist on this, —are the psychological and essential characteristics of the hystericals. These characteristics, it is evident, are found more or less similar among other patients, but it is not a sufficient reason for neglecting them with the hysterical.

These weaknesses of attention are so great that they not only interfere with the intellectual works, but even modify the normal life, the ordinary thinking, which requires continually a certain effort of attention. The patient perceives imperfectly the things happening about him; he takes no account of all the situations of life, and he perceives only a very small portion of the facts; he seems always to forget the major part of the impressions which ought to strike him. If we try to verify this mental state in a more precise way, we establish that a hysterical woman cannot experience several sensations at the same time. As soon as she experiences a feeling of any kind she becomes indifferent to all the other excitations made on parts of the body and on organs ordinarily sensitive. She presents the same absence of mind for remembrances, and while she thinks of one idea she forgets all the contrary notions which she knew quite well a moment before. Lastly, we establish the same character in her acts and movements; voluntarily she makes but one movement at a time and loses the power of doing it the moment her attention is diverted by a sensation or another movement. . . .

We endeavoured formerly not to explain, but to summarize, all these many facts into a simple formula. Psychological life not only consists of a succession of phenomena coming one after the other, and forming a long series in one direction, but each of these successive states is in reality a complex state; it contains a multitude of more elementary facts and owes its apparent unity to synthesis alone, to the systematization of all these elements. We have proposed to call *"field of consciousness,* or maximum extension of consciousness," the largest number of simple, or relatively simple, phenomena, which might be gathered at every moment, which might be simultaneously connected with our personality in one and the same personal perception. . . .

To bring together, compare, and classify is not to confound; on the contrary, we do not mean entirely to identify a simple hysterical, with her anaesthesia, her attacks, and her contractures, with a psychasthenic, who presents nothing but doubts, impulsions, and fixed ideas. There is not, however, between these two categories of facts, the great difference which was formerly supposed to exist, when it was said that the first were physical phenomena and the others moral phenomena. Really, these factors are psychological, the one as well as the other; but important differences may exist even between psychological factors. The lack of mental synthesis, the disintegration of the mind, does not present itself the same way in the two cases. In hysteria the psychological phenomena, not being of a nature to be fully reunited, clearly separate into several groups in a way independent of each other. The personality cannot perceive all phenomena; it does, indeed, sacrifice a few; it is a kind of autonomy, and these abandoned phenomena develop separately without the subject's having any knowledge of their activity. The anaesthesia is, therefore, clear, the amnesia absolute, the attack and the somnambulistic sleep well distinguished from the waking state; the fixed ideas are not expressed, nor even known by the subject. The delirium exists in the mind of the subject without his being conscious of it, and while he goes on talking very reasonably. A hysterical patient spits out her food as soon as she puts it in her mouth, and yet she seems to make every reasonable effort to eat. Nevertheless, she rejects the food in spite of herself, without meaning to do so, or thinking of doing it; you think, while watching her, and she thinks, herself, that the trouble lies in deglutition or in some accident purely physical; you would be wrong to say that she is crazy. She is, notwithstanding, in full delirium. Since her last attack she has been constantly dreaming that her mother in heaven invites her to join her, and tells her to let herself die of hunger as fast as possible, and her vomiting is provoked by nothing else than this delirium. But this delirium is separated from the normal consciousness; it is subconscious; the bystanders and the patient herself are ignorant of it.

"Hystericals," say MM. Breuer and Freud, "are reasonable beings when awake, and crazy in their hypnoid state." This clear separation of the psychological phenomena may be expressed schematically by saying that in hysteria there is the formation of two independent personalities. The disintegration takes the form of the undoubling (dédoublement) of the personality.

It is quite otherwise with the psychasthenics. Their mental disintegration does not occur in the same way; it seems that their personality does not resign itself to the necessary sacrifices and that it abandons the phenomena to their automatic development in part only. There is no longer any very clear anaesthesia or amnesia. They are always incomplete and take the form of an absence of mind and of a continuous doubt. Instead of passing readily from one idea to another, forgetting wholly the preceding one, the psychasthenic remains always undecided between the different ideas. Deliriums, unfortunately for the patient, do not remain subconscious; they invade consciousness every instant; they mix with the other thoughts and create a much more considerable and general disturbance of thought. The patient, therefore, who comes complaining, whining, that it is in spite of herself that she thinks of betraying her husband, and that she is obsessed by this continuous idea, appears to us much more crazy than the hysterical who vomits. The subject herself feels much more ill, and never displays the fine indifference of the hystericals. Sometimes, although less frequently, the disintegration with this patient goes so far as to form different personalities, but they are never independent as with the hysterical. The patient feels this development of another personality within herself, and she talks constantly about possession, while the hysterical, the most undoubled (dédoublé), the most possessed in reality, is generally ignorant of this division of her mind.

We cannot study here this new form of mental disintegration which characterizes the psychasthenics, nor indicate its degree of gravity and its consequences. It will be sufficient to remark that it is different from that which has been established for the hystericals. . . . It is not necessary to deny the moral character of hysteria to preserve for it its place; it is enough to distinguish mental diseases from each other.

It is useless to take up again a discussion we have already often had concerning the relations of hysteria to the normal state. We have shown that in absence of mind, habits, passions, in the psychological automatism of the normal man, we find again the germ of all hysterical phenomena. Some authors have been surprised at it and make use of remarks of the same sort to represent as normal persons decided hystericals, or *vice versa*. This comparison need cause no surprise. "We must admit in a moral sense the great principle universally admitted in a physical sense since M. Claude Bernard —namely, that the laws of disease are the same as those of health, and that there is in the former but the exaggeration or the diminution of the phenomena which were already found in the latter." It is these degrees of the phenomena which we must be willing to recognize in order to distinguish an absence of the mind from an anaesthesia, an emotion from an attack, a dream from a somnambulic sleep. The distinction will always be difficult if one is merely satisfied with studying uncertain and doubtful cases, and easy if willing to begin studying the "type cases," and compare the former with the latter.

We have enlarged, upon one point, the conception of hysteria in connecting with it somnambulisms and subconscious acts; but we have limited the extent of this disease in distinguishing it from deliriums and the alienations which appear to come nearest to it. Mental disintegration is more permanent in hysteria than in deliriums; it is much clearer and more complete in this malady than in the psychasthenic states.

Resumé

There is no call in this work for dwelling on the etiology or the evolution of hysteria; it suffices to recall well-established notions. Pathological heredity plays in hysteria, as in all other mental maladies, a role absolutely preponderant. A very great number of circumstances play the part of "provocative agents," and manifest by accidents this latent predisposition; they are haemorrhages, wasting and chronic diseases, infectious diseases, typhoid fever in particular, and, in certain cases, the autointoxications, the organic diseases of the nervous system; various intoxications, physical or moral shocks, overwork, either physical or moral, painful emotions, and especially a succession of that sort of emotions the effects of which are cumulative, etc. It is easy to see that all these provocative agents are of the same character; they weaken the organism and increase the depression of the nervous system. There is, above all, an age which in this respect is particularly critical—the age of puberty. We speak here not of physical puberty, which has, however, a great influence, but of a state which comes a little later and which might justly be called moral puberty. It is an age slightly variable according to countries and surroundings, when all the greatest problems of life present themselves simultaneously; the choice of a career and the anxiety about making a living; all the problems of love, and for some the religious problems. These are preoccupations which invade the mind of young people and completely absorb their feeble power of thought. These thousand influences manifest a *psychological insufficiency* which remains latent during the less difficult periods. In a mind predisposed by hereditary influences, this psychological insufficiency develops, takes a special form, and presently manifests itself by an ensemble of symptoms which we call hysteria.

The word "hysteria" should be preserved, although its primitive meaning has much changed. It would be very difficult to modify it nowadays, and, truly, it has so great and so beautiful a history that it would be painful to give it up; but since every epoch has given it a different meaning, let us try to find out what meaning it has to-day. In order to try to summarize what we have borrowed from all these recent studies concerning hysteria, it is sufficient to gather up the conclusions of our foregoing paragraphs.

Hysteria,—we can say,—is a mental disease belonging to the large group of the diseases due to weakness, to cerebral exhaustion; it has only rather vague physical symptoms, consisting especially in a general diminution of nutrition; it is above all characterized by moral symptoms, the principal one being a weakening of the faculty of psychological synthesis, an abulia, a contraction of the field of consciousness manifesting itself in a particular way; a certain number of elementaty phenomena, sensations and images, cease to be perceived and appear suppressed by the personal perception; the result is a tendency to a complete and permanent division of the personality, to the formation of several groups independent of each other; these systems of psychological factors alternate some in the wake of the others or co-exist; in fine, this lack of synthesis favours the formation of certain parasitic ideas which develop completely and in isolation under the shelter of the control of the personal consciousness and which manifest themselves by the most varied disturbances, apparently only physical.

If we would sum up in two words this rather complex definition, we should say:

Hysteria is a form of mental disintegration characterized by a tendency toward the permanent and complete undoubling (dedoublement) of the personality.

Permit us, in closing, to repeat what we have said at the outset. A definition of this kind does not pretend to explain phenomena, but simply to summarize the greatest possible number of them. It will soon, we hope be superseded by a more comprehensive definition, one that will contain all the preceding facts and add to them still more phenomena—such as the physiological modifications which accompany and provoke this cerebral insufficiency. We only hope that this wholly provisional definition may now render some service and give somewhat greater precision to the innumerable remarks made during a long period by physicians and psychologists regarding the mental state of hystericals.

chapter 19

Freud and the Advent
of the Scientific Method
in Psychotherapy

Sigmund Freud's (1856-1939) early experiments in hypnosis and hypno-therapy follow in the footsteps of Liébeault, Bernheim and Charcot. But his major achievement, the psychoanalytic system of thought and the psycho-analytic method of treatment, is without precedent. Pierre Janet, the French psychiatrist who preceded him in catching a glimpse of unconscious factors —so-called psychological automatisms—in the causation of hysteria, fell short of recognizing the part played by sexual drives and their repression in the origin of the disease. On the theoretical side Freud ventured into territo-ry previously explored by the philosopher Edward von Hartmann and the psychologist Th. Lipps. Some of his general conclusions were anticipated by the German physician and romanticist C. G. Carus half a century before him. Again, Frederick Myers, the classical scholar and founder of the Eng-lish Society for Psychical Research, hit upon the concept of the "subliminal self" some fifteen years prior to Freud, without, however, realizing its far-reaching clinical implications. The noted Viennese physician, Josef Breuer, was Freud's early guide and mentor in the hypnotic treatment of hysteric patients. Yet Freud's daring attack upon sexual problems caused the two men to part company, as it alienated him from many more of his former teachers, friends and associates.

His discoveries have been likened to those of Copernicus or Galileo in the field of the physical sciences. It is true that Freud did not start experiment-ing by throwing objects from the leaning tower of Pisa as did Galileo in the early seventeenth century, but he was not satisfied to shut himself off from the facts of life in the ivory tower of the scholastic philosophers and moral therapists of a past age. He based his theories—and his new method of treat-ment—upon painstaking observation and therapeutic experimentation in case after case. There are the published case histories of Emmy von N.; Lucy R.; of Dora; of little Hans; of the Wolf Man; of the Schreber case, and many more. They are the raw material which went into the making of his system of thought and into the psychoanalytic method of treatment.

Seen in historical perspective, his work thus stands like a vast mountain range rising above the plains and foothills of the preceding centuries. There is no shortcut to the methodical exploration of its rugged peaks, winding valleys and dark underground caves. The tourist carried to the top by cable car or by such guided tours as can be provided by this anthology is barely able to catch a glimpse of Freud's contribution to psychiatry.

Fortunately, in the selections that follow, Freud himself plays the role of the tourist guide. They are taken from An Outline of Psychoanalysis, first published in 1940, one year after his death in London, and from his Autobiographical Study, first published in 1925. In these slim volumes Freud surveys the ground he covered in the course of a brilliant career as neuropathologist, psychoanalyst and student of the human mind in its dynamic, cultural and anthropological aspects. He sketches in broad outline what amounts to the anatomy of the psychic apparatus; his libido theory; his theory of instincts, of repression, and of infantile sexuality. He explains the need for distinguishing between conscious and unconscious mental functions, and in so doing arrives at a better understanding of the dream, the neurotic symptom and mental disorders in their genetic and dynamic aspects. The principles of psychoanalytic therapy follow cogently from these theoretical propositions.

It should be noted that this fact is in itself a new departure in the history of mental healing. It is true that both magic and religion had sought before to evolve a theory of their own upon which the healing approach was based. Yet since the theories of magic were of an essentially spurious nature, all attempts at their verification and application in practice were of necessity doomed to failure. Again, the premises of religion, derived as they are from experience outside the range of empirical observation, were no less difficult to reconcile with the scientific method. Religion, it has been said, has something of an extraterritorial status in relation to science. By contrast, Freud's approach brings the basic supposition of psychotherapy within the realm of science. He regards the psychic apparatus as subject to the same laws of cause and effect that govern the world at large. In such a picture, nothing is left to chance. Every slip of the tongue, every dream fragment, every neurotic symptom, can be traced back to a cause and viewed against the background of the patient's personal experience, conscious or unconscious.

Therapy, then, consists of undoing the damage done by the cumulative effects of harmful life experiences, especially those stemming from early childhood. The therapist helps the patient to relive his past and to readjust faulty reactions he established in his relations to parents, siblings and other persons in his early environment. The patient, in his relationship to the analyst, duplicates his early patterns of interpersonal relationships. This is *what Freud describes as psychoanalytic transference. The concept of trans-ference thus takes the place of the mysterious "rapport" which was once supposed to exist between the Mesmerist and his subject. According to Freud—and his disciple, the Hungarian analyst Sandor Ferenczi—the hyp-notic state itself is but a special case of the transference situation, in which the hypnotized subject surrenders to the control of a kindly—or authoritar-ian—parent figure.*

This analytic interpretation of the hypnotic state was another milestone in the history of psychotherapy. It seemed to remove the last element of magic from the therapist's approach. This being accomplished, the deck was cleared for what appeared to be a thoroughly rational method of mental healing, based on the technique of free association, the interpretation of dreams and the gradual reintegration of repressed mental content with the patient's personality.

These, in a nutshell, are the ingredients from which the new psychoana-lytic method has evolved. It undoubtedly comes close to the goal of a truly scientifically oriented psychotherapy: to describe, to explain and to re-adjust a person's deviant mental processes and bodily states, and to do this guided by a dynamic understanding of his symptoms, his personality and his interrelations with his fellow men.

Introductory Note

The aim of this brief work is to bring together the doctrines of psycho-analysis and to state them, as it were, dogmatically—in the most concise form and in the most positive terms. Its intention is naturally not to compel belief or to establish conviction.

The teachings of psychoanalysis are based upon an incalculable number of observations and experiences, and no one who has not repeated those observations upon himself or upon others is in a position to arrive at an independent judgment of it.

The Psychical Apparatus

Psychoanalysis makes a basic assumption, the discussion of which falls within the sphere of philosophical thought, but the justification of which lies in its results. We know two things concerning what we call our psyche or mental life: firstly, its bodily organ and scene of action, the brain (or nervous system), and secondly, our acts of consciousness, which are im-mediate data and cannot be more fully explained by any kind of descrip-tion. Everything that lies between these two terminal points is unknown to us and, so far as we are aware, there is no direct relation between them. If it existed, it would at the most afford an exact localization of the processes of consciousness and would give us no help toward understanding them.

Our two hypotheses start out from these ends or beginnings of our knowledge. The first is concerned with localization. We assume that mental life is the function of an apparatus to which we ascribe the characteristics of being extended in space and of being made up of several portions—which we imagine, that is, as being like a telescope or microscope or something of the sort. The consistent carrying through of a conception of this kind is a scientific novelty, even though some attempts in that direction have been made previously.

We have arrived at our knowledge of this psychical apparatus by studying the individual development of human beings. To the oldest of these mental provinces or agencies we give the name of *id*. It contains everything that is inherited, that is present at birth, that is fixed in the constitution— above all, therefore, the instincts, which originate in the somatic organization and which find their first mental expression in the id in forms unknown to us.

Under the influence of the real external world which surrounds us, one portion of the id has undergone a special development. From what was originally a cortical layer, provided with organs for receiving stimuli and with apparatus for protection against excessive stimulation, a special organization has arisen which henceforward acts as an intermediary between the id and the external world. This region of our mental life has been given the name of ego.

The principal characteristics of the ego are these. In consequence of the relation which was already established between sensory perception and muscular action, the ego is in control of voluntary movement. It has the task of self-preservation. As regards *external* events, it performs that task by becoming aware of the stimuli from without, by storing up experiences of them (in the memory), by avoiding excessive stimuli (through flight), by dealing with moderate stimuli (through adaptation) and, finally, by learning to bring about appropriate modifications in the external world to its own advantage (through activity). As regards *internal* events, in relation to the id, it performs that task by gaining control over the demands of the instincts, by deciding whether they shall be allowed to obtain satisfaction, by postponing that satisfaction to times and circumstances favorable in the external world or by suppressing their excitations completely. Its activities are governed by consideration of the tensions produced by stimuli present within it or introduced into it. The raising of these tensions is in general felt as *unpleasure* and their lowering as *pleasure*. It is probable, however, that what is felt as pleasure or unpleasure is not the *absolute* degree of the tensions but something in the rhythm of their changes. The ego pursues pleasure and seeks to avoid unpleasure. An increase in unpleasure which is expected and foreseen is met by a *signal of anxiety*; the occasion of this increase, whether it threatens from without or within, is called a *danger*. From time to time the ego gives up its connection with the external world and withdraws into the state of sleep, in which its organization undergoes far-reaching changes. It may be inferred from the state of sleep that that organization consists in a particular distribution of mental energy.

The long period of childhood, during which the growing human being lives in dependence upon his parents, leaves behind it a precipitate, which forms within his ego a special agency in which this parental influence is prolonged. It has received the name of *superego*. In so far as the superego is differentiated from the ego or opposed to it, it constitutes a third force which the ego must take into account.

Thus, an action by the ego is as it should be if it satisfies simultaneously the demands of the id, of the superego and of reality, that is to say if it is able to reconcile their demands with one another. The details of the relationship between the ego and the superego become completely intelligible if they are carried back to the child's attitude toward his parents. The parents' influence naturally includes not merely the personalities of the parents themselves but also the racial, national, and family traditions handed on through them as well as the demands of the immediate social *milieu* which they represent. In the same way, an individual's superego in the course of his development takes over contributions from later successors and substitutes of his parents, such as teachers, admired figures in public life, or high social ideals. It will be seen that, in spite of their fundamental difference, the id and the superego have one thing in common: they both represent the influences of the past (the id the influence of heredity, the superego essentially the influence of what is taken over from other people), whereas the ego is principally determined by the individual's own experience, that is to say by accidental and current events.

This general pattern of a psychical apparatus may be supposed to apply equally to the higher animals which resemble man mentally. A superego must be presumed to be present wherever, as in the case of man, there is a long period of dependence in childhood. The assumption of a distinction between ego and id cannot be avoided.

Animal psychology has not yet taken in hand the interesting problem which is here presented.

One of the corner stones of psychoanalysis is Freud's theory of instincts. Instincts (or drives) are described as "the forces behind the tensions caused by the needs of the id." In his later years Freud distinguished between two instincts: Eros and Thanatos—love and death—or the instincts of procrea-

tion and destruction. His concept of the death instinct has caused considerable controversy even among his closer associates. But Freud's libido theory has become one of the principal propositions of his system of thought. This is how, in one of his early works, Three Contributions to the Theory of Sex (1905), *he describes the part played by infantile sexuality:*

The Neglect of the Infantile. It is a part of popular belief about the sexual instinct that it is absent in childhood and that it appears in the period of life known as puberty. This, though a common error, is serious in its consequences and is chiefly due to our ignorance of the fundamental principles of the sexual life. A comprehensive study of the sexual manifestations of childhood would probably reveal to us the essential features of the sexual instinct and would show us its development and its compositions from various sources.

It is quite remarkable that those writers who endeavor to explain the qualities and reactions of the adult individual have given so much more attention to the ancestral period than to the period of the individual's own existence—that is, they have attributed more influence to heredity than to childhood. As a matter of fact, it might well be supposed that the influence of the latter period would be easier to understand, and that it would be entitled to more consideration than heredity. To be sure, one occasionally finds in medical literature notes on the premature sexual activities of small children, about erections and masturbation and even reactions resembling coitus, but these are referred to merely as exceptional occurrences, as curiosities, or as deterring examples of premature perversity. No author has, to my knowledge, recognized the normality of the sexual instinct in childhood, and in the numerous writings on the development of the child the chapter on "Sexual Development" is usually passed over.

Infantile Amnesia. The reason for this remarkable negligence I see partly in conventional considerations, which influence writers because of their own bringing up, and partly to a psychic phenomenon which thus far has remained unexplained. I refer to the peculiar amnesia which veils from most people (not from all) the first years of their childhood, usually the first six or eight years. So far it has not occurred to us that this amnesia should surprise us, though we have good reasons for it. For we are informed that during those years which have left nothing except a few incomprehensible memory fragments we have vividly reacted to impressions, that we have manifested human pain and pleasure, and that we have expressed love, jealousy and other passions as they then affected us. Indeed, we are told that we have uttered remarks which proved to grown-ups that we possessed understanding and a budding power of judgment. Still we know nothing of all this when we become older. Why does our memory lag behind all our other psychic activities? We really have reason to believe that at no time of life are we more capable of impressions and reproductions than during the years of childhood.

On the other hand we must assume, or we may convince ourselves through psychological observations of others, that the very impressions which we have forgotten have nevertheless left the deepest traces in our psychic life, and acted as determinants for our whole future development. We conclude therefore that we do not deal with a real forgetting of infantile impressions but rather with an amnesia similar to that observed in neurotics for later experiences, the nature of which consists in their being kept away from consciousness (repression). But what forces bring about this repression of the infantile impressions? He who can solve this riddle will also explain hysterical amnesia.

We shall not, however, hesitate to assert that the existence of the infantile amnesia gives us a new point of comparison between the psychic states of the child and those of the psychoneurotic. We have already encountered another point of comparison when confronted by the fact that the sexuality of the psychoneurotic preserves the infantile character or has returned to it. May there not be an ultimate connection between the infantile and the hysterical amnesias?

The connection between infantile and hysterical amnesias is really more than a mere play of wit. Hysterical amnesia which serves the repression can only be explained by the fact that the individual already possesses a sum of memories which were withdrawn from conscious disposal and which by associative connection now seize that which is acted upon by the repelling forces of the repression emanating from consciousness. We may say that without infantile amnesia there would be no hysterical amnesia.

I therefore believe that the infantile amnesia which causes the individual to look upon his childhood as if it were a *prehistoric* time and conceals from him the beginning of his own sexual life—that this amnesia is responsible for the fact that one does not usually attribute any value to the infantile period in the development of the sexual life. One single observer cannot fill the gap which has been thus produced in our knowledge. As early as 1896, I had already emphasized the significance of childhood for the origin of certain important phenomena connected with the sexual life, and since then I have not ceased to put into the foreground the importance of the infantile factor for sexuality.

The Sexual Latency Period of Childhood and Its Interruptions

The extraordinary frequent discoveries of apparently abnormal and exceptional sexual manifestations in childhood, as well as the discovery of infantile reminiscences in neurotics which were hitherto unconscious, allow us to sketch the following picture of the sexual behaviour of childhood. It seems certain that the newborn child brings with it the germs of sexual feelings which continue to develop for some time and then succumb to a progressive suppression, which may in turn be broken through by the regular advances of the sexual development or may be checked by individual idiosyncrasies. Nothing is known concerning the laws and periodicity of this oscillating course of development. It seems, however, that the sexual life of the child mostly manifests itself in the third or fourth year in some form accessible to observation.

Sexual Inhibition. It is during this period of total or at least partial latency that the psychic forces develop which later act as inhibitions on the sexual life, and narrow its direction like dams. These psychic forces are loathing, shame, and moral and esthetic ideal demands. We may gain the impression that the erection of these dams in the civilized child is the work of education; and surely education contributes much to it. In reality, however, this development is organically determined and can occasionally be produced without the help of education. Indeed education remains properly within its assigned domain if it strictly follows the path laid out by the organic, and only imprints it somewhat cleaner and deeper.

Reaction Formation and Sublimation. What are the means that accomplish these very important constructions so important for the later personal culture and normality? They are probably brought about at the cost of the infantile sexuality itself. The influx of this sexuality does not stop even in this latency period, but its energy is deflected either wholly or partially from sexual utilization and conducted to other aims. The historians of civilization seem to be unanimous in the opinion that such deflection of sexual motive powers from sexual aims to new aims, a process which merits the name of *sublimation*, has furnished powerful components for all cultural accomplishments. We will, therefore, add that the same process acts in the development of every individual, and that it begins to act in the sexual latency period.

We can also venture an opinion about the mechanisms of such sublimation. The sexual feelings of these infantile years would on the one hand be unusable, since the procreating functions are postponed—this is the chief character of the latency period; on the other hand, they would as such be perverse, as they would emanate from erogenous zones and from impulses which in the individual's course of development could only evoke a feeling of displeasure. They, therefore, awaken psychic counterforces (feelings of reaction), which build up the already mentioned psychical dams of disgust, shame and morality.

The Interruptions of the Latency Period. Without deluding ourselves as to the hypothetical nature and deficient clearness of our understanding regarding the infantile period of latency and delay, we will return to reality and state that such a utilization of the infantile sexuality represents an ideal bringing up from which the development of the individual usually deviates in some measure, often very considerably. A part of the sexual manifestation which has withdrawn from sublimation occasionally breaks through, or a sexual activity remains throughout the whole duration of the latency period until the reinforced breaking through of the sexual instinct in puberty. In so far as they have paid any attention to infantile sexuality, the educators behave as if they shared our views concerning the formation of the moral defense forces at the cost of sexuality. They seem to know that sexual activity makes the child uneducable, for they consider all sexual manifestations of the child as an "evil" in the face of which little can be accomplished. We have, however, every reason for directing our attention to those phenomena so much feared by the educators, for we expect to find in them the solution of the primary structure of the sexual instinct.

The Manifestations of Infantile Sexuality

Thumbsucking. For reasons which we shall discuss later, we will take as a model of the infantile sexual manifestations thumbsucking, to which the Hungarian pediatrist, Lindner, has devoted an excellent essay.

Thumbsucking, which manifests itself in the nursing baby and which may be continued till maturity or throughout life, consists in a rhythmic repetition of sucking contact with the mouth (the lips), wherein the purpose of taking nourishment is excluded. A part of the lip itself, the tongue, which is another preferable skin region within reach, and even the big toe—may be taken as objects for sucking. Simultaneously, there is also a desire to grasp things, which manifests itself in a rhythmical pulling of the ear lobe and which may cause the child to grasp a part of another person (generally the ear) for the same purpose. The pleasure-sucking is connected with a full absorption of attention and leads to sleep or even to a motor reaction in the form of an orgasm. Pleasure-sucking is often combined with a rubbing contact with certain sensitive parts of the body, such as the breast and external genitals. It is by this path that many children go from thumbsucking to masturbation.

Lindner himself clearly recognized the sexual nature of this activity and openly emphasized it. In the nursery, thumbsucking is often treated in the same way as any other sexual "naughtiness" of the child. A very strong objection was raised against this view by many pediatrists and neurologists, which in part is certainly due to the confusion between the terms "sexual" and "genital." This contradiction raises the difficult question, which cannot be avoided, namely, in what general traits do we wish to recognize the

sexual expression of the child. I believe that the association of the manifestations into which we have gained an insight through psychoanalytic investigation justifies us in claiming thumbsucking as a sexual activity. Through
thumbsucking we can study directly the essential features of infantile sexual
activities.

Autoeroticism. It is our duty to devote more time to this manifestation.
Let us emphasize the most striking character of this sexual activity, which is
that the impulse is not directed to other persons but that the child gratifies
himself on his own body; to use the happy term invented by Havelock Ellis,
we will say that he is *autoerotic.*

It is, moreover, clear that the action of the thumbsucking child is determined by the fact that he seeks a pleasure which he has already experienced
and now remembers. Through the rhythmic sucking on a portion of the skin
or mucous membrane, he finds gratification in the simplest way. It is also
easy to conjecture on what occasions the child first experienced this pleasure
which he now strives to renew. The first and most important activity in the
child's life, the sucking from the mother's breast (or its substitute) must have
acquainted him with this pleasure. We would say that the child's lips behaved like an *erogenous zone,* and that the stimulus from the warm stream
of milk was really the cause of the pleasurable sensation. To be sure, the
gratification of the erogenous zone was at first united with the gratification
of the need for nourishment. The sexual activity leans first on one of the
self-preservative functions and only later makes itself independent of it. He
who sees a satiated child sink back from its mother's breast and fall asleep
with reddened cheeks and blissful smile, will have to admit that this picture
remains as typical of the expression of sexual gratification in later life. But
the desire for repetition of sexual gratification is then separated from the
desire for taking nourishment; a separation which becomes unavoidable
with the appearance of teeth when the nourishment is no longer sucked but
chewed. The child does not make use of a strange object for sucking but
prefers his own skin, because it is more convenient, because it thus makes
him independent of the outer world which he cannot control, and because
in this way he creates for himself, as it were, a second, even if an inferior,
erogenous zone. This inferiority of this second region urges him later to seek
the same parts, the lips of another person. ("It is a pity that I cannot kiss
myself," might be attributed to him.)

Not all children suck their thumbs. It may be assumed that it is found
only in children in whom the erogenous significance of the lip-zone is con-
stitutionally reinforced. If the latter is retained in some children, they develop into kissing epicures with a tendency to perverse kissing, or, as men,
they show a strong desire for drinking and smoking. But should repression
come into play, they then show disgust for eating and evince hysterical

vomiting. By virtue of the community of the lip-zone, the repression encroaches upon the instinct of nourishment. Many of my female patients showing disturbances in eating, such as *hysterical globus*, choking sensations and vomiting, have been energetic thumbsuckers in infancy.

In thumbsucking or pleasure-sucking, we are already able to observe the three essential characters of an infantile sexual manifestation. It has its origin in an *anaclitic* [from the verb, *anaclino*, leaning on] relation to a physical function which is very important for life; it does not yet know any sexual object, that is, it is *autoerotic*, and its sexual aim is under the control of an *erogenous zone*. Let us assume for the present that these characteristics also hold true for most of the other activities of the infantile sexual instinct.

The Sexual Aim of the Infantile Sexuality

Characteristic Erogenous Zones. From the example of thumbsucking, we may gather a great many points useful for distinguishing an erogenous zone. It is a portion of skin or mucous membrane in which stimuli produce a feeling of pleasure of definite quality. There is no doubt that the pleasure-producing stimuli are governed by special conditions; as yet we do not know them. The rhythmic characters must play some part and this strongly suggests an analogy to tickling. It does not, however, appear so certain whether the character of the pleasurable feelings evoked by the stimulus can be designated as "peculiar," and in what part of this peculiarity the sexual factor consists. Psychology is still groping in the dark when it concerns matters of pleasure and pain, and the most cautious assumption is therefore the most advisable. We may perhaps later come upon reasons which seem to support the peculiar quality of the sensation of pleasure.

The erogenous quality may adhere most notably to definite regions of the body. As is shown by the example of thumbsucking, there are predestined erogenous zones. But the same example also shows that any other region of skin or mucous membrane may assume the function of an erogenous zone, hence it must bring along a certain adaptability for it. The production of the sensation of pleasure therefore depends more on the quality of the stimulus than on the nature of the bodily region. The thumbsucking child looks around on his body and selects any portion of it for pleasure-sucking, and becoming accustomed to this particular part, he then prefers it. If he accidentally strikes upon a predestined region, such as breast, nipple or genitals, it naturally gets the preference. A very analogous tendency to displacement is again found in the symptomatology of hysteria. In this neurosis the repression mostly affects the genital zones proper, and they in turn transmit their excitability to the other zones which are usually dormant in adult life, but then behave exactly like genitals. But besides this, just as in thumbsucking, any other region of the body may become endowed with the excitation of the genitals and raised to an erogenous zone. Erogenous and hysterogenous zones show the same characters.

The Infantile Sexual Aim. The sexual aim of the infantile impulse consists in the production of gratification through the proper excitation of this or that selected erogenous zone. To have a desire for its repetition, this gratification must have been previously experienced, and we may be sure that nature has devised definite means so as not to leave this experience of gratification to mere chance. The arrangement which has fulfilled this purpose for the lip-zone, we have already discussed; it is the simultaneous connection of this part of the body with the taking of nourishment. We shall also meet other similar mechanisms as sources of sexuality. The state of desire for repetition of gratification can be recognized through a peculiar feeling of tension which in itself is rather of a painful character, and through a *centrally-conditioned* feeling of itching or sensitiveness which is projected into the peripheral erogenous zone. The sexual aim may therefore be formulated by stating that the main object is to substitute for the projected feeling of sensitiveness in the erogenous zone that outer stimulus which removes the feeling of sensitiveness by evoking the feeling of gratification. This external stimulus consists usually in a manipulation which is analogous to sucking.

It is in full accord with our physiological knowledge, if the need happens to be awakened also peripherally, through an actual change in the erogenous zone. The action is puzzling only to some extent, as one stimulus seems to want another applied to the same place for its own abrogation.

The Masturbatic Sexual Manifestations ESTATIONS

It is a matter of great satisfaction to know that there is nothing further of great importance to learn about the sexual activity of the child, after the impulse of one erogenous zone has become comprehensible to us. The most pronounced differences are found in the action necessary for the gratification, which consists in sucking for the lip-zone, and which must be replaced by other muscular actions in the other zones, depending on their situation and nature.

The Activity of the Anal Zone. Like the lip-zone, the anal zone is, through its position, adapted to produce an anaclisis of sexuality to other functions of the body. It should be assumed that the erogenous significance of this region of the body was originally very strong. Through psychoanalysis one finds, not without surprise, the many transformations that normally take place in the sexual excitations *emanating* from here, and that this zone often retains for life a considerable fragment of genital irritability. The intestinal catarrhs which occur quite frequently during infancy produce sensitive irritations in this zone, and we often hear it said that intestinal catarrh at this delicate age causes "nervousness." In later neurotic diseases, they exert a definite influence on the symptomatic expression of the neurosis, placing at its disposal the whole sum of intestinal disturbances. Considering the erogenous significance of the anal zone which has been retained at least in transformation, one should not laugh at the hemorrhoidal influences to which the old medical literature attached so much weight in the explanation of neurotic states.

Children utilizing the erogenous sensitiveness of the anal zone can be recognized by their holding back of fecal masses until through accumulation there result violent muscular contractions; the passage of these masses through the anus is apt to produce a marked irritation of the mucous membranes. Besides the pain, this must also produce a sensation of pleasure. One of the surest premonitions of later eccentricity or nervousness is when an infant obstinately refuses to empty his bowel when placed on the chamber pot by the nurse, and controls this function at his own pleasure. It naturally does not concern him that he will soil his bed; all he cares for is not to lose the subsidiary pleasure in defecating. Educators have again shown the right inkling when they designate children who withhold these functions as naughty.

The content of the bowel which acts as a stimulus to the sexually sensitive surface of mucous membrane, behaves like the precursor of another organ which does not become active until after the phase of childhood. In addition, it has other important meanings to the nursling. It is evidently treated as an additional part of the body; it represents the first "donation," the disposal of which expresses the pliability while the retention of it can express the spite of the little being towards his environment. From the idea of "donation," he later derives the meaning of the "babe," which according to one of the infantile sexual theories is supposed to be acquired through eating, and born through the bowel.

The retention of fecal masses, which is at first intentional in order to utilize them, as it were, for masturbatic excitation of the anal zone, is at least one of the roots of constipation so frequent in neurotics. The whole significance of the anal zone is mirrored in the fact that there are but few neurotics who have not their special scatologic customs, ceremonies, etc., which they retain with cautious secrecy.

Real masturbatic irritation of the anal zone by means of the fingers, evoked through either centrally or peripherally supported itching, is not at all rare in older children.

The Activity of the Genital Zone. Among the erogenous zones of the child's body, there is one which certainly does not play the first role, and which cannot be the carrier of the earliest sexual feeling, which, however, is destined for great things in later life. In both male and female, it is connected with the voiding of urine (penis, clitoris), and in the former it is enclosed in a sack of mucous membrane, probably in order not to miss the irritations caused by the secretions which may arouse sexual excitement at an early age. The sexual activities of this erogenous zone, which belongs to the real genitals, are the beginning of the later "normal" sexual life.

Owing to the anatomical position, the overflowing of secretions, the washing and rubbing of the body, and to certain accidental excitements (the wandering of intestinal worms in the girl), it happens that the pleasurable feeling which these parts of the body are capable of producing makes itself noticeable to the child, even during the sucking age, and thus awakens a desire for repetition. When we consider the sum of all these arrangements and bear in mind that the measures for cleanliness hardly produce a different result than uncleanliness, we can scarcely ignore the fact that the infantile masturbation, from which hardly anyone escapes, forms the foundation for the future primacy of this erogenous zone for sexual activity. The action of removing the stimulus and setting free the gratification consists in a rubbing contiguity with the hand or in a certain previously formed pressure reflex, effected by the closure of the thighs. The latter procedure seems to be the more common in girls. The preference for the hand in boys already indicates what an important part of the male sexual activity will be accomplished in the future by the mastery impulse (Bemaechtigungstrieb).

In his Autobiographical Study (1925) Freud gives the following account of his method of psychoanalytic therapy based as it is on overcoming the patient's resistances to facing unconscious material and on the handling of the transference relationships:

The means which I first adopted for overcoming the patient's resistance, by pressing and encouraging him, had been indispensable for the purpose of giving me a first general survey of what was to be expected. But in the long run it proved to be too much of a strain upon both sides, and further it seemed open to certain obvious criticisms. It therefore gave place to another method which was in one sense its opposite. Instead of urging the patient to say something upon some particular subject, I now asked him to abandon himself to a process of *free association*, i.e., to say whatever came into his head, while ceasing to give any conscious direction to his thoughts. It was essential, however, that he should bind himself to report literally everything that occurred to his self-perception and not to give way to critical objections which sought to put certain associations on one side on the ground that they were not sufficiently important or that they were irrelevant or that they were altogether meaningless. There was no necessity to repeat explicitly the insistence upon the need for candour on the patient's part in reporting his thoughts, for it was the precondition of the whole analytic treatment.

It may seem surprising that this method of free association, carried out subject to the observation of the *fundamental rule of psychoanalysis*, should have achieved what was expected of it, namely the bringing into consciousness of the repressed material which was held back by resistances. We must, however, bear in mind that free association is not really free. The patient remains under the influence of the analytic situation even though he is not directing his mental activity on to a particular subject. We shall be justified in assuming that nothing will occur to him that has not some reference to that situation. His resistance against reproducing the repressed material will now be expressed in two ways. Firstly it will be shown by critical objections; and it was to deal with these that the fundamental rule of psychoanalysis was invented. But if the patient observes that rule and so overcomes his reticences, the resistance will find another means of expression. It will so arrange it that the repressed material itself will never occur to the patient but only something which approximates to it in an allusive way; and the greater the resistance, the more remote will be the substitutive association which the patient has to report from the actual idea that the analyst is in search of. The analyst, who listens composedly but without any constrained effort to the stream of associations and who, from his experience, has a general notion of what to expect, can make use of the material brought to light by the patient according to two possibilities. If the resistance is slight he will be able from the patient's allusions to infer the unconscious material itself; or if the resistance is stronger he will be able to recognize its character from the associations as they seem to become more remote from the subject, and will explain it to the patient. Uncovering the resistance, however, is the first step towards overcoming it. Thus the work of analysis involves an *art of interpretation*, the successful handling of which may require tact and practice but which is not hard to acquire. But it is only in the saving of labour that the method of free association has an advantage over the earlier method. It exposes the patient to the least possible amount of compulsion, it never allows of contact being lost with the actual current situation, it guarantees to a great extent that no factor in the structure of the neurosis will be overlooked and that nothing will be introduced into it by the expectations of the analyst. It is left to the patient in all essentials to determine the course of the analysis and the arrangement of the material; any systematic handling of particular symptoms or complexes thus becomes impossible. In complete contrast to what happened with hypnotism and with the urging method, interrelated material makes its appearance at different times and at different points in the treatment. To a spectator, therefore—though in fact there can be none—an analytic treatment would seem completely obscure.

Another advantage of the method is that it need never break down. It must theoretically always be possible to have an association, provided that no conditions are made as to its character. Yet there is one case in which in fact a breakdown occurs with absolute regularity; from its very uniqueness, however, this case too can be interpreted.

I now come to the description of a factor which adds an essential feature to my picture of analysis and which can claim, alike technically and theoretically, to be regarded as of the first importance. In every analytic treatment there arises, without the physician's agency, an intense emotional relationship between the patient and the analyst which is not to be accounted for by the actual situation. It can be of a positive or of a negative character and can vary between the extremes of a passionate, completely sensual love and the unbridled expression of an embittered defiance and hatred. This *transference*—to give it its shortened name—soon replaces in the patient's mind the desire to be cured, and so long as it is affectionate and moderate, becomes the agent of the physician's influence and neither more nor less than the mainspring of the joint work of analysis. Later on, when it has become passionate or has been converted into hostility, it becomes the principal tool of the resistance. It may then happen that it will paralyze the patient's powers of associating and endanger the success of the treatment. Yet it would be senseless to try to evade it; for the analysis without transference is an impossibility. It must not be supposed, however, that transference is created by analysis and does not occur apart from it. Transference is merely uncovered and isolated by analysis. It is a universal phenomenon of the human mind; it decides the success of all medical influence, and in fact dominates the whole of each person's relations to his human environment. We can easily recognize it as the same dynamic factor that the hypnotists have named "suggestibility," which is the agent of hypnotic *rapport* and whose incalculable behaviour led to such difficulties with the cathartic method. When there is no inclination to a transference of emotion such as this, or when it has become entirely negative, as happens in dementia praecox or paranoia, then there is also no possibility of influencing the patient by psychological means.

It is perfectly true that psychoanalysis, like other psychotherapeutic methods, employs the instrument of suggestion (or transference). But the difference is this: that in analysis it is not allowed to play the decisive part in determining the therapeutic results. It is used instead to induce the patient to perform a piece of mental work—the overcoming of his transference-resistances—which involves a permanent alteration in his mental economy. The transference is made conscious to the patient by the analyst, and it is resolved by convincing him that in his transference-attitude he is *re-experiencing* emotional relations which had their origin in his earliest object-attachments during the repressed period of his childhood. In this way the transference is changed from the strongest weapon of the resistance into the best instrument of the analytic treatment. Nevertheless, its handling remains the most difficult as well as the most important part of the technique of analysis.

Freud's letters, especially those written to his friend, Wilhelm Fliess, give a fascinating insight into the inner workshop of genius. They reveal his hopes, his doubts, his remorseless self-criticism. Some of them contain fragments of his self-analysis which in effect paved the way for most of his discoveries. A letter written by a struggling young physician, aged 39, unknown beyond a small circle of friends, but "certain that the core of the matter"—the problem of neuroses—was within his grasp, reads as follows:

(25.5.1895)

Dear Wilhelm,

I have had an inhuman amount to do, and after ten or eleven hours with patients I have been incapable of picking up a pen to write you even a short letter, though I had a great deal to tell you. But the chief reason was this: a man like me cannot live without a hobby-horse, a consuming passion—in Schiller's words, a tyrant. I have found my tyrant, and in his service I know no limits. My tyrant is psychology; it has always been my distant, beckoning goal and now, since I have hit on the neuroses, it has come so much the nearer. I am plagued with two ambitions: to see how the theory of mental functioning takes shape if quantitative considerations, a sort of economics of nerve-force, are introduced into it; and secondly, to extract from psychopathology what may be of benefit to normal psychology. Actually a satisfactory general theory of neuropsychotic disturbances is impossible if it cannot be brought into association with clear assumptions about normal mental processes. During recent weeks I have devoted every free minute to such work; the hours of the night from eleven to two have been occupied with imaginings, transpositions, and guesses, only abandoned when I arrived at some absurdity or had so truly and seriously overworked that I had no interest left for the day's medical work. . . . I get great satisfaction from the work on neuroses in my practice. Nearly everything is confirmed daily, new pieces are added, and it is a fine thing to feel certain that the core of the matter is within one's grasp. . . .

Your Sigm.

Freud was an indefatigable letter writer. His early letters to his fiance, his later correspondence with Fliess, with Binswanger, with Thomas Mann are invaluable human documents. The Freud-Jung letters in particular, published in 1974, throw more light on their stormy relationship: from its idyllic onset, through the years of fruitful cooperation, to their tragic break.

Freud died in London in 1939, an exile from Vienna, the city of his early struggles and setbacks and of the subsequent triumphs which carried his fame all over the civilized world. In fact, it was his exile and the dispersal of most of his followers to the English-speaking countries which greatly contributed to the world-wide success of the psychoanalytic movement.

Yet this success has by no means brought to an end the opposition to so-called Freudian analysis either without or within the psychoanalytic camp. Academic psychology and psychiatry—to say nothing of the Catholic Church—have for decades been critical of Freud's teachings. But so have a number of his closest associates. The controversy has led to various rival schools of psychoanalysis, some of whose members refuse even to be known as psychoanalysts and prefer to call themselves "individual psychologists," "analytic psychotherapists"—or simply psychotherapists.

However, despite the growing fragmentation of the Freudian patrimony and despite the inroads of behaviorist and biochemical shortcuts to psychiatric treatment, the basic principles of psychoanalysis have entered the mainstream of twentieth century thought. Like the basic theorems of Euclidian geometry, they are here to stay under terrestrial conditions, even though most people may no longer feel it necessary to acknowledge their indebtedness to his labors.

chapter 20

Adler's Individual Psychology

Alfred Adler (1870-1937) was the first of Freud's early associates to rebel against the master. Adler's rebellion was directed against the very heart of the psychoanalytic doctrine as it had evolved by the year 1911: it challenged Freud's thesis of sex as the prime mover of human behavior, and of sexual conflict as the prime cause of neurosis. Adler placed his main emphasis on the individual's innate urge to assert himself as a self-contained, independent being in his own right, and to compensate—and overcompensate—for any weaknesses that may exist in his physical or mental make-up. To Adler, the feeling of inferiority based on such weaknesses is at the root of every neurosis. Character is molded by the way in which a person seeks to overcome his inferiority feelings; neurosis from a faulty way of doing so. Freud's castration complex becomes just one example of inferiority feelings; the Oedipus complex, nothing but the pampered child's desperate attempt to hold on to and to control the parent of the opposite sex; and the manifestations of early infantile sexuality, special instances of how the child may be able to play upon the anxieties of an over-solicitous parent.

In Adler's view the unconscious is comparatively unimportant. He describes it as "that which was as yet unknown" to a person. Similarly, dreams reveal only little more than what has all the time been on the dreamer's mind: his quest for power and for the realization of his particular "style of life." The main themes running through Adler's Individual Psychology are thus in an unmistakably contrapuntal relationship to Freud's doctrine. It may well be that it was in part the sheer momentum of the younger man's rebellion against the older man that carried Adler further afield in his crusade for desexualizing psychoanalysis than would otherwise have been the case. Perhaps this clash of personalities and doctrines also helped to make psychoanalysis itself slow in allowing for what Adler described as the individual's quest for power and self-assertion. Psychoanalysis had dealt with this aspect of personality under the heading of ego functions but had originally paid more attention to the unconscious or the

Freudian id. It was Freud's daughter, Anna Freud, and his associates Wilhelm Reich, Otto Rank, Paul Federn, Heinz Hartman, Rudolf Loewenstein and others, who in effect broke the ice when they called for a more intensive study of the functions—and defenses—of the ego.

Recent years have seen the gradual loosening of the barriers between the two respective systems of thought. C. G. Jung has gone far to integrate Freudian and Adlerian ideas in his system, and Paul Schilder, Karen Horney, Erich Fromm and Harry Stack Sullivan have sought to reconcile Adler's "quest for power" with the original psychoanalytic doctrine. The new existentialist school of psychotherapy, which emerged during the post-war years in Europe, has adopted many of Adler's teachings while repudiating most of their remaining analytic implications.

This selection is from Alfred Adler's book What Life Should Mean To You, *published in 1931.*

Since the meaning given to life works out as if it were the guardian angel or pursuing demon of our careers, it is very clearly of the highest importance that we should understand how these meanings come to be formed, how they differ from one another, and how they can be corrected if they involve big mistakes. This is the province of psychology, as distinct from physiology or biology—the use for human welfare of an understanding of meanings and the way in which they influence human actions and human fortunes. From the first days of childhood we can see dark gropings after this "meaning of life." Even a baby is striving to make an estimate of its own powers and its share in the whole life which surrounds it. By the end of the fifth year of life a child has reached a unified and crystallized pattern of behavior, its own style of approach to problems and tasks. It has already fixed its deepest and most lasting conception of what to expect from the world and from itself. From now on, the world is seen through a stable scheme of apperception: experiences are interpreted before they are accepted, and the interpretation always accords with the original meaning given to life. Even if this meaning is very gravely mistaken, even if the approach to our problems and tasks brings us continually into misfortunes and agonies, it is never easily relinquished. Mistakes in the meaning given to life can be corrected only by reconsidering the situation in which the faulty interpretation was made, recognizing the error and revising the scheme of apperception. In rare circumstances, perhaps, an individual may be forced by the consequences of a mistaken approach to revise the meaning he has given to life and may succeed in accomplishing the change by himself. He will never do it, however, without some social pressure, or without finding that if he proceeds with the old approach he is at the end of his tether: and for the most part the approach can best be revised with the assistance of some one trained in the understanding of these meanings, who can join in discovering the original error and help to suggest a more appropriate meaning.

Let us take a simple illustration of the different ways in which childhood situations may be interpreted. Unhappy experiences in childhood may be given quite opposite meanings. One man with unhappy experiences behind him will not dwell on them except as they show him something which can be remedied for the future. He will feel, "We must work to remove such unfortunate situations and make sure that our children are better placed." Another man will feel, "Life is unfair. Other people always have the best of it. If the world treated me like that, why should I treat the world any better?" It is in this way that some parents say of their children, "I had to suffer just as much when I was a child, and I came through it. Why shouldn't they?" A third man will feel, "Everything should be forgiven me because of my unhappy childhood." In the actions of all three men their interpretations will be evident; and they will never change their actions unless they change their interpretations. It is here that individual psychology breaks through the theory of determinism. No experience is a cause of success or failure. We do not suffer from the shock of our experiences—the so-called *trauma*—but we make out of them just what suits our purposes. We are *self-determined* by the meaning we give to our experiences; and there is probably something of a mistake always involved when we take particular experiences as the basis for our future life. Meanings are not determined by situations, but we determine ourselves by the meanings we give to situations.

There are, however, certain situations in childhood from which a gravely mistaken meaning is very frequently drawn. It is from children in these situations that the majority of failures come. First, we must take children with imperfect organs, suffering from diseases or infirmities during their infancy. Such children are overburdened, and it will be difficult for them to feel that the meaning of life is contribution. Unless there is some one near them who can draw their attention away from themselves and interest them in others, they are likely to occupy themselves mainly with their own sensations. Later on, they may become discouraged by comparing themselves with those around them, and it may even happen, in our present civilization, that their feelings of inferiority are stressed by the pity, ridicule or avoidance of their fellows. These are all circumstances in which they may turn in upon themselves, lose hope of playing a useful part in our common life, and consider themselves personally humiliated by the world.

I was the first person, I think, to describe the difficulties that confront a child whose organs are imperfect or whose glandular secretions are abnormal. This branch of science has made extraordinary progress, but hardly along the lines in which I should have liked to see it develop. From the beginning I was seeking a method of overcoming these difficulties, and not a ground for throwing the responsibility for failure upon heredity or physical condition. No imperfection of organs compels a mistaken style of life. We never find two children whose glands have the same effects on them. We can often see children who overcome these difficulties and who, in overcoming them, develop unusual faculties for usefulness. In this way Individual Psychology is not a very good advertisement for schemes of eugenic selection. Many of the most eminent men, men who made great contributions to our culture, began with imperfect organs; often their health was poor and sometimes they died early. It is mainly from those people who struggled hard against difficulties, in body as in outer circumstances, that advances and new contributions have come. The struggle strengthened them and they went further ahead. From the body we cannot judge whether the development of the mind will be bad or good. Hitherto, however, the greatest part of children who started with imperfect organs and imperfect glands have not been trained in the right direction; their difficulties have not been understood and they have mainly become interested in their own persons. It is for this reason that we find such a great number of failures amongst those children whose early years were burdened with imperfect organs.

The second type of situation which often provides the occasion for a mistake in the meaning given to life is the situation of the pampered child. The pampered child is trained to expect that his wishes will be treated as laws. He is granted prominence without working to deserve it and he will generally come to feel this prominence as a birthright. In consequence, when he comes into circumstances where he is not the center of attention and where other people do not make it their chief aim to consider his feelings, he will be very much at a loss: he will feel that his world has failed him. He has been trained to expect and not to give. He has never learned any other way of facing problems. Others have been so subservient to him that he has lost his independence and does not know that he can do things for himself. His interest was devoted to himself and he never learned the use and the necessity of cooperation. When he has difficulties before him, he has only one method of meeting them—to make demands on other people. It seems to him that if he can regain his position of prominence, if he can force others to recognize that he is a special person and should be granted everything he wants, then and then only will his situation improve.

These grown-up pampered children are perhaps the most dangerous class in our community. Some of them may make great protestations of good will; they may even become very "lovable" in order to secure an opportunity to tyrannize; but they are on strike against cooperating, as ordinary human beings, in our ordinary human tasks. There are others who are in more open revolt: when they no longer find the easy warmth and subordination to which they were accustomed, they feel betrayed; they consider society as hostile to themselves and try to revenge themselves upon all their fellows. And if society shows hostility to their way of living (as it almost undoubtedly will) they take this hostility as a new proof that they are *personally* ill-treated. This is the reason why punishments are always ineffective; they can do nothing but confirm the opinion, "Others are against me." But whether the spoiled child goes on strike or openly revolts, whether he tries to dominate by weakness or to revenge himself by violence, he is in fact making much the same mistake. We find people, indeed, who try both methods at different times. Their goal remains unaltered. They feel, "Life means—to be the first, to be recognized as the most important, to get everything I want," and so long as they continue to give this meaning to life, every method they adopt will be mistaken.

The third situation in which a mistake can easily be made is the situation of a neglected child. Such a child has never known what love and cooperation can be: he makes up an interpretation of life which does not include these friendly forces. It will be understood that when he faces the problems of life he will overrate their difficulty and underrate his own capacity to meet them with the aid and good will of others. He has found society cold to him and he will expect it always to be cold. Especially he will not see that he can *win* affection and esteem by actions which are useful to others. He will thus be suspicious of others and unable to trust himself. There is really no experience which can take the place of disinterested affection. The first task of a mother is to give her child the experience of a trustworthy other person: later she must widen and enlarge this feeling of trust until it includes the rest of the child's environment. If she has failed in the first task—to gain the child's interest, affection and cooperation—it will be very difficult for the child to develop social interest and comradely feeling towards his fellows. Everybody has the capacity to be interested in others; but this capacity must be trained and exercised or its development will be frustrated.

If there were a pure type of neglected or hated or unwanted child we should probably find that he was just blind to the existence of cooperation; that he was isolated, unable to communicate with others and completely ignorant of everything that would help him to live in association with human beings. But, as we have already seen, an individual in these circumstances would perish. The fact that a child lives through the period of infancy is proof that he has been given some care and attention. We are therefore never dealing with pure types of neglected children: we are dealing with those who had less than usual consideration, or who were neglected in some respects, though not in others. In short, we need only say that the neglected child is one who never quite found a trustworthy other person. It is a very sad comment on our civilization that so many failures in life come from those children who were orphans or illegitimate; and that we must group such children, on the whole, amongst the neglected children.

These three situations—imperfect organs, pampering, and neglect—are a great challenge to give a mistaken meaning to life; and children from these situations will almost always need help in revising their approach to problems. They must be helped to a better meaning. If we have an eye for such things—which really means, if we have a true interest in them and have trained ourselves in this direction—we shall be able to see their meaning in everything they do. Dreams and associations may prove useful: the personality is the same in dreaming life as in waking life, but in dreams the pressure of social demands is less acute and the personality will be revealed with fewer safeguards and concealments. The greatest of all helps, however, in gaining a quick comprehension of the meaning an individual gives to himself and to life comes through his memories. Every memory, however trivial he may think it, represents to him something *memorable*. It is memorable because of its bearing on life as he pictures it; it says to him, "This is what you must expect," or "This is what you must avoid," or "Such is life!" Again we must stress that the experience itself is not so important as the fact that just this experience persists in memory and is used to crystallize the meaning given to life. Every memory is a memento.

The memories of early childhood are especially useful in showing how long standing is the individual's own peculiar approach to life, and in giving the circumstances in which he first crystallized his life-attitude. For two reasons the earliest memory of all has a very notable place. First, the fundamental estimate of the individual and his situation is contained in it; it is his first totalling-up of appearances, his first more or less complete symbol of himself and the demands made of him. Secondly, it is his subjective starting point, the beginning of the autobiography he has made up for himself. We can often find in it, therefore, the contrast between a position of weakness and inadequacy in which he felt himself and the goal of strength and security which he regards as his ideal. It is indifferent for the purposes of psychology whether the memory which an individual considers as first is really the first event which he can remember—or even whether it is a memory of a real event. Memories are important only for what they are "taken as"; for their interpretation and for their bearing on present and future life. . . .

What is new in the outlook of Individual Psychology is our observation that the feelings are never in contradiction to the style of life. Where there is a goal, the feelings always adapt themselves to its attainment. We are no longer, therefore, in the realm of physiology or biology; the rise of feelings cannot be explained by chemical theory and cannot be predicted by chemical examination. In Individual Psychology we must presuppose the physiological goal. It is not so much our concern that anxiety influences the sympathetic and parasympathetic nerves. We look, rather, for the purpose and end of anxiety.

With this approach anxiety cannot be taken as rising from the supression of sexuality, or as being left behind as the result of disastrous birth-experiences. Such explanations are beside the mark. We know that a child who is accustomed to be accompanied, helped and supported by its mother may find anxiety—whatever its source—a very efficient weapon for controlling its mother. We are not satisfied with a physical description of anger; our experience has shown us that anger is a device to dominate a person or a situation. We can take it for granted that every bodily and mental expression must be based on inherited material; but our attention is directed to the use which is made of this material in striving to achieve a definite goal. This, it seems, is the only real psychological approach.

In every individual we see that feelings have grown and developed in the direction and to the degree which were essential to the attainment of his goal. His anxiety or courage, cheerfulness or sadness, have always agreed with his style of life: their proportionate strength and dominance has been exactly what we could expect. A man who accomplishes his goal of superiority by sadness cannot be gay and satisfied with his accomplishments. He can only be happy when he is miserable. We can notice also that feelings appear and disappear at need. A patient suffering from agoraphobia loses the feeling of anxiety when he is at home or when he is dominating another person. All neurotic patients exclude every part of life in which they do not feel strong enough to be the conqueror.

The emotional tone is as fixed as the style of life. The coward, for example, is always a coward, even though he is arrogant with weaker people or seems courageous when he is shielded by others. He may fix three locks on his door, protect himself with police dogs and mantraps and insist that he is full of courage. Nobody will be able to prove his feeling of anxiety; but the cowardice of his character is shown sufficiently by the trouble he has taken to protect himself.

The realm of sexuality and love gives a similar testimony. The feelings belonging to sex always appear when an individual desires to approach his sexual goal. By concentration, he tends to exclude conflicting tasks and incompatible interests; and thus he evokes the appropriate feelings and functions. The lack of these feelings and functions—as in impotence, premature ejaculation, perversion and frigidity—is established by refusing to exclude inappropriate tasks and interests. Such abnormalities are always induced by a mistaken goal of superiority and a mistaken style of life. We always find in such cases a tendency to expect consideration rather than to give it, a lack of social feeling, and a failure in courage and optimistic activity. . . .

Feelings of Inferiority and Superiority

The "inferiority complex," one of the most important discoveries of Individual Psychology, seems to have become world-famous. Psychologists
of many schools have adopted the term and use it in their own practice. I
am not at all sure, however, that they understand it or use it with the right
meaning. It never helps us, for example, to tell a patient that he is suffering
from an inferiority complex; to do so would only stress his feelings of inferiority without showing him how to overcome them. We must recognize
the specific discouragement which he shows in his style of life; we must encourage him at the precise point where he falls short in courage. Every neurotic has an inferiority complex. No neurotic is distinguished from other
neurotics by the fact that he has an inferiority complex and the others have
none. He is distinguished from the others by the kind of situation in which
he feels unable to continue on the useful side of life; by the limits he has put
to his strivings and activities. It would no more help him to be more courageous if we said to him, "You are suffering from an inferiority complex,"
than it would help some one with a headache if we said, "I can tell you what
is wrong with you. You have a headache!" . . .

The so-called Oedipus Complex is in reality nothing more than a special
instance of the "narrow stable" of the neurotic. If an individual is afraid to
meet the problem of love in the world at large, he will not succeed in ridding
himself of this problem. If he confines his field of action to the family circle,
it will not surprise us to find that his sexual strivings also are elaborated
within these limits. From his feeling of insecurity he has never spread his interest outside the few people with whom he is most familiar. He fears that
with others he would not be able to dominate in his accustomed way. The
victims of the Oedipus Complex are children who were pampered by their
mothers, who were trained to believe that their wishes carried with them a
right to fulfillment, and who never say that they could win affection and
love by their independent efforts outside the bounds of the home. In adult
life they remain tied to their mothers' apron strings. In love they look, not
for an equal partner, but for a servant; and the servant of whose support
they are surest is their mother. We could probably induce an Oedipus Complex in any child. All we should need is for its mother to spoil it, and refuse
to spread its interest to other people, and for its father to be comparatively
indifferent or cold. . . .

Adler was more concerned with the ripples caused by the contending
forces and tensions on the psychic surface of the individual and his society
than with trying to gauge the currents and eddies swirling in the depth of the
mind. But he was keenly aware of the hidden meaning of a wide variety of

security operations and subtle maneuvering for power which form the woof and warp of the social fabric. Yet his playing down of sexual matters tended to blunt the revolutionary impact of his approach and made it appear drab and lackluster in comparison with Freud's.

Nevertheless, many sociologists, psychologists, and educators found this expurgated version of psychoanalysis more congenial. Others felt Adler's emphasis on the purposeful, teleological nature of human conduct more to their liking, and preferred its philosophical implications to Freud's causal reductive thinking. They include C. G. Jung, Erich Fromm, Karen Horney, Eric Erikson, H. S. Sullivan, and a number of transactional and existential analysts. Yet Adler had more borrowers who helped themselves to the rich store of his insights than followers prepared to identify with his cause.

chapter 21

Focus on Culture and Interpersonal Relationships

H. S. SULLIVAN, E. FROMM,
K. HORNEY, AND H. KELMAN

The importance of Freud's contribution to the field of mental healing can be gauged from the fact that the teachings of some of the dissenting schools of psychoanalysis look like so many segments lifted from the broad spectrum of his system of thought. They seem to focus attention on one particular aspect of the human mind, while paying less attention to the others. It may well be that twenty-five hundred years from now they will all be lumped together under the heading "Freudian Writings," as it happened to what is now known as the Hippocratic Collection.

But at the present juncture, the work of such pioneers of psychoanalysis as Alfred Adler, Sándor Ferenczi, Wilhelm Stekel, Otto Rank, Karen Horney, Franz Alexander, Karl Menninger, Ernest Jones, Edward Glover, Melanie Klein and many others is outstanding enough to justify their occupying a separate niche in the psychoanalytic Hall of Fame. Still, this anthology must be satisfied with a few representative samples from the wealth of contributions made by both followers and dissenters who came in the wake of Sigmund Freud.

We have seen how one of Alfred Adler's major objections to Freud was his overemphasis on sexual factors. But a younger generation of psychoanalysts found further shortcomings in the orthodox Freudian position. Viewing the personality of Freud himself against his cultural and socio-economic background, they felt that this had unduly colored, if not distorted, his concept of man. Man, they argued, cannot be studied in isolation from his culture. Freud's overemphasis on sex may thus have been largely due to the repressive attitude of the Victorian and Francisco-Josephinian era toward such matters. Some of his generalizations were therefore true for his time and for his society, but not for another.

Recent years have brought an increasing awareness of cultural problems to the practicing psychotherapist, especially when he himself has been subjected to the experience of emigration and to the need to adjust himself to a new culture.

Harry Stack Sullivan (1892-1949) is one of the leading figures of the culturalist school of psychoanalysis. He shares with Horney and Fromm his emphasis on cultural factors and the part played by interpersonal relationships. But by contrast to Fromm he is inclined to lay much less stress on the individual set apart from his social environment and his culture. Sullivan is known as the founder of the Washington School of psychiatry. He was the son of a farmer of Irish descent, brought up in unhappy family conditions and has been described as a withdrawn and lonely child. A disciple of Adolph Meyer and William Alanson White, he deviated in many ways from orthodox analysts. His contribution to modern dynamic psychiatry, especially to the treatment of psychotics, have gained wide recognition in this country and abroad.

Psychiatry, according to Sullivan, is the study of interpersonal relationships by what he calls the psychiatrist's "participant observation." The psychoanalytic approach, he asserts, focuses attention on the individual and his drives or instincts and only in the second place on his interaction with his fellow men. Sullivan shifts his focus to communication, interaction, interpersonal relationships and other aspects of social psychology. He does so to such an extent that he has, according to his critics, at times lost sight of personality itself. In effect, Sullivan sees in personality nothing but the "enduring pattern" of social interactions. To him the self is made up of "reflected appraisals" brought to bear on the child by parent figures and other significant adults. An excess of "depreciatory" attitudes on their part results in similar attitudes of the child toward himself as well as toward others. It is one of the major sources of anxiety. Conversely, loving attitudes communicated to him by emotional contagion or empathy make the child capable of love, fellowship and good social adjustment in general.

Needless to say, Sullivan does not deny the importance of biological factors. He recognizes the part played by the bodily organization of man. It supplies the driving forces in his quest for satisfaction. The other major factor in man's mental functioning is what Sullivan describes as the maintenance of security. It is this pursuit which is responsible for his adjustment to culture and society.

Despite major divergencies, Sullivan has thus incorporated two principles of psychoanalysis and Individual Psychology into his system of thought: the principle of gratification of instinctual needs, usually attributed to Freud; and the principle of self-assertion and other security operations, usually attributed to Adler. But his emphasis on interpersonal relationships, on cultural and sociological aspects is largely his own.

This selection is from Sullivan's book Conception of Modern Psychiatry, *first published in 1940.*

Psychiatry is the study of processes that involve or go on between people. The field of psychiatry is the field of interpersonal relations, under any and all circumstances in which these relations exist. It was seen that *a personality* can never be isolated from the complex of interpersonal relations in which the person lives and has his being. . . .

Human performances, the subject of our study, including revery processes and thought, are susceptible of a two-part classification which is based on the end states, the end conditions toward which these processes are obviously moving, or which our provision has reached. In other words, now and then you set out to start for somewhere. You preview the steps which will be necessary to get there and we can foresee the whole process on the basis of your reaching that place.

The most general basis on which interpersonal phenomena, interpersonal acts, may be classified, is one which separates the sought end states into the group which we call satisfactions and those which we call security or the maintenance of security. Satisfactions in this specialized sense are all those end states which are rather closely connected with the bodily organization of man. Thus the desire for food and drink leads to certain performances which are in this category. The desire for sleep leads to such performances. The state of being which is marked by the presence of lust is in this group; and finally, as the most middling example, the state of being which we call loneliness. All these states lead to activity which is the pursuit of satisfaction.

On the other hand, the pursuit of security pertains rather more closely to man's cultural equipment than to his bodily organization. By "cultural" I mean what the anthropologist means—all that which is man-made, which survives as monument to preexistent man, that is the cultural. And as I say, all those movements, actions, speech, thoughts, reveries and so on which pertain more to the culture which has been imbedded in a particular individual than to the organization of his tissues and glands, is apt to belong in this classification of the pursuit of security.

The thing which many people if they were quite honest with themselves would say that they were after when they are showing a process of this type is prestige, and one of my long-acquainted colleagues, Harold D. Lasswell, a political scientist, worked out a statement for this field in three terms: security, income, and deference. All these pertain to the culture, to the social institutions, traditions, customs, and the like, under which we live, to our social order rather than to the peculiar properties of our bodily or somatic organizations.

This second class, the pursuit of security, may be regarded as consisting of ubiquitous artifacts—again in the anthropological sense, man-made— evolved by the cultural conditioning or training; that is, education of the impulses or drives which underlie the first class. In other words, given our biological equipment—we are bound to need food and water and so on— certain conditioning influences can be brought to bear on the needs for satisfaction. And the cultural conditioning gives rise to the second group, the second great class of interpersonal phenomena, the pursuit of security.

To follow this line of thought profitably, however, one must look closely at this conception of conditioning, and one must consider especially the states characterized by the feeling of ability or power. This is ordinarily much more important in the human being than are the impulses resulting from a feeling of hunger, or thirst, and the fully developed feeling of lust comes so very late in biological maturation that it is scarcely a good source for conditioning.

We seem to be born, however, with something of this power motive in us. An oft-told story beautifully illustrates the early appearance of what I am discussing as the motive toward the manifestation of power or ability. The infant seeing for the first time the full moon, reaches for it. Nothing transpires. He utters a few goos and nothing transpires; then he starts to cry in rage, and the whole household is upset. But he does not get the moon, and the moon becomes 'marked' unattainable.

This is an instance of the frustration of the manifestation of power; one has failed at something which you might say one expects oneself to be able to achieve—not that the infant does much thinking, but the course of events indicates the application of increasingly complex techniques in the effort to achieve the object.

The full development of personality along the lines of security is chiefly founded on the infant's discovery of his powerlessness to achieve certain desired end states with the tools, the instrumentalities, which are at his disposal. From the disappointments in the very early stages of life outside the womb—in which all things were given—comes the beginning of this vast development of actions, thoughts, foresights, and so on, which are calculated to protect one from a feeling of insecurity and helplessness in the situation which confronts one. This accultural evolution begins thus, and when it succeeds, when one evolves successfully along this line, then one respects oneself, and as one respects oneself so one can respect others. That is one of the peculiarities of human personality that can always be depended on. If there is a valid and real attitude toward the self, that attitude will manifest as valid and real toward others. It is not that as ye judge so shall ye be judged, but as you judge yourself so shall you judge others; strange but true so far as I know, and with no exception.

The infant has as perhaps his mightiest tool the cry. The cry is a performance of the oral apparatus, the lips, mouth, throat, cheeks, vocal cords, intercostal muscles, and diaphragm. From this cry is evolved a great collection of most powerful tools which man uses in the development of his security with his fellow man. I refer to language behavior, operations including words.

Originally the infant's magical tool for all sorts of purposes, all too many of us still use vocal behavior as our principal adaptive device; and while none of you, of course, would do this, you must all know some people who can do in words practically anything and who have a curious faith that having said the right thing, all else is forgiven them. In other words, they are a little more like the infant than we are; they figure that a series of articulate noises turns any trick. We have, of course, learned that many other acts, performances, and foresights are necessary for success in living. None the less, denied our language behavior and the implicit revery processes that reach their final formulations in words, we would be terribly reduced in our competence and materially diminished in our security in dealing with other people.

At this point, I wish to say that if this series of lectures is to be reasonably successful, it will finally have demonstrated that there is nothing unique in the phenomena of the gravest functional illness. The most peculiar behavior of the acutely schizophrenic patient, I hope to demonstrate, is made up of interpersonal processes with which each one of us is or historically has been familiar. Far the greater part of the performances, the interpersonal processes of the psychotic patient are exactly of a piece with processes which we manifest some time every twenty-four hours. Some of the psychotic performances seem very peculiar indeed, and, as I surmised in 1924, for the explanation and familiarization of these performances, we have to look to the interpersonal relations of the infant, to the first eighteen months or so of life after birth. In most general terms, we are all much more simply human than otherwise, be we happy and successful, contented and detached, miserable and mentally disordered, or whatever.

To return to the epoch of infancy, first let me state that this is the period of maturation, of experimentation, of empathic 'observation,' and of autistic invention in the realm of power. Two of these terms may need some explanation.

From birth it is demonstrable that the infant shows a curious relationship or connection with the significant adult, ordinarily the mother. If the mother, for example, hated the pregnancy and deplores the child, it is a pediatric commonplace that there are feeding difficulties, unending feeding difficulties, with the child. If a mother, otherwise deeply attached to the infant, is seriously disturbed by some intercurrent event around nursing time, is frightened by something or worried about something around the time of nursing, then on that occasion there will be feeding difficulty or the infant has indigestion. All in all we know that there is an emotional linkage between the infant and the significant adult.

Empathy is the term that we use to refer to the peculiar emotional linkage that subtends the relationship of the infant with other significant people—the mother or the nurse. Long before there are signs of any understanding of emotional expression, there is evidence of this emotional contagion or communion. This feature of the infant-mother configuration is of great importance for an understanding of the acculturation or cultural conditioning to which I have referred.

We do not know much about the fate of empathy in the developmental history of people in general. There are indications that it endures throughout life, at least in some people. There are few unmistakable instances of its function in most of us, however, in our later years; I find it convenient to assume that the time of its great importance is later infancy and early childhood—perhaps age six to twenty-seven months. So much for empathy.

The other strange term in our statement about the epoch of infancy is *autistic*, an adjective by which we indicate a primary, unsocialized, unacculturated state of symbol activity, and later states pertaining more to this primary condition than to the conspicuously effective consensually validated symbol activities of more mature personality. The meaning of the autistic will become clearer in my discussion of language.

We see our infant, then, expanding as a personality through the exercise of ability or power. We see him using the magic tool of the cry. We now see him acquiring another tool, which in turn also becomes magical. I refer here to his expression of satisfaction. It is biological for the infant when nourished to show certain expressive movements which we call the satisfaction-response, and it is probably biological for the parent concerned to be delighted to see these things. Due to the empathic linkage, this, the reaction of the parent to the satisfaction-response of the infant, communicates good feeling to the infant and thus he learns that this response has power. Actually, this may be taken to be the primitive root of human generosity, the satisfaction in giving satisfaction and pleasure: another thing learned by some people in infancy.

I shall pass infancy now, to return presently to one aspect of it. As soon as the infant has picked up a vocal trick, saying perhaps "ma" and getting a tremendous response from the significant adult, without any idea of precisely what has happened but catching on the second time it happens, as soon as the rudiments of language habits have appeared, we say that infancy as a state of personality development has ceased and that the young one has become a child.

Childhood includes a rapid acculturation, but not alone in the basic acquisition of language, which is itself an enormous cultural entity. By this I mean that in childhood the peculiar mindlessness of the infant which seems to be assumed by most parents passes off and they begin to regard the little one as in need of training, as being justifiably an object of education; and what they train the child in consists of select excerpts from the cultural heritage, from that surviving of past people, incorporated in the personality of the parent. This includes such things as habits of cleanliness—which are of extremely good repute in the Western culture—and a great many other things. And along with all this acculturation, toilet habits, eating habits, and so on and so forth, there proceeds the learning of the language as a tool for communication. . . .

Along with learning of language, the child is experiencing many restraints on the freedom which it had enjoyed up till now. Restraints have to be used in the teaching of some of the personal habits that the culture requires everyone should show, and from these restraints there comes the evolution of the self system—an extremely important part of the personality—with a brand-new tool, a tool so important that I must give you its technical name, which unhappily coincides with a word of common speech which may mean to you anything. I refer to *anxiety*.

With the appearance of the self system or the self-dynamism, the child picks up a new piece of equipment which we technically call anxiety. Of the very unpleasant experiences which the infant can have we may say that there are generically two, pain and fear. Now comes the third.

It is necessary in the modification of activity in the interest of power in interpersonal relations, including revery and elementary constructive revery—that is, thought—that one focus, as it were, one's interest into certain fields that work. It is in learning this process that the self is evolved and the instrumentality of anxiety comes into being.

As one proceeds into childhood, disapproval, dissatisfaction with one's performances becomes more and more the tool of the significant adult in educating the infant in the folk ways, the tradition, the culture in which he is expected to live. This disapproval is felt by the child through the same empathic linkage which has been so conspicuous in infancy. Gradually he comes to perceive disapproving expressions of the mother, let us say; gradually he comes to understand disapproving statements; but before this perception and understanding he has felt the disapproval which he was not able to comprehend through the ordinary sensory channels.

This process, coupled with the prohibitions and the privations that he must suffer in his education, sets off the experiences that he has in this education and gives them a peculiar coloring of discomfort, neither pain nor fear but discomfort of another kind. Along with these experiences there go in all well regulated homes and schools a group of rewards and approbations for successes. These, needless to say, are not accompanied by this particular type of discomfort, and when that discomfort is present and something is done which leads to approbation, then this peculiar discomfort is assuaged and disappears. The peculiar discomfort is the basis of what we ultimately refer to as anxiety.

The self dynamism is built up out of this experience of approbation and disapproval, of reward and punishment. The peculiarity of the self dynamism is that as it grows it functions, in accordance with its state of development, right from the start. As it develops, it becomes more and more related to a microscope in its function. Since the approbation of the important person is very valuable, since disapprobation denies satisfaction and gives anxiety, the self becomes extremely important. It permits a minute focus on those performances of the child which are the cause of approbation and disapprobation, but, very much like a microscope it interferes with noticing the rest of the world. When you are staring through your microscope, you don't see much except what comes through that channel. So with the self dynamism. It has a tendency to focus attention on performances with the significant other person which get approbation or disfavor. And that peculiarity, closely connected with anxiety, persists thenceforth through life. It comes about that the self, that to which we refer when we say "I," is the only thing which has alertness, which notices what goes on, and, needless to say, notices what goes on in its own field. The rest of the personality gets along outside of awareness. Its impulses, its performances, are not noted.

Not only does the self become the custodian of awareness, but when anything spectacular happens that is not welcome to the self, not sympathetic to the self dynamism, anxiety appears, almost as if anxiety finally became the instrument by which the self maintained its isolation within the personality.

Needless to say, the self is extremely important in psychiatry and in everyday life. Not only does anxiety function to discipline attention, but it gradually restricts personal awareness. The facilitation and deprivations by the parents and significant others are the source of the material which is built into the self dynamism. Out of all that happens to the infant and child, only this 'marked' experience is incorporated into the self, because through the control of personal awareness the self itself from the beginning facilitates and restricts its further growth. In other words, it is self-perpetuating, if you please, tends very strongly to maintain the direction and characteristics which it was given in infancy and childhood.

For the expression of all things in the personality other than those which were approved and disapproved by the parent and other significant persons, the self refuses awareness, so to speak. It does not accord awareness, it does not notice; and these impulses, desires, and needs come to exist disassociated from the self, or *dissociated*. When they are expressed, their expression is not noticed by the person.

Our awareness of our performances, and our awareness of the performances of others are permanently restricted to a part of all that goes on and the structure and character of that part is determined by our early training; its limitation is maintained year after year by our experiencing anxiety whenever we tend to overstep the margin.

Needless to say, limitations and peculiarities of the self may interfere with the pursuit of biologically necessary satisfactions. When this happens, the person is to that extent mentally ill. Similarly, they may interfere with security, and to that extent also the person is mentally ill.

The self may be said to be made up of reflected appraisals. If these were chiefly derogatory, as in the case of an unwanted child who was never loved, of a child who has fallen into the hands of foster parents who have no real interest in him as a child; as I say, if the self dynamism is made up of experience which is chiefly derogatory, the the self dynamism will itself be chiefly derogatory. It will facilitate hostile, disparaging appraisals of other people and it will entertain disparaging and hostile appraisals of itself.

As I have said, the peculiarity exists that one can find in others only that which is in the self. And so the unhappy child who grows up without love will have a self dynamism which shows great capacity for finding fault with others and, by the same token, with himself. That low opinions of oneself are seldom expressed with simple frankness can also be explained.

So difficult is the maintenance of a feeling of security among his fellows for anyone who has come to have a hostile-derogatory self, that the low self-appreciation must be excluded from direct communication. A person who shrewdly attacks the prestige of sundry other people can scarcely add to each such performance, a statement to the effect that he knows, because he has the same fault or defect. At the same time, we know that that which is in the self is not dissociated from the self; in other words, if it shows in the witting performances towards others, it is within the limits of personal awareness and not outside, resisted, so to say, by anxiety.

The relative silence about the low self-appraisal is achieved in part by the clamor of derogating others, in part by preoccupation with implicit revery processes that dramatize the opposite of one's defects, or protest one's rights, or otherwise manifest indirectly one's feeling of unworthiness and inferiority.

Let us rest this matter here for the time being, and review what has been said. We have seen something of the origin and organization of the self and of its marked tendency to stabilize the course of its development. We have seen that if, for example, it is a self which arose through derogatory experience, hostility toward the child, disapproval, dissatisfaction with the child, then this self more or less like a microscope tends to preclude one's learning anything better, to cause one's continuing to feel a sort of limitation in oneself, and while this can not be expressed clearly, while the child or the adult that came from the child does not express openly self-depreciatory trends, he does have a depreciatory attitude toward everyone else, and this really represents a depreciatory attitude toward the self.

The stabilizing influence of past experience is due to the fact that when it is incorporated in the organization of the self, the structure of the self dynamism, it precludes the experience of anything corrective, anything that would be strikingly different. The direction of growth in the self is maintained by the control exercised over personal awareness and by the circumscribing of experience by anxiety when anything quite different from one's prevailing attitude tends to be noticed.

We have seen how the self can be a derogatory and a hateful system, in which case the self will inhibit any experience of friendliness, of positive attitude toward other persons, and thus continue to go on derogatory, hostile, negative, in its attitude toward others.

This selective exclusion of experience which leads to one's being occupied with or noticing only the hostile unfriendly aspect of living not only is manifested in one's attitude toward others, but also is represented in the attitude toward the self. No matter how well the outward manifestations of self-contempt may be disguised, we may be assured that they are there. We see here the explanation of one of the greatest mysteries of human life, how some unfortunate people carry on in the face of apparently overwhelming difficulties, whereas other people are crushed by comparatively insignificant events, contemplate suicide, perhaps actually attempt it.

This is to be understood on the basis not of the particular 'objective' events which bring about the circumstance of success under great hardship or self-destruction; it is to be understood on the basis of the experience which is the foundation of the self system, the organization of experience reflected to one from the significant people around one—which determines the personal characteristics of those events. In no other fashion can we explain the enormous discrepancy between people's reactions to comparable life situations.

Despite his emphasis on the importance of communication, H. S. Sullivan unfortunately lacked the gift of presenting his ideas in clear and simple terms. His difficulties were partly due to his predilection for newly coined words, such as self-system, to replace the Freudian concept of the ego, and self-dynamism, to designate its functional aspect. Again, he uses the word anxiety in a new sense, that is, merely to denote any kind of danger threatening the self-system, and the word revery as a synonym of waking phantasy life.

Yet his concept of the psychiatrist's participant observation in the treatment situation is highly original and forms a link with propositions of modern theoretical physics concerning the effects upon the object observed by the observer's monitoring instruments. In a similar vein, Sullivan's emphasis on interpersonal fields and interpersonal relationships is closely akin to modern field theoretical concepts in both the behavioral and natural sciences.

More problematical is his tendency to deny the reality of an independent and self-contained personality structure in the Freudian sense, which he replaces with "interpersonal operations" and "reflected appraisals" by significant others. In so doing, the egos of both the patient and the therapist are apt to be lost in the shuffle.

Indeed, as with other pioneers in the field of psychiatry, some of Sullivan's contributions carry the imprint of his personal pathology. He has a history of hospitalization with what may have been a schizophrenic episode. His friends and former associates describe his emotional coldness and detachment, his fear of closeness and intimacy, and other telltale signs of social maladjustment. He was certainly able to speak about mental disease with the authority of one who knew it inside out—long before the advent of LSD or other psychotomimetic drugs.

Erich Fromm (1900-   ), who came to this country from Germany, is one of the foremost advocates of the new cultural orientation of psychoanalysis. Fromm took objection to what he considered Freud's one-sided emphasis on the biological aspects of human nature. Human nature, according to Fromm, differs from animal nature in the decisive part played by cultural factors in the making of man. Man himself is both the product and the maker of his culture. All that is specifically human is the result of an interplay between social, economic and psychological factors, brought to bear upon the individual in a given society. Neither man's sexual behavior nor his lust for power—nor his tendency to submission—is solely determined by his fixed biological needs. Each is molded by his response to his training and upbringing, to existing environmental factors. Accordingly his neurotic reactions vary from culture to culture. So also does the part played by the Oedipus complex, by castration fears, by Adler's "masculine protest," and so on.

Western man living in present-day industrial society is apt to respond with a particular type of neurotic conflict. It derives from what Fromm calls the historical dichotomy of human nature on the one hand, and from such inescapable "existential" dichotomies as the inevitability of death and man's quest for immortality, on the other. Above all, modern man has broken his ties with the rest of nature. As a result he may seek to re-establish his lost solidarity with her, and with his fellow men, by resorting to various neurotic methods of relating to the group. He may develop certain sadomasochistic patterns of behavior. He may assume an attitude of lifeless, automatic conformiy. He may try to solve his problems by an irrational destructive *trend. This is what Fromm describes as the various mechanisms of escape, representing so many types of neurotic reactions in modern man.*

Fromm's therapeutic approach is guided by these basic principles. He lays great stress on helping the patient to re-establish his sense of personal identity, his self-awareness and self-realization. By contrast to the noncommittal, detached attitude of the orthodox analyst toward the world of values and religion, Fromm is greatly concerned with ethical problems. Some of his critics have charged him—as well as C. G. Jung, Karen Horney and other culturally oriented therapists—with being overly directive, with wanting to set the clock back to pre-Freudian "moral therapy" and its undue emphasis on conscious factors, while neglecting the deeper strata of the human mind.

The following selections are taken from Fromm's book Escape from Freedom.

Contrary to Freud's viewpoint, the analysis offered in this book is based on the assumption that the key problem of psychology is that of the specific kind of relatedness of the individual towards the world and not that of the satisfaction or frustration of this or that instinctual need per se; furthermore, on the assumption that the relationship between man an society is not a static one. It is not as if we had on the one hand an individual equipped by nature with certain drives and on the other, society as something apart from him, either satisfying or frustrating these innate propensities. Although there are certain needs, such as hunger, thirst, sex, which are common to man, those drives which make for the differences in men's characters, like love and hatred, the lust for power and the yearning for submission, the enjoyment of sensuous pleasure and the fear of it, are all products of the social process. The most beautiful as well as the most ugly inclinations of man are not part of a fixed and biologically given human nature, but result from the social process which creates man. In other words, society has not only a suppressing function—although it has that too—but it has also a creative function. Man's nature, his passions, and anxieties are a cultural product; as a matter of fact, man himself is the most important creation and achievement of the continuous human effort, the record of which we call history.

It is the very task of social psychology to understand this process of man's creation in history. Why do certain changes of man's character take place from one historical epoch to another? Why is the spirit of the Renaissance different from that of the Middle Ages? Why is the character structure of man in monopolistic capitalism different from that in the nineteenth century? Social psychology has to explain why new abilities and new passions, bad or good, come into existence. Thus we find, for instance, that from the

Renaissance up until our day, men have been filled with a burning ambition for fame, while this striving which today seems so natural was little present in man of the medieval society. In the same period men developed a sense for the beauty of nature which they did not possess before. Again, in the Northern European countries, from the sixteenth century on, man developed an obsessional craving to work which had been lacking in a free man before that period.

But man is not only made by history—history is made by man. The solution of this seeming contradiction constitutes the field of social psychology. Its task is to show not only how passions, desires, anxieties change and develop as a result of the social process, but also how man's energies thus shaped into specific forms, in their turn become productive forces, molding the social process. Thus, for instance, the craving for fame and success and the drive to work, are forces without which modern capitalism could not have developed; without these and a number of other human forces, man would have lacked the impetus to act according to the social and economic requirements of the modern commercial and industrial system. . . .

Most psychiatrists take the structure of their own society so much for granted that to them the person who is not well adapted assumes the stigma of being less valuable. On the other hand, the well-adapted person is supposed to be the more valuable person in terms of a scale of human values. If we differentiate the two concepts of normal and neurotic, we come to the following conclusion: the person who is normal in terms of being well a-dapted is often less healthy than the neurotic person in terms of human values. Often he is well adapted only at the expense of having given up his self in order to become more or less the person he believes he is expected to be. All genuine individuality and spontaneity may have been lost. On the other hand, the neurotic person can be characterized as somebody who was not ready to surrender completely in the battle for his self. To be sure, his attempt to save his individual self was not successful, and instead of expressing his self productively he sought salvation through neurotic symptoms and by withdrawing into a phantasy life. Nevertheless, from the standpoint of human values, he is less crippled than the kind of normal person who has lost his individuality altogether. Needless to say, there are persons who are not neurotic and yet have not drowned their individuality in the process of adaptation. But the stigma attached to the neurotic person seems to us to be unfounded, and justified only if we think of neurotic in terms of social efficiency. As for a whole society, the term neurotic cannot be applied in this latter sense, since a society could not exist if its members did not function socially. From a standpoint of human values, a society could be called neurotic in the sense that its members are crippled in the growth of their personality. Since the term neurotic is so often used to denote lack of social functioning we would prefer not to speak of a society in terms of its being neurotic, but rather in terms of its being adverse to human happiness and self-realization.

The mechanisms we shall discuss in this chapter are mechanisms of escape, which result from the insecurity of the isolated individual.

Once the primary bonds which gave security to the individual are severed, once the individual faces the world outside of himself as a completely separate entity, two courses are open to him since he has to overcome the unbearable state of powerlessness and aloneness. By one course he can progress to "positive freedom"; he can relate himself spontaneously to the world in love and work, in the genuine expression of his emotional, sensuous, and intellectual capacities; he can thus become one again with man, nature, and himself, without giving up the independence and integrity of his individual self. The other course open to him is to fall back, to give up his freedom, and to try to overcome his aloneness by eliminating the gap that has arisen between his individual self and the world. This second course never reunites him with the world in the way he was related to it before he emerged as an "individual," for the fact of his separateness cannot be reversed; it is an escape from an unbearable situation which would make life impossible if it were prolonged. This course of escape, therefore, is characterized by its compulsive character, like every escape from threatening panic; it is also characterized by the more or less complete surrender of individuality and the integrity of the self. Thus it is not a solution which leads to happiness and positive freedom; it is, in principle, a solution which is to be found in all neurotic phenomena. It assuages an unbearable anxiety and makes life possible by avoiding panic; yet it does not solve the underlying problem and is paid for by a kind of life that often consists only of automatic or compulsive activities.

Some of these mechanisms of escape are of relatively small social import; they are to be found in any marked degree only in individuals with severe mental and emotional disturbances. . . .

The first mechanism of escape from freedom I am going to deal with is the tendency to give up the independence of one's own individual self and to fuse one's self with somebody or something outside of oneself in order to acquire the strength which the individual self is lacking. Or, to put it in different words, to seek for new, "secondary bonds" as a substitute for the primary bonds which have been lost.

The more distinct forms of this mechanism are to be found in the striving for submission and domination, or, as we would rather put it, in the masochistic and sadistic strivings as they exist in varying degrees in normal and neurotic persons respectively. We shall first describe these tendencies and then try to show that both of them are an escape from an unbearable aloneness.

The most frequent forms in which masochistic strivings appear are feelings of inferiority, powerlessness, individual insignificance. The analysis of persons who are obsessed by these feelings shows that, while they consciously complain about these feelings and want to get rid of them, unconsciously some power within themselves drives them to feel inferior or insignificant. Their feelings are more than realizations of actual shortcomings and weaknesses (although they are usually rationalized as though they were); these persons show a tendency to belittle themselves, to make themselves weak, and not to master things. Quite regularly these people show a marked dependence on powers outside themselves, on other people, or institutions, or nature. They tend not to assert themselves, not to do what they want, but to submit to the factual or alleged orders of these outside forces. Often they are quite incapable of experiencing the feeling "I want" or "I am." Life, as a whole, is felt by them as something overwhelmingly powerful, which they cannot master or control.

In the more extreme cases—and there are many—one finds besides these tendencies to belittle oneself and to submit to outside forces, a tendency to hurt oneself and to make oneself suffer.

This tendency can assume various forms. We find that there are people who indulge in self-accusation and self-criticism which even their worst enemies would scarcely bring against them. There are others, such as certain compulsive neurotics, who tend to torture themselves with compulsory rites and thoughts. In a certain type of neurotic personality we find a tendency to become physically ill, and to wait, consciously or unconsciously, for an illness as if it were a gift of the gods. Often they incur accidents which would not have happened had there not been at work an unconscious tendency to incur them. These tendencies directed against themselves are often revealed in still less overt or dramatic forms. For instance, there are persons who are incapable of answering questions in an examination when the answers are very well known to them at the time of the examination and even afterwards. There are others who say things which antagonize those whom they love or on whom they are dependent, although actually they feel friendly toward them and did not intend to say those things. With such people, it almost seems as if they were following advice given them by an enemy to behave in such a way as to be most detrimental to themselves.

Besides these masochistic trends, the very opposite of them, namely, sadistic tendencies, are regularly to be found in the same kind of characters. They vary in strength, are more or less conscious, yet they are never missing. We find three kinds of sadistic tendencies, more or less closely knit together. One is to make others dependent on oneself and to have absolute and unrestricted power over them, so as to make of them nothing but instruments, "clay in the potter's hand." Another consists of the impulse not only to rule over others in this absolute fashion, but to exploit them, to use them, to steal from them, to disembowel them, and, so to speak, to incorporate anything eatable in them. This desire can refer to material things as well as to immaterial ones, such as the emotional or intellectual qualities a person has to offer. A third kind of sadistic tendency is the wish to make others suffer or to see them suffer. This suffering can be physical, but more often it is mental suffering. Its aim is to hurt actively, to humiliate, embarrass others, or to see them in embarrassing and humiliating situations.

Sadistic tendencies for obvious reasons are usually less conscious and more rationalized than the socially more harmless masochistic trends. Often they are entirely covered up by reaction formations of over-goodness or over-concern for others. Some of the most frequent rationalizations are the following: "I rule over you because I know what is best for you, and in your own interest you should follow me without opposition." Or, "I am so wonderful and unique, that I have a right to expect that other people become dependent on me." Another rationalization which often covers the exploiting tendencies is: "I have done so much for you, and now I am entitled to take from you what I want." The more aggressive kind of sadistic impulses finds its most frequent rationalization in two forms: "I have been hurt by others and my wish to hurt them is nothing but retaliation," or "By striking first I am defending myself or my friends against the danger of being hurt."

What is the root of both the masochistic perversion and masochistic character traits respectively? Furthermore, what is the common root of both the masochistic and the sadistic strivings?

The direction in which the answer lies has already been suggested in the beginning of this chapter. Both the masochistic and sadistic strivings tend to help the individual to escape his unbearable feeling of aloneness and powerlessness. Psychoanalytic and other empirical observations of masochistic persons give ample evidence (which I cannot quote here without transcending the scope of this book) that they are filled with a terror of aloneness and insignificance. Frequently this feeling is not conscious; often it is covered by compensatory feelings of eminence and perfection. However, if one only penetrates deeply enough into the unconscious dynamics of such a person, one finds these feelings without fail. The individual finds himself "free" in the negative sense, that is, alone with his self and confronting an alienated, hostile world. In this situation, to quote a telling description of Dostoevski, in *The Brothers Karamasov*, he has "no more pressing need than the one to find somebody to whom he can surrender, as quickly as possible, that gift of freedom which he, the unfortunate creature, was born with." The frightened individual seeks for somebody or something to tie his self to; he cannot bear to be his own individual self any longer, and he tries frantically to get rid of it and to feel security again by the elimination of this burden: the self.

Masochism is one way toward this goal. The different forms which the masochistic strivings assume have one aim: to get rid of the individual self, to lose oneself; in other words, to get rid of the burden of freedom. This aim is obvious in those masochistic strivings in which the individual seeks to submit to a person or power which he feels as being overwhelmingly strong. (Incidentally, the conviction of superior strength of another person is always to be understood in relative terms. It can be based either upon the actual strength of the other person, or upon a conviction of one's own utter insignificance and powerlessness. In the latter event a mouse or a leaf can assume threatening features.) In other forms of masochistic strivings the essential aim is the same. In the masochistic feeling of smallness we find a tendency which serves to increase the original feeling of insignificance. How is this to be understood? Can we assume that by making a fear worse one is trying to remedy it? Indeed, this is what the masochistic person does. As long as I struggle between my desire to be independent and strong and my feeling of insignificance or powerlessness, I am caught in a tormenting conflict. If I succeed in reducing my individual self to nothing, if I can overcome the awareness of my separateness as an individual, I may save myself from this conflict. To feel utterly small and helpless is one way toward this aim; to be overwhelmed by pain and agony another; to be overcome by effects of intoxication still another. The phantasy of suicide is the last hope if all other means have not succeeded in bringing relief from the burden of aloneness. . . .

What is the essence of the sadistic drives? Again, the wish to inflict pain on others is not the essence. All the different forms of sadism which we can observe go back to one essential impulse, namely, to have complete mastery over another person, to make of him a helpless object of our will, to become the absolute ruler over him, to become his God, to do with him as one pleases. To humiliate him, to enslave him, are means to this end and the most radical aim is to make him suffer, since there is no greater power over another person than that of inflicting pain on him, to force him to undergo suffering without his being able to defend himself. The pleasure in the complete domination over another person (or other animate objects) is the very essence of the sadistic drive.

It seems that this tendency to make oneself the absolute master over another person is the opposite of the masochistic tendency, and it is puzzling that these two tendencies should be so closely knitted together. No doubt with regard to its practical consequences, the wish to be dependent or to suffer is the opposite of the wish to dominate and to make others suffer. Psychologically, however, both tendencies are the outcomes of one basic need, springing from the inability to bear the isolation and weakness of one's own self. I suggest calling the aim which is at the basis of both sadism and masochism: symbiosis. Symbiosis, in this psychological sense, means the union of one individual self with another self (or any other power outside of the own self) in such a way as to make each lose the integrity of its own self and to make them completely dependent on each other. The sadistic person needs his object just as much as the masochistic needs his. Only instead of seeking security by being swallowed, he gains it by swallowing somebody else. In both cases, the integrity of the individual self is lost. In one case I dissolve myself in an outside power; I lose myself. In the other case I enlarge myself by making another being part of myself and thereby I gain the strength I lack as an independent self. It is always the inability to stand the aloneness of one's individual self that leads to the drive to enter into a symbiotic relationship with someone else. It is evident from this why masochistic and sadistic trends are always blended with each other. Although on the surface they seem contradictions, they are essentially rooted in the same basic need. People are not sadistic or masochistic, but there is a constant oscillation between the active and the passive side of the symbiotic complex, so that it is often difficult to determine which side of it is operating at a given moment. In both cases individuality and freedom are lost.

Karen Horney (1885-1952) started her career as a Freudian analyst, but her emphasis on the part played by interpersonal relationships and cultural factors in the origin of neuroses soon brought her into conflict with her more orthodox confreres. At the same time, she attracted a growing number of followers with whose assistance she founded the Horneyan school of psychoanalysis. Her work shows a close affinity to that of H. S. Sullivan, Erich Fromm, and the Washington school of psychiatry. She also leaned heavily on Alfred Adler's Individual psychology, though she emphasized that her interpretations still rested on Freudian grounds. Yet her allegiance to psychoanalysis did not prevent her from taking issue with Freud's concept of penis envy and his general bias against women. Her studies of female sexuality made her a pioneer of the women's liberation movement. In her later years, Horney showed a growing interest in Zen Buddhism and existential philosophy.

The selection that follows is taken from the first chapter of her bestselling book The Neurotic Personality of Our Time.

We use the term *neurotic* quite freely today without always having, however, a clear conception of what it denotes. Often it is hardly more than a slightly highbrow way of expressing disapproval: one who formerly would have been content to say lazy, sensitive, demanding or suspicious, is now likely to say instead "neurotic." Yet we do have something in mind when we use the term, and without being quite aware of it we apply certain criteria to determine its choice.

First of all, neurotic persons are different from average individuals in their reactions. We should be inclined to consider neurotic, for example, a girl who prefers to remain in the rank and file, refuses to accept an increased salary and does not wish to be identified with her superiors, or an artist who earns thirty dollars a week but could earn more if he gave more time to his work, and who prefers instead to enjoy life as well as he can on that amount, to spend a good deal of his time in the company of women or in indulging in technical hobbies. The reason we should call such persons neurotic is that most of us are familiar, and exclusively familiar, with a behavior pattern that implies wanting to get ahead in the world, to get ahead of others, to earn more money than the bare minimum for existence.

These examples show that one criterion we apply in designating a person as neurotic is whether his mode of living coincides with any of the recognized behavior patterns of our time. If the girl without competitive drives, or at least without apparent competitive drives, lived in some Pueblo Indian culture, she would be considered entirely normal, or if the artist lived in a village in Southern Italy or in Mexico he, too, would be considered normal, because in those environments it is inconceivable that anyone should want to earn more money or to make any greater effort than is absolutely necessary to satisfy immediate needs. Going farther back, in Greece the attitude of wanting to work more than one's needs required would have been considered positively indecent.

Thus the term *neurotic*, while originally medical, cannot be used now without its cultural implications. One can diagnose a broken leg without knowing the cultural background of the patient, but one would run a great risk in calling an Indian boy psychotic because he told us that he had visions in which he believed. In the particular culture of these Indians the experience of visions and hallucinations is regarded as a special gift, a blessing from the spirits, and they are deliberately induced as conferring a certain prestige on the person who has them. With us a person would be neurotic or psychotic who talked by the hour with his deceased grandfather, whereas such communication with ancestors is a recognized pattern in some Indian tribes. A person who felt mortally offended if the name of a deceased relative were mentioned we should consider neurotic indeed, but he would be absolutely normal in the Jicarilla Apache culture. A man mortally frightened by the approach of a menstruating woman we should consider neurotic, while with many primitive tribes fear concerning menstruation is the average attitude.

The conception of what is normal varies not only with the culture but also within the same culture, in the course of time. Today, for example, if a mature and independent woman were to consider herself "a fallen woman," "unworthy of the love of a decent man," because she had had sexual relationships, she would be suspected of a neurosis, at least in many circles of society. Some forty years ago this attitude of guilt would have been considered normal. The conception of normality varies also with the different classes of society. Members of the feudal class, for example, find it normal for a man to be lazy all the time, active only at hunting or warring, whereas a person of the small bourgeois class showing the same attitude would be considered decidedly abnormal. This variation is found also according to sex distinctions, as far as they exist in society, as they do in Western culture, where men and women are supposed to have different temperaments. For a woman to become obsessed with the dread of growing old as she approaches the forties is, again, "normal," while a man getting jittery about age at that period of life would be neurotic.

To some extent every educated person knows that there are variations in what is regarded as normal. We know that the Chinese eat foods different from ours; that the Eskimos have different conceptions of cleanliness; that the medicine-man has different ways of curing the sick from those used by the modern physician. That there are, however, variations not only in customs but also in drives and feelings, is less generally understood, though implicitly or explicitly it has been stated by anthropologists. It is one of the merits of modern anthropology, as Sapir has put it, to be always rediscovering the normal.

For good reasons every culture clings to the belief that its own feelings and drives are the one normal expression of "human nature," and psychology has not made an exception to this rule. Freud, for example, concludes from his observations that woman is more jealous than man, and then tries to account for this presumably general phenomenon on biological grounds. Freud also seems to assume that all human beings experience guilt feelings concerning murder. It is an indisputable fact, however, that the greatest variations exist in the attitude toward killing. As Peter Freuchen has shown, the Eskimos do not feel that a murderer requires punishment. In many primitive tribes the injury done a family when one of its members is killed by an outsider may be repaired by presenting a substitute. In some cultures the feelings of a mother whose son has been killed can be assuaged by adopting the murderer in his place.

Making further use of anthropological findings we must recognize that some of our conceptions about human nature are rather naive, for example the idea that competitiveness, sibling rivalry, kinship between affection and sexuality, are trends inherent in human nature. Our conception of normality is arrived at by the approval of certain standards of behavior and feeling within a certain group which imposes these standards upon its members. But the standards vary with culture, period, class and sex.

These considerations have more far-reaching implications for psychology than appears at first impression. The immediate consequence is a feeling of doubt about psychological omniscience. From resemblances between findings concerning our culture and those concerning other cultures we must not conclude that both are due to the same motivations. It is no longer valid to suppose that a new psychological finding reveals a universal trend inherent in human nature. The effect of all this is to confirm what some sociologists have repeatedly asserted: that there is no such thing as a normal psychology, which holds for all mankind.

These limitations, however, are more than compensated by the opening up of new possibilities of understanding. The essential implication of these anthropological considerations is that feelings and attitudes are to an amazingly high degree molded by the conditions under which we live, both cultural and individual, inseparably interwoven. This in turn means that if we know the cultural conditions under which we live we have a good chance of gaining a much deeper understanding of the special character of normal feelings and attitudes. And inasmuch as neuroses are deviations from the normal pattern of behavior there is for them, too, a prospect of better understanding.

In part, taking this way means following Freud along the path that led him ultimately to present the world with a hitherto unthought-of understanding of neuroses. While in theory Freud traced back our peculiarities to biologically given drives he has emphatically represented the opinion—in theory and still more in practice—that we cannot understand a neurosis without a detailed knowledge of the individual's life circumstances, particularly the molding influences of affection in early childhood. Applying the same principle to the problem of normal and neurotic structures in a given culture means that we cannot understand these structures without a detailed knowledge of the influences the particular culture exerts over the individual.

For the rest it means that we have to take a definite step beyond Freud, a step which is possible, though, only on the basis of Freud's revealing discoveries. For although in one respect he is far ahead of his own time, in another—in his over-emphasis on the biological origin of mental characteristics—Freud has remained rooted in its scientific orientations. He has assumed that the instinctual drives or object relationships that are frequent in our culture are biologically determined "human nature" or arise out of unalterable situations (biologically given "pregenital" stages, Oedipus complex).

Freud's disregard of cultural factors not only leads to false generalizations, but to a large extent blocks an understanding of the real forces which motivate our attitudes and actions. I believe that this disregard is the main reason why psychoanalysis, inasmuch as it faithfully follows the theoretical paths beaten by Freud, seems in spite of its seemingly boundless potentialities to have come into a blind alley, manifesting itself in a rank growth of abstruse theories and the use of a shadowy terminology.

We have seen now that a neurosis involves deviation from the normal. This criterion is very important, though it is not sufficient. Persons may deviate from the general pattern without having a neurosis. The artist cited above, who refused to give more time than necessary to earning money, may have a neurosis or he may simply be wise in not permitting himself to be pulled into the current of competitive struggle. On the other hand, many persons may have a severe neurosis who according to surface observation are adapted to existing patterns of life. It is in such cases that the psychological or medical point of view is necessary.

Curiously enough, it is anything but easy to say what constitutes a neurosis from this point of view. At any rate, as long as we study the manifest picture alone, it is difficult to find characteristics common to all neuroses. We certainly cannot use the symptoms—such as phobias, depressions, functional physical disorders—as a criterion, because they may not be present. Inhibitions of some sort are always present, for reasons I shall discuss later, but they may be so subtle or so well disguised as to escape surface observation. The same difficulties would arise if we should judge from the manifest picture alone the disturbances in relations with other people, including the disturbances in sexual relations. These are never missing but they may be very difficult to discern. There are two characteristics, however, which one may discern in all neuroses without having an intimate knowledge of the personality structure: a certain rigidity in reaction and a discrepancy between potentialities and accomplishments.

Both characteristics need further explanation. By rigidity in reactions I mean a lack of that flexibility which enables us to react differently to different situations. The normal person, for instance, is suspicious where he senses or sees reasons for being so; a neurotic person may be suspicious, regardless of the situation, all the time, whether he is aware of his state or not. A normal person is able to discriminate between compliments meant sincerely and those of an insincere nature; the neurotic person does not differentiate between the two or may discount them altogether, under all conditions. A normal person will be spiteful if he feels an unwarranted imposition;

a neurotic may react with spite to any insinuation, even if he realizes that it is in his own interest. A normal person may be undecided, at times, in a matter important and difficult to decide; a neurotic may be undecided at all times.

Rigidity, however, is indicative of a neurosis only when it deviates from the cultural patterns. A rigid suspicion of anything new or strange is a normal pattern among a large proportion of peasants in Western civilization; and the small bourgeois' rigid emphasis on thrift is also an example of normal rigidity.

In the same way, a discrepancy between the potentialities of a person and his actual achievements in life may be due only to external factors. But it is indicative of a neurosis if in spite of gifts and favorable external possibilities for their development the person remains unproductive; or if in spite of having all the possibilities for feeling happy he cannot enjoy what he has; or if in spite of being beautiful a woman feels that she cannot attract men. In other words, the neurotic has the impression that he stands in his own way.

Leaving aside the manifest picture and looking at the dynamics effective in producing neuroses, there is one essential factor common to all neuroses, and that is anxieties and the defenses built up against them. Intricate as the structure of a neurosis may be, this anxiety is the motor which sets the neurotic process going and keeps it in motion. The meaning of this statement will become clear in the following chapters, and therefore I refrain from citing examples now. But even if it is to be accepted only tentatively as a basic principle it requires elaboration.

As it stands the statement is obviously too general. Anxieties or fears— let us use these terms interchangeably for a while—are ubiquitous, and so are defenses against them. These reactions are not restricted to human beings. If an animal, frightened by some danger, either makes a counterattack or takes flight, we have exactly the same situation of fear and defense. If we are afraid of being struck by lightning and put a lightning-rod on our roof, if we are afraid of the consequences of possible accidents and take out an insurance policy, the factors of fear and defense are likewise present. They are present in various specific forms in every culture, and may be institutionalized, as in the wearing of amulets as a defense against the fear of the evil eye, the observation of circumstantial rites against the fear of the dead, the taboos concerning the avoidance of menstruating women as a defense against the fear of evil emanating from them.

These similarities present a temptation to make a logical error. If the factors of fear and defense are essential in neuroses, why not call the institutionalized defenses against fear the evidence of "cultural" neuroses? The fallacy in reasoning this way lies in the fact that two phenomena are not necessarily identical when they have one element in common. One would not call a house a rock merely because it is built out of the same material as a rock. What, then, is the characteristic of neurotic fears and defenses that makes them specifically neurotic? Is it perhaps that the neurotic fears are imaginary? No, for we might also be inclined to call fear of the dead imaginary; and in both cases we should be yielding to an impression based on lack of understanding. Is it perhaps that the neurotic essentially does not know why he is afraid? No, for neither does the primitive know why he has a fear of the dead. The distinction has nothing to do with gradations of awareness or rationality, but it consists in the following two factors.

First, life conditions in every culture give rise to some fears. They may be caused by external dangers (nature, enemies), by the forms of social relationships (incitement to hostility because of suppression, injustice, enforced dependence, frustrations), by cultural traditions (traditional fear of demons, of violation of taboos) regardless of how they may have originated. An individual may be subject more or less to these fears, but on the whole it is safe to assume that they are thrust upon every individual living in a given culture, and that no one can avoid them. The neurotic, however, not only shares the fears common to all individuals in a culture, but because of conditions in his individual life—which, however, are interwoven with general conditions—he also has fears which in quantity or quality deviate from those of the cultural pattern.

Secondly, the fears existing in a given culture are warded off in general by certain protective devices (such as taboos, rites, customs). As a rule these defenses represent a more economical way of dealing with fears than do the neurotic's defenses built up in a different way. Thus the normal person, though having to undergo the fears and defenses of his culture, will in general be quite capable of living up to his potentialities and of enjoying what life has to offer to him. The normal person is capable of making the best of the possibilities given in his culture. Expressing it negatively, he does not suffer more than is unavoidable in his culture. The neurotic person, on the other hand, suffers invariably more than the average person. He invariably has to pay an exorbitant price for his defenses, consisting in an impairment in vitality and expansiveness, or more specifically in an impairment of his capacities for achievement and enjoyment, resulting in the discrepancy I have mentioned. In fact, the neurotic is invariably a suffering person. The only reason why I did not mention this fact when discussing the characteristics of all neuroses that can be derived from surface observation is that it is not necessarily observable from without. The neurotic himself may not even be aware of the fact that he is suffering.

Talking of fears and defenses, I am afraid that by this time many readers will have become impatient about such an extensive discussion of so simple a question as what constitutes a neurosis. In defending myself I may point out that psychic phenomena are always intricate, that while there are seemingly simple questions there is never a simple answer, that the predicament we meet here at the beginning is no exceptional one, but will accompany us throughout the book, whatever problem we shall tackle. The particular difficulty in the description of a neurosis lies in the fact that a satisfactory answer can be given neither with psychological nor with sociological tools alone, but that they must be taken up alternately, first one and then the other, as in fact we have done. If we should regard a neurosis only from the point of view of its dynamics and psychic structure we should hypostatize a normal human being: he does not exist. We run into more difficulties as soon as we pass the borderline of our own country or of countries with a culture similar to our own. And if we regard a neurosis only from the sociological point of view as a mere deviation from the behavior pattern common to a certain society, we neglect grossly all we know about the psychological characteristics of a neurosis, and no psychiatrist of any school or country would recognize the results as what he is accustomed to designate a neurosis. The reconcilement of the two approaches lies in a method of observation that considers the deviation both in the manifest picture of the neurosis and in the dynamics of the psychic processes, but without considering either deviation as the primary and decisive one. The two must be combined. This in general is the way we have gone in pointing out that fear and defense are one of the dynamic centers of a neurosis, but constitute a neurosis only when deviating in quantity or quality from the fears and defenses patterned in the same culture.

We have to go one step further in the same direction. There is still another essential characteristic of a neurosis and that is the presence of conflicting tendencies of the existence of which, or at least of the precise content of which, the neurotic himself is unaware, and for which he automatically tries to reach certain compromise solutions. It is this latter characteristic which in various forms Freud has stressed as an indispensable constituent of neuroses. What distinguishes the neurotic conflicts from those commonly existing in a culture is neither their content nor the fact that they are essentially unconscious—in both respects the common cultural conflicts may be identical—but the fact that in the neurotic the conflicts are sharper and more accentuated. The neurotic person attempts and arrives at compromise solutions—not inopportunely classified as neurotic—and these solutions are less satisfactory than those of the average individual and are achieved at great expense to the whole personality.

Reviewing all these considerations, we are not yet able to give a well-rounded definition of a neurosis, but we can arrive at a description: a neurosis is a psychic disturbance brought about by fears and defenses against these fears, and by attempts to find compromise solutions for conflicting tendencies. For practical reasons it is advisable to call this disturbance a neurosis only if it deviates from the pattern common to the particular culture.

Harold Kelman (b. 1906), a past president of the American Academy of Psychoanalysis, was a close associate of Karen Horney's and for years the editor of the American Journal of Psychoanalysis, *a forum and sounding board for the Horneyan school of thought. Like Horney, Kelman felt a growing affinity to ancient Far Eastern schools of philosophy and to existential analysis. His major work,* Helping People, *is an exposition of Horney's approach, enriched with his own experience. His articles on* Kairos *(the Favorable Moment) hark back to the classical Hippocratic tradition. The following selection (1960) shows Kelman as a builder of bridges between the wisdom of the East and the modern intellectual approach to the challenge of healing: It is taken from "Psychoanalytic Thought and Eastern Wisdom" by Harold Kelman in* Science and Psychoanalysis, Vol. 3, *edited by J. Masserman, Copyright Grune and Stratton, New York.*

Eastern wisdom is not alien to the West. The West is becoming more aware of and congruent with it. Eastern and Western civilization are descendants of the magic world to which the East remained closer than the West. In evolving from the magic world East and West dealt differently with reference to the subject and object. "The Western mind fixes the object as the *ob-jectum*—that which is thrown against the subject—in a word, the opposite. It is independent of the subject. What corresponds to the object in the West, in the East is better named—the other." The distinct cleavage, as in the subject-object dualism, does not occur. "A certain bond and affinity thus persists . . . embracing equally the grim and friendlier aspects of world and nature." What characterizes the East is the subjectifying attitude, the West, the objectifying one. "*Eastern cognition is interested in consciousness itself. Western cognition is interested in the objects of consciousness.*"

The guiding principle of the Eastern mind structure is juxtaposition and identity. In the West it is unity in variety. The East is essentially concerned with life in its intuitive and aesthetic immediacy and produced the world's religions. The West is primarily interested in the theoretically designated and inferred factors in nature and produced science. Wisdom, for the West, is what can be conceptualized. Reality is what can be explained by theories. "The East attempts to establish immediate contact with the Real. This communion and what derives from it is, to the man of the East—wisdom." The Western absolute is an abstraction or a deity so that even in "*unio mystica*" a distinction between the human and divine remains, a dualism persists. The Eastern absolute is the Real. With its subjectifying attitude in the subject-other relation, by a process of dismantling consciousness of its contents, "the subject meets and experiences itself, freed from the interference of otherness altogether." Then all is pure subject, pure consciousness, pure being. The subject and all otherness are identical as is the absolute and the Real. Then there is "awareness without anything of which awareness is aware—hence a state of pure lucidity."

East and West differ in their attitudes toward time. "Time is the arch-enemy of all living." The West attempts to define it explicitly, to oppose and dominate it, only to become its victim. The East shows pronounced discretion toward time. The West postulates abstract and absolute time. In the East time is ever filled, concrete time. It has not reality other than as time experienced. In the West emphasis is on the past and the future, i.e., away from here-now. In the East time is the absolute present. Past and future are absorbed into it. In China, time is experienced as succession. Past and future are absorbed in the eternal presence of the ancestral family. India's attitude toward time is almost ahistorical. "What reality there is in this world resides in the individual, not as a link and member of the historical process, but in him as such."

Some essential differences between East and West can be explicitly pointed at through an exercise in which the body is used and breathing is of central importance. Yogic exercises or Buddhist meditation in the lotus position are Eastern examples and for the West any form of sport. The disciple sits on the floor, cross-legged. He is actively at rest in the most solidly contained and earth-rooted position a human being can be. His attention is directed inward toward his breathing and its rhythmicity. His orientation is centripetal. Gradually he lets go of his attachments to time, place, person, causality, teleology, materiality, thinking, action, willing, the guiding notions of the West. In time he becomes less affected by thirst, hunger, fullness of bowel and bladder and other bodily sensations and feelings. By attending to his breathing he becomes his breathing, its rhythmicity, its spontaneity. These exercises guide him. They are a stream that carries him into his depths, to control of his heart rate, breathing and ultimately consciousness itself.

In the West exercise means being in the erect position, locomoting, centrifugally oriented and dominated by dualisms, will, thought, feeling and action, i.e., focusing on winning. Breathing is disregarded until the anguish prior to getting second wind obtrudes itself. The experience of breathing and playing being one (i.e., being the breathing or the piano playing without the experience of an I doing it) is not unknown to Western athletes and artists. Good teachers are good gurus. Roger Bannister experienced the being run rather than running and Leopold Auer helped his pupils become the "method of no method" and play brilliant violin with effortless effort. . . .

Only those who have become steeped in and explored what the West has and is contributing can be open to what the East can offer. They must be aware of the uniqueness of this time in human history. Also they must have experienced the limitations of dualistic thinking and sense impressions. And finally, their anxiety responses to Existentialism, the work of Martin Buber and Zen Buddhism must not be of such intensity that they are driven to be antagonistic, indifferent or to swallow one or all whole. That man has proselytized and prostituted love, religion and in recent times science cannot be held against them. That fads and frauds have been made out of the teachings of Existentialism, Buber, Zen and psychoanalysis does not discredit them. Man has always gone through phases of besmirching his dignity with indignities.

There are certain blocks to our being open and receptive for what the East has to offer. To the extent we are aware, they will stand less in our way. Our language is noun-oriented. We make propositions about things. Languages which are verb oriented make propositions about events. They are more suitable for communicating immediacies. Our language, subject-predicate in form, creates a dualism and a hypostatization of processes. Process languages facilitate experiencing. Our language is phonetic alphabetic, the ultimate in abstraction. Ideographic languages, like Chinese, which are painting, are close to the intuitive and esthetic, and better communicate feeling. The most expressing language I know is the sign-language of mutes. It uses the whole body as a brush and for touching. Finally our Western mind-structure, with its emphasis on conceptualization and its built-in dualisms, blocks communicating, experiencing and being, on which the East focuses.

Freud in forcing Western rational man to pay more attention to his feelings, symbolized by sex and 'the unconscious,' unwittingly moved him closer to the East. When patients came to Freud, as physician, he was relying on an ancient tradition. It started with the priest being also physician. After a period of separation of functions, it is the physician who is now becoming the priest. The patient came to Freud much as a disciple seeks out a master or guru. To this extent psychoanalysis is nonproselytizing, i.e., non-Western. At the deepest level, it is spiritual anguish which brings the sufferer to seek the helper, better named the more experienced one in self investigation, in contemplation. In these regards, psychoanalysis is closer to Buddhism, Hinduism, and Taoism than to Judaism, Christianity or Mohammedanism.

Once in the analyst's office the patient is required to become even more non-Western. He is told, "Say whatever goes through your mind." To spell out, he is required to be nonconventional, nonproselytizing, nonteleological, nonrational, nonlogical, nonconceptual, nontime-bound, nonspacebound, nonmaterialistic, passively alert, choicelessly aware and threshold conscious. In short he is required to adopt a whole range of attitudes not only contrary to usual Western forms but quite consonant with many Eastern ones.

Freud asked the analyst to assume the same attitude in his "self-observation." He recommended that he model himself after "the surgeon who puts aside all his own feelings, including that of human sympathy, and concentrates his mind on one single purpose, that of performing the operation as skillfully as possible. . . . The justification for this coldness in feeling in the analyst is that it is the condition which brings the greatest advantage to both persons involved."

Freud's model was the pure research viewpoint of nineteenth century science. That he was caught in a dualism is evident in his opposites of sympathy and coldness. But if we take him literally when he suggests putting "aside all his own feelings," in a sense, he is defining the impersonal attitude of the guru or master which is the ultimate in being personal. Freud's limited interest in therapy and greater one in psychoanalysis as an investigative tool is almost Eastern. The basic premise of the East is that experiencing is understanding, is knowing, is enlightenment, is therapy carried to its ultimate.

Menninger requires of the analyst, " 'The will-power of desirelessness': in other words, how to free himself from *the desire to cure*. . . . Elsewhere it was implied that the physician must sincerely want to get the patient well." The paradoxes and dualisms remain and also the nonteleological attitude.

Psychoanalysis carried to its logical conclusion is Eastern in its techniques and Eastern in its ultimate aims and aspirations. It is not Eastern in its theories because the East does not theorize in a Western sense. Psychoanalysis and its theories are a product of the West and of the subject-object dualism. Between theory and technique there is a built-in dichotomy. Freud's theory fits the nineteenth century scientific materialistic, rationalistic, dualistic man. With each contribution to psychoanalysis an additional facet to the image of man was added. Jung added a collective unconscious; Rank the creative will; Adler the masculine protest and social factors; and Reich, character. Recently, Sullivan, Fromm and Horney have emphasized in different ways cultural, social, interpersonal, intrapersonal and moral factors and the human situation.

Theories of man have shifted from the individualistic toward the interpersonal, holistic and the unitary. Instead of being posed as an object that must change and being opposed to a society that will not, man became a participant-observer and an aspect of the unitary process, individual-environment.

Concomitantly changes in the therapist's function occurred. Freud's pure research viewpoint, when applied to human beings, had to give way before countertransference. Ferenczi positively wanted the therapist to be symbol, surrogate and human being. As the therapist became participant observer, the comprehensive concept of interpersonal transactions and the doctor-patient relationship became necessary. With the being of therapist and patient participating, the concept of *Begegnung* became essential for Existentialism.

The emergence of and interest in Existentialism, the work of Buber and Zen, to me are evidence that Western man is aware that his philosophic roots are inadequate. I feel these interests are a current phenomenon of the West and a phase on the way toward something different which will unify the contributions of East and West in ways heretofore not existent or envisaged. Existentialism is the formulated awareness of the emptiness, meaninglessness and nothingness of our previous ways of being on the basis of the subject-object dualism and the tragedy of it. It points at the experienced despair and hopelessness of hanging on to an outmoded way of being. It defines the fear of the responsibility of choosing to let go into freedom, a freedom with which the West has little experience. In terms of my notion of the symbolizing process and the self system, Western man's present situation is experiencing the struggle involved in hanging on to and in letting go of the formed aspects of his self system in which are imbedded the old and familiar individual, family, group, societal and Western forms of being. He is struggling against and hanging on to the underpinnings of Western civilization which Copernicus in an obvious way began to undermine. The difference between a Westerner and a disciple and master is that the Westerner, and maybe his analyst, still have their eyes on heaven and hell, and are centrifugally oriented and hanging on. The Occidental is being pushed off the precipice into the unknown, into formlessness, against his will, in terror, dread and despair. The Easterner makes this leap into formlessness through choice, in the natural course of his discipleship.

To the extent that the analyst can be the subject-other relation of the East, he can be the ultimate of the impersonal which is the ultimate in the personal. Then truly he will experience juxtaposition and identity and that pain is pain and pleasure is pleasure, neither to be exalted nor degraded. He will be aware that his patient is both identical with him in essentials and different from him in those aspects that enrich the essentials. He will feel him continuous with himself in identity and contiguous with him, as each experiences his own identity in his own right. To the extent this obtains, there will be more meditating, looking inward and being centripetally oriented, until centripetal and centrifugal become one, inward and onward become one and only different ways of looking at and naming the same process, being.

The analyst will have to be aware that the only place we can ever be and experience is here; that the only time we can ever be and experience is now; and that the only feelings we can ever be, not have, are present feelings. This means the only time and place we live is the moment. This being the moment, being it totally, is vastly different from the Western experience of urgency and emergency that demands relief and release and in which each moment is experienced as a matter of life and death but on quite a different plane. Total acceptance of the Western notion that we have to die to be re-born is more possible and widespread in the East. Each moment we die and are reborn. Each moment is new. This notion is not alien to us. Goldstein says, "If the organism is 'to be,' it always has to pass again from moments of catastrophe to states of ordered behavior." And in quantum physics energy exchange is discontinuous.

With the feeling of the subject-object relation, the absolute now, reality indicated by the Chinese notion of hsing, pointed at by Northrop's concept of pure fact and Gabriel Marcel's Being and being guided by the unifying hypothesis of the symbolizing process, I feel vaster and deeper possibilities are now open to what is now called psychoanalysis which can and does move more in the direction of the Eastern master-disciple relation.

chapter 22

Transactional Analysis:
Therapy Without Tears

ERIC BERNE AND T. A. HARRIS

Transactional analysis is one of the latest offshoots of the psychoanalytic movement. Its founder, Eric Berne (1910-1970), was a prominent California psychiatrist who set out in the 1960s to found a school of his own.

While the culturalist approach tends to project interpersonal conflict into the outside world, with the patient's relatives and friends acting as the chief protagonists, transactional analysis carries the conflict back into the patient's personality structure, where, according to analytic doctrine, it all started in the first place. In doing so, Berne has chased the three shadowy tenants—Ego, Id and Superego—from the house that Freud built and proceeded to replace them with a new cast of lively and sometimes mischievous characters engaged in the games people play: Parent, Adult and Child. Still, they can readily be recognized as reincarnations, first, of the introjected parent figure—the "parental introject"; second, of the patient's mature ego; and third, of residues of his early childlike identity or "ego state."

Using these three dramatis personae for his scenario, Berne arrives at an intriguing formulation of interpersonal transactions, games, pastimes, rituals, and their commonly seen distortions.

These ingredients are supplemented by suitably transcribed versions of Freud's Oedipus conflict and regression; of Adler's "fictitious" life styles (as contrasted with more authentic existential modes of existence), and by Skinner's operant reinforcements, which are reintroduced in terms of what Berne describes as the give and take of "strokes." Such "strokes," he declares, are the fundamental units of social transactions.

Berne succeeds admirably in blending these sundry ingredients into a consistent system of thought. Focusing on interpersonal transactions and "strokes" as the elementary units of social intercourse, transactional analysis seeks to diagnose which ego state in the agent—Child, Parent or Adult—

gives rise to the transaction, and which ego state in the respondent controls the response. On a deeper level, Berne aims at uncovering the unconscious script or life plan—the Adlerian "life style," or the Daseinsanalytic "mode of existence"—which forms the matrix for the ongoing games. Thus script analysis and game analysis are the two guiding principles of his approach.

The detailed structural study of the game plan (who is responding to whom?) is subordinate to this dual objective. Specifically, Berne asks: Who is, at a given moment, engaged in the transaction—Mother? Father? Child? Adult? Whose influence is, in turn, superimposed on the Parent in question? The Parent's Father or Mother? Alternatively, is there a grownup telescoped into the Child's reaction? (If so, he is colloquially referred to as the "Professor.")

It is these colloquialisms and metaphors, the use of everyday English, and deceptively simple formulations that make Berne's presentation so appealing and which may account for the sustained popular success of his books. Critics have argued that his method is largely confined to ego psychology; that it fails to come to grips with the deeper, unconscious aspects of personality, and thereby caters to the patient's resistances, his tendency to denial, and other defensive maneuvers. Yet Berne's witty, urbane, and at times playful approach seems to have carried the day with all but the most disturbed patients, and it seems well suited to disarm less deeply entrenched ego defenses in the rest.

The following passages are taken from Bern's best-selling The Games People Play *(1967).*

Observation of spontaneous social activity, most productively carried out in certain kinds of psychotherapy groups, reveals that from time to time people show noticeable changes in posture, viewpoint, voice, vocabulary, and other aspects of behavior. These behavioral changes are often accompanied by shifts in feeling. In a given individual, a certain set of behavior patterns corresponds to one state of mind, while another set is related to a different psychic attitude, often inconsistent with the first. These changes and differences give rise to the idea of *ego states*.

In technical language, an ego state may be described phenomenologically as a coherent system of feelings, and operationally as a set of coherent behavior patterns. In more practical terms, it is a system of feelings accompanied by a related set of behavior patterns. Each individual seems to have available a limited repertoire of such ego states, which are not roles but psychological realities. This repertoire can be sorted into the following categories: (1) ego states which resemble those of parental figures (2) ego states which are autonomously directed toward objective appraisal of reality and (3) those which represent archaic relics, still-active ego states which were fixated in early childhood. Technically these are called, respectively, exteropsychic, neopsychic, and archaeopsychic ego states. Colloquially their exhibitions are called Parent, Adult and Child, and these simple terms serve for all but the most formal discussions.

The position is, then, that at any given moment each individual in a social aggregation will exhibit a Parental, Adult or Child ego state, and that individuals can shift with varying degrees of readiness from one ego state to another. These observations give rise to certain diagnostic statements. "That is your Parent" means: "You are now in the same state of mind as one of your parents (or a parental substitute) used to be, and you are responding as he would, with the same posture, gestures, vocabulary, feelings, etc." "That is your Adult" means: "You have just made an autonomous, objective appraisal of the situation and are stating these thought-processes, or the problems you perceive or the conclusions you have come to, in a non-prejudicial manner." "That is your Child" means: "The manner and intent of your reaction is the same as it would have been when you were a very little boy or girl."

The implications are:

1. That every individual has had parents (or substitute parents) and that he carries within him a set of ego states that reproduce the ego states of those parents (as he perceived them), and that these parental ego states can be activated under certain circumstances (exteropsychic functioning). Colloquially: "Everyone carries his parents around inside of him."

2. That every individual (including children, the mentally retarded and schizophrenics) is capable of objective data processing if the appropriate ego state can be activated (neopsychic functioning). Colloquially: "Everyone has an Adult."

3. That every individual was once younger than he is now, and that he carries within him fixated relics from earlier years which will be activated under certain circumstances (archaeopsychic functioning). Colloquially: "Everyone carries a little boy or girl around inside of him." . . .

Before we leave the subject of structural analysis, certain complications should be mentioned.

1. The word "childish" is never used in structural analysis, since it has come to have strong connotations of undesirability, and of something to be stopped forthwith or gotten rid of. The term "childlike" is used in describing the Child (an archaic ego state), since it is more biological and not prejudicial. Actually the Child is in many ways the most valuable part of the personality, and can contribute to the individual's life exactly what an actual child can contribute to family life: charm, pleasure and creativity. If the Child in the individual is confused and unhealthy, then the consequences may be unfortunate, but something can and should be done about it.

2. The same applies to the words "mature" and "immature." In this system there is no such thing as an "immature person." There are only people in whom the Child takes over inappropriately or unproductively, but all such people have a complete, well-structured Adult which only needs to be uncovered or activated. Conversely, so-called "mature people" are people who are able to keep the Adult in control most of the time, but their Child will take over on occasion like anyone else's, often with disconcerting results.

3. It should be noted that the Parent is exhibited in two forms, direct and indirect: as an active ego state, and as an influence. When it is directly active, the person responds as his own father (or mother) actually responded ("Do as I do"). When it is an indirect influence, he responds the way they wanted him to respond ("Don't do as I do, do as I say"). In the first case he becomes one of them; in the second, he adapts himself to their requirements.

4. Thus the Child is also exhibited in two forms: the *adapted* Child and the *natural* Child. The adapted Child is the one who modifies his behavior under the Parental influence. He behaves as father (or mother) wanted him to behave: compliantly or precociously, for example. Or he adapts himself by withdrawing or whining. Thus the Parental influence is a cause, and the adapted Child an effect. The natural Child is a spontaneous expression: rebellion or creativity, for example. A confirmation of structural analysis is seen in the results of alcohol intoxication. Usually this decommissions the Parent first, so that the adapted Child is freed of the Parental influence, and is transformed by release into the natural Child. . . .

The Adult is necessary for survival. It processes data and computes the probabilities which are essential for dealing effectively with the outside world. It also experiences its own kinds of setbacks and gratifications. Crossing a busy highway, for example, requires the processing of a complex series of velocity data; action is suspended until the computations indicate a high degree of probability for reaching the other side safely. The gratifications offered by successful computations of this type afford some of the joys of skiing, flying, sailing, and other mobile sports. Another task of the Adult is to regulate the activities of the Parent and the Child, and so mediate objectively between them.

The Parent has two main functions. First, it enables the individual to act effectively as the parent of actual children, thus promoting the survival of the human race. Its value in this respect is shown by the fact that in raising children, people orphaned in infancy seem to have a harder time than those from homes unbroken into adolescence. Secondly, it makes many responses automatic, which conserves a great deal of time and energy. Many things are done because "That's the way it's done." This frees the Adult from the necessity of making innumerable trivial decisions, so that it can devote itself to more important issues, leaving routine matters to the Parent.

Thus all three aspects of the personality have a high survival and living value, and it is only when one or the other of them disturbs the healthy balance that analysis and reorganization are indicated. Otherwise each of them, Parent, Adult, and Child, is entitled to equal respect and has its legitimate place in a full and productive life.

The unit of social intercourse is called a transaction. If two or more people encounter each other in a social aggregation, sooner or later one of them will speak, or give some other indication of acknowledging the presence of the others. This is called the *transactional stimulus*. Another person will then say or do something which is in some way related to this stimulus, and that is called the *transactional response*. Simple transactional analysis is concerned with diagnosing which ego state implemented the transactional stimulus, and which one executed the transactional response. The simplest transactions are those in which both stimulus and response arise from the Adults of the parties concerned. The agent, estimating from the data before him that a scalpel is now the instrument of choice, holds out his hand. The respondent appraises this gesture correctly, estimates the forces and distances involved, and places the handle of the scalpel exactly where the surgeon expects it. Next in simplicity are Child-Parent transactions. The fevered child asks for a glass of water, and the nurturing mother brings it.

Both these transactions are *complementary*; that is, the response is appropriate and expected and follows the natural order of healthy human relationships. . . .The first rule of communication is that communication will proceed smoothly as long as transactions are complementary; and its corollary is that as long as transactions are complementary, communication can, in principle, proceed indefinitely. These rules are independent of the nature and content of the transactions; they are based entirely on the direction of the vectors involved. As long as the transactions are complementary, it is irrelevant to the rule whether two people are engaging in critical gossip (Parent-Parent), solving a problem (Adult-Adult), or playing together (Child-Child or Parent-Child). . . .

The converse rule is that communication is broken off when a *crossed transaction* occurs. The most common crossed transaction, and the one which causes and always has caused most of the social difficulties in the world, whether in marriage, love, friendship, or work . . . is the principal concern of psychotherapists and is typified by the classical transference reaction of psychoanalysis. The stimulus is Adult-Adult: e.g., "Maybe we should find out why you've been drinking more lately," or, "Do you know where my cuff links are?" The appropriate Adult-Adult response in each case would be: "Maybe we should. I'd certainly like to know!" or, "On the desk." If the respondent flares up, however, the responses will be something like "You're always criticizing me, just like my father did," or, "You always blame me for everything." These are both Child-Parent responses, and as the transactional diagram shows, the vectors cross. In such cases the Adult problems about drinking or cuff links must be suspended until the vectors can be realigned. This may take anywhere from several months in the drinking example to a few seconds in the case of the cuff links. Either the agent must become Parental as a complement to the respondent's suddenly activated Child, or the respondent's Adult must be reactivated as a complement to the agent's Adult. If the maid rebels during a discussion of dishwashing, the Adult-Adult conversation about dishes is finished; there can only ensue either a Child-Parent discourse, or a discussion of a different Adult subject, namely her continued employment. . . .

Simple complementary transactions most commonly occur in superficial working and social relationships, and these are easily disturbed by simple crossed transactions. In fact a superficial relationship may be defined as one which is confined to simple complementary transactions. Such relationships occur in activities, rituals and pastimes. More complex are *ulterior transactions*—those involving the activity of more than two ego states simultaneously—and this category is the basis for games. Salesmen are particularly adept at *angular transactions*, those involving three ego states. A crude but dramatic example of a sales game is illustrated in the following exchange:

Salesman: "This one is better, but you can't afford it."
Housewife: "That's the one I'll take."

The salesman, as Adult, states two objective facts: "This one is better" and "You can't afford it." At the ostensible, or *social*, level these are directed to the Adult of the housewife, whose Adult reply would be: "You are correct on both counts." However, the ulterior, or *psychological*, vector is directed by the well-trained and experienced Adult of the salesman to the housewife's Child. The correctness of his judgment is demonstrated by the Child's reply, which says in effect: "Regardless of the financial consequences, I'll show that arrogant fellow I'm as good as any of his customers." At both levels the transaction is complementary, since her reply is accepted at face value as an Adult purchasing contract.

A *duplex* ulterior transaction involves four ego states, and its commonly seen in flirtation games. . . .

At the social level this is an Adult conversation about barns, and at the psychological level it is a Child conversation about sex play. On the surface the Adult seems to have the initiative, but as in most games, the outcome is determined by the Child, and the participants may be in for a surprise.

Transactions may be classified, then, as complementary or crossed, simple or ulterior, and ulterior transactions may be subdivided into angular and duplex types.

Thomas A. Harris a psychiatrist affiliated with the Institute for Transactional Analysis in Sacramento, California, uses essentially the same ingredients as Eric Berne in his approach. Thus there is a marked moralistic, if not religious, slant to Harris' version of transactional analysis. "The therapist is here to teach," he declares. "The patient is here to learn."

His formula "I'm OK—You're OK" is a capsule statement of the therapeutic goals pursued by Harris' method of transactional analysis. In view of the striking popular success of this formula, it may therefore be no coincidence if it evokes distant echos of Émile Coué's once celebrated prescription for mental health: "Every day in every way I'm feeling better and better."

chapter 23

Jung in Search of the Soul

GLOVER ON FREUD OR JUNG? . . .
EHRENWALD: FREUD VERSUS JUNG: THE MYTHOPHOBIC
VERSUS THE MYTHOPHILIC TEMPER

C. G. Jung's (1875-1961) position in the history of psychotherapy cannot be defined by merely contrasting his work with Freud's system of thought. Like Adler, Stekel and Otto Rank, Jung was an early associate of Freud. He shared with him the dawning insight into the dynamics of mental processes; into the part played by unconscious motivations in health and disease; into the deeper meaning of dreams. He, too, considered the transference relationship one of the most important factors in every form of psychotherapy. But in matters of basic philosophy there was a wide gulf between Freud and Jung. This made the breach between the two men inevitable. In 1911 Jung openly severed his ties with the psychoanalytic movement and founded what has since been known as the Zurich School of analytic psychotherapy. Apart from occasional bouts of controversy, Jungian and Freudian analysts have not, since then, been on speaking terms.

Jung, like Adler, rejected Freud's thesis of sexuality as the principal factor in neurotic disorders. It is true, he said, that neurosis is often due to a disturbance in the dynamics of the patient's libido organization. But to Jung libido is no longer identical with sex. It embraces the sum total of the vital energies of man. It is the life force itself. In a similar bold generalization, he extended the scope of the unconscious beyond that which has been repressed by the individual. The individual unconscious, he holds, merges into the collective unconscious, common to men of all races and all historical periods. The collective unconscious itself is the repository of what he described as the primordial images or archetypes. It forms the universal power house from which man's creative energies, myths and religious experiences are derived. Their occasional break-through into individual consciousness may give rise to mental illness, especially schizophrenia. Otherwise there exists a well-balanced complementary relationship between the conscious and unconscious parts of the personality. This balance, in conjunction with the particular way in which the individual is wont to relate to the outside world, is responsible for the two major types of personality

*described by Jung, the extrovert and the introvert type, and the various
subgroups which can be discerned within these two classes.*

*These are, however, only some of the features of Jung's system of
thought, those which can readily be compared—or contrasted—with
Freud's theories. But the major cleavage between Freud and Jung is of a
deeper, philosophical nature. Freud's system has evolved from strictly
scientific propositions. It is committed to an essentially mechanistic outlook
on the world, governed by the laws of cause and effect: it is deterministic.
Not so the universe of C. G. Jung. Jung's archetypes transgress the barriers
of time and space. More than that: they are capable of breaking the
shackles of the law of causality. They are endowed with frankly mystical
"prospective" faculties. The soul itself, according to Jung, is the reaction of
the personality to the unconscious and includes in every person both male
and female elements, the animus and the anima, as well as the persona or
the person's reaction to the outside world. Jung has reached what his critics
describe as an essentially mystical attitude late in his career. But he has
steadily moved toward it from the outset. In one of his latest works, he
contrasts the laws governing nature at large with an acausal or noncausal
principle which, he feels, applies to the psychic realm and accounts for such
unorthodox happenings as telepathy, clairvoyance and occasional prophetic dreams.*

*In the view of his adversaries, Jung has thus broken faith with the scien-
tific method and has reverted to the ancient belief in magic, alchemy and
astrological correspondences between Man and the Universe, as it was held
by the mystery cults, by Plato and the Neoplatonists, and by his great pre-
decessor, Paracelsus of Hohenheim. There is reason to believe that Jung
himself would have little quarrel with such a verdict.*

*In the selection that follows, Jung gives, among other things, a concise ex-
position of his own teachings as contrasted with those of Freud and Adler. It
is taken from* Two Essays on Analytic Psychology, *published in 1953. They
represent a late version of earlier essays dealing with the same problem.*

Fate willed it that one of Freud's earliest disciples, Alfred Adler, should
formulate a view of neurosis based exclusively on the power principle. It is
of no little interest, indeed singularly fascinating, to see how utterly different the same things look when viewed in a contrary light. To take the main
contrast first: with Freud everything follows from antecedent circumstances
according to a rigorous causality, with Adler everything is a teleological
"arrangement." Here is a simple example: A young woman begins to have
attacks of anxiety. At night she wakes up from a nightmare with a blood-
curdling cry, is scarcely able to calm herself, clings to her husband and im-
plores him not to leave her, demanding assurances that he really loves her,

etc. Gradually a nervous asthma develops, the attacks also coming on during the day.

The Freudian method at once begins burrowing into the inner causality of the sickness and its symptoms. What were the first anxiety dreams about? Ferocious bulls, lions, tigers, and evil men were attacking her. What are the patient's associations? A story of something that happened to her before she was married. She was staying at a health resort in the mountains. She played a good deal of tennis and the usual acquaintances were made. There was a young Italian who played particularly well and also knew how to handle a guitar in the evening. An innocent flirtation developed, leading once to a moonlight stroll. On this occasion the Italian temperament "unexpectedly" broke loose, much to the alarm of the unsuspecting girl. He gave her "such a look" that she could never forget it. This look follows her even in her dreams: the wild animals that pursue her look at her just like that. But does this look in fact come only from the Italian? Another reminiscence is instructive. The patient had lost her father through an accident when she was about fourteen years old. Her father was a man of the world and travelled a good deal. Not long before his death he took her with him to Paris, where they visited, among other places, the Folies-Bergère. There something happened that made an indelible impression on her. On leaving the theatre, a painted hussy jostled her father in an incredibly brazen way. Looking in alarm to see what her father would do, she saw this same look, this animal glare, in his eyes. This inexplicable something followed her day and night. From then on her relations with her father changed. Sometimes she was irritable and subject to venomous moods, sometimes she loved him extravagantly. Then came sudden fits of weeping for no reason, and for a time, whenever her father was at home, she suffered at table from a horrible gulping accompanied by what looked like choking-fits, generally followed by loss of voice for one or two days. When the news of the sudden death of her father reached her, she was seized by uncontrollable grief, which gave way to fits of hysterical laughter. However, she soon calmed down; her condition quickly improved, and the neurotic symptoms practically vanished. A veil of forgetfulness was drawn over the past. Only the episode with the Italian stirred something in her of which she was afraid. She then abruptly broke off all connection with the young man. A few years later she married. The first appearance of her present neurosis was after the birth of her second child, just when she made the discovery that her husband had a certain tender interest in another woman.

This history gives rise to many questions: for example, what about the mother? Concerning the mother the relevant facts are that she was very nervous and spent her time trying every kind of sanatorium and method of cure. She too suffered from nervous asthma and anxiety symptoms. The marriage had been of a very distant kind as far back as the patient could remember. Her mother did not understand the father properly; the patient always had the feeling that she understood him much better. She was her father's confessed darling and was correspondingly cool at heart towards her mother.

These hints may suffice to give us an over-all picture of the illness. Behind the present symptoms lie fantasies which are immediately related to the experience with the Italian, but which clearly point back to the father, whose unhappy marriage gave the little daughter an early opportunity to secure for herself the place that should properly have been filled by the mother. Behind this conquest there lies, of course, the fantasy of being the really suitable wife for the father. The first attack of neurosis broke out at a moment when this fantasy received a severe shock, probably the same shock that the mother had also received, though this would be unknown to the child. The symptoms are easily understandable as an expression of disappointed and slighted love. The choking is due to the feeling of constriction in the throat, a well-known concomitant of violent affects which cannot be quite "swallowed down." (The metaphors of common speech, as we know, frequently relate to such physiological phenomena.) When the father died, her conscious mind was grieved to death, but her shadow laughed, after the manner of Till Eulenspiegel, who was doleful when things went downhill, but full of merry pranks on the weary way up, always on the look-out for what lay ahead. When her father was at home, she was dejected and ill; when he was away, she always felt much better, like the innumerable husbands and wives who hide from each other the sweet secret that neither is altogether indispensable to the other.

That the unconscious had at this juncture some justification for laughing is shown by the supervening period of good health. She succeeded in letting her whole past sink into oblivion. Only the episode with the Italian threatened to resurrect the underworld. But with a quick gesture she flung the door to and remained healthy until the dragon of neurosis came creeping back, just when she imagined herself safely over the mountain, in the perfect state, so to speak, of wife and mother.

Sexual psychology says: the cause of the neurosis lies in the patient's fundamental inability to free herself from her father. That is why that experience came up again when she discovered in the Italian the mysterious "something" which had previously made such an overwhelming impression on her in connection with her father. These memories were naturally revived by the analogous experience with her husband, the immediate cause of the neurosis. We could therefore say that the content of and reason for the neurosis was the conflict between the infantile-erotic relation to her father and her love for her husband.

If, however, we look at the same clinical picture from the point of view of the "other" instinct, the will to power, it assumes quite a different aspect. Her parents' unhappy marriage afforded an excellent opportunity for the childish urge to power. The power-instinct wants the ego to be "on top" under all circumstances, by fair means or foul. The "integrity of the personality" must be preserved at all costs. Every attempt, be it only an apparent attempt, of the environment to obtain the slightest ascendency over the subject is met, to use Adler's expression, by the "masculine protest." The disillusionment of the mother and her withdrawal into neurosis created the desired opportunity for a display of power and for gaining the ascendency. Love and good behavior are, from the standpoint of the power-instinct, known to be a choice means to this end. Virtuousness often serves to *compel* recognition from others. Already as a child the patient knew how to secure a privileged position with her father through especially ingratiating and affectionate behavior, and to get the better of her mother—not out of love for her father, but because love was a good method of gaining the upper hand. The laughing-fit at the time of her father's death is striking proof of this. We are inclined to regard such an explanation as a horrible depreciation of love, not to say a malicious insinuation, until we reflect for a moment and look at the world as it is. Have we not seen countless people who love and believe in their love, and then, when their purpose is accomplished, turn away as though they had never loved? And finally, is not this the way of nature herself? Is "disinterested" love at all possible? If so, it belongs to the highest virtues, which in point of fact are exceedingly rare. Perhaps there is in general a tendency to think as little as possible about the purpose of love; otherwise we might make discoveries which would show the worth of our love in a less favorable light.

The patient, then, had a laughing-fit at the death of her father—she had finally arrived on top. It was an hysterical laughter, a psychogenic symptom, something that sprang from unconscious motives and not from those of the conscious ego. That is a difference not to be made light of, and one that also tells us whence and how certain human virtues arise. . . .

The first outbreak of neurosis in our patient occurred the moment she realized that there was something in her father which she could not dominate. And then a great light dawned: she now knew what was the purpose of her mother's neurosis, namely that when you encounter an obstacle which cannot be overcome by rational methods and charm, there is still another method, hitherto unknown to her, which her mother had already discovered beforehand, i.e., neurosis. So from now on she imitates her mother's neurosis. But what, we may ask in astonishment, is the good of a neurosis? What can it do? Anyone who has in his neighborhood a definite case of neurosis knows well enough what it can "do." There is no better method of tyrannizing over the entire household. Heart attacks, choking fits, spasms of all kinds, produce an enormous effect that can hardly be surpassed. Oceans of sympathy are let loose, there is the anguish of worried parents, the running to and fro of servants, telephone bells, hurrying doctors, difficult diagnoses, elaborate examinations, lengthy treatments, heavy expenses, and there in the midst of all the hubbub lies the innocent sufferer, with everybody overflowing with gratitude when at last he recovers from his "spasms."

This unsurpassable "arrangement"—to use Adler's expression—was discovered by the little one and applied with success whenever her father was there. It became superfluous when the father died, for now she was finally on top. The Italian was dropped overboard when he laid too much emphasis on her femininity by an appropriate reminder of his virility. But when a suitable chance of marriage presented itself, she loved and resigned herself without a murmur to the fate of wife and mother. So long as her revered superiority was maintained, everything went swimmingly. But once her husband had a little bit of interest outside, she had recourse as before to that exceedingly effective "arrangement" for the indirect exercise of her power, because she had again encountered the obstacle—this time in her husband—which previously in her father's case had escaped her mastery.

This is how things look from the point of view of power psychology. I fear the reader must feel like the *cadi* who, having heard the counsel for the one party, said, "Thou has well spoken. I perceive that thou art right." Then came the other party, and when he had finished, the *cadi* scratched himself behind the ear and said, "Thou hast well spoken. I perceive that thou also art right." It is unquestionable that the urge to power plays an extraordinarily important part. It is correct that neurotic symptoms and complexes are also elaborate "arrangements" which inexorably pursue their aims, with incredible obstinacy and cunning. Neurosis is teleologically oriented. In establishing this Adler has won for himself no small credit.

Which of the two points of view is right? That is a question that might lead to much brain racking. One simply cannot lay the two explanations side by side, for they contradict each other absolutely. In the one, the chief and decisive fact is Eros and its destiny; in the other, it is the power of the ego. In the first case, the ego is merely a sort of appendage to Eros; in the second, love is just a means to the end, which is ascendency. Those who have the power of the ego most at heart will revolt against the first conception, but those who care most for love will never be reconciled to the second.

THE PROBLEM OF THE ATTITUDE-TYPE

The incompatibility of the two theories discussed in the preceding chapters requires a standpoint superordinate to both, in which they could come together in unison. We are certainly not entitled to discard one in favor of the other, however convenient this expedient might be. For, if we examine the two theories without prejudice, we cannot deny that both contain significant truths, and, contradictory as these are, they should not be regarded as mutually exclusive. The Freudian theory is attractively simple, so much so that it almost pains one if anybody drives in the wedge of a contrary assertion. But the same is true of Adler's theory. It too is of illuminating simplicity and explains just as much as the Freudian theory. No wonder, then, that the adherents of both schools obstinately cling to their onesided truths. For humanly understandable reasons they are unwilling to give up a beautiful, rounded theory in exchange for a paradox, or, worse still, lose themselves in the confusion of contradictory points of view.

Now, since both theories are in a large measure correct—that is to say, since they both appear to explain their material—it follows that a neurosis must have two opposite aspects, one of which is grasped by the Freudian, the other by the Adlerian theory. But how comes it that each investigator sees only one side, and why does each maintain that he has the only valid view? It must come from the fact that, owing to his psychological peculiarity, each investigator most readily sees that factor in the neurosis which corresponds to his peculiarity. It cannot be assumed that the cases of neurosis seen by Adler are totally different from those seen by Freud. Both are obviously working with the same material; but because of personal peculiarities they each see things from a different angle, and thus they evolve fundamentally different views and theories. Adler sees how a subject who feels suppressed and inferior tries to secure an illusory superiority by means of "protests," "arrangements," and other appropriate devices directed equally against parents, teachers, regulations, authorities, situations, institutions, and such. Even sexuality may figure among these devices. This view lays undue emphasis upon the subject, before which the idiosyncrasy and significance of object entirely vanishes. Objects are regarded at best as vehicles of suppressive tendencies. I shall probably not be wrong in assuming that the love relation and other desires directed upon objects exists equally in Adler as essential factors; yet in his theory of neurosis they do not play the principal role assigned to them by Freud.

Freud sees his patient in perpetual dependence on, and in relation to, significant objects. Father and mother play a large part here; whatever other significant influences or conditions enter into the life of the patient go back in a direct line of causality to these prime factors. The *pièce de résistance* of his theory is the concept of transference, i.e., the patient's relation to the doctor. Always a specifically qualified object is either desired or met with resistance, and this reaction always follows the pattern established in earliest childhood through the relation to father and mother. What comes from the subject is essentially a blind striving after pleasure; but this striving always acquires its quality from specific objects. With Freud objects are of the greatest significance and possess almost exclusively the determining power, while the subject remains remarkably insignificant and is really nothing more than the source of desire for pleasure and a "seat of anxiety." As already pointed out, Freud recognizes ego-instincts, but this term alone is enough to show that his conception of the subject differs *toto coelo* from Adler's, where the subject figures as the determining factor.

Certainly both investigators see the subject in relation to the object; but how differently this relation is seen! With Adler the emphasis is placed on a subject who, no matter what the object, seeks his own security and supremacy; with Freud the emphasis is placed wholly upon objects, which, according to their specific character, either promote or hinder the subject's desire for pleasure.

This difference can hardly be anything else but a difference of temperament, a contrast between two types of human mentality, one of which finds the determining agency pre-eminently in the subject, the other in the object. A middle view, it may be that of common sense, would suppose that human behaviour is conditioned as much by the subject as by the object. The two investigators would probably assert, on the other hand, that their theory does not envisage a psychological explanation of the normal man, but is a theory of neurosis. But in that case Freud would have to explain and treat some of his patients along Adlerian lines, and Adler condescend to give earnest consideration in certain instances to his former teacher's point of view—which has occurred neither on the one side nor on the other.

The spectacle of this dilemma made me ponder the question: are there at least two different human types, one of them more interested in the object, the other more interested in himself? And does that explain why the one sees only the one and the other only the other, and thus each arrives at totally different conclusions? As we have said, it was hardly to be supposed that fate selected the patients so meticulously that a definite group invariably reached a definite doctor. For some time it had struck me, in connection both with myself and with my colleagues, that there are some cases which make a distinct appeal, while others somehow refuse to "click." It is of crucial importance for the treatment whether a good relationship between doctor and patient is possible or not. If some measure of natural confidence does not develop within a short period, then the patient will do better to choose another doctor. I myself have never shrunk from recommending to a colleague a patient whose peculiarities were not in my line or were unsympathetic to me, and indeed this trait is in the patient's own interests. I am positive that in such a case I would not do good work. Everyone has his personal limitations, and the psychotherapist in particular is well advised never to disregard them. Excessive personal differences and incompatibilities cause resistances that are disproportionate and out of place, though they are not altogether unjustified. The Freud-Adler controversy is simply a paradigm and one single instance among many possible attitude-types.

I have long busied myself with this question and have finally, on the basis of numerous observations and experiences, come to postulate two fundamental attitudes, namely introversion and extraversion. The first attitude is normally characterized by a hesitant, reflective, retiring nature that keeps itself to itself, shrinks from objects, is always slightly on the defensive and prefers to hide behind mistrustful scrutiny. The second is normally characterized by an outgoing, candid, and accommodating nature that adapts easily to a given situation, quickly forms attachments, and, setting aside any possible misgivings, will often venture forth with careless confidence into unknown situations. In the first case obviously the subject, and in the second the object, is all-important.

Naturally these remarks sketch the two types only in the roughest outline. As a matter of the empirical fact the two attitudes, to which I shall come back shortly, can seldom be observed in their pure state. They are infinitely varied and compensated, so that often the type is not at all easy to establish. The reason for variation—apart from individual fluctuations—is the predominance of one of the conscious functions, such as thinking or feeling, which then gives the basic attitude a special character. The numerous compensations of the basic type are generally due to experiences which teach a man, perhaps in a very painful way, that he cannot give free rein to his nature. In other cases, for instance with neurotics, one frequently does not know whether one is dealing with a conscious or an unconscious attitude because, owing to the dissociation of the personality, sometimes one half of it and sometimes the other half occupies the foreground and confuses one's judgment. This is what makes it so excessively trying to live with neurotic persons.

The actual existence of far-reaching type differences, of which I have described eight groups, has enabled me to conceive the two controversial theories of neurosis as manifestations of a type-antagonism.

Here Jung discusses the problem of transference and its correlation with his theory of the archetypes:

The transference is in itself no more than a projection of unconscious contents. At first the so-called superficial contents of the unconscious are projected, as can be seen from symptoms, dreams, and fantasies. In this state the doctor is interesting as a possible lover. Then he appears more in the role of the father: either the good, kind father or the "thunderer," according to the qualities which the real father had for the patient. Sometimes the doctor has a maternal significance, a fact that seems somewhat peculiar, but is still within the bounds of possibility. All these fantasy projections are founded on personal memories.

Finally there appear forms of fantasy that possess an extravagant character. The doctor is then endowed with uncanny powers: he is a magician or a wicked demon, or else the corresponding personification of goodness, a saviour. Again, he may appear as a mixture of both. Of course, it is to be understood that he need not necessarily appear like this to the patient's conscious mind; it is only the fantasies coming to the surface which picture him in this guise. Such patients often cannot get it into their heads that their fantasies really come from themselves and have little or nothing to do with the character of the doctor. This delusion rests on the fact that there are no personal grounds in the memory for this kind of projection. It can sometimes be shown that similar fantasies had, at a certain period in childhood, attached themselves to the father or mother, although neither father nor mother provided any real occasion for them. . . .

In this further stage of treatment, then, when fantasies are produced which no longer rest on personal memories, we have to do with the manifestations of a deeper layer of the unconscious where the primordial images common to humanity lie sleeping. I have called these images or motifs "archetypes," also "dominants" of the unconscious.

The discovery means another step forward in our understanding: the recognition, that is, of the two layers in the unconscious. We have to distinguish between a personal unconscious and an impersonal or transpersonal unconscious. We speak of the latter also as the collective unconscious because it is detached from anything personal and is entirely universal, and because its contents can be found everywhere, which is naturally not the case with the personal contents. The personal unconscious contains lost memories, painful ideas that are repressed (i.e., forgotten on purpose), subliminal perceptions, by which are meant sense-perceptions that were not strong enough to reach consciousness, and finally, contents that are not yet ripe for consciousness. It corresponds to the figure of the shadow so frequently met with in dreams.

The primordial images are the most ancient and the most universal "thought-forms" of humanity. They are as much feelings as thoughts; indeed, they lead their own independent life rather in the manner of part-souls, as can easily be seen in those philosophical or Gnostic systems which rely on awareness of the unconscious as the source of knowledge. The idea of angels, archangels, "principalities and powers" in St. Paul, the archons of the Gnostics, the heavenly hierarchy of Dionysius the Areopagite, all come from the perception of the relative autonomy of the archetypes.

We have now found the object which the libido chooses when it is freed from the personal, infantile form of transference. It follows its own gradient down into the depths of the unconscious, and there activates what has lain slumbering from the beginning. It has discovered the hidden treasure upon which mankind ever and anon has drawn, and from which it has raised up its gods and demons, and all those potent and mighty thoughts without which man ceases to be man. . . .

The archetype is a kind of readiness to produce over and over again the same or similar mythical ideas. Hence it seems as though what is impressed upon the unconscious were exclusively the subjective fantasy-ideas aroused by the physical process. Therefore we may take it that archetypes are recurrent impressions made by subjective reactions. Naturally this assumption only pushes the problem further back without solving it. There is nothing to prevent us from assuming that certain archetypes exist even in animals, that they are grounded in the peculiarities of the living organism itself and are therefore direct expressions of life whose nature cannot be further explained. Not only are the archetypes, apparently, impressions of ever-repeated typical experiences, but, at the same time, they behave empirically like agents that tend towards the repetition of these same experiences. For when an archetype appears in a dream, in a fantasy, or in life, it always brings with it a certain influence or power by virtue of which it either exercises a numinous or a fascinating effect, or impels to action.

Freud himself avoided public controversy on a larger scale with his former associates. His followers, however, have shown less restraint in this respect. In 1950 Edward Glover (1888-   ), one of the leaders of the British psychoanalytic movement, published his book, Freud or Jung? *It gives an uncompromising statement of the orthodox psychoanalytic position as opposed to the teachings of the Zurich School. The selection that follows is from the concluding chapter of Glover's book.*

At the risk of appearing unduly partisan, and thereby arousing the reader's sympathy for an oppressed cause, it is necessary to restate in conclusion the reasons why the Freud-Jung issue cannot be blanketed by eclectic compromises.

In the first place it should be made clear that when basic principles are at stake, there can be no question of arriving at a gentleman's agreement. It is not hard to imagine what astronomical confusion would have arisen had the eclectics of the period insisted on supporting compromises between the Ptolomaic and the Copernican systems. As Jung himself remarked, 'He whose sun still revolves around the earth is a different person from him whose earth is the satellite of the Sun.' The issue between Freud and Jung is of a similar degree of magnitude and is as refractory to compromise. If Freud is right, Jung is nothing more or less than an academic (conscious) psychologist masquerading as the apostle of a new dynamic psychology. If Jung is right, Freud's system should be dismissed as the symptomatic expression of a psychopathological character, valid only for those who suffer from similar obsessions.

Throughout this essay, attention has been concentrated on those basic concepts of the Freudian and Jungian systems which illustrate their mutual incompatibility; and an endeavor has been made to set forth as simply as possible the technical reasons why they are so incompatible. In summing up these arguments, it is desirable however to restate the position in more general terms.

Freud's discovery of the dynamic unconscious, his formulation of the laws that govern this part of the psychic apparatus, his description of the origin and development of the unconscious ego and of the various components of primitive instinct which it seeks to regulate, were the first and decisive steps towards the building up of a scientific psychology. For the first time it was possible to understand the part played by psychic conflict in accelerating the development of specifically human characteristics; for the first time the staggering achievements of child-development could be assessed at their proper value, and the majority of adult mental disorders recognized as measures of the failure of the child to overcome the odds with which it is faced; for the first time it was possible to hold out some hope that by adjustment of earlier difficulties, the adult mind might be freed to carry out its tasks of adaptation.

As we have seen the most consistent trend of Jungian psychology is its negation of every important part of Freudian theory. The Freudian unconscious is abolished and in its place we are presented with that shallow preconscious system described by Jung as the Personal Unconscious. Having eliminated the dynamic unconscious and being unable to discover in his Personal Unconscious forces and mechanisms that would account for man's psychic activities, Jung looks for the mainspring of mind in a purely constitutional factor—the Collective Unconscious. By so doing he closes the door against any possibility of discovering the unconscious ego, and at the same time abolishes the concept of individual unconscious conflict. Conflict is reduced to an opposition between constitutional tendencies and the volitional aspects of consciousness. To make assurance doubly sure, a system of opposites and compensations is postulated which abolishes any dynamic distinction between the Collective Unconscious and consciousness.

This nihilistic approach to the facts of mental development is further reinforced by the Jungian concept of mental energy which does away with the necessity of investigating infantile life and at the same time reduces conflict to the level of a conscious problem. With the introduction of his monistic *elan vital*, moving like a neutral force from one position to another, from the Collective Unconscious to the Persona and back, the whole concept of instinctual modification and with it the concept of infantile conflict goes by the board. Inevitably, unconscious psychic mechanisms lose any distinctive characteristics they possess and are reduced to mere centripetal and centrifugal movements of mental energy in a closed system. In any case there is no room in the Jungian psychology for concepts such as repression which are totally incompatible with the automatic operation of laws of opposites and compensations.

This, then, is a sample of the controversy which has engaged the rival schools of psychoanalysis in the course of the past decades. Glover's position leaves no room for a compromise between the Freudian and the Jungian approach. To him the two are worlds (or rather world views) apart, like the Ptolemaic and the Copernican systems of astronomy. But the question is whether the Freudian, the Jungian or, for that matter, any one of the modern schools of psychotherapy, has actually attained the status of such an exact natural science as astronomy, and whether they are qualified to make assertions of equal assurance. The partisan answer to this question may conceivably be in the affirmative. The faithful follower may consider the Freudian, the Jungian or any one particular system the ultimate truth. But the reader who has seen the many views presented in the pages of this anthology may perhaps prefer to suspend judgment.

Jung's posthumous Dreams, Memories, Reflections, *edited by Aniela Jaffe and first published in 1961, has provided new dramatic insights into his enigmatic personality. Above all, it throws light on the contrasting personalities of Jung and Freud, and on their relationship. It contains, among other things, Jung's account of the "poltergeist" incident in Freud's study, which Freud dismissed as a "beautiful delusion," while Jung claimed it as evidence of his own mediumistic powers.*

The selection that follows is taken from a Freud memorial lecture, delivered by Jan Ehrenwald, the editor of this anthology, to the Israeli Psychoanalytic Society, May 5, 1967: * Freud versus Jung—the Mythophobic versus the Mythophilic Temper in Psychotherapy.

---

*A Freud Memorial Lecture, delivered to the Israel Psychoanalytic Society, May 5, 1967.

Are we capable of weighing the respective contributions of Freud and Jung in a spirit of objective inquiry, sine ire et studio, without being tempted to measure Jung by Freudian or Freud by Jungian standards? . . .

The issue, as I see it, is the striking contrast between two personalities tied together by dedication to the same cause, confronted with the same psychic reality. Yet each man tried to meet the challenge of exploration and discovery in his own way, arriving at conflicting, if not mutually incompatible, theories of the human mind.

Freud's exploration of the unconscious was predicated on his belief in the supremacy of reason over the heritage of primitive mentality: magic and myth. Jung pinned his faith on the superiority and ultimate truth value of myth. Myths, to Jung, were of a higher order of reality than science and scientific theory. The same contrast applies to their respective attitudes towards religion. Freud was deeply committed to a code of personal ethics and morality, but he considered religion as a collective neurosis of mankind —an illusion without a Future—and he protested, perhaps too much, his innocence of all "oceanic feelings." Jung, the son of a protestant clergyman, with eight more parsons in his family, remained equally committed to religion and ultimately to mysticism of his own brand. Freud, the rationalist and agnostic, resorted to myth and metaphor as figures of speech—with apologies for their continued usage. He tolerated no compromise in his adherence to the principles of the natural sciences. To Jung, Freud's figures of speech came alive as archetypes, springing from the depth of his prodigious "mythopoetic" imagination— a faculty which, to his regret, "had vanished from our age."

Yet on closer scrutiny vestiges of his own mythopoetic imagination can still be discovered in Freud's system of thought. Freud's tripartite picture of the "mental apparatus" has been compared with the three constituent parts of the soul postulated by the Jewish Kabbalah, or with the tripartite structure of the medieval Christian universe in which the Superego stands for Heaven, the abode of the Divinity; the Ego for Earth, and the Id for Hell.

On taking a closer look at Freud's diagram of personality structure in the Ego and the Id, I was struck by the similarity of the outlines of the Horkappe —the forerunner of the Superego—sitting jauntily on top of the ego, like the yarmulke, the skull-cap worn all day by the orthodox Jew except in the bathroom or while he is asleep. Confronted with this similarity one may well ask whether it does not amount to a pictorial representation of a "return of the repressed"—in this case of the religious underpinnings of the Freudian Superego?

I do not think Freud would have looked favorably at such an interpretation, but turning from religion to myth, the master himself has commented on the relationship of his dualistic theory of instinct—of the Instincts of

Love and Death—to the mythos of Eros and Thanatos propounded by Empedocles. Likewise, he noted the similarity of his concept of intrapsychic conflict with Plato's fable of the Charioteer and his Two Horses. It certainly was no coincidence that Freud chose the lines: *Flectere si nequeo Superos Acheronta movebo* (If I cannot sway the Superior Powers, I will bend those of the Netherworld to my will) as the motto for his magnum opus, *The Interpretation of Dreams*.

On the other hand, Freud's challenge of the "Acherontic Powers" has to be viewed against the background of his analytic exposure and radical rejection of the quest for magic omnipotence as a throwback to primitive mentality or a regression to the level of the neurotic or the child. Yet despite his protestations, Freud's attitude towards myth, magic and the quest for omnipotence was not entirely free from ambivalence. Indeed, on closer scrutiny, his own attitude shows evidence of what psychoanalysis describes as reaction formations against repudiated "mental content."

If magic is made up of three main ingredients: (1) the ritual, (2) the spell, and (3) the magician's impact upon his client, Freud might be said to have shown excessive zeal in purging all three from his analytic approach. Together with religion, he banished rites and rituals from the psychoanalytic situation—unless we regard the couch as the last remnant of the temple sleep or incubation used by the ancients in their shrines of healing.

Freud repudiated magical spells and incantations and made mandatory the analyst's silence in the therapeutic situation. However, here again, we can discover vestiges of magic in those therapists who are still inclined to overrate the power of words used in analytic interpretations. As for the therapist's quest for omnipotence, Freud's correspondence and early writings testify to his dismay over his own unexpected personal impact upon his patients. This may in effect have been one of the reasons for his abandoning hypnosis as a therapeutic tool.

Yet the conflict between Freud and Jung was more than a clash of philosophies, of scientific doctrines or methods of treatment. The cleavage between the two men was of a more deeply personal and idiosyncratic nature. It involved their respective "archetypal" images of themselves—and of the other: their "styles of life" or "modes of existence." Freud saw in Jung his "beloved son," the heir apparent to whom he wanted to bequeath, his scientific legacy. He was to be a replacement for his lost friend and "love object," the imaginative and mystically inclined Wilhelm Fliess. Freud to Jung was a mentor, revered and resented at the same time: a reincarnation of his beloved and hated father, with all its attending Oedipal implications, which even Jungian analysts tend to attach to relationships of this order.

In one of Jung's dreams, recorded in his *Memories, Dreams, Reflections*, the dreamer sees Freud as a "peevish looking petty customs official,"

searching for contraband in luggage which people try to smuggle over the
Swiss-Austrian border—or from the unconscious into the conscious realm.
Someone remarks on the little man in the dream: "He is nothing but a
ghost . . . one of those who cannot die properly." It is a remark betraying
both the dreamer's death wishes and the aura of immortality surrounding
Freud, the petty Austrian customs official of lowly birth. By contrast, Jung
sees himself in another fragment of the dream as Siegfried, Lohengrin or
Parsival—a knight in shining armour, a crusader "full of life, completely
real."

Sinister premonitions of Jung's Oedipal conflict with his father are contained in one of the earliest dreams recorded in his memoirs. In the dream
Jung saw himself descending a staircase into an underground chamber.
There he came face to face with a huge tree trunk, fifteen feet high, made of
skin and naked flesh. It had an eye on top, emitted a dim light and was
seated on a magnificent throne. He heard his mother's voice call to him:
"Yes, just look at him. That is the man-eater!" Jung conjectures that the
awesome creature was connected with the apparition of a Jesuit priest and
of the Lord Jesus, who had frightened him in his early childhood years.

In a variation on the same theme it was God who sat on the throne. The
throne was placed on top of a big, shiny cathedral, representing the world.
To his horror Jung could not suppress the thought of God suddenly defecating on his cathedral in such an explosive manner that the feces shattered its
roof and broke the walls asunder.

To the Freudian analyst the latent meaning of these images is envy, fear
and hatred of the powerful, Godlike father possessed of superhuman phallic
and anal prowess. Jung remarks that not until the age of sixty-five had he
been able to tell anybody of these guilt-laden dreams and fantasies.

The same conflict, thoroughly disguised and stripped of its anal ingredients, appears again in a dream dreamt at the time of his close association
with Freud. In the dream Jung sees himself in the upper stories of a house
representing his own personality. He descends deeper and deeper and, ultimately, to prehistoric levels of the building. On the deepest level he discovers two human skulls "obviously very old and half disintegrated." Jung
related this dream to Freud and remarks: "What chiefly interested Freud in
this dream were the two skulls. He returned to them repeatedly and urged
me to find a wish in connection with them. What did I think about those
skulls? And who were they? I knew, perfectly well, of course, what he was
driving at: that secret death wishes were concealed in the dream. 'But what
does he really expect of me?' I thought to myself. Toward whom would I
have death wishes? I felt violent resistance to any such interpretation. But I
did not then trust my own judgment and wanted to hear Freud's opinion. I
wanted to learn from him. Therefore I submitted to his intention and said:

'My wife and my sister-in-law'—after all I had to name someone whose death was worth the wishing."

In Jung's interpretation the dream represents a structual diagram of the human psyche merging into the Collective Unconscious. Thus it foreshadows one of his major ideas, with all its far-reaching metaphysical implications. Unfortunately, this "Jungian" reading of the dream still leaves the theme of the two skulls unaccounted for. But in the light of Freudian theory their meaning is rather transparent. By his own account, Jung's relationship with his father had always been precarious; at times it was openly hostile. The same ambivalence had marred his relationship with Freud. Viewed against this background, the two skulls, "very old and half disintegrated," are those of Jung's father and of Freud himself. They are the *corpora delicti* of double patricide, not of the flippantly admitted and subsequently discounted murder of his wife and sister-in-law.

Freud did not go on record with his interpretation of Jung's dream. But its hidden meaning must have left him with no doubt as to his "beloved son's" secret death wishes against him. It may be no coincidence that two of Freud's fainting fits occurred in Jung's presence and that in both cases they were triggered off by indications of open conflict between the two men. Yet on one of these occasions it was Jung, husky and strong-armed, who carried the older man to a sofa to rest. Ernest Jones, reporting the incident, notes that on regaining consciousness, Freud mumbled under his breath: "How sweet must it be to die. . . ."

Whatever the dynamics of Freud's reaction to the impending break with his "beloved son," Jung has made his "violent resistance" to one of the cornerstones of Freud's theories perfectly clear. He was totally unprepared to face his unresolved ambivalence conflict with Freud, much in the same way that he closed his mind to facing the depth of his resentment and death wishes against his father.

On the other hand Jung was quite explicit concerning the guilt feelings connected with his obsessive fantasies of God-Father defecating upon his shiny cathedral. Yet in this instance his defenses were not confined to the familiar device of denial or displacement as described in his *Memories*. They amount to a spectacular tour de force, testifying to his theological acumen. After much soul-searching and obsessive rumination, Jung concluded that his very blasphemic thoughts must have come from God himself; that God who had permitted Adam and Eve to fall into sin had also made him, Jung, dream the blasphemic dreams. But in so doing God had absolved him of the responsibility for the unspeakable crime committed by the dreamer. In the last analysis it lay outside his province and could be placed squarely on the doorstep of what he later was to describe as the archetypes, which were themselves instruments of both God's cruelty and

God's grace. This insight came to Jung with the power of sudden illumination. It may in effect have been one of the sources of his celebrated theory of the Collective Unconscious teeming with a wealth of numinous archetypal images. Once the idea had dawned on him, Jung's conviction of its validity became unshakable. It has become the cornerstone of Jung's system of thought, of his personal myth—and of his "anti-Freudian" ego defenses. Put in psychoanalytic terms, at least part of his doctrine was in effect an ingenious system of rationalizations, reaction formations and secondary elaborations. It was a system intended to explain, or explain away, his hostility against his father, his unconscious incestuous drives, and his anal-sadistic impulses, and thus to allay the tormenting guilt feelings associated with them. That his defenses gradually reached proportions of cosmic magnitude and striking philosophical profundity was obviously due to Jung's unique personality, his vast ego resources, and his undeniable genius.

Needless to say, no Jungian analyst is likely to agree with such a causal-reductive "Freudian" interpretation of Jung's theories. He may object that whatever be their purported oedipal or preoedipal implications, they must not obscure the broader vistas opened up by his discovery of the Collective Unconscious and by the awesome imagery of his archetypal dreams and fantasies. Although Glover emphatically denies the feasibility of a compromise between the Freudian and Jungian approaches, the possibility must indeed be granted that Jung's fantasies were "overdetermined" in both the Freudian and Jungian senses. They were meaningful as elaborate rationalizations and reaction formations against raw impulse and unresolved guilt. At the same time they may well be considered creations of a prodigious mythopoetic imagination which, as Jung put it, has vanished from our rational age.

There is another series of incidents described in Jung's memoirs which strikes a more ominous note. Throughout his life Jung had a marked interest in the occult. His doctoral thesis dealt with the psychological interpretation of a spiritualistic medium who was incidentally a distant relative. He himself relates a number of seemingly telepathic incidents that had taken place in his childhood and later years. His book on synchronicity was an attempt to bring observations of this kind within a scientifically consistent frame of reference. One of his most spectacular accounts of this order is the splitting, with a loud report, and for no apparent reason, of a solid walnut tabletop in his and his mother's presence. Both he and his mother were convinced that such a mysterious event must have had a deeper meaning. Shortly thereafter a big bread knife snapped and, with an equally loud report, broke into several pieces, Jung adds to this story that he had carefully kept the pieces "to this day."

A later incident of this kind gains added significance from the fact that it was witnessed by Freud. During one of his visits in Vienna Jung had asked

Freud's views concerning "occult" phenomena. "Because of his materialistic prejudice," writes Jung in his memoirs, "he rejected this entire complex of questions as nonsensical and did so in terms of so shallow a positivism that I had difficulty in checking the sharp retort on the tip of my tongue. . . ." And he continues: "While Freud was going on this way I had a curious sensation. It was as if my diaphragm were made of iron and were becoming red-hot, a glowing vault. At that moment there was such a loud report in the bookcase which stood right next to us that we both started up in alarm, fearing that the thing was to topple over us. I said to Freud 'There, that is an example of a so-called catalytic exteriorization phenomenon,' "i.e., a case of what parapsychologists today would call telekinesis. "Oh come," he exclaimed, Jung goes on to say: "Oh come, that is sheer bosh," was Freud's retort to Jung's excursion into the occult.

A few weeks later, in a letter to Jung dated April 6, 1909, Freud came back to the incident. After assuring him that he had given the phenomenon serious thought, Freud writes: "My credulity . . . vanished along with your personal presence. Once again for various inner reasons it seems to me wholly implausible that anything of the sort should occur. The furniture stands before me spiritless and dead, like nature silent and godless before the poet after the passing of the gods of Greece." And he adds: "I therefore don once more my hornrimmed paternal spectacles and warn my dear son to keep a cool head and rather not understand something than make such great sacrifice for the sake of understanding."

At the end of his letter Freud seeks to soften this rebuke with this remark: "I . . . look forward to hearing more about your new investigations of the spook complex, my interest being the interest one has in a lovely delusion which one does not share oneself."

The tone of the letter is as cordial as ever, but from then on the ominous word *delusion* must have stood between the two men like an invisible wall. We know from Jung's own account that he himself was at times plagued by doubts as to his sanity—a fact obviously unsuspected on the conscious level by either Freud or Ernest Jones, however critical they may have been of Jung since the parting of their ways. But Jung confesses in his *Memories* that following his break with Freud he had lived under constant pressure, at times so strong that he thought "there was some psychic disturbance" in him.

Jung's account of what he himself described as psychotic episodes belongs among the striking human documents of our age. It is a mine of wealth for the student of mental disorder, based as it is on a unique combination of inside experience and authoritative description of the disorder itself. If Freud had to rely for his studies of schizophrenia on such secondhand information as the autobiographical account of the Schreber case, Jung was in the unique position of having descended in person to the netherworld of the human mind and of returning from it virtually unscathed so as to give the world a firsthand report of his experiences. By contrast, all Freud was destined to do to match such exploits may have been the inner experience of his own obsessive-compulsive neurosis, or a lifelong obsessive-compulsive trend.

But Jung undoubtedly had to pay a high price for his brush with mental disorder. At times his hallucinations and delusional experiences assumed all the hallmarks of reality to him. The line between his projections and the emergence of a motley group of mythological personages became blurred. His collective unconscious was more than a mere theoretical construct surpassing Freud's individual unconscious in both broadness and depth. It was crowded with the creations of Jung's mythopoetic imagination. The archetypes of the Great Mother, of the Wise Man, of Salome, and of the Prophet Elijah became living companions of his days and nights of seclusion in the tower of his estate in Bollingen. Jung came close to falling victim to his externalized introjects, as G. Bychowski put it.

But here, again, Jung developed an elaborate system of defenses that helped him to hold his own and to emerge victorious from his ordeal. His seclusion in the tower, we are told, had "sensitized" him to such an extent that he was able to perceive the presence of all sorts of "departed folk": to communicate with the dead—and at times with the living—in a telepathic way. Communications of this order were to him added evidence of his mediumistic or paranormal faculties as postulated by modern parapsychology or psychical research. In short, Jung turned what would generally be considered delusional experiences into cases of extrasensory perception, of psychokinesis, of precognition, retrocognition or the like: he tried to cast them into the mold of traditional "occult" or paranormal occurrences. Ultimately Jung, in collaboration with W. Pauli, formulated his celebrated theory of synchronicity as a "new principle of nature." Whatever its merits as a philosophical contribution in its own right, it bears all the features of another spectacular feat of rationalization seeking to explain—or explain away—an otherwise well-camouflaged delusional trend.

In a similar vein, his unfortunate thesis, proposed in 1934, of a *Jewish* versus an *Arian* unconscious, calling for an "Arian" versus a "Jewish" psychology, may be largely due to Jung's need to maintain his defenses in the face of the intolerable "Freudian" truths. Freud's obscene propositions, he stated, may have been valid for the Jewish psyche; but they were inapplicable to the Arian soul. If this interpretation of Jung's embarrassing anti-Jewish pronouncement is correct, his apparent puzzlement over being called anti-Semitic is not so surprising. They were not meant as insults against the Jews. Like G. B. Shaw's Warwick, sending Joan of Arc to her death at the stake, Jung too seemed to imply that his disparaging statements were merely a political—or in this case—a psychological necessity.

Do we have to assume that Jung's indisputably anti-Jewish position during World War II had left him without a feeling of guilt? His *Memories* gloss over this point without a clue. The book includes a brief case history of "a Jewish woman who had lost her faith." It is a report which, it appears, was largely intended to show his attempts to be objective and free of prejudice in treating a Jewish patient. "It all began with a (premonitory) dream of mine," we are told. It was a dream of a woman whom "I did not understand at all." Next day a young woman patient came to seek his help. "She was a well-adapted, westernized Jewess . . . enlightened to her bones. . . ." Jung "could not understand" her at all—until it dawned on him: "Good Lord, it is the little girl in my dream." It turned out that the grandfather of this "wholly westernized, chic, elegant and highly intelligent young lady had been a Zaddic, a Chassidic rabbi." Jung insisted that the patient's father had been an apostate to the Jewish faith: that he had betrayed "the secret" and turned his back on God. "And you have your neurosis," he stated, "because the fear of God has got into you." That statement, Jung goes to say, had struck her "like a bolt of lightning" and put her well on the way of her recovery.

Next night, we are told, Jung had another dream. "A reception was taking place in my house, and behold, the girl was there too. She came up to me and asked 'Haven't you got an umbrella? It's raining so hard.' I actually found an umbrella, fumbled around with it to open it and was on the point of giving it to her. But what happened instead? I handed it to her on my knees as if she was a goddess. . . ."

Jung told this patient about his dream. And he adds: "In a week her neurosis had vanished."

It is a pity we know so little about the circumstances surrounding the dreamer and his dream at the time the dream occurred. It was first published in 1954 so that it may well have happened in the postwar years. If so, the Jewish girl seeking refuge in Jung's house from the rainstorm may have stood for all those who had asked for protection under his "umbrella" while he, Jung, had "fumbled around to open it." Still, as if trying to do penance for what he had done—or had failed to do—he handed it to her on his knees "as if she was a goddess."

Be that as it may, reaction formations, rationalizations, and frank denial were unmistakable ingredients of Jung's system of thought in reference to both the "Jewish problem" and to his own delusional trend.

Yet all but the supposedly most uncompromising "orthodox" psychoanalysts are likely to grant that trying to sum up Jung's work and Jung's personality in such terms would fail to do justice to his contributions to psychiatry. It certainly runs counter to this "inner vision" of himself: to what he had appeared to himself sub specie aeternitatis. This vision, he asserted, was one "which cannot be expressed in the language of science, but only by way of myth." Myth, to him, is in effect the ultimate arbiter of truth, and this is why he describes his *Memories* as an undertaking that tries to tell his "personal myth."

By contrast, Freud's attitude to the irrational, toward the raw, untrammeled forces of human nature—of *homo natura*, as Binswanger put it—was one of awe, suspicion and dread. Dreams, mental disorder, myth and even religion were manifestations of those Acherontic powers he had set out to expose, to bend to his will: to neutralize by psychoanalysis and, if need be, to keep at bay by supreme efforts of the Ego, the "charioteer" of Plato's two horses.

To Freud mythological forces of this order were only figures of speech. They were necessary scientific constructs, to be discarded as soon as they could be replaced by more precise language and less mythological concepts. Myth to Freud was that which had to be overcome in order to establish the primacy of reason in human affairs. By contrast, myth to Jung had to maintain its supremacy and ultimate control over reason. Freud, in the end, disowned most of his own mythological constructs in order to ensure the integrity of knowledge. Little wonder, therefore, that in his estimate Jung's excessive preoccupation with myth was a symptom of regression, presaging the return of the repressed.

It is true that what Jung had to say about the power of the archetypes, about the occult, about prophecies and poltergeists had struck sympathetic chords in Freud's mind. But for this very reason Freud was loath to listen to the voice of the younger man. It was a voice intoning a siren song, full of danger and secret appeal. Like Ulysses, Freud tied himself to the mast of his scientific knowledge in order to maintain his foothold on the ship. We do not know whether he realized how close his companion had come to being swept overboard.

Part 4

BEYOND PSYCHOANALYSIS
or the Quest
for New Solutions

chapter 24

Existential Therapies:
The Quest for Transcendence

SELECTIONS FROM L. BINSWANGER, M. BOSS, R. MAY . . .
R. D. LAING'S KINGSLEY HALL

*The diverse schools of existential philosophy originating in Europe before
and after the Second World War represent a major pendulum swing of ideas
from the essentially materialistic position of the natural sciences. They are
associated with the Danish thinker Søren Kierkegaard and with Jean-Paul
Sartre in France, Martin Heidegger in Germany, Martin Buber in Israel, and
José Ortega y Gasset in Spain. They had a profound influence on the work
of such psychiatrists and psychotherapists as Karl Jaspers in Germany,
Victor Frankl in Austria, and Ludwig Binswanger and Medard Boss in Switzerland. Rollo May, H. M. Ruitenbeek, Harold Kelman and Carl Rogers are
perhaps the most important representatives of the same trend in this country.*

*Ludwig Binswanger (b. 1881), a disciple of Eugen Bleuler, succeeded his
father as medical director of the Sanatorium Bellevue in Kreuzlingen, Switzerland. Binswanger, one of the early followers of Freud, defected, like
Adler, Jung, and Rank before him, from the analytic camp. Yet unlike other
dissenters, he maintained a friendly and indeed respectful relationship with
the master. This is reflected in the following passage from his* Freud and the
Magna Charta of Clinical Psychiatry *(1955):*

It was on a September morning of the year 1927. Having broken away
from the Congress of German Neurologists and Psychiatrists that was meeting in Vienna, I hurried to Semmering, full of impatience to return the un-
forgettable visit he [Freud] had paid me in those difficult times. I was about
to leave and we were talking about the old days. Soon, however, the conversation turned to that which twenty years ago had brought us together
and which in spite of clear differences of opinion had held us together,
namely his life's work, his "great idea." With respect to a concrete clinical
example—a serious case of compulsion neurosis—that had occupied us both
a good deal, I threw out the question as to how we were to understand the
failure of this patient to take the last decisive step of psychoanalytic insight

and thus to continue in his misery in spite of all previous efforts and technical progress. As a contribution to the solution of the problem, I suggested that such a failure might only be understood as the result of something which could be called a deficiency of spirit [Geistigkeit], that is, an inability on the part of the patient to raise himself to the level of spiritual communication with the physician. Thus the patient was barred by his own lack from encompassing and overcoming his unconscious instinctual impulses at the last decisive point. I could barely believe my ears when the answer came: "Yes, spirit [Geist] is everything." I presumed that by spirit, Freud meant something like intelligence. But then he continued: "Man has always known he possessed spirit: I had to show him there is such a thing as instinct. But men are always unsatisfied, they cannot wait, they always want something whole and finished; but one has to begin somewhere and very slowly move forward."

Encouraged by this concession, I went a step further, explaining that I found myself forced to recognize in man something like a basic religious category; that, in any case, it was impossible for me to admit that "the religious" is somehow and from somewhere a derivative phenomenon. (I was thinking, of course, not of the origin of a particular religion or even of religion in general but of something which I have since learned to call the religious I-thou relation.) But I had stretched the bow of agreement too far and began to feel its resistance. "Religion arises," so Freud declared, quickly and curtly, "out of the helplessness and anxiety of childhood and early manhood. Indisputably." With that he went to the drawer of his desk: "This is the moment for me to show you something," laid before me a finished manuscript that bore the title "The Future of an Illusion," and looked laughingly and questioningly at me. I easily guessed from the situation what the title meant. Meanwhile the moment of farewell had come. Freud accompanied me to the door. His last words, spoken with a knowing, lightly ironic smile, were: "Forgive me that I cannot satisfy your religious needs."

The following article contains a condensed outline of Binswanger's approach. It leans heavily on Edmund Husserl's phenomenological method and his attempt to grasp the "intuitional essences" of the world without preconceived ideas. At the same time Binswanger discards the traditional Cartesian dichotomy of subject and object, rejects Freud's topographic picture of personality structure, and replaces it with Heidegger's concept of man's "being-in-the-world," his Dasein—or what can be termed his "existential presence." In a similar vein, he rejects Freud's causal-reductive, deterministic description of mental mechanisms and emphasizes man's "finite" freedom of choice, his attendant personal responsibility and propensity to guilt and anxiety. Like Alfred Adler, he takes issue with postulating "behind" the

conscious self an autonomous unconscious province of the mind. Accord-
ing to Binswanger, the unconscious has no world of its own. As for dreams,
he holds that they represent a particular world design or being-in-the-world,
when the dreamer is wholly immersed in his Eigenwelt *or private experi-*
ence, as opposed to his Umwelt *or external environment, and to his* Mitwelt
or the world of his fellow men, as conceived by Heidegger. Like E. Min-
kowski and other existentialists, Binswanger regards mental illness as
twisted, distorted modes of experience in their own right. Above all, he de-
mands that man should not be viewed as an object of the analyst's detached
scientific inquiry. Their meeting should amoung to a spiritual "encounter"
between two Daseins *or existential presences. It is this mutual understand-*
ing and interpenetration on the level of shared, authentic and undistorted ex-
perience that holds the promise of cure. The following is from "Existential
Analysis and Psychotherapy" by Ludwig Binswanger, in Progress in Psychotherapy, *Vol. 1, edited by Frieda Fromm-Reichman and J. L. Moreno,*
1956, by permission of Grune and Stratton, New York, 1956.

Zurich is the birthplace of existential analysis (*Daseinsanalyse*) as a psy-
chiatric-phenomenologic research method. I emphasize the term *research
method*, for if the psychoanalytic theory of Freud or the teaching of Jung
arose out of a dissatisfaction with preceding psychotherapy, thus owing
their origin and development predominantly to psychotherapeutic impulses
and aims, the existential research orientation in psychiatry arose from dissatisfaction with the prevailing efforts to gain scientific understanding in
psychiatry; so that existential analysis owes its origin and development to
an attempt to gain a new scientific understanding of the concerns of psychiatry, psychopathology and psychotherapy, on the basis of the analysis
of existence (*Daseinsanalytik*) as it was developed in the remarkable work
of Martin Heidegger: "Being and Time" (*Sein und Zeit*), in the year 1927.
Psychology and psychotherapy, as sciences, are admittedly concerned with
"man," but not at all primarily with mentally *ill* man, but with *man as such.*
The new understanding of man, which we owe to Heidegger's analysis of
existence, has its basis in the new conception that man is no longer
understood in terms of some theory—be it a mechanistic, a biologic or a
psychological one—but in terms of a purely phenomenologic elucidation of
the total structure or total articulation of existence as Being-In-The-World
(*In-der-Welt-sein*). What this expression, fundamental for existential analysis, means, I unfortunately cannot develop here; be it only emphasized
that it encompasses alike the individual's own world and the simultaneous
and coextensive relationships with and to other people and things. Nor can I
go into the difference between an ontologic-phenomenologic analysis of
existence, and empiric-phenomenologic existential analysis, and an empiric
discursive description, classification and explanation.

Once, in his interpretation of dreams, Freud said that psychiatrists had "forsaken the stability of the psychic structure too early." Existential analysis could say the same thing, albeit with an altogether different meaning. Freud, as is well known, had in mind the stability of the articulation of the life-history with the psychic structure, in contrast to the psychiatrists of his day who, at the very first opportunity, considered the psychic structure to be disrupted, and who resorted instead to physiologic processes in the cerebral cortex. Existential analysis, on the other hand, does not have in mind the solidity of the structure of the inner life-history, but rather the solidity of the transcendental structure preceding or underlying, a priori, all psychic structures as the very condition of this possibility. I regret that I cannot explain in fuller detail these philosophic expressions, already employed by Kant but here used in a much wider sense; those among you conversant with philosophy will readily understand me. I want to emphasize only that philosophy is not here in any way being introduced into psychiatry or psychotherapy, but rather that the philosophic bases of these sciences are being laid bare. Obviously, this in turn has an effect upon one's understanding of what constitutes their scientific object or field. This effect reveals itself in the fact that we have learned to understand and to describe the various psychoses and neuroses as specific *deviations* of the a priori, or the transcendental, structure of man's humanity, of the *condition humaine*, as the French say.

Be it noted in passing that the existential-analytic research method in psychiatry had to investigate the structure of existence as being-in-the-world, as Heidegger had outlined and delineated it still further and along various new paths. Such, for instance, are its studies of various existential "dimensions," i.e., height, depth and width, thingness and resistance (*Materialität*), lighting and coloring of the world, fullness or emptiness of existence, etc. The investigation of psychotic or neurotic world-projects and existential structures such as, for example, those which we designate as manic, depressive, schizophrenic, or compulsive, have so occupied all of us who are engaged upon this work that only suggestions are at hand with regard to the significance of existential-analytic research for psychotherapy. I should like now very cursorily to indicate a few of the main trends of this relationship.

1. A psychotherapy on existential-analytic bases investigates the life-history of the patient to be treated, just as any other psychotherapeutic method, albeit in its own fashion. It does not explain this life-history and its pathologic idiosyncrasies according to the teachings of any school of psychotherapy, or by means of its preferred categories. Instead, it *understands* this life-history as modifications of the total structure of the patient's being-in-the-world, as I have shown in my studies "On Flight of Ideas" (*Uber Ideenflucht*), in my studies of schizophrenia, and most recently in the case of "Suzanne Urban."

2. A psychotherapy on existential-analytic bases thus proceeds *not* merely by showing the patient where, when and to what extent he has failed to realize the fullness of his humanity, but it tries to make him *experience* this as radically as possible—how, like Ibsen's master-builder, Solness, he has lost his way and footing in "airy heights" or "ethereal worlds of fantasy." In this case the psychotherapist could be compared to someone who is informed, e.g., a mountain guide, familiar with the particular terrain, who attempts the trip back to the valley with the unpracticed tourist who no longer dares either to proceed or to return. And inversely, the existential-analytically oriented therapist seeks to enable the depressed patient to get out of his cavernous subterranean world, and to gain footing "upon the ground" once more, by revealing it to him as being the only mode of existence in which the fullness of human possibilities can be realized. And further, the existential-analytically oriented therapist will lead the twisted schizophrenic out of the autistic world of distortion and askewness in which he lives and acts, into the shared worlds, the *koinos kosmos* of Heraclitus; or he will strive to help a patient who, in her own words, lives "in two speeds" to "synchronize" these (again using her own expression). Yet, another time the therapist will see (as happened in one of Roland Kuhn's cases of anorexia mentalis) that the goal may be reached much more rapidly if one explores not the temporal but the spatial structures of a particular patient's world. It came as a surprise to us to find how easily some otherwise not particularly intelligent or educated patients proved accessible to an existential-analytic kind of exploration, and how thoroughly they felt understood by it in their singularity. This is, after all, an altogether indispensable prerequisite for any kind of psychotherapeutic success.

3. Regardless of whether the existential analyst is predominantly psychoanalytic or predominantly Jungian in orientation, he will always stand on the same plane with his patients—the plane of common existence. He will therefore not degrade the patient to an object toward which he is subject, but he will see in him an existential partner. He will therefore not consider the bond between the two partners to be as that of two electric batteries— a "psychic contact"—but as an *encounter* on what Martin Buber calls the "sharp edge of existence," an existence which *essentially* "is in the world," not merely as a self but also as a being-together with one another—relatedness and love. Also what has, since *Freud*, been called transference is, in the existential-analytic sense, a kind of encounter. For encounter is a being-with-others in *genuine presence*, that is to say, in the present which is altogether continuous with the *past* and bears within it the possibilities of a *future*.

4. Perhaps you will also be interested in hearing what is the position of existential analysis toward the *dream*, and this again particularly with re-

gard to psychotherapy. Here again it is removed from any theoretic "explanation" of the dream, especially from the purely sexual exegesis of dream contents in psychoanalysis; rather, it understands the dream, as I emphasized a long time ago, as a specific way of being-in-the-world, in other words, as a specific world and a specific way of existing. This amounts to saying that in the dream we see the whole man, the *entirety* of his problems, in a different existential modality than in waking, but against the background and with the structure of the a priori articulation of existence, and therefore the dream is also of paramount therapeutic importance for the existential analyst. For precisely by means of the structure of dreams he is enabled first of all to show the patient the structure of his being-in-the-world in an over-all manner, and secondly, he can, on the basis of this, free him for the *totality* of existential possibilities of being, in other words, for open resoluteness (*Enischlossenheit*); he can, to use Heidegger's expression, "retrieve" (*zuruckholen*) existence from a dream existence to a genuine capacity for being itself. For the time being, I will refer you to Roland Kuhn's paper, "On the Existential Structure of a Neurosis" in Gebsattel's *Jahrbuch fur Psychologie und Psychotherapie*. I only ask of you not to imagine existential structure as something static, but as something undergoing constant change. Similarly, what we call neurosis represents a changed existential *process*, as compared with the healthy. Thus, existential analysis understands the task of psychotherapy to be the opening up of new structural possibilities to such altered existential processes.

As you see, existential analysis, instead of speaking in theoretic concepts, such as "pleasure principle" and "reality principle," investigates and treats the mentally ill person with regard to the structures, structural articulations, and structural alterations of his existence. Hence, it has not, by any means, consciousness as its sole object, as has been erroneously stated, but rather the whole man, prior to any distinction between conscious and unconscious, or even between body and soul; for the existential structures and their alterations permeate man's entire being. Obviously, the existential analyst, insofar as he is a therapist, will not, at least in the beginning of his treatment, be able to dispense with the distinction between conscious and unconscious, deriving from the psychology of consciousness and bound up with its merits and its drawbacks.

5. Taking stock of the relationship between existential analysis and psychotherapy, it can be said that existential analysis cannot, over long stretches, dispense with the traditional psychotherapeutic methods; that, however, it can, as such, be therapeutically effective only insofar as it succeeds in opening up to the sick fellow man an understanding of the structure of human existence, and allows him to find his way back from his neurotic or psychotic, lost, erring, perforated or twisted mode of existence and

world, into the freedom of being able to utilize his own capacities for existence. This presupposes that the existential analyst, insofar as he is a psychotherapist, not only is in possession of existential-analytic and psychotherapeutic competence, but that he must dare to risk committing his own existence in the struggle for the freedom of his partner's.

On the occasion of Freud's eightieth birthday, Binswanger joined in the eulogies acclaiming the octogenarian who gave the world the definitive picture of man viewed as homo natura—*Man shorn of his spiritual aspects. He sent a copy of his lecture to Freud. This is part of Freud's reply to Binswanger:*

Dear Friend: A sweet surprise, your lecture. . . .
But, of course, I don't believe a word of what you say. I've always lived only in the parterre and basement of the building. You claim that with a change of viewpoint one is able to see an upper story which houses such distinguished guests as religion, art, etc. You're not the only one who thinks that, most cultured specimens of *homo natura* believe it. In that you are conservative, I revolutionary. If I had another lifetime of work before me, I have no doubt that I could find room for these noble guests in my little subterranean house. . . .

Medard Boss (b. 1903) is professor of psychoanalysis at the University of Zurich. He studied under Freud and Jung and is the author of a number of books on psychotherapy, psychosomatic medicine and dream analysis. His Psychoanalysis and Daseinanalysis, *published in 1963 in this country, is a major attempt at bringing about a rapprochement between the two schools of thought. The following section is taken from Chapter 4 of* Psychoanalysis and Daseinsanalysis *by Medard Boss, © 1963 by Basic Books Publishing Co., Inc., New York.*

Even a superficial and general comparison of the descriptions Freud gave of the events during a psychoanalytic cure and of our foregoing portrayal of *Dasein* leads to an unexpected discovery. All important passages in Freud's work pertaining to practical advice for the analyst contain the same basic terms which Heidegger, twenty years later, used to characterize human being. Both Freud and Heidegger talk again and again of "understanding," of "meaningfulness," "openness," "clarity," "language," "truths," and "freedom." To be sure, Freud speaks here from the basis of his "natural," unreflected-upon, everyday experience of man, while Heidegger has deliberately worked his experience of man into a fundamental ontology and has articulated the basic nature of man most carefully. Nevertheless, these two pioneers of the science of man are talking about exactly the same phenomena. Therefore, their findings and interpretations are certainly comparable, unless one is still caught in the neo-Platonic, artificial dichotomizing of the world into two "ontic-ontological" levels, which we have already refuted.

In order to enter into particulars as to the intrinsic harmony of the tacit understanding of man on which Freud's practical therapeutic activities are based and of the Daseinsanalytic insights into man's very nature, we had best recall first Freud's fundamental therapeutic rule, which stands above all other rules in psychoanalytic therapy: the patient must be absolutely honest and truthful with himself and the analyst. He is obliged to confess everything, whatever may pass through his mind or through his heart, and this without any exception. If this rule is followed, it means that all those possibilities of awareness, all feeling, thinking, imagining, dreaming, and acting relationships with the world which either had been fought against until then, or had not even been discovered up to then, are now accepted, realized freely, and appropriated with responsibility at constituting one's own existence, so that they may then be at the analysand's disposal and may be carried out in the future, "if . . . after her cure life makes that demand on her." In other words, all of Freud's practical advice aims at enabling the patient to unveil himself and to unfold into his utmost openness.

Freud, however, would never have been able to create this basic rule of his treatment at all if he had not secretly shared the Daseinsanalytic insight into man's existence as being of the nature of a primordial openness and lucidity. No thought of unveiling hidden phenomena could have occurred in Freud's mind without his tacit awareness of man's existence as an open, lucid realm into which something can unveil itself and shine forth out of the dark.

The same basic rule of psychoanalytic therapy implies a specific conception of truth. Current epistemologies are apt to define truth in terms of the adequacy of the representation of the external world in man's consciousness. In psychoanalytic therapy, however, truthfulness is clearly understood to be the shining forth of the emerging, unveiled phenomena in the specifically Daseinsanalytic sense of the ancient Greek *aletheia*, to which analysis of *Dasein* always refers when speaking of the essence of "truth."

In this connection even Freud's insistence on the patient's reclining—making it impossible for him to see the therapist—reveals his deep, though unarticulated, awareness of man's basic condition, as Daseinsanalysis has brought it to light, regardless of the seemingly extraneous reasons he gave for this rule. For to let the patient lie down in the analytic situation takes cognizance of the human body itself as a sphere of human existence; it is not merely an apparatus or an organism attached in some enigmatic way to a psyche. For this reason an analysand does not comply fully with the demand to let himself become aware of all his characteristics without censoring them beforehand (as being of higher or lower value) unless he loosens up physically, too, while lying horizontally, so that all his limbs are also on the same level. The conventional arrangement in which physician and patient sit facing each other corresponds—as far as the respective bodily spheres of their existences are concerned—to the traditional conception of two subjects, separate and standing opposite each other. Thus the physical juxtaposition implicitly preserves the conception of rank and value systems which the patient brings into the therapeutic situation. Sitting opposite the therapist enforces the patient's tendency to resist the basic rule of psychoanalytic therapy, by leaving "above" (in the widest sense) what always has been "above," and leaving "below" what always was "below." Furthermore, erect stature is the position *par excellence* of self-assertion. It accentuates self-glorification, as much as the supremacy of everything that belongs to the head, the elevation of the spirit (the higher and lighter) raised *above* the lower and sensual pole (base, animalistic, abysmal).

The mutual control of two individuals who sit opposite each other also often robs the patient of the opportunity to be, for once, totally delivered up to himself, without getting support from the behavior (particularly the facial expressions and gestures) of another. Many patterns of behavior which the patient tries to ward off will not emerge into his reflections at all if he sits facing the therapist. But if they do not show themselves openly, it is impossible, of course, that they can be uttered, be admitted to full reality thereby and in so doing be *overcome*. However, it goes without saying that the rule to lie down, like all other psychoanalytic rules, must never be rigidly enforced. Lying down robs the analysand of the visual support of the physician, and leaves the patient to himself. For this reason, it often constitutes a frustration. According to Freud's instructions, the whole analytic cure has to be carried out in an atmosphere where immediate satisfactions are frustrated. But such frustration may stay within the realm of the possible and must not overtax the limitations of a given analysand. The more immature a patient is emotionally at the beginning of treatment, the more the treatment has to resemble a child analysis at the start. In the analysis of a child, lying down is not possible either. We have, however, rarely encountered an analysand for whom it did not turn out to be beneficial to lie down during long phases of the analytic process.

Freud himself has pointed out that the mere visual perception of the concrete presence of the therapist who sits opposite the patient insurmountably obstructs the rise of all possibilities of behaving which are too infantile, and are therefore repulsed. Actually the situation then appears to be a dialogue between two equally grown-up partners. This means that the position of the partners' bodily realms of existence in no way corresponds to the childlike nature of much of the patient's being, which is especially in need of psychotherapy and which needs to be openly and responsibly integrated and appropriated into an essential being-myself. For this reason, a situation in which the two partners in the dialogue conventionally face each other prevents in itself the less mature partner from becoming aware of his more childlike strivings.

Freud objected to sitting and facing the patient for yet another reason. He felt that the mutual observation inevitable in such an arrangement leads to self-control on the part of the therapist as well, thereby interfering with his ability to maintain his evenly hovering attention. But precisely this attitude is the indispensable basis for the psychoanalyst's ability to be silent. In silent listening, the analyst opens himself to, and belongs to, the patient's as yet concealed wholeness; and this silence alone can free the patient for his own world by providing him with the necessary interhuman mental openness. The less a physician is capable of being silent in such a fashion, the more he is in danger of setting up obstacles to the unfolding of the patient's own potential, of pressing him in pseudopedagogic fashion into the physician's own matrix.

When we take into account the real meaning of lying down during therapy, the counterarguments of those psychotherapists who, on principle, treat a patient only if he sits facing them sound shallow indeed. They claim that letting the patient lie down makes him feel all the more sick; one should appeal to what is healthy in him, above all to his common sense. But is it not, often, the first therapeutic task to enable the patient to acknowledge his being ill, so that he may realize with full awareness the nature of his illness? Once an individual has been cured by responsibly and honestly accepting his wholeness, he will also be well when he lies down. The counterarguments apparently stem from the same attitude of concealing and covering up that the old persuasion therapies were based upon.

Furthermore, Freud as early as 1900 has started his *Interpretation of Dreams* with a most "daring assumption," to use his own expression. His fundamental work began with the proud announcement that, if his technique of dream interpretation is employed, "every dream reveals itself as a psychical structure which has a meaning. . . ." Soon Freud gained the insight that not only dreams but *all* human phenomena were meaningful, including the most bizarre mental and physical symptoms of neurotics. By this discovery Freud opened a completely new dimension of thought to the healing science and lifted our understanding of illness from the conception of "meaningless" natural causal connections and sequences of "facts" to a level where everything makes "sense." This all-decisive deed of Freud's genius, however, again presupposes the basic Daseinsanalytic insight that there is a luminated realm into the lucidity of which the meaningfulness of our world's phenomena can disclose itself, shine forth, and that it is nothing else than the human existence itself which serves as this necessary, elucidating, world-openness.

Freud's proud introduction to his *Interpretation of Dreams*, however, did not stop by asserting only the meaningfulness of every dream. It asserted also that every dream also can "be inserted at an assignable point in the chain of the mental activities of waking life." To regard human phenomena as having their particular, meaningful spot in the course of a man's unfolding is not the attitude of a natural scientist but exactly that of a genuine historian, if "history" is understood in the Daseinsanalytic sense. For "history," in analysis of *Dasein*, always means a sequence of meaningful world disclosures as they are sent into being by destiny, engaging, in an equally primordial way, human existence as the lucid world-openness as well as the emerging particular phenomena shining forth therein.

Freud, it is true, restricted his historical interest almost exclusively to the individual life histories of his patients whenever he made the transition from pure natural scientist to historian. It is even more true that he was always in a hurry to become a natural scientist again as soon as he began to theorize about his patients' life histories. In his role as a natural scientist he felt he owed it to himself (as a serious investigator and searcher for truth) to transform intellectually the temporal succession of experiences and actions occurring during the course of a life into an assumed sequence of cause and effect. His procedure shows plainly that he had not yet reached a full understanding of the original historicity and temporality of man's existence in the Daseinsanalytic sense. He was still a long way from the insight that each man's life history by way of a continuous disclosure of the particular beings which are sent to shine forth, to come to pass, in the light of the meaning-disclosing relationships which constitute human existence. Nevertheless, Freud was able to get glimpses of man's fundamental temporality, an insight which later was to become the turning point of Heidegger's analysis of *Dasein*. These glimpses occurred with particular clarity when Freud realized that even the seemingly most meaningless phenomena of dreams have their place in the sequence of events of the total life history of a man. They also occurred when Freud talked of the necessity to regard the past of man not as a piece of him which has fallen off, like something which no longer belonged to him and was merely a matter of history (in this word's ordinary, classifying sense), but as a force pervading the present. In the case of neurotic patients, Freud had even discovered that the power of the past is indeed so great that it pushes both present and future aside, a dismissal evident in the patient's symptomatology and behavior. Therefore, he could state that these patients "suffer from their reminiscences." If, then, the

intention of the psychoanalytic cure is to make an analysand aware of the
historic occurrence of the symptoms, how can it be anything else, fundamentally, than an attempt to heal neuroses by an elucidation of the life history? Such an elucidation, however, must make it possible for the patient to
recapture his past openly, to bring it into the present and make it his own by
possessing the memory of it; it thus liberates the analysand for a free acceptance of his future.

These statements of Freud contain nothing less than the discovery that
any single feature of man's existence can be comprehended fully only if it is
regarded, not as merely momentarily present in a chain of separated
"nows," but as a phenomenon embedded in an individual's life history, including his past, present, and future.

This understanding of time and history in human life, which pervades all
of psychoanalytic therapy more or less implicitly, corresponds to a great
extent to the original temporality of human existence which Heidegger elu-
cidated explicitly for the first time. We need only recall Heidegger's statement that man's existence always emerges in the unity of the three temporal
"ekstases," i.e., man's past, present, and future.

The intrinsic harmony of psychoanalytic therapy and analysis of *Dasein*
becomes particularly evident in their common underlying conception of
human freedom. Heidegger discovered that man's existence is a realm of
lucid openness, so that all that is to be and to become finds its necessary
realm of lucidity into which it can shine forth, appear, and become a "phenomenon" (in this word's original Greek meaning). In other words, human
existence emerges only through and as man's possibilities of meaning-
disclosing relationships to the particular beings of our world. Man's freedom, then, consists in his being able to choose either to obey this claim and
carry out his possibilities of relating to, and caring for, what he encounters,
or not to obey this claim.

If Freud had not had this Daseinsanalytic insight into human beings when
actually treating his patients (regardless of whether he put it into words or
not, and regardless of his theoretical formulations), he could not have gone
beyond Breuer and Janet to become the father of modern psychotherapy.
Only because Freud sensed what human freedom really means was he able
to overcome the objective and purely biological theory of repression of his
predecessors. Freedom in the Daseinsanalytic sense is the condition for the
possibility of psychoanalytic practice as taught by Freud. Freud's writings,
insofar as they deal with practical psychoanalytic technique, abound with
references to freedom. These references differ grossly from the strongly deterministic point of view he proclaims in his theoretical works. It is at least
as true to call Freud the discoverer of the importance of human freedom for
the etiology of man's illnesses as to see in him the scientific discoverer of

sexuality. Both Heidegger and Freud define human freedom as being able to choose. They mean choice between two decisions. One choice consists in the responsible, conscientious adoption of all "functions," "abilities," "character traits," and "behavior possibilities" constituting man's essence. Such adoption amounts to a congregation of all possibilities for relating to the particular phenomena of our world. It leads to an independent self. The other choice consists in denial and nonrecognition of essential manners of behaving. Man then falls prey to the anonymous, unauthentic mentality of "tradition," to "authoritarian commands" foreign to him. Thus he misses assembling all his possibilities of relating toward the world into the wholeness of an authentic, free selfhood. If man does not choose the first of these alternatives, he cannot reach the goal of therapy as Freud formulated it: full capacity for work and enjoyment. For both capacities presuppose that any given person has all possibilities of living at his disposal. For this reason, Freud explicitly states the human qualifications he considers to be indispensable for psychoanalytic treatment. He mentions factors such as natural intelligence and ethical development; deep-rooted malformation of character and traits of a degenerate constitution he considers counterindications. In Daseinsanalytic terminology, such statements amount to an insistence that one select patients capable of choosing in terms of human freedom.

Heidegger's analysis of *Dasein* led him to regard man as one who basically and customarily avoids independent, responsible selfhood. Freud's development of his psychoanalytic therapy into an analysis of resistance indicates that secretly he must have shared Heidegger's insights in this respect. Obviously, both of them knew that the abilities to be free and to be unfree belong necessarily together. Man is inclined to flee from being his real own self in responsibility. He is prone to let himself be swallowed up by the anonymity of his surroundings and everyday pursuits. It is for this reason that Freud is so insistent that psychoanalytic therapy must focus, in the beginning and throughout the whole cure, on the patient's resistances against standing openly and foursquare with all that he actually is.

Freud did not, however, consider his discovery (that *Dasein* is historical and that it is capable of either freely taking over or denying given possibilities of behavior) to be the decisive characteristic of his new psychotherapy. To him, the departure from Breuer's hypnotic technique and the institution of free association in its place marked the birth of psychoanalysis; the consistent application of this method was its basis. Source and center of Heidegger's thinking is the insight into man's primary awareness of Being-ness, the basic dimension of nonobjectifiable human *Dasein*. Nothing could be further from Heidegger's thinking than a method directly resulting from the domination of eighteenth- and nineteenth-century associational psychology. The positions of the two thinkers seem incompatible. On the one hand, a conception based on the simplest, immediately given, and indisputable phenomenon—the primary awareness of Being-ness and the freedom it grants to man; on the other, a completely unfree, deterministic psychology based on unreal intellectual abstractions. We need hardly mention that associationism was proven untenable long before Heidegger; it was, indeed, refuted almost simultaneously with Freud's basic discoveries.

Open agreement exists between Freud and Heidegger insofar as both consider language to be man's habitat. Heidegger refers to language as the "home of Being-ness." Freud admonishes the patients to put all thoughts and emotions into words, in detail and without selecting. To do so is to assure that the process of becoming aware of myself does not stop at the halfway goal of a pseudohonesty, confined to myself and therefore easily lost again. Instead, this process is to achieve an open, continuous adherence to being-whole, i.e., to accept and to take over all of one's possibilities of existing, to stand up to them—as one's own belongings—with responsibility. Freud emphasized verbalization again and again, because what *is* exists, in fact, only—and is undeniably preserved only—when it is verbally articulated.

Finally, *Daseinsanalysis* never loses sight of primary awareness of Being-ness and of the fact that man's existence is claimed to serve as the luminated realm into which all that is to be may actually shine forth, emerge, and appear as a phenomenon, i.e., as that which shows itself. These are the conditions for the possibility that man can permit (to the best of his ability) everything that claims him (by being encountered) to unfold in the light of his existence. To understand man in this fashion (namely, as servant and guardian of the truth inherent in things as they are permitted to come into being) is to free him from the egocentric self-glorification, the autonomy and autarchy, of subjectivistic world views. The Daseinsanalytic point of view gives back man's dignity: he is the emissary of the ground of everything that is; an emissary who is sent into his life history entrusted with the task of letting the truth of particular beings become apparent to the extent that this is possible at a given time and place. On the basis of this fundamental feature of man's existence, all so-called ethical values become self-evident.

Freud's analytic therapy implies the same view of man. We have only to focus our attention once more on what separated Freud from his predecessors Janet and Breuer. At first glance the differences may seem insignificant. Breuer had considered hypnoid states to be the causes of pathogenic forgetting of certain emotions and memories. To account for the same phenomena, Janet had assumed a constitutional weakness of the capacity for psychic synthesis. Freud, however, recognized that the true motive for repression of mental content was that such content could not be squared with the moral attitude or the self-esteem of the patient. He found that "repression . . . [always] proceeds from the self-respect of the ego." "Everything that had been forgotten had in some way or other been painful: it had been either alarming or disagreeable or shameful by the standards of the subject's personality. . . . That was precisely why it . . . had not remained conscious."

The discovery that repression always has something to do with moral values again opened up a completely new dimension to medical science. For to say that repression can result from a moral attitude, or from shame, is to imply that man can distinguish between right and wrong, beauty and ugliness, good and evil. Good and evil in psychoanalytic therapy, however, are determined in a strict Daseinsanalytic sense. The analysand is called upon completely to relinquish his conceit, in particular his vainglorious conviction that either he or the pseudomoralistic traditions of his environment have a right to determine who he is and how things should disclose themselves to him. From the analyst the practice of psychoanalysis demands above all selfless care and cherishing of the patient. For months and years on end, the analyst must concentrate on just one fellow being, week after week, hour after hour, and all this mostly in receptive silence. He must accept the other fully the way he is, with all his physical and mental beauties as well as blemishes. All the patient's possibilities must be given a chance to emerge. He must become free, regardless of the personal ideas, wishes, or judgments of the analyst. Such an undertaking, Freud stated, can succeed only if the analyst allows the relation of analyst to patient to become an almost limitless "playground" [*Tummelplatz*], a place where all of the patient's possibilities for relating could freely come out into the open. This is the only way by which the patient can achieve new confidence in his world. The analyst must, of course, restrain himself so as not to derive any personal advantage from any behavior of the patient in the transference situation.

Freud had, it is true, expressly said that the physician should "be impenetrable to the patient, and, like a mirror, reflect nothing but what is shown to him." The comparison of the physician to a mirror is one of the most frequently mentioned "proofs" for the dehumanization and mechanization of Freud's psychoanalytic practice. Those, however, who personally experienced the mirror called "Freud" know beyond doubt that he was opaque only in his own imagination and that to his patients and disciples his unusual kindness, warmth, and humaneness shone through even from a distance. Actually Freud thought of the "opaqueness" of the analyst primarily as an extreme reserve which, in turn, was due to his respect for the individuality of the analysand. His concern was to enable the patient to *become himself* totally out of his own resources, without being influenced by the physician at all, and certainly without being overpowered by the therapist's personality.

Rollo May (b. 1909) is a clinical psychologist, sensitive critic of the contemporary scene and American values, author of such best-sellers as Love and Will *and* Power and Innocence *and editor (with E. Angel and H. F. Ellenberger) of the anthology* Existence: A New Dimension in Psychiatry and Psychology, *which has made an important contribution to the Americanization of existential analysis.*

The following section is taken from Chapter 2 of Existence: A New Dimension in Psychiatry and Psychology, *ed. Rollo May, Ernest Angel, Henri F. Ellenberger, © 1958 by Basic Books, Inc., New York.*

Those who read works on existential analysis as handbooks of technique are bound to be disappointed. They will not find specifically developed practical methods. The chapters in this book, for example, have much more the character of "pure" than of applied science. The reader will also sense that many of the existential analysts are not greatly concerned with technical matters. Part of the reason for this is the newness of the approach. Since existential analysis is a relatively new discipline, it has not yet had time to work out its therapeutic applications in detail.

But there is another, more basic reason for the fact that these psychiatrists are not so concerned with formulating technique and make no apologies for this fact. Existential analysis is a way of understanding human existence, and its representatives believe that one of the chief (if not *the* chief) blocks to the understanding of human beings in Western culture is precisely the overemphasis on technique, an overemphasis which goes along with the tendency to see the human being as an object to be calculated, managed, "analyzed." Our Western tendency has been to believe that *understanding follows technique*; if we get the right technique, then we can penetrate the riddle of the patient, or, as said popularly with amazing perspicacity, we can "get the other person's number." The existential approach holds the exact opposite; namely, that *technique follows understanding*. The central task and responsibility of the therapist is to seek to understand the patient as a being and as being-in-his-world. All technical problems are subordinate to this understanding. Without this understanding, technical facility is at best irrelevant, at worst a method of "structuralizing" the neurosis. With it, the groundwork is laid for the therapist's being able to help the patient recognize and experience his own existence, and this is the central process of therapy. This does not derogate disciplined technique; it rather puts it into perspective. . . .

It is clear at the outset that what distinguishes existential therapy is not what the therapist would specifically do, say, in meeting anxiety or confronting resistance or getting the life history and so forth, but rather the *context* of his therapy. How an existential therapist might interpret a given dream, or an outburst of temper on the patient's part, might not differ from what a classical psychoanalyst might say, if each were taken in isolated fashion. But the context of existential therapy would be very distinct; it would always focus on the questions of how this dream throws light on this particular patient's existence in his world, what it says about *where* he is at the moment and what he is moving toward, and so forth. The context is the patient not as a set of psychic dynamisms or mechanisms but as a human being who is choosing, committing, and pointing himself toward something right now; the context is dynamic, immediately real, and present.

I shall try to block out some implications concerning therapeutic technique from my knowledge of the works of the existential therapists and from my own experience of how their emphases have contributed to me, a therapist trained in psychoanalysis in its broad sense. Making a systematic summary would be presumptuous to try and impossible to accomplish, but I hope the following points will at least suggest some of the important therapeutic implications. It should be clear at every point, however, that the really important contributions of this approach are its deepened understanding of human existence, and one gets no place talking about isolated techniques of therapy unless the understanding we have sought to give in the earlier portions of these chapters is presupposed at every point.

The *first* implication is the variability of techniques among the existential therapists. Boss, for example, uses couch and free association in traditional Freudian manner and permits a good deal of acting out of transference. Others would vary as much as the different schools vary anyway. But the critical point is that the existential therapists have a definite reason for using any given technique with a given patient. They sharply question the use of techniques simply because of rote, custom, or tradition. Their approach also does not at all settle for the air of vagueness and unreality that surrounds many therapeutic sessions, particularly in the eclectic schools which allegedly have freed themselves from bondage to a traditional technique and select from all schools as though the presuppositions of these approaches did not matter. Existential therapy is distinguished by a sense of reality and concreteness.

I would phrase the above point positively as follows: existential technique should have flexibility and versatility, varying from patient to patient and from one phase to another in treatment with the same patient. The specific technique to be used at a given point should be decided on the basis of these questions: What will best reveal the existence of this particular patient at this moment in his history? What will best illuminate his being-in-the-world? Never merely "eclectic," this flexibility always involves a clear understanding of the underlying assumptions of any method. Let us say a Kinseyite, for example, a traditional Freudian, and an existential analyst are dealing with an instance of sexual repression. The Kinseyite would speak of it in terms of finding a sexual object, in which case he is not talking about sex in human beings. The traditional Freudian would see its psychological implications, but would look primarily for causes in the past and might well ask himself how this instance of sexual repression *qua* repression can be overcome. The existential therapist would view the sexual repression as a holding back of *potentia* of the existence of this person, and though he might or might not, depending on the circumstances, deal immediately with the sex problem as such, it would always be seen not as a mechanism of repression as such but as a limitation of this person's being-in-his-world.

The *second* implication is that psychological dynamisms always take their meaning from the existential situation of the patient's own, immediate life.

Take, also, the ways of behaving known as *repression* and *resistance*. Freud saw repression as related to bourgeois morality, specifically, as the patient's need to preserve an acceptable picture of himself and therefore to hold back thoughts, desires, and so forth which are unacceptable according to bourgeois moral codes. Rather, says Boss, the conflict must be seen more basically in the area of the patient's acceptance or rejection of his own potentialities. We need to keep in mind the question—What keeps the patient from accepting in freedom his potentialities? This may involve bourgeois morality, but it also involves a lot more: it leads immediately to the existential question of the person's freedom. Before repression is possible or conceivable, the person must have some possibility of accepting or rejecting —that is, some margin of freedom. Whether the person is aware of this freedom or can articulate it is another question; he does not need to be. To repress is precisely to make one's self unaware of freedom; this is the nature of the dynamism. Thus, to repress or deny this freedom already presupposes it as a possibility. Boss then points out that psychic determinism is always a secondary phenomenon and works only in a limited area. The primary question is how the person relates to his freedom to express potentialities in the first place, repression being one way of so relating.

With respect to *resistance*, Boss again asks the question: What makes such a phenomenon possible? He answers that it is an outworking of the tendency of the patient to become absorbed in the *Mitwelt*, to slip back into *das man*, the anonymous mass, and to renounce the particular unique and original potentiality which is his. Thus "social conformity" is a general form of resistance in life; and even the patient's acceptance of the doctrines and interpretations of the therapist may itself be an expression of resistance.

We do not wish here to go into the question of what underlies these phenomena. We want only to demonstrate that at each point in considering these dynamisms of transference, resistance, and repression Boss does something critically importants for the existential approach. *He places each dynamism on an ontological basis.* Each way of behaving is seen and understood in the light of the existence of the patient as a human being. This is shown, too, in his conceiving of drives, libido, and so forth always in terms of *potentialities* for existence. Thus he proposes "to throw overboard the painful intellectual acrobatic of the old psychoanalytic theory which sought to derive the phenomena from the interplay of some forces or drives behind them." He does not deny forces as such but holds that they cannot be understood as "energy transformation" or on any other such natural science model but only as the person's *potentia* of existence. "This freeing from unnecessary constructions facilitates the understanding between patient and doctor. Also it makes the pseudo-resistances disappear which were a justified defense of the analysands against a violation of their essence." Boss holds that he thus can follow the "basic rule" in analysis—the one condition Freud set for analysis, namely, that the patient give forth in complete honesty whatever was going on in his mind—more effectively than in traditional psychoanalysis, for he listens with respect and takes seriously and without reserve the contents of the patient's communication rather than sieving it through prejudgments or destroying it by special interpretations. Boss holds himself to be entirely loyal to Freud in all of this and to be simply engaged in bringing out the underlying meaning of Freud's discoveries and placing them on their necessary comprehensive foundation. Believing that Freud's discoveries have to be understood below their faulty formulation, he points out that Freud himself was not merely a passive "mirror" for the patient in analysis, as traditionally urged in psychoanalysis, but was "translucent," a vehicle and medium through which the patient saw himself.

The *third* implication in existential therapy is the emphasis on *presence.* By this we mean that the relationship of the therapist and patient is taken as a real one, the therapist being not merely a shadowy reflector but an alive human being who happens, at that hour, to be concerned not with his own problems but with understanding and experiencing so far as possible the being of the patient. . . . Existentially, truth always involves the relation of the person to something or someone, and the therapist is part of the patient's relationship "field." This is not only the therpist's best avenue to understanding the patient but he cannot really *see* the patient unless he participates in the field.

Several quotations will make clearer what this presence means. Karl Jaspers has remarked, "What we are missing! What opportunities of understanding we let pass by because at a single decisive moment we were, with all our knowledge, lacking in the simple virtue of a *full human presence!*" . . .

Presence is not to be confused with a sentimental attitude toward the patient but depends firmly and consistently on how the therapist conceives of human beings. It is found in therapists of various schools and differing beliefs—differing, that is, on anything except one central issue—their assumptions about whether the human being is an object to be analyzed or a being to be understood. Any therapist is existential to the extent that, with all his technical training and his knowledge of transference and dynamisms, he is still able to relate to the patient as "one existence communicating with another," to use Binswanger's phrase. In my own experience, Frieda Fromm-Reichmann particularly had this power in a given therapeutic hour; she used to say, "The patient needs an experience, not an explanation." . . .

The *fourth* implication for technique in existential analysis follows immediately from our discussion of presence: therapy will attempt to "analyze out" the ways of behaving which destroy presence. The therapist, on his part, will need to be aware of whatever in him blocks full presence. I do not know the context of Freud's remark that he preferred that patients lie on the couch because he could not stand to be stared at for nine hours a day. But it is obviously true that any therapist—whose task is arduous and taxing at best—is tempted at many points to evade the anxiety and potential discomfort of confrontation by various devices. . . . Real confrontation between two people can be profoundly anxiety-creating. Thus it is not surprising that it is much more comfortable to protect ourselves by thinking of the other only as a "patient" or focusing only on certain mechanisms of behavior. The *technical* view of the other person is perhaps the therapist's most handy anxiety-reducing device. This has its legitimate place. The therapist is presumably an expert. But technique must not be used as a way of blocking presence. Whenever the therapist finds himself reacting in a rigid or preformulated way, he had obviously best ask himself whether he is not trying to avoid some anxiety and as a result is losing something existentially real in the relationship. The therapist's situation is like that of the artist who has spent many years of disciplined study learning technique; but he knows that if specific thoughts of technique preoccupy him when he actually is in the process of painting, he has at that moment lost his vision; the creative process, which should absorb him, transcending the subject-object split, has become temporarily broken; he is now dealing with objects and himself as a manipulator of objects.

The *fifth* implication has to do with the goal of the therapeutic process. The aim of therapy is that the patient *experience his existence as real*. The purpose is that he become aware of his existence fully, which includes becoming aware of his potentialities and becoming able to act on the basis of them. The characteristic of the neurotic is that his existence has become "darkened," as the existential analysts put it, blurred, easily threatened and clouded over, and gives no sanction to his acts; the task of therapy is to illuminate the existence. The neurotic is overconcerned about the *Umwelt*, and underconcerned about *Eigenwelt*. As the *Eigenwelt* becomes real to him in therapy, the patient tends to experience the *Eigenwelt* of the therapist as stronger than his own. Binswanger points out that the tendency to take over the therapist's *Eigenwelt* must be guarded against, and therapy must not become a power struggle betwen the two *Eigenwelten*. The therapist's function is to *be there* (with all of the connotation of *Dasein*), present in the relationship, while the patient finds and learns to live out his own *Eigenwelt*.

An experience of my own may serve to illustrate one way of taking the patient existentially. I often have found myself having the impulse to ask, when the patient comes in and sits down, not *"How* are you?" but *Where* are you?" The contrast of these questions—neither of which would I probably actually ask aloud—highlights what is sought. I want to know, as I experience him in this hour, not just how he feels, but rather *where he is,* the "where" including his feelings but also a lot more—whether he is detached or fully present, whether his direction is toward me and toward his problems or away from both, whether he is running from anxiety, whether this special courtesy when he came in or appearance of eagerness to review things is really inviting me to overlook some evasion he is about to make, where he is in relation to the girl friend he talked about yesterday, and so on. I became aware of this asking "where" the patient was several years ago, before I specifically knew the work of the existential therapists; it illustrates a spontaneous existential attitude. . . .

The *sixth* implication which distinguishes the process of existential therapy is the importance of *commitment*. The basis for this was prepared at numerous points in our previous sections, particularly in our discussion of Kierkegaard's idea that "truth exists only as the individual himself produces it in action." The significance of commitment is not that it is simply a vaguely good thing or ethically to be advised. It is a necessary prerequisite, rather, for seeing truth. This involves a crucial point which has never to my knowledge been fully taken into account in writings on psychotherapy, namely, that *decision precedes knowledge.* We have worked normally on the assumption that, as the patient gets more and more knowledge and insight about himself, he will make the appropriate decisions. This is a half truth. The second half of the truth is generally overlooked, namely, that *the patient cannot permit himself to get insight or knowledge until he is ready to decide, takes a decisive orientation to life, and has made the preliminary decisions along the way.*

Ronald D. Laing (b. 1927) is another contemporary psychiatrist whose approach has been molded by both psychoanalytic principles and existentialist philosophy. Yet he is not likely to feel comfortable in the company of the staid, academically more exalted figures whose work is sampled in this chapter. He won fame and a growing number of followers through his fresh, unconventional approach to the problem of sanity versus madness; through his unorthodox attempts to treat so-called schizophrenics at his therapeutic community in Kingsley Hall, a dilapidated three-story building in a London suburb; and through his two best-selling books, The Divided Self *and* The Politics of Experience.

His followers—both patients and psychiatrists—were attracted to him by his open-minded, essentially relativistic stance regarding mental illness. He does not regard schizophrenia as a well-defined or even definable disease entity, mental or physical, but as the individual's legitimate response to a mad society. It is in effect a person's idiosyncratic reaction to a bad family situation, to an alienated culture, or to the flawed network of communication in which he is enmeshed: it is his particular mode of existence, as Heidegger, Binswanger, or Boss would put it. It is this basic philosophy, this nonjudgmental attitude toward individual or social aberration that stamps Laing as an existentialist. But his radical posture as a social reformer, his missionary zeal combined with a hard-nosed, pragmatic approach distinguishes him from the older, pre-World War II generation of existential psychiatrists. Like Thomas Szasz, his fellow campaigner for the same cause in this country, he attacks the psychiatric establishment and what he calls the coercive position of his psychiatric confreres. These attacks, combined with his knack for hyperbole and pungent paradoxes, have made him the mouthpiece of the disaffected young on both sides of the Atlantic and a champion of a disadvantaged minority that our culture is wont to stigmatize as schizophrenics.

Whether his therapeutic results are in any way superior to those of his colleagues has been questioned. William Sargant, chief of psychiatry at a prominent London hospital, complained that he had to take care of Laing's failures, and Hans Eysenck, the psychologist and critic of psychoanalysis, accused him and his associates of using patients as a captive audience for his "pseudophilosophical" arguments. Other critics have noted that Laing's theory of a purely societal origin of schizophrenia is incompatible with evidence of hereditary transmissions with the schizophrenic reactions seen in users of LSD, and with his own imaginative references to the regression of the patient in terms of a journey to "primal man," if not to his phylogenetic past. In the meantime, Kingsley Hall, the experimental proving-ground of his ideas, had to close down as a noble failure—or yet another victim of a dysfunctioning society. Still, there can be no doubt that Laing's ideas themselves have had a major impact on the contemporary psychiatric scene and its growing disenchantment with the medical model of mental illness.

The following section is taken from Chapter 5 of The Politics of Experience *by R. D. Laing, Copyright © R. D. Laing 1967, (Penguin Books 1967), pp. 85-87, 88, 89, 90, 91, 93-96, 98-100, 106-107 in the Penguin Edition.*

In the last decade, a radical shift of outlook has been occurring in psychiatry. This has entailed the questioning of old assumptions, based on the attempts of nineteenth-century psychiatrists to bring the frame of clinical medicine to bear on their observations. Thus the subject matter of psychiatry was thought of as mental illness; one thought of mental physiology and mental pathology, one looked for signs and symptoms, made one's diagnosis, assessed prognosis and prescribed treatment. According to one's philosophical bias, one looked for the etiology of these mental illnesses in the mind, in the body, in the environment, or in inherited propensities.

The term "schizophrenia" was coined by a Swiss psychiatrist, Bleuler, who worked within this frame of reference. In using the term schizophrenia, I am not referring to any condition that I suppose to be mental rather than physical, or to an illness, like pneumonia, but to a label that some people pin on other people under certain social circumstances. The "cause" of "schizophrenia" is to be found by the examination, not of the prospective diagnosee alone, but of the whole social context in which the psychiatric ceremonial is being conducted.

Once demystified, it is clear, at least, that some people come to behave and to experience themselves and others in ways that are strange and incomprehensible to most people, including themselves. If this behavior and experience fall into certain broad categories, they are liable to be diagnosed as subject to a condition called schizophrenia. By present calculation almost one in every 100 children born will fall into this category at some time or other before the age of forty-five, and in the United Kingdom at the moment there are roughly 60,000 men and women in mental hospitals, and many more outside hospitals, who are termed schizophrenic.

A child born today in the United Kingdom stands a ten times greater chance of being admitted to a mental hospital than to a university, and about one fifth of mental hospital admissions are diagnosed schizophrenic. This can be taken as an indication that we are driving our children mad more effectively than we are genuinely educating them. Perhaps it is our way of educating them that is driving them mad.

Most but not all psychiatrists still think that people they call schizophrenic suffer from an inherited predisposition to act in predominantly incomprehensible ways, that some as yet undetermined genetic factor (possibly a genetic morphism) transacts with a more or less ordinary environment to induce biochemical-endocrinological changes which in turn generate what we observe as the behavioral signs of a subtle underlying organic process.

But it is wrong to impute a hypothetical disease of unknown etiology and undiscovered pathology to someone unless *he* can prove otherwise.

The schizophrenic is someone who has queer experiences and/or is acting in a queer way, from the point of view usually of his relatives and of ourselves. . . .

That the diagnosed patient is suffering from a pathological process is either a fact, or an hypothesis, an assumption, or a judgment.

To regard it as fact is unequivocally false. To regard it as an hypothesis is legitimate. It is unnecessary either to make the assumption or to pass judgment.

The psychiatrist, adopting his clinical stance in the presence of the pre-diagnosed person, whom he is already looking at and listening to as a patient, has tended to come to believe that he is in the presence of the "fact" of schizophrenia. He acts as if its eixstence were an established fact. He then has to discover its cause or multiple etiological factors, to assess its prognosis, and to treat its course. The heart of the illness then resides outside the agency of the person. That is, the illness is taken to be a process that the person is subject to or undergoes, whether genetic, constitutional, endogenous, exogenous, organic or psychological, or some mixture of them all.

Many psychiatrists are now becoming much more cautious about adopting this starting point. But what might take its place?

In understanding the new viewpoint on schizophrenia, we might remind ourselves of the six blind men and the elephant: one touched its body and said it was a wall, another touched an ear and said it was a fan, another a leg and thought it was a pillar, and so on. The problem is sampling, and the error is incautious extrapolation.

The old way of sampling the behavior of schizophrenics was by the method of clinical examination. The following is an example of the type of examination conducted at the turn of the century. The account is given by the German psychiatrist Emil Kraepelin in his own words.

Gentlemen, the cases that I have to place before you today are peculiar. First of all, you see a servant-girl, aged twenty-four, upon whose features and frame traces of great emaciation can be plainly seen. In spite of this, the patient is in continual movement, going a few steps forward, then back again; she plaits her hair, only to unloose it the next minute. *On attempting to stop her movement*, we meet with unexpectedly strong resistance; *if I place myself in front of her with my arms spread out* in order to stop her, if she cannot push me on one side, she suddenly turns and slips through under my arms, so as to continue her way. *If one takes firm hold* of her, she distorts her usually rigid, expressionless features with deplorable weeping, that only ceases so soon as one lets her have her own way. We notice besides that she holds a crushed piece of bread spasmodically clasped in the fingers of the left hand, which she absolutely *will not allow to be forced from her.* The patient does not trouble, in the least about her surroundings so long as you leave her alone. *If you prick her in the forehead with a needle,* she scarcely winces or turns away, and leave the needle quietly sticking there without letting it disturb her restless, beast-of-prey-like wandering backwards and forwards. *To questions* she answers almost nothing, at the most shaking her head. But from time to time she wails: "O dear God! O dear God! O dear mother! O dear mother!" always repeating uniformly the same phrases.

Here are a man and a young girl. If we see the situation purely in terms of Kraepelin's point of view, it all immediately falls into place. He is sane, she is insane; he is rational, she is irrational. This entails looking at the patient's actions out of the context of the situation as she experienced it. But if we take Kraepelin's actions (in italics)—he tries to stop her movements, stands in front of her with arms outspread, tries to force a piece of bread out of her hand, sticks a needle in her forehead, and so on—out of the context of the situation as experienced and defined by him, how extraordinary *they* are!

A feature of the interplay between psychiatrist and patient is that if the patient's part is taken out of context, as is done in the clinical description, it might seem very odd. The psychiatrist's part, however, is taken as the very touchstone for our common-sense view of normality. The psychiatrist, as *ipso facto* sane, shows that the patient is out of contact with him. The fact that he is out of contact with the patient shows that there is something wrong with the patient, but not with the psychiatrist.

But if one ceases to identify with the clinical posture and looks at the psychiatrist-patient couple without such presuppositions, then it is difficult to sustain this naive view of the situation.

Psychiatrists have paid very little attention to the *experience* of the patient. Even in psychoanalysis there is an abiding tendency to suppose that the schizophrenic's experiences are somehow unreal or invalid; one can make sense out of them only by interpreting them; without truth-giving interpretations the patient is enmeshed in a world of delusions and self-deception. Kaplan, an American psychologist, in an introduction to an excellent collection of self-reports on the experience of being psychotic, says very justly:

> With all virtue on his side, he (the psychiatrist or psychoanalyst) reaches through the subterfuges and distortions of the patient and exposes them to the light of reason and insight. In this encounter between the psychiatrist and patient, the efforts of the former are linked with science and medicine, with understanding and care. What the patient experiences is tied to illness and irreality, to perverseness and distortion. The process of psychotherapy consists in large part of the patient's abandoning his

false subjective perspectives for the therapist's objective ones. But the essence of this conception is that the psychiatrist understands what is going on, and the patient does not.

H. S. Sullivan used to say to young psychiatrists when they came to work with him, "I want you to remember that in the present state of our society, the patient is right, and you are wrong." This is an outrageous simplification, I mention it to loosen any fixed ideas that are no less outrageous, that the psychiatrist is right, and the patient wrong. I think, however, that schizophrenics have more to teach psychiatrists about the inner world than psychiatrists their patients.

A different picture begins to develop if the interaction between patients themselves is studied without presuppositions. One of the best accounts here is by the American sociologist Erving Goffman.

Goffman spent a year as an assistant physical therapist in a large mental hospital of some 7,000 beds, near Washington. His lowly staff status enabled him to fraternize with the patients in a way that upper echelons of the staff were unable to do. One of his conclusions is:

> There is an old saw that no clearcut line can be drawn between normal people and mental patients; rather there is a continuum with the well-adjusted citizen at one end and the full-fledged psychotic at the other. I must argue that after a period of acclimatization in a mental hospital, the notion of a continuum seems very presumptuous. A community is a community. Just as it is bizarre to those not in it, so it is natural, even if unwanted, to those who live it from within. The system of dealings that patients have with one another does not fall at one end of anything, but rather provides one example of human association, to be avoided, no doubt, but also to be filled by the student in a circular cabinet along with all of the other examples of association that he can collect.

It is on account of their behavior outside hospitals, however, that people get diagnosed as schizophrenic and admitted to hospitals in the first place.

There have been many studies of social factors in relation to schizophrenia. These include attempts to discover whether schizophrenia occurs more or less frequently in one or another ethnic group, social class, sex, ordinal position in the family and so on. The conclusion from such studies has often been that social factors do not play a significant role in the "etiology of schizophrenia." This begs the question, and moreover such studies do not get close enough to the relevant situation. If the police wish to determine whether a man has died of natural causes, or has committed suicide, or has been murdered, they do not look up prevalence or incidence figures. They investigate the circumstances attendant upon each single case in turn. Each investigation is an original research project, and it comes to an end when enough evidence has been gathered to answer the relevant questions.

It is only in the last ten years that the immediate interpersonal environment of "schizophrenics" has come to be studied in its interstices. This work was prompted, in the first place, by psychotherapists who formed the impression that, if their patients were *disturbed*, their families were often very *disturbing*. Psychotherapists, however, remained committed by their technique not to study the families directly. At first the focus was mainly on the mothers (who are always the first to get the blame for everything), and a "schizophrenogenic" mother was postulated, who was supposed to generate disturbance in her child.

Next, attention was paid to the husbands of these undoubtedly unhappy women, then to the parental and parent-child interactions (rather than to each person in the family separately), then to the nuclear family group of parents and children, and finally to the whole relevant network of people in and around the family, including the grandparents of patients. By the time our own researches started, this methodological breakthrough had been made and, in addition, a major theoretical advance had been achieved.

This was the "double-bind" hypothesis, whose chief architect was the anthropologist Gregory Bateson. The theory, first published in 1956, represented a theoretical advance of the first order. The germ of the idea developed in Bateson's mind while studying New Guinea in the 1930s. In New Guinea the culture had, as all cultures have, built-in techniques for maintaining its own inner balance. One technique, for example, that served to neutralize dangerous rivalry was sexual transvestism. However, missionaries and the occidental government tended to object to such practices. The culture was therefore caught between the risk of external extermination or internal disruption.

Together with research workers in California, Bateson brought this paradigm of an insoluble "can't win" situation, specifically destructive of self-identity, to bear on the internal communication pattern of families of diagnosed schizophrenics.

The studies of the families of schizophrenics conducted at Palo Alto, California, Yale University, the Pennsylvania Psychiatric Institute and the National Institute of Mental Health, among other places, have all shown that the person who gets diagnosed is part of a wider network of extremely disturbed and disturbing patterns of communication. In all these places, to the best of my knowledge, *no* schizophenic has been studied whose disturbed pattern of communication has not been shown to be a reflection of, and reaction to, the disturbed and disturbing pattern characterizing his or her family of origin. This is matched in our own researches.

In over 100 cases where we studied the actual circumstances around the social event when one person comes to be regarded as schizophrenic, it seems to us that *without exception* the experience and behavior that gets labeled schizophrenic is *a special strategy that a person invents in order to live in an unlivable situation.* In his life situation the person has come to feel he is in an untenable position. He cannot make a move, or make no move, without being beset by contradictory and paradoxical pressures and demands, pushes and pulls, both internally from himself, and externally from those around him. He is, as it were, in a position of checkmate.

This state of affairs may not be perceived as such by any of the people in it. The man at the bottom of the heap may be being crushed and suffocated to death without anyone noticing, much less intending it. The situation here described is impossible to see by studying the different people in it singly. The social system, not single individuals extrapolated from it, must be the object of study.

We know that the biochemistry of the person is highly sensitive to social circumstance. That a checkmate situation occasions a biochemical response which, in turn, facilitates or inhibits certain types of experience and behavior is plausible *a priori.*

The behavior of the diagnosed patient is part of a much larger network of disturbed behavior. The contradictions and confusions "internalized" by the individual must be looked at in their larger social contexts.

Something is wrong somewhere, but it can no longer be seen exclusively or even primarily "in" the diagnosed patient.

From an ideal vantage point on the ground, a formation of planes may be observed in the air. One plane may be out of formation. But the whole formation may be off course. The plane that is "out of formation" may be abnormal, bad or "mad," from the point of view of the formation. But the formation itself may be bad or mad from the point of view of the ideal observer. The plane that is out of formation may also be more or less off course than the formation itself is.

The "out of formation" criterion is the clinical positivist criterion.

The "off course" criterion is the ontological. One needs to make two judgments along these different parameters. In particular, it is of fundamental importance not to confuse the person who may be "out of formation" by telling him he is "off course" if he is not. It is of fundamental importance not to make the positivist mistake of assuming that, because a group are "in formation," this means they are necessarily "on course." This is the Gadarene swine fallacy. Nor is it necessarily the case that the person who is "out of formation" is more "on course" than the formation. There is no need to idealize someone just because he is labeled "out of formation." Nor is there any need to persuade the person who is "out of formation" that cure consists in getting back into formation. The person who is "out of formation" is often full of hatred toward the formation and of fears about being the odd man out.

If the formation is itself off course, then the man who is really to get "on course" must leave the formation. But it is possible to do so, if one desires, without screeches and screams, and without terrorizing the already terrified formation that one has to leave.

In the diagnostic category of schizophrenic are many different types of sheep and goats.

"Schizophrenia" is a diagnosis, a label applied by some people to others. This does not prove that the labeled person is subject to an essentially pathological process, of unknown nature and origin, going on *in* his or her body. It does not mean that the process is, primarily or secondarily, a psychopathological one, going on *in* the *psyche* of the person. But it does establish as a social fact that the person labeled is one of Them. It is easy to forget that the process is a hypothesis, to assume that it is a fact, then to pass the judgment that it is biologically maladaptive and, as such, pathological. But social adaptation to a dysfunctional society may be very dangerous. The perfectly adjusted bomber pilot may be a greater threat to species survival than the hospitalized schizophrenic deluded that the Bomb is inside him. Our society may itself have become biologically dysfunctional, and some forms of schizophenic alienation from the alienation of society may have a sociobiological function that we have not recognized. This holds even if a genetic factor predisposes to some kinds of schizophrenic behavior. Recent critiques of the work on genetics and the most recent empirical genetic studies, leave this matter open. . . .

There is no such "condition" as "schizophrenia," but the label is a social fact and the social fact a *political event*. This political event, occurring in the civic order of society, imposes definitions and consequences on the labeled person. It is a social prescription that rationalizes a set of social actions whereby the labeled person is annexed by others, who are legally sanctioned, medically empowered and morally obliged, to become responsible for the person labeled.

Describing the schizophrenic experience as a journey from outer—that is, consensually validated—space and time into inner space and time, "back through one's personal life, in and back and beyond into the experience of mankind, of the primal man, of Adam and perhaps even further, into the being of animals, vegetables and minerals," Laing suggests that the healing process in schizophrenia amounts to a journey back from the "infinite reaches of the inner space."

What is entailed then is:
  (i) a voyage from outer to inner,
  (ii) from life to a kind of death,
  (iii) from going forward to going back,
  (iv) from temporal movement to temporal standstill,
  (v) from mundane time to eonic time,
  (vi) from the ego to the self,
  (vii) from outside (post-birth) back into the womb of all things (pre-birth),
and then subsequently a return voyage from
  (1) inner to outer,
  (2) from death to life,
  (3) from the movement back to a movement once more forward,
  (4) from immortality back to mortality,
  (5) from eternity back to time,
  (6) from self to a new ego,
  (7) from a cosmic fetalization to an existential rebirth.

I shall leave it to those who wish to translate the above elements of this perfectly natural and necessary process into the jargon of psychopathology and clinical psychiatry. This process may be one that all of us need, in one form or another. This process could have a central function in a truly sane society.

The controversy about Laing's theories—especially about the societal origin of schizophrenia—is still in progress. Yet the growing evidence of biochemical and genetic factors involved in schizophrenic reactions is apt to weaken Laing's more radical claims. The same is true for Thomas Szasz's spirited attacks against the medical model of mental illness in general. An early formulation of his views will be found in Chapter 26, featuring the controversy concerning modern behavior therapy.

Reverting to our preceding selections, the gulf between Freudian and existential therapists seems indeed difficult to bridge. Freud's detached, uncompromisingly scientific attitude cannot be reconciled with the existentialists' highly subjective, personally involved, value-oriented—if not religiously inspired—philosophy. Added to this is the basic difference of personal styles and the characteristic language of existential writings. Critics have pointed to their turgid style, copious verbiage, the endless repetition of essentially inspirational pronouncements reminiscent of ancient oracles or poetic diction. Yet others note that despite their emphasis on a new philosophical approach, existential analysts continue to see their patients two or three times a week, listening to their troubles in the spirit of sympathetic understanding, looking for deeper meanings in their dreams, symptoms or fantasies, and trying to convey to them a better understanding of their own neurotic or otherwise warped, eccentric or extravagant modes of existence. Indeed, most psychoanalysts will protest that they too deal with their patients according to such principles whenever this is possible and clinically desirable. They will note that failing to do so would be merely indicative of their own unresolved countertransference.

The fact is that Medard Boss in Switzerland and Ronald Laing in England, and Harold Kelman, Karen Horney, and Rollo May and their associates in this country have gone a long way in their attempts to reconcile the differences between the two camps.

chapter 25

Parapsychology:
Magic Lost and Regained?

FREUD, SERVADIO, EHRENWALD, EISENBUD . . .
ULLMAN'S REM EXPERIMENTS

The intellectual ferment of any given time tends to surface in the religious movements of the period; in the crosscurrents of philosophical debate; in the area of political controversy; in the waves and eddies of its artistic and literary expression. At the time of this writing, it is brought into focus in the current trends of psychology and psychotherapy. We have seen that existential analysis is challenging the essentially materialistic, positivistic, causal-reductive position of psychoanalysis. The diverse contemporary attempts at rediscovering and recapturing long-forgotten, seemingly lost magico-mythical aspects of the human mind carry the pendulum swings of ideas even further away from the firmly entrenched, computerized but fragmented and compartmentalized picture of the world. The focus is on the privacy of altered states of consciousness, on ecstasy, on mystical experiences, self-induced or triggered by psychedelic drugs.

Champions of the new dispensation argue that modern man's alienation and spiritual malaise is due to his loss of religious values, to the demythologization of his myths and to the death of God. As an antidote to what can be described as the ensuing myth-deprivation, he resorts to diverse techniques of transcendental meditation, to esoteric cults such as Zen Buddhism, Taoism, Sufism, borrowed from a past era or from Far Eastern philosophies. Such spiritual disciplines, it is hoped, should restore man's control over deeper levels of his personality, restore his lost unity with the symbiotic matrix of his existence, and counteract the dominance of reason, of the intellect, and of a miscarried science and technology in our culture.

Paradoxically, science itself is being mobilized to assist in this new development. There are the various techniques of biofeedback aiming at the control of alpha waves, of autonomic functions, of primitive learning, and the like. Modern parapsychology, which grew out of J. B. Rhine's statistical experiments with ESP cards and PK dice, is spearheading the advance into this new frontier of the mind. At the other end of the spectrum are the contributions of a growing number of psychoanalysts and psychiatrists demonstrat-

ing the part played by telepathy, clairvoyance and related psi phenomena in the clinic and consulting room.

To the chagrin of some of his more orthodox followers, Freud himself went on record with a few observations that he more or less reluctantly interpreted in parapsychological terms. Other analysts who made important contributions to the field are Wilhelm Stekel, Istvan Hollós, Emilio Servadio, Nando Fodor, Jan Ehrenwald, and Jule Eisenbud, to say nothing of C. G. Jung's lifelong interest in the mystical or "occult" which ultimately led to his break with Freud.

The selection below is taken from Freud's "Dreams and the Occult," originally published in 1933. It shows how telepathy and related phenomena essentially obey the same principles that underlie the psychodynamics of dreams, neurotic symptoms and primary process functioning in general. Nevertheless, in discussing one of his most impressive examples—the case of Dr. Forsyth—he warns his readers not to take the reality of "occult" phenomena unconditionally for granted:

Ladies and Gentlemen—You have heard what dream interpretation and psychoanalysis in general can do for occultism. You have seen by means of examples that, through the application of psychoanalytic theory, occult phenomena have been revealed which would otherwise have remained unrecognized. The question which doubtless interests you most, whether we ought to believe in the objective reality of the phenomena, is one which psychoanalysis cannot answer directly; but at least the material which it has helped to bring to light is favorable to an affirmative reply. But your interest will not stop there. You will want to know to what conclusion that far richer vein of material, with which psychoanalysis has nothing whatever to do, leads us. There, however, I cannot follow you; it is no longer my province. The only thing I can do, is to tell you of some observations, which at any rate have something to do with psychoanalysis in the sense that they were made during analytical treatment, and were perhaps rendered possible by means of it. I will give you one example, the one which left the strongest impression with me; it will be long-winded, and you will have to keep a number of details in your minds, and even so a great deal will have to be omitted which increased the evidential value of the observation. It is an instance in which the phenomena in which we are interested came to light quite obviously and did not have to be brought out by analysis. In discussing it, however, we shall not be able to do without analysis. But I ought to warn you beforehand that even this example of apparent thought transference in the analytic situation is not proof against all objections, and does not warrant unconditional acceptance of the reality of occult phenomena.

The story is this. One autumn day in the year 1919, at about 10:45 A.M., Dr. David Forsyth, who had just arrived from London, sent in his card while I was working with a patient. (My respected colleague from the University of London will, I feel sure, not think I am being indiscreet if I tell you that he came to me for some months to be initiated into the mysteries of psychoanalytical technique.) I had only time to say "How do you do?" and arrange an appointment for later on. Dr. Forsyth had a special claim upon my interest; for he was the first foreigner who came to me after the isolation of the war years, and seemed to be a harbinger of better times. Soon after this, at eleven o'clock, my next patient arrived, a Mr. P., an intelligent and charming man of between forty and fifty, who had come to me because he experienced difficulties in sexual intercourse with women. In his case there was no prospect of bringing about a cure, and I had long ago suggested that he should break off the treatment; but he had preferred to continue it, obviously because he felt comfortable in a well-tempered father transference upon myself. Money played no part at this time, because there was too little of it about. The hours I spent with him were stimulating for me as well, and a relaxation, and so, setting aside the strict rules of medical etiquette, we were going on with the analytic treatment for a specified length of time.

On this particular day P. reverted to his attempts at sexual intercourse with women, and mentioned once more the pretty, piquante girl, in poor circumstances, with whom he might have been successful if only the fact of her virginity had not frightened him off from taking any serious steps. He had often spoken of her, but that day he told me for the first time that she, though naturally she had not the slightest idea of the real grounds of his difficulty, used to call him Mr. Foresight (*Vorsicht*). I was much struck by this piece of information; Dr. Forsyth's card was beside me, and I showed it to him.

These are the facts. I dare say they will seem to you to be rather thin; but if you will have patience you will find that there is more to come.

P. had spent some years of his youth in England, and had retained a lasting interest in English literature. He possessed a well-stocked library of English books, which he used to lend me, and it is to him that I owe my acquaintance with authors such as Arnold Bennett and Galsworthy, of whose works I had so far read but little. One day he lent me a novel by Galsworthy called *The Man of Property*, the subject of which is an imaginary family named Forsyte. Galsworthy's imagination was obviously captured by this creation of his, because in the later stories he repeatedly went back to members of this family, and eventually collected all the stories which had to do with them under the heading of *The Forsyte Saga*. Only a few days before the event I am telling you about, P. had brought me a new volume out of this series. The name Forsyte and all that it typified for the author, had played a part in my conversations with P.; it had become a part of the private language which so easily grows up between two people who see each other regularly. Now the same Forsyte out of the novels is not very different from that of my visitor Forsyth (as pronounced by a German, indeed, they are hardly distinguishable), and the expressive English word "foresight," which means *"Voraussicht"* or *"Vorsicht,"* would be pronounced in the same way. P. had, therefore, produced from his own personal experiences a name that was in my mind at the same time on account of a circumstance quite unknown to him.

As you see, we are making some progress. But I think we shall be even more strongly impressed by this remarkable occurrence and get some sort of insight into the conditions of its origin, if we turn the light of analysis onto two other associations which P. brought up during the same hour.

First: One day in the preceding week I was expecting Mr. P. at 11 o'clock, but he had not appeared, and I went out to pay a call on Dr. Anton v. Freund at his pension. I was surprised to find that Mr. P. lived on another floor of the same house in which the pension was. Referring to this later, I told P. that I had in a sense paid him a visit at his house; but I am absolutely certain that I did not mention the name of the person whom I had visited in the pension, and now, soon after the mention of Mr. Foresight, he asked me the following question: "Is the lady called Freud-Ottorego who gives the English course at the Volksuniversitat your daughter by any chance?" And for the first time in our long acquaintance he let slip the distorted form of my name, to which officials, clerks, and printers have accustomed me; instead of Freud, he said Freund.

Secondly: At the end of the hour he told me a dream, out of which he had woken with a feeling of anxiety, a regular *"Alptraum"* ("nightmare") he called it. He added that he had recently forgotten the English word for it, and had told someone who had asked him, that the English for *"Alptraum"* was "a mare's nest." That is of course, absurd, because "a mare's nest" means nothing of the sort, and the correct translation of *"Alptraum"* is "nightmare." This association seemed to have nothing more in common with the others than the element of "English"; but he reminded me of a trivial occurrence which had happened about a month before. P. was sitting in my room with me, when there appeared quite unexpectedly another welcome guest from London, Dr. Ernest Jones, whom I had not seen for a long time. I nodded to him to go into my other room until I had finished with P. The latter recognized him at once, however, from a photograph of him which hung in the waiting room, and even asked to be introduced to him. Now Jones is the author of a monograph on the nightmare (109). I did not know whether P. was acquainted with the book; he avoided reading analytical literature.

At this point I should like to consider what analytical understanding we can obtain of P.'s associations and their motivations. P. had the same attitude toward the same Forsyte as I had; it meant the same to him as it did to me, and in fact it was to him that I owed my knowledge of the name. The remarkable thing was that he brought this name into the analysis immediately after it had acquired another meaning for me through a recent experience, namely the arrival of the physician from London. But perhaps not less interesting is the *way* in which the name came up in his analytical hour. He did not say: "Now the name Forsyte, out of the novels you have read, comes into my mind," but, without any conscious reference to this source, he managed to weave it into his own personal experiences and brought it to the surface in that way—a thing which might have happened long before, but which had not as a matter of fact occurred until now. At this juncture, however, he said: "I am a Forsyte, too, for that is what the girl called me." One cannot mistake the mixture of exacting jealousy and plaintive self-depreciation which finds expression in this utterance. We shall not go far wrong if we complete it thus: "I am hurt that your thoughts should be so much wrapped up in this newcomer. Come back to me; after all, I am a Forsyth too—or rather only a Mr. Foresight, as the girl called me." And now, starting from the idea of "English," his train of thought worked back to two earlier situations, which might very well have aroused the same jealousy in him. "A few days ago you paid a visit at my house, but, alas, it was not to me, it was to a Herr v. Freund." This idea made him distort the name Freud into Freund. The name Freud-Ottorego from the lecture list came in, because as the name of a teacher of English it paved the way for the manifest association. And now the memory of another visitor of a few weeks back presented itself, a visitor toward whom he certainly felt just as jealous, this visitor (Dr. Jones) was at the same time in a superior position to him, because he could write a book about nightmares, while the best he could do was to have nightmares himself. The allusion to his mistake about the meaning of a "mare's nest" belonged to the same connection; it must mean: "I am not a proper Englishman after all, any more than I am a proper Forsyth."

Now it could not be said that his jealous feelings were either inappropriate or incomprehensible. He had already been made aware that his analysis, and with it our relations, would come to an end as soon as foreign pupils and patients began to return to Vienna; and this is actually what happened shortly afterward. But what we have just been doing has been a piece of analytical work: the explanation of three ideas which were brought up in the same hour and were determined by the same motivation. This has not much to do with the question whether these ideas could have been produced without thought transference or not. The latter question applies to each of the three ideas, and can thus be divided into three separate questions. Could P. have known that Dr. Forsyth had just paid his first visit to me? Could he have known the name of the person whom I visited in his house? Did he know that Dr. Jones had written a book about nightmares? Or was it only my knowledge of these things which was displayed in the ideas that came into his head? Whether this observation of mine leads to a conclusion in favor of thought transference depends on the answer which is given to these separate questions. Let us leave the first question aside for the moment, as the two others are easier to deal with. The case of the visit to the pension strikes one at first sight as being very convincing. I am quite sure that in my short humorous mention of my visit to his house I did not mention any name; I think it is most improbable that P. made inquiries in the pension to discover the name of the person I had called on; in fact, I believe that he never knew of his existence. But the evidential value of this case is undermined by a chance factor. The man whom I had been to see in the pension was not only *called* Freund, but was indeed a true friend to us all. It was he whose generosity had made possible the founding of our publishing house. His early death, and that of Karl Abraham a few years later, were the most serious misfortunes which have befallen the development of psychoanalysis. It is possible, therefore, that I said to Mr. P.: "I have been visiting a *friend* at your house," and with this possibility the occult interest of the second association evaporates.

The impression made by the third association, too, soon fades. Could P. have known that Jones had published a monograph on the nightmare, seeing that he never read analytical literature? Yes, he could. He possessed books issued by our publishing house, and he might certainly have seen the titles of new publications printed on the covers. It cannot be proved, but it cannot be disproved. Along this road, then, we can come to no decision. This example of mine, I regret to say, is open to the same objections as so many others. It was written down too late, and came up for discussion at a time when I was not seeing Mr. P. any more, and could not ask him any further questions.

Let us return to the first association, which even by itself would support the alleged occurrence of thought transference. Could P. have known that Dr. Forsyth had been with me a quarter of an hour before him? Could he even have known of his existence or of his presence in Vienna? We must not give way to the temptation to answer both questions straight off in the negative. I might very well have told Mr. P. I was expecting a physician from England for training in analysis, the first dove after the deluge. This might have happened in the summer of 1919; Dr. Forsyth had made arrangements with me by letter, months before his arrival. I may even have mentioned his name, though that is most improbable. In view of the other association which the name had for us both, the mention of it would inevitably have led to a conversation of which some trace at least would have been preserved in my memory. Nevertheless such a conversation may have taken place and I may have totally forgotten it, so that it became possible for the mention of Mr. Foresight in the analytical hour to strike me as miraculous. If one regards oneself as a skeptic, it is as well from time to time to be skeptical about one's skepticism. Perhaps I too have that secret leaning toward the miraculous which meets the production of occult phenomena halfway.

Even if one part of this miraculous occurrence is thus explained away, we still have another part on our hands, and that the most difficult part of all. Granted that Mr. P. knew that there was such a person as Dr. Forsyth and that he was expected in Vienna in the autumn, how was it that my patient became sensitive to him on the very day of his arrival and immediately after his first visit? We might say that it was chance, that is, we might leave it unexplained; but I have mentioned the two other ideas which occurred to Mr. P. precisely in order to exclude the chance, in order to show you that he really was occupied with jealous thoughts directed against people who visited me, and whom I visited. Or, if we are anxious not to overlook anything even remotely possible, we might suppose that P. noticed that I was in a state of unusual excitement, a state of which I was certainly not aware, and that he drew his inference from that. Or that Mr. P., who after all had arrived only a quarter of an hour after the Englishman, had met him in the immediate neighborhood of my house, that he had recognized him from his typically English appearance, and with his jealous feelings on the alert, had immediately thought: "Ah, there is Dr. Forsyth, whose arrival means the end of my analysis; and probably he has just left the Professor." I cannot go any further into these rationalistic hypotheses. We are left once more with a *non liquet*, but I must confess that here too I feel that the balance is in favor of thought transference. For the matter of that, I am certainly not the only person who has met with "occult" phenomena in the analytic situation. Helene Deutsch in 1926 (*XII*) reported some observations of the same kind, and studied the way in which they were conditioned by the relation of transference between the patient and the analyst.

Emilio Servadio (b. 1904) is a prominent Italian psychoanalyst, past president of the Italian Psychoanalytic Association and author of several books and many articles in the field of parapsychology. Together with Freud, Hollos, Eisenbud, and others mentioned earlier, Servadio is among the pioneers of a psychoanalytic approach to telepathy and related phenomena.

The selection that follows (1955) deals with an apparently telepathic-precognitive dream in which the patient seems to peek into his analyst's

*private life, to "unmask" emotionally colored psychic material in his mind
and, as it were, to "throw it in his face":*

The following is an example of a "paranormal" occurrence during a-
nalysis such as has been repeatedly observed and reported by Freud, Hollos, H. Deutsch, Burlingham, Ehrenwald, Fodor, Eisenbud, Pederson-
Krag, Gillespie, Rubin, myself, and others. I consider it particularly interesting for the following main reasons: (1) Because of the admixture of
"telepathic" and "precognitive" elements in the analytic material (a dream);
(2) because it seems to me that the material itself can be satisfactorily explained and fully justified in a psychodynamic frame of reference *only* if
we take the aforesaid elements into account; (3) because the case shows
once more that the "paranormal" material which inserts itself into a psychological situation is submitted—as Freud first indicated—to the laws
and mechanisms of the primary process; and (4) because the case itself
shows the particular importance in such occurrences of the transference-
countertransference relation.

The dreamer, whom I shall call A, is a patient in his thirties, suffering
from an obsessional neurosis and labouring under the delayed influence
of an emotionally 'dry' childhood. His main symptomatic defences and
fantasies concern ideas of contamination and infection by "worms" and
other intestinal parasites, of venereal diseases, etc. When he had the dream,
analysis had just started afresh after an interval of about one month due
to my summer holidays. A is in a phase of negative transference, and his
main complaint is that the analyst is "distant," "aloof," "academic," etc.,
and is not getting really deep into his problems. Interpretations of this
attitude as being an unconscious repetition of his infantile dissatisfaction
concerning his father (whose ways of thinking and behaving in fact indicated a notable lack of contact with reality) and his mother (who gave
the patient plenty of food and material comfort, but little emotional
warmth and very little understanding) have so far been unsuccessful.

The dream occurred on the night between 27 and 28 August, 1953. It
was reported to me by the patient on the evening of the twenty-ninth, as
follows:

I was near your house, but it was not the real one. It was like a cottage in a suburb of a California city, with a small garden in the front.
It seemed to me that your maid, N, had placed a bowl of Italian noodles
near the garden gate. I went for this dish, feeling hungry, cold, and
miserable. I was wearing only a pair of shorts. While I was approaching
the bowl, I saw a car coming. I knew that you and your wife were inside. I got alarmed, and ran away.

The dream then changes. I was inside the house, seeing your wife from behind. She had three daughters with her: one I knew to be your fourteen-year-old daughter, whom I have seen once or twice (she was prettier than in reality). The others were two very pretty blonde girls: one looked about eight years old, the other about three or four. I still felt miserable and neglected, although I seemed to know that your family was nice and had nothing particular against me.

The associations produced by A immediately after telling me his dream were the following:

Noodles: "Italian *vermicelli*, meaning literally 'little worms.' I have avoided eating noodles lately, because they are fattening."

California cottage: "A small house in California near the sea. It belonged to my uncle E. I was there in 1931 or 1932. It was very small and uncomfortable, with many promiscuous people coming and going. I was sick while I was staying there. This reminds me of another severe illness which occurred when I was three and a half years old. I seemed 'Christianly resigned' to die, and was showing this attitude to my mother. Once I woke up in a panic, at night, and said I knew that my father wanted to murder me."

The maid N: "Of course, I see her every time I come here. I have never dreamt about her before."

Analyst's wife: No associations.

The three girls: No associations.

If we were to interpret this dream along the usual lines, without taking into account several elements which will be mentioned later, it might be possible to state that the patient has transferred into the analytical setting (involving the analyst's family and milieu) his oral infantile claims and is complaining that he is being neglected and emotionally starved by his parents. The "parents" (analyst and wife in the transference) go around in a car (=have sexual and other pleasures) while their "son" is left starving, half-naked, and is treated like a dog. They even disturb his very timid attempts to reach the food so ungraciously offered. The "mother" (analyst's wife) is busy with other children (the patient has several siblings) and turns her back on him. What can a child do but feel miserable and wish he were dead?

One could implement this interpretation by introducing the well-known symbolic relation house = woman (mother) and by stating that in all probability the "bowl of noodles" is a symbolic representation of the (unsatisfactory) breast. The "garden" near the house is, of course, a feminine "area," where genital and anal representations seem to overlap. Seeing my wife from behind, in the second part of the dream, can also mean, besides the charge against a mother who "turns her back" to her child, a libidinal wish concerning her "behind." The dream shows, among other things, that the patient's preoccupations about "worms," etc., have—as well as the obvious anal implications—an oral origin. They are, in the final analysis, the first disturbing or dangerous, although unavoidable, "incorporated objects" (milk, feces, etc.).

However, many elements of the aforesaid dream seem still to remain quite unaccounted for. I shall mention them one by one: (1) the bowl of noodles (why just this symbol and not another?—the association with "vermicelli" does not seem to explain it in full); (2) the little house with the garden (it does not correspond to the analyst's house, is not the house of A's parents, and is only superficially compared to a house in California); (3) the three girls (the analyst has only one daughter; the patient's siblings do not correspond to the "sisterly images" of the dream, either in number or sex or age); and (4) the analyst, his wife, his maid, etc. (their behaviour, as far as the patient's conscious knowledge goes, does not in the least resemble, or justify, the details of the manifest content of the dream).

Let us now consider a few facts on which the patient had no information whatsoever, either because they were completely outside his knowledge, or because they had not yet occurred when he had his dream.

1. As was pointed out, when A had his dream I had just come back from my holidays, which I had spent with my wife travelling in various foreign countries. A had no reason to suppose that my wife had left home again; even less, that she had actually gone to a place near the sea, where she was living in a small house with a little garden, together with our daughter and two little nieces, very pretty and blonde, one of eight, the other of three and a half years of age—exactly as pictured in his dream!

2. On my coming back to Rome, I had several personal and domestic problems to face, and—my wife having left again almost immediately —no one with whom to discuss them. The fact that my wife has her own office-work during the day, and has to keep to a regular routine, limits our relations to little more than mealtimes and from night to morning. I do not like taking my meals alone, but I had to do so while my wife and daughter were absent, and I was certainly not indifferent to the fact that *for about a week it was a maidservant, and not my wife, who attended to my alimentary needs* according to her own judgment, offered me the dishes, and exchanged a few casual words with me at lunch or at dinner. To this particular deprivation caused by my wife's absence, I should add of course the frustration of my affectionate feelings and sexual wishes. In a way, I might have felt somewhat "abandoned" and ill-treated, although this did not consciously affect me in any noticeable way, and did not prevent me in the least from carrying on my daily work.

3. On the evening of 27 August, I had had the pleasure of asking my

American colleague, Dr. L. E., and Mrs. E. (who were spending a couple of days in Rome), to have dinner with me the following night. I was especially eager for them to have *some very special Italian noodles* in a particular Roman restaurant, internationally known for this dish. Two other members of the Italian Psychoanalytical Society joined me in this reception of our distinguished guests: a reception which, as I have indicated, was planned on the evening before the night of the dream (while I was dining with Dr. and Mrs. E. at their hotel). It will be remembered that the dream of my patient occurred during the night between 27 and 28 August.

4. In order to be in time for my engagement with Dr. E., I had to cancel my appointment with A, which had been scheduled for 28 August at 8 p.m. After having tried unsuccessfully to get in touch with A by telephone, at about 5 p.m. on 28 August *I finally sent my maid N to his flat* with a message, asking him not to come at the appointed hour. This was the first and only time I had ever sent my maid to A's place, during the two years of our relationship. In A's dreams, as already stated, my maid had never appeared before. She did appear, however, in the dream he had immediately before the exceptional occurrence just described.

Summarizing the last points: the patient could have had no notion: (*a*) about the absence of my wife; (*b*) about her sojourn near the sea, in a small house with garden; (*c*) about the fact that she was staying with our daughter, plus two little girls of just eight and three and a half years of age, respectively; (*d*) about my own emotional reactions to having been "neglected"; (*e*) about my offer of noodles to people I liked; (*f*) about the imminent interference of my maid in our relation; or (*g*) about the fact that I would "neglect" him (cancel his session) just *because* I wanted to offer a dish of noodles to others!

From a parapsychological viewpoint, I am inclined to classify items (*a*), (*b*), (*c*), (*d*) and (*e*) as telepathic, whereas items (*f*) and (*g*) seem to me not fully understandable in purely "telepathic" terms, and to contain some "precognitive" factor. It is possible, of course, that on the night of 27 August I may have thought vaguely of cancelling A's session; but most certainly I had *not* thought of sending my maid to him with this announcement. I did so, as stated, only after having vainly tried to call him on the telephone.

In order to see in a clearer light to what extent the acknowledgment of the telepathic-precognitive elements in A's dream can help us toward a fuller understanding of the dream itself, and of its significance in the analytic situation, let us suppose that the aforesaid elements had been known to A through the usual sensory channels. In such a case, the psychodynamics of the dream would appear completely justified in every respect. It would be as if the patient, on the basis both of actual impressions *and* of the reactivation of childhood patterns, were complaining to parental substitutes (and to the analyst in the first place) that he was being neglected; that the "father" (analyst) was thinking intensely and affectionately about the "mother" (analyst's wife), but not about him, the patient (to whom, in fact, I had sent *only* my maid!); that he (the patient) was offered "food" in a condescending fashion, as if he were a dog, through a servant, and then prevented by the "parents" from eating it, whereas the "father" (analyst) was quite ready to offer the same food to strangers; that "mother" (analyst's wife), though not hating him, was neglecting him and favouring his "sisters"; etc.

Now the fact is that A did *not* consciously know all this. His unconscious apparently supplemented his conscious notions with extrasensorily perceived material, in order to build up a dream which could thus make perfect and complete sense.

We might be satisfied with this, accepting once more the fact that telepathic and/or precognitive dreams do exist, and that the dream-work can utilize "paranormal" information just as it does day-remnants and other perceptual material. However, in my opinion there is more to be noted. The dynamics of such a dream reveal, as do similar cases reported in the psychoanalytic literature, what was defined by Hollos and myself as an *unmasking* by the patient of emotional psychic material pertaining to the analyst's mind—material which is thus thrown, as it were, in the analyst's face. Viewed from this angle, the dream is a challenge to the analyst's attempt to conceal, or to repress, something which might have appeared—or to a certain extent may have actually been—unfriendly or hostile to the patient (Hollós says that it is the patient who carries out a sort of vicarious parapraxis, substituting himself for the analyst and "betraying" *him*). I have no difficulty in admitting that in my countertransference to this patient hostile feelings must have been present. These feelings, as far as I can understand them, were due first of all to the fact that the patient, as previously stated, was in a prolonged phase of resistance, practically frustrating all my efforts to make him aware of the transference elements in his repeated "attacks" and criticisms concerning myself. But besides "unmasking" this hostility of mine (and exaggerating it considerably because of his own unresolved infantile claims), the patient has in my opinion also "unmasked" some particular emotional motives of my own, namely: my own reactions to having been "abandoned" by my wife, my resentment at being attended by a servant, perhaps even some disappointment at having to invite my colleague and his wife to a restaurant and not to my own home, and to appeal to "servants" to cater for them and for me instead of having my wife's help for this purpose. This "dovetailing" of my own emotional patterns with those of the patient can be described as an unconscious dynamical configuration *à deux* (including elements of transference and countertransference, as well as of identification and counteridentification, both normal *and* paranormal), which, as I and other observers have remarked, seems to be a very strong precondition for the occurrence of psi phenomena.

In short, it all sounds as if A, in the emotional language of his dream, had been saying: "Don't I know that you think more about your wife than about myself? Don't I know that you offer nice food to strangers and not to me? Don't I know that your wife giver her love and affection to young people, while *I* have no motherly woman who cares or has cared for me? Don't I know that you are going to neglect my needs, sending your maid to me and pretending that you 'give me something,' whereas in reality you disturb and prevent my 'feeding'? Don't I know that all this goes in parallel with similar feelings and reactions of yours, which are *your own* and should not interfere with my treatment? Well, yes: just as I felt my father's 'murderous' wishes when I was a child, so I can feel, and describe in detail, all this information, your hostility, your neglect of me, and the emotional drives which have been and are yours, that you have attempted to conceal from me. Yes: in spite of your efforts to 'keep me out' of all this, here you are: I *do* KNOW!"

Jan Ehrenwald (b. 1900), the editor of this anthology, was, together with Jule Eisenbud, Montague Ullman, Joost Meerloo, Geraldine Pederson-Krag, Gotthard Booth, Robert Laidlaw, and others, a charter member of the Medical Section of the American Society for Psychical Research, dedicated to the study of psi phenomena.

The selection below is taken from New Dimensions of Deep Analysis *by Jan Ehrenwald, © Copyright 1955 by Grune and Stratton, New York. It describes in some detail a dream whose presumed telepathic nature was based on the appearance of a number of specific features or "tracer elements" contained in its manifest content. The tracer elements seemed to originate in the therapist's emotionally charged preoccupations at the time the patient's dream occurred. Note that it is the specificity of such correspondences, combined with the psychological significance or meaningful nature of a telepathic interpretation, that lends support to the telepathy hypothesis in such cases.*

Ruth, the dreamer, was an unmarried woman of thirty-eight who had lost her mother when she was an infant. Brought up by a housekeeper and a moody, alcoholic father, she always felt that an older sister and brother were her father's favorites. Analysis showed a masochistic fixation on her father which she had carried over to her therapist. Her positive transference soon ushered in a symptomatic improvement in her condition. At that time, on March 10, 1948, she reported the following dream:

"I went to my dressmaker's apartment. The dressmaker showed me her place and said the apartment was to let. I looked at it. It consisted of a beautiful long, well-shaped living room, spacious, with high ceiling. It opened out to a nice open terrace where the sun shone. It was long; it stretched along the whole building across the front . . . some fifty feet or so. It had a brick wall and the floor was made of planks with cracks in between. There was not much furniture in the room, not so much as you would have if you would furnish it yourself. There was quite a lot of space left between the things. It was not a cluttered room. There was no carpet, only oriental rugs, a big one in the middle with figures like the one you have here in the office. There were smaller rugs at either end. But they covered only part of the floor, much of it was showing. There were also a few mahogany chairs and an open fireplace. A French door and two French windows opened to the terrace. A dingy little hall led into the bedroom and into a bathroom. I thought this would be the apartment I would like to live in, except that it did not have a maid's room and no extra bathroom. Still, I was wondering how that little dressmaker could afford such a nice apartment. . . ."

The patient's associations shed little light on the deeper meaning of the dream. . . . More light can be thrown on the dream by considering the psychological situation on my side of the picture. A week before the dream occurred, on March 3, I had moved into a new apartment in a residential suburb of New York. It was in a large unfinished apartment house and I had been glad to settle down in it comfortably after nearly ten years of nomadic existence during World War II. Let me add that on the night of the dream my brother and his wife had arrived from the country to visit us for the first time in our new home. The shared my enthusiasm. It was a dark rainy night but we stepped out on the terrace which belonged to the apartment. A French door and two French windows opened to the terrace from the living room. It ran across the whole building from one end to the other—between two street blocks—though only a stretch of about fifty by twenty-two feet was our own. The living room extending into the hall was spacious and high, thirty-four by twelve feet. It was only scantily furnished at the time the dream occurred. In the hall, there was only a studio couch and a large unpainted wooden chest. There was no carpet in the apartment, but the floor of the living room was covered by one larger and two smaller oriental rugs, leaving much of the wooden floor uncovered. These rugs were of the same type as I had in my office. A small dingy hall led from the living room to the bedroom. It also opened to the bathroom and a second bedroom, occupied by my daughter. The furniture was modern, functional bleached walnut. There were no mahogany chairs, no fireplace. The main entrance was not from the dingy hall but from the staircase into the hall-living room. . . . The terrace formed the ceiling of the garages belonging to the house. It had a brick wall. At the time the dream occurred the wooden casing of its cemented roof had not yet been removed. It was unfinished and covered with a layer of tarred paper. At one place there was a gaping hole in the floor.

I have to add here that the dreamer located the apartment she saw on the second floor. She made a drawing of its layout which corresponded startlingly with the floor plan of my apartment. It should be noted, however, that some details in her sketch were at variance with the reality. . . . Ruth had lived as a child with her father in a self-contained house of the Colonial type. The mahogany furniture seen in her dream was the same, she said, as they had at home. The fireplace, too, reminded her of their sitting room. There was no terrace.

In spite of these differences, the similarity of the apartment seen by the patient in her dream and my own apartment is striking enough. The majority of the elements mentioned are independent features of whatever apartment they may belong to, although it may be stated that some are interrelated (several rugs—the floor showing in between; location of bedroom and bathroom, etc.). On the other hand, the whole layout of the place, the references to the large terrace with the parapet running across the house, the French door and windows opening onto it, the oriental rugs, etc., are so specific that the correspondences cannot reasonably be attributed to chance alone. Indeed, the chance hypothesis would explain nothing in our case. On the contrary, it would rather bar the way for a proper understanding even of the familiar psychoanalytic aspects of the dream.

The corresponding features can be listed in the table below:

Dream	*Reality*
(1) Spacious high living room.	(1) Spacious high living room.
(2) French door and windows to terrace.	(2) French door and windows to terrace.
(3) Very large terrace running across the house.	(3) Very large terrace running across the house.
(4) Brick parapet on terrace.	(4) Brick parapet on terrace.
(5) Scanty furniture in living room, "not as you would furnish it yourself."	(5) Scanty furniture in living room (European taste).
(6) Oriental rugs "like here in the office."	(6) Oriental rugs of the identical type.

(7) One large rug, two smaller ones on both sides.	(7) One large rug, two smaller ones on both sides.
(8) Floor uncovered in places.	(8) Floor uncovered in places.
(9) Bedroom located to the east of living room.	(9) Bedroom located to the east of living room.
(10) Bathroom located to the east of living room	(10) Bathroom located to the east of living room.
(11) Dingy little hall connecting (9) and (10) with living room.	(11) Dingy little hall connecting (9) and (10) with living room.
(12) No maid's room.	(12) No maid's room.
(13) No second bathroom	(13) No second bathroom.

For the sake of the record I have to add here that the patient had been completely ignorant of my personal circumstances before and during the whole course of the treatment. She did not know my private address or telephone number, she had been unaware of my moving to a new apartment and could by no conceivable "normal" way of communication have learned about its size, layout, and furnishings.

Despite some correspondence there are, however, a number of points of difference between the dream and reality. I need only recall the mahogany chairs and the fireplace which reminded her of her father's apartment. This indicates that the apartment seen in the dream represents something like a composite picture of her own childhood home and my residence. It is a product of the dream work in which what I described as *autopsychic* material, derived from early recollections, is condensed with *heteropsychic* material of telepathic origin.

This interpretation accounts for both the correspondences and divergences found in the manifest dream content as compared with its two sources: autopsychic and heteropsychic. In this way—and in this way only —we can arrive at a better understanding of the dream. I hinted that the patient's associations left a major part of its manifest content unaccounted for. But once we realize the origin of that material from outside, that is, from a heteropsychic source, we are able to close the gap. More than that: we arrive at a better understanding of the patient's attitude towards myself and towards the treatment at the time the dream occurred. It quite obviously dramatizes her wish to move into my apartment and to live there with me as she did with her father during her childhood years. It expresses Ruth's positive transference upon the therapist. The presence of Anne, the sister of the man to whom she had clung for many years as to another father substitute, completes the picture. Anne is the replica of her own sister Mary, who had usurped her place in her father's affection. Now the apartment with the large terrace and the fireplace was to become hers, and Anne, the rival, is just an onlooker. By taking sole possession of her dream house, she made one of her cherished childhood dreams come true.

At this point I should like to insert a few remarks about the psychological setting on "my end" at the time of Ruth's dream. I mentioned that it coincided with my brother's arrival from the country. Yet, as it happened, seeing my new home was not the sole purpose of his coming. We had just learned from our mother in England that she had suddenly been taken ill and that operation had become necessary. We had therefore good reason to try to hasten her coming to this country—a project that met with considerable difficulties. We had also agreed that on her arrival here she should live in my new home until better arrangements could be made for her permanent accomodation. This plan touched on the problem of where my daughter, aged thirteen, would live on my mother's arrival; on my concern over the way in which relationships in our extended little family group were to work out; and on a host of other rather personal problems which need not be discussed here in greater detail.

However, tracer elements or specifically identifiable features of a dream are by no means the only telltale signs of telepathy in the psychoanalytic situation. Telepathic cues emanating from the therapist may influence the patient's productions in many other ways. He may oblige a Freudian analyst by producing "Freudian" dreams, a Jungian analyst by weaving mythological motives into the fabric of his dreams, and so on. This is described as "doctrinal compliance." As a third alternative, the patient may respond to his analyst's therapeutic motivations with a genuine improvement in his condition, instead of merely producing tracer effects or doctrinal compliance in order to meet the therapist's need to prove a point or to validate a hypothesis close to his heart. Such a direct telepathic impact of the practitioner's therapeutic wishes and expectations meeting halfway, as it were, the patient's hopes to be cured, may well serve as an elementary model of the therapist-patient relationship in unorthodox healing.

It is needless to say that in the absence of clear-cut tracer elements, such a hypothesis with regard to unorthodox healing is difficult to prove. Nevertheless, the vast array of historical and anthropological reports, of clinical observations and anecdotal material reviewed in Part I of this book, can no longer be brushed aside. They gain indirect support by recent attempts to provide an experimental basis for alleged cases of unorthodox healing in the laboratory in animals, plants and chemical agents. The biologist Bernard Grad, of McGill University in Montreal, reported a statistically significant acceleration of wound healing in mice treated by a "healer" as compared with a control group of mice.

In the following selection, I deal with clinical-psychiatric aspects of psi phenomena. Entitled "The Telepathy Hypothesis and Schizophrenia", published in the Journal of the American Academy of Psychoanalysis

(1974), it calls attention to the embarrassing similarity of the hypotheses proposed by parapsychologists and paranoid patients. I also stress the therapeutic implications of the patient's delusional system and the apparent restitutional value of his belief in the reality of telepathy: it makes him feel he is "sane," after all.

Early advocates as well as informed critics of parapsychology have called attention to the embarrassing similarity of some of its basic propositions to the paranoid schizophrenic's delusions of grandeur, of thought and action at a distance. There is a no less embarrassing similarity to what anthropologists of the Victorian era described as the "monstrous farrago" of magic and animism or with preliterate man's paleological patterns of thinking. A third parallel is with the child's and the neurotic's fantasies of omnipotence and omniscience, especially in relation to the symbiotic mother. As a result, telepathy and related incidents—so-called psi phenomena—still tend to be relegated to the lunatic fringe of our culture.

Men of classical antiquity, to say nothing of ancient Far Eastern cultures, were less squeamish about such resemblances. Occasional veridical features, real or imaginary, in the ravings of the insane, in the ecstasies of saints or seers, in the fabric of dreams, struck the observer with awe, reverence, or fear. The ancient Greeks considered epilepsy as a sacred disease and Plato distinguished divine madness from other types of insanity. Similar notions are still reflected in the writings of Aldous Huxley, Allan Watts, Timothy Leary, and John Lilly.

But what about schizophrenic reactions or the full-fledged picture of paranoid schizophrenia of modern clinical psychiatry? What about such drug-induced alterations of consciousness as LSD, mescaline, or major marijuana trips? Do they lend substance to the widely held belief that they are positively correlated with demonstrable psi phenomena? We shall see that the clinical evidence available so far is inconclusive. Freud has repeatedly commented on the paranoid patient's uncanny capacity to probe for the weak spots in the analyst's unconscious. According to Otto Fenichel, the paranoid individual is selectively sensitive to the unconscious of his fellow man "where such perception can be utilized to rationalize his tendency to projection." Frieda Fromm-Reichmann, Silvano Arieti, Gustav Bychowski, and many others have likewise stressed the schizophrenic's propensity to ferret out repressed or subdued hostility in his social environment. Yet all this can still be accounted for by reference to unconscious expressive movements or other familiar means of nonverbal communication.

Nevertheless, the clinical observer keeping an open mind about the phenomena is occasionally faced with spontaneous incidents strongly suggestive of the patient's telepathic sensitiveness to clearly identifiable and emotionally charged features or "tracer elements" seemingly "picked" from the therapist's mind.

Two of my clinical observations go back to the early years of my career as a psychiatrist. The first concerned Florence C., a schizophrenic at an advanced stage of the process, with marked catatonic features. She was negativistic, given to impulsive outbursts, exposed herself, and exhibited various mannerisms and antics. I first saw her on June 21, 1942, shortly after I had commenced work in an institution in England. I was about to make the routine six-monthly notes in her case-sheet and cast a brief glance at her particulars before proceeding to her room. The case-sheet contained the usual data—her name, age, address, date of admission, etc. Admitted in 1935, she was 30 years of age at that time, and 37 at the time of the interview. However, in a moment of absent-mindedness I mistook the significance of "1935" and jumped to the wrong conclusion that she was 35 years old, that is, seven years my junior. This mistake will perhaps be better understood if I mention that having been born in 1900 I had made it a habit to calculate other person's ages by comparing their birth date with my own year of birth. After my casual glance at her papers, I entered the patient's room and put the usual question: "How old are you?" No answer. She wanders about the room, grimaces. "How old are you?" "Don't ask silly questions . . . you are seven years older than me. . . ." No further conversation was possible. She took no notice of my presence and remained resistive to examination. Her apparent reference to the erroneous result of my calculation struck me only after I had left the patient. Her statement about our respective ages was certainly off the mark. Yet it was all the more significant in that it reflected my own absent-minded error in figuring.

The next observation was made shortly afterwards in the same institution. Catherine J., age 24, a schizophrenic with marked paranoid features, had watched a fellow patient of about her own age, Betty H., breaking out of her room, smashing a window pane, and sustaining slight cuts on her wrist which necessitated stitching. Betty was a difficult patient and had failed to respond to insulin shock treatment. The day before I had remarked to the ward sister that I felt even my cautious attempts at humoring her might have had a paradoxical effect and helped to bring about her recent outbursts. After attending to Betty's wounds I found Catherine waiting for me at the door. Reproachfully she turned to me and said, "*You* have done that to her. . . . You made her do it!" She ignored my explanations and maintained her charge. "You should have the courage to admit that you have made her do it. Why don't you admit it?"

The telepathic interpretation of this case is open to the usual objections. But accepting it for the sake of argument, we have to assume that it was an ill-founded (though psychologically intelligible) feeling of guilt on my part which was "sensed" and picked up by Catherine.

There are several more cases of this order in my files. They all involve references made by schizophrenic patients to more or less emotionally charged preconscious material in my mind. This factor played a particularly significant part in the two incidents described above. They occurred in 1942, during my wartime exile in England. It was a time when I had barely recovered from the shock of emigration, and from the hardships imposed on my family and myself by the London Blitz. The war was going badly. I had just found employment as an assistant medical officer in a state mental hospital and I felt my job was a letdown from more prestigious positions I had held in the Old Country. My English was poor. I disliked the rigid, authoritarian ways in which the hospital was run. To make matters worse, on my first day in the wards I was physically attacked by one of the assaultive patients. All this contributed to my feeling of insecurity and heightened vulnerability in the new situation. It must have been this state of affairs, with its attendant anxiety, which was picked up by the patients. Here, for once, they were faced with a doctor who fell grievously short of the image of the smug, self-assured professional man, and they let him know about it in no uncertain terms. By the same token, it was the unusual circumstances surrounding the two cases which may have accounted for the paucity of telepathic incidents of this order in my own later experience—or, for that matter, in the well-ordered routine of my psychiatric confreres.

This may also be the reason for the altogether different complexion of telepathic incidents involving schizophrenic patients which occurred at a later period of my career when I was safely ensconced again in more congenial hospital positions and engaged in private practice in this country. The following observation is a case in point.

Mr. M. is a commercial artist of 29 who developed a paranoid trend and phobic symptoms which on one occasion made a brief hospitalization necessary. He felt persecuted by big, burly men who spied on him and tried to break into his apartment while he was with a girl friend. He said they kept him awake at night by making suspicious noises. He showed a slight disorder of thinking and flatness of affect suggestive of a latent or borderline schizophrenia.

M. had previously been treated by Dr. Y., a distinguished psychiatrist, who referred him to me for further therapy. As it happened, M. made excellent progress while under my care, which seems to have prompted Dr. Y to refer his own son, Peter, age 25, for psychotherapy with me. On the evening of April 1, 1957, Dr. Y. made a surprise call to my office in order to discuss his son's problems. They were, in effect, in many ways similar to those of the patient, Mr. M. whom Dr. Y had referred to me a few months earlier.

I may note at this point that it was Dr. Y's first visit in the course of many years of our professional association, and that during our conversation I was greatly inconvenienced by a small blister which had just developed on my left eyelid. Dr. Y. first inquired about Mr. M., the patient he had first referred to me for treatment. I informed him that he continued to make good progress, that I had reduced the frequency of his visits, but that he was still coming to see me "off and on." I also pointed out that success in M.'s case might have been partly due to my more permissive, nonauthoritarian approach. "In the patient's eyes I am the passive, permissive one, you are the active, forceful one," I remarked. What I did not tell Dr. Y. was that I considered this very difference in our personalities as a good augury for my work with his son.

Two days later I saw Mr. M. in my office. He reported a dream which had occurred the night after my meeting with Dr. Y. These are the salient points of M.'s dream.

"I came to see a psychiatrist. But in fact there were two of them, a woman and a man. The woman had a pimple or mole on her left eye. I was very mad at her because she said I did not come regularly for my sessions whereas I had only missed a couple of sessions during a whole year. The woman reminded me of Aunt Sally, mother's sister, who always had gotten on my nerves. The male psychiatrist reminded me of Charlton Heston, who played the role of Janus in the Broadway play of the same name."

Without going into the deeper dynamics of this dream, it shows certain unmistakable correspondences with some of the details of my meeting with Dr. Y. the night before: (1) the dreamer's reference to two psychiatrists amounts to a statement of actual fact; (2) his reference to one *woman* and one *man* psychiatrist seems to paraphrase my reference to myself as the passive, permissive one and Dr. Y. as the active, forceful one; (3) the patient's mention of Janus, the two-faced mythological figure, appears to lend further emphasis to my remarks concerning our contrasting personalities; (4) the dreamer seems to have caught me at telling at half-truth about him and expressed his resentment in no uncertain terms. The truth is that he had always been irregular in keeping his appointments with Dr. Y., but had been coming regularly to see me throughout the past year. His main objection was apparently to my phrase "He was still coming to see me off and on"; and (5) the dreamer seemed to be aware of the discomfort caused by the blister on my left eyelid.

So much for the presumed telepathic aspect and the specific "tracer elements" contained in M.'s dream. Yet if we are satisfied with the reality of this aspect, we arrive at the same time at a fairly satisfactory understanding of its underlying dynamics. First and foremost, the dreamer seems to inject himself into my meeting with Dr. Y. as a "participant observer." He is greatly annoyed with my reference to his alleged irregular attendance. His annoyance is in effect out of keeping with the harmlessness of my remark and may in part be due to his paranoid trend.

Yet his annoyance is more readily understandable if we assume that M. became telepathically aware of the intrusion of a sibling figure, Dr. Y.'s son, Peter, into our relationship. The fact is that one of M.'s problems did spring from an intense sibling rivalry with his older brother. To add to this similarity, both M., and Peter, his "sibling rival," had grown up in the shade of a stern, authoritarian father and a controlling, possessive mother.

Calling attention to the mother-child relationship as the "Cradle of ESP," I note that schizophrenic reactions may emerge from this universal matrix of human experience:

Here too, the child is apt to feel he is magically controlled by all-powerful and all-knowing parental figures, while he may harbor corresponding fantasies of exercising control over them. Indeed, we have learned from child analysts that the boundaries of the newborn child's personality have not as yet been delineated and that his ego is still fused with that of his mother. This is what Benedek has described as the primary unit: mother-child. . . .

Yet I also noted that a schizophrenic child may respond to influences of this order—telepathic or otherwise—in an exaggerated fashion. He may respond in terms of either autistic withdrawal or passive compliance and surrender to the overpowering parent figure. It is these two contrasting reactions which Margaret Mahler has described as the autistic versus the symbiotic child psychosis. . . .

In effect, the adult patient may show all shades and gradations between these two contrasting reaction types. They may include varying degrees of resistance and/or sensitiveness to psi phenomena. They may range from thinly veiled paranoid, violently hostile to passive compliant reactions—or a combination of both. This is illustrated by the distinctly ambivalent attitudes of the subjects of the five clinical cases discussed here to apparent telepathic influences emanating from the therapist. Obviously he too represented a magically endowed parent figure to these patients.

In the light of these considerations, one might well expect a wealth of telepathic incidents to come to our notice in schizophrenic patients. However, in my experience, as well as in that of other observers with an open mind to psi phenomena, this is by no means the case. Experimental ESP tests, as well as my own observations, indicate that by and large paranoid schizophrenics are neither more nor less susceptible to demonstrable psi phenomena than are nonschizophrenics.

At first sight, such a conclusion tends to cast doubt on our thesis that there is a close affinity between psi phenomena and schizophrenic reactions; that the patient's delusional system shows striking correspondences with the psychic reality of his family situation—if not with that of a potentially "schizophrenogenic" society at large; and that his underlying pathology is in effect conducive to increased sensitiveness to telepathy in general.

However, the relative paucity of verifiable clinical and experimental data in support of such a thesis is only apparent. The available evidence suggests that the schizophrenic's potentially increased sensitiveness to telepathy—to what can be described as "psi pollution"—tends to be canceled out by his reaction formations against it. He may mobilize a wide variety of ego or perceptual defenses, including Freud's *Reizschutz* or screening functions of the ego, and Reich's "armor plating" of the schizoid character, resulting in the familiar withdrawn, shut in, autistic traits of the schizophrenic personality. Thus the individual's reactions to psi may amount to a paradoxical blend of the Princess on the Pea or of the Indian yogi resting serenely on his bed of nails.

As a general rule, however, the schizophrenic is desperately anxious to resist the lure, or to ward off the threat, of being engulfed in the symbiotic matrix of his existence. In this respect his is in effect an exaggerated version of Western man's compulsive need to repress that which is incompatible with his prevailing sociocultural mode of existence. Indeed, the roots of our resistance to psi may well go deeper than culturally acquired attitudes: they may be due to what Sigmund Freud described as an *organic repression*, that is, to a tendency inherent in the evolutionary process itself. Viewed in this light, the schizophrenic breakdown signals the failure of the process of organic repression. It is contingent, among other things, on the breakdown of ego barriers designed to prevent the intrusion of ego-alien material into the patient's consciousness. In the longitudinal perspective the struggle against this contigency is lifelong and unrelenting. We have seen that it may culminate in the patient's total surrender to a possessive, engulfing or devouring mother figure. Alternatively, it may lead to the disruption of communication with her and with the rest of his social environment, to autistic withdrawal or catatonic stupor. Yet we have also seen that this shifting balance between compliance and resistance is not merely confined to overt verbal and nonverbal cues, pressures and prohibitions. It includes the same alternatives in relation to psi influences impinging upon the infant or the growing child, even though, in the absence of tracer elements, the part played by such stimuli is difficult to determine.

It may be well to realize, however, that the psi factor comprises only one—presumably narrow—segment of the psychic reality to which the schizophrenic patient responds in his characteristic way. We know that human closeness and intimacy in any form and on any level of experience are potential threats to his vulnerable ego. To him the outside world—including the unconscious of his fellow men—is fraught with the same dangers as are his own unconscious drives. Both the outside world and the unconscious of his fellow men have become immediately transparent to him, merging imperceptibly with his own personality. The therapist himself cannot help being caught up in this fateful pattern of lost boundaries, of shifting and overlapping perspectives. Whatever he seeks to convey to his patient on the level of ordinary discourse is apt to be contaminated by psi pollution or drowned out by "noise" in the schizophrenic's overloaded channels of communication. To the schizophrenic the therapist's unconscious speaks louder than his words. This is why communication between the two is the greatest challenge to the therapist's skill and the supreme test of his personal integrity and dedication to his calling.

Jule Eisenbud (b. 1908) of Denver, Colorado, is perhaps the leading analyst whose work has been chiefly devoted to the psychoanalytic aspects of telepathy and related phenomena. One of his books, The World of Ted Serios *(1967), is a controversial study of a case of "thoughtography," or the apparent impact of thoughts or visual imagery upon Polaroid film.*

His major work, Psi and Psychoanalysis *(1970), contains a wealth of observations on telepathy in the psychoanalytic situation and references to the "psi-pathology" of everyday life. It includes a number of presumptively precognitive dreams and ingenious attempts to unravel telepathic "cross-dreaming" among his patients. Eisenbud considers the psi hypothesis an important exploratory tool and he does not hesitate to use it with his patients.*

The following passages, quoted from Chapter 16, "The Use of the Psi Hypothesis in Interpretation," from Psi and Psychoanalysis *by Jule Eisenbud, 1970, reprinted by permission of Grune and Stratton, New York, and the author, illustrate Eisenbud's approach:*

Once the analyst has accepted the value of the psi hypothesis in attempting to structure the data of analysis, the issue arises as to the extent to which this new dimension can be fruitfully introduced into interpretations communicated to patients. I would like to add here to what was said about this in earlier chapters.

Shortly following the publication in 1946 of the paper in which I first touched upon the question of interpretations in which presumptively psi-cognized data are utilized, I received a cautionary letter from one of the acknowledged deans of the psychoanalytic community, whose writings on technique were widely cited. He began by confessing to a long-standing interest in the subject of telepathy and admitted that he was far from discounting its possible reality. "However," he went on, "it clearly can have no place in analysis."

What clearly should have no place in analysis are, of course, ex cathedra pronouncements. The place of psi—or anything else—in analysis, particularly in interpretation, can be decided only empirically. However, few analysts have reported interpreting presumptively psi-conditioned material to patients. Ehrenwald states that "such material should be treated in exactly the same manner as material derived from the autopsychic sphere," but adds a couple of reservations. One is that "interpretations involving *psi* incidents should only be given at an advanced stage of analysis, when all aspects of the transference relationship have been thoroughly worked through and when the therapist feels safe to expose whatever hidden evidence of his own countertransference is contained in the telepathic material under review." The other, having to do with marked negative transference (which the author feels does not favor the emergence of psi anyway), is that "any reference to the occurrence of telepathy has to be carefully avoided under such conditions. This is particularly true," he adds, "for the advanced schizophrenic who may easily use interpretations involving *psi* factors as added confirmation of his delusional trend."

As a rule I have found that if an event or series of events can be meaningfully structured with the aid of the psi hypothesis, the issue of what or what not to communicate to the patient, of how and when to do so, is best decided—with special reservations soon to be noted—in terms of the empirical rules that would ordinarily apply to the interpretation of resistance, defense and material defended against, and not in terms of anything relating to the psi hypothesis itself. The precise type of presumptive psi mechanism required for meaningfully structuring the analytically garnered material— that is, unconscious telepathy or clairvoyance (or even, for that matter, precognition)—or questions of what ordinary barriers to cognition might exist (time, distance, presumed limits of unconscious organizing abilities, and so forth) seem to have little bearing on whether or not to impart to the patient interpretations based on the general assumption of a broadly conceived psi capacity. Where I introduce the notion of psi for the first time, I find it sufficient to acquaint patients with it in the simplest and most flexible terms. I do not enter into a history of the subject, or discuss the types of data it comprises. I find that even those patients—and they are a majority— who have never done any thinking about or reading in the subject seem to know intuitively what I am talking about. I do not recall, surprisingly, ever having had a question of a theoretical nature asked about the subject (and I have had my share of bright patients, including a few in the hard sciences).

As the reader may already have perceived, all types of material may be thrown into the spotlight along psi-conditioned pathways, and all types of patients have, at one time or another in my experience, shown some capacity to behave in a psi-conditioned way.[1] I have worked with a few individuals who seem never to have come up with any extraordinary correspon-

---

[1] Coleman, who holds that "any person [in analysis] is potentially capable of paranormal perception under proper transference conditions," writes: "Another impression I have gained is that paranormal productions tend to herald a particular turning point in the treatment of withdrawn borderline patients."

dences that I could make dynamic sense of with the aid of the psi hypothesis, but these have not fallen into any single diagnostic or characterological category. In my experience it has been, in general, the least disturbed people who have shown the greatest amount of manifest, utilizable psi activity in analysis. This tends to square with the personality studies that have been made on high and low scorers in ESP tests.

I have yet to find a contraindication to acquainting patients with the psi hypothesis and its usefulness in connection with specific types of analytic material. It is, of course, helpful to be able to show a patient that a given group of data cannot be adequately understood *without* the assumption of psi (if it can be structured at all thus); but even where there appears at first to be only a slight advantage to the use of the psi hypothesis over ordinary clinical hypotheses, I have found no categorical reason not to adduce it. Let us recall that one cannot know in advance what significant pathways will be opened by this maneuver, what fresh or confirmatory material elicited. In general, the only limitation I have found on the use of the psi hypothesis in interpretation, other than what I would find in the case of *any* interpretative intervention, is the extent to which I might be loath to reveal details of my own presumptive involvement in a patient's material, or the extent to which I might deem it inappropriate—for reasons not connected with psi factors *per se*, however—to disclose to one patient the details of another's material.

As I have already indicated, patients to whom I have communicated interpretations based upon presumptive psi factors, whether involving triangulating data or not, seem for their part to be able intuitively to comprehend what is going on. They tend to respond with the well-known confirmatory signs of an effective interpretation—laughter, pleasant excitement, astonishment, the disappearance of a symptom or resistance and the release of further material—which are characteristically seen in the case of ordinary interpretations that hit the mark. There may be a slightly greater sense of awe at the omnipotence and omniscience of the unconscious, but I have never known a patient to exhibit signs of anxiety referable to the use in interpretation of the psi hypothesis itself or to the analyst's readiness to think in such terms. I have, finally, never seen this type of communication stimulate delusional trends in patients or reinforce such trends in overtly psychotic persons, although it has given some of my patients the feeling of being in an exclusive and favored relationship to me. In certain instances this may have led them to produce psi-conditioned material in great profusion, but one deals with such a development just as one would with any other type of reenactment in the transference. The charge, in any event, of "lifelong damage to . . . intellectual and emotional powers" of patients to whom "a psychoanalyst blinded by his beliefs (imputes) magical powers" is not supported by any evidence of which I am aware.

In instances . . . in which I selectively communicate certain psi-based constructions to the patient while withholding others that I may judge to be equally valid from a purely dynamic point of view, I am seldom able to justify my differential handling of the data solely in terms of technical considerations. I must presume that my reluctance to reveal to the patient one or another aspect of the emerging material is a reflection of the very neurotic hang-ups that may have found their way into the dreams and associations of the patients in the first place, and undoubtedly betoken resistances in me as specific as those of the patient in a given area. This is true, I have noticed, even to the extent of my finding it easier to deal in the abstract and the long ago than in the concrete here and now in my relationship to the patient. However much I may tell myself that it is sufficient for me to use my insights mainly for the bailing out and the stabilization of the countertransference, the fact is that I have very little to go on to justify such a presumptive rationalization. In cases, on the other hand, where I have gone the whole or a good part of the distance in bringing my own countertransference attitudes to the attention of the patient, I have never observed that my candor has jeopardized the conduct of the analysis; and in only one or two instances has a patient seized upon information I might have supplied about myself for purposes of further resistance. Such trends can, of course, be analyzed in the ordinary way.

In the handling of conceivably psi-conditioned correspondences between the dreams or other material of different patients, or between my own material and that of patients, I have tried generally to proceed on the principle that the actual mechanics of interpretative cross-fertilization be guided primarily by the overall requirements of the analytic situation, with all other considerations subordinated to the clinical value of a given step. As I have said before, there is little point in the demonstration of psi for psi's sake. I have generally found it best to proceed stepwise, imparting just so much of the material of one patient to another or others—what Ehrenwald calls "heteropsychic" material—as I judge to be necessary to raise a question or bring into focus something that might otherwise not emerge, or in the hopes of flushing out further data when a patient's associations seem to have come to a standstill. However, it is not always easy to assure oneself in advance that cross-fertilization is an indispensable maneuver, even if one feels that, for purposes of theoretical formulation, the applicability of the psi hypothesis in a given situation is in itself fully justified. But by the same token, the clinical penalties of waiting overlong for clear-cut grounds to arise spontaneously may be equally difficult to assess—just as difficult, in fact, as the grounds for the application and timing of conventional interpretative measures.

Here is an example of Eisenbud's psychoanalytic interpretation of a patient's dream:

A man in analysis reported the following dream: *I was reading in a newspaper the account of the crash of a Rainbow plane, but I could not make out the details.*

Two or three days previously one of the patient's friends had begged a favor of him in connection with an airline known as The Rainbow Line, which operated between Rochester, N.Y. and New York City. The friend, who represented the line promotionally, asked if the patient would not approach a large dye manufacturing firm in Rochester with the idea of retaining a certain amount of space on the line for the use of its executives. He felt that the patient was in a particularly favorable position to handle this matter because he was a research consultant to the company, was well acquainted with most of its executives, and had mentioned, as a matter of fact, that he had shortly to visit Rochester to look into some new developments in the dye processes in which he was involved.

The patient was to leave for Rochester on the day following his dream. He was somewhat anxious about the trip because he was planning to approach the company with the idea involving a fundamental technical improvement in the design and manufacture of its color dyeing process, and he felt that his entire future hinged on the success of this visit.

In the dream on the eve of his trip the patient appears to substitute for his anxiety about his color process project—his primary concern and the chief reason for his trip—a lesser anxiety about his friend's project, which, of the two, he would rather see crash. The link is in the symbol "rainbow," which ostensibly refers to the friend's project of that name but which could also refer to the color process project which was the patient's major source of anxiety at the moment. One may suspect on the part of the patient a certain resentment against his friend at being burdened by him with an added obligation at a time when he was worried enough about the outcome of his own affairs. "The devil with it," he would appear to be saying about his friend's Rainbow Airline project, "let it crash!"

Ordinarily, in the practice of analysis, we are satisfied if we get this much out of a dream. There seem to be fairly clear lines of connection between the main elements in the manifest content and what, in terms of the known concerns of the patient at the time of the dream, we can comfortably construe to be the latent thoughts out of which the dream was presumably elaborated. Generally, if we are able to do this much with a dream, we don't pursue the matter further.

Now let us consider the item which appeared in the New York Times on the morning after the dream:

Rochester, N.H., May 5 (U.P.). Leslie L. ——, ——, his wife and their pilot, Robert C. ——, were killed today when their plane rammed into Parker Mountain in a rainstorm and burned.

The event referred to in this news item occurred on the day of the dream but upon inquiry was found not to have appeared on the local news broadcasts of that day. However, let us imagine for a moment that the patient had had access to this information through some ordinary means before he went to sleep that night; and let us suppose that this was one of the associations he brought up during the discussion of his dream with me on the following morning. Under these circumstances we would clearly feel justified in making use of the fact of this additional information by bringing it into relation with the other data we had and formulating the presumptive latent thoughts behind the dream as follows: "It is not *my* Rochester color project that was fated to crash, nor was it even my friend's irksome Rochester Rainbow project; it was someone else entirely, someone I don't know and about whom I have no feelings whatever, who happened to crash in a rainstorm around Rochester; this crash, furthermore, didn't even occur at Rochester, New York, but at Rochester, New Hampshire."

From a purely configurational and dynamic point of view, the fact of an actual plane crash in a rainstorm at a place named Rochester would seem to provide an excellent solution for the dreamer as he is casting about, as it were, to find a simple, economical way of dealing symbolically with the concerns of the outside world as they crowd in upon his sleep. (For the sake of simplification I am not going to deal with the possible relationship between this occurrence and the patient's earlier history and personality development.) But we know that the dreamer had no "normal" way of gaining information about this event—barring, of course, the possibility that he had, despite his claim to the contrary, seen the newspaper item between the time of his awakening and his analytic session several hours later, having in the meantime elaborated a "dream" which he retrospectively misidentified as a dream of the preceding night. (We can consider this as representative of all hypotheses having to do with so-called normal information getting processes in this situation.) Neglecting this possibility, since we have no way at this point of evaluating it as an independent probability,* we are then presented with two alternatives: (1) to consider the relationship between the actual plane crash (or at least the newspaper item referring to it) and the dream to be a purely chance one, which then provides no basis whatsoever for any inferences regarding the meaning of the dream; or (2) to consider the relationship to be a nonchance one, permitting certain psychodynamic inferences and constructions. If we utilize the latter alternative we have then to assume that the patient had gained the information in question through means other than the so-called normal ones.

At this point we may call upon the psi hypothesis as formulated earlier. It will not be out of the way to remark again, however, that from the standpoint of formal procedure we are not citing the events described as evidence bearing upon the psi hypothesis. We are merely taking the position that in view of the cumulative evidence, considered in its own right and independently of the present situation, bearing on the hypothesis that it is possible for an individual to gain information about events which he cannot apprehend directly or indirectly by normal sensory means, we may justifiably consider the possibility in the present case. We may then hypothesize that my patient became aware of and utilized information that was relevant to his needs of the moment although he appears not to have had normal means of access to this information.

This is all that is meant by the application of the psi hypothesis to a given set of data. It does not imply the proposition that psi necessarily *was* the means whereby the patient got his information, since we are not in a position absolutely to rule out one or more ways of accounting along conventional lines for the data described. The mere application of the psi hypothesis, furthermore, does not *per se* commit us to any particular degree of confidence or belief in the relative probability of this hypothesis being correct in the situation described; it simply places psi among several hypotheses which are logically conceivable under the circumstances, such as the possibility, considered earlier, that the patient's alleged dream was a retrospective falsification of which he was consciously unaware; or that he was acquainted with the family of the pilot of the plane that had crashed and had, before his dream, received news of the event by telephone or wire; or that the data in the case were falsified or invented by me. The only hypothesis we have so far ruled out is that of chance, and this we have done, it will be recalled, not because we were able to take certain steps to insure universal agreement that what we call chance could have played little or no part in the events described, but simply because we made the *decision* to treat these events as if chance were not in the picture. We made this decision, let us remember, chiefly on the grounds that to consider the chance hypothesis a good one would deprive the data of a kind of meaning that, with the aid of certain psychoanalytic assumptions, we might otherwise be able to ascribe to them.

This is what Eisenbud has to say about the larger role of psi in the universe:

It is one thing for organisms with efficient neuro-humoral means of information transmission and feedback to maintain homeostasis and quite another for a multitude of separate entities with a sharply limited number of mechanisms of information exchange between them, and without a central governing "brain," to arrange themselves into orderly self-correcting systems able to operate within relatively narrow limits of optimum functioning. Neither the "law of large numbers" nor general systems theory, on which ecologists are wont to rely (conveniently leaving the details, however, up to nature herself) can take care of this, any more than can the postulation of equally vague (if not downright demonological) "organizers" or "organizing fields" in the cellular domain or, getting down to today's fundamentals, of electrons to which individual wills are ascribed by way of getting out of the theoretical jam. What is clearly needed, besides a "brain" of some sort, is a means of communication between entities, be they particles, cells, organisms or even inanimate aggregates (which indeed are already held to "communicate" in a universal gravitational system).

But by the same token it becomes apparent why, if something like psi is postulated as the basic means of communication between entities and events in nature, it is not necessarily used in the pursuit of the purely egoistic goals the individual normally holds desirable. The answer is that the goals psi serves are primarily not those of the individual at all but of an ascending hierarchy of interrelated systems in which the individual is merely a messenger of sorts. Psi serves, as it were, as part of the vegetative nervous system of nature (just as it provides at the same time a sort of psychic counterpart of the vegetative nervous system of the individual, where it operates within the constraints and boundary conditions imposed by a higher system).

Here, at any rate, we arrive at another segment of the seemingly unbridgeable moat separating man's theoretical concepts from things as they are. How, without something like psi communication in the broadest sense (in which our physical and biological laws would be viewed merely as special "force" cases that have "hardened" out of the ur-field over billions of years of progressive structuralization, like footpaths worn into the village green), could order come at all into a universe which, solely according to conventional notions of physics, should have come to a dead halt long before the birth of the first amino acids?

Montague Ullman (b. 1916), a psychiatrist and psychoanalyst leaning toward the cultural school, is another founder of the Medical Section of the ASPR who has had a longtime interest in the study of psi phenomena.

Ullman was not satisfied with a purely clinical, phenomenological approach to the problem, and together with Stanley Krippner, Charles Honorton, and others at the Dream Laboratory (now the Division of Parapsychology and Psychophysics) of the Maimonides Medical Center in Brooklyn, he developed an ingenious experimental technique for the study of telepathic dreams under laboratory conditions.

This is the way Professor Gardner Murphy, who has served as a mentor and guide for several generations of aspiring parapsychologists, introduces Ullman's Dream Telepathy (1973, written in collaboration with S. Krippner and A. Vaughan):

This volume takes a giant step into the unknown. A prominent psychiatrist, a versatile and ingenious psychologist, and a collaborator in the laboratory from which their work has come present us with a broad, clear, specific, and highly challenging approach to the telepathy of the dream. Dreams can carry a message through channels other than the channels of the senses. This has long been suspected. Indeed, it has been the subject of both theory and practice from the ancient civilizations of China and Egypt to the period of modern parapsychology.

For several decades, attempts to study telepathy in the dream have appeared in the research of psychiatrists and psychologists. Sigmund Freud, having introduced the scientific world to the obscure and intriguing messages of the dreams of his patients, his colleagues, and himself, referred at times to the problem of telepathy in the dream, and a considerable body of psychoanalytic studies of dream telepathy is scattered through reports of his clinical work with patients.

In recent years the need for an experimental method has clearly been shown. Dreams are so complicated, their symbolism so involved, that the likelihood of coincidence of dreams with actual events is very great, and no "master key" is likely to open the fortress of scientific incredulity but planned experiments. The authors give us, after their extensive historical survey of dream studies, a detailed and disciplined account of the experimental methods they have developed over the years at the Dream Laboratory at the Maimonides Medical Center in Brooklyn. Over a hundred published studies have shown the real payoff which follows from a strict experimental method in which normal, genuine, real dreams of ordinary human beings are studied with full attention to the rigorous techniques of electrophysiology.

In such studies, it is necessary to bring an experimental subject to the laboratory in the evening to become familiar with the setting and with the procedure to be followed. The subject prepares for sleep, and electrodes are fastened to his scalp. He goes to sleep; he dreams—as is shown both by the rapid eye movements and the brain-wave changes which go with the sleeping process. When the records show he has been dreaming, he is awakened. He tells what he dreamed and gives free associations to what he has reported. A distant experimenter, nearly a hundred feet away and beyond three closed doors, has been attempting to guide the course of the sleeper's dream thoughts in accordance with a randomly chosen target, following a procedure which would exclude any possibility of the subject's normal knowledge of what was being beamed to him.

Later the data are evaluated by comparing the contents of the subject's dreams with the contents of the message which was beamed to him. Results have demonstrated that the resemblances are significantly greater than would be expected by chance. Along the lines of an improved method of evaluating successes and failures much more work remains to be done. Enough, however, has been done to show that in a span of a half-dozen years with over a hundred subjects, there is a significant relation between what is "sent" and what is "received."

Following a broad survey of the available evidence about telepathic dreams and a detailed discussion of his experimental procedure, Ullman summarizes his principal conclusions as follows:

Of all the altered states of consciousness investigated by parapsychologists as being favorable to ESP, dreaming is the only one which happens to each of us every day, in a regular physiological rhythm, occurring about every ninety minutes throughout the night's sleep. At these times the eyes move rapidly back and forth (Rapid Eye Movement periods or REM). Other physiological changes, i.e., changes in respiration, pulse rate, penile erection, also occur. The REM periods increase in duration through the night. While dreaming, the brain shows electrical activity that is closest to the waking pattern as compared with other stages of sleep. It is during this REM period that sleeping subjects are also most likely to have transitory awakenings.

These correlations are both intriguing and puzzling. Does the eye movement represent scanning activity? Or is some unknown biological mechanism at work? Do the penile erections represent a state of sexual arousal? Or is this part of a non-specific effect of generalized tissue irritability? Does the electrical activity of the brain represent arousal? Or is this a special state unrelated to the arousal mechanism?

The interpretation of these data are widely disputed, especially when considered in the context of psychoanalytic thinking.

In addition to providing well-substantiated evidence of telepathy in the REM state, Ullman concludes by offering a theory of the presumed biological functions of telepathy in dreams and in man's mental makeup in

general. Its function is what he describes as psi vigilance. As senior author,
he refers to himself in the third person.

Ullman, in the mid-1950s, postulated that dreaming states represented a
heightened state of vigilance and extended the idea of vigilance to include
parapsychological data. The dreamer generally dreams about a recent event
that has some disturbing quality. Ullman suggested that, in addition to
scanning his own past for experiences related to the theme of the dream, the
dreamer can on occasion span both time and space to pick up information
that is of importance to him.

The experimental discovery of the REM effect was supportive of the vigilance theory of dreaming to the extent that it suggested that there was a
built-in, physiologically controlled mechanism producing recurrent states
of brain arousal and activity. Awakening could occur if the intensity and
quality of feelings generated during these periods were great enough. During these repetitive bouts of brain activity, the dreamer, focusing on the
most recent disturbing experience, engages in two kinds of operation to
determine whether the disturbance is one that would warrant awakening.
He reviews his own past history for the historical roots of his response to
the present disturbance, and he mobilizes his characteristic strategies of defense against anxiety and change. Only if these mechanisms cannot contain
and resolve the anxiety does awakening take place. The dreamer, in effect,
has made an emotionally determined decision as to whether or not it is safe
to continue sleeping. This is the central idea of the vigilance theory of
dreaming.

The "psi vigilance" theory (a term initiated by Dr. Rex Stanford) postulates that during the REM dreaming state the human mind is most susceptible to psi impressions, which are in turn incorporated into the dream. At
these times, the dreamer is scanning not only his internal environment but
also his "psi field" to see if any hostile or threatening influences external to
himself must be dealt with. During sleep, man is at his most helpless and is
most vulnerable to attack. Animals who live in constant threat of their lives
may perhaps deal with this by a REM mechanism whereby they periodically
come close to waking. Man apparently has a more sophisticated system of
vigilance, one that responds to symbolic threats rather than physical
threats to his social existence. The dreaming state, perhaps because of its
possible linkage to a primitive danger sensing mechanism, provides the
most favorable altered state of consciousness for ESP.

Ullman also suggests that this dreaming state of "psi vigilance" can, in
some individuals, result in creative dream solutions to problems at hand
and, in the light of precognition dream studies, to problems on their way.
Examples of dream creativity run the gamut from the solution of everyday

problems to creative breakthroughs, although the latter are as rare as truly creative ideas themselves.

Ullman's emphasis on the factor of vigilance in dreaming and its relationship to psi effects has by no means been generally accepted by the psychological and psychiatric community. Neither has it won complete approval of the parapsychological community—which seldom reaches agreement on anything—all of which makes for stimulating controversies. . . .

Our main surmise is that the psyche of man possesses a latent ESP capacity that is most likely to be deployed during sleep, in the dreaming phase. Psi is no longer the exclusive gift of rare beings known as "psychic sensitives," but is a normal part of human existence, capable of being experienced by nearly everyone under the right conditions. It took many hundreds of thousands of years before man learned to write his language. How much longer will it take before he learns to use his psi? We are optimistically inclined to say that the time lag between "discovery" and "application" will be considerably shortened in the coming years and that a deeper understanding of psi will profoundly influence our way of looking at our place in the universe. We may discover ourselves to be less alienated from each other, more capable of psychic unity and more capable of closeness in ways never before suspected.

Whether this will come about depends largely on how realistically we try to understand ourselves and the world we have created—not merely our "parapsychological" self but our whole self, our whole psyche as well as our ability to realize a planetary concern that crosses national boundaries. The future direction of man depends on the future direction not only of his sciences and technologies, but also of his philosophies. If technology and its concomitant philosophy of mastery over nature continue to crowd out a philosophical humanism based on a congruence between man and nature our problems will grow worse: pollution, decay, wars, alienation. If such a humanistic philosophy guides our technology, we have a chance. Man's psychic potential suggests that in the basic fabric of life everything and everyone is more closely linked than our discrete physical boundaries would seem to suggest. Perhaps all forms of life are vitally interrelated in ways we do not yet clearly understand.

Kirlian photography is a recent technical innovation which, rightly or wrongly, has been associated with the field of parapsychology. Discovered by a Russian husband and wife research team, it is based on photographing auralike emanations from parts of the human body or other living tissue—for instance, finger tips or leaves from a tree—under the influence of a high-powered electrical current similar to alternating currents generated by the Tesla coil.

The pictures obtained are often quite spectacular and have given rise to a wealth of imaginative interpretations by viewers and experimenters. Some of them are inspired by similarities to the halos of saints or to the auras claimed to be seen by so-called psychics or sensitives. Some experimenters noted that the emanations issuing from psychic healers carry specific "signatures," that the auras of patients are disease-specific and show striking changes under the influence of "laying on hands" by a gifted healer.

The findings themselves are certainly impressive. But trying to attribute the photographic artifacts to the arcane powers of a would-be healer, to mysterious fluctuations of a life-force, or to correlate them with certain personality traits of an ill-defined healer, or an ill-defined disease entity is merely apt to confound the issue and to discredit a promising procedure.

Stripped of its aura of the occult and mysterious connotations, Kirlian photography may well find its place alongside the psychogalvanic reflex or diverse polygraph techniques in the hands of qualified investigators.

chapter 26

Behavior Modification: Psychotherapy Without a Psyche

H. J. EYSENCK, J. WOLPE, T. KRAFT, T. SZASZ, I. BIEBER,
J. MASSERMAN, J. MARMOR . . . SAMPLES OF A CONTROVERSY

Turning from existential analysis, ESP and attempts at unorthodox healing to the new methods of behavior modification, we find ourselves at the opposite end of the therapeutic spectrum. Behavior modification as a therapeutic tool is an offspring of the marriage of a philosophy and a technique. The philosophy is frankly materialistic, positivistic, causal-reductive, and is based on Pavlovian, Watsonian, and Skinnerian principles of conditioned reflexes, operant reinforcement, and learning theory. B. F. Skinner makes no bones about his aim to formulate a technology of behavior without reference to man's goals and purposes or to the human "mind." In his view, Plato, Thomas Aquinas, Descartes, Locke, and Kant were preoccupied with incidental, if not irrelevant, by-products of behavior. Behavior is determined by genetic and environmental factors such as operant reinforcements, aversive or punitive interventions, and their consequences. The self —or the sense of self—is merely the product of our sociocultural environment generating self-knowledge and self-control. Freedom and dignity are illusions and autonomous man is a mythical animal.

The technique is derived from laboratory experiments with animals and humans. It includes conditioned reflex therapy, reciprocal inhibition, aversion or implosion therapy, desensitization, "hypnotic flooding," assertiveness training, and diverse "token economies" used in mental institutions to reinforce appropriate behavior.

H. J. Eysenck (b. 1916), the German-born British psychologist, has become perhaps the most articulate and most controversial advocate of the behaviorist position in psychotherapy. At the same time he has spearheaded the most virulent attacks against the rationale and therapeutic efficacy of the diverse Freudian and non-Freudian schools. Eysenck is no clinician and his knowledge of the field is secondhand, based on painstaking studies of the literature. In a 1952 survey of results claimed by various schools of psychotherapy, he came to the conclusion that none could substantiate recovery rates by reference to objective criteria; that few reports included adequate controls; and that symptomatic improvements obtained by attempts *at behavior modification were in effect the only reliable indicators of thera-peutic success. In a monograph entitled* The Effects of Psychotherapy *(1966)* *he reconsiders his earlier position and draws the following conclusions:*

1. When untreated neurotic control groups are compared with experi-mental groups of neurotic patients treated by means of psychotherapy, both groups recover to approximately the same extent.

2. When soldiers who have suffered a neurotic breakdown and have not received psychotherapy are compared with soldiers who have received psy-chotherapy, the chances of the two groups returning to duty are approxi-mately equal.

3. When neurotic soldiers are separated from the Service, their chances of recovery are not affected by their receiving or not receiving psychotherapy.

4. Civilian neurotics who are treated by psychotherapy recover or im-prove to approximately the same extent as similar neurotics receiving no psychotherapy.

5. Children suffering from emotional disorders and treated by psycho-therapy recover or improve to approximately the same extent as similar children not receiving psychotherapy.

6. Neurotic patients treated by means of psychotherapeutic procedures based on learning theory, improve significantly more quickly than do pa-tients treated by means of psychoanalytic or eclectic psychotherapy, or not treated by psychotherapy at all.

7. Neurotic patients treated by psychoanalytic psychotherapy do not im-prove more quickly than patients treated by means of eclectic psychother-apy, and may improve less quickly when account is taken of the large pro-portion of patients breaking off treatment.

8. With the single exception of the psychotherapeutic methods based on learning theory, results of published research with military and civilian neurotics, and with both adults and children, suggest that the therapeutic effects of psychotherapy are small or nonexistent, and do not in any demonstrable way add to the nonspecific effects of routine medical treat-ment, or to such events as occur in the patients' everyday experience.

These conclusions go a little beyond those which resulted from the writ-er's original survey of the literature, published in 1952. The conclusion then was simply that published research failed to disprove the null-hypothesis with respect to psychotherapeutic effectiveness. The additional studies which have come to hand since, particularly those making use of a control group, have been so uniformly negative in their outcome that a somewhat stronger conclusion appears warranted. Methodologically, of course, it is impossible to prove that any treatment has no effect whatsoever, and no such conclusion is implied. The results do show that whatever effects psychotherapy may have are likely to be extremely small; if they were large as compared with the effects of nonspecific treatments and events it seems reasonable to suppose that some effects would have been found in the studies quoted. It is possible, of course, that effects were looked for in the wrong quarter; psychotherapy may affect personality traits and behavior patterns other than those relevant to psychiatric improvement as ordinarily understood. In the absence of specific hypotheses and experimental research there is no fruitful way of discussing such a possibility. The writer must admit to being somewhat surprised at the uniformly negative results issuing from all this work. In advancing his rather challenging conclusion in the 1952 report, the main motive was one of stimulating better and more worthwhile research in this important but somewhat neglected field; there was an underlying belief that while results to date had not disproved the null-hypothesis, improved methods of research would undoubtedly do so. Such a belief does not seem to be tenable any longer in this easy optimistic form, and it rather seems that psychologists and psychiatrists will have to acknowledge the fact that current psychotherapeutic procedures have not lived up to the hopes which greeted their emergence fifty years ago.

The following article from the Medical Tribune, April 4, 1973, in which Eysenck summarizes his latest position, is another sample of the controversy.

At the turn of the century, Freud's contributions to the understanding and treatment of neurosis (and, to a smaller extent, psychosis) rightly excited admiration and hope; we may still admire his intellectual ardor, but any hopes that his theories and methods would have practical effects on the treatment of these disorders vanished long ago—as he himself acknowledged shortly before his death. Equally, the scientific status of his work has been undermined by the criticism of experimental psychologists and of philosophers such as Popper and Kuhn. The latter pointed out that Freud's system did not possess the essential property of *falsifiability*. It was impossible to carry out any specifiable experimental observational procedures which could conceivably prove his theories to be wrong; Freud could explain everything and predict nothing.

Freud's distrust and dislike of experimental study of his concepts was vividly expressed in his famous postcard to Rosenzweig, who had told him of his attempts to carry out experimental studies of repression: "I cannot put much value on these confirmations because the wealth of reliable observations on which these assertions rest make them independent of experimental verification." Many investigators tried to rephrase his theories in such a way that deductions could be made and experimentally tested. The outcome has not been very positive; as I pointed out at the end of a review of such efforts: "I would conclude that no such verification is possible, nor has it been accomplished." Psychoanalysis still rests, as it has always done, on subjective impressions and interpretations, unrelated to observable behavior and unverifiable by any objective method whatever. Any apparent prediction it makes can immediately be turned into its opposite by invoking the process of "reaction formation," and appeals to the patient's own words can be countered by positing unconscious ideas the very opposite to those voiced. If there were at least agreement among psychoanalysts on major points, one might take the method more seriously; as it is, we have a case of "quot homines, tot sententiae," and no accepted method of deciding between them.

If psychoanalysis could be shown to work—i.e., to be instrumental in curing neurotic patients—then these criticisms might appear purely academic; in medicine we often have to work with methods whose rationale we do not understand. But the evidence is completely unanimous: if psychoanalysis has any effects, then these have never been empirically demonstrated.

This statement depends for its acceptance on a chain of reasoning which goes like this: neurotic disorders are subject to spontaneous remission; extensive studies show that seriously ill patients receiving no psychiatric treatment of any kind show considerable improvement, or cure, to the extent of 70 percent recovering after two years and 90 percent after five years. Any treatment claiming to be effective must do better than this, or else incorporated a control group in the experimental design which does not receive the treatment under investigation.

When I first reviewed the published literature in 1952, I discovered that the efficacy claimed for different methods of psychotherapy and psychoanalysis was almost exactly that found for spontaneous remission; there were no studies using control groups of any kind. I concluded that there was no evidence for the effectiveness of psychoanalysis; I indicated also that the design and execution of the studies summarized were unimpressive, so that it was not possible to conclude definitely that the methods of all psychotherapy were in fact useless. The Scottish verdict of "not proven" was the only possible one. Since then a large number of studies have been published, some of which did include control groups; on the whole, the level of these studies is still unsatisfactory, but as far as they go they bear out my original conclusion.

An excellent summary of the evidence, with critical reviews of individual studies, has been published by Rachman; his conclusion is in agreement with my own. He draws particular attention to the fact that patients treated with psychoanalysis are very highly selected, on the basis of criteria of "suitability" which emphasize factors favorable for the treatment—i.e., youth, wealth, intelligence, and education.

Yet, in spite of this preselection, psychoanalysis can do no better than "no treatment" of random groups of patients not distinguished by youth, intelligence, wealth, or education. These facts now seem to be widely acknowledged even by psychoanalysts; Rachman quotes a study undertaken by the American Psychoanalytic Association itself which shows that even under optimal conditions, with highly selected patients, many psychoanalysts do not in fact hold out any hopes of being able to help their patients.

Several studies have recently appeared suggesting, but not establishing, that it is the personality of the therapist that is important; warmth and genuineness, for instance, are therapeutic; coldness and aloofness are counterproductive. The typical, remote psychoanalyst, interpreting dreams and other fantasy material but not showing much empathy or giving much help, would apparently have negative rather than positive effects.

If success is due to the man, not the method, then the method as such cannot be implicated in success or failure—particularly when different methods all show this dependence on the personal qualities of the therapist. If the findings can be confirmed, they may also explain spontaneous remission; neurotics not in treatment are known to discuss their troubles with friends, relatives, priests, and other sympathetic listeners, and these might play the part of the "good' therapist—with equal success.

Psychoanalysts have gradually given up the claims that used to be made for their method of treatment; we hear less and less about "cures" and more and more about enabling the patient to "live with his symptoms" and about improving the patient's "personality." These aims are difficult to check, and in any case they are appropriate only if there are no methods in existence which can in fact produce a cure. This is no longer so; the recently perfected methods of behavior therapy have already amply justified the early hopes for their effectiveness. Rachman gives a cautious but not unfavorable review of the available evidence. It should also be noted that these studies are of a much higher caliber scientifically than those dealing with psychoanalysis; proper control groups are much more common, and efforts have been made to quantify the "symptoms" to be treated, and to measure with some precision their disappearance.

Comparisons have been made, not only with "no treatment" controls but also with groups receiving different types of treatment; in general, the conclusion is that methods of behavior therapy (desensitization, modeling, "flooding," aversion therapy) not only work better than alternative treatments (or no treatment) but also work much more quickly. Considering the fact that these methods have been widely used only in the last dozen years, this success is surprising. It also demonstrates that it is possible to carry out properly controlled comparisons between different methods of therapy, or between therapy and no therapy, a point often denied by Freudians. Even with psychotics, important successes have been demonstrated; thus the "token economy" appears to be a very powerful instrument for reversing deterioration of long-term psychotic patients in mental institutions.

Mention has been made of behavior therapy, not only because it demonstrates the possibilities of experimental investigations in this complex field but also because it enables us to put to the test one of the few Freudian theories which appear sufficiently definite to escape the philosophers' criticisms that they are not falsifiable. Freud argued that neurotic "symptoms" arise from some disease process which he identified as a "complex," usually stemming from repression of infantile material (the Oedipus complex or the Electra complex). Hence the only method of treatment was an attack on the cause, rather than on the symptom; purely symptomatic treatment, he thought, would lead to relapse and symptom substitution.

Behavior therapy is based on a quite different conception; "symptoms," so called, are not really symptoms of anything but are simply conditioned emotional reactions, and behavior processes evolved as reactions to these conditioned emotional reactions. There are no "complexes" or other hidden "causes" for the neurotic illness; hence a direct attack on the "symptom," leading to its extinction, is all that is needed. No relapses, and no symptom substitution, are expected in this theory. Here, then, we have two quite distinct theories, giving rise to quite different predictions; experiment should be able to decide between them.

The outcome has been quite clear-cut; behavior therapy usually succeeds quite quickly in eliminating the "symptom," but there is no evidence of any relapse, or of any symptom substitution. It seems that in this respect spontaneous remission, too, is contrary to Freudian theory; no such remission should be possible, certainly not without relapse or symptom substitution. Yet the existence of such remission is probably the best-documented fact we have about neurosis, as Rachman amply demonstrates. We may perhaps conclude, without doing him an injustice, by stating that Freud's theory, on the one important point where it leads to a definite prediction, has been shown not to be in accord with the facts. The evidence is against any view of neurosis as based on unconscious "complexes," and in good accord with the view of neurotic "symptoms" as conditioned emotional reactions. Under these conditions, it ill becomes psychoanalysts who cannot *even* cure "symptoms" to accuse behavior therapists of *only* curing "symptoms"!

To be fair to psychoanalysts, however, it should be said that they have, for the most part, taken to heart the published evidence and have ceased to argue about the inevitability of relapses. As we have already noted, they have also ceased to make the kinds of claims for psychoanalytic treatment which used to be made twenty or thirty years ago. And many analysts, and philosophers friendly to psychoanalysis have ceased to argue that psychoanalysis is a science, or proceeds by scientific argument and observation; they now conceive of it as an aid to "understanding." Even so, however, we are given no indication of how we might test the truth or otherwise of the "understanding" so achieved; it would take us too far to trace and criticize this particular development, especially so since it does not alter the position with respect to the effectiveness of psychotherapy.

It has become pretty obvious, even before the effectiveness of psychotherapy came under criticism, that psychoanalysis could never be the answer to neurotic illness—the duration and cost of the treatment, as well as the difficulty of training analysts in any number, restricted treatment effectively to a small percentage of wealthy patients. Here, too, behavior therapy compares favorably with psychoanalysis. Duration of treatment is short; no medical expertise is required, as the psychological reeducation of patients involved has no medical rationale; psychologists can be trained more readily and quickly than medical analysts.

We are probably at the threshold of a great step forward; the possibility now exists of giving effective treatment for neurotic disorders to thousands of people who previously had to rely on spontaneous remission. The reduction of human misery which could be effected in this way is staggering; at last, the hopes raised early on by psychoanalysis look like being fulfilled by behavior therapy.

Freud drew attention to the problem, and devoted his life to finding the answer; unfortunately, he failed to apply the critical methods of science to curb his tremendous imagination. From his tragic failure have sprung other approaches, more closely linked with the psychological laboratory, and with modern theories of learning. We can still venerate Freud as a great pioneer; we would be very wrong in still believing in his gospel, and following in his footsteps.

Joseph Wolpe (b. 1915), a South African-born psychiatrist now at the University of Virginia School of Medicine, is the foremost pioneer of clinical behavior therapy and challenger of psychoanalysis as a method of treatment. Focusing as he does on overt behavior, he feels fully justified in disregarding the individual's private experience or inner conflicts. To Wolpe the unconscious is an unnecessary hypothesis and most psychoanalytic propositions are not "falsifiable," since they can be neither proved nor disproved. Behavior modification must therefore be satisfied with removing overt symptoms—that is, extinguishing faulty habits or attitudes. In so doing, it sets the stage for the acquisition of new, more appropriate or socially desirable patterns of behavior.

Having said that symptomatic improvement is the only criterion of improvement of neuroses that must be taken into account in every case, I must make my meaning clear. Baldly stated, symptomatic improvement simply means that the patient has less discomfort. Discomfort can be diminished in a variety of ways. One method consists of the use of appropriate drugs. Although drugs are a valuable *aid* to treatment of many cases, for several reasons it is unsatisfactory to base treatment solely on them. The alleviation of symptoms is often only partial, there may be side effects, there are risks of toxicity and addiction, and, above all, the need for treatment may well continue indefinitely. Psychoanalysts and conditioning therapists are at one in comparing this with treating a slipped spinal disc with analgesics; they rightly disparage it, favoring the superior therapeutic objective of removing the underlying state of affairs upon which the symptoms depend. In other words, they both advocate aiming at a *radical* cure of neurosis, to render the patient free from his symptoms without the use of drugs or other means of palliation. Among other palliative measures I include taking the patient away from a disturbing environment, or manipulating the environment so as to ameliorate stressful features. Clearly, if the underlying basis of his symptoms were to be removed, the patient would be symptom-free without drugs in all circumstances in which symptoms were previously evoked. The crucial question, then, in comparing the clinical status of the conditioning therapies with that of psychoanalysis is: how effective is each of them in achieving this result?

While directing our minds to this practical question, we must be aware that at bottom the conflict is one of *concepts.* The comparison is not between this and that batch of methods that are merely empirically different, like some of the remedies for warts, but between two different conceptions of the nature of neurosis, each of which generates methods of treatment consistent with it. The different theories of neurosis suggest different requirements for recovery, and therefore different therapeutic maneuvers. In carrying out appropriate therapeutic maneuvers one is in fact performing operations that test predictions from the respective theories. As always in science, a theory becomes questionable when its predictions fail to be supported by experience.

Psychoanalytic Therapy

With the foregoing as orientation we may proceed to evaluate the clinical status of psychoanalytic therapy. The conception of neurotic symptoms that leads to this therapy is that they are the consequences of emotional forces that have been repressed, taking the form of compromises between partial discharges of these forces and various defenses resisting their discharge. In 1922 Freud put it in the following words:

> The neuroses are the expression of conflicts between the ego and such of the sexual impulses as seem to the ego incompatible with its integrity or with its ethical standards. . . . Symptoms are in the nature of compromise-formations between the repressed sexual instincts and the repressive ego instincts. . . .

Although some analysts may protest that this statement is out of date, modern deviators from Freud, such as Horney, Fromm, and Alexander, differ from his mainly in the direction of ascribing greater importance to unconscious conflicts related to the immediate situation of the patient. The core of the theory remains, and with it, quite naturally, a broad basis of agreement upon what needs to be done in therapy, this being a logical deduction from the theory. The psychoanalytic objective is to overcome a neurosis by making repressed impulses conscious, using various tactics to overcome the resistances that oppose this. Munroe has said that the crux of the therapeutic process not only for Freud, but also for Adler, Horney, Fromm, and Sullivan "may be stated as the development of insight," not mere intellectual insight, but "the actual *experiencing* of aspects of one's personality which have been made defensively unconscious."

We need to consider to what extent the therapeutic procedures based on psychoanalytic theory have been effective in bringing about recovery from neurosis. It must be said at once that the evidence available is remarkable for its paucity, considering that psychoanalysis has been practiced for sixty years. It is also remarkable that, as far as I have been able to discover, not a single individual psychoanalyst has ever published a statistical survey of his own practice. Is it unreasonable to ask if this may be at least partly because they have not been very happy with their results? . . .

The Conditioning Therapies

Now let us consider the conditioning therapies. These methods stem from the conception that neuroses are persistent unadaptive habits that have been conditioned (that is, learned). If this conception is correct, the fundamental overcoming of a neurosis *can* consist of nothing but deconditioning—or undoing the relevant habit patterns.

The most characteristic and common feature of neurotic habits is anxiety. There is persuasive evidence, both experimental and clinical, that the great majority of neuroses are fundamentally conditioned autonomic responses. The individual has persistent habits of reacting with anxiety to situations that, objectively, are not dangerous. Typical stimuli to which the response of anxiety may be regarded as neurotic are the sight of a bird, the interior of an elevator, asking a favor, or receiving a compliment. Experimentally it is possible to condition an animal to respond with anxiety to any stimulus one pleases merely by arranging for that stimulus, on a number of occasions, to appear in an appropriate time relation to the evocation of anxiety; and by manipulating various factors one can obtain an emotional habit that is utterly refractory to extinction in the ordinary way. In human neuroses one can usually elicit a history of similar kinds of conditioning. Human neuroses, too, are characterized by the same remarkable resistance to extinction. Since neurotic reactions are, as a rule, autonomic reactions first and foremost, this resistance is in keeping with Gantt's observations of the great refractoriness of cardiovascular conditioned responses to extinction.

It is implicit in conditioning theory that recovery from neurosis should be achieved by applying the learning process in a reverse direction: whatever undesirable behavior has been learned may be unlearned. In experiments performed about fourteen years ago I demonstrated in cats that had been made neurotic experimentally how this unlearning can be brought about. Anxiety reactions had been strongly conditioned to a small confining cage and to other stimuli, and could not be made to extinguish despite repeated exposure to the stimuli. The anxiety response habits could, however, be overcome in piecemeal fashion by counterposing feeding to weak anxiety responses. At first, stimuli distantly similar to the conditioned stimuli were used, until anxiety decreased to zero, and then, step by step, stimuli closer in resemblance to the original conditioned stimuli were introduced, until even the strongest eventually lost its power to evoke anxiety. These findings led to the framing of the reciprocal inhibition principle of psychotherapy, which is that *if a response inhibitory of anxiety can be made to occur in the presence of anxiety-evoking stimuli it will weaken the bond between these stimuli and the anxiety.*

Experience with human neuroses indicates that the principle has quite general validity; in addition to feeding, a good many other kinds of responses, each of which, empirically, appears to inhibit anxiety, have been successfully used to weaken neurotic anxiety-response habits and related neurotic habits. The reciprocal inhibition principle also affords an explanation for the therapeutic effects of interviewing as such (which is seemingly the main basis of the successes of the traditional therapies) and for so-called spontaneous recoveries.

I have described elsewhere the deliberate therapeutic use of a considerable range of anxiety-inhibiting responses. I shall briefly review those most widely employed—assertive, relaxation, and sexual responses.

Assertive responses are used where there is a need to overcome neurotic anxieties that arise irrationally in the course of interpersonal relationships —such anxieties as prevent a person from expressing his opinions to his friends lest they disagree, or from reprimanding inefficient underlings. The essence of the therapist's role is to encourage appropriate assertiveness, the outward expressions, wherever it is reasonable and right to do so, of the feelings and action tendencies that anxiety has in the past inhibited. In other words, the therapist instigates "acting out." Each act of assertion to some extent reciprocally inhibits the anxiety, and in consequence somewhat weakens the anxiety response habit. The assertion required is not necessarily aggressive, and behavior in accordance with affectionate and other feelings may need to be instigated. The maneuvers involved are largely similar to those described by Salter, though the rationale upon which he bases them is different.

Relaxation responses were first used on a scientific basis by Jacobson, who demonstrated that they have autonomic accompaniments opposite to those of anxiety. His method of intensive training in relaxation for use in the life situation, though of great value, is rather cumbersome. More economical and clearly directed use of relaxation is made in the technique known as *systematic desensitization.*

Lang reports its use in the context of snake phobias, but its range of application is very wide indeed. The therapist has to identify the categories of stimuli to which the patient reacts with anxiety, and then rank the stimuli of each category in order of intensity of evoked anxiety. In the course of about six interviews the patient is given training in relaxation in parallel with this. When the preliminaries have been completed, the patient is made to relax as deeply as possible (in some cases under hypnosis), and then instructed to imagine the weakest of the anxiety-evoking stimuli for a few seconds. The instruction is repeated at short intervals, and if the response to the stimulus has been weak initially, it declines, on repetition, to zero. Under these circumstances, what apparently happens is that on each occasion the relaxation inhibits the anxiety, to some extent, and somewhat weakens the anxiety-evoking potential of the stimulus concerned. With repetition this potential is brought down to zero.

Recent studies have demonstrated:

—that the effects of desensitization are due to the procedure itself and not to suggestion or transference;

—that after one or two sessions it can be predicted with virtual certainty whether a patient will respond to this treatment or not; and

—that in phobias with independently measurable parameters, such as acrophobia, the numbers of therapeutic operations involved show consistent mathematical relationships to the stages of decrement of the phobia that are suggestively similar to the psychophysical law proposed by Stevens.

Sexual responses are used to inhibit anxiety responses conditioned to sexual situations. By manipulating the conditions of sexual approaches so that anxiety is never permitted to be strong, reciprocal inhibition of anxiety by sexual arousal is effected, and the anxiety response habit is progressively weakened. It is usually possible to overcome impotence or premature ejaculation in a few weeks. Sexual responses have generally only a secondary role in the treatment of frigidity. . . .

Using the whole range of available methods according to their indications, I have reported between 1952 and 1958 three series of results embracing 210 neurotic patients. Every patient in whom the reciprocal inhibition techniques had been given a fair trial was included in the series. Nearly 90 percent of these patients were . . . either apparently cured or much improved after an average of about 30 therapeutic interviews. The cases were unselected in the sense that no case diagnosed as neurotic was ever refused treatment. Psychotics and psychopaths were not accepted for treatment unless by error of diagnosis.

Until recently, there were no other studies involving considerable number of patients, although numerous accounts had been published describing the successful treatment of individuals or small groups. One noteworthy small group comprised 18 cases of phobias in children treated by Lazarus. All the patients recovered in a mean of 9.5 sessions; follow-up from six months to two and a half years showed no relapses. . . .

A critical question is, of course, the durability of the results obtained by conditioning methods. The answer appears to be that they are practically always long-lasting. In 1958 I was able to report only one relapse among forty-five patients who had been followed up for periods ranging from two to seven years. Published communication from other conditioning therapists indicates that their experience is essentially the same. Furthermore, whenever resurgence of symptoms has occurred, and could be investigated, it has always been found to be related to specific events that could clearly have reconditioned the neurotic emotional habit. Learning theory predicts that *unless* there are intervening events that directly recondition neurotic reactions, recovery from neurosis that is radical . . . will be lasting, no matter by what maneuvers it has been obtained.

Besides Wolpe, S. Rachman, A. Salter, and A. A. Lazarus, a growing number of other workers have made important contributions to the field. The areas of application of behavior therapy range from phobias and anxiety reactions to such sexual deviations as homosexuality, impotence, frigidity, and fetishism, from obsessive-compulsive states to hysterical tics or drug addiction. Its literature includes such topics as "orgasmic reconditioning to change sexual object choice through controlled masturbation fantasies" and the application of learning theory to the treatment of bedwetting, somnambulism, and anorexia nervosa.

The selection below is taken from "The Use of Behavior Therapy in a Psychotherapeutic Context," a contribution by the British psychiatrist Thomas Kraft to A. A. Lazarus's Clinical Behavior Therapy (1972). Kraft's paper contains a graphic example of constructing "hierarchies" of imaginary situations aimed at desensitizing the patient against the type of experiences which are known to trigger anxiety attacks or phobic reactions. The paper shows at the same time how the behavior therapist combines relaxation exercises, hypnosis, or narcohypnosis in his armamentarium.

Constructing the Hierarchy for Systematic Desensitization

It is unwise to use a standardized hierarchy for all patients even though they may be suffering from a similar type of disorder, and it is recommended that a hierarchy should be especially constructed to meet the needs of each individual patient.

Some patients find it quite easy to construct a hierarchy of their own and know which situations cause little distress and which are extremely anxiety-provoking, but his is certainly not true of all. The author has found that many patients are prepared to begin treatment using an easy item at a time when a hierarchy has not yet been developed, and then to progress towards more difficult situations, offering helpful suggestions to the therapist as treatment proceeds. This allows the patient to participate in the treatment program rather than being a passive agent to whom treatment is administered. This is extremely important because eventually the patient must learn to conduct his own affairs without the assistance of a therapist.

A patient who has a fear of heights may be able to construct a suitable hierarchy of increasing height quite easily. He has a ladder at home and feels that he can climb a little higher each day. On the other hand, many patients find it very difficult or even impossible to construct any sort of hierarchy, and need a lot of assistance from the therapist. One patient who had a severe dog phobia could not think of any situation involving dogs which would not provoke maximum anxiety, so it was suggested that she look at a picture of a dog in a children's picture book, which was quite acceptable to her. Soon she was able to hug a toy dog, and gradually she learned to cope with dogs in the street. A neighbor who owned a dog was very helpful in her treatment in that she gave her a graded series of situations, first when the dog sat still, then walking away from her, towards her, cuddling and feeding the dog. Another patient who had a fear of water learned to swim and later dive with the assistance of a life guard who happened to be an in-patient in the same ward at that time.

It may be necessary to construct two hierarchies and these can often be offered to the patient concurrently. For example, a male homosexual patient who had difficulty passing urine in public toilets was given one hierarchy involving heterosexual situations leading to sexual intercourse, and a second hierarchy for using urinals in public toilets.

It might be helpful at this stage to give some examples of hierarchies used in particular patients. The first patient was absolutely terrified of dogs, a fear which developed at the age of five when she was running down an alley and an Alsatian dog grabbed her by the hair and dragged her along the alley, though finally she managed to get away. Her friends called her mother, but she was reluctant to come and fetch her as she too was frightened of dogs. The hierarchy was very carefully constructed and the patient has made a very good recovery.

Dog Phobia

1. Looking at a picture of a dog in a children's picture book.
2. Cuddling the children's toy dog.
3. Seeing a poodle on a lead (a) 10 yards away.
                            (b) 5 yards away.
                            (c) A woman passing by her.
4. Touching a puppy behind a wire mesh in the market.
5. Looking at the neighbor's spaniel, Kim, held in the arms of its mistress.
6. Touching Kim when the dog is quiet, held in the arms of its mistress.
7. Touching Kim when the dog is quiet.
8. Stroking Kim.
9. Kim putting up her paws.
10. Looking at an Alsatian dog.
11. Watching Kim jumping on the road when she is indoors and the windows are closed.
12. Watching Kim walk round the room.
13. Feeding Kim with a biscuit.
14. Kim held by its mistress, and then jumping on the ground.
15. Kim running.

16. Kim jumping from a chair onto the floor.
17. Kim jumping on the floor and then putting up her paw.
18. Kim wagging her tail.
19. Kim wagging her tail and then putting her paw up.
20. Kim running down the corridor.
21. Kim running away from her.
22. Kim running towards her.
23. Kim roaming round the house without a lead.
24. Knocking on the door of the neighbor, and Kim running towards her, barking.
25. Dogs fighting.

This hierarchy was completed in 21 sessions.

The second patient was a 38-year-old docker who became phobic to water and heights after a serious accident at his work. He often stepped on and off ships without the safety precaution of a gangplak, but on this occasion, he missed the quay, fell onto a wooden fender and then dropped into the water below. Once in the water, he knew that the tide here was strong and that he could drown or be crushed to death between the ship and the quay. He was given two hierarchies and the first of these will be given in full.

Fear of Water and Heights

1. Taking a bath at home.
2. Taking a shower at home.
3. Going into the shallow end of the swimming pool.
4. Starting to swim at the shallow end of the swimming pool, breast stroke only.
5. Swimming at the shallow end, doing the crawl.
6. Jumping into the swimming pool at the shallow end.
7. Jumping into the pool and then doing the crawl.
8. Swimming at the shallow end, first breast stroke, then the crawl.
9. Pushing himself away from the bars and causing a splash.
10. Swimming in the middle of the pool at a depth of 5 ft. 3 ins.
11. Swimming at the shallow end and then at the deep end (10 ft. 3 ins).
12. Going into the deep end of the swimming pool.
13. Watching people jump from the diving boards.
14. Standing on a step at the deep end of the pool and making a "little jump" into the water.
15. Backstroke at the shallow end of the pool.
16. Jumping into the water at the shallow end of the pool ("belly flop dive").

17. "Belly flop dive" at the deep end of the pool.
18. Racing dive at shallow end of the pool.
19. Racing dive at the deep end of the pool.
20. Swimming three times across the deep end of the pool without stopping
    (a) breast stroke
    (b) crawl
    (c) backstroke
21. Jumping into the pool at a depth of:
    (a) 5 ft. 3 ins.
    (b) 6 ft.
    (c) 7 ft.
22. Several jumps at 6 ft., 7 ft., alternating these, and then remaining at the 7 feet depth.
23. Going onto the 1st diving board and jumping into the water.
24. Jumping off the 1st diving board, then diving from the 1st board.
25. Diving off the 1st board.
26. Jumping from the 1st diving board, jumping from 2nd diving board, then diving from the 1st diving board.
27. Jumping off the 1st, 2nd, and 3rd diving boards, then diving from the 1st diving board.
28. Jumping off the 1st, 2nd, and 3rd diving boards, then diving from the 1st, and then the 2nd diving board.
29. Jumping off the 4th diving board, then diving off the 2nd diving board.
30. Jumping off the 5th diving board, then diving off the 3rd diving board.
31. Jumping off the 5th diving board, then diving off the 4th diving board.
32. Jumping off the top board, then diving off the 4th diving board.
33. Jumping off the top board, then diving off the 5th diving board.
34. Diving off the top diving board.
35. Random stimuli.
36. Looking round before jumping off the 3rd diving board.
37. Looking round before jumping off the 4th diving board.
38. Looking round before jumping off the 5th diving board.
39. Diving from the 5th diving board and looking round before diving.
40. Diving from the top board and looking round before diving.

This hierarchy was completed in 40 sessions, each lasting half an hour. He then started the second part of the desensitization program which involved standing near a lake, rowing on a lake, and crossing viaducts, bridges, canals, rivers, and finally going down the vertical ladder to the water's edge at the original site of the accident. This patient received 107 treatment sessions in all, and he has made a complete recovery, which has been maintained for over three years.

Systematic Desensitization
Under Conditions of Relaxation

Most patients who are given systematic desensitization are given some form of relaxation, but little is said about this aspect of the treatment situation in the articles which are published. The author offers two forms of relaxation, either hypnosis or intravenous injections of Methohexital sodium, but in the case of drug addicts they are only offered hypnosis, since it is felt that injections should not be encouraged by the treatment. Other patients are given the choice, and some prefer hypnosis, particularly if they are afraid of injections, while others prefer injections which they regard as more "medical."

The patient is asked to lie on a bed, but if he feels very threatened by this, he can be hypnotized sitting in a comfortable chair. Intravenous injections of Methohexital sodium must not be given to a patient in the sitting position as this may prove dangerous.

For those patients who receive hypnosis, the author tends to used the hand levitation technique, which will be described in detail at the end of this section. Some patients, particularly adolescents, respond to a very quiet voice, while others respond better to loud instructions, and this varies from one patient to another. When the patient is hypnotized, he is given the first item on the hierarchy. A patient who is being treated for her frigidity might be asked to imagine being in the kitchen at home, talking to her husband. At first, she may find it difficult to imagine this scene and here the therapist helps to produce visual images. He can assist her in this by additional cues such as seeing the kettle boil, making a cup of tea, asking the patient to describe the clothes worn by her husband, and sooner or later the patient will say that she can see her husband quite clearly. The patient may say that she feels perfectly alright provided that her husband is two feet away from her. The scene is then withdrawn and the patient is told to stop thinking about it and relax. The second scene to be presented might be sitting with her husband watching television, and the third, saying goodnight to him, without any physical contact. The therapist suggests that she will reach a deeper level of relaxation next time, and that with practice, she will obtain stronger visual images as the treatment proceeds. Unfortunately, not all patients have the capacity to form visual images, but desensitization can occur in the absence of either visual or auditory imagery, providing there is the appropriate emotional component. Some patients find it helpful to be given a relief response between items, and this aids anxiety-relief. One patient might like to think of roses, another of strawberries, and young people often like to think of a favorite pop record.

If the patient is presented with a scene which she finds very disturbing, it may be necessary to withdraw it, because if the patient comes out of the hypnotic state at this point, she may refuse to be hypnotized again, either on this or on a subsequent occasion.

As each scene is presented, it is quite easy to see from the facial expression whether the patient feels comfortable in this situation. On the first presentation, the patient may bite his lip, or furrow his brow or show a pained expression, and the therapist may have to present the scene several times before he remains perfectly calm and relaxed when visualizing it. Although it is quite satisfactory to present the next scene when the patient shows no evidence of anxiety, the author continues to present it until the patient is so happy with it that he can smile and dismiss it as though it had never been a problem at all. This is based on the principle of over-learning. At the beginning of each session, patients find it very helpful to start with a scene which has been well rehearsed, as this increases their confidence, but this is not essential.

Before bringing the patient out of the hypnotic state, it is important to give a strong counter-suggestion that he will be able to open his eyes, be wide awake, and perfectly fresh, because otherwise he may remain in a semi-hypnotized state for the rest of the day. One patient could not understand why he was not fully awake and said that he felt confused and as if walking through clouds, and further counter-suggestions were given later. It has been the author's experience that drug-addicted adolescents are particularly resistant to the counter-suggestion, and this may be due to a reluctance to come out of the hypnotic state, which they say is somewhat similar to the drug-induced state. . . .

Thomas Szasz (b. 1920), professor of psychiatry at Syracuse University Upstate Medical Center, is no stranger to controversy. His book The Myth of Mental Illness *(1967) proclaims his complete break with the medical model in psychiatry. At the same time, he declares war against the coercive aspects of psychiatric treatment. In this respect, he is a counterpart of the equally antiestablishment orientation of R. D. Laing in England.*

In the article quoted below, Szasz rejects the coercive medical model underlying the behavioral approach as against the moral aspect of the therapeutic encounter. Psychotherapy and psychoanalysis, he holds, are predicated on the freedom and responsibility of the individual, while behavior therapy is based on "authority, coercion and mystification." At best, he says, it may help people whose goal is to attain "nonfreedom."

However diverse in form, all psychotherapies have one thing in common: Each seeks to bring some type of influence to bear on the patient. The question is: To what end?

Psychotherapeutic practices may be divided into two large classes—one fostering the subject's socialization, the other encouraging a client's individuation. Pre-Freudian therapies were repressive; their purpose was to transform an "abnormal patient" into a "normal person." In contrast, psychoanalysis was to be expressive; its aim was to help the client become authentic and free, not "normal." (To be sure, sometimes Freud, as well as his followers, deviated from this principle; nevertheless, personal autonomy was—and remains—the ideal of psychoanalysis.)

This dichotomy, which was basic to Freud's thought and ought to be basic to our understanding of the varied methods of psychotherapy, has become obscured, primarily by the medical conceptualization of mental illness and psychiatric treatment. So long as we consider the "cure of souls" to be a medical and therapeutic activity rather than a human relationship and moral encounter, we shall not be able to unravel the tangled skein—the claims and counterclaims of rival psychiatric ideologies, theories, and "therapies."

The dialogue in psychiatry began with the publication, in 1893-95, of Breuer and Freud's *Studies in Hysteria*. Until then, psychiatrists spoke one language only. In it, the psychiatric patient is mad; his ideas and his beliefs are nonsense. Since then, some psychiatrists have learned another language. In it, the psychiatric patient is a reasonable person; his ideas and beliefs, though sometimes different from those of the psychiatrist, make sense.

In principle, the former perspective is medical, objective, positivistic, and statistical; the latter is nonmedical, subjective, humanistic, and individualistic. In practice, the former treats the mental patient as a defective object needing repair by the psychiatrist who is a medical-technological expert acting therapeutically on the patient; the latter treats the mental patient as a dignified and responsible person who enters with the psychiatrist into a human relationship significant for both.

The dialogue between adherentes of these two conflicting approaches has continued for more than seven decades. If it often generates more heat than light, and thereby more confusion than clarification, it is because the contenders do not fully realize the conceptual and ethical gulf that divides them.

Professor Eysenck's contributions to psychotherapy, and especially his writings on behavior therapy, are among the most cogent articulations of the medical approach.

By his own account, Eysenck is not interested in the personal life of the patients he describes, and, apparently, he does not himself practice psychotherapy. The accounts of behavior therapy he cites provide no description of the patients as human beings; they are merely the bearers of neurotic symptoms. He is interested mainly in whether the persons in question *have symptoms* (in which case they are "patients") or whether they *no longer have symptoms* (in which case they are "cured ex-patients").

To Eysenck, psychotherapy is just another variety of medical treatment. ". . . The study of the effects of psychotherapy," he proposes, "should be similar in methodology and experimental treatment to the study of the effects of any other therapeutic agent. . . ." He describes behavior therapy in the language of medicine: illness, symptom, neurosis, patient, treatment, recovery, cure, success rate, phobic disorder, booster dose are the words that recur constantly. This semantics is the more significant inasmuch as Eysenck asserts that ". . . neurotic disorders are not innate or caused by cortical lesions"; that neurosis is "learned," and that therapy is a process of "unlearning." Thus a person afraid of cats or spiders may be transformed into one who is not; a homosexual into a heterosexual; a philandering husband into a faithful one; and so forth.

To me, the most significant thing about Eysenck's theoretical and semantic scheme is not so much what it contains as what it omits—namely, ethical and political considerations.

Webster defines *ethics* as "the discipline dealing with what is good and bad or right and wrong . . ." and as "the principles of conduct governing an individual. . . ." Since all human conduct involves considerations of good and bad or right and wrong, how can we ignore moral values in studying such conduct? Yet this is precisely what Eysenck does. Many of his critics do the same. He "demoralizes" conduct by "medicalizing" morals. He accomplishes this, first, by means of a medical rhetoric; second, by avoiding the use of ordinary English words with moral and political meanings; and third, by accepting the conventional definitions of who is a psychiatric patient and what constitutes mental symptoms and diseases.

The lack of a morally and politically significant vocabulary in Eysenck's writings can be demonstrated by noting all the words conspicuous by their absence: money, power, coercion, domination, submission, equality, freedom, oppression, force, choice, decision, truth, falsehood, good, bad, agreement, contract, promise, and many more.

Eysenck's favorite examples of patients cured by behavior therapy are persons suffering from "phobic disorders." In plain English, these are persons who fear and avoid certain ordinary objects or situations; through behavior therapy, they are changed into persons more favorably disposed toward these things.

Fear, however, is a ubiquitous affect, and avoidance of what is feared, a common disposition. Not all instances of fearful avoidance are considered "phobic" and undesirable; indeed, most are considered "normal." Many persons abhor and avoid eating pork; many more detest the idea of slaughtering cattle and eating beef. We do not, however, say that Orthodox Jews suffer from a pork phobia, or Hindus from a beef phobia. Why not? Because we consider such avoidance behavior a matter of religious preference, rather than one of psychiatric compulsion.

The phobic person avoids what he fears for *his* reasons, which may be idiosyncratic. The religious person avoids what he fears for *his* reasons, which may be culturally shared. Here is the crux of the psychiatric dilemma: Should we accord moral standing only to group values, and treat personal values as psychiatric problems? Or should we accord moral significance to personal values as well? If we say yes to the first question—as do traditional psychiatrists and behavior therapists—we commit ourselves to a collectivistic bias. If we say yes to the second question—as do psychoanalysts and existential psychiatrists—we commit ourselves to an individualistic bias. Therapist and patient cannot have it both ways simultaneously.

It may be argued that the distinction between a typical phobia and a religious avoidance is simpler than I have drawn it. The individual experiences the former as "ego dystonic" and seeks to relinquish it, whereas he experiences the latter as "ego syntonic" and seeks to retain it. This criterion is of great practical value. But it not clearly articulated by behavior therapists, nor consistently followed by them. If it were, it would preclude the treatment of nonconsenting patients. In his discussion of behavior therapy, however, Eysenck does not distinguish between voluntary and involuntary patients. Some of the most impressive "successes" cited for behavior therapy are from studies conducted on children and delinquents, whose treatment is perforce coerced.

Although the proponents and opponents of behavior therapy disagree on many details, they agree on certain fundamental premises: That neurosis is an illness for which psychotherapy is a treatment, and that such treatment may be effective or ineffective. As during the Renaissance, warring Catholics and Protestants were at bottom united by their belief in a Christian divinity and its "diagnostic" and "therapeutic" corollary, the existence of witches and the duty of the clergy to combat witchcraft; so today, behavior therapists, psychoanalysts, and the adherents of most other "schools" of psychiatric thought are united by their belief in the myth of a mental illness and its diagnostic and therapeutic corollary, the psychiatrist's duty to cure such illness.

Formerly, contending religious groups tried to enlist the power of the state, each seeking exclusive support for its principles and practices as those of the only "true faith" and the suppression of all others as heresies. Today, contending psychiatric groups do likewise, each seeking exclusive support for its theories and methods as the only ones that are "scientifically valid" and the suppression of all others as "quackeries."

Totalitarian states have already abolished psychoanalysis and put their stamp of approval on suggestive psychotherapies similar to behavior therapy. Some authorities now advocate the suppression of psychoanalysis in the United States. According to the principles of ethics of the American

Medical Association, says Henry Davidson, psychoanalysis might qualify as a "cult." The justification for suppressing psychoanalysis is pushed still further in a recent letter to the Editor of *Science* (10 February 1967). "If the hypothesis is correct," asks the writer, ". . . that psychoanalysis does not in fact contribute to the cure of mental disease or to measurable improvement in mental health, what should the scientific community do about it?" He then draws a parallel between claims for psychoanalysis and for Krebiozen, the Hoxsey cancer cure, and worthless battery additives, and suggests that "If typical psychoanalysis is basically a fraud, . . . then surely something should be done about it."

Santayana observed that he who cannot remember history is destined to repeat it. In recommending and rejecting behavior therapy, we are treading a path Freud himself had traveled. He described his journey well enough. Shouldn't we try to learn from his experiences?

Freud began his psychiatric work by practicing a kind of behavior therapy. In a paper published in 1892-93, he relates the case of young woman he "cured" by hypnosis. The "illness" consisted of the woman's inability to nurse her children. Her first child, delivered three years before Freud was called in, had to be fed by a wet nurse. After the birth of the second child, Freud recounts, "external circumstances added to the desirability of avoiding a wet nurse. But the mother's attempts at feeding the child herself seemed even less successful and to provoke even more distressing symptoms than the first time. She vomited all her food, became agitated when it was brought to her bedside, and was completely unable to sleep." At last, on the recommendations of Breuer and Lott, two prominent Viennese physicians who had cared for the patient, Freud was called in to try hypnosis.

"I made use of suggestion," he writes, "to contradict all her fears and the feelings on which those fears were based: 'Have no fear! You will make an excellent nurse and the baby will thrive. Your stomach is perfectly quiet, your appetite is excellent, you are looking forward to your next meal, etc.!' "

The symptoms immediately disappeared. The patient slept well, ate well, and fed the baby well. But the difficulty recurred the following day. Freud returned and hypnotized the patient a second time. When he visited the family the third evening, ". . . the patient refused to have any further treatment. There was nothing more wrong with her, she said. She had an excellent appetite and plenty of milk for the baby; there was not the slightest difficulty when she was put to the breast, and so on."

"There was," Freud concludes, with what seems a trace of sadness, "nothing more for me to do. The mother fed her child for eight months; and I had many opportunities of satisfying myself in a friendly way that they were both doing well. I found it hard to understand, however, as well as annoying, that no reference was ever made to my remarkable achievement."

Why did Freud give up hypnosis if he was so successful with it? Because he disliked the ethics of suggestive therapy—the deceit, the coercion, the ignorance. He abandoned hypnosis and instead strove to develop a novel type of psychotherapeutic relationship—one in which he and the patient could comprehend the meaning of the patient's "illness" by understanding the patient's life; and in which the patient would not be ordered to behave in any particular way but would be free to conduct himself as he saw fit.

The result was the psychoanalytic situation characterized by mutual agreement between any two persons who freely consent to the relationship; by complete confidentiality on the part of the analyst; by the payment of a fee on the part of the analysand; and by the limitation of the therapist's role to listening and talking to the patient. The goal of this procedure was not the relief of a symptom or the cure of a disease. On the contrary, in 1923, Freud asserted that "analysis does not set out to make pathological reactions impossible, but to give the patient's ego *freedom* to decide one way or the other."

To oppose psychoanalysis, therefore, is to refuse individuals the freedom to make such decisions about their lives. There are persons, both in and out of psychiatry, who would readily deny this freedom to those who hold opinions differing from theirs—especially to so-called mental patients.

In formulating psychoanalysis as a "therapeutic instrument," Freud tacitly assumed that, like himself, neurotic patients wanted to be independent and free. Psychoanalysis often helps such people to strive more effectively toward this goal.

To Be Unfree

However, not everyone loves freedom. Some people, as Erich Fromm long ago noted, fear it and try to escape from it. Behavior therapy, like older psychotherapies based on authority, coercion, and mystification, may well help such persons attain their goal of nonfreedom.

In view of the historical record, it is curious that Eysenck criticizes psychoanalysis for failing to accomplish something it deliberately avoids, that is, "curing symptoms." "Behavior therapists consider it a trifle odd," he wrote, "that they should be criticized for *only* curing 'symptoms' by those who cannot *even* cure 'symptoms'!" Eysenck is, however, partly right. Behavior therapy should no more be criticized as a *bad method* of therapy than psychoanalysis should be praised as a *good method*. The important question for both is: To achieve what end? The end can, of course, be stated only in moral terms.

If my foregoing analysis is correct, then the difference between the effectiveness of behavior therapy and of psychoanalysis in the treatment of neurosis is not like the difference between penicillin and aspirin in the treatment of pneumonia. They are not competitive therapeutic methods whose relative value is a matter of medical judgment. Instead, the difference between them is more like that between closed and open societies, or between religious orthodoxy and scientific rationalism. Behavior therapy and psychoanalysis are essentially two rival systems of belief—one full of order, simplicity, and oppression; the other full of diversity, complexity, and freedom—whose relative value is a matter of moral judgment. Which state is more admirable, Sparta or Athens? Which man, Napoleon or Camus?

Perhaps another qualification is necessary here. Behavior therapy may be, but need not be, used coercively. Its use *could* be limited to situations in which the patient is free to begin or to stop treatment as he sees fit. Such a patient would, of course, be no more coerced than any person who purchases a dentist's services, which may also be unpleasant. But I am not aware that behavior therapists seek such limitations on the use of their method.

In contrast, psychoanalysis cannot, in my opinion, be used coercively. As soon as it is, it ceases to be psychoanalysis. To be sure, the word "psychoanalysis," like other good words such as "liberty" and "love," is often misemployed to describe and legitimize coercive methods of psychotherapy; such is the fate of words. Freud's position on this issue is, however, clearly on record: ". . . There must be some limits set to the extent to which psychological influence may be used," he wrote in 1905, "and I respect as one of these limits the patient's own will and understanding." This unconditional respect for the patient's "own will and understanding" is what distinguishes psychoanalysis, both ethically and in practice, from other methods of psychotherapy.

To Be Uncoerced

The overenthusiastic advocates of both behavior therapy and psychoanalysis may, in their zeal, injure the dignity and retard the self-determination of man. Each is willing, indeed eager, to enlist the police power of the state to ensure the supremacy of his doctrines and practices. Neither is content to offer his ideas and services in the free marketplace and allow the consumer uncoerced choice from a variety of competing "therapeutic wares."

Our Founding Fathers sought to protect the society they were building from just this kind of mischief. They decreed that Church and State be separated by an invisible but impenetrable wall. It now behooves the people to protect themselves from alliances between psychiatric creeds and the state, lest a monopolistic mental-health ethic be brought into being by the majority, and imposed on the minority. If we want the consumer of mental health services to be free to choose what he wants for himself—rather than be forced to submit, at the hands of experts backed by the police power of the state, to what the government wants for him—then we must erect a wall separating Psychiatry and the State.

It will be noted that behavior therapists, despite their exclusive reliance on the streamlined techniques of learning theory, lean heavily on such time-tested methods as suggestion, muscle relaxation, hypnosis, and even narco-hypnosis as parts of their therapeutic approach. Having chased the magic element from their temples of healing, they have permitted its return through the back door. Nor can they dispense with the all-important factor of a wholesome doctor-patient relationship, including the contraband of positive transference smuggled into the treatment situation. This is attested also by followers and friendly critics familiar with Wolpe's approach to his patients. They have pointed to his forceful, dynamic personality, and to his strong faith in the validity of his principles and procedure—which is in turn apt to inspire the same faith in his patients. In short, he is depicted as a charismatic healer in disguise. It is interesting to note Wolpe's retort to such a charge: "If faith were all that is responsible for the results of behavior therapy, such results would occur under all conditions and not only in the conditions our theory predicts."

A few more examples of the controversy touched off by the behaviorist challenge are appropriate here. Predictably, criticisms issuing from the psychoanalytic camp vary according to the critic's position vis-a-vis a by now more or less defunct Freudian orthodoxy.

E. L. Zetzel, formerly of Maudsley Hospital, London, is honorary secretary of the International Psychoanalytic Association. Following are some of her remarks in H. J. Eysenck's monograph The Effects of Psychotherapy:

It is common knowledge that many neurotic conditions appear to improve without formal therapeutic intervention. For example, the rapid symptomatic improvement of neurotic soldiers removed from combat areas is too well known to merit comment. Do we, however, accept symptomatic improvement contingent on substantial retreat from the physical, emotional, and intellectual challenges intrinsic to human growth and development as evidence for recovery from neurotic illness? The young girl who becomes anxious on receiving her first proposal may indeed master her conflict and go on to a successful marriage. Sometimes she develops severe neurotic symptoms which may or may not respond to psychotherapy. She may, however, also "recover spontaneously" by increased inhibition. Though her symptoms disappear, she avoids men. She never marries; she supports her aging mother, and goes to an occasional movie with similar "girls" in her office. Is this recovery, or an unnecessary, even tragic waste?

The human mind is capable of a wide range of response to both internal and external challenge. Some of these constitute genuine growth and substantial mastery of conflict. Some involve symptom formation. Some, finally, lead to substantial retreat and constriction of horizons. Symptoms which include manifest anxiety or depression typically characterize developmental, situational, or regressive emergencies. They seldom persist indefinitely but tend towards a state in which homeostasis on a higher, equal, or lower plane of adaptation is achieved. This typically includes amelioration of subjective distress. It need not, however, imply genuine improvement in respect to emotional maturity or realistic achievement.

Such considerations present serious problems in the evaluation of Dr. Eysenck's quoted 70 percent spontaneous improvement. The studies he quotes, for example, make no differentiation between the nature and severity of presenting symptoms and the quality and rate of spontaneous recovery. The very fact, for example, that neurotic patients could be included in an untreated control group is not without significance. That these patients were capable of remaining in the community without treatment or support suggests a bias towards the milder forms of symptomatic distress. A question must therefore be asked as to whether the effects of therapy should be tested against an undifferentiated rate of spontaneous symptomatic remission. Is it not, rather, essential that the patients subjected to therapy be compared with a strictly comparable control group? Dr. Eysenck makes this very suggestion in his discussion of behavior therapy but does not apply it to the evaluation of psychoanalysis and related methods. What is sauce for the goose is sauce for the gander! Validation of a therapeutic tool depends on objective investigation of the prognosis of the course of illness in the absence of treatment. If a significant number of patients marked as "controls" are biased in one or the other direction, the null hypothesis may not justifiably be cited. To be specific, if the patients treated by a method of therapy belong not in the happy 70 percent but in the less fortunate 30 percent group who do not recover spontaneously, a control group weighted towards the 70 percent end of the scale would be misleading as a basis for evaluation.

Psychoanalysis is no panacea. Its success is not to be measured by one-word definitions such as "improvement" or "recovery." Successful analysis, moreover, does not safeguard the individual from future anxiety, depression, or transient symptom formation. It implies, rather, a positive attitude towards human experience both painful and pleasant. It may be agreed that evaluation of results which relate not to specific symptoms but to a wide range of functions presents a difficult challenge. The criteria in essence concern the degree to which treated individuals have become more capable of reaching their own potential for achievement, personal relations, and the capacity for happiness. The complexity of this task does not justify the use of such simple criteria as symptomatic remission and superficial adaptation, which may be meaningless in the light of these considerations.

Despite this reservation I would not be willing to dismiss studies using certain objective criteria of improvement if the other prerequisites for a satisfactory experimental design were carefully carried out. To be specific, if the success of therapeutic psychoanalysis in respect to disabling neurotic symptoms is the variable under investigation, several conditions must be fulfilled. First, the definition of "psychoanalysis" must be correctly formulated. It is here that Dr. Eysenck's misrepresentation of psychoanalysis must be considered. He presents an erroneous definition, implying that psychoanalysts consider that since neurotic symptoms derive from early childhood experience they are to be regarded as relatively permanent. He suggests that psychoanalysts believe: "They can only be treated by psychotherapy which uncovers the root of the disorder, using psychoanalysis, a method based on Freudian theory." While the contemporary psychoanalyst would agree that certain neurotic disorders might conform to this definition, he would by no means agree with an inference which suggested either that all of them could profit by this difficult therapeutic method. Provided, however, that the selection of patients in a statistical investigation had been made by experienced psychoanalysts—provided, in addition, that the treatment of patients included had also been carried out by satisfactory analytic technique, and provided, finally, that at least one year had elapsed subsequent to the completion of treatment before a follow-up study was commenced, I do not believe that most research-minded psychoanalysts would be averse to an objective study.

According to the above criteria, there are many pitfalls in Dr. Eysenck's interpretation of available statistics relevant to the results of psychoanalysis. Some of the evidence he presents may be considered briefly, using as a framework of reference his own comments on the interpretation of the results reported in respect to the behavior therapy which he advocates. I quote: "Referral for behavior therapy during the years in question was frequently on the basis of using it as a last resort, and after everything else had failed. This would necessarily bias the outcome against behavior therapy." With two exceptions, all the figures relevant to psychoanalysis antedated World War II. During the period in question, referrals to psychoanalytic clinics comprised in general severely disturbed patients who had not responded to other methods of therapy. It may be retrospectively suggested that this too might bias the outcome against the method of therapy under investigation. Dr. Eysenck, however, prefers to compare these results against the 70 percent spontaneous rate of remission.

"The psychologists who carried out behavior therapy were only just beginning to experiment with the technique and had not received any satisfactory form of training in these methods. Results achieved, therefore, are not representative of what well-trained behavior therapists would be able to achieve at the present time." The psychoanalytic studies reported referred to clinic results. Surely Dr. Eysenck knows that psychoanalytic clinics are mainly concerned with evaluating patients who will be psychoanalyzed by candidates in training. Such candidates have had little if any previous experience in this technique. The results reported may therefore have been influenced not only by the disturbance of the patients but also by the inexperience of the analysts. They may not be representative of the results obtainable by qualified psychoanalysts in the treatment of carefully selected patients today.

Jules Masserman, professor of psychiatry and neurology at Northwestern University Medical School and past president of the American Academy of Psychoanalysis, is less sanguine in his defense of the analytic cause. In the debate sponsored by the Psychiatric Tribune *(April 18, 1973, p. 16) he notes that psychiatric theory is indeed "capable of exploring or predicting human conduct. It therefore proves of great heuristic value." Yet he readily admits that "psychoanalytic metapsychology has not fulfilled its early promise"; psychoanalysis as a clinical theory is difficult to evaluate because "no two practitioners conduct therapy in accordance with the cult or school to which they profess to belong." Masserman therefore takes issue with the term "schools" of psychoanalysis and suggests the term "biodynamics" as the overall designation of his brand of treatment. Nevertheless, he still considers himself a psychoanalyst, provided that the term no longer implies "a rigid dogma, eliticist pretensions and stereotyped therapy." He also feels that with "comprehensive revisions, what can be retained as rational and applicable in psychoanalytic research, theory and therapy will become integrated in the broader medical and social disciplines of psychiatry."*

The contributions to the Tribune controversy of such prominent representatives of the old school as Lawrence Kubie and Edward Glover are surprisingly restrained and avoid coming to grips with the major objections raised by the behaviorists. Kubie confines his remarks to attempts at conceptual clarification and concludes that "it is not yet possible to identify with precision the nature of change in the psychoanalytic process." Glover's remarks are largely polemical and add little to the substance of the debate.

Judd Marmor, professor of psychiatry at the Southern California School of Medicine and also a past president of the American Academy of Psychoanalysis, holds out the olive branch to the challengers. In his view, there need be no sharp dividing line between the analytic and the behaviorist camps. He gives the behaviorists credit for having opened the door to a new strategy of treatment and thereby enriching its effectiveness. He pleads in favor of integrating both traditions: the psychodynamic and the experimental approaches.

The following selection is from "Dynamic Psychotherapy and Behavior Therapy" by Judd Marmor, © Copyright 1971, Archives of General Psychiatry, *Vol. 24, Jan. 1971, pp. 22-28.*

In the course of psychiatric training and practice our professional identities become so intimately linked to what we have learned and how we practice that we are prone to extol uncritically the virtues of our own techniques and to depreciate defensively those techniques that are different. The dialogue that has gone on between most behavior therapists and dynamic psychotherapists has been marred by this kind of bias, and claims as well as attacks have been made on both sides that are exaggerated and untenable. Science is not served by such emotional polemics but rather by objective efforts to evaluate and extend our knowledge.

Part of the discussion that exists in discussing these two basic approaches to therapy is that they are often dealt with as though each group represents a distinct entity when, in fact, they are anything but monolithic. The various schools of thought among the dynamic psychotherapists are too well known to require elaboration. They cover a wide range from classical Freudians, to adherents of other major theorists, to eclectics who borrow from all of them, to still others who try to adapt their concepts to correspond with modern learning theories, information theory, game theory, or general systems theory.

What is less well known is that among behavior therapists also there is a broad range of differences, from adherents of Pavlov and Hull, to Skinnerians, to eclectics, and to those who lean toward information theory and general systems theory. At one end of each spectrum the theories of behavioral and dynamic psychotherapists tend to converge, while at the other end their divergence is very great. It is because adherents of these two approaches tend to define each other stereotypically in terms of their extremes that so much misunderstanding and heat are often generated between them.

It would further serve to clarify the discussion of this problem if we distinguish between investigative methods, therapeutic techniques, and theoretical formulations. A good investigative technique is not necessarily a good therapeutic technique, nor is the reverse true. By the same token, as we have long known, the success of a psychotherapeutic method for any particular condition does not in itself constitute a validation of its theoretical framework; indeed, exactly why and how any particular psychotherapeutic method works and what it actually accomplishes within the complex organization of drives, perception, integration, affect, and behavior that we call personality, is itself a major research challenge.

In the remarks that follow, therefore, I shall not concern myself with the knotty issues of the comparison of results between behavior and psychodynamic therapies or of their validation. The problem of how to measure or evaluate psychotherapeutic change is still far from clear, and a matter for much-needed research. Moreover, comparisons of results between these two approaches are unsatisfactory because different criteria of efficacy are applied, and different techniques of investigation are employed, even if complete objectivity on the part of the various protagonists could be assumed—which is doubtful!

In addition, I shall not get into the oft-argued issue of whether or not simple symptom removal inevitably leads to symptom substitution. Long before behavior therapists began to question this hoary assumption, hypnotherapists had presented evidence that symptom substitution did not always take place when a symptom was removed by hypnosis. Indeed, I would agree, on purely theoretical grounds, that symptom substitution is *not* inevitable. Earlier psychoanalytic assumptions concerning symptom substitution were based on what we now know was an erroneous closed-system theory of personality dynamics. If the conflictual elements involved in neurosis formation are assumed to be part of a closed system, it follows logically that removal of the symptomatic consequences of such an inner conflict without altering the underlying dynamics should result in some other symptom manifestation. If, however, personality dynamics are more correctly perceived within the framework of an open system, then such a consequence is not inevitable. Removal of an ego-dystonic symptom may, on the contrary, produce such satisfying feedback from the environment that may result in major constructive shifts within the personality system, thus leading to modification of the original conflictual pattern. Removal of a symptom also may lead to positive changes in the perception of the self, with resultant satisfying *internal* feedbacks, heightening of self-esteem, and a consequent restructuring of the internal psychodynamic system.

Psychodynamic theorists have been aware of this possibility for many years, dating back at least to 1946 when Alexander and French published their book entitled *Psychoanalytic Therapy*. In this volume a number of cases of brief psychotherapy are described, some of them involving only one to three interviews, following which the patients were not only dramatically relieved of their presenting symptoms but were then able to go on to achieve more effective adaptive patterns of functioning than they had previously displayed. In the years that followed this important publication, dynamic psychotherapists have become increasingly involved with techniques of brief psychotherapy and of crisis intervention, with a growing body of evidence that in many instances such interventions can have long-lasting positive consequences for personality integration.

Where I part company with most behavior therapists is not in questioning their therapeutic claims—although I would offer the caution that many of them are repeating the error of the early psychoanalysts of promising more than they can deliver— but in what I consider to be their oversimplified explanations of what goes on in the therapeutic transaction between patient and therapist. The explanations to which I refer are those which assume that the essential and central core of their therapeutic process rests on Pavlovian or Skinnerian conditioning and, incidentally, is therefore more "scientific" than the traditional psychotherapies. With these formulations often goes a conception of neurosis that seems to me to be quite simplistic. Thus, according to Eysenck, "Learning theory [note that he uses the singular—actually there are many theories of learning] regards neurotic symptoms as simply learned habits; there is no *neurosis* underlying the symptom but merely the symptom itself. *Get rid of the symptom and you have eliminated the neurosis.*" Such an explanation is like evaluating the contents of a package in terms of its wrapping, and represents a regrettable retrogression from the more sophisticated thinking that has begun to characterize dynamic psychiatry in recent years; an approach that recognizes that "psychopathology" does not reside solely in the individual but also has significant roots in his system of relationships with his milieu and with other persons within his milieu. Hence the growing emphasis on family therapy, on conjoint marital therapy, on group therapy, and on dealing with the disordered socio-economic conditions which constitute the matrix of so many personality disorders. To see the locus of psychopathology only in the individual leads to an emphasis on techniques of adjusting the individual to his environment regardless of how distorted, intolerable, or irrational that environment might be. Such an emphasis brings us uncomfortably close to the dangerous area of thought and behavior control.

However, I do not wish to overemphasize this ethical issue. The fact that a technical method may lend itself to being misused does not constitute an argument against its scientific validity. My major point is that the *theoretical* foundation of Eysenck's formulation is scientifically unsound. Even if we deliberately choose to restrict our focus only to what goes on within the individual himself, the Eysenckian point of view has profound limitations. It overlooks all of the complexities of thought, symbolism, and action which must be accounted for in any comprehensive theory of psychology and psychopathology. To assume that what goes on subjectively within the patient is irrelevant and that all that matters is how he behaves is to arbitrarily disregard all of the significant psychodynamic insights of the past 75 years. In saying this, I am not defending all of psychoanalytic theory. I have been as critical as anyone of certain aspects of classical Freudian theory and I am in full accord with those who argue that psychodynamic theory needs to be reformulated in terms that conform more closely to modern theories of learning and of neurophysiology. Current researches strongly suggest that the brain functions as an extremely intricate receiver, retriever, processor,

and dispatcher of information. A stimulus-response theory of human behavior does not begin to do justice to this complex process. It is precisely
what goes on in the "black box" *between* stimulus and response that is the
central challenge of psychiatry, and no theory that ignores the complexities
of the central processes within that "black box" can be considered an adequate one. It is to Freud's eternal credit, regardless of the limitations of some
of his hypotheses, that he was the first to develop a rational investigative
technique for, and a meaningful key to, the understanding of this uncharted
realm that exerts so profound an influence on both our perceptions and our
responses.

Evidence from learning theories themselves reveals that neurotic disorders are not necessarily the simple product of exposure to traumatic conditioning stimuli or to the operant conditioning of responses. The work of
Pavlov, Liddell, Masserman, and others has clearly demonstrated that neurotic symptoms can ensue when an animal is faced with incompatible
choices between simultaneous approach and avoidance reactions, or with
confusing conditioned stimuli which it is unable to differentiate clearly.
This corresponds to the psychodynamic concept of conflict as being at the
root of the vast majority of human neurotic disorders. Once such a neurotic
conflict is set up in a human being, secondary elaborations, defensive adap-
tations, and symbolic distortions may become extensively and indirectly
intertwined with almost every aspect of the individual's perceptual, cognitive, and behavioral process.

A behavioral approach alone cannot encompass these complexities.
Granting that Skinnerians include verbal speech as an aspect of behavior
that may require modification, what shall we say about subjective *fantasies*,
concealed *thoughts*, and hidden *feelings?* Are they totally irrelevant? What
about problems involving conflicts in value systems, disturbances in self-
image, diffusion of identity, feelings of anomie, or even concealed delusions
and hallucinations? Are they less important than specific symptom entities
of a behavioral nature? No comprehensive theory of psychopathology or of
the nature of the psychotherapeutic process can properly ignore these aspects of man's subjective life.

To illustrate my point that much more goes on between therapist and patient than most behavior therapists generally recognize, I should like now to
briefly focus on three contrasting behavioral therapeutic approaches: (1)
Wolpe's technique of reciprocal inhibition, (2) aversive conditioning treatment of homosexuality, and (3) the Masters and Johnson technique of treating sexual impotence and frigidity. In discussing these three approaches, I
wish to emphasize that it is not my intention to denigrate their usefulness as
therapeutic modalities or to question their results, but solely to present
some of the diverse variables that I believe are involved in their therapeutic
effectiveness.

Wolpe has elaborated his technique in many publications as well as in at least one film that I have seen. Although he considers the crux of his technique to be the development of a hierarchical list of graded anxieties which are then progressively dealt with by his technique of "reciprocal inhibition," the fact is that a great deal more than this takes place in the patient-therapist transaction in the Wolpe technique. Most significantly, in the orientation period of the first session or two the patient is not only informed of the treatment method per se, but also of the fact that it has yielded successful results with comparable patients, and it is indicated implicitly, if not explicitly, that the patient can expect similar success for himself if he is cooperative. Wolpe, moreover, is warm, friendly, and supportive. At the same time he is positive and authoritative in such a way as to reinforce the patient's expectations of therapeutic success. During this introductory period a detailed history is taken and even though the major emphasis is on the symptom with all of its manifestations and conditions for appearance, a detailed genetic history of personality development is usually taken also.

Following this a hierarchical list of the patient's anxieties is established. The patient is then taught a relaxation technique which is remarkably similar to what is traditionally employed in inducing hypnosis. After complete relaxation is achieved, the patient is instructed to create in fantasy these situations of graded anxiety beginning at the lowest level of anxiety, and is not permitted to go to the next level until he signals that he is completely relaxed. This procedure is repeated over and over again in anywhere from 12 to 60 or more sessions until the patient is able to fantasy the maximally phobic situation and still achieve muscular relaxation. Throughout this procedure the patient receives the strong implication, either explicitly or implicitly, that this procedure will cause his symptoms to disappear.

Wolpe attributes the success of his technique to "systematic desensitization" and explains it on the basis of Pavlovian counterconditioning. He asserts that any "activities that might give any grounds for imputations of transference, in sight, suggestion, or de-depression," are either "omitted or manipulated in such a way as to render the operation of these mechanisms exceedingly implausible." This kind of claim that Wolpe repeatedly makes in his writings clearly reflects his failure to appreciate the complexity of the variables involved in the patient-therapist transaction. I cannot believe that anyone who watches Wolpe's own film demonstration of his technique would agree that there are no elements of transference, insight, or suggestion in it. Indeed, one could make as plausible a case for the overriding influence of suggestion in his technique as for the influence of desensitization. In saying this I am not being pejorative about Wolpe's technique. Suggestion, in my opinion, is an integral part of every psychotherapeutic technique, behavioral or psychodynamic. It need not be overt; indeed, it probably works most potently when it is covert. Suggestion is a complex process in which elements of transference, expectancy, faith, and hope all enter. To the degree that a patient is receptive and perceives the therapist as a powerful help-giving figure, he is more likely to accept the suggestions he is being given and to try to conform to them. This process is most obvious in hypnosis but it is equally present in all psychotherapeutic techniques, where the suggestion is usually more covert. Wolpe's technique abounds in covert as well as overt suggestion. It is questionable, moreover, whether the fantasies that Wolpe has his patients create are actual substitutes for the phobic reality situations, as he would have us believe. It may well be that what is really taking place is not so much desensitization to specific stimuli, as repeated reassurance and strong systematic suggestion, within a setting of heightened expectancy and faith.

However, even the combination of *desensitization* (assuming that it is taking place) and *suggestion* do not begin to cover all the elements that are present in the Wolpe method. There is also the *direct transmission of values* as when Wolpe says to a young patient, "You must learn to stand up for yourself." According to Ullman and Krasner, Wolpe hypothesizes that if a person can assert himself, anxiety will automatically be inhibited. (Parenthetically, one might question whether this is inevitably so. One frequently sees patients who assert themselves regularly, but always with enormous concomitant anxiety.) In any event, Ullman and Krasner say: "The therapist provides the motivation by pointing out the irrationality of the fears and encouraging the individual to insist on his legitimate human rights." Obviously this is not very different from what goes on in dynamic psychotherapy and it is not rendered different by virtue of the fact, according to Ullman and Krasner, that it is "given a physiological basis by Wolpe who refers to it as excitatory." Still another variable which cannot be ignored is Wolpe's manner, which, whether he realizes it or not, undoubtedly facilitates a "positive transference" in his patients. In his film he is not only kindly and empathic to his female patient, but occasionally reassuringly touches her. Does Wolpe really believe that a programmed computer repeating his instructions to a patient who had had no prior contact with the doctor himself would achieve the identical therapeutic results?

The second behavioral technique that I would like to briefly consider is that of the aversion treatment of homosexuals. I had occasion to explore this technique some time ago with Dr. Lee Birk, of the Massachusetts Mental Health Center, who was kind enough to demonstrate his technique and go over his results with me.

Dr. Birk's method is based on the anticipatory avoidance conditioning technique introduced by Feldman and MacCulloch. The patient is seated in a chair in front of a screen with an electrode cuff attached to his leg. The method involves the use of patient-selected nude and semi-nude male and female pictures which are flashed onto the screen. The male pictures (and presumably the fantasies associated with them) become aversive stimuli by linkage with electic shocks which are administered to the leg whenever these pictures appear on the screen. On the other hand, the female pictures become discriminative stimuli signalling the safety, relief, and protection from the shocks.

In Dr. Birk's hands, as in others, the use of this method has apparently produced a striking reversal of sexual feelings and behavior in more than one half of the male homosexuals so treated. On the face of it, this would seem to be the result of a relatively simple negative conditioning process to aversive "male" stimuli, with concomitant positive conditioning to "female" stimuli.

Closer inspection will reveal, however, that the process is considerably more complex. I wonder whether most psychiatrists realize what is actually involved in such aversive conditioning. I know that I, for one, did not, until I asked Dr. Birk to permit me to experience the kind of shock that he administered to his patients—the least intense, incidentally, of the graded series that he employed. I can only say that if that was a "mild" shock, I never want to be subjected to a "severe" one! I do not have a particularly low threshold for pain, but it was a severe and painful jolt—much more than I had anticipated—and it made me acutely aware of *how strongly motivated toward change a male homosexual would have to be to subject himself to a series of such shocks visit after visit.*

The significance of this variable cannot be ignored. Once it is recognized, the results of aversive therapy, although still notable, become less remarkable. The fact is that if other forms of psychotherapy were limited only to such a select group of exceptionally motivated homosexuals, the results also would be better than average. Although one might assume that in dynamic psychotherapies the cost of therapy in itself should insure equally good motivation, this is not always the fact. Costs of therapy may not be sacrificial, or they may be borne or shared by others, but no one else can share the pain involved in the aversive conditioning process.

Again, then, it becomes clear that we are dealing with something that is much more complicated than a simple conditioning process. The patient's intense wish to change, and his faith and expectation that this very special technique will work for him—as the doctor himself implicitly or explicitly suggests—are important factors in the total therapeutic gestalt of this aversive technique, as they are in successful dynamic psychotherapies also.

But more than this, the transference-countertransference transaction between therapist and subject is also of paramount importance. Dr. Birk communicated two interesting experiences he had which underline this point. Two of his subjects who had had very favorable responses to the "conditioning" procedure suffered serious relapses immediately after becoming

angry at him. The first patient became upset because of what he considered
a breach in the privacy of his treatment. Before this, he had not only been
free from homosexual contacts for the first time in many years, but also of
conscious homosexual urges. When he became angry, he immediately went
and sought out a homosexual partner because he wanted to see "how really
good" the treatment was. Dr. Birk was aware that his patient obviously
wanted to show him up and prove that the treatment was no good. Although the patient remained improved as compared to his previous homosexual behavior, *he was never again*, despite many more conditioning
treatments, completely free from conscious homosexual urges and continued to act them out although less frequently than in the past. The second
patient became angry with Dr. Birk because he concluded that the therapist
seemed to be more interested in the results he was obtaining than he was in
the patient as a person. Immediately after expressing this irritation the patient regressed to a series of homosexual encounters.

These striking examples illustrate that a simple conditioning explanation
does not fit the complex process that goes on in such techniques of therapy.
Aversive conditioning that has been solidly established would not be expected to disappear on the basis of such experiences unless there is something that goes on centrally in the patient that is a very important factor in
the therapeutic modifications achieved. A basic aspect of this central process is in the patient-physician interpersonal relationship and it cannot and
must not be ignored even in behavior therapies. I have recently encountered
a number of instances where patients who were referred to behavior therapists failed to return to them after the initial sessions because the behavior
therapists involved ignored this essential factor and related to the patients
as though they were dealing with experimental animals.

Let us now turn to a consideration of the Masters and Johnson technique
of treating disorders of sexual potency. In many ways this technique falls
midway between a behavioral and a psychodynamic approach and illustrates one of the ways in which a fusion of both can be successfully employed. The Masters and Johnson technique is behavioral in the sense that it
is essentially symptom-focused, and that one of its most important technical
tools is desensitization of the performance anxieties of the patients.

Conceptually, however, the Masters and Johnson approach to their patients goes considerably beyond simple conditioning or desensitization processes. For one thing, Masters and Johnson recognize that the problem of
impotency or frigidity does not exist merely in the symptomatic individual
but in his relationship with his partner. Therefore, they insist on treating the
couple as a unit, and the symptom as a problem of the unit. This constitutes
a systems approach in contrast to a strictly intrapsychic or behavioral one.

Secondly, Masters and Johnson are acutely aware of the influence of psychodynamic factors on the sexual behavior of their couples. In their preliminary interviews they carefully assess and evaluate the importance of these factors, and if they consider the neurotic components or interpersonal difficulties to be too great, they may refuse to proceed with their method and will refer the couple back to their physicians for appropriate psychotherapy.

This kind of selective procedure has an effect, of course, on their percentage of successful results, as does the high degree of motivation that their patients must have to come to St. Louis (who, after all, goes to St. Louis for a two-week vacation?) and to commit themselves to the considerable expense and inconvenience that is involved.

The fact, also, that Masters and Johnson insist that the therapeutic team consist of a man and a woman reveals their sensitivity to the transference implications of their relationship to their couples. They function as a sexually permissive and empathic mother-surrogate and father-surrogate who offer not only valuable technical advice and suggestions concerning sexual behavior, but also a compassion and understanding that constitute a corrective emotional experience for their patients.

Finally, the tremendous charisma and authority of this highly publicized therapeutic team must inevitably have an enormous impact on the expectancy, faith, and hope with which their patients come to them. This cannot help but greatly accentuate the suggestive impact of the given instructions in facilitating their patients' therapeutic improvement. This improvement is then reinforced by subsequent follow-up telephone calls which, among other things, confirm to the patient the empathic interest, concern, and dedication of these parent-surrogates.

I am all too aware that these brief and summary remarks cannot begin to do justice to the three above-mentioned behavioral techniques. I hope, however, that I have succeeded in making the point that in each of these instances, complex variables are involved that go beyond any simple stimulus-response conditioning model.

The research on the nature of the psychotherapeutic process in which I participated with Franz Alexander beginning in 1958, has convinced me that all psychotherapy, regardless of the techniques used, is a learning process. Dynamic psychotherapies and behavior therapies simply represent different teaching techniques, and their differences are based in part on differences in their goals and in part on their assumptions about the nature of psychopathology. Certain fundamental elements, however, are present in both approaches.

In any psychotherapeutic relationship, we start with an individual who presents a problem. This problem may be in the form of behavior that is regarded as deviant, or it may be in the form of subjective discomfort, or in certain distortions of perception, cognition, or affect, or in any combination of these. Usually, but not always, these problems motivate the individual or someone in his milieu to consider psychiatric treatment. This decision in itself establishes an *expectancy* in the individual which is quite different than if, say, "punishment" rather than "treatment" were prescribed for his problems. This expectancy is an essential part of *every* psychotherapeutic transaction at its outset, regardless of whether the patient presents himself for behavioral or dynamic psychotherapy. The patient, in other words, is *not* a neutral object in whom certain neurotic symptoms or habits have been mechanically established and from whom they can now be mechanically removed.

Expectancy is a complex process. It encompasses factors that Frank has demonstrated as being of major significance in psychotherapy—the degree of faith, trust, and hope that the patient consciously or unconsciously brings into the transaction. It is based in large part on previously established perceptions of authority or help-giving figures, perceptions that play a significant role in the degree of receptivity or nonreceptivity that the patient may show to the message he receives from the psychotherapist. Psychoanalysts have traditionally referred to these presenting expectations as aspects of "transference," but regardless of what they are called, they are always present. Transference is not, as some behavior therapists seem to think, something that is "created" by the therapist—although it is true that transference distortions may be either increased or diminished by the technique the therapist employs. The way in which the therapist relates to the patient may reinforce certain maladaptive perceptions or expectations, or it may teach the patient that his previously learned expectations in relation to help-giving or authority figures are incorrect. The latter teaching is part of what Alexander and French called the "corrective emotional experience."

Even in "simple" conditioning studies, experimenters like Liddell, Masserman, and Pavlov have called attention to the significance of the relationship between the experimental animal and the experimenter. In humans the problem is more complex, however. Thus, a therapist who behaves in a kindly but authoritarian manner may confirm the patient's expectancies that authority figures are omnipotent and omniscient. This increases the patient's faith and may actually facilitate his willingness to give up his symptoms to please the powerful and good parent-therapist, but it does *not* alter his childlike self-image in relation to authority figures. Depending on the therapist's objectives, this may or may not be of importance.

What I am indicating, in other words, is that a positive transference facilitates symptom removal, but if the patient's *emotional maturation, rather than just symptom removal, is the goal of therapy*, what is necessary eventually is a "dissolution" of this positive transference—which means teaching the patient to feel and function in a less child-like manner, not only in relation to the therapist but also to other authority figures.

Closely related and interacting with the patient's motivations and expectancies is the therapist's social and professional role, by virtue of which the help-seeking patient endows him with presumptive knowledge, prestige, authority, and help-giving potential. These factors play an enormous role in strengthening the capacity of the therapist to influence the patient, and constitute another element in the complex fabric that makes up the phenomenon of positive transference.

Also, the *real persons* of both patient and therapist, their actual physical, intellectual, and emotional assets, and liabilities, and their respective *value systems* enter into the therapeutic transaction. Neither the patient nor the therapist can be regarded as stereotypes upon whom any particular technique will automatically work. Their idiosyncratic variables are always an important part of their transaction.

Given the above factors, a number of things begin to happen more or less simultaneously, in varying degrees, in behavior therapies as well as in dynamic psychotherapies. I have discussed these factors in detail elsewhere and will merely summarize them here. They are:

(1) *Release of tension* through catharsis and by virtue of the patient's hope, faith, and expectancy. (2) *Cognitive learning*, both of the trial-and-error variety and of the gestalt variety. (3) Reconditioning by virtue of *operant conditioning*, by virtue of subtle reward-punishment cues from the therapist, and by corrective emotional experiences. (4) Identification with the therapist. (5) Repeated *reality testing*, which is the equivalent of *practice* in the learning process. These five elements encompass the most significant factors on the basis of which change takes place in a psychotherapeutic relationship.

As I have mentioned above, suggestion takes place in all of these, covertly or overtly. Furthermore, as can be seen, a conditioning process takes place in dynamic psychotherapies as well as in behavior therapies, except that in the latter this process is intentional and more structured, while in the former it has not been generally recognized. In focusing on this conditioning process, behavior therapists have made a valuable contribution to the understanding of the therapeutic process. It is the thrust of this paper, however, that in so doing they have tended to minimize or ignore other important and essential elements in the therapeutic process, particularly the subtle but critical aspects of the patient-therapist interpersonal relationship.

In the final analysis, the technique of therapy that we choose to employ must depend on what aspect of man's complex psychic functioning we address ourselves to. If we choose to focus on the patient's overt symptoms

THE HISTORY OF PSYCHOTHERAPY

or behavior patterns, some kind of behavior therapy may well be the treatment of choice. On the other hand, if the core of his problems rests in symbolic distortions of perception, cognition, affect, or subtle disturbances in interpersonal relationships, the source and nature of which he may be totally unaware, then the more elaborate reeducational process of dynamic psychotherapy may be necessary.

Moreover, indications for one approach do not necessarily rule out the other. Marks and Gelder, and Brady, among others, have demonstrated that the use of both behavior therapy and dynamic therapy in the same patient either concurrently or in sequence often brings about better therapeutic results than the use of either approach alone. Indeed, many dynamic psychotherapists have for years been unwittingly using such a combination of approaches when they prescribe drugs for the direct control of certain symptoms while concurrently pursuing a psychotherapeutic approach.

To conclude, then, in my opinion behavior therapies and dynamic psychotherapies, far from being irreconcilable, are complementary psychotherapeutic approaches. The line of demarcation between them is by no means a sharp one. As Breger and McGaugh and others have shown, behavior therapists do many things in the course of their conditioning procedures that duplicate the activities of dynamic psychotherapists including ". . . discussions, explanation of techniques and of the unadaptiveness of anxiety and symptoms, hypnosis, relaxation, 'nondirective cathartic discussions,' and 'obtaining an understanding of the patient's personality and background.' " The process in both approaches is best explicable in terms of current theories of learning which go beyond simple conditioning explanations and encompass central cognitive processes also. The fact that in some disorders one or the other approach may be more effective should not surprise us and presents no contradiction. Just as there is no single best way of teaching all pupils all subjects, there is no single psychotherapeutic technique that is optimum for all patients and all psychiatric disorders.

Within this total context, it seems to be that behavior therapists deserve much credit for having opened wide the armamentarium of therapeutic strategies. By so doing they have forced dynamic psychotherapists into a reassessment of their therapeutic techniques and their effectiveness—a reassessment that in the long run can only be in the best interests of all psychiatrists and their patients. The psychotherapeutic challenge of the future is to so improve our theoretical and diagnostic approaches to psychopathology as to be able to most knowledgeably and flexibly apply to each patient the particular treatment technique and the particular kind of therapist that together will most effectively achieve the desired therapeutic goal.

Since completing this paper, I have come across the excellent article by Klein et al. in which many of the conclusions I have set forth are confirmed by them as a result of five days of direct observation of the work of Wolpe and his group at the Eastern Pennsylvania Psychiatric Institute. The authors also point out that as a consequence of their increasing popularity, behavior therapists are now beginning to treat a broader spectrum of more "difficult" patients (complex psychoneurotic problems, character neuroses, or border-line psychotic problems) with the result that their treatment procedures are "becoming longer and more complicated, with concomitant lowering of success rates."

Irving Bieber (b. 1908), professor of psychiatry at New York Medical College and an authority on the psychoanalytic exploration and treatment of homosexuality, made a critical appraisal of behavior therapy the topic of his presidential address to the Academy of Psychoanalysis in 1972. He noted that psychoanalysis as treatment and science cannot ignore the contributions made by other approaches. Yet he pointed to several flaws in the behaviorist position, for example, to Wolpe's notion that anxiety is the cause of neurosis, rather than a symptom. By contrast, psychoanalysis holds that anxiety itself is due to irrational ideas. The therapist's goal, therefore, is to extinguish such ideas—not just to eliminate anxiety. Side-stepping the high improvement rates claimed by the behaviorists, Bieber takes issue with Wolpe's technique of desensitization and assertiveness training and pleads for the integration of psychodynamic and pragmatically useful behavioristic principles into the psychotherapeutic approach.

The following passages are taken from his presidential address.

[Wolpe] maintains that phobias may be alleviated through self-assertion. Illustrative is his report of a 32-year-old woman who developed a phobia of knives when she was 26 years old while still in the hospital following the birth of a son. She had the persistent fear that she might use a knife to injure her child. All knives had to be removed from her home. Wolpe concluded that her fear of knives was based on her inability to assert anger; why she was so angry seemed beside the point, but she first had to learn to assert it before being desensitized about her fear of knives. As a psychoanalyst, my assumption would be that the patient had had a postpartum, depressive reaction with an accompanying fear of injuring her child, a common symptom in postpartum reactions. A frequently noted fear during the pregnancies of such women is that something will be wrong with the child. Many normal women have such a dread but it evaporates with the birth of a normal baby. The later postpartum psychiatric syndrome may include the fear of injuring one's child. In my clinical experience with patients having a reaction like the one Wolpe described, the psychodynamics almost invariably involve a masochistic need to injure a highly valued object. The masochistically derive destructiveness is a defense against unconscious expectations of hostility and predation from the mother, a fear usually generalized to include other women. Wolpe's failure to associate the symptom with a post-partum reaction especially since the symptom appeared so soon after the delivery, and his exclusion of the psychodynamic process inherent in post-partum reactions, led him to an erroneous interpretation and, I think, inappropriate therapy.

On the other hand, Wolpe has described in detail a patient with a traumatic neurosis following an auto accident. His personal dedication to her therapy and the success he achieved with her are impressive. Once a traumatic neurosis becomes chronically established, it is incredibly intractible to most other types of therapy. But it is also clear that in this patient-therapist relationship, there were present those psychoanalytic variables that Wolpe denies exist in his procedures. Marmor has pointed out that Wolpe's disclaimer against any psychoanalytic variables appearing in his work merely reflect his failure to appreciate the complexity of variables involved in the patient-therapist relationship. Says Marmor, "I cannot believe that anyone who watches Wolpe's own filmed demonstration of his technique would agree that there are no elements of transference, insight, or suggestion in it. Indeed, one could make as plausible a case for the overriding influence of suggestion in his technique as for the influence of desensitization."

If we turn the problem around and ask whether psychoanalysts, as part of everyday practice, use behavioral techniques, I would say we do—at least I do. For example, I have a patient who had never felt at ease in the presence of others, never free and relaxed except when alone. He is now in a relationship with a woman who is in love with him and completely accepts him. I have worked out with him all those private behaviors he considers to be unacceptable and I have been encouraging him to express in her presence those behaviors he is ashamed of. They are, of course, quite normal, including singing which his mother actively discouraged despite his good voice. Until recently, the patient had been unable to spend a complete night with his sweetheart. Of late, he has been able to spend weekends with her and feel comfortable. The psychoanalytic process was never even slightly disturbed by direct efforts to modify certain of the patient's anxiety-ridden behavior.

With certain obsessional patients I employ techniques that could also be described as operant conditioning. As the analysis proceeds, most obsessive patients can begin to recognize their obsessions as diversionary symptoms. I encourage them to search for the real fears being concealed by their obsessions and I teach them to approach the obsessional content as one would the manifest content of a dream; however, when a patient obsessively and repetitively produces the same unproductive material, I deliberately do not respond. This deliberate lack of response may be viewed, I suppose, as negative reinforcement: it is calculated to stimulate the patient to produce material to which I will respond. obsessive patients often attempt to engage the therapist in sterile dialogues about their intellectualized rationalizations; the more experienced analyst usually avoids these defensive quagmires by a judicious silence.

In the last decade, Skinnerian principles have been adopted in treating male homosexuality; aversive conditioning as a technique proceeds as follows: A homosexual subject is shown slides depicting erotic homosexual situations which the subject himself has chosen as particularly arousing cues. He views the scene for a given period, say 8 seconds, and is then given a rather painful electric shock through electrodes attached to his arms. The patient can prevent the shock if he presses a switch that turns off the homoerotic slide before the 8-second period is up. In the next stage of treatment, the subject cannot guarantee shock avoidance simply by switching off the slide, since shock may occur at any point during the viewing. Shock can be avoided only by immediately replacing the slide by a heteroerotic one. This technique purportedly extinguishes homosexuality and institutes heterosexuality.

The idea that the extinction of homosexuality automatically establishes heterosexuality is neither theoretically sound nor is it supported by clinical evidence. It may be compared with the spurious notion of a fixed energy system, as exemplified by the libido theory which proposes that if sexual energy does not flow into homosexual channels, it will, of necessity, flow into heterosexual channels. This same idea is reflected in the supposition that if a patient stops masturbating, he will more likely have intercourse. From psychoanalytic experience, we find that only when a homosexual patient resolves his fears about heterosexuality can he make a heterosexual adaptation. An enforced termination of homosexuality merely establishes an *asexual* adaptation.

The results reported from the treatment of homosexuality are indeed extraordinary. Feldman and McCulloch claim a 50 percent rate of reversal to heterosexuality within 5-28 sessions of aversive therapy with 8-10 booster sessions the following year. Marmor suggests that electric shock is so painful, that only those homosexuals very strongly motivated to change would undergo this treatment and that given such intense motivation for change, any procedure could be successful. The long-term homosexuality study by Bieber et al. established a positive correlation between a patient's expressed wish to change his sexual adaptation and achieve change with psychoanalytic therapy. . . .

The most recent technique to be claimed by the behavior therapists is the treatment of sexual inadequacy. The work of Masters and Johnson is too well known to warrant a description. There is no question that they and others who have replicated their work, with or without modification, are able to obtain positive results in secondary impotence and frigidity in relatively short periods. The Masters and Johnson techniques are easily learned and applied; these procedures include establishing a more intimate and sexually accomodating attitude between patient and spouse. It also seems clear that the support and permissiveness of a respected authority figure of either sex helps in the resolution of sexual anxieties. Masters and Johnson refer to their work as psychotherapy, not behavior therapy. "The basic means of treating the sexually distraught marital relationship is, of course, to reestablish communication . . . attaining skill at physical stimulation is of minor moment compared to the comprehension that this is but another more effective means of marital unit communication."

One might well ask why the behavior therapists have included Masters and Johnson's work under the rubric of behavior therapy. Is it because they take a directive, instructive approach in treating sexual inadequacy? If so, why are their methods considered behavioral while conventional supportive, directive therapy is not? Does the fact that Masters and Johnson engage the patient in direct behavioral experience classify their methods as behavior therapy? Analytic group therapy also engages the patient in direct experience. . . .

Bieber closes his critique of behavior therapy with the credo of the psychoanalyst:

From its earliest history, psychoanalysis opted for more than symptom removal. As it developed, psychoanalytic therapy became progressively longer in duration. Psychoanalysis is oriented to a maximum reparative achievement and to reaching the maximum potential for the individual in his functioning and happiness. Ours is a humanistic therapy based on the importance of the individual. This is not to minimize the significance of removing symptoms. A physician who is called in to treat a patient suffering from pneumonia and who successfully treats her for this condition but does not examine the patient totally, might miss a small breast neoplasm which, one year later, would be inoperable. In behavioral treatment, the therapist "contracts" to treat an isolated symptom; in psychoanalysis, the thrust is to resolve as much of existing psychopathology in total personality as is possible—a critical difference between the two methods.

A sociopsychiatric paradox exists today. As a result of the immense contribution psychoanalysis has made to psychiatry, everyone now is aware of the widespread prevalence of psychiatric illness and of the urgent need for extensive therapeutic intervention. With governmental agencies looking toward limited budgets for health expenditures on the one hand, and their being put under pressure to supply broad psychiatric coverage on the other, they are necessarily directed to rapid solutions. Understandably, people are attracted to get-cured-quick therapies but, in general, only the more unrealistic sacrifice reason to wish fulfillment and seriously pursue the shortcut route. Psychoanalysis has been accused of being an antisocial and an unrealistic method because of its emphasis on the importance of the individual. Behavior therapy has made rapid gains because of its claims of a quick cure. The get-cured-quick type of climate has tended to produce a therapeutic polarization: quality therapy, which is psychoanalysis at the one end— and, on the other, the poor man's therapy, which can be almost anything else.

As I stated at the outset, we psychoanalysts welcome innovations that promise to facilitate treatment, and behavior therapy has developed ways of treating discrete sequences of pathological behaviors, i.e., symptoms. Stimulus-response learning theory may be of value to some of us as a way of ordering our observations or planning therapeutic strategies. Some of the behaviorist practices are easy to incorporate into existing psychoanalytic theory and practice. This sort of influence, however, has only to do with technique and is conceptually quite periphereal to dynamic psychiatry. Psychoanalysis is not likely to be significantly altered by the techniques of behavior therapy.

A disconcerting feature of this controversy is the lack of meaningful communication between the two camps. Psychoanalysis, humanistic psychologists, and existentialists are apparently loath to tangle with the formidable statistical arguments marshaled by Eysenck and his associates. This may be one of the reasons the analysts have failed to take issue with one of the basic premises of the challengers. They seem tacitly to accept the proposition that behavior therapy is indeed as good as psychoanalysis in effecting symptom removal, if not better. In failing to come to grips with this argument, analysts may appear to admit that symptom removal is the only available indicator of change amenable to quantitative evaluation and that it is indeed this question that the controversy is all about.

However, every experienced therapist—and every patient who has experienced relief as a result of psychotherapy—knows full well that quantifiable criteria are not the only ones by which the success or failure of a given treatment, psychoanalytic or otherwise, may be measured. Psychotherapy has made it its business to reach aspects of human personality which are beyond the scope of the behaviorist approach. The behaviorist views the patient by tunnel vision, as it were, or through the narrow peephole of laboratory observation to which he is geared. In so doing, he cannot possibly encompass the totality of man. Thus Eysenck and his followers are caught in a predicament of their own making. It is the kind of plight in which a nineteenth-century physicist would find himself if he were to try to measure atomic radiation with a fever thermometer. On failing to register any change in temperature, he would jump to the conclusion that atomic radiation is ineffectual—or indeed nothing but an illusion or fraud.

Another consequence of the deliberately restricted behaviorist frame of reference is the difficulty in doing justice to the ever present element of suggestion or doctrinal compliance, to Robert Rosenthal's "Pygmalion effect," arising from their approach. (See also the Epilogue to this volume.) To be sure, Wolpe and his associates know full well how to make the best use of the dynamics of transference and countertransference in their approach, but these phenomena have remained largely outside their simplified stimulus-response scheme. As a result, behaviorists are apt to ignore the fact that such "extraneous" influences as transference or doctrinal compliance may become significant sources of error in their attempts to arrive at an objective assessment of the different results obtained in control groups, in placebo procedures, and in self-reports elicited from patients.

It should be recalled that much the same tendency to contamination by doctrinal compliance has vitiated the bona fide claims made by generations of psychotherapists of a past era.

A valiant attempt at an objective study of the effects of behavior therapy has been made by a task force instituted in 1973 by the American Psychiatric Association. Their report came out with a cautiously favorable verdict, without trying, however, to sort out the part played by primarily behaviorist strategies versus such nonspecific factors as suggestion or doctrinal compliance.

On the negative side, the task force called attention to the short period of follow-up observations available so far, to the need for more rigorous training of behavioral therapists, to the ethical problems of coercive control, and to the nontherapeutic use of punishment with its attendant risk of rationalizing sadistic behavior on the part of the therapist. The report also noted the limitations of behavior therapy in patients going through existential crisis. Their conclusion: "Certain kinds of problems treated by dynamic psychotherapy are simply not appropriate candidates for behavior therapy."

chapter 27

Psychoanalysts
Rediscover the Body

SELECTIONS FROM W. REICH AND F. PERLS

Wilhelm Reich (1897-1951), one of Freud's early followers, discovered the body in a circuitous way. While Freud described neurosis as a result of intrapsychic conflict and focused his attention on the "psychic apparatus," Reich was struck by the somatic concomitants of the inner struggle. Sexual tension, rage or anxiety are expressed in a variety of vegetative symptoms and, above all, in the patient's skeletomuscular system. This is apt to develop over the years into what Reich termed the "armor-plating" of character. In effect, this armor-plating becomes one of the major features of character neuroses and a key to the formation of diverse characterological types. However, the principal source of frustration and neurotic disturbance is the damming up of libido—of what Reich later described as "orgasmic" or "orgone energy." If unrelieved, such a stasis leads to orgasmic impotence and calls for special techniques of orgone therapy and indeed for a radically new departure of "sexual economy" in society at large.

The further pursuit of these ideas led Reich to the invention of his notorious "orgone box," to his clash with the Food and Drug Administration, to his imprisonment, and to his ultimate psychotic breakdown. Nevertheless, Reich's work had a major impact on a whole generation of "Reichian" analysts and helped to usher in the sexual revolution of the sixties and seventies.

The following selection is taken from Chapter XIII of Character Analysis, *third enlarged edition, by Wilhelm Reich, translated by R. Carfagno, reprinted by permission of Farrar, Straus and Giroux, Inc., 1945, 1949, and 1972, by Mary Boyd Higgins, as Trustee of the Wilhelm Reich Infant Trust Fund.*

Pleasure, Anxiety, Anger, and Muscular Armor

In character-analytic practice, we discover the armor functioning in the form of a chronic, frozen, muscular-like bearing. First and foremost, the identity of these various functions stands out; they can be comprehended on the basis of *one* principle only, namely *of the armoring of the periphery of the biopsychic system.*

Sex-economy approaches these problems from the point of view of the psychic function of the armor and, in this respect, it has something to say. It proceeds from the practical demand of restoring the patient's freedom of vegetative movement.

In addition to the two primary affects, sexuality and anxiety, we have a third affect, *anger* or, more accurately, *hate.* As in the first two affects, here too we must assume that, in expressions such as "boiling with anger" and "consuming anger" to describe anger which is not discharged, the vernacular reflects an actual biophysiological process. It is our opinion that the full scale of affects can be comprehended on the basis of these three basic affects. All more complicated affect impulses can be deduced from these three. However, it will have to be proven whether and to what extent the anger affect can be deduced from the vicissitudes of the first two affect impulses.

We found that sexual excitation and anxiety can be comprehended as two antithetical directions of current. How is the function of hate related to the two primary affects?

Let us proceed from the clinical study of the *character armor.* This concept was created to offer a dynamic and economic comprehension of the character's basic function. According to the sex-economic view, the ego assumes a definite form in the conflict between instinct (essentially libidinal need) and fear of punishment. To carry out the instinctual inhibition demanded by the modern world and to be able to cope with the energy stasis which results from this inhibition, the ego has to undergo a change. The process we have in mind, though we are talking about it in absolute terms, is definitely of a causal nature. The ego, i.e., that part of the person that is exposed to danger, becomes rigid, as we say, when it is continually subjected to the same or similar conflicts between need and a fear-inducing outer world. It acquires in this process a chronic, automatically functioning mode of reaction, i.e., its "character." It is as if the affective personality armored itself, as if the hard shell it develops were intended to deflect and weaken the blows of the outer world as well as the clamoring of the inner needs. This armoring makes the person less sensitive to *unpleasure* but also restricts his libidinal and aggressive motility and thus reduces his capacity for achievement and pleasure. We say the ego has become less flexible and more rigid; and that the ability to regulate the energy economy depends upon the extent of the armoring. We regard orgastic potency as a measure of this ability, since it is a direct expression of vegetative motility. The character armoring requires energy, for it is sustained by continual consumption of libidinal or vegetative forces, which otherwise (under the condition of their motor inhibition) would produce anxiety. This is how the character armor fulfills its function of absorbing and consuming vegetative energy.

When the character armor is broken down through character analysis, bound aggression regularly rises to the surface first. But is the oft-mentioned binding of aggression or anxiety *concretely* represented?

If, further along in the character analysis, we succeed in freeing the aggression bound in the armor, the result is that anxiety becomes free. Anxiety, then, can be "transformed" into aggression and aggression into anxiety. Is the relation between anxiety and aggression analogous to that between anxiety and sexual excitation? It is not easy to answer this question.

To begin with, our clinical investigations reveal a number of peculiar facts. The inhibition of aggression and psychic armor go hand in hand with increased tonus; sometimes there is even a rigidity of the musculature of the extremities and the trunk. Affect-blocked patients lie on the couch as still as boards, wholly rigid and immobile. It is not easy to bring about a change in this kind of muscle tension. If the analyst tries to persuade the patient to relax, the muscle tension is replaced by restlessness. In other cases, we observe that patients make various involuntary movements, the inhibition of which immediately engenders feelings of anxiety. On the basis of these observations, Ferenczi was inspired to develop his "active technique of interference." He recognized that the hindering of the chronic muscular reactions increases the stasis. We agree with this, but we feel that there is more to be inferred from these observations than quantitative changes in excitation. It is a matter of a functional identity between character armor and muscular hypertonia or muscular rigidity. *Every increase of muscular tonus and rigidification is an indication that a vegetative excitation, anxiety, or sexual sensation has been blocked and bound.* When genital sensations arise, some patients succeed in eliminating or weakening them through motor restlessness. The same holds true in the absorption of feelings of anxiety. In this connection, we are reminded of the great importance motor restlessness has in childhood as a means of discharging energy.

It is often observed that there is a *difference* in the state of muscular tension *before* and *after* a severe repression has been resolved. Usually, when patients are in a state of resistance, i.e., when an idea or an instinctual impulse is barred from consciousness, they sense a tension in the scalp, the upper thighs, the musculature of the buttocks, etc. If they succeed in overcoming this resistance on their own or it is resolved by the analyst through correct interpretation, they feel suddenly relieved. In such a situation a female patient once said: "It is as if I had experienced sexual gratification."

We know that every remembrance of the content of a repressed idea also brings about psychic relief. However, this alleviation does not constitute a cure, as the uninitiated believe. How does this alleviation come about? We have always contended that it is brought about by a discharge of previously bound psychic energy. Let us disregard the alleviation and the feeling of gratification which are connected with every new realization. Psychic tension and alleviation cannot be without a somatic representation, for tension and relaxation are biophysical conditions. Until now, apparently, we have merely carried over these concepts into the psychic sphere. Now it has to be proven that we were right in doing this. But it would be wrong to speak of the "transfer" of physiological concepts to the psychic sphere, for what we have in mind is not an analogy but a real identity: the unity of psychic and somatic function.

Every neurotic is muscularly dystonic, and every cure is directly manifested in a "relaxation" or improvement of the tonus of the musculature. This process can be observed best in the compulsive character. His muscular rigidity is expressed in awkwardness; unrhythmical movements, particularly in the sexual act, lack of mimetic movement, a typically taut facial musculature which often gives him a slightly mask-like expression. Also common to this character type is a wrinkle stretching from above the side of the nose to the corner of the mouth, as well as a certain rigidity in the expression of the eyes, caused by the rigidity of the eyelid musculature. The musculature of the buttocks is almost always tense. The typical compulsive character develops a general muscular rigidity; in other patients this rigidity is paired with a flabbiness (hypotonus) of other muscle areas, which does not, however, reflect relaxation. This is frequently seen in passive-feminine characters. And then, of course, there is the rigidity in catatonic stupor which accompanies complete psychic armoring. This is ordinarily explained as disturbances of extrapyramidal innervations. We have no doubt that the related nerve tracts are always involved in changes of muscular tonus. In this innervation, however, we again perceive only a general disturbance of function which is expressed through it. It is naive to believe that something has been explained when the innervation or its path has been ascertained.

The psychic rigidity of post-encephalitics is not the "expression" of muscular rigidity, nor does it result from it. Muscular rigidity *and* psychic rigidity are a unit, the sign of a disturbance of the vegetative motility of the biological system as a whole. And it is an open question whether the disturbance of the extrapyramidal innervation is not itself a result of something, effective at a primary level, which has already damaged the vegetative apparatus itself, not just the affected organs. Mechanistic neurology, for example, explains a spasm of the anal sphincter on the basis of the continual excitation of the nerves belonging to it. The difference between the mechanistic-anatomical and the functional view can be easily demonstrated here: sex-economy conceives of the nerves only as the transmitters of general vegetative excitation.

The spasm of the anal sphincter, which is the cause of a number of very severe intestinal disturbances, is brought about by a fear of defecation acquired in childhood. It constitutes a block. Explaining it on the basis of the pleasure derived from holding back one's bowel movements does not appear to get to the core of the matter. Berta Bornstein describes the holding back of evacuation in a one-and-a-half-year-old child. For fear of soiling the crib, the child was in a continual state of spasm and was able to sleep at night only in a crumpled-up sitting position with clenched hands. The muscular pushing back and holding back of feces is the prototype for repression in general and is its initial step in the anal zone. In the oral zone, repression is manifested as a tightening of the musculature of the mouth and a spasm in the musculature of the larynx, throat, and breast; in the genital zone, it is manifested as a continual tension in the pelvic musculature.

The freeing of vegetative excitation from its fixation in the tensions of the musculature of the head, throat, jaws, larynx, etc., is one of the indispensable presuppositions for the elimination of oral fixations in general. According to our experiences in character analysis, neither the remembrance of oral experiences and desires nor the discussion of genital anxiety can have the same therapeutic value. Without it, the patient remembers but he does not experience the excitations. These are usually very well concealed. They escape notice by concealing themselves in conspicuous modes of behavior which appear to be part of the person's natural makeup.

The most important secrets of pathological displacements and the binding of vegetative energy are usually contained in phenomena such as the following: a toneless, languid, or high-pitched voice; speaking with a tight upper lip; a mask-like or immobile facial expression; even slight suggestions of a so-called baby face; an inconspicuous wrinke of the forehead; drooping eyelids; tensions in the scalp; a concealed, undetected hypersensitivity in the larynx; a hurried, abrupt, constrained manner of speech; faulty respiration; noises or movements in the act of speaking which appear to be merely incidental; a certain way of hanging one's head, of shaking it, of lowering it when looking, etc. Nor is it difficult to persuade oneself that the anxiety of genital contact does not appear so long as these symptoms in the regions of the head and neck have not been uncovered and eliminated. Genital anxiety in particular is, in most cases, displaced toward the upper part of the body and bound in the contracted musculature of the neck. A fear of a genital operation in a young girl was expressed in the way she held her head while lying on the couch. After she had been made aware of this peculiar way of holding her head, she herself said: "I am lying here as if my head were nailed to the couch." As a matter of fact, she did give the appearance of being held down by the hair by an invisible force and was not able to move.

It will be asked, and justifiably, whether these concepts do not contradict another assumption. The increased tonus of the musculature is of course a *parasympathetic*-sexual function; the decreased tonus and paralysis of the musculature, on the other hand, are a *sympathetic*-anxious function. How does this tie in with the fact than an apprehensive holding back of feces or a speech inhibition in a child go hand in hand with a muscular *contraction*? In going over the theory relating to these facts, I had to ask myself this question and, for a long time, was not able to find an explanation. However, as always happens when such difficulties crop up in the investigation of various relations, it was precisely its puzzling aspect that led to a deepening of the insight.

First of all, it had to be understood that the process of muscular tension in sexual excitation could not be the same as the process of muscular tension in anxiety. In *expectation of danger*, the musculature is tense, as if *ready for action*. Visualize a deer on the verge of taking flight. In a *state of fright*, the musculature is suddenly depleted of excitation ("paralyzed with fright"). The fact that, in the case of fright, an involuntary evacuation can take place as a result of the sudden relaxation of the anal sphincter also fits in with our concept of the relation between anxiety and the sympathetic function. In this way, a sympathetic, fear-induced diarrhea in the case of fright can be distinguished from a parasympathetic diarrhea produced by pleasure in the case of sexual excitation. The former is based on the paralysis of the sphincter (sympathetic function); the latter on increased peristalsis of the intestinal musculature (parasympathetic function). In sexual excitation, the musculature is contracted, i.e., prepared for motor action, for further contraction and relaxation. In an expectation fraught with anxiety, on the other hand, the musculature is gripped in a *continual tension* until it is released by some form of motor activity. Then, either it gives way to paralysis if the fright reaction takes place, or it is replaced by a reaction of motor flight. The musculature can, however, remain tense, i.e., not resolve itself in either of the two forms. In this event, that condition sets in which, in contrast to *fright paralysis*, can be designated as *fright rigidity* ("scared stiff"). Observation shows that, in fright *paralysis*, musculature becomes flaccid, is exhausted by excitement; the vasomotor system, on the other hand, reaches a state of full excitation; acute palpitations, profuse perspiration, pallidness. In the case of fright *rigidity*, the peripheral musculature is rigid, the sensation of anxiety is missing or is only partially developed; one is "apparently calm." In reality, one cannot move and is as incapable of physical flight as of vegetative escape into the self.

What is the lesson of these facts? *Muscular rigidity can take the place of the vegetative anxiety reaction*. To express it another way, the same excitation which, in the fright *paralysis*, takes flight internally uses, in the case of fright *rigidity*, the musculature to form a *peripheral armoring of the organism*.

It can be observed that a person operated upon under local anesthesia displays the same muscular rigidity. If voluntary efforts are made to relax, anxiety is immediately intensified in the form of palpitations and perspiration. Thus, the muscular tension that is present and is not resolved in a motor discharge consumes excitation which would otherwise appear as anxiety; in that way the anxiety is retained. In this process we recognize the prototype of the binding of anxiety through aggression which, when it too is inhibited, leads to an *affect-block*. This binding of anxiety is very familiar to us from neurotic formations.

These clinical findings are of great importance for the theory of affects. Now we have a better comprehension of the interrelation of:

1. *Character block or armor and muscular rigidity*
2. *Loosening of the muscular rigidity and the liberation of anxiety*
3. *Binding of anxiety and the establishment of muscular rigidity*
4. *Muscular tension and libidinal inhibition*
5. *Libidinal relaxation and muscular relaxation*

Before we formulate a theoretical conclusion on the basis of these findings, let us cite further clinical facts that pertain to the relation between muscle tonus and sexual tension. When, in the course of character analysis, the muscular tension begins to give way because of the loosening of the character encrustation, then—as we have pointed out—what comes to the surface is anxiety and/or aggression, or libidinal impulse. We conceive of the libidinal impulse as a flowing of excitation and body fluids toward the *periphery*, and we conceive of anxiety as a flowing of excitation and body fluids toward the *center*. The aggressive excitation also corresponds to an excitation directed toward the *periphery*, but one relating *solely* to the musculature of the extremities. If the excitation flowing in all *three* directions can be liberated from the muscular rigidity, from the increased chronic muscular tonus, then we must conclude that *chronic muscular hypertonicity represents an inhibition of the flow of every form of excitation (pleasure, anxiety, rage) or at least a significant reduction of vegetative streaming*. It is as if the inhibition of the life functions (libido, anxiety, aggression) was brought about by the formation of a muscular armor around a person's biological core. If the formation of the character has such a close relation to the tonus of the musculature, we can assume that there is a functional identity between neurotic character and muscular dystonus. We will cite additional findings which confirm this assumption; we will also cite findings that might perhaps limit the validity of the functional identity of character armor and muscular armor.

From a purely phenomenological standpoint, it is clear that *attractiveness*, i.e., sexual appeal, can be chiefly described by the relaxed quality of a person's musculature which accompanies flowing psychic agility. The rhythmicity of one's movements, the *alternation* of muscular tension and relaxation in movement, go together with the capacity for linguistic modulation and general musicality. In such people, one also has the feeling of direct psychic contact. The sweetness of children who have not been subject to any severe repressions, particularly in the anal zone, has the same basis. On the other hand, people who are physically stiff, awkward, without rhythm, give us the feeling that they are also psychically stiff, wooden, immobile. They speak in a monotone and they are seldom musical. Many of them never "loosen up"; others are induced "to let go a bit" only under conditions of intimate friendship. In this event, the trained observer can immediately ascertain a change in the tonus of the musculature. Psychic and somatic rigidity, then, are not analogous manifestations; they are functionally identical. Men and women of this kind give us the impression of being deficient in eroticism as well as anxiety. Depending upon the depth of such armoring, the rigidity can go together with more or less strong *inner* excitation.

In observing melancholic or depressive patients, one finds that they betray a stiffness in their speech and facial expressions, as if every movement were possible only through the overcoming of a resistance. In manic patients, on the other hand, all impulses appear to flood the entire personality precipitately. In catatonic stupor, psychic and muscular rigidity coincide completely; for this reason, the dissolution of this condition restores psychic and muscular mobility.

From this vantage point, it is also possible to pave the way to an understanding of laughter (the "joyous" facial expression) and sorrow (the depressive facial expression). In laughter, the facial musculature contracts; in depression, it becomes flaccid. This is entirely in keeping with the fact that muscular contraction (clonus of the diaphragm in the case of laughter, "belly-shaking laugh") is parasympathetic and libidinal, while muscular flaccidity is sympathetic and anti-libidinal.

In the so-called genital character who does not suffer from any stasis of excitation or chronic inhibition of excitation, the question arises whether he does not or cannot develop a muscular armor. This would be an argument against my thesis that, fundamentally, the character armor is functionally identical with muscular armor. For the genital character, too, has developed a "character." The investigation of such character types shows that they, too, *can* develop an armor, that they, too, have the ability to immure themselves against unpleasure and to spare themselves anxiety through an encrustation of the periphery. When this is the case, however, there is a greater austerity in bearing and facial expression. Under such conditions, sexual excitation and the capacity for sexual pleasure are negatively affected, but not necessarily the capacity for work. However, work which is usually performed effortlessly and with a feeling of pleasure is replaced by a mechanical, pleasureless performance. Therefore, a gratifying sexual life provides the best structural basis for productive achievement. The difference between the armor of the neurotic character and the armor of the genital character lies in the fact that, in the former, muscular rigidity is chronic and automatic, whereas in the latter it can be used or dispensed with at will.

The following example will illustrate the functional relationship between a character attitude and muscular tension and vegetative excitation. The character analysis of a patient was marked by a superficiality of communication; the patient himself felt it to be "mere chatter," even when he was discussing the most serious matters. This superficiality, it soon became clear, had become the central character resistance. What better means of destroying every affective impulse! To begin with, the analysis revealed that the "chatter" and "superficiality" represented an identification with his stepmother, who had the same character traits. This identification with the mother figure contained the passive-feminine attitude to the father; and the chattering was an attempt to win the homosexual object, to amuse it, to dispose it favorably, to "pet" it as one would a dangerous lion. But it also functioned as a substitute contact, for, while identifying with the mother figure, the patient had no relationship whatever to his father. He felt estranged from him, a fact which did not come out until late in the analysis. The repression of a strong aggression toward the father lay at the root of and sustained this estrangement. Hence, chattering was also the expression of passive-feminine wooing (vegetative function), the warding off of aggressive tendencies (armor function), and a compensation for the contactlessness. The psychic content of the superficiality could be formulated somewhat as follows: "I want and have to win my father over to my side, I have to please him and amuse him; but I don't at all like having to do this; I don't care a hoot about him—I hate him, deep down. I have no relationship to him at all, but I can't let this come out." In addition to these psychic attitudes, the patient's awkwardness and muscular rigidity were immediately obvious. He lay there in a way very familiar to the character analyst: stiff as a board, rigid and immobile. It was clear that every analytic effort would be hopeless until this muscular armor had been loosened. Though he gave the impression of being afraid, the patient said he was not aware of having any anxieties. In addition to the above traits, he exhibited severe states of depersonalization, and he had a lifeless feeling about himself. His highly interesting childhood experiences were not important as such or in their relation to his neurotic symptoms; at this point, solely their relationship to this armor interested us. It was a question of breaking through this armor, of extracting from it the childhood experiences as well as the moribund vegetative excitations.

To begin with, the superficiality turned out to be a "fear of depth," specifically a fear of falling. In this connection, the patient produced convincing reports that the fear of falling had indeed dominated his life. He was afraid of drowning, of falling into a mountain gorge, of falling overboard from the deck of a ship; he was afraid of riding on a toboggan, etc. It soon became clear that these anxieties were connected with and rooted in an avoidance of the typical sensations experienced in the region of the diaphragm while swinging and descending in the elevator. In my book *Die Funktion des Orgasmus* I was able to demonstrate that, in some instances, the fear of orgastic excitation is concretely experienced as a fear of falling. It will not surprise us, therefore, that the patient suffered precisely from a severe orgastic disturbance of this kind. In short, the superficiality was more than a passive attitude or an "inborn" character trait; it had a very definite function in the patient's psychic operations. It was an *active* attitude, a warding off of the "fear of depth" and the sensations of vegetative excitation. There had to be a connection between these two warded-off conditions. I reflected that *the fear of falling had to be identical with the fear of vegetative excitation*. But how?

The patient remembered that, when as a child he was on a swing, he immediately made himself stiff, i.e., cramped his muscles as soon as he sensed the diaphragmatic sensations. His muscular habitus, characterized by awkwardness and a lack of coordination, stemmed from this period. It will be of interest to the musicologist that he appeared to have no ear for music whatever. But this lack of musicality could also be traced back to other childhood experiences. In connection with the history of his contactlessness and his muscular armor, the analysis produced proof that this defect also served to ward off vegetative excitation. He remembered that his mother was in the habit of singing sentimental songs to him which tremendously excited him, put him in a state of tension, caused him to be restless. When the libidinal relationship to his mother was repressed because of disappointment in her, musicality also fell victim to repression. This was the case not only because the relationship to the mother was essentially sustained by musical experiences but also because he could not endure the vegetative excitations aroused by her singing. And this was related to excitation which he experienced in childhood masturbation and which had lead to the development of acute anxiety.

In their dreams, patients often represent their resistance to uncovering unconscious material as a fear of going into a cellar or of falling into a pit. We know that this resistance and its representation in the dream are connected, but we do not as yet understand it. Why should the unconscious be associated with depth, and fear of the unconscious with the fear of falling? This puzzling situation was solved in the following way: the unconscious is the reservoir of repressed vegetative excitations, i.e., excitations not allowed to discharge and flow freely. These excitations are experienced in one of two forms:

(1) sexual excitement and feelings of gratification, as in the case of healthy men and women; or (2) feelings of anxiety and constriction, growing more and more unpleasant, in the region of the solar plexus in the case of people who suffer from disturbances of vegetative motility. They are similar to the sensations in the region of the heart and diaphragm and in the musculature which are experienced in fright or during a rapid descent. Also to be mentioned in this connection are the sensations experienced in the region of the genitalia when one is standing on the edge of a steep precipice looking down. In this situation, a feeling of genital contraction usually accompanies the idea of falling. The fact is that, at the mere thought of danger, the organism acts as if the dangerous situation were real and withdraws into itself. In the case of fright, as I explained earlier, energy cathexes in the form of body fluids flow toward the center of the organism and thus create a stasis in the region of the genitalia and the diaphragm. In the case of falling, furthermore, this physiological process is an automatic reaction on the part of the organism. Hence, *the idea of depth and the idea of falling must be functionally identical with the sensation of central excitation in the organism.* This also enables us to understand the otherwise incomprehensible fact that swinging, rapid descents, etc., are experienced by so many people with a mixture of anxiety and pleasure. According to sex-economic theory, anxiety and pleasure are twins, sprung from one stem and later opposed to one another. To return to our patient: it is objectively justified to describe his fear of the unconscious as being identical with his fear of depth. From the point of view of sex-economy, therefore, we see that our patient's superficiality was an active character attitude for the avoidance of vegetative excitations of both anxiety and pleasure.

The affect-block also falls into this category. The relation between muscular rigidity on the one hand and character superficiality and contactlessness on the other still remains to be explained. It can be said that, physiologically, the muscular armor fulfills the same function that contactlessness and superficiality fulfill psychically. Sex-economy does not conceive of the primal relation between the physiological and the psychic apparatus as one of mutual dependency but as one of functional identity with simultaneous antithesis, i.e., it conceives of the relation *dialectically.* Hence, the further question arises whether muscular rigidity is not functionally identical with character armor, contactlessness, affect-block, etc. The antithetical relationship is clear: the physiological behavior determines the psychic behavior, and vice versa. The fact that the two mutually influence one another, however, is far less important for the comprehension of the psychophysical relation than everything which supports the view of their functional identity.

I want to cite one more clinical example which shows unmistakably how the vegetative energy can be precisely liberated from the psychic and muscular armor.

This patient was characterized by his intense phallic-narcissistic warding off of the passive-homosexual impulses. This central psychic conflict was revealed in his external appearance: he had a gaunt leathery body, and his character was aggressive in a compensatory way. Great analytic effort was required to make him aware of this conflict, for he put up strong resistance to the recognition and breakthrough of the anal-homosexual impulses. When the breakthrough finally occurred, the patient suffered, to my surprise, a vegetative shock. One day he came to the analysis with a stiff neck, severe headache, dilated pupils, his skin alternating between mottled redness and pallor, and severe oppression. The pressure in his head subsided when he moved it and grew worse when he held it still. Severe nausea and feelings of giddiness completed the picture of sympaticotonia. The patient recovered quickly. The incident was a glaring confirmation of the validity of my views on the relation between character, sexual stasis, and vegetative excitation. It seems to me that these findings also provide an insight into the problem of schizophrenia, for it is precisely in psychoses that the functional relations between the vegetative and the characterological components are so typical and so conspicuous. And there is good reason to believe that the new perspective which we have outlined here will one day provide a consistent and satisfactory explanation of these relations. What is new here is not the knowledge that psychic apparatus and vegetative system are related to one another, or that they have a mutual functional relation. What is new is:

1. The basic function of the psyche is of a sex-economic nature.

2. Sexual excitation and sensations of anxiety are identical and antithetical at one and the same time (i.e., they derive from the same source of the biopsychic organism but flow in opposing directions) and they represent the irreducible basic antithesis of vegetative functioning.

3. The formation of the character is the result of a *binding* of vegetative energy.

4. Character armor and muscular armor are functionally identical.

5. Vegetative energy can be liberated, i.e., reactivated from the character armor and muscular armor with the help of a definite technique and, at present, only with this technique.

I should like to make it quite clear that this theory which we have developed on the basis of the clinical data derived from character analysis represents merely an initial step toward a comprehensive presentation of the functional psychophysical relations, that the still unsolved problems are incomparably more complicated, extensive, and difficult than what we have thus far achieved in the way of a solution. However, I feel that I have definitely succeeded in arriving at some fundamental formulations concerning the whole complex of problems that may very well serve to advance our knowledge of the psychophysical relations. I feel that my attempt to apply the functional method of investigation has been successful and is justified by the results. This method is diametrically opposed to the metaphysical-idealistic or mechanistic-causal-materialistic methods applied in the attempt to arrive at an applicable knowledge of psychophysical relations. At this point, however, it would lead us too far afield to set forth the fundamental epistemological objections to these methods. The sex-economic approach differs from the recent efforts to comprehend the psychophysical organism as a "totality" and "unity" in that it makes use of a functional method of investigation and regards the function of the orgasm as the central problem.

Frederick Perls received his M.D. in Berlin in 1921. Like Wilhelm Reich, he started out as a Freudian analyst, but under the influence of Kohler, Wertheimer and Kurt Goldstein developed his own school of analysis: Gestalt therapy. Neurosis, in Perls's view, results from a disorganization of an appropriate fluid balance between "figure" and "ground." What should be figure may recede into the background and what should be ground may come to the fore. This may shift an intrapsychic conflict to the somatic level, e.g., to an imbalance between agonists and antagonists in the muscular system, and lead to immobilization and "choking off" of behavior. Gestalt therapy is an extension of academic Gestalt psychology, Perls stated, which "adds the need for better bodily awareness to the Gestalt forming process." In so doing, it utilizes the insights gained to "unblock" the individual's "need-fulfilling patterns."

Perls's personal charisma, his emphasis on the here and now, on the joy of self-fulfillment and self-actualization, made him one of the prophets— and bearded gurus—to young people in the sixties and seventies. His seminars on gestalt therapy and group treatment at Esalen have greatly contributed to his reputation as a radical innovator. It was marred, however, by his intemperate attacks against psychoanalysis. A typical example is the dictum: "It took us a long time to debunk the whole Freudian crap."

The following selection is from Gestalt Therapy: Excitement and Growth in the Human Personality, *by Frederick Perls, Ph.D., M.D., Ralph F. Hefferline, Ph.D., and Paul Goodman, Ph.D., New York: Julian Press, 1951, Delta paperback 1964. It shows Perls's emphasis on the somatic concomitants of inner conflict. "Retroflexion" is one of the ways in which pent-up emotion may redirect an individual's energies "toward himself." What Perls describes as "experiments" are attempts at calling his readers' attention to uncalled-for muscular tension, lack of awareness, and so on:*

Experiment 12: Investigating Misdirected Behavior

To retroflect means literally "to turn sharply back against." When a person retroflects behavior, he does to himself what originally he did or tried to do to other persons or objects. He stops directing various energies outward in attempts to manipulate and bring about changes in the environment that will satisfy his needs; instead, he redirects activity inward and *substitutes himself in place of the environment* as the target of behavior. To the extent that he does this, he splits his personality into "doer" and "done to."

Why did he not persist as he started—that is, directing outward toward the environment? Because he met what was for him at that time insuperable opposition. The environment—mostly other persons—proved hostile to his efforts to satisfy his needs. They frustrated and punished him. In such an unequal contest—he was a child—he was sure to lose. Consequently, to avoid the pain and danger entailed in renewed attempts, he gave up. The environment, being stronger, won out and enforced its wishes at the expense of his.

However, as has been demonstrated repeatedly in recent years by a number of experiments, punishment has the effect, not of annihilating the need to behave in the way that met with punishment, but of teaching the organism to *hold back* the punishable responses. The impulse or the wish remains as strong as ever and, since this is not satisfied, it is constantly organizing the motor apparatus—its posture, pattern of muscular tonus, and incipient movements—in the direction of overt expression. Since this is what brings punishment, the organism behaves toward its own impulse as did the environment—that is, it acts to suppress it. Its energy is thus divided. Part of it still strains toward its original and never satisfied aims; the other part has been retroflected to hold this outgoing part in check. The holding back is achieved by tensing muscles which are antagonistic to those which would be involved in expressing the punishable impulse. At this stage two parts of the personality struggling in diametrically opposite directions are in a clinch. What started as conflict between organism and environment has come to be an "inner conflict" between one part of the personality and another part—between one kind of behavior and its opposite.

Do not jump to the conclusion that we imply that it would be fine if we could all without further ado "release our inhibitions." In some situations holding back is necessary, even life-saving—for instance, holding back inhaling while under water. The important question is whether or not the person has *rational grounds* for presently choking off behavior in given circumstances. While crossing a street it certainly is to his advantage if he quells any urge to contest the right-of-way with an oncoming truck. In social situations it is usually advantageous to suppress a tendency to go off half-cocked. (But if fully cocked, aimed and ready, it may be quite a different matter!)

When retroflection is under aware control—that is, when a person in a current situation suppresses particular responses which, if expressed, would be to his disadvantage—no-one can contest the soundness of such behavior. It is only when the retroflection is habitual, chronic, out of control, that it is pathological; for then it is not something done temporarily, perhaps as an emergency measure or to await a more suitable occasion, but is a deadlock perpetuated in the personality. Furthermore, since this stabilized battle-line does not change, it ceases to attract attention. We "forget" it is there. This is *repression*—and neurosis.

If it were true that the social environment remained adamant and uncompromising—if it were just as dangerous and punishable to express certain impulses now as it was when we were children—then repression ("forgotten" retroflection) would be efficient and desirable. But the situation has changed! We are not children. We are bigger, stronger, and we have "rights" which are denied children. In these drastically changed circumstances it is worth having another try at getting what we need from the environment!

When we suppress behavior, we are aware both of what we are suppressing and the fact that we are suppressing; in repression, on the contrary, we have lost awareness both of what is repressed and the process by which we do the repressing. Psychoanalysis has stressed recovery of awareness of what is repressed—that is, the blocked impulse. We, on the other hand, emphasize recovery of awareness of the blocking, the feeling that one is doing it and *how* one is doing it. Once a person discovers his retroflecting action and regains control of it, the blocked impulse will be recovered automatically. No longer held in, it will simply come out. The great advantage of dealing with the retroflecting part of the personality—the active repressing agent—is that this is within fairly easy reach of awareness, can be directly experienced, and does not depend upon guessed-at interpretations.

Theoretically, the treatment of retroflection is simple: merely reverse the direction of the retroflecting act from inward to outward. Upon doing so, the organism's energies, formerly divided, now once more join forces and discharge themselves toward the environment. The impulse which had been blocked is given the chance at last to express and complete itself and is satisfied. Then, as is the case when any genuine need of the organism is fulfilled, there can be rest, assimilation and growth. In practice, however, the undoing of a retroflection is not so straightforward. Every part of the personality comes to its defense as if to head off catastrophe. The person is overcome with embarrassment, fear, guilt and resentment. The attempt to reverse the self-aggression, to differentiate the clinch of the two parts of the personality, is responded to as if it were an attack on his body, his "nature," on his very life. As the clinched parts begin to loosen and come apart, the person experiences unbearable excitement, for the relief of which he may have to go temporarily into his clinch again. These are unaccustomed feelings which are being resurrected and he has to make approaches to them and gradually learn to tolerate and use them. At first he becomes anxious and would rather retreat into his deadened state of unawareness.

A main reason for the fear and guilt in reversing retroflections is that most retroflected impulses are aggressions, from the mildest to the cruelest, from persuasion to torture. To let these loose even into awareness is terrifying. But aggression, in the broad sense of its clinical usage, is indispensable to happiness and creativity. Furthermore, reversing the retroflection does not manufacture aggression that was not already there. It was there—but applied against the self instead of against the environment! We are not denying that aggression may be pathologically misused against objects and other persons, just as it is pathologically misused when directed steadfastly against the self. But until one can become aware of what one's aggressive impulses are and learn to put them to constructive use, they are *certain* to be misused! As a matter of fact, it is the act of repressing them—the setting up and maintenance of the grim clinch of the musculature—that makes these aggressions seem so wasteful, "anti-social," and intolerable. Once they are allowed to develop spontaneously in the context of the total personality, rather than being squeezed and suffocated in the remorseless clinch of retroflection, one puts quite a different and more favorable evaluation upon his aggressions.

What is also feared in releasing a blocked impulse is that one will then be completely frustrated—for retroflection does give at least partial satisfaction. A religious man, for instance, unable to vent his wrath on the Lord for his disappointments, beats his own breast and tears his own hair. Such self-aggression, obviously a retroflection, nevertheless *is* aggression and it *does* give some satisfaction to the retroflecting part of the personality. It is aggression that is crude, primitive, undifferentiated—a retroflected childish temper tantrum—but the part of the personality that is attacked is always there and available for attack. Self-aggression can always be sure of its victim!

To reverse such a retroflection in one fell swoop would mean that the person would then attack others in ways just as ineffectual and archaic. He would rouse the same overwhelming counter-aggression that led him to retroflect in the first place. It is some realization of this which makes even the imagined reversal of retroflections productive of so much fear. What is overlooked is that the change can be made in easy stages which gradually transform the whole situation as they proceed. One can, to start with, discover and accept the fact that he does "take it out on himself." He can become aware of the emotions of the retroflecting part of his personality— notably, the grim joy taken in administering punishment to himself. This, when he achieves it, represents considerable progress, for vindictiveness is so socially disesteemed as to be most difficult to acknowledge and accept even when supposedly one spares others and directs it solely against oneself. Only when accepted—that is, when it is reckoned with as an existing, dynamic component of one's functioning personality—does one reach the possibility of modifying, differentiating, redirecting it into healthy expression. As one's orientation in the environment improves, as one's awareness of what one genuinely wants to do becomes clearer, as one makes approaches which are limited try-outs to see what will happen, gradually one's techniques for expression of previously blocked impulses develop also. They lose their primitive, terrifying aspect as one differentiates them and gives them a chance to catch up with the more grown-up parts of the personality. Aggression will then still be aggression, but it will have been put to useful tasks and will no longer be blindly destructive of self and others. It will be expended as the situation demands, and not accumulated until one feels that he sits precariously atop a seething volcano.

Experiment 13: Mobilizing the Muscles

In this experiment we come to grips with the mechanics of retroflection. When your approaches to objects and persons in the environment are frustrated or evaluated as too dangerous to continue, so that you turn your aggressions inward against yourself, the muscular motions by which you do this may retain their form or be modified to conform to the substitute objects. If with your fingernails you scratch your own flesh, this is precisely what, without the retroflection, you would do to someone else. On the other hand, when you control an urge to pound someone with your fist by contracting the antagonistic muscles and thus immobilizing your arm and shoulder, the retroflection does not consist of pounding yourself; it is instead, a statically maintained counteraction. It is a doing of one thing and also its opposite at the same time in such fashion as to achieve a net effect of zero. So long as the conflict endures, the use of the arm for other purposes is impaired, energies are squandered, and the state of affairs is the same as the military situation of a stabilized battleline. Here the battleline is within the personality.

Retroflections are manipulations of your own body and impulses as substitutes for other persons and objects. Such self-manipulation is unquestionably useful and healthy when it constitutes withholding, biding your time, adjusting yourself to the surroundings, in situations where you need to exercise prudence, caution, selectivity, in the service of your own over-all best interests. The neurotic abuse is when you have once and for all *cen-sored* a part of yourself, throttled and silenced it, so that it may no longer lift its voice in your aware personality. But no matter how squeezed, choked off, clamped down upon this censored part may be, it still exerts its pressure. The struggle goes on. You have simply lost awareness of it. The end-result of such censoring, whether recognized or not, is invariably a more or less serious psychosomatic dysfunction: impairment of powers of orientation or manipulation, ache, weakness, or even degeneration of tissues.

Consider how ineffectual is retroflection in the following example. A patient undergoing treatment may display an extraordinary frequency and amount of weeping, perhaps several outbursts in a single session. The crying occurs whenever one might expect the patient to come forth with a reproach or some other kind of attack. What happens is this: the patient feels like attacking, but, not daring to, retroflects the attack against himself, feels hurt, and bursts into tears as if to say, "See how harmless and how abused I am." The original aim, of course, is to make some Person X, perhaps the therapist, cry. When this cannot be achieved, the crying spells and the chronic resentment persists until the aggression can be reorganized and turned outward.

Other cases may have frequent headaches which are, as the Freudians would say, "converted" crying. Here the mystery of the "conversion-process" is readily solved when one recognizes that the headaches, like most other psychosomatic symptoms, are retroflected motor activity. They are produced by *muscular tensing against a swelling impulse.*

If you open a water tap slightly and attempt with a finger to hold back the water against the pressure in the pipe, you find this increasingly difficult. There is a strict analogy between this and many internal conflicts where you squeeze or hold back an urge to defecate, to have an erection or to become tumescent, to vomit or belch, etc. If you clench your fist hard, after a while it will ache from cramp. The "psychogenic" headache—or, as it used to be well called, the "functional" headache—is the same type of phenomenon. In a given instance, you start to cry, but then you control the impulse by squeezing your own head so as not to be a sissy or to give others the satisfaction of seeing they have made you cry. You would like to squeeze the life out of Person X who has so upset you, but you retroflect the squeezing and use it to hold back your crying. Your headache is nothing but your experience of the muscular straining. If you de-tense the muscles, you will start to cry and, simultaneously, the headache will disappear. (Not all headaches, of course, are produced in this way; also, crying may be inhibited by tensions other than those in the head—for example, by tightening the diaphragm against the clonic movements of sobbing.)

We repeat once more our opposition to premature relaxation. Suppose you manage to relax the muscles of your neck, brow, and eyes and burst out crying. This by no means solves the original conflict. It merely by-passes it. An important part of the symptom—namely, the tendency to aggressive squeezing—goes unanalyzed. When someone has hurt you, there is the wish to retaliate by hurting him. This tendency gets some expression—you do some hurting—even if it is but the retroflected squeezing which makes you the victim of your own aggression as well as of that of the other person. If, instead of reversing the retroflection, you simply give up the retroflecting behavior—in this case, your self-squeezing—you can succeed only by somehow also getting rid of your proneness to be hurt. This requires a technique more serious than retroflection, namely desensitization. Not wanting to hurt depends on not being hurt, which depends on ceasing to respond emotionally to the environment. This process can go as far as depersonalization. Admittedly, one may be *hyper*sensitive and "have one's feelings hurt" by almost everything; one has, correspondingly, a heightened urge to "hurt back." The solution for this condition is reorganization of the personality, not further disorganization in the form of going numb. *The healthy organism, when genuinely attacked, fights back in a way and to a degree appropriate to the situation.*

Furthermore, when muscles are willfully relaxed, they are less at your disposal even for behavior not involved in the conflict. You lose agility, grace, and mobility of feature. This accounts for the relaxed facelessness of some "analyzed" persons. They have "mastered" their problems by becoming aloof—too aloof to be fully human.

In the healthy organism the muscles are neither cramped nor relaxed (flaccid), but in middle tone, ready for the execution of movements which maintain balanced posture, provide locomotion, or manipulate objects. In beginning the motor-muscular work of this experiment, do not relax. Later we shall amend this by saying do not relax until you can cope with the excitement which will thereby be released. If relaxation occurs prematurely and you are surprised and frightened by unblocked excitement, you will clamp against it harder than ever and experience great anxiety. With correct concentration, however, on the motor manipulation of yourself, slowly and methodically adjusting to pressures as you feel yourself exerting them, the loosening of tension will often take place as a matter of course.

From the beginning be prepared for sudden urges to break out in rage, to cry, vomit, urinate, behave sexually, etc. But such urges as you experience at the start will come from the near surface of awareness and you will be

quite able to cope with them. Nevertheless, to spare yourself possible embarrassment, it is advisable at first to perform the muscular experiments in
solitude. Furthermore, if you are prone to anxiety attacks, before attempting intensive muscular concentration, work through what you are going to
do by internally verbalizing it.

*Perls' impact on the American scene has been due more to his colorful
personality than to his theoretical pronouncements. Like an Indian guru, he
attracted a growing number of disciples to his seminars in the Esalen Institute in Big Sur, California, and in other human potential centers elsewhere teaching the individual's awareness of the here and now. His principles of gestalt therapy have been adopted by countless encounter and sensitivity groups.*

chapter 28

Group Therapies: Mental Health for the Small Consumer

SELECTIONS FROM A. WOLF, S. H. FOULKES, J. L. MORENO

Groups of people were banding together for mutual support and relief from anxiety long before they knew what they were engaged in. Group therapy, like the prose diction of Moliere's Bourgeois Gentilhomme, came into being only when its grammar and syntax were spelled out and its name duly entered in the registry of available therapeutic facilities. This done, the hitherto nameless foundling had many fathers: psychoanalysts, "individual" psychologists, psychodramatists, Gestaltists and transactional analysts. Yet the proliferation of assorted group therapy movements is more than a mere fad. On the face of it, it is meant to bring the benefits of psychiatric treatment down to the level of the small consumer. It has been argued that it is in effect a product of modern marketing techniques, an attempt to meet the need for mental health care at a price the majority of patients can afford, and to do so with the limited number of professionals and paraprofessionals available for the purpose. Others have noted that the major benefit of group therapy, especially encounter groups, is derived from the closeness and intimacy the group experience can afford to the lonely, isolated city dweller in the depersonalized and alienated urban society of our age.

There is another, often neglected aspect of group therapy. It reflects the dramatic shift of authority, of the role of leadership, from parental figures to peer groups. Adolescents and young adults switch their allegiance from the paterfamilias, the school principal, and the Establishment to classmates, to the Walden II type of commune, to the "guys in the locker room," even to street gangs like Hell's Angels or the Ghetto Brothers in the Bronx. By the same token, the role once delegated to the parish priest, the religious counselor, or the supposedly all-knowing and infallible psychoanalyst is being transferred to the Group—writ large—discretely guided or even left to its own resources by a self-effacing "facilitator" or group leader.

Among the more innovative examples of the group movement are the attempts to bring about cathartic release through the acting out in a more or *less symbolic form of repressed instinctual drives through intimate body contact, as in Esalen in California, or through letting go of repressed anger or frustrated sexual impulses, as in certain forms of Reichian therapy and in Janov's "screaming cure." On the lunatic fringe, uninhibited nude marathons may serve as rationalizations for officially sanctioned group sex, heterosexual or homosexual coition, gang bangs or organized wife swapping. In these cases the scenario seems to duplicate the Dionysian revels, the Witches' Sabbath or the Black Mass of the Middle Ages—staged against the backdrop of the frenzied rock festivals of the Now Generation in Woodstock or Haight Ashbury.*

The diverse forms of the modern group therapy movement are, however, inspired by four principal schools of thought: (1) psychoanalysis; (2) eclectic, interpersonal, or Adlerian psychology; (3) existential analysis; and (4) psychodrama.

S. R. Slavson and Alexander Wolf, (with his associates E. K. Schwartz), H. Durkin, M. Grotjahn, and H. Spotnitz, are regarded as the paramount representatives of psychoanalytic group therapy in this country. For technical reasons, S. R. Slavson's pioneering works on psychoanalytic group therapy with both adults and children, e.g., The Fields of Group Therapy *(1956), and a more recent textbook* Group Therapies for Children, *published jointly with M. Schiffer (1974) cannot be included in this anthology.*

Alexander Wolf (b. 1907) has been involved in psychoanalytic group therapy since 1947. He is coauthor of Psychoanalysis in Groups *and* Beyond the Couch, *as well as of numerous articles published jointly with E. K. Schwartz, many of which have been collected by Zanvel Liff in* The Leader in the Group. *Wolf emphasizes the differences between psychoanalytic and nonanalytic group therapy. In nonanalytic therapy, the patient may submit to the group leader in terms of his early experiences with parental figures. In group analysis, such tendencies are brought out into the open, unconscious processes revealed, and the emergence of his "repressed ego" encouraged.*

The following selection, taken from Wolf's paper "The Psychoanalysis of Groups" and published in 1950, is a concise statement of principles and procedures to be followed in psychoanalytic group therapy.

The Size of the Group

The size of the group is important. It should number eight or ten. With fewer than eight members there is often not enough interpersonal provocation and activity. This will lead to lulls or dead spots in spontaneous interreaction and lessen the effectiveness of the group procedure. However, with more than ten it is difficult for both patient and analyst to keep up with what is going on. An overly large group is especially bad for the patient's morale. He is likely to feel threatened and "lost" in such a setting; what little "security" he has had in his relationship to the analyst would disappear. Too large a group might, then, immediately produce immobility. Four or five men and an equivalent number of women make up a practical working group. In my experience ninety minute sessions, meeting three times weekly are most effective.

Closed or Continuous Groups

Groups are self-perpetuating. Although there is infrequent transplanting of patients, the group never disbands entirely. Patients join and leave groups by permission of their members as well as that of the analyst. However, I shall discuss these points later in more detail.

Resistance to Joining a Group

The attitude of the prospective member is of considerably more importance than such generalizations on group formation. If he does not already know it, the analyst soon discovers that the average person views with prompt alarm the mere suggestion that he affiliate himself with eight or nine unknown neurotic patients. For the purposes of this discussion we can assume that candidates for group membership fall into three classes: the resistant (the majority), the enthusiastic, and the curious or open-minded. The latter commonly approach group analysis with the healthiest attitude. In preliminary individual treatment the therapist must study and gradually break down particular resistances to joining a group. The enthusiastic may be variously motivated: from honest need for social contact to exhibitionism, voyeurism, and a search for foils for neurotic destructiveness directed toward the group. Whatever the motive, it emerges and is analyzed in the group setting.

Patients who resist entry into a group should not be pushed too hard. Their premature introduction may precipitate such anxiety or resistance that after one or two meetings they fail to return. It is wiser to inquire into and analyze their opposition beforehand. In time the majority express a willingness to give a group method a trial. Usually in the first visit I propose to the patient that at a mutually agreeable time he will join a group for further analysis.

Specifically, among the most frequently encountered objections to group affiliation are the following:

Patients shrink from what they regard as a mortifying invasion of their privacy. The idea of baring their motives and acts to strangers is so completely alien that I imagine forcing them into a nudist camp might be less abhorrent. Suspicion that their revelations might be circulated by the indiscreet augment their fears.

Certain patients want exclusive neurotic possession of the therapist. Alone with him they can relive and realize the repressed affect originally directed toward early familial figures; they will not willingly agree to share him with others.

To some the word "group" unconsciously connotes the original family, and they refuse to subject themselves once again to its trying influence. Their difficulties started years ago in a nightmarish family, and it is the epitome of a social constellation from which they once escaped. Why return to it?

Those to whom a friendly glance or an unfriendly word is devastating, who are shaken by the slightest sign of criticism, coolness or warmth, who shun the give and take of social living, resist group analysis. Why, they reason, should one sacrifice the gentle, detached, earnest and expert consideration of a private doctor for the blundering crudities and rough handling one would probably get in a group?

Some patients are unconsciously afraid that they will have to relinquish a secretly cherished neurotic trend, which the analyst will allow but the group would not tolerate. They cling to the illusion that the therapist will permit them to retain this gratifying obsessive design; they may even hope that the analyst will augment the obsession.

Others will protest at transfering from individual to group treatment because they "will get only one tenth the attention." Although member contributions may not be as professionally sound as those of the analyst, they are so intuitively significant and increasingly valid analytically that, in a sense, treatment is really multiplied by ten.

Some patients project such painful or terrifying masks onto other people that they cannot easily enter group analysis. Such individuals require a relatively long period of individual preparation. And after entering a group they have to be desensitized in stages by permitting them to enter and leave the group at frequent intervals. Usually they are able to remain for longer periods of time following each successive absence.

And finally, there are some patients who experience intolerable pangs of anxiety at the freedom with which sexual material is discussed in the group. They too must be more thoroughly prepared in individual sessions by the therapist. He must gradually and persistently probe for the affect-laden unconscious conflict whose emergence they prohibit. This should be executed so delicately that anxiety is not created. After a while the succeeding increments of insight enable patients to attend group sessions with less alarm.

The analyst must do his best to allay these and other fears. He assures the prospective group member that, initially, he is under no obligation to reveal embarrassing facts and that his privacy will, in any event, be held strictly inviolate. Group patients, he is told, know each other by their first names only. They function under a rigorous injunction of anonymity and discretion. Patients are warned against gossip with the threat of discharge from the group. While such admonition early in treatment guards against exposure outside the group, as time goes on, mutual regard and respect for the members' privacy play a major role in preserving ethical secrecy. The exclusion of psychopaths is a further guarantee that confidences will not be betrayed. The patient is always advised that, in the therapist's eleven years of group analytic experience, no member has been dropped for disclosing intimate group affairs.

For the patient who prefers to have the analyst to himself the therapist may have to clarify, in stages, the infantile demand for the possession of the isolated parent or sibling in the person of the analyst; the transferred rivalry with other group members for his exclusive attention and, the necessity, at last, of sharing with other members of this "new family" in the group a more satisyfing mutual devotion and affection. For those to whom the group unconsciously represents the traumatic original family, the therapist tries to create a most permissive atmosphere. He interrupts any early possibility of cumulative interpersonal hostility and if a clash is imminent, he intervenes gently, asking for ventilating and cathartic material like dreams, fantasies, personal difficulties, and even biographical data. He emphasizes the fact that all the members are present because, for some time earlier in their lives, they were not allowed to express their feelings; that if the group plays a prohibitive role now, it will only underscore old traumatic influences; that we must try to permit particular irrationality and not play a prohibiting role. In this manner the therapist attempts to influence each patient toward becoming an ally of the liberating, creative, expansive, and social forces in every other member and also an enemy of the repressive, destructive, contracting, and antisocial trends.

For those who fear emotional contact the therapist may have to spend considerable time in prior individual analysis building up rapport and using this tentative affective closeness as a bridge to the group. Some patients are so afraid of the possibility of a positive or negative transference to the therapist, which painfully evokes for them repressed incestuous conflict, that they try to run eagerly into group sessions after just a few individual interviews. All of this is done in the hope of damming back what appears to them to be dangerous, emerging trends. Such members try to "hide out" in the group and attempt to use the group to resist the uncovering of affect.

With regard to the supposed expertness of the therapist and the clumsiness and misguidance of the group, patients cannot be underestimated for their intuitive perception, and adjunct analytic facility. The analyst must use these qualities to common advantage. The members should be made increasingly aware of their considerable usefulness to one another. They are inclined to overestimate the parental authority in the person of the therapist and to underestimate their own production. The analyst continuously rewards each participant for spontaneous and intuitive speculation and points out how very often such prospecting leads to deep insight. Furthermore, he does not permit crude blundering which might distress others. He plays a moderating role. Gradually, as patients are rewarded with insight and respect for one another's feelings, mutual regard for what each has to offer develops.

Sometimes the benevolence of the therapist in individual treatment permits the patient to cling compulsively and for too long to a treasured neurotic pattern. The group has less of this tolerance for illness. It more vigorously demands, and usually gets a more rapid healthy response. When it puts too much pressure on a patient to abandon old forms for new, before he is able to relinquish them, the analyst must use his position to intercede in the patient's interest.

When a patient requests a description of the group he is about to join, its members are portrayed for him, as he has in turn been anonymously introduced to them. It is explained that the association may be regarded as tentative by either party. Some patients gain solace from the assurance that they may leave the group if they become overanxious or unduly disturbed while undergoing treatment. From time to time patients do drop out temporarily after a clash of transference and countertransference, but normally a few private interviews will recondition them for a return. . . .

Destructive Patterns in Group Analysis

An unfavorable situation which may arise in a group is the development of intense generalized neurotic resistance, accompanied by hostile transference and countertransference, and the formation of allies in groups of two or three, leaving some individuals pretty well isolated except for a relatively warm relationship to the therapist. Sometimes even this association becomes strained, because the patient blames the therapist for having exposed him to such a trying, antagonistic environment. Such a group must be tackled vigorously by the analyst. Otherwise it may fall apart. Attendance may become low and demoralize those present. The therapist, while taking an analytic view of absenteeism, must threaten those who stay away with being dropped. He must study transferences that force aggressors into belligerent roles and point out their illusory character. He must be equally vigilant with regard to projective devices that impel the compulsively withdrawn to retreat further or to submit to the domination of other members.

He must discover the causes for resistance to participation on deeper levels, pointing out explicitly the destructive character of particular defenses and encouraging free emotional ventilation. If the situation is unwholesome enough, he may for a while, suggest no "going around" in order to interrupt unanalyzed, aggressive attacks and propose a retreat to the second stage of treatment: the exclusive presentation of dreams and fantasies. A return to the airing of the personal, unconscious material which is interpreted with the help of the group is preparation for a new unity. All else failing, the analyst may be obliged to remove a patient here and there, one at a time, at varying intervals, introducing each retired member into a more cohesive group. Such a crisis can usually be avoided by not organizing a group with a majority of strongly sadomasochistic patients. Too many such members in the same milieu provide an unfavorable climate for the evolution of the fraternal good will that should be established early if the group is to proceed efficiently.

In my early experience with group analysis I felt a good deal of uncertainty as to the practicality of using free association and of trying to handle transference and countertransference reactions among numbers of patients. Might not a patient's resources be paralyzed by the "attacks" of others? Might his feelings of anxiety, exaggerated by mounting neurotic aggression in the group, force him into further withdrawal or irrelevant countersorties of his own? With a weak ego structure to start with, would he not beat a further psychic retreat in a setting that encourages free interpersonal, affective responses, some of which are bound to be charged with hostility? How easily might he tolerate an atmosphere in which sexual matters are freely discussed, without running for cover? However, repeated clinical experience reassured me. For a patient under inappropriate fire inevitably finds allies in the therapist and some other member or members of the group. Their support fortifies him against hurt and isolation. If a penetrating remark made in free association hits a target and makes him falter, the other members sustain him fraternally, until he can usefully tolerate insight. If an acute observation is lost on him, because it is aggressively colored and he hears only the hostility, the therapist or patients dissect what is valid from what is neurotic attack. Then the group analyses both his peculiar attention to ill-will that compels him to lose sight of what may be useful to him in terms of further self-understanding (i.e., his countertransference), and the character trend of the aggressor in terms of his projection that impels him to design his comments in such a destructive way that it becomes difficult for others to extract what is very valuable from them and to accept them. This calls for analysis of the constructive and destructive content of the latter's comments. And it also involves study of his provocative role and transference devices. Attention to these details tends to dispel anxiety. The group finds that careful exploration of psychic recesses is ultimately less terrifying than shutting its eyes to them, so that the therapist's insistence on frankness is bound to be rewarding. Spectres of the past vanish when the unconscious closet is thoroughly inspected.

Another occasionally troubling problem is the temptation of some patients to consummate intimate sexual relations. Sporadically, a couple will have intercourse within the first half dozen meetings. If the analyst forbids such intimacy, he duplicates the original parental proscription against incest. Besides, men and women who become so engaged do so compulsively and generally drift into physical familiarity whether the physician prohibits it or not. Then the therapist is faced with their sense of guilt, a tendency to hide aspects of the relationship and a secret defiance that complicates and obscures the significance of the act. Furthermore, patients who leap into bed with one another do so rather extensively with people outside the group. In the therapeutic setting the repetition of the sexual act has the advantage of subjecting compulsive promiscuity to examination under the microscope. Whenever members reach out for one another in sexual release, the relationship is inevitably brought up for group discussion and analysis within a few sessions. But the therapist does not encourage sexual intercourse. He takes a neutral position. In the beginning of group treatment he presents the position I have outlined above, and thus guards as best he can against playing the repressive role of original familial figures. If in spite of the points outlined by the analyst, patients still indulge in intercourse, the analyst and the group simply try to understand the full meaning of the act. Later on in the course of treatment, when patients' embryonic, libidinous urgings emerge in healthier give and take, a more wholesome union can take place. Here certainly the therapist can be encouraging. For as long as affective yearnings are the expression of genuine affection or love, he must not match the original, castrating parent, but play a permissive if not promoting part. However, for the majority of patients, taboos against incest are so strong and the family unit so sharply reanimated in the group that excursions into sexual contact are forbidden to them by old and stringent incorporated disciplines.

What may be regarded by some therapists as a danger is the quick penetration of a facade and the sudden, premature presentation to a patient of deep, unconsciou material by the intuitive association of another member. In over eleven years of clinical experience with the group analytic method no one has been driven into a psychosis by such precocious insight. I have always found that, if a patient is not ready to assimilate profound understanding, his resistance disposes of it. If a member seems on the verge of great anxiety or instability as a result of being exposed too precipitously to insight, he may be withdrawn temporarily into individual analysis for reassurance, repression and ego strengthening until he is able to withstand intensive analysis.

Constructive Patterns in Group Analysis

A constructive use to which group analysis is put, is the demonstration to each patient that he shares his problems with others. He loses the illusion of the uniqueness of his neurosis. How many times has the analyst working alone with a patient heard him inquire whether the therapist has ever encountered such an unusual and complex case before. It is the discovery of common difficulties that leads to freer self-exposure. The group milieu is also a buffer against despair of recovery. If the patient falters or is set back, the improvement and recovery of others encourages him to go on. His fear that he will receive only a fraction of the attention available in individual treatment is dissipated by the actual experience when he is transferred from private to group analysis. Here he finds himself scrutinized by the searching inquiry of people whose analytic skill multiplies with successive visits. The group comes very quickly and accurately to the heart of a problem by progressive increments of cross-association and intuition. The penetrating powers of the therapist are limited by his character structure. Alone with the patient, the analyst evokes circumscribed responses in him determined by the physician's particular personality. For the rest the therapist must rely on his knowledge of unconscious forces and artificial and sometimes awkward devices to evoke all the unconscious facets of a patient's transference responses. The group makes this much easier. By providing a number of disparate character structures it spontaneously elicits in each member different aspects of himself. The divergent personalities provoke more varied sides of the individual that would perhaps otherwise remain unseen. Numbers of patients provide more agents to facilitate spontaneous interreaction and intuitive penetration of facades.

There are social rewards obtainable in a group that are not as accessible to a patient who chooses private analysis. The group appreciates proffered insight and acknowledges such favors with regard and affection. Besides, the patient who intuitively produces a bit of valuable information, hitherto unseen, learns to respect his inner reserves out of the esteem of others. This approval does not encourage compulsively brilliant performance which excludes affect. Rather it values unplanned, emotional responses that gratify all the members concerned. In this way a patient learns to appreciate his natural and uninhibited resources at the same time as he cultivates them along social lines. The group method also rewards the participant by making him feel increasingly helpful as an adjunct analyst, a function he cannot so easily play in individual treatment.

The group has a constructive effect in recreating the family—but with a new look. By cultivating a permissive atmosphere in which mutual tolerance and regard can flourish, the earlier prohibitive character of the original family is projected with less intensity and is more easily dispersed. Furthermore, the general acceptance and sense of belonging that follow make it possible to achieve similarly easy transition to correspondingly untroubled social relations beyond the confines of the group. The other patients, out of their numbers, provide more familial surrogates for transference evocation. Each member comes to a realization of the extent to which he recreates his own childhood family in every social setting and invests others with inappropriate familial substitute qualities. The number of participants also clarifies the variety and multiplicity of central and penumbral transferences. While in individual analysis the therapist tries to see clearly what perceptual distortions the patient makes of outer reality and what internal factors contribute to this social disfigurement, the analyst is often misled, because he does not see the patient in action. In group analysis the physician is interested primarily in what is happening at the moment so that the patient's unconscious warping of the fact can be observed in motion. He can then be confronted with his projective technics and the inciting role he plays in precipitating the environmental disturbances he resents so much.

The group facilitates the emergence and acceptance of insight by confronting each member with his disparate investments of other patients and the therapist. In individual analysis it is most trying to persuade the patient to regard his endowing the physician with parental or sibling characteristics as a projective phenomenon rather than a true estimate of fact. When, however, he joins a group, he finds that each patient unconsciously warps his perception of the therapist and of the other patients as well. He begins to question the reality of his view of people in the group. As he studies his transferences, he becomes aware too of his provocative role. In individual analysis the therapist does not often react spontaneously to the patient. But the group always does—until the final stage of analysis. Each member tells him frankly what effect he produces, so that the character of his neurotic provocation and the part he plays in creating environmental responses becomes clear to him. Nowhere in individual analysis is there such a microscopic laboratory in which the patient can discover in action the interplay of unconscious forces. If occasional individual sessions are indicated because insight has been imposed too quickly and the patient cannot easily handle his newly exposed conflicts, the therapist merely offers repressive support in a temporary return to individual treatment. If deep insight is tolerated, the analyst underlines that trend in the conflict, which has a healthy social as well as personally gratifying objective.

The group has a curious explosive effect in the way it stirs the unconscious into activity. The analyst alone with a single patient appears to gain access to the repressed by probing analysis that is slower and more painstaking. The group, by its interreactive spontaneous free association, bursts the seams of resistance in a sort of chain reaction. It is as if the presentation of a nightmare to an assemblage had a socially agitating effect on unconscious energy, until now in check, that forces it into release. This animation in turn vitalizes others, and so on. It is startling to see one patient after another getting flashes of insight from the fantasies and dreams of successive free associators. The stimulating power of each member's provocative inner self rakes up repressed trends all around him. Evidently there is so much closely shared unconscious material that the uninhibited imagery of one man stirs the deepest levels of another. The comments of the therapist are sometimes too interpretation-loaded and intellectual. This may remove him, if he is not careful, from an essential affective connection with the patient. No such dangers of emotional detachment can prevail in the group. Here the freely interreacting unconscious excitation of patient on patient is an endless source of provocation and passionate interconnection, that furnishes material for analysis and good will. The effect of exposure to the naked, unconscious trends of other people cannot be resisted. "Going around" establishes a freely flowing generalized absence of restraint, so that resistances break down and deeply conflictful material is exposed. The awareness of another's buried impulses and contradictory strivings agitate the observer profoundly and force him to participate on his own deepest levels of emotional conflict. If, as rarely happens, the patient insists on not exposing some of these personal matters to the group, he discusses them with the physician in private. . . .

In conclusion, it seems to me that group analysis, even at its present state of development, is a natural outcome from the previous theory and practice of psychoanalysis. It enables the therapist who possesses an adequate understanding of the social character of man to unite this awareness with .iis methods of treatment of individuals who have been immobilized by the conflicts of our culture. It provides a means for the elimination of interpersonal dominance and exploitation among patients. It teaches them that appropriation of one another, the incorporation of our societal criterion, is immobilizing to all concerned. They learn, at least on this level, to throw off the binding sense that self-aggrandizement is the means to security and happiness. The patient socializes himself as best he can on the level of interpersonal relationships. Rid of our vapid cultural illusions which he had embodied, he is better able to attune himself with reality. By training each participant to be sensitive to the unconscious strivings in himself as well as in others, group analysis provides a practice ground for deep rapport with others. This ability to establish an inner attunement provides group analysands with psychic antennae which are a social asset to the extent to which they help to establish a profound emotional closeness among themselves and subsequently with strangers outside the analytic circle. Group analysis is a balance between self-study and social study. Their dynamic interrelation reveals and promotes the whole man.

S. H. Foulkes (b. 1923) is one of the leaders of the group therapy movement in England. While his colleague Joshua Bierer introduced the method of "situational treatment" in social clubs and Maxwell Jones developed facilities of milieu therapy in his therapeutic communities, Foulkes founded the Group-Analytic Society at Maudsley Hospital in London. Though essentially based on psychoanalytic tenets, his approach is eclectic and combines principles of individual psychology and learning theory. At the same time, his network theory of neuroses shows his affinity to modern communication theory. In contrast to A. Wolf and E. K. Schwartz in this country, Foulkes does not insist on the sharp separation of group dynamics from group therapy in a strict sense.

The following selection comes from Foulkes's introductory chapter in Practicum of Group Therapy, *jointly authored by Asya Kadis, Jack D. Krasner, and Charles Winik (1963).*

Patients in a group are the focus of this book. The particular kind of group in which we are interested is concerned with psychotherapy. If you wish to treat a patient by psychotherapy, you must assume that he is expected to change. Here at once a number of questions arise: *who* expects him to change? If only you or someone of his surroundings, e.g., his family, expect him to change, this is obviously not enough. Therefore you must claim that he himself wants to change. If so, why does he want to change? In what respect does he want to change? In what way does he think that the change is to come about? Why does he come to you for this? We well know that all of these questions have a conscious and an unconscious aspect. It is, therefore, of limited value to ask the patient these questions, and you cannot expect to get answers from him that will lead you far.

Rather it is a matter of finding out the answers to all these questions by inference, based on all sorts of communications, responses, and attitudes which the patient presents or betrays. The same is true for his entire attitude toward the proposed treatment procedure and toward you. In judging these, too, your own conclusions must be based not merely and, probably, not mainly on what is manifest and conscious. You will form impressions as to how difficult it is for him to become aware of something previously unperceived, how long a way he may have to go to accept parts of himself which hitherto he had not realized. In this way, among others, you gain some appreciation of his capacity for insight, integration, as well as other factors. You also get a first inkling of the strength and mode of his defenses —that is to say, the strength and way in which he will resist change.

If you have arrived at a fair picture concerning these points and find the situation on the whole quite favorable for change, you have assessed something which is largely comprised in the term "motivation." This is perhaps the most significant factor for indication for psychotherapy and is more important than the diagnosis. If the formal diagnosis is meaningful and not a mere label, it will correspond to the psychopathological dynamics fairly well, at least in a general way.

A conversional hysteric, for instance, might present you with some physical complaint, say being sick and vomiting. This may appear quite unrelated to any situation. If he is confident enough of his defenses, he may be very eager for treatment, he may be free from anxiety, pleasant and cooperative. You would not be surprised if you found that while this patient adhered to a belief in the ultimate physical nature of his disturbance, he came to you readily on the authoritative advice of his physician. He might expect a purely symptomatic cure from you, maybe on a magical basis—and he would readily bestow magical powers on you so long as you maintain this fiction with him. On the other hand, he may pay lip service to psychological causation (preferably in early childhood) which he will expect you to discover and thus cure him.

A patient with a phobia, such as being afraid to go out alone, or travel in a train, perhaps under some specified circumstances, will have a much more frankly psychological approach. His defenses will be expressed correspondingly in different ways and his own theory of treatment will be correspondingly different.

In these simple examples, the psychopathology and the diagnosis correspond and indicate the task and the nature of the therapeutic process. Even here, however, the mere diagnostic label would not tell us enough. For instance, the hysteric mentioned might soon show deep hypochondriacal fears or he might or might not relate himself in a more or less central or vital way to the therapist, thus throwing the field wide open for a therapeutic approach; or he might soon find a way of breaking up the treatment situation. Most diagnostic labels, however, are not dynamically significant or they cover too large a ground. It follows from all this that we cannot well express suitability for psychotherapy in terms of diagnoses and still less can we construe a differential indication as to the form of psychotherapy as, for instance, whether better in an individual (two-personal) or in a group situation. Motivation and capacity for change seem more important.

Symptoms and Change

We must, therefore, make a psychodynamic assessment of the problem with which the patient presents us. Such a psychodynamic profile has multidimensional aspects and should include at least a provisional idea of the strength of the various positions (e.g., paranoid) according to the level of regression and corresponding defense. In the light of this, we may have some tentative answers to the questions: Can he change? How far? By what means? What can we do about it? It is important that these questions be answered in the light of the practical situation in which you and the patient find yourselves and that the aims you hope to achieve are consistent with the limitations set by the reality in which you work.

The patient's own conclusions and manifest ideas may correspond fairly well with your conception of his real problem or, on the contrary, they may be poles apart.

Meantime, on our part, we have made a basic assumption. We have assumed or, better perhaps, accepted, that a symptom is a symptom and not the true disturbance which causes the patient to come to us. Furthermore, we have accepted that the disturbance is not a disease in the sense of a process which has descended upon our patient from outside of himself. Rather we have learned from the experience of half a century, an experience confirmed in every single case over again, that this disturbance is brought about by unresolved conflicts often referred to as "problems." From this it follows that our idea of therapy is that the *patient* must change, himself, not something outside himself, and not that something must be changed for him. What the conflicts are and why they are not resolved and why, for all the suffering, change is so desperately resisted, cannot be gone into here. For this, I would have to recall the whole psychoanalytic body of observation.

Our concept of the nature of the change which is desired differs, therefore, fundamentally from the patient's concept. If it did not differ, he would not need to consult us. We can confidently say that if, as a result of our treatment, the patient comes around, by genuine conviction based on his own experience, from his original idea as to what is wrong with him, and how it could be cured, to our idea as just formulated, he must be on the way to recovery. The first essential and general aim of all psychotherapy is thus clear. I like to refer to it as *the move from the symptom to the problem*. This is major progress in psychotherapy though only part of the process.

The individual steps which bring about such change could also be called "learning," but this term could easily be misleading. Learning suggests an intellectual process and this is not at all what is wanted primarily, just as insight is largely useless if it is intellectual—rather it should follow from change. Learning of facts or of information as, for instance, how to operate an engine, can be largely intellectual, but learning in the sense it would apply here, that is vital learning, presupposes a change of attitude concerning the whole person. If used in this sense, there appears to be no clear-cut difference between the learning and the therapeutic processes. (For this reason group teaching has special merits. This is also confirmed in psychiatric teaching and it is borne out that experience as a patient—either in individual or group-analytic psychotherapy—has proved to be a powerful means of learning.)

Resistance to Change

Another point should be kept in mind: In psychotherapy as we have it in mind here, and in particular insofar as it is analytic in orientation, the process of *unlearning* is particularly important.

We must never lose sight of the fact that resistances to change, to learning, and to unlearning, are not merely caused by the inherent difficulties in doing so. Even the well-motivated patient—both consciously and unconsciously—has very strong powers working actively in himself against change, a change which would be in his favor. These powerful forces are for the most part unconscious. In the last resort, they must be self-destructive but they are not necessarily so in a straightforward way. It may be, for instance, that the patient is afraid of success or not allowed to enjoy himself. There is much self-deception operating here as in the case of hidden passionate desires. Projections onto fate or bad luck, onto others, onto the past, are favorite mechanisms. There is also a kind of projection into reality and into the body. On this level, I have in mind real reality ("realization" one might call it) and "real" physical illness, which the doctor or the laboratory test would confirm. Such projections induce other people to act and react in the ways in which the patient anticipated. In the face of such self-deceptions, locating these dark forces within one's own mind is among the most difficult tasks. The profundity of insight required for doing so is given only to few individuals, particularly gifted in this respect.

Strange to say, in my experience, insight sufficient to be workable and effective in practical terms can be achieved not infrequently. Some of the most decisive therapeutic changes occur just in this area. It is here that insight achieves its major triumphs. Since this discussion must be limited, I cannot enter into the theoretical reasons beyond indicating that they stem from the curative agent being not so much the undoing of repression and its allied defense mechanisms as it is the undoing of self-deception in relation to one's own ego identity. A change of heart, of attitude here pays immediate dividends even though the deep sources from which these self-destructive energies flow may remain unconscious.

In addition to all these resistances to change, there is yet another set of resistances which goes beyond the individual as an isolated person. This set leads us to the need for a group pathological and group therapeutic viewpoint as the only appropriate one. The human individual never exists in isolation, least of all in a deep psychological sense. It is as though he had for his well-being, not only to maintain an equilibrium within his own system but also within a system which comprises a number of significant people. These are the representatives of the community and culture in which his life is spent. These representatives may be past or present, physically or otherwise, they may appear to be within or without himself; in their total concert they perform over and over again the tragedy and comedy of love and hatred, of life and death, of all human existence. The individuals are but nodal points in this play of forces and the equilibrium of each is interdependent with that of the others. I like to call this a "network" of interaction. It is inevitable that any change in any one of the members of such a network causes change in any one of the others to a greater or lesser degree and is, therefore, resisted by them. It is not possible here to go further into the consequences of such an insight, both practical and theoretical, and I must refer to some of my own writings concerning this "network" theory of the neuroses and allied disturbances. I believe that this view will ultimately prevail and will provide an end to the distinction between psychology, biology, and sociology, more particularly between "individual" and "social" psychology as well as between psychology and psycho-pathology.

Suffice it here to say that in any individual case this network can be reduced to a relatively few relevant persons. These will almost certainly include members of the family but will most probably not be confined to them. It is in this respect that my network approach differs from the family treatment which has, more recently, begun to come into its own, especially in the United States, but which is nevertheless a step in the right direction. Group treatment that has as its object the therapeutic analysis of such a primary group is one essential form of group psychotherapy. It has great difficulties and holds great dangers as well as promise.

Interaction in Group Psychotherapy

The other major form of group psychotherapy, on the contrary, takes each individual right out of his primary network and mixes him with others, thus forming a new field of interaction in which each individual has a fresh start. The situation is unprejudiced as to his own reactions and contributions as well as those of the other members to himself. He is therefore forced to realize—or to defend himself against such realization—to what extent and depth he is conditioned by imprints of his former and present primary networks. He also has a first-hand opportunity of comparing and contrasting his own ways with those of others; he can see that what he thought peculiar in himself is usual and that what he thought usual is peculiar to him ("mirror reaction"). He also becomes familiar with new ways of suffering and new ways of solution as represented by real persons in the same room with him. This whole new encounter, ever developing and ever changing, is or should be as far as possible, confined to the therapeutic meeting in the presence of the therapist. The therapist's task is to keep the situation thus confined, to keep it therapeutic, that is to say, to preserve individuals from harm through excessive reactions or incompatible selection, to see that what is learned is made meaningful and can be used constructively.

This whole volume is concerned with this second form of group psychotherapy. In the last few sentences, I have only tried to circumscribe some of the essential foundations upon which therapy in groups rests. To go into detail is not my task here, and I can confidently leave that in the hands of the distinguished experts who are your guides.

If we now proceed to our last question, namely, *how* do people change, whether this be generally in life or in this particular situation, we have already given some general answer in the foregoing. A few words may be added: the first condition seems to be experience, vital involved experience, especially in relation to other people.

The therapeutic character of these meetings is personified and maintained by the therapist. I propose that we define clearly the main factors which account for this therapeutic character and, insofar as they are realized, we may call it a T-situation. Such a situation is differently defined according to the material in which we work, including ourselves and our limitations (for example, the time available). The important over-all principle is that our aims are in accordance with these limitations. For our purpose, it is important that the T-situation allows, encourages, and demonstrates repetition of significant behavior and response in transference, that it focuses on the psychological level, gives full recognition to unconscious processes, whether these are manifested intrapersonally or interpersonally. In pure form this can be done in the group-analytic situation, the main ingredient of which is the consistent analytical attitude of the conductor. Only the therapist who is fully trained and experienced as a psychoanalyst and a group analyst can maintain this level and should do so.

However, much valuable group psychotherapy—it may indeed be of greater practical importance—can be done by using the constructive effects of group participation, of didactic influences, and of opening up channels for corrective experiences, which to some extent regulate themselves. This latter type of group psychotherapy leaves the therapist considerable flexibility according to his purpose and inclinations.

In all of these situations it would, however, seem advisable that the therapist does not too readily fulfill the group's wish to be led or to be taught and that he remain relatively nondescript as to his own person. Furthermore, while it is important that newly won and liberated capacities for action and response should be practiced, it is nevertheless necessary to watch that such carrying over into life should not be too hot. Indeed, it is of therapeutic importance to learn *not* to act upon impulses but to keep them in suspense and thus allow for recognition, reflection, and correction. This applies to patient and therapist alike.

The long and distinguished career of J. L. Moreno (1898-1974) as a psychiatrist and psychotherapist has been studded with successes, setbacks, and controversy. He has claimed—and has been credited with—many firsts, ranging from his informal "rap sessions" with groups of prostitutes on park benches in imperial Vienna to his blueprint of a "theater of spontaneity" in Berlin, to his monograph Invitation to an Encounter *(which he considered the curtain raiser for the advent of existential therapy), and to his sociometric investigations in this country. But his most significant contribution was his founding of the Institute for Psychodrama in Beacon, New York, and, subsequently, similar groups elsewhere in the United States and abroad. He described psychodrama as "the depth therapy of the group" and elaborated on this theme in many publications, among them his magnum opus* Who Shall Survive? Foundations of Sociometry and Sociodrama *(1953). Moreno plunged into all these enterprises as author, showman, and stage manager, and was his own impresario and historian. His virulent attacks against psychoanalysis and rival schools of group therapy embroiled him in endless controversies. Yet workshops, seminars, and periodicals devoted to psychodrama, sociodrama, and sociometry have sprung up all over the Western world, as well as in the U.S.S.R. and Eastern Europe.*

The following is a selection from Progress in Psychotherapy, *Vol. 1, 1956, "The Philosophy of the Third Psychiatric Revolution with Special Emphasis on Group Psychotherapy and Psychodrama," by J. L. Moreno, Beacon House, Inc., and Grune and Stratton, New York, 1956.*

Psychodrama

Psychodrama explores the truth by means of dramatic methods. It is the *depth* therapy of the group. It starts where group psychotherapy ends, and extends it in order to make it more effective. The expressed aim of the therapy group is to function for its members as a miniature society to which they can adapt themselves more harmoniously than heretofore. If this aim is taken seriously, other methods besides conversation, interview or analysis have to be added in order that such an objective—a catharsis of integration—can be fulfilled. The need of going beyond the level of abreaction and discussion and structuring the inner and outer events becomes imperative. It is not enough if we react to private and collective ideologies of group sessions in a symbolic fashion; we must structure these abreactions and relate our feelings and thoughts to embodiment of these principles and to concrete personages.

Frequently, in the course of typical verbal interactional group sessions, one member of the group may experience a problem with such intensity that words alone are unsatisfactory. He has the urge to act out the situation, to structure an episode; to act out means to "live it," to structure it more thoroughly than life outside would permit. The problem he has is often shared by all the members of the group. He becomes their embodiment in action. At such moments, the group spontaneously gives him space, for space is the first thing he needs. He moves into the center or in front of the group, so he can communicate with all. One or another member of the group may be equally involved in a counterrole, and steps upon the scene to coact with him. This is the natural and spontaneous transformation of a simple group therapy session into a group psychodrama. Authoritarian group psychotherapists may try to hinder this development, and they may be aided at times by the resistance of the group against spontaneous acting out and the exposure of its deeper dynamics. But the history of the last twenty years shows that the development cannot be stopped. It became logical in the course of time that one should not leave the realization of acting out to chance, and be resigned to verbal discussion because of lack of facilities. Putting a platform or a stage in the room, or designating a special area for production, gave "official" license to a tacitly accepted practice. It was then understood by the group that when its deep emotions were striving for dramatic expression, this place could be used for production. The stage is not outside by inside of the group.

As long as only a single individual entered into therapy, the therapeutic process could be limited to a dialog between two, facing each other. The world could be left outside, but once the group entered into therapy, the whole world—its anguishes and values—had to become part of the therapeutic situation. As long as we treated the individual by individual methods, we could let him find a test of the success of treatment in the reality outside. But now that we have brought the whole world into the therapeutic situation, the adequacy of his behavior within it can be tested within the framework of therapy itself. The problem of human society, as well as the problem of the individual—the portrayal of human relations, love and matrimony, sickness and death, war and peace, describing the panorama of the world at large—now can be presented in miniature within a setting removed from reality, within the framework of the group.

Technology. The locus of a psychodrama, if necessary, may be designated anywhere, wherever the patients are—the field of battle, the hospital ward, the classroom or the private home. But the ultimate resolution of deep group conflicts benefits from an objective setting, the therapeutic theater. The stage provides the patient with a living space which is multidimensional and flexible to the maximum. The living space of reality is often narrow and restraining; he may easily lose his equilibrium. On the stage he may find it again, due to its methodology of freedom—freedom from unbearable stress and freedom for experience and expression. The stage space is an extension of life beyond the reality test of life itself. Reality and fantasy are not in conflict, but both are functions within a wider sphere—the psychodramatic world of objects, persons and events. In its logic, the ghost of Hamlet's father is just as real, and permitted to exist as Hamlet himself. Delusions and hallucinations are given flesh—embodiment on the stage—and an equality of status with normal sensory perceptions. The architectural design of the stage is made in accord with therapeutic requirements. The stage's circular forms and levels—levels of aspiration—point up the vertical dimension, stimulate relief from tensions and permit mobility and flexibility of action. High above the stage is the balcony level from where the megalomaniac, the Messiah, the hero, communicates with the group. The space surrounding the stage is designed to contain the group. The architectural structure allows every member of the group to see every other, so that interaction and participation is secured. The group has two functions: it may serve to help the patients on the stage, or become the patient itself. The vehicle permits the supplementation of the production with psychodrama, psychomusic, psychodance, sound recording, and the influence of light and color. Just as a surgeon requires a special table, special lights, instruments, and nurses, such devices as a special stage, circular forms, lights and colors serve only the purpose of helping to create an atmosphere to attaining maximum therapeutic effects, and performance with a minimum risk.

Psychodrama of a Psychotic World. Christs and Napoleons are frequently embodied by mental patients, but I do not recall that a pseudo-Hitler has ever been reported in the literature. It was my good fortune to treat such a case at the beginning of World War II. In order to illustrate the theory and technique of psychodrama, here follow a few highlights of the case.

I am in my office. The door opens, the nurse comes in. "Doctor," she says, "there is a man outside; he wants to see you." "You know I can't see anyone, because I am about to give a session in the theater and the students are waiting." "He claims he has an appointment. He does not want to give his name." "Try to find out who he is and what he wants." Nurse leaves and returns: "He insists that he has an appointment with you. He won't go away." "Well, let him come in." The door opens; a man enters; he is in his early forties. We look at each other, our eyes meet. He looks familiar. Now he looks challengingly at me, says: "Don't you know who I am?" "I'm sorry, I don't." "Well," he exclaims sharply, "my name is Adolf Hitler." I was taken aback; indeed, he looked the part—the same hypnotic look, the way of brushing his hair, the moustache. I rise from my seat; he carries his body the same way, makes the same gestures, speaks in the same shrieking, penetrating voice. "Of course, now I recognize you." I am flustered and uneasy, sit down again and try to be as formal as possible. "Won't you sit down, Mr. Hitler?" He takes a seat. I open my record book: "Your first name, please?" "But don't you know? Adolf!" "Oh, yes, Adolf Hitler. Where do you live?" He replies with a gesture of surprise and annoyance: "In Berchtesgaden, of course." "In Berchtesgaden, oh yes. But why have you come to me?" "Don't you know? Didn't she tell you?" "Who? My wife?" "Oh, yes, now I remember." In fact, I recall that not so long ago a woman had come to see me; she spoke of her husband who owns a meat market on Third Avenue in the heart of Yorkville. It flashes through my mind that she was depressed and cried. She said: "My husband has changed; he is sick; his real name is Karl and now he calls himself Adolf. He believes he is Hitler. I don't know what to do with him." "Why don't you let him come to see me?"

About three months have elapsed since she came; now, here he is. Adolf speaks to me again, "Is there anything you can do for me?" "I may, but first tell me what happened." "But didn't she tell you?" He becomes excited again: "I organized the party for him, he took my name; I wrote *Mein Kampf* but he took it away from me. I was in jail for him for two years; he took everything I have, my inspiration, my brainpower, my energy. Right now, as I'm sitting here, he takes it all from me, every minute. That scoundrel! I can't stop him, maybe you can." He puts his head on my shoulder and weeps. "Oh, help me, help me! I will make you the chief of all the doctors in the Third Reich."

I begin to feel more at home in the situation, reach for the telephone and speak to the nurse. A moment later two men come in—one fat, one skinny. I perform the introductions: "Mr. Goering, Mr. Hitler; Mr. Goebbels, Mr. Hitler." Remarkably, Adolf accepts them without question, is happy to see them, and shakes hands with them. They are two male nurses, trained auxiliary egos. Hitler seems to know them well. "Gentlemen," I suggest, "let us all go into the theater. Mr. Hitler wishes to make an announcement." All four of us proceed to the psychodrama theater. A group of students are waiting.

(The opening session is crucial for the course of psychodramatic treatment. I had a clue which his wife had given me. She came home after a short vacation and saw the walls of their apartment covered with Hitler's pictures. All day long, Karl stood before a mirror, trying to imitate Hitler's speech, the way he eats and walks. He neglected the business and took a job as doorman of a motion picture house, so he could wear a uniform and make converts for the cause. He and his wife no longer sleep in the same bedroom; now he has his own. He does not seem to care for her anymore. She asked him what all this meant, but he only got angry. Theoretically, this would have been an excellent clue for the first episode, but it might have thrown off the whole production, because "at this moment" the wife had no reality for him; speaking in psychodramatic jargon, he was not warmed-up to this episode. But he was intrigued with the fellows who portrayed Goering and Goebbels; therefore, I followed his own clue. . . .)

Karl steps forward and makes an announcement to the German people, speaking over a public address system. He states that he is the real Hitler; the other is an impostor. The German people should eject the impostor! He will return triumphantly to Germany to take over the helm. The group receives his proclamation with spontaneous applause. A few scenes follow swiftly: Hitler returns to Germany on a boat. He calls a meeting of the war cabinet, planning with his ministers the future of the Third Reich. He ends the first session with a moving scene at the grave of his mother, whom he lost at the age of eighteen.

For many weeks we had sessions with Hitler at regular intervals. We provided him with all the characters he needed to put his plans of conquering the world into operation (technique of self-realization). He seemed to know everything in advance; many things he presented on the stage came very close to what actually took place years later. He appeared to have a special sense for fitting himself into moods and decisions which were made thousands of miles apart from him. In fact, at times we speculated whether he, the patient, was not the real Hitler and the other in Germany his double. We had the strange experience of feeling the real Hitler among us, working desperately on finding a solution for himself. We saw him often with his mother or sweetheart alone, bursting out in tears, fighting with astrologists for an answer when he was in doubt, praying in his solitude to God for help, knocking his head on the wall, fearing that he might become insane before he could attain the great victory. At other times, he portrayed moods of great desperation, feelings that he had failed and that the Reich would be conquered by its enemies. In one of these moods, he stepped upon the stage and declared that the time had come for him to end his life. He asked all the Gestapo leaders who filled the audience—from Goering, Goebbels, Ribbentrop, Hess, down to the last man—to die with him. He ordered that the music of *Gotterdammerung* be played to accompany the death orgy. He shot himself in from of the audience. Many years later, when the real Hitler killed himself and his wife in some Berlin underground, I recalled the strange coincidence that the poor butcher of Yorkville should have anticipated the future of world history so closely. Many times, he and I stood alone on the stage, eye to eye, involved in a conversation. "What's the matter with me?" he said, "Will this torture never end? Is it real or is it a dream?" Such intimate dialogs prove to be of unique value for the progress of therapy. It is at the height of psychodramatic production that rare levels of intensive reflection are reached.

Hospitalization did not seem indicated because his wife provided excellent supervision; she employed the two nurses who took the parts of Goering and Goebbels. Outside the sessions, while with his constant companions, he acted very distant in the beginning. But one day, due to the intimate rapport he established with them in the production of his inner life, he began to become more intimate with them. During an intermission of one session he said to Goering: "Hello, Goering, what do you think of the joke which I made on the stage today?" And they laughed together. But suddenly Hitler swatted Goering. Goering responded in kind and a regular fistfight took place on the spot, during which Hitler took a bad beating. Later they enjoyed a glass of beer together. From then on the ice gradually began to melt.

(Physical contact and physical attack—from caressing and embracing, to pushing and hitting—is permissible in psychodramatic therapy if it is of benefit to the patient. It is obvious that here the utmost caution has to be practiced to prevent excesses, or to prevent the auxiliary ego from taking advantage of the patient in order to satisfy his own needs. A great responsibility rests upon the ego. It is natural that the auxiliary ego who portrays the part of a brutal father may really have to hit his son, not only "as if," in order to provoke in the son the responses in action, the perception and feelings he has for his father. It is customary in psychodramatic logic that a sick soldier who comes back home from war should embrace and caress his auxiliary mother or wife on the stage, if that is what he would do in real life. It is also psychodramatic logic that if some auxiliary ego takes the part of an older brother who is suddenly attacked by the patient, a real physical encounter may ensue upon the stage, or in the living quarters of the patient if it is there where the session takes place.

The result of the physical contact between Hitler and Goering was that Hitler permitted his auxiliary ego to call him by his first name, Adolf, and he called him Herman. They acted like pals; their relation was full of homosexual undertones. From then on Herman began to get an inside hold on Hitler's thoughts and feelings. We began to use this relationship as a therapeutic guide, for now Hitler was able to accept correction from Herman. Our productions on the stage were greatly facilitated by getting clues from the auxiliary ego (Herman) as to how to direct the production.

The point is that a therapist who is unable to establish a working rapport with a noncooperative patient, in a physician-patient situation, may be able to produce one by means of the psychodramatic method. For instance, in the case of our pseudo-Hitler, who was noncooperative to an extreme, it was possible to warm him up to a level of communication when an auxiliary ego portrayed the role of Goering in an episode relevant to his psychotic world. Once he had established rapport with the auxiliary therapist on the psychodramatic stage, he was later able to develop a relationship to the private person behind Goering, just a plain therapeutic nurse, with whom he began to communicate spontaneously on a realistic level. This was the turning point in the therapeutic process.)

Approximately three months after treatment first began, a strange event occurred. The group was gathered in the theater waiting for Hitler's next session. Goering came to me and said: "Adolf wants a haircut." "Well," I replied, "call a barber." It was the first time since he fell ill that he had allowed anyone to touch his hair. A barber came, and cut his hair according to Adolf's instructions—on stage. When the ceremony was over, the barber started to pack his instruments, getting ready to leave. Suddenly, Hitler looked sharply at the group, at me, then at the barber, and said: "Take this off!" He pointed at his moustache. The barber immediately soaped his face, applied the razor, and the moustache was gone! A very tense silence had descended upon the audience. Hitler rose from his chair, pointed at his face: "It's gone, it's gone, it's over!" Then he commenced to weep: "I lost it, I lost it! Why did I do it? I shouldn't have done it!"

Gradually, a change took place; from session to session we saw his body and behavior changing—the look in his eyes, his smile, the words he spoke. Still later he asked to be called "Karl" and not "Adolf." He asked his wife to come to the sessions. For the first time in many months, he kissed her in a scene on the stage.

(These episodes are from a large psychodramatic protocol, illustrating the rapid diagnostic picture given by protagonists, often within a single psychodramatic session.)

The patient made a good social recovery and returned to the fatherland a few years later. His case illustrates the hypothesis that "acting-out techniques" are the treatment of choice for "acting out syndromes."

chapter 29

Encounter and Intimacy
versus
Alienation and Detachment

SELECTIONS FROM C. ROGERS, M. A. LIEBERMAN, M. B. MILES,
AND I. B. YALOM, WITH A NOTE OF CAUTION BY K. W. BAK

The dividing line between therapy groups and encounter groups is fuzzy. Partisans of the encounter movement may claim that, although they do not realize it, participants in therapy groups—Freudian or otherwise—are in effect engaged in existential encounters, while champions of group therapy may point out that encounter groups, whatever their avowed purpose, function according to psychodramatic principles that can be understood only in psychoanalytic terms. According to this precept, therapy groups conform to the medical model of helping people, while encounter groups meet the more general need for the fellowship, intimacy, and mutual support offered by an intensive group experience, without reference to specific therapeutic goals or attempts at psychoanalytic probing.

Among the more utilitarian purposes pursued by encounter groups are so-called sensitivity training or "T-groups" designed to enhance human relationship skills; sensory awareness groups; task-oriented groups; team-building groups; organizational development groups; Gestalt groups; and creative workshops.

The existential aspects of the group experience have largely been inspired by Martin Buber and his concept of the "I-Thou" relationship and the dialogic existence; by Hans Trueb and his thesis of the "healing encounter" (Heilung als Begegnung); and by J. L. Moreno and his concept of Zweifuhlung—that is, of empathy or Einfuhlung embracing two or more persons.

The growing need for such forms of group experience is reflected in the mushrooming of innumerable communes or other projects for community living, ranging from B. F. Skinner's Walden Two in this country to R. D. Laing's Kingsley Hall in a London suburb. They became prominent features of the counterculture of the 1960s and 1970s and were apparently hit upon as antidotes for Western man's growing alienation, detachment, and isolation in an impersonal urban civilization.

Carl Rogers (b. 1902), resident fellow at the Center for Studies of the Person, La Jolla, California, is one of the major figures in clinical psychology and in the encounter movement in this country. He combines a sensitive, empathetic attitude toward people with a strong moral commitment and the pragmatic approach of a social reformer. His original orientation was toward individual counseling or nondirective, client-centered psychotherapy. His compassion for the individual who is struggling with the problems of living and of self-actualization is reflected in his book On Becoming a Person *and in numerous other publications. One of his major contributions is to the encounter movement, which is perhaps one of the most idiosyncratically American offshoots of European existentialist philosophy.*

The following selection is from Carl Rogers on Encounter Groups *by Carl R. Rogers,* © *Copyright 1970 by Carl Rogers, reprinted by permission of Harper and Row, Publishers, Inc., New York, 1970. It presents Rogers' concept of the basic encounter, which he characterizes as one of the most important social conventions of our time, and contains graphic descriptions of the growth process, self-reports and follow-up studies of participants in encounter groups.*

What really goes on in an encounter group? This is a question often asked by persons who are contemplating joining one, or who are puzzled by the statements of people who have had the experience. The question has been of great interest to me also, as I have tried to understand what appear to be common elements in the group experience. I have come to sense, at least dimly, some of the patterns or stages a group seems to go through and will describe them as best I can.

My formulation is simple and naturalistic. I am not attempting to build a high-level abstract theory, nor to make profound interpretations of unconscious motives or of some developing group psyche. You will not find me speaking of group myths, or even of dependence and counterdependence. I am not comfortable with such inferences, correct though they may be. At this stage of our knowledge I wish merely to describe the observable events and the way in which, to me, these events seem to cluster. In doing so I am drawing on my own experience and that of others with whom I have worked, upon written material in this field, upon the written reactions of many individuals who have participated in such groups, and to some extent upon recordings of such group sessions, which we are only beginning to tap and analyze.

As I consider the terribly complex interactions that arise in twenty, forty, or sixty or more hours of intensive sessions, I believe I see certain threads which weave in and out of the pattern. Some of these trends or tendencies are likely to appear early, some later in the group sessions, but there is no clear-cut sequence in which one ends and another begins. The interaction is best thought of, I believe, as a rich and varied tapestry, differing from group to group, yet with certain kinds of trends evident in most of these intensive encounters and with certain patterns tending to precede and others to follow. Here are some of the process patterns I see developing, briefly described in simple terms, illustrated from tape recordings and personal reports and presented in roughly sequential order.

1. *Milling around.* As the leader or facilitator makes clear at the outset that this is a group with unusual freedom and not one for which he will take directional responsibility, there tends to develop a period of initial confusion, awkward silence, polite surface interaction, "cocktail-party talk," frustration, and great lack of continuity. The individuals come face to face with the fact that "there is no structure here except what we provide. We do not know our purposes, we do not even know each other, and we are committed to remain together over a considerable period of time." In this situation, confusion and frustration are natural. Particularly striking to the observer is the lack of continuity between personal expressions. Individual A will present some proposal or concern, clearly looking for a response from the group. Individual B has obviously been waiting for his turn and starts off on some completely different tangent as though he had never heard A. One member makes a simple suggestion such as, "I think we should introduce ourselves," and this may lead to several hours of highly involved discussion in which the underlying issues appear to be: Who will tell us what to do: Who is responsible for us? What is the purpose of the group?

2. *Resistance to personal expression or exploration.* During the milling-around period some individuals are likely to reveal rather personal attitudes. This tends to provoke a very ambivalent reaction among other members of the group. One member, writing of his experience afterward, says, "There is a self which I present to the world and another one which I know more intimately. With others I try to appear able, knowing, unruffled, problem-free. To substantiate this image I will act in a way which at the time or later seems false or artificial or 'not the real me.' Or I will keep to myself thoughts which if expressed, would reveal an imperfect me."

"My inner self, by contrast with the image I present to the world, is characterized by many doubts. The worth I attach to this inner self is subject to much fluctuation and is very dependent on how others are reacting to me. At times this private self can feel worthless."

It is the public self that members tend to show each other, and only gradually, fearfully, and ambivalently do they take steps to reveal something of the private self.

Early in one intensive workshop, the members were asked to write anonymously a statement of some feeling or feelings they had which they were not willing to tell in the group. One man wrote, "I don't relate easily to people. I have an almost impenetrable facade. Nothing gets in to hurt me but nothing gets out. I have repressed so many emotions that I am close to emotional sterility. This situation doesn't make me happy but I don't know what to do about it." This individual is clearly living in a private dungeon, but except in this disguised fashion he does not even dare to send out a call for help.

In a recent workshop, when one man started to express the concern he felt about an impasse he was experiencing with his wife, another member stopped him, saying essentially, "Are you sure you want to go on with this, or are you being seduced by the group into going further than you want to go? How do you know the group can be trusted? How will you feel about it when you go home and tell your wife what you have revealed, or when you decide to keep it from her? It just isn't safe to go further." It seemed quite clear that in his warning this second member was also expressing his own fear of revealing *himself*, and *his* lack of trust in the group.

3. *Description of past feelings.* In spite of ambivalence about the trust-worthiness of the group, and the risk of exposing oneself, expression of feelings does begin to assume a larger proportion of the discussion. The executive tells how frustrated he feels by certain situations in his industry; the housewife relates problems she has with her children. A tape-recorded exchange involving a Roman Catholic nun occurs early in a one-week workshop, when talk has turned to a rather intellectualized discussion of anger:

Bill: What happens when you get mad, Sister, or don't you?
Sister: Yes, I do—yes I do. And I find when I get mad, I, I almost get, well, the kind of person that antagonizes me is the person who seems so unfeeling toward people—now I take our dean as a person in point because she is a very aggressive woman and has certain ideas about what the various rules in a college should be; and this woman can just send me into high "G"; in an angry mood. *I mean this.* But then I find, I . . .
Facilitator: But what, what do you do?
Sister: I find that when I'm in a situation like this, I strike out in a very sharp *tone* or else I refuse to respond—"all right, this happens to be her way"—I don't think I've ever gone into a tantrum.
Joe: You just withdraw—no use to fight it.
Facilitator: You say you use a sharp tone. To *her*, or to other people you're dealing with?
Sister: Oh no! To *her*.

This is a typical example of a *description* of feelings which in a sense are obviously current in her but which she is placing in the past and describes as being outside the group in time and place. It is an example of feelings existing "there and then."

4. *Expression of negative feelings.* Curiously enough, the first expression of genuinely significant "here and now" feeling is apt to come out in negative attitudes toward other group members or the group leader. In one group in which members introduced themselves at some length, one woman refused, saying that she preferred to be known for what she was in the group and not in terms of her status outside. Very shortly after this, a man in the group attacked her vigorously and angrily for this stand, accusing her of failing to cooperate, of keeping herself aloof from the group, of being unreasonable. It was the first *current personal feeling* brought into the open in that group.

Frequently the leader is attacked for his failure to give proper guidance. One vivid example of this comes from a recorded account of an early session with a group of delinquents, where one member shouts at the leader, "You'll be licked if you don't control us right at the start. You have to keep order here because you are older than us. That's what a teacher is supposed to do. If he doesn't do it we'll make a lot of trouble and won't get anything done. (Then, referring to two boys in the group who were scuffling, he continues) Throw 'em out, throw 'em out! You've just *got* to make us behave!"*

An adult expresses his disgust at people who talk too much, but points his irritation at the leader. "It's just that I don't understand why someone doesn't shut them up. I would have taken Geral and shoved him out the window. I'm an authoritarian. I would have told him he was talking too much and he had to leave the room. I think the group discussion ought to be led by a person who simply will not recognize these people after they've interrupted about eight times."*

Why are negatively toned expressions the first current feelings to be expressed? Some speculative answers might be the following. This is one of the best ways to test the freedom and trustworthiness of the group. Is it *really* a place where I can be and express myself, positively and negatively? Is this *really* a safe place, or will I be punished? Another quite different reason is that deeply positive feelings are much more difficult and dangerous to express than negative ones. If I say I love you, I am vulnerable and open to the most awful rejection. If I say I hate you, I am at best liable to attack, against which I can defend myself. Whatever the reasons, such negatively toned feelings tend to be the first "here and now" material to appear.

5. *Expression and exploration of personally meaningful material.* It may seem puzzling that, following such negative experiences as the initial confusion, the resistance to personal expression, the focus on outside events, and the voicing of critical or angry feelings the event most likely to occur next is for some individual to reveal himself to the group in a significant way. The reason for this no doubt is that the individual member has come to realize

---

*T. Gordon, *Group Centered Leadership* (Boston: Houghton Mifflin & Co., 1955), p. 214.

that this is in part *his group*. He can help to make of it what he wishes. He has also experienced the fact that negative feelings have been expressed and accepted or assimilated without catastrophic results. He realizes there is a freedom here, albeit a risky freedom. A climate of trust is beginning to develop. So he begins to take the change and the gamble of letting the group know some deeper facet of himself. One man tells of the trap in which he finds himself, feeling that communication between himself and his wife is hopeless. A priest tells of the anger he has bottled up because of unreasonable treatment by one of his superiors. What should he have done? What might he do now? A scientist at the head of a large research department finds the courage to speak of his painful isolation, to tell the group that he has never had a single *friend* in his life. By the time he finishes, he is letting loose some of the tears of sorrow for himself which I am sure he has held in for many years. A psychiatrist tells of the guilt he feels because of the suicide of one of his patients. A man of forty tells of his absolute inability to free himself from the grip of his controlling mother. A process which one workshop member has called "a journey to the center of self," often a very painful process, has begun.

A recorded example of such exploration is found in a statement by Sam, member of a one-week workshop. Someone had spoken of his strength.

Sam: Perhaps I'm not aware of or experiencing it that way, as strength. (Pause) I think, when I was talking with, I think it was the first day, I was talking to you, Tom, when in the course of that, I expressed the *genuine surprise* I had, the first time I realized that I could *frighten* someone——It really, it was a discovery that I had to just kind of look at and feel and get to know, you know, it was such a *new* experience for me. I was so used to the feeling of being frightened by *others* that it had never occurred to me that anyone could be—I guess it *never had*—that anyone could be frightened of *me*. And I guess maybe it has something to do with how I feel about myself.

Such exploration is not always an easy process, nor is the whole group receptive to such self-revelation. In a group of institutionalized adolescents, all of whom have been in difficulty of one sort or another, one boy reveals an important aspect of himself and is immediately met by both acceptance and sharp nonacceptance from other members.

George: This is the thing. I've got too many problems at home—um, I think some of you know why I'm here, what I was charged with.
Mary: I don't.
Facilitator: Do you want to tell us?

George: Well—uh—it's sort of embarrassing.

Carol: Come on, it won't be so bad.

George: Well, I raped my sister. That's the only problem I have at home and I've overcome that, I think. (Rather long pause.)

Freda: Oooh, that's weird!

Mary: People have problems, Freda, I mean ya know . . .

Freda: Yeah, I know, but *yeOUW!!!*

Facilitator: (To Freda) You know about these problems, but they still are weird to you.

George: You see what I mean; it's embarrassing to talk about it.

Mary: Yeah, but it's OK.

George: It *hurts* to talk about it, but I know I've got to so I won't be guilt-ridden for the rest of my life.

Clearly Freda is completely shutting him out psychologically, while Mary in particular is showing a deep acceptance. George is definitely willing to take the *risk*.

6. *The expression of immediate interpersonal feelings in the group.* Entering into the process, sometimes earlier, sometimes later, is the explicit bringing into the open of feelings experienced in the immediate moment by one member toward another. These are sometimes positive, sometimes negative. Examples would be: "I feel threatened by your silence." "You remind me of my mother, with whom I had a tough time." "I took an instant dislike to you the first moment I saw you." "To me you're like a breath of fresh air in the group." "I like your warmth and your smile." "I dislike you more every time you speak up." Each of these attitudes can be, and usually is, explored in the increasing climate of trust.

7. *The development of a healing capacity in the group.* One of the most fascinating aspects of any intensive group experience is to observe the manner in which a number of the group members show a natural and spontaneous capacity for dealing in a helpful, facilitating, and therapeutic fashion with the pain and suffering of others. As one rather extreme example of this I think of a man in charge of maintenance in a large plant who was one of the low-status members of an industrial executive group. As he informed us, he had "not been contaminated by education." In the initial phases the group tended to look down on him. As members delved more deeply into themselves and began to express their own attitudes more fully, this man came forth as without doubt the most sensitive member of the group. He knew intuitively how to be understanding and accepting. He was alert to things which had not yet been expressed but were just below the surface. While the rest of us were paying attention to a member who was speaking, he would frequently spot another individual who was suffering silently and

in need of help. He had a deeply perceptive and facilitating attitude. This kind of ability shows up so commonly in groups that it has led me to feel that the ability to be healing or therapeutic is far more common in human life than we suppose. Often it needs only the permission granted—or freedom made possible—by the climate of a free-flowing group experience to become evident.

8. *Self-acceptance and the beginning of change.* Many people feel that self-acceptance must stand in the way of change. Actually, in these group experiences as in psychotherapy, it is the *beginning* of change.

Some examples of the kinds of attitude expressed would be these: "I *am* a dominating person who likes to control others. I do want to mold these individuals into the proper shape." "I really have a hurt and overburdened little boy inside of me who feels very sorry for himself. I *am* that little boy, in addition to being a competent and responsible manager."

I think of one government executive, a man with high responsibility and excellent technical training as an engineer. At the first meeting of the group he impressed me, and I think others, as being cold, aloof, somewhat bitter, resentful, cynical. When he spoke of how he ran his office he appeared to administer it "by the book" without warmth or human feeling entering in. In one of the early sessions, when he spoke of his wife a group member asked him, "Do you love your wife?" He paused for a long time, and the questioner said, "OK, that's answer enough." The executive said, "No, wait a minute! The reason I didn't respond was that I was wondering if I ever loved anyone. I don't think I have *ever* really *loved* anyone." It seemed quite dramatically clear to those of us in the group that he had come to accept himself as an unloving person.

A few days later he listened with great intensity as one member of the group expressed profound personal feelings of isolation, loneliness, pain, and the extent to which he had been living behind a mask, a facade. The next morning the engineer said, "Last night I thought and thought about what Bili told us. I even wept quite a bit by myself. I can't remember how long it has been since I've cried and I really *felt* something. I think perhaps what I felt was love."

It is not surprising that before the week was over he had thought through new ways of handling his growing son, on whom he had been placing extremely rigorous demands. He had also begun genuinely to appreciate his wife's love for him, which he now felt he could in some measure reciprocate.

9. *The cracking of facades.* As the sessions continue, so many things tend to occur together that it is hard to know which to describe first. It should again be stressed that these different threads and stages interweave and overlap. One of the threads is the increasing impatience with defenses. As

time goes on the group finds it unbearable that any member should live behind a mask or front. The polite words, the intellectual understanding of
each other and of relationships, the smooth coin of tact and cover-up—
amply satisfactory for interactions outside—are just not good enough. The
expression of self by some members of the group has made it very clear that
a deeper and more basic encounter is *possible*, and the group appears to
strive intuitively and unconsciously, toward this goal. Gently at times,
almost savagely at others, the group *demands* that the individual be himself, that his current feelings not be hidden, that he remove the mask of ordinary social intercourse. In one group there was a highly intelligent and
quite academic man who had been rather receptive in his understanding of
others but revealed himself not at all. The attitude of the group was finally
expressed sharply by one member when he said, "Come out from behind
that lectern, Doc. Stop giving us speeches. Take off your dark glasses. We
want to know *you*."

In Synanon, the fascinating group so successfully involved in making
persons out of drug addicts, this ripping away of facades is often dramatic.
An excerpt from one of the "synanons" or group sessions makes this clear:

Joe: (Speaking to Gina) I wonder when you're going to stop sounding so
good in synanons. Every synanon that I'm in with you, someone asks you
a question and you've got a beautiful book written. All made out about
what went down and how you were wrong and how you realized you
were wrong and all that kind of bullshit. When are you going to stop doing that? How do you feel about Art?
Gina: I have nothing against Art.
Will: You're a nut. Art hasn't got any damn sense. He's been in there, yell-
ing at you and Moe, and you've got everything so cool.
Gina: No, I feel he's very insecure in a lot of ways but that has nothing to
do with me . . .
Joe: You act like you're so goddamn understanding.
Gina: I was *told* to act as if I understand.
Joe: Well, you're in a synanon now. You're not supposed to be acting like
you're such a goddamn healthy person. Are you so well?
Gina: No.
Joe: Well, why the hell don't you quit acting as if you were?*

If I am indicating that the group is quite violent at times in tearing down a
facade or defense, this is accurate. On the other hand, it can also be sensitive and gentle. The man who was accused of hiding behind a lectern was

---

*D. Casriel, *So Fair a House* (Englewood Cliffs, N.J.: Prentice Hall, 1963), p. 81.

deeply hurt by this attack, and over the lunch hour looked very troubled, as though he might break into tears at any moment. When the group reconvened, the members sensed this and treated him very gently, enabling him to tell us his own tragic personal story, which accounted for his aloofness and his intellectual and academic approach to life.

10. *The individual receives feedback.* In the process of this freely expressive interaction, the individual rapidly acquires a great deal of data as to how he appears to others. The hail-fellow-well-met finds that others resent his exaggerated friendliness. The executive who weighs his words carefully and speaks with heavy precision may discover for the first time that others regard him as stuffy. A woman who shows a somewhat excessive desire to be of help to others is told in no uncertain terms that some group members do not want her for a mother. All this can be decidedly upsetting, but so long as these various bits of information are fed back in the context of caring which is developing in the group, they seem highly constructive.

11. *Confrontation.* There are times when the term *feedback* is far too mild to describe the interactions that take place—when it is better said that one individual *confronts* another, directly "leveling" with him. Such confrontations can be positive, but frequently they are decidedly negative, as the following example will make abundantly clear. In one of the last sessions of a group, Alice had made some quite vulgar and contemptuous remarks to John, who was entering religious work. The next morning, Norma, who has been a very quiet person in the group, takes the floor:

Norma: (Loud sigh) Well, I don't have *any* respect for you, Alice. *None!* (Pause) There's about a hundred things going through my mind I want to say to you, and *by God* I hope I get through 'em all! First of all, if you wanted us to respect you, then why couldn't you respect *John's* feelings last night? *Why have you been on him today?* H'mm? Last night—*couldn't you* —*couldn't you* accept—*couldn't you* comprehend in any way at all that— that *he felt* his unworthiness in the service of God? *Couldn't you accept this* or did you have to dig into it today to find something *else* there? H'mm? I personally don't think John has any problems that are *any* of *your damn business!* ... Any real woman that I know wouldn't have acted as you have this week, and particularly what you said this afternoon. That was so *crass!!* It just made me want to puke, right there!!! And—I'm just *shaking* I'm so mad at you—I don't think you've been real once this week! ... I'm so infuriated that *I want to come over and beat the hell out of you!! I want to slap you across the mouth so hard and*—oh, and you're so, you're many years above me—and I respect age, and I respect people who are older than me, *but I don't respect you, Alice. At all!!* (A startled pause.)

It may relieve the reader to know that these two women came to accept each other, not completely but much more understandingly, before the end of the session. But this *was* a confrontation!

12. *The helping relationship outside the group sessions.* No account of the group process would be adequate, in my opinion, if it did not mention many ways in which group members assist each other. One of the exciting aspects of any group experience is the way in which, when an individual is struggling to express himself, or wrestling with a personal problem, or hurting because of some painful new discovery about himself, other members give him help. This may be within the group, as mentioned earlier, but occurs even more frequently in contacts outside the group. When I see two individuals going for a walk together, or conversing in a quiet corner, or hear that they stayed up talking until 3:00 a.m. I feel it is quite probable that at some later time in the group we will hear that one was gaining strength and help from the other, that the second person was making available his understanding, his support, his experience, his caring—making himself *available* to the other. An incredible gift of healing is possessed by many persons, if they only feel freed to give it, and experience in an encounter group seems to make this possible.

Let me offer an example of the healing effect of the attitudes of group members both outside and within the group meetings. This is taken from a letter written by a workshop member to the group one month later. He speaks of the difficulties and depressing circumstances he has met during that month and adds,

> I have come to the conclusion that my experiences with you have profoundly affected me. I am truly grateful. This is different than personal therapy. None of you *had* to care about me. None of you had to seek me out and let me know of things you thought would help me. None of you had to let me know I was of help to you. Yet you did, and as a result it has far more meaning than anything I have so far experienced. When I feel the need to hold back and not live spontaneously, for whatever reasons, I remember that twelve persons just like those before me now said to let go and be congruent, be myself and of all unbelievable things they even loved me more for it. This has given me the *courage* to come out of myself many times since then. Often it seems my very doing of this helps the others to experience similar freedom.

13. *The basic encounter.* Running through some of the trends I have just been describing is the fact that individuals come into much closer and more direct contact with each other than is customary in ordinary life. This appears to be one of the most central, intense, and change-producing aspects

of group experience. To illustrate, I should like to draw an example from a recent workshop group. A man tells, through his tears, of the tragic loss of his child, a grief which he is experiencing *fully* for the first time, not holding back his feelings in any way. Another says to him, also with tears in his eyes, "I've never before felt a real physical hurt in me from the pain of another. I feel completely with you." This is a basic encounter.

From another group, a mother with several children who describes herself as "a loud, prickly, hyperactive individual," whose marriage has been on the rocks and who has felt that life was just not worth living, writes,

> I had really buried under a layer of concrete many feelings I was afraid people were going to laugh at or stomp on which, needless to say, was working all kinds of hell on my family and on me. I had been looking forward to the workshop with my last few crumbs of hope. It was really a needle of trust in a huge haystack of despair. [She tells of some of her experiences in the group, and adds,] the real turning point for me was a simple gesture on your part of putting your arm around my shoulder one afternoon when I had made some crack about you not being a member of the group—that no one could cry on your shoulder. In my notes I had written the night before, "There is no man in the world who loves me!" You seemed so genuinely concerned that day that I was overwhelmed . . . I *received* the gesture as one of the first feelings of acceptance—of me, just the dumb way I am, prickles and all—that I had ever experienced. I have felt needed, loving, competent, furious, frantic, anything and everything but just plain *loved*. You can imagine the flood of gratitude, humility, release that swept over me. I wrote with considerable joy, "*I* actually felt *loved*." I doubt that I shall soon forget it.

Such I-Thou relationships (to use Buber's term again) occur with some frequency in these group sessions and nearly always bring a moistness to the eyes of the participants.

One member, trying to sort out his experiences immediately after a workshop, speaks of the "commitment to relationship" which often developed on the part of two individuals—not necessarily individuals who have liked each other initially. He goes on to say, ". . . the incredible fact experienced over and over by members of the group was that when a negative feeling was fully expressed to another, the relationship grew and the negative feeling was replaced by a deep acceptance for the other. . . . Thus real change seemed to occur when feelings were experienced and expressed in the context of the relationship. 'I can't *stand* the way you talk!' turned into a real understanding and affection for you the *way* you talk." This statement seems to capture some of the more complex meanings of the term *basic encounter*.

14. *The expression of positive feelings and closeness.* As indicated in the last section, an inevitable part of the group process seems to be that when feelings are expressed and can be accepted in a relationship, then a great deal of closeness and positive feeling results. Thus as the sessions proceed, an increasing feeling of warmth and group spirit and trust is built up, not out of positive attitudes only but out of a realness which includes both positive and negative feeling. One member tried to capture this in writing shortly after a workshop by saying that if he were trying to sum it up, ". . . it would have to do with what I call confirmation—a kind of confirmation of myself, of the uniqueness and universal qualities of men, a confirmation that when we can be human together something positive can emerge."

Some may be very critical of a "leader" so involved and so sensitive that she weeps at the tensions in the group which she has taken into herself. For myself it is simply another evidence that when people are real with each other, they have an astonishing ability to heal a person with a real and understanding love, whether that person is "participant" or "leader."

15. *Behavior changes in the group.* It would seem from observation that many changes in behavior occur in the group itself. Gestures change. The tone of voice changes, becoming sometimes stronger, sometimes softer, usually more spontaneous, less artificial, with more feeling. Individuals show an astonishing amount of thoughtfulness and helpfulness toward each other.

Our major concern, however, is with the behavior changes that occur following the group experience. This constitutes the most significant question, on which we need much more study and research. One person gives a catalog which may seem too pat, but which is echoed in many other statements, of the changes he sees in himself. "I am more open, spontaneous. I express myself more freely. I am more sympathetic, empathic, and tolerant. I am more confident. I am more religious in my own way. My relations with my family, friends, and coworkers are more honest and I express my likes and dislikes and true feelings more openly. I admit ignorance more readily. I am more cheerful. I want to help others more."

Another says, ". . . Since the workshop there has been found a new relationship with my parents. It has been trying and hard. However, I have found a greater freedom in talking with them, especially my father. Steps hae been made toward being closer to my mother than I have ever been in the last five years." Another says, "It helped clarify my feelings about my work, gave me more enthusiasm for it, made me more honest and cheerful with my coworkers and also more open when I was hostile. It made my relationship with my wife more open, deeper. We felt freer to talk about anything and we felt confident that anything we talked about we could work through."

Sometimes the changes described are very subtle. "The primary change is the more positive view of my ability to allow myself to *hear*, and to become involved with someone else's 'silent scream.' "

At the risk of making the outcomes sound too good, I will add one more statement written shortly after a workshop by a mother. She says, "The immediate impact on my children was of interest to both me and my husband. I feel that having been so accepted and loved by a group of strangers was so supportive that when I returned home my love for the people closest to me was much more spontaneous. Also, the practice I had in accepting and loving others during the workshop was evident in my relationships with my close friends."

M. A. Lieberman, M. B. Miles and I. B. Yalom are representatives of a newly emerging tendency to carry out teamwork in the social and behavioral sciences. The following selection, from Chapter 2 of Encounter Groups: First Facts, *by Morton A. Lieberman, Irvin D. Yalom, and Matthew B. Miles, © 1973 by Morton A. Lieberman, Irvin D. Yalom and Matthew B. Miles, Basic Books, Inc., Publishers, New York, describes a joint research project involving psychological studies of 18 encounter groups, of their leaders, and of 210 college students who served as subjects and participated in the group experience. The groups ranged all the way from T-groups, Gestalt groups, transactional analysis groups, and Esalen-type eclectic groups to marathon groups and leaderless groups. The study also includes a discussion of control groups, follow-up reports, self-reports, and ranking by participants of group leaders according to their competence.*

The following selection from Encounter Groups *describes the operation of a sensitivity-training or T-group. It is followed by a Gestalt group, described as a "love fest, letting it all hang out, pretend the pillow is her and let her have it, everything goes, fun, funny. . . ." [sic!]*

T-GROUP

Classic, old school, sensitivity group, members frustrated, straining at bit; leader patient, firmly holding reins. . . .

Group #2 met seven times. The first and the fourth meetings were six hours long, the other five were three hours long. The first two meetings were in a dormitory lounge, and the last five in the living room of a member's on-campus apartment. The setting was informal; all sat on the floor. The three women and seven men in the group attended regularly.

Leader #2 was a clinical psychologist who had been deeply involved in sensitivity training for eleven years, and was nationally recognized as an expert in the area of group function and group dynamics. He stressed the importance of molding the group and of the members' participation and understanding of the process of group formation so that they could begin to understand other social environments in which they had to function. He said it was important for him that individuals in the group work toward greater humaneness toward others and more openness and honesty with themselves; he wanted them to enjoy the others in the group. He described himself as deliberately less active than many leaders because he felt that a group should struggle with its internal problems and have the satisfaction of resolving them, rather than being constantly removed from the cocoon of group forces by a well-meaning but too active and tantalizing leader. He saw himself as both leader and member: "I am somewhere between a teacher in the broadest sense, and a member of the community which develops."

Observers rated Leader #2 third among the leaders in the attention he focused on the entire group, second in attention to interpersonal material. Observers reported that he often invited members to participate, questioned them, or reflected something back to them, but he rarely directly challenged or confronted them. He provided cognitive structure by comparing members one to another or inviting them to seek feedback from the other members, although he did not often explain, or summarize, or offer members a specific suggestion about how to understand themselves. He did support members of the group occasionally, but rarely explicitly protected or befriended a member. He did not participate as a member of the group, and he rarely revealed his own personal values or his own here-and-now feelings, but he did tend to draw attention to himself as a leader.

The observers found him a "social engineer and releaser of emotions by suggestion." He attempted to focus attention on how the group as a whole should move ahead, rather than on the private problems of individual members. He often was seen to manage the group by stopping it, or blocking something, or focusing on a particularly important thing, or pacing the group, or by calling attention to a decision that the group had to make.

These statements come from the beginning of the first meeting:

Does anybody have any ideas how we might start? Shall we have introductions? . . . How do you feel about what's going on so far? . . . How did you feel as this was going on? . . . Gee, I didn't have that feeling at all. I was touched by what you said. How do you feel about that?

I think we should bring this thing into the present, into the now, instead of thinking about it as just a discussion we are having. It sounded like you had a lot of feelings about me. . . . I don't know yet if I want to be a member of the group. . . . I guess the leader is always the assumed central part of a group somehow. . . .

From Session 5:

Is a discussion about getting involved here a kind of red hot topic? . . . Do you feel any ties here at all, I'm asking each of you? Is it hard to talk about them, about how you feel toward people in the room?

Do you think that you can react physically with this group? I'll ask you if there's any physical technique that you'd want to use if you don't want to react verbally with the group. . . . I'm sure that each person will find his own way to express himself, I don't care how. We're not limited to verbal expression. There's your face, your body, anyway. I wouldn't make a game or a gimmick out of it, but if you actually want to express yourself, by all means it's open to you.

Jim, can I share a feeling I have about you? I have the impression that you're just bursting to be the leader of this group. In one way or another that would make you happy. . . . I'd like to check this out with you. How do you feel about being the leader of this group, because it's a hunch on my part? . . . I don't know of a simple lecture to give you.

. . . I want to describe my role as I do it, and I think I reserve the option to do this. From time to time I'll offer what I think are suggestions, about the way in which I think you can work usefully. It may not work, but I will do what I can along that line. The other important thing is I think it's useful to you individually and collectively to find out where I am because I really can't tell you. . . . I know I don't want to lead you. I think the responsibility is with each of you. . . . I want to feel free to make suggestions and do things to increase the way in which you can learn here. . . . I still don't know where I am in my relationship to you. . . . I think you're fighting the position that reflects your attitudes toward me. I looked around and I saw you and Ted lying down and everybody else except Ted was up on his elbows conscious.

Leader #2 used approximately twenty-three exercises during the life span of the group, about midway among the seventeen leaders. Examples of his exercises:

Close your eyes. Visualize the people in the group. Who would be easy to communicate with? Who difficult? Now, go up to the person and tell them why you could or couldn't communicate with them.

Everyone shout somebody's name . . . whose name was shouted the most? Okay, Jan, if you're talking about being straight, can you go around and identify the straight people in this group?

Can you say it with more bite? Can you tell them how you really feel?

Don't move. Everyone look at Bill. Tell him what it says to you. Describe him.

Would you all take some partner and step outside and share one thing with that partner that you've censored here in the group.

Everybody space out, close your eyes, feel the space around you and push it aside. Now curl up in the tiniest space you can, slowly come out, shake your shell off.

Looking Back

Immediately after the group ended, the members rated it in the top third of the seventeen groups on these dimensions: they found it a pleasant experience, were turned on by it, thought it constructive, and felt they learned a great deal. They did not rate their leader highly. He ranked slightly below the average—thought him competent, would like to be in a group with him again, admired him as a person, approved of his techniques and effectiveness. He rated slightly above average on understanding his group. The members felt that he was too remote and passive. As with Leader #1, the observers rated him as much more competent than did the group members. Only three leaders were rated higher.

GESTALT GROUP

Love fest, letting it all hang out, pretend the pillow is her and let her have it, everything goes, fun, funny. . . .

Group #3 met for three time-extended meetings. The first six-hour meeting was followed a week later by another. The last meeting, two weeks later, was for eighteen hours. The first meetings were held in a dormitory lounge; the last in a reading room. The eleven members sat on the floor on pillows or mattresses; they attended regularly.

Leader #3 was a clinical psychologist who had been running therapy groups for about eight years. One innovation of his has been the open sharing of his own fantasies and dreams. He reported that he pays careful attention to posture shifts, and helps members get in touch with themselves through these observations. He prefers to do group work because he finds it more exciting. He considers himself innovative and radical. He wants each member to have increased awareness about his own behavior and greater understanding of the "why" of such behaviors. He hopes that each member of the group will be able to choose to make of his life what he wishes. He feels that it's important to frustrate members of the group in order to help them assume responsibility for their own acts. He tends to focus as much as possible on the here-and-now.

Leader #3 was a very high support, high challenge, antiintellectual leader who revealed himself freely, as observers saw him. The focus of his attention was fairly evenly distributed among interpersonal, intrapersonal, and group behaviors and midway among the leaders. He often invited questions and confronted members in an effort to "open them up." However, he gave a great deal of support. . . . He revealed his here-and-now feelings and his own personal values, often drew attention to himself as a person and as a leader, and in many ways participated as a member of the group.

He gave less attention than any other leader to any type of coherence-aiding statement, whether explanation, clarification, or interpretation. He managed the group by focusing on members or issues, or by suggesting some type of structural procedure.

The observer rated his global style as "challenger," or "releaser of emotions by demonstration," and as a "personal leader," one who expressed considerable warmth, acceptance, genuineness, and caring for other human beings.

These remarks were selected from the beginning of the first meeting:

Let's begin. I'm. . . . Can you tell me your expectations for our group? I'll tell you what my ground rules are: (1) there's no subgrouping, and subgrouping is bad. If you have something to say, say it. I hear some of you whispering. (2) No drugs. No dope, tranquilizers. (3) The last rule is no physical violence that will be injurious. . . .

I Haven't the foggiest idea what the research is about. I am as much in doubt as you are. . . . I filled out the same forms, by the way. . . . I'm in favor of getting all the hidden agendas out in the open. If you have something to say, say it. I'll lay it right out and I hope you do the same. . . .

This is what I do. I lead groups. I lead groups on a regular basis. . . . One of the things I don't do is give lectures on what groups are like and stuff like that.

Let's go around the room and each of you find somebody that you think is interesting. Go sit by the person. . . . When you get together with your partner, get a little space between you, don't cram together. Just sit together for a few minutes and get to know the person you're sitting with without using any words.

This is a little experiment in awareness. Don't go somewhere else. Get in touch with what you're thinking. Let your attention go there. Keep in touch with your awareness. Don't try and change anything. Just stay in touch. We're going to take a little trip together. Innerspace travel, like you are shrunk down and traveling in your blood stream. Imagine a little tiny you entering your body. . . .

We've got about seven more minutes. I'd like you to experiment by telling the other three people in your group something you've been holding back, something like a secret.

Excerpts from the final session:

What are you experiencing right now? . . . There is heavy stuff going on here and there's a lot not being said. I can feel it. A cloud is hanging over it. . . . You're gossiping. . . . You're still gossiping. . . . You're pussy-footing. It's obvious you have very different points of view but you're saying it so carefully like maybe she's going to fall apart.

Make believe your girlfriend is sitting right here, and talk to her. . . . Stay with it. . . . You're holding back. . . . Keep telling her. . . . Okay, now switch seats, and you play your girlfriend and see what she says. . . . Yell back if you want to. . . . Pound your fists. . . . Louder . . . Louder . . . Why don't you tell her, "I give you the power to make me feel guilty"? . . Do you resent that? . . . Say, "I'm just putty in your hands."

What do you mean, being crazy? . . . How would you be like if you went crazy? What's your fantasy? . . . And then? . . . Bullshit . . . you're being so calm and collected. . . . I'm entitled not to believe you. . . . I think you're a prick. . . . Because when I tell you that I don't believe you you're so calm . . . and so nice. . . . Now, what's going on inside? I think you want to drive me crazy. . . . Well, I don't feel like explaining myself. . . . Tough. I don't want to do it. I'd rather drive you crazy than have you drive me crazy. . . . I am being obnoxious. . . . I'm a rat. You're a rat. He's a rat. . . . He's not a rat. Is that what I said? I never heard me say that. . . . You're an elephant. . . . I'd like to see you two guys drive each other crazy. You're both the same way. I'm getting out of here.

Leader #3 used a high number of structured exercises, approximately sixty. Only two leaders used as many or more:

Form small groups of four people. Take turns introducing yourselves nonverbally. Take five minutes to decide how you want to do it. Try to come up with a name for your group.

Be a little metal box. Imagine you're empty: you're a shell. How do you feel?

I'd like some feedback. Tell me what you feel. Go around on me, on the leader.

Let's all try to bring you to a boil. I'd like to hear what the mind-fuck sounds like out loud.

Get in touch with your headache. Be your headache and talk to him. Say that's your headache.

Group Processes

The members of Group #3 spent much of their time discussing inside, here-and-now material. When the group did discuss outside material, it was generally a discussion of personal current events. Past historical material, or abstract issues, or current social issues were rarely discussed. The inside here-and-now material was fairly evenly distributed between interpersonal and intrapersonal issues. . . . The group spent a relatively high proportion of time discussing its feelings toward the leader, both as a leader and as a person.

The members spent much of their time in leader-organized subgroup discussions. Not infrequently, they discussed one particular member. Rarely were there prolonged monologues or dialogues. The leader himself was quite active. The members disclosed a great deal about their here-and-now feelings; in only two groups was there more self-disclosure. Self-disclosure was very high in the very first meeting and then tapered off. The observers noted that Group #3 was unusually harmonious, unusually informal, and highly open. . . . The cohesion was higher at the eighth meeting than at the fourth.

Intense emotional expression (kissing, touching, expressing caring, commenting on likeability, crying, pleading for help) was much approved. Sexual, dream/fantasy material, problems with outsiders, were seen as appropriate content. Group #3 was also high on approval of advice-giving, trying to convince others, judging another's behavior as wrong, telling another he was unlikeable, and shouting with anger.

Much more frequently than in most groups, members of Group #3 frequently cited situations which involved expressing a positive ("warm," "close") feeling as the most important events in group meetings. Insight or some type of cognitive gain were very infrequently mentioned. Group #3 emphasized understanding their impact on others and expressing their feelings as primary learnings. . . . They reported that they also gained from understanding why they felt and thought the way they did, and from discovering previously unknown parts of themselves.

Looking Back

At the end of the group, the members were exceedingly enthusiastic. They found their group a pleasant experience . . . they were "turned on" by the group . . . they considered it to be a constructive experience . . . they felt that they learned a great deal. . . .

Lieberman, Yalom, and Miles found that roughly one third of participants derived some benefit from their experiences, the rest did not, dropped out or had untoward reactions. The study classes some ten percent as "casualties." The authors conclude: "When one strips away the excesses and the frills, the ability of such groups to provide a meaningful emotional setting in which individuals can overtly consider previously prohibited issues cannot be ruled out as an important means for facilitating human progress."

A recent report by a Task Force on Group Psychotherapy (in the New York State Journal of Medicine, October 1973) under the auspices of the New York District Branch of the American Psychiatric Association, has made the distinction between group therapy and encounter groups more specific. It emphasizes the nonmedical, largely educational character of encounter groups, as contrasted with group psychotherapy, which is fashioned after the medical model. Encounter groups focus on problem solving, self-improvement, self-betterment, increased awareness, "and other such goals." Participants are not labelled as patients; leaders are "facilitators"; the experience is not considered therapy. The report cautions that patients should not be referred to encounter groups and, conversely, those seeking merely education and instruction should not be exposed to the emotional stress of group psychotherapy.

Our final selection is taken from an article by Kurt W. Bak, professor of sociology and psychiatry at Duke University and recipient of a Russell Sage Foundation grant for the study of sensitivity training as a social phenomenon. Titled "The Group Can Comfort but It Can't Cure" (Psychology Today, 1972), the article discusses the merits of the encounter movement and sounds a note of caution about the hazards and possible harmful effects of the group experience upon more vulnerable participants.

Encounter groups propose to reduce man's alienation from other persons, from nature, and from genuine emotion. Leaders are working out purportedly scientific techniques to make man more involved with others. Other purveyors of scientific techniques have been chastened out and controlled when their procedures turned out to be irresponsible—as with DDT, and the SST. But, ironically, now that encounter advocates' own techniques are widespread, producing effects that cannot be predicted, they have retreated to the morality of the marketplace; they cater to public demand and look with dismay at consumer protection.

System. The ideas underlying sensitivity training are not new; intensive group experiences have long been part of human society. But earlier cultures kept them under strict social control. They worked up the techniques as part of an intricate system of beliefs, not just for the worth of the experience. Such institutionalized belief systems are now in decline. Today's leaders in sensitivity training have assumed some of the functions performed by healers, priests and shamans in earlier societies. With these functions, they also should have assumed certain responsibilities. Past societies controlled the individuals who exercised this kind of influence, through selection, training and supervision. Modern techniques are as intense as religious and healing experiences, and they leave similar marks on participants. But social controls are lacking.

Encounter groups concern themselves only with the here and now; discussions and actions relate only to the present situation. More important, the relationships within the groups last only as long as the group lasts. Characteristically, these groups are made up of strangers who have come together for a weekend or a few weeks, or for a few hours a week, who have never seen each other before, have not selected each other, and presumably will not see each other again.

Survival. The striking feature of all sensitivity training is how persons come to care for each other in these groups and how they seem to become important to each other for the time the group lasts. It may become a strong experience that leaves memories to be cherished, but it all ends with the group.

Carl Rogers is an advocate of such limited intense relationships. He says that in the highly mobile, high-density society of the future, the ability to make short-range, strong, effective relationships and to relinquish them easily—that is, to invest in the meaning of brief encounters—will be one of the preconditions of psychic survival, and that a society of this kind will have its special beauties and charms. Perhaps. Nevertheless, advocates claim that this intense experience produces beneficial, measurable change in the individual. These claims are not met.

Search. Traditionally, the practitioner, the companion through the process of change, assumed a special responsibility to guide the person into this new status and to help him through any unforeseen consequences. In encounter groups, however, the responsibility ends with the final session.

Nor does the scientific rhetoric that often is used to justify the action in encounter groups seem to create professional responsibility. The social scientist has succeeded the priest as the guide to personal change and even to spiritual search. Scientific authority enforces its own rules and sanctions, and these offer society protection against abuse of special power and knowledge. Those who organize encounter groups claim competence in the scientific method, which they apply as the essence of their profession. The ethics of their practice should come from scientific and professional codes.

The client must be able to believe that the practitioner is well qualified, that a definite service can be performed, that possible dangers are kept at a minimum, and that these dangers stand in sensible relation to the possible benefits. The professional encounter-group organizer assumes responsibility within the framework of behavioral science. Psychology, social psychology, sociology and psychiatry provide the basis on which he can rest his procedure and activities.

Skeptic. Encounter groups aim to do more, however, than most scientific professions. The practitioners' use of intense emotional experiences and ritualistic exercises, and their talk of treating alienation and existential despair, make them spiritual advisers as well. The sensitivity trainer combines the religious healer's charisma with the scientist's language. Thus, he assumes both the competent professional's responsibility and the guru's compassion of shared emotion.

The double role makes it hard to judge a group leader's performance. If a skeptic challenges the scientific basis of sensitivity training, citing the danger of the procedures in comparison with the low evidence of success, the leader can deprecate these concerns as being picayune in the context of spiritual regeneration. Or he may come back by comparing sensitivity training with such other procedures as psychoanalysis and point to the lack of hard research proving their effectiveness. Between claiming to be beyond evaluation and quibbling over the relative merit of his own and others' research results, the sensitivity-training leader leaves the question of his responsibility unanswered.

Stance. The issue of responsibility was raised in New York in 1969 when the weekly paper, *The Village Voice*, refused to advertise groups whose claims implied therapy. The paper said that advertising therapy was against professional standards and, in general, unethical. The sponsors of encounters argued that they did not conduct therapy or aim at changing the psychological state of participants in a fundamental way; a committee of encounter-group leaders said they aimed only "to provide a *social environment* for people who prefer not to relate to others in the distracting and sometimes artificial environments of bars, parties, dances, etc." Such a statement suggests little concern for scientific competence.

The whole stance of the movement stresses feeling, the strong experience as *experience*, and the gratifications that come out of this experience. Despite the scientific language, there has been little systematic evaluation of encounter processes. Many persons in the movement have become impatient with the lack of evaluation techniques and the lack of attempts to standardize results.

So we have people undergoing a strong experience that historically has been controlled and frequently has been part of the sacred aspect of society. This has been taken over as pure technique, with few, if any, professional controls. It has become a general social problem to be dealt with by the larger society.

But evaluation is not easy; there is little hard evidence about either benefits or dangers. The benefits of encounter groups usually are defined negatively. The group is an experience unlike ordinary life; in it, persons may shed their old restraints and try out new patterns of behavior and experience. Encounter techniques seem to work best either as recreation or as

limited adjuncts to specific training programs. Benefits are possible, but the
ways that they are derived and the goals that are achieved are unknown.
Testimony on the good effects of encounters are similar to testimony on the
good effects of drug usage. There is nothing wrong with feeling good, but
we should weigh it against the possible danger.

Students. Data on danger has been collected even less systematically than
that on benefits. There are occasional serious emotional breakdowns. One
of the lower estimates is one in 1,500; a study at Yale showed that the incidence of psychiatric disorders was lower among students who participated
in sensitivity training than a general sample of students. Other estimates,
however, are much higher. George Odiorne has stated that there is likely to
be one person with a serious problem in practically every encounter group,
and Juan Rosello, for several years psychiatrist for the National Training
Laboratories (NTL), estimates that there are about five serious problems
there each summer. NTL's data show 25 serious psychiatric incidents among
11,000 participants in 22 years of summer programs and eight incidents
among 3,000 participants in 13 years of industrial laboratory programs.

M. A. Lieberman, Irvin D. Yalom and M. B. Miles deal with identification and estimation of psychiatric casualities in a recent evaluation. They
found a casualty rate of 9.6 percent, compared to none in a control group.
They defined casualty as evidence of definite harm occurring as a consequence of the sessions. Grave as it seems, this finding itself is less important
thar their finding that the persons *least* able to identify casualties were the
group leaders; trainees, peers, or associates all were more able to identify
casualties. This casts doubt on many of the low estimates that are given
elsewhere, mainly derived from leaders or from organizations that conduct
the programs.

Stress. There are many anecdotal reports of complete breakdowns in persons who previously had been functioning quite effectively. Almost everyone who has been involved in encounter groups knows of at least one case
of serious breakdown.

But while psychotic breakdowns are the most visible casualties, they are
unlikely to be the only ones. The anguish of a person who is excluded from
the group can be quite traumatic; just as traumatic can be the situation of a
group member who does not conform to the group norms of openness,
spontaneity, and involvement. This group-induced stress might be justifi-
able in a technique in which definite gain can be expected, or in which the
training follows a procedure whose workings the practitioner understands.
But, as Rodney Luther said, "We are concerned that 25 to 40 percent of persons sent to sensitivity gain nothing and very possibly lose some highly valuable behavioral assets. Even in actual war, win-loss ratios of this order of
magnitude are impossible to justify.

Another subtle but pervasive problem is invasion of privacy. Encounter groups often regard privacy as obnoxious, and there is social pressure to surrender it. But there is little concern with how the person reconstructs his defenses afterward.

Standards. When we weigh the dangers against the limited and vague benefits of encounter techniques, the balance is not encouraging. It might be most useful to look at encounter groups as frankly experimental. Benefits cannot be established in more than a tentative way, but the leaders and organizers of the groups believe that they have discovered a new dimension of human experience that has potential value for today's mass society. They also believe that their new techniques are worth experimenting with, even if there is little underlying theory in the rigorous sense of the word.

If we accept this, then we must consider encounter groups in the same way that we consider any other experimentation with human subjects. The ethics or experimentation have been a controversial subject, but gradually some standards have emerged. The three main principles that guide experimentation with human subjects are 1) voluntary participation, 2) informed consent, and 3) compensating value.

The first principle, voluntary participation, states that nobody should be forced to be an experimental subject. But not everyone who participates in an encounter group does so voluntarily. For example, an entire business or school may accept an encounter-group program as a training procedure, in which case it is difficult for an individual to refuse to participate. Defective screening aggravates this problem. Even with our limited knowledge, it may be possible to screen out people who obviously could be harmed. But this simple precaution—so seldom observed—is made more difficult to enforce if pressure of any kind brings whole groups involuntarily to an encounter.

The second principle, informed consent, brings up another knotty problem. Since the workings of encounter groups are so little understood, even by practitioners, it is extremely difficult to describe to a layman what is involved. The principal safeguard is the professional competence of the experimenter. The prospective subject trusts that the experimenter has learned what is harmful and is sufficiently ethical to want to avoid doing harm.

Frequently it is the case that trained and responsible professionals lead encounter groups. But even they cannot know much about the factors that operate in encounter groups, because so little is known. There are no provisions for introducing participants to the encounter experience, guiding them through the difficulties they face in the group, or providing suitable closure. In addition, there are few requirements or professional standards for leaders of encounter groups. They have a variety of backgrounds and no common fund of knowledge or experience, nor do they have a common set of professional ethics. The fact is, unfortunately, that the prospective participant generally has little knowledge about the professional background of his trainer.

The third principle, compensating value, stipulates that the subject must receive either personal benefit from the experiment or social benefit through the creation of knowledge that might help him or others in similar circumstances. Personal benefits are hard to define and hard to promise to participants. If encounters then are looked on as broad social research, it is just at this point that the orientation of the group leader becomes important. In exchange for the invasion of privacy, temporary anguish, and risk of danger, the group leader cannot promise anything like a personal reward, as a physician does when he uses an experimental, high-risk treatment. If the group leader is a serious researcher, he must, therefore, commit himself to a valid study design that can give possible future benefit, and help in understanding the strong emotional forces he releases in his groups.

Stake. The problem of responsibility has faced sensitivity training for a long time. On the one hand, the leaders can point to examples of novel developments in human culture that advocates of the established order have suppressed; they assert a freedom to experiment with new ways of feeling, encounter, and human organization. Clearly, no critic wants to be part of a modern inquisition. On the other side, society has a stake in protecting the public from untested and potentially dangerous techniques that the layman may be unable to judge. One has only to compare the care and supervision demanded for the introduction of a new drug. The need for the activity of the Food and Drug Administration is not often questioned. If sensitivity training can have effects of comparable strength, there should be comparable protection of the public.

There have been Governmental hearings, but no legislation has yet been passed. The American Psychological Association has established a standing committee to study the ethical implications of sensitivity training. And the organizations involved in sensitivity training have taken steps to police their own activities. The National Training Laboratories have been in the forefront of this effort; they have publicized a set of standards to guard against untoward incidents, to make group leaders responsible, and to establish qualifications for the trainers themselves.

Structure. Even the professional group leaders have a *laissez-faire* attitude toward possible breakdowns and other detrimental effects. Jane Howard, in *Please Touch*, has noted the casual acceptance of many events, such as death or psychotic commitment, which are considered traumatic in most circumstances. In a magazine account of the encounter-group training of the Company of Young Canadians in which six members developed serious troubles and two were hospitalized, the psychiatrist in charge was quoted as saying, "There is always a danger in bringing people from a structured society into an unstructured society where there are no rules, no authority." In the therapy method closest to encounter groups, Gestalt therapy, the same unconcern prevails. Fritz Perls states in his book, "Sir, if you want to go crazy, commit suicide, improve, get turned on, or get an experience that would change your life, that is up to you. You came here out of your own free will."

Self. The personal-growth centers, and especially Esalen, have elaborated the concept of responsibility. This builds on Perls's ideas and has been worked out by William Schutz. His statement to a New York workshop gives the general idea. ". . . whatever happens, you are responsible for yourself. That is, if during the course of these things you want to become physically injured, then you can do that if you want to; if you want to bow to group pressure, you can do that. If you want to not bow to group pressure, you can also do that. But I want to underline clearly at the outset that you are responsible for whatever happens to you here."

Given this basic philosophy, the task of the trainer is only to do what he thinks is best; his responsibility ends there, and the responsibility of the group member who came to the session on his own takes over. This interpretation of responsibility goes so far that one hears of opposition to having resident psychiatrists or counselors available.

But recently, Esalen had to disassociate itself from some practitioners who claimed that they had "Esalen training" and who got involved in malpractice suits. Thereby Esalen implied that its mark of approval meant something and referred to a specific training; this may be a first step along the road to certification similar to what the more conservative NTL has done.

Sequence. One way or the other, through external or internal policing, protection for the consumer is on its way. Sensitivity training is at the end of an era. Its ideas are no longer new. The glamor has faded. Social scientists are waiting for hard-research results, and even the popular media are abandoning the wide-eyed picture of the breakthrough in human relations and the equally exaggerated picture of the sinister manipulative group leader.

In the future, most of the more disciplined techniques of the encounter movement are likely to be absorbed by traditional scientific enterprises. The more extreme aspects probably will become purely religious or recreational exercises. Some sensitivity groups are coming more and more to approximate religious retreats, Sufi and Yoga centers, halfway houses, and singles' weekends at mountain and beach resorts. These gatherings will become more esoteric and attract a tighter and tighter clique of true believers.

Synthesis. Already social psychologists are showing more interest in the nature of affection, love and trust, as well as hate and aggression. Psychophysiologists are beginning to do laboratory studies of meditation and its

effects and are returning to experimental psychology's heritage of intro-
spection to describe meditation and similar exercises in their own terms.
Therapists have begun to incorporate into orthodox therapy groups some
exercises that were first used in sensitivity training. Management has
adopted some intensive techniques without buying the whole sensitivity-
training approach.

It has been the fate of many new belief systems to have a few of their new
techniques accepted selectively. After some testing, society finds virtue in a
few parts of the system and incorporates them into the older framework.
Instead of breaking through with massive change, we take in a few useful
tools—differential calculus came into being as an important aspect of a
philosophy of the perfection of God.

Surrender. What of the future of sensitivity training in the history of
ideas? It is hazardous to predict the future of the movement as ideology
rather than as technique. Proponents of the more mystical side of the movement frequently rely on analogies with previous times, most often with the
breakdown of classical civilization. The see sensitivity training as the cutting edge of a movement that brings forth new beliefs, new values, new
ways of life that would be as radically different from the existing system as
Christianity was from classicism.

Perhaps. But it is always a little presumptuous to regard oneself as being
located at the moment of supreme crisis at the start of a new era. Other
historical analogies may be less grandiose. One that comes to mind is the
"splendid century" in France when the aristocracy had amassed great af-
fluence but had lost its function and purpose and thereby gained a great
amount of leisure. Aristocrats spent their time in sensual play and in close
examination and discussion of the minutiae of interpersonal relations,
which they endowed with enormous meaning. They also sought less innocent diversions, such as occultism. In time there was a revolution.

In the same vein, Peter Berger has predicted that the meaning of the
"counterculture" is "the blueing of America"—the surrender of power positions by upper-class youth to the lower-middle and lower classes. He maintains that for the ones who do not want to drop out completely, there will
always be jobs available as T-group leaders.

Sensibility. Neither of the two analogies fits exactly. We do not have the
social or economic conditions of the Roman Empire or of Louis XIV's
France. Our wealth and our leisure are based on the rapid rise of technology
and science, and much of our spirituality springs from our need to face the
implications of science. Sensitivity training is a movement within this context. We can be sure that it will not be the last of its kind. But whether it
represents a transition to a new era or merely the sensibility of the new af-
fluence and leisure, only future historians can tell.

epilogue

The Therapeutic Triad
and the Power of Insight

Man's quest for relief from his irrational fears, inner conflicts and emotional discomfort is ceaseless and unremitting. He does not realize that his demons are within and not without, or that the perils of the soul may be just as real as the menace of wild beasts lurking at the entrance to his cave or of the mugger at the door of his brownstone house. Like the restless sleeper, he keeps tossing and turning in his bed to assuage his malaise and existential anxieties. He switches from his bed to the couch, to the hammock or the bare floor. Having tried the Temple Sleep of ancient Egypt or Greece, he turns to James Graham's Celestial Bed in eighteenth-century London, to James Braid's neurohypnology, to Wilhelm Reich's orgone box, to the Indian yogi's lotus position. He moves from magic to religion, from spells and incantations to prayer and priestly mediation with the divinity. He tries the medieval dirt pharmacy, Paracelsus' weapon salve and Sir Kenelm Digby's powder of sympathy. He experiments with Mesmer's animal magnetism and Mary Baker Eddy's Christian Science. He moves on to Charcot and Janet; to Freudian, Adlerian, or Jungian psychotherapy; and from there to Sullivan or Fromm; to transactional analysis, Gestalt therapy, or Janov's screaming cure. Sick to death of loneliness and isolation in the spiritual wasteland of Western industrialized society, he seeks closeness and intimacy in the encounter groups and communes that have proliferated in the contemporary American scene.

Paradoxically, the city dweller or villager of the Indian subcontinent, tired of the milling crowds of his community or smothered by the omnipresence of his extended family, takes to the road to seek the solitude of the recluse, the hermit, the anchorite, while his Western counterpart tries to find solace and peace of mind in such esoteric cults or religions as Zen Buddhism, yoga, Kundalini, and Sufism.

He experiments with transcendental meditation; with biofeedback techniques to produce alpha or theta waves to still the electric activity of his restless brain—a modern King Canute commanding ocean waves to cease beating against the shore. He enlists the latest gimmicks of electronic technology to gain control over his vegetative functions: his heartbeat, blood pressure, skin temperature, or gastric acidity. As his latest venture, he mobilizes the latter-day magic of parapsychology to effect unorthodox cures by telepathy or psychokinesis.

The fact is that most of these attempts have had a modicum of success. Some were passing fads that did not outlast their failures. Some were more enduring and flourished for decades before they were supplanted by others. The life span of Freudian analysis has by now come close to three quarters of a century, although its critics have already pronounced it dead or dying.

Is it possible, on reviewing the broad historic canvas of the healing arts, to account for the ephemeral nature of one school and the longevity of another? This question has been pondered by such students of the history of psychotherapy and anthropology as Pierre Janet (1929), Gregory Zilboorg, (1941), Henri Ellenberger (1970), J. D. Frank (1963), Hans Strupp (1973), and Claude Levi-Strauss (1967). The current consensus is that there is indeed a specific set of psychodynamic, interpersonal, and cultural factors or variables present in virtually all forms of psychotherapy which have passed the test of time. It is made up of (1) the personality of the healer, (2) the personality of the patient, and (3) the culture or subculture in which they are both immersed.

The foremost characteristics of the healer are his authentic therapeutic motivations, his confidence in his ability to help, to relieve the patient's suffering, to cure. His therapeutic motivations are in turn met halfway, as it were, by the patient's corresponding hopes and expectations that he will be cured—by his trust in the personality of the healer. A third variable is a favorable cultural setting: a vicariously participating tribal, cultist or sectarian group; a devout, prayerful congregation getting in on the act and sharing in the experience. The ensuing circular pattern of mutual reinforcements involving healer, patient and community then serves as the vehicle for the therapeutic process. It can indeed be found at the core of all the forms of prescientific psychotherapy mentioned in this book.

Depending on personal predilection, professed doctrine, and cultural context, such a scenario may call for a miracle performed by a charismatic healer, assisted by worshipful disciples, with the patient as a passive recipient of grace. Alternatively, the main action is shifted to the group: to a frantic band of dancing dervishes; to inspired members of a revivalist meeting; to devout pilgrims at a holy shrine with no healer present in the flesh. Or else both healer and the group are replaced by the projections of a patient whose imagination conjures up an awestruck audience, a Greek chorus or a milling crowd of "extras" doing their bit and bearing witness to a cure by divine intervention. Even the case of a modern psychotherapist working in the privacy of his office can be regarded as a *forme fruste* of our therapeutic triad, with the reputation of his school, of his professional affiliations, his publications, and the plaudits of his confreres serving to bolster the faith of his patients and to reinforce whatever personal charisma he may be able to muster.

Yet this diagrammatic picture cannot do justice to the more complicated state of affairs in scientific psychotherapy. The scientific psychotherapist adds to our triad the pragmatic knowledge and experience accrued to his specialty. He tempers belief in his omnipotence by insight and better reality testing. He is trained to base his diagnosis and prognosis on his observations of the patient's behavior, not on clues derived from the entrails of animals or the movement of heavenly bodies. He studies personality traits, psychodynamics, transference-countertransference configurations; his interventions aim at reaching catharsis through insight and at consolidating gains through working-through and reeducation. Or else he may remove symptoms by methodical desensitization, or conditioned reflex or aversion therapy; through reciprocal inhibition, "token economies," or milieu therapy. He may work with groups guided by psychoanalytic, transactional, Gestaltist or existential principles, and he may add relaxation exercises or diverse physical or chemical nostrums—energizers or tranquilizers—to his armamentarium.

All these efforts to apply to the healing arts the principles of scientific method have led to three rather disconcerting and seemingly paradoxical conclusions concerning scientific psychotherapy. First, they have shown that the propositions of virtually all schools are borne out by the actual findings of their protagonists. Second, they suggest that the therapeutic results obtained or claimed by the rival schools are roughly the same. And third, they bring home to us the difficulty of demonstrating conclusively the superiority of scientific psychotherapy over its primitive forerunners.

As far as validation of basic propositions is concerned, the comparative study of Freudian, Jungian, Adlerian, Rankian, Horneyan, or existentialist case reports indicates that the productions of the patients invariably confirm the hypotheses promulgated by their therapists. Freudian patients tend to bring their analysts "Freudian" dreams, Jungian patients feature "Jungian" themes in the manifest content of their dreams, and so on. Each school of thought seems to supply its own corroborative evidence, even though their respective propositions are at variance and mutually incompatible. Each amounts to a virtually self-sealing system of thought—at least so long as it is not punctured by hostile criticism from outsiders relying on a different set of premises.

It is the spectacle of these contradictions and inconsistencies that I have described as doctrinal compliance by the patient with the therapist's cherished theoretical presuppositions and theories (1966). Robert Rosenthal (1969), approaching the same problem from the angle of the experimenter, arrived at similar conclusions. He found that the clinical or educational psychologist's observations are subject to contamination by observer bias, the experimenter's expectations or the preconceived ideas of the classroom teacher. All this may have a profound effect on the subjects' or the students' performances. It may affect their scores in I.Q. or projective tests as well as their behavior in the classroom. This is what Rosenthal has described as the Pygmalion effect.

Apparently this tendency to ward doctrinal compliance, toward Rosenthal's Pygmalion effect, accounts for the inner consistency, the record of unfailing self-validation, and the attendant persuasiveness of the diverse schools of psychotherapy, regardless of the mutual incompatibility of their theories.

It should also be noted that, according to the figures made available by representatives of the diverse schools, their therapeutic results are roughly identical. They all claim improvements or recoveries in the range of 70 to 80 percent. Such critics as H. J. Eysenck, J. Wolpe, T. Szasz and others have gone so far as to claim that their results are no better—and in some cases worse—that those seen in spontaneous remissions. I noted in chapter 26 that such statements have to be taken with a grain of salt. The behaviorist critic focuses on mere symptom removal, which is indeed a criterion of change readily amenable to quantitative treatment. By contrast, the psychoanalyst, the Jungian, the Adlerian, or the existential therapist is dealing with aspects of human personality which so far have defied attempts at statistical evaluation. The changes effected in patients emerging from under the cloud of alienation, existential anxiety, emotional frustration, or intellectual stagnation do not lend themselves to registration in the appropriate holes of an IBM card. Nor can the therapeutic claims made by fledgling schools appearing on the psychiatric scene stand comparison with clinical improvements seen in patients or families observed over a period of years or decades. The case history of Freud's Wolf Man extends over a period of more than fifty years (1971), and my own studies of the Obscomp clan have covered therapeutic results observed in four generations of this obsessive-compulsive family (1963, 1976).

Indeed, Thomas Szasz (1961), R. D. Laing (1961), and many existentialists have questioned the usefulness of a purely medical model applied to mental illness and its purported cure. If man does not live by bread alone, his illness or cure, his suffering or salvation, cannot be measured by reference to mere symptom removal or to the reduction of the number of days spent in a mental hospital. It requires a scale of values not included in current statistical manuals and a multidimensional model of man, who is still waiting in the wings to be admitted to the deliberations of the scientific community.

This leads us to our third paradox. If a major portion of success obtained by a given therapeutic procedure is contingent on a proper blend of the patient's, the therapist's and the group's dovetailing and interlacing wishes, hopes, and expectations regarding the efficacy of the procedure, it is readily understood that a healer engaged in scientific psychotherapy yet "sicklied o'er with the pale cast of thought" may lose much of his charismatic impact on the patient. On the other hand, the value of an informed, scientifically guided approach has been amply demonstrated. It has been brought home by clinical observations, anthropological findings and documentary evidence not contaminated by doctrinal compliance or the Pygmalion effect. It has become abundantly clear, even though it is not amenable to statistical verification. Thus statistical evaluation, supposedly the acid test of the scientific method, fails to bear out the claims of the superiority of scientific psychotherapy over primitive healing.

Nevertheless, what can be called the existential validation of both primitive healing and scientific psychotherapy is here for everyone to see. It is borne out by chapters 2 through 11 of this anthology, and by the persistent demands of patients, families and the community at large for guidance, counseling, and psychotherapy—for the healing encounter with a benevolent, supportive parent figure. In our civilization the scientific psychotherapist is evidently best equipped to cater to these needs and to meet both the patient's and the group's hopes and expectations within their common cultural context. Indeed, his therapeutic impact on his patients is contingent on his ability to do so. On the other hand, his failure to meet their hopes and expectations with authentic therapeutic motivations of his own, and to inspire corresponding attitudes in them, is bound to defeat his purpose as a healer regardless of his professional skills and expertise. His patient may respond in terms of doctrinal compliance or of Rosenthal's Pygmalion effect; his productions may bear out the therapist's pet scientific hypotheses. But this will not improve the patient's condition or allay his suffering. He will look for a therapist ready to try a novel approach, to experiment with new and, if necessary, "far out" techniques or procedures. Failing this, the patient will do what so many before him have done: he will turn to a helper who is able to offer what the expert has failed to deliver—to a latter-day magician, medicine man or guru—or he may fall into the hands of a charlatan.

What, then, can we learn from our guided tour of the history of psychotherapy? First, it suggests that, other things being equal, a highly motivated charismatic healer may have a powerful therapeutic impact even with little help from the patient or his group. This is illustrated by some of the healing miracles of the Bible. Second, it shows that, given a devoutly trusting patient, even a thoroughly skeptical agent ministering to the sick may succeed in his ministry, in spite of himself, as it were. This is exemplified by the apparent cures effected by the "royal touch" of such reluctant healers as some of the kings of old England. In this case, it was the patient's faith that, though unable to move mountains, was at least capable of removing warts or other minor defects or disabilities. Third, it appears that, given an equally strong faith animating a devout group or congregation, similar cures can be effected without the presence of a charismatic person. Classic examples are the cures attributed to such healing shrines as Epidaurus, Lourdes, and St. Anne de Beaupre. Fourth, we have seen that the judicious manipulation of transference, suggestion, insight, reeducation, desensitization, and other means of scientific psychotherapy is apt to achieve what seems to be superior and more enduring results even without a charismatic healer and in the absence of anything like blind faith or implicit trust on the part of the patient or his friends and relations.

But we have also noted that the absence of such purportedly irrational factors in scientific psychotherapy is only apparent. Here, too, personal integrity, authentic therapeutic motivation, a hopeful attitude on the part of the patient, and a propitious cultural climate are indispensable ingredients of an effective therapeutic formulary or helping situation. Indeed, only a reasonable balance of all four ingredients attuned to existing personal idiosyncrasies and geared to the prevailing sociocultural conditions can claim to be truly "scientific."

Bibliography

The references marked by asterisks (*) refer to publications selections from which are included in this anthology. Other titles are mentioned in the editor's comments or are quoted as further recommended reading.

Abell, R. G. (1966). Group psychoanalysis. In *Handbook of Psychoanalytic Therapies*, ed. J. Masserman. New York: Aronson.

*Adler, A. (1931). *What Life Should Mean to You*. New York: Grosset & Dunlap.

Arieti, S. (1955). *Interpretation of Schizophrenia*. New York: Brunner-Mazel.

*Avicenna (1952). Book of salvation. In *Avicenna's Psychology*, ed. F. Rahman. Oxford University Press.

*Bak, K. W. (1972). The group can comfort but it can't cure. In *Psychology Today*. New York: Russell Sage Foundation, Basic Books.

Baker Eddy, M. (1906). *Science and Health*. 1st ed. 1875, with key to the scriptures. Trustees under the will of Mary Baker Eddy.

Beckett, W. (1732). *Laying on of Hands*. Quoted from Thompson (1946).

*Berne, E. (1967). *Games People Play*. New York: Grove Press.

*Bernheim, H. (1889). *Suggestive Therapeutics: A Treatise on the Nature of Uses of Hypnotism*. trans. C. A. Herter. New York: Putnam.

*Bieber, I. (1973). On behavior therapy: A critique. *Journ. Am. Academy of Psychoanalysis* (1973): 43-46.

*Binswanger, L. (1956). Existential analysis and psychotherapy. In *Progress in Psychotherapy, Vol. I*, eds. F. Fromm-Reichmann and J. L. Moreno. New York: Grune & Stratton.

*———(1963). Freud and the magna charta of clinical psychiatry. In *Being-in-the-World: Selected Papers, Part II*, trans. J. Needleman. New York: Basic Books.

Bierer, J. (1948). *Therapeutic Social Clubs.* ed. H. K. Lewis. London.

*Boissarie (1911). *Lourdes, Les Guerisons* (*The Cures of Lourdes*). Editor's translation.

*Boss, M. (1963). *Psychoanalysis and Daseinsanalysis* (Chapter 4). New York: Basic Books.

*Braid, J. (1843). *Neurypnology or the Rationale of Nervous Sleep Considered in Relation with Animal Magnetism.* London: I. Churchill.

Buber, M. (1958). *I and Thou.* New York: Scribner.

*Carrel, A. (1950). *The Voyage to Lourdes.* New York: Harper and Row.

*Carter, M. E. and McGarey, M.D. (1972). *Edgar Cayce on Healing.* New York: Paperback Library.

Cayce, E. (1972). *On Healing.* See Carter and McGarey.

*Charcot, J. M. (1889). *Clinical Lectures on the Diseases of the Nervous System.* Trans. T. Savill. London: New Sydenham Society.

Coue, E. (1927). *How to Practice Suggestion and Autosuggestion.* New York: American Library Service.

*Digby, Sir Kenelm (1658). *A Late Discourse Made in a Solemne Assembly of Notables and Learned Men at Montpellier in France.* Trans. R. White. London.

*Ehrenwald, J. (1955). *New Dimensions of Deep Analysis.* New York: Grune & Stratton. Also, London: Allen and Unwin, 1954; New York: Arno, 1975.

*———(1966). The telepathy hypothesis and schizophrenia. *Journal of the American Academy of Psychoanalysis* 2: 159-169.

*———(1968). Freud versus Jung: The mythophobic versus the mythophilic temper in psychotherapy. *Israel Annals of Psychiatry* 6.

*———(1974). Family dynamics and the transgenerational treatment effect. *Yearbook of Group Therapy 1974.* Ed. L. Wolberg and M. Aronson. New York: Stratton Intercontinental.

*———(1976). *Parapsychiatry: A Study of Psi Functions and Dysfunctions.* New York: Putnam.

*Eisenbud, J. (1970). *Psi and Psychoanalysis.* New York: Grune & Stratton.

Ellenberger, H. (1970). *The Discovery of the Unconscious.* New York: Basic Books.

*Epicurus (1654). *Morals.* Trans. W. Charlton. London: P. Davis, 1926.

Erikson, E. (1950). *Childhood and Society.* New York: Norton.

*Eysenck, H. J. (1966). *The Effects of Psychotherapy.* New York: International Science Press.

*———(1973). Evaluating psychoanalysis. *New Medical Tribune*, April.

———(1973). *The Experimental Study of Freudian Theories.* London: Methuen.

Fodor, N. (1953). Telepathy in analysis. *Psychoanalysis and the Occult.* Ed. G. Devereux. New York: International Universities Press.

Frank, J. D. (1973). *Persuasion and Healing*. Baltimore: Johns Hopkins University Press.

Frankl, V. (1955). *The Doctor and the Soul*. Trans. R. and C. Winston. New York: Knopf.

*Frazer, J. (1890). *The Golden Bough*. New York: Macmillan.

Freud, S. (1913). *The Interpretation of Dreams*. New York: Macmillan.

*———(1916). *Three Contributions to the Theory of Sex*. Trans. A. A. Brill. New York: Nervous and Mental Disease Monographs.

———(1927). *The Ego and the Id*. London: Hogarth Press.

*———(1934). Dreams and the occult. *New Introductory Lectures on Psychoanalysis*. London: Hogarth Press.

*———(1940). *An Outline of Psychoanalysis*. New York: Norton.

*———(1950). *Totem and Taboo*. New York: Norton.

———(1952). *Autobiographical Study*. New York: Norton.

———(1954). *The Origins of Psychoanalysis: Letters to Wilhelm Fliess*. New York: Basic Books.

———(1971). *The Wolf Man: by the Wolf Man*. Ed. M. Gardiner. New York: Basic Books.

Freud-Jung Letters (1974). Ed. W. McGuire. Trans. R. Manheim and R. F. C. Hull. Princeton, N.J.: Bollingen Series, Princeton University Press.

*Fromm, E. (1941). *Escape from Freedom*. New York: Rinehart.

Galen (1963). *On the Passions and Errors of the Soul*. Trans. P. W. Harkins. Columbus, Ohio: Ohio State University Press.

*Glover, E. (1950). *Freud or Jung*. New York: Norton.

Grad, B., Cadoret, R., and Paul, G. (1961). The influence of an unorthodox method of treatment on wound healing in mice. *International Journal of Parapsychology* 9: 5-24.

Graham, J. *Celestial Bed*. Quoted from Thompson, C. J. S.

Harris, T. A. (1967). *I'm O.K.—You're O.K.* New York: Avon Books, Harper and Row.

Hartmann, H. (1964). *Essays on Ego Psychology*. New York: International Universities Press.

Heidegger, M. (1963). *Being and Time*. New York: Harper and Row.

*Hippocrates (no date). *Genuine Works*. 3 Vols. With a preliminary discourse and annotations. Translated by Francis Adams. New York: William Wood.

Hollos, I. (1953). A summary of Istvan Hollos' theories. *Psychoanalysis and the Occult*. Ed. G. Devereux. New York: International Universities Press.

*Horney, K. (1937). *The Neurotic Personality of Our Time*. New York: Norton.

*Janet, P. (1901). *The Mental State of Hystericals*. Trans. C. R. Carson. New York: Putnam.

Janet, P. (1929). *Psychological Healing*. Trans. E. and C. Paul. New York: Macmillan.

Janov, A. (1970). *The Primal Scream*. New York: Putnam.

Jaspers, K. (1949). *The Perennial Scope of Philosophy*. New York: Philosophical Library.

Jones, E. (1957). *The Life and Works of Sigmund Freud*. New York: Basic Books.

Jones, M. (1962). *Social Psychiatry*. Springfield, Ill.: Charles C Thomas.

*Jung, C. G. (1953). *Two Essays on Analytic Psychology*. Princeton, N.J.: Bollingen Series, Princeton University Press.

———(1961). *Memories, Dreams, Reflections*. Ed. A. Jaffe. New York: Pantheon Books.

*Kadis, A. L., Krasner, J. D., Winnick, C., and Foulkes, S., (1963). *A Practicum of Group Psychotherapy*. New York: Harper and Row.

*Kelman, H. (1960). Psychoanalytic thought and eastern wisdom. *Science and Psychoanalysis*. Vol. 3. Ed. J. Masserman. New York: Grune and Stratton.

———(1971). *Helping People: A Karen Horney Psychoanalytic Approach*. New York: Jason Aronson.

Kielholz, A. (1956). Von Kairos zum Problem der Kurpfuscherei. *Schweizer Mediz. Wochenshcrift* 86, 35.

Kiev, A., ed. (1964). *Magic, Faith and Healing*. New York: Free Press.

Kierkegaard, S. (1953). *Fear and Trembling*. New York: Doubleday Anchor.

Kovel, J. (1976). *A Complete Guide to Therapy: From Psychoanalysis to Behavior Modification*. New York: Pantheon.

*Kraft, T. (1972). The use of behavior therapy in a psychotherapeutic context. *Clinical Behavior Therapy*. Ed. A. A. Lazarus. New York: Brunner-Mazel.

*Kramer, H. and Sprenger, J. (1951). *Malleus Maleficarum or Witches' Hammer, 1484*. London: Pushkin Press.

*Laing, R. D. (1967). *The Politics of Experience*. London: Penguin.

Levi-Strauss, C. (1967). *Structural Anthropology*. New York: Doubleday Anchor.

*Liebeault, A. A. (1881). Concerning sleep and analogous states considered from the angle of the mind-body relationship. *Journal du Magnetism*, June.

Liebman, J. (1965). *Peace of Mind*. New York: Simon and Schuster.

*Lieberman, M. A., Yalom, I. B., and Miles, M. B. (1973). *Encounter Groups: First Facts*. New York: Basic Books.

Liff, Zanvel (1975). *The Leader in the Group*. New York: Aronson.

*Maimonides, M. (1912). *The Eight Chapters of Maimonides on Ethics*. Ed. J. J. Corfinde. New York: Columbia University Press.

*Malinowski, B. (1958). *Magic, Science and Religion*. Garden City, N.Y.: Doubleday Anchor.

Marcel, G. (1948). *The Philosophy of Existence*. London: Harwell.

Malmsbury, W. *The Royal Touch*. Quoted from Thompson, C. G. S.

*Marmor, J. (1971). Dynamic psychotherapy and behavior therapy. *Archives of General Psychiatry* 24: 22-28.

Masserman, J. H. (1955). *Practice of Dynamic Psychiatry*. Philadelphia: W. B. Saunders.

———(1957). Evolution vs. "revolution" in psychotherapy: A biodynamic integration. *Progess in Psychotherapy*, Vol. II. Ed. J. H. Masserman and J. L. Moreno. New York: Grune and Stratton.

———(1966). The timeless therapeutic trinity. *Handbook of Psychiatric Therapies*. New York: Jason Aronson.

*May, R., Angel, E., and Ellenberger, H. F. (1958). *Existence: A New Dimension in Psychiatry and Psychology*. New York: Basic Books.

Menninger, K. et al. (1963). *The Vital Balance: The Life Process in Mental Health and Illness*. New York: Viking.

*Mesmer, A. (1948). *Dissertation on Animal Magnetism*. Trans. V. R. Myers. Ed. Gilbert Frankau. London: A. P. Watt.

Michelet, J. (1939). *Satanism and Witchcraft*. New York: Citadel.

Minkowski, E. (1958). Findings in a case of schizophrenic depression. *Existence*. Ed. R. May et al. New York: Basic Books.

Moreno, J. L. (1953). *Who Shall Survive: Foundations of Sociometry, Group Psychotherapy and Sociodrama*. New York: Beacon.

*———(1956). The philosophy of the third psychiatric revolution with special emphasis on group psychotherapy and psychodrama. *Progress of Psychotherapy*. Vol. 1. New York: Grune and Stratton.

*Murphy, G. (1973). Foreword to M. Ullman, S. Krippner and A. Vaughan, *Dream Telepathy*. New York: Macmillan.

———(1949). *Historical Introduction to Modern Psychology*. New York: Harcourt Brace; London: Routledge, Kegan Paul.

Myers, F. W. H. (1954). *Human Personality and its Survival of Bodily Death*. New York: Longmans Green.

Nolen, W. A. (1974). *Healing: A Doctor in Search of a Miracle*. New York: Random House.

Ortega y Gasset, J. (1973). *Interpretation of Universal History*. New York: Norton.

*Paracelsus (1941). *On Diseases that Deprive Men of Health and Reason*. Trans. G. Zilboorg. Baltimore: Johns Hopkins University Press.

Pell, R. (1958). *Christian Science: Its Encounter with American Culture*. New York: Henry Holt.

*Perls, F., Hefferline, R., and Goodman, P. (1964). *Gestalt Therapy*. New York: Julian Press, Delta.

*Pinel, P. (1801). *Traite Medico-Psychologique sur l'Alienation Mental.* Paris: Richard Caille et Ravoir.

*———(1806). *Treatise on Insanity.* Trans. D. D. Davis. Sheffield, England: W. Todd.

*Plato (1937). *The Dialogues.* Trans. B. Jowett. 2 Vols. New York: Random House.

*Reich, W. (1972). *Character Analysis.* Trans. R. Carfagno. New York: Farrar, Straus and Giroux.

Rhine, J. B. (1953). *New World of the Mind.* New York: W. Sloane Assoc.

*Rogers, C. (1970). *Carl Rogers on Encounter Groups.* New York: Harper and Row.

Rosenthal, R. (1969). Interpersonal expectations: Effects of the experimenter's hypothesis. *Artifacts in Behavior Research.* Ed. R. Rosenthal et al. New York: Academic Press.

———(1971). The silent language of classroom and laboratory. *Proceedings of the Parapsychology Association,* pp. 95-116.

———(1973). The pygmalion effect lives. *Psychology Today,* September.

Ruitenbeek, H. M., ed. (1962). *Psychoanalysis and Existential Philosophy.* New York: Dutton.

Sartre, J.-P. (1953). *Existential Psychoanalysis.* New York: Philosophical Library.

*Schweitzer, A. (1965). Black magic reborn. *Tomorrow Magazine.*

*Servadio, E. (1955). A presumptively telepathic-precognitive dream during analysis. *International Journal of Psycho-Analysis* 36: 1-4.

Slavson, S. R. (1956). *The Fields of Group Therapy.* New York: International Universities Press.

Skinner, B. F. (1972). *Beyond Freedom and Dignity.* New York: Bantam, Vintage.

Skinner, B. F. (1948). *Walden Two.* New York: Macmillan.

Spotnitz, H. (1961). *The Couch and the Circle.* New York: Knopf.

Stekel, W. (1921). Der Telepathische Traum. Berlin: J. Braun Verlag.

Strupp, H. (1973). *Psychotherapy: Clinical Research and Theoretical Issues.* New York: Aronson.

*Sullivan, H. S. (1947). *Conceptions of Modern Psychiatry.* New York: Norton.

Szasz, T. (1961). *The Myth of Mental Illness.* New York: Hoeber, Harper and Row.

*———(1967). Behavior therapy and psychoanalysis. *Medical Opinion and Review,* June, pp. 24-26.

*Thompson, C. J. S. (1946). *Magic and Healing.* London: Rider.

Tillich, P. (1959). *The Courage to Be.* New Haven, Conn.: Yale University Press.

*Twain, M. (S. L. Clemens) (1907). *Christian Science with Notes Containing Corrections to Date*. New York: Harper Brothers.

*Ullman, M., Krippner, S. and Vaughan, A. (1973). *Dream Telepathy*. New York: Macmillan.

*Veith, I., trans.(1949). *The Yellow Emperor's Classic on Internal Medicine*. Baltimore: Williams and Wilkins.

*Weatherhead, L. (1951). *Psychology, Religion and Healing*. New York: Abingdon Press.

Werfel, F. (1943). *The Song of Bernadette*. Trans. R. Lewisohn. New York: Viking.

West, D. (1957). *Eleven Lourdes Miracles*. London: G. Tuckworth.

*Weyer, J. (1917). De Praestigiis Daemonicum 1563, Dr. John Weyer and the witch mania. *Studies in the History and Method of Science*. Ed. C. Singer. Oxford.

Wolberg, L. R. (1954). *The Technique of Psychotherapy*. New York: Grune and Stratton.

*Wolf, A. (1949-1950). The psychoanalysis of groups. *American Journal of Psychotherapy* 3: 5-9; and 4: 58-65.

*Wolpe, J., Salter, A. and Reyna, L. J. (1964). *The Conditioning Therapies*. New York: Holt, Rinehart and Winston.

*Zetzel, E. L. (1966). Remarks on Eysenck's *The Effects of Psychotherapy*. See Eysenck, 1966.

*Zilboorg, G. (1935). *The Medical Man and the Witch During the Renaissance*. Baltimore: Johns Hopkins University Press.

*———, and Henry, G. W. (1941). *A History of Medical Psychology*. New York: Norton.

*Zweig, S. (1932). *Mental Healers*. Trans. E. and C. Paul. New York: Viking.

Index